Data Structures and Algorithms in C++

Michael T. Goodrich
Department of Information & Computer Science
University of California, Irvine

Roberto Tamassia
Department of Computer Science
Brown University

David M. Mount
Department of Computer Science
University of Maryland

John Wiley & Sons, Inc.

ACQUISITIONS EDITOR	Paul Crockett
SENIOR MARKETING MANAGER	Katherine Hepburn
SENIOR PRODUCTION EDITOR	Ken Santor
SENIOR COVER DESIGNER	Dawn Stanley

About the cover: *Yala Yala Gibbs Tjungurrayi, Tingari Cycle,* 1986. Acrylic on canvas (121 cm. × 181 cm.). Private Collection. Image from *Songlines and Dreamlines: Contemporary Australian Aboriginal Painting*, Lund Humphries Publishers, London, 1996. Photograph provided courtesy of Nicholas Corbally Stourton and Patrick Corbally Stourton, Corbally Stourton Contemporary Art, Australia.

This book was set in LaTeX by the authors and printed and bound by Von Hoffmann, Inc. The cover was printed by Von Hoffmann, Inc.

This book is printed on acid free paper. ∞

ISBN 0-471-20208-8

Printed in the United States of America

10 9 8 7 6 5 4 3 2 1

To Karen
  – *Michael T. Goodrich*

To Isabel
  – *Roberto Tamassia*

To Jeanine
  – *David M. Mount*

Contents

Preface

This book provides a comprehensive introduction to data structures and algorithms, including their design, analysis, and implementation. In terms of the computer science and computer engineering curricula, we have written this book to be primarily focused on the Freshman-Sophomore level Data Structures (CS2) course.

This is a "sister" book to Goodrich-Tamassia, *Data Structures and Algorithms in Java (DSAJ)*, but uses C++ as the basis language instead of Java. This present book maintains the same general structure as DSAJ, so that CS/CE programs that teach data structures in both C++ and Java can share the same core syllabus, with one course using DSAJ and the other using this book.

While this book retains the same pedagogical approach and general structure as DSAJ, the code fragments have been completely redesigned. Because the C++ language supports almost all of Java's basic constructs, it would be tempting to simply translate the code fragments from Java to the corresponding C++ counterparts. We have been careful, however, to make full use of C++'s capabilities and design code in a manner that is consistent with modern C++ usage. In particular, whenever appropriate, we use elements of C++ that are not part of Java, including templated functions and classes, the C++ Standard Template Library (STL), C++ memory allocation and deallocation (and we discuss the associated tricky issues of writing destructors, copy constructors, and assignment operators), virtual functions and virtual class destructors, stream input and output, and C++'s safe run-time casting. However, we have avoided some of C++'s more arcane or easily misused elements, such as pointer arithmetic.

Highlights of this book include:

- Review of basic features of the C++ programming language
- Introduction to object-oriented design with C++ and design patterns
- Consistent object-oriented viewpoint throughout the book
- Comprehensive coverage of all the data structures taught in a typical CS2 course, including vectors, lists, heaps, hash tables, and search trees
- Detailed explanation and visualization of sorting algorithms
- Coverage of graph algorithms and pattern-matching algorithms for more advanced CS2 courses
- Visual justifications (that is, picture proofs), which make mathematical arguments more understandable for students, appealing to visual learners
- Motivation of algorithmic concepts with Internet-related applications, such as Web browsers and search engines
- Accompanying Web site http://datastructures.net with a special password-protected area for instructors

About the Authors

Professors Goodrich, Tamassia, and Mount are well-recognized researchers in data structures and algorithms, having published many papers in this field, with applications to Internet computing, information visualization, geographic information systems, computer security, and computer graphics. They have an extensive record of research accomplishments and have served as principal investigators in several projects sponsored by the National Science Foundation, the Army Research Office, and the Defense Advanced Research Projects Agency. They are also active in educational technology research, with special emphasis on algorithm visualization.

Michael Goodrich received his Ph.D. in Computer Science from Purdue University in 1987. He is currently a professor in the Department of Information and Computer Science at University of California, Irvine. Prior to this service, he was a professor of Computer Science at Johns Hopkins University and codirector of the Hopkins Center for Algorithm Engineering. He is an editor for the *International Journal of Computational Geometry & Applications* and *Journal of Graph Algorithms and Applications*.

Roberto Tamassia received his Ph.D. in Electrical and Computer Engineering from the University of Illinois at Urbana-Champaign in 1988. He is currently a professor in the Department of Computer Science and the director of the Center for Geometric Computing at Brown University. He serves as an editor for *Computational Geometry: Theory and Applications* and as editor-in-chief of the *Journal of Graph Algorithms and Applications*. He previously served on the editorial board of *IEEE Transactions on Computers*.

David Mount received his Ph.D. in Computer Science from Purdue University in 1983. He is currently a professor in the Department of Computer Science at the University of Maryland with a joint appointment in the University of Maryland's Institute for Advanced Computer Studies. He is an associate editor for *Pattern Recognition*.

In addition to their research accomplishments, the authors also have extensive experience in the classroom. For example, Dr. Goodrich has taught data structures and algorithms courses at Johns Hopkins University and at the University of California, Irvine since 1987, including Data Structures as a freshman-sophomore level course and Introduction to Algorithms as an upper-level course. He has earned several teaching awards in this capacity. His teaching style is to involve the students in lively interactive classroom sessions that bring out the intuition and insights behind data structuring and algorithmic techniques, as well as in formulating solutions whose analysis is mathematically rigorous. Dr. Tamassia has taught Data Structures and Algorithms as an introductory freshman-level course at Brown University since 1988. He has also attracted many students to his advanced course on Computational Geometry. One thing that has set his teaching style apart is his effective use of interactive hypermedia presentations, continuing the tradition of Brown's "electronic classroom." The carefully designed Web pages of the courses taught by Dr. Tamassia have been used as reference material by students and professionals worldwide. Dr. Mount has taught both the Data Structures and the Algorithms courses at the University of Maryland since 1985. He has won a number of teaching awards from Purdue University, the University of Maryland, and the Hong Kong University of Science and Technology. His lecture notes and homework exercises for the courses that he has taught are widely used as supplementary learning material by students and instructors at other universities.

Use as a Textbook

The study of data structures is part of the core of every collegiate computer science and computer engineering major program we are familiar with. Typically, in programs based upon semesters, elementary data structures are briefly introduced in the first programming or introduction to computer science course (CS1), and this is followed by a more in-depth data structures (CS2) course (possibly preceded by an intermediate programming and introduction to data structures course, CS1.5). Furthermore, the CS2 course is typically listed as a prerequisite for a host of other courses, and is often followed at a later point in the curriculum by a more in-depth study of data structures and algorithms (CS7). We feel that this book provides a strong foundation for a CS2 course, with the companion book, *Algorithm Design: Foundations, Analysis, and Internet Examples*, being a good text for a CS7 course. The importance of data structure design and analysis in the curriculum is fully justified, given the importance of efficient data structures in most software systems, including operating systems, databases, compilers, and scientific simulations.

With the emergence of the object-oriented paradigm as the framework of choice for the implementation of robust and reusable software, we have tried to take a consistent object-oriented viewpoint throughout this text. One of the main ideas of the object-oriented approach is that data should be presented as being encapsulated with the methods that access and modify them. That is, rather than simply viewing data as a collection of bytes and addresses, we think of data as instances of an *abstract data type* (***ADT***) that includes a repertory of methods for performing operations on the data. Likewise, object-oriented solutions are often organized utilizing common ***design patterns***, which facilitate software reuse and robustness. Thus, we present each data structure using ADTs and their respective implementations and we introduce important design patterns as means to organize those implementations into classes, methods, and objects.

Prerequisites

We have written this book assuming that the reader comes to it with certain knowledge. Namely, we assume that the reader is at least vaguely familiar with a high-level programming language, such as C, C++, Pascal, or Java, and that he or she understands the main constructs from such a high-level language, including:

- Variables and expressions
- Functions and procedures
- Decision structures (such as if-statements and switch-statements)
- Iteration structures (for-loops and while-loops).

For readers who are familiar with these concepts, but not with how they are expressed in C++, we provide a primer on the C++ language in the first two chapters. Because we expect that some readers will come to this book with a knowledge of Java, in this primer we explain a few of the subtle differences between these two languages. For readers already familiar with C++ this material may be skipped, but it can be read to provide a quick refresher to this material. We do not assume, however, that the reader is necessarily familiar with object-oriented design or with linked structures, such as linked lists, for these topics are covered in the core chapters of this book.

In terms of mathematical background, we assume the reader is somewhat familiar with topics from high-school mathematics, including exponents, logarithms, and elementary probability. Even so, we review most of these facts in Chapter 3, including exponents, logarithms, and summations, and we give a summary of other useful mathematical facts, including elementary probability, in Appendix A.

For the Instructor

As mentioned above, this book is intended primarily as a textbook for a Freshman-Sophomore Data Structures (CS2) course using C++ as its implementation language. This book contains many C++-code and pseudo-code fragments, and over 500 exercises (with roughly 200 having solutions that are posted at the instructor's area of the web site), which are divided with roughly 40% being reinforcement exercises, 40% being creativity exercises, and 20% being projects. The code fragments have all been successfully compiled and tested on major C++ compilers including GNU g++, Borland C++-Builder, and Microsoft Visual C++.

This book is also structured to allow the instructor a great deal of freedom in how to organize and present the material. For example, we include optional material, that is somewhat mathematically more advanced, in several chapters. Such optional sections are indicated with a star ($\star$).

In Table 0.1, we illustrate possible options for this book in a CS2 course.

Chapter	Possible Options
1. C++ Programming	skip if students know it already
2. Object-Oriented Design	skip if students know it already
3. Analysis Techniques	omit justification methods
4. Stacks, Queues & Deques	provide alternate case study
5. Vectors, Lists, and Sequences	omit amortized analysis
6. Trees	omit general trees
7. Priority Queues	omit bottom-up heap construction, locators
8. Dictionaries	omit skip lists, locators
9. Search Trees	omit (2,4) and red-black trees
10. Sorting, Sets, and Selection	omit sorting lower bound
11. Text Processing	omit tries, compression, & LCS
12. Graphs	omit directed graphs

Table 0.1: Options for a Freshman-Sophomore Data Structures course (CS2).

Web Site

This book comes accompanied by an extensive Web site maintained by the authors:

http://datastructures.net

(See also the publisher's site http://www.wiley.com/college/goodrich.) This Web site provided an extensive collection of educational aids that augment the topics of this book, for both students and instructors. Specifically for students we include:

- All the C++ source code fragments in this book
- Presentation handouts (four-per-page) in PDF format for most topics in the book
- Interactive animations illustrating fundamental data structures and algorithms
- Links to other data structures and algorithms resources.

The interactive animations should be of particular interest, since they allow readers to interactively "play" with different data structures, which leads to better understanding of the different ADTs and the way they can be implemented.

For instructors using this book, there is a password-protected portion of the Web site that includes the following additional teaching aids:

- Solutions to selected exercises
- Presentation slides in PowerPoint and PDF format.

Data Structures in C++

As mentioned earlier, the implementation language used in this book is C++. The reader interested in a data structures book using Java, is encouraged to consider the companion text, *Data Structures and Algorithms in Java*. C++ and Java are clearly the most widely used languages in the modern computer science curriculum. The two languages share a similar syntax and a number of important elements, such as an emphasis on object-oriented program design and strong type checking. Hence, they both incorporate important software-engineering concepts.

These two languages have advantages and disadvantages relative to each other. Java is arguably the simpler and cleaner of the two languages. It has better automatic run-time error checking, it is platform-independent, it provides automatic garbage collection, and is generally friendlier to the programmer. C++ provides a number of desirable features that are not available in Java, however. It includes stronger compile-time type checking, through the use of the **const** type modifier, and namespaces to achieve better control of the visibility of shared data. It provides efficient compile-time type polymorphism through templates, and run-time polymorphism through abstract classes and virtual functions. It includes additional data types such as enumerations and pointers. It allows explicit control over the deallocation of free-store data and destruction of class objects. For low-level code efficiency, it permits the programmer to provide hints to the compiler through inline functions and register variables. In general, C++ provides much greater control for the programmer, but it places a much greater burden of responsibility as well.

C++ was designed with the philosophy of providing a complete set of features for a procedural, object-oriented programming language, while allowing the compiler to produce very efficient code with minimal run-time overhead. Given its emphasis on efficiency, C++ continues to be a popular language for developing modern software systems. This book will help provide an understanding of the wide spectrum of skills ranging from sound algorithm and data structure design to clean and efficient implementation and coding of these designs in C++.

Acknowledgments

There are a number of individuals who have made contributions to this book. Many students have used the related textbook DSAJ, and their experiences and responses have helped shape it. We are grateful to all our research collaborators and teaching assistants who provided feedback on early drafts of book chapters and have helped us in developing exercises, programming assignments, and algorithm animation systems. In particular, we would like to thank Jeff Achter, James Baker, Ryan Baker, Benjamin Boer, Lubomir Bourdev, Stina Bridgeman, Bryan

Cantrill, Yi-Jen Chiang, Robert Cohen, Jody Fanto, Ashim Garg, Natasha Gelfand, Mark Handy, Michael Horn, Benoît Hudson, Jovanna Ignatowicz, Seth Padowitz, Michael Shapiro, Galina Shubina, Nikos Triandopoulos, and Luca Vismara.

There have been a number of friends and colleagues whose comments have lead to improvements in the text. We are particularly thankful to Evan Golub, Karen Goodrich, Larry Herman, Charles Lin, Art Moorshead, Nelson Padua-Perez, and Scott Smith for their insightful comments. We are also truly indebted to the outside reviewers and readers for their comments and constructive criticism.

We are grateful to our editors, Paul Crockett and Bill Zobrist, for their enthusiastic support of this project. The production team at Wiley has been great. Many thanks go to Simon Durkin, Katherine Hepburn, Ken Santor, Jeri Warner, and Jovan Yglecias.

The advanced computing environments and excellent technical staff in our departments at UCI, Brown, and UMD gave us a reliable working environment. This manuscript was prepared with LaTeX for the text and Adobe FrameMaker® and Microsoft Visio® for the figures. Code fragments were processed using lgrind.

Finally, we would like to warmly thank Isabel Cruz, Karen Goodrich, Jeanine Mount, Giuseppe Di Battista, Franco Preparata, Ioannis Tollis, and our parents for providing advice, encouragement, and support during the preparation of this book. We also thank them for reminding us there are things in life beyond writing books.

Michael T. Goodrich
Roberto Tamassia
David M. Mount

Chapter

1

Basic C++ Programming

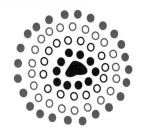

Contents

The first digital computer, ENIAC, did not use any data structures to speak of. Its primary function was to perform long sequences of mathematical calculations at speeds that were truly remarkable for its time. As important an achievement as this was, the major impact of ENIAC is not in the actual calculations it performed, but in the computational era it ushered in.

Computers are utilized today in myriad different ways. For consumers, computers provide real-time control of washing machines, automobiles, and ovens. For scientists and engineers, computers are used to design new airplanes, to model complex molecules, and to simulate galaxies. And computers are essential for modern-day commerce, as they are employed to perform most financial transactions and to facilitate a host of different modes of communication, including the Internet. Indeed, we have come a long way since 1945 when ENIAC was first built.

Modern computers routinely have memory capacities that are tens of millions of times larger than ENIAC ever had,[1] and memory capacities continue to grow at astonishing rates. This growth in capacity has brought with it a new and exciting role for computers. Rather than simply being fast calculators, modern computers are ***information processors***. They store, analyze, search, transfer, and update huge collections of complex data. Quickly performing these tasks requires that data be well organized and that the methods for accessing and maintaining data be fast and efficient. In short, modern computers need good data structures and algorithms.

Specifying these data structures and algorithms requires that we communicate instructions to a computer, and an excellent way to perform such communication is using a high-level computer language, such as C++, which is the programming language we use in this book. C++ evolved from the programming language C, and has, over time, undergone further evolution and development from its original definition. It has incorporated many features that were not part of C, such as symbolic constants, in-line function substitution, reference types, parametric polymorphism through templates, and exceptions (which will all be discussed later). As a result, C++ has grown to be a complex programming language. Fortunately, we do not need to know every detail of the language in order to use it effectively.

In this chapter and the next, we will present a quick tour of the C++ programming language and its features. It would be impossible to present a complete presentation of the language in this short space, however. Since we assume that the reader is already familiar with programming with some other language, such as C, Pascal, or Java, our descriptions will be short and will sometimes highlight the differences between C++ and these other languages. This chapter will present the language's basic features, and in the following chapter, we will concentrate on those features that are important for object-oriented programming.

---

[1]ENIAC's memory was upgraded around 1952 to be able to store a program of 1,800 two-digit instructions and a data set of 100 ten-digit numbers.

1.1 Basic C++ Programming Elements

C++ is a powerful and flexible programming language, which was designed to build upon the constructs of the C programming language. Thus, with minor exceptions, C++ is a superset of the C programming language. C++ shares C's ability to deal efficiently with hardware at the level of bits, bytes, words, addresses, etc. In addition, C++ adds several enhancements over C (which motivates the name "C++"), with the principal enhancement being the object-oriented concept of a ***class***.

A class is a user-defined type that encapsulates many important mechanisms such as guaranteed initialization, implicit type conversion, control of memory management, operator overloading, and polymorphism (which are all important topics that will be discussed later in this book). A class also has the ability to hide its underlying data. This allows a class to conceal its implementation details and allows users to conceptualize the class in terms of a well-defined interface. Classes enable programmers to break an application up into small, manageable pieces, or ***objects***. The resulting programs are easier to understand and easier to maintain.

The C++ Programming Model

Like many programming languages, creating and running a C++ program requires several steps. First, we create a file, such as "CoolProgram.cpp," and we type in the lines of our program. After we save this file, we then run a program, called a ***compiler***, which creates a machine-code interpretation of this program. Another program, called a ***linker*** (which is typically invoked automatically by the compiler), includes any required library code functions needed and produces an machine-executable file, which might be called "a.out." A user wishing to then run our program, simply executes this program. We illustrate this process in Figure 1.1.

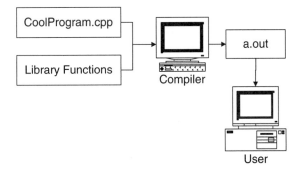

Figure 1.1: An example compilation of a C++ program.

1.1.1   A Simple C++ Program

We begin our presentation of C++ with a very simple program to illustrate some of the language's basic elements, so don't worry if some elements in this example are not fully explained. We will discuss them in greater depth later in this chapter. This program inputs two integers, x and y, and then computes and outputs their sum. Incidentally, the line numbers are not part of the program; they are just for our reference so that we can discuss the main components of this program line by line.

```
1  #include <cstdlib>
2  #include <iostream>
3  /* This program inputs two numbers x and y and outputs their sum */
4  int main( ) {
5     int x, y;
6     std::cout << "Please enter two numbers: ";
7     std::cin >> x >> y;                    // input x and y
8     int sum = x + y;                       // compute their sum
9     std::cout << "Their sum is " << sum << std::endl;
10    return EXIT_SUCCESS;                   // terminate successfully
11 }
```

A few things about this C++ program should be fairly obvious. First, comments are indicated with two slashes (//). Each such comment extends to the end of the line. As with C and Java, longer block comments are enclosed between /* and */. Block comments may extend over multiple lines. This program uses three integer variables, x, y, and sum. Notice that variables may be declared anywhere in the program, not just at the start.

Highlighting the C++ Elements

Let us consider some of the elements of the above program that are more particular to C++. Lines 1 and 2 input the two **header files**, "cstdlib" and "iostream." The first provides some standard system definitions and the second provides definitions needed for input and output.

The initial entry point for C++ programs is the function main. The statement "int main( )" on line 4 declares main to be a function that takes no arguments and returns an integer result. (In general, the main function may be called with the command-line arguments, but we will not discuss this.) The ***function body*** is given within curly braces ({...}). The program terminates when the return statement on line 10 is executed.

By convention, the function main returns the value zero to indicate success and returns a nonzero value to indicate failure. The include file cstdlib defines the constant EXIT_SUCCESS to be 0. Thus, the return statement on line 10 returns 0, indicating a successful termination.

The statement on line 6 prints a string using the output operator ("<<"), and the statement on line 7 inputs the values of these variables using the input operator (">>"). These values could be supplied, for example, from the person running our program. The name std::cout indicates that output is to be sent to the **standard output stream**. This convention is analogous to stdout in C and System.out in Java. There are two other important I/O streams in C++: **standard input** is where input is typically read, and **standard error** is where error output is written. These are denoted std::cin and std::cerr, respectively.

The prefix "std::" indicates that these objects are from the system's **standard library**. We should include this prefix whenever referring to objects from the standard library. Nonetheless, it is possible to inform the compiler that we wish to use objects from the standard library—and so omit this prefix—by utilizing the "using" statement, as shown below.

```cpp
#include <iostream>
using namespace std;                        // makes std:: available
// ...
cout << "Please enter two numbers: ";   // (std:: is not needed)
```

We will discuss the using statement later in Section 1.1.4. In order to keep our examples short, we will often omit the include and using statements when displaying C++ code. We will also use " //..." to indicate that some code has been omitted.

Returning to our simple example C++ program, we note that the statement on line 9 outputs the value of the variable sum, which in this case stores the computed sum of x and y. By default, the output statement does not produce an end of line. The special object std::endl generates a special end-of-line character. Another way to generate an end of line is to output the special character '\n' or equivalently the single-character string "\n". If run interactively, that is, with the user inputing values when requested to do so, this program's output would appear as shown below. The user's input is indicated below in blue.

```
Please enter two numbers:   7 35
Their sum is 42
```

1.1.2   Fundamental Types

We continue our exploration of C++ by discussing the language's basic data types and how these types are represented as constants and variables. The fundamental types are the basic building blocks from which more complex types are constructed. They include the following.

bool	Boolean value, either true or false
char	character
short	short integer
int	integer
long	long integer
float	single-precision floating-point number
double	double-precision floating-point number

There is also an enumeration, or enum, type to represent a set of discrete values. Together, enumerations and the types bool, char, and int are called ***integral types***. Finally, there is a special type void, which explicitly indicates the absence of any type information. We now discuss each of these types in greater detail.

Characters

A char variable holds a single character. A char in C++ is typically 8-bits, but the exact number of bits used for a char variable is dependent on the particular implementation. By allowing different implementations to define the meaning of basic types, such as char, C++ can tailor its generated code to each machine architecture and so achieve maximum efficiency. This flexibility can be a source of frustration for programmers who want to write machine-independent programs, however.

A ***literal*** is a constant value appearing in a program. Character literals are enclosed in single quotes, as in 'a', 'Q', and '+'. A backslash (\ ) is used to specify a number of special character literals, as shown below.

'\n'	newline	'\t'	tab
'\b'	backspace	'\r'	return
'\0'	null	'\''	single quote
'\"'	double quote	'\\'	backslash

Every character is associated with an integer code. The function int(ch) returns the integer value associated with a character variable ch.

Integers

An int variable holds an integer. Integers come in three sizes: short int, (plain) int, and long int. The terms "short" and "long" are synonyms for "short int" and "long int," respectively. Decimal numbers such as 0, 25, 98765, and -3 are of type int. The suffix "l" or "L" can be added to indicate a long integer, as in 123456789L. Octal (base 8) constants are specified by prefixing the number with the zero digit, and hexadecimal (base 16) constants can be specified by prefixing the number with "0x."

When declaring a variable, we have the option of providing a **definition**, or initial value. If no definition is given, the initial value is zero. Variable names may consist of any combination of letters, digits, or the underscore (_) character, but the first character cannot be a digit. Here are some examples of declarations of integral variables.

```
short n;                                    // default value = 0
int   octalNumber = 0400;                   // 400 (base 8) = 256 (base 10)
char  newline_character = '\n';
long  BIGnumber = 314159265L;
short _aSTRANGE__1234_variABIE_NaMe;
```

C++ does not specify the exact number of bits in each type, but a short is at least 16 bits, and a long is at least 32 bits. In fact, there is no requirement that long be strictly longer than short (but it cannot be shorter!). Given a type T, the expression sizeof(T) returns the size of type T, expressed as some number of multiples of the size of char.

Enumerations

An enumeration is a user-defined type that can hold any of a set of discrete values. Once defined, enumerations behave much like an integer type. A common use of enumerations is to provide meaningful names to a set of related values. Each element of an enumeration is associated with an integer value. By default, these values count up from 0, but it is also possible to define explicit constant values.

```
enum Color { RED, GREEN, BLUE };
enum Mood { HAPPY = 3, SAD = 1, ANXIOUS = 4, SLEEPY = 2 };

Color skyColor = BLUE;            // skyColor is of type Color
Mood myMood = SLEEPY;            // myMood is of type Mood
```

In this case RED, GREEN, and BLUE would be associated with the values 0, 1, and 2, respectively. As a hint to the reader, we will write enumeration names and other constants with all capital letters.

Floating Point

A variable of type float holds a single-precision floating-point number, and a variable of type double holds a double-precision floating-point number. As it does with integers, C++ leaves undefined the exact number of bits in each of the floating point types. By default, floating point literals, such as 3.14159 and -1234.567 are of type double. Scientific or exponential notation may by specified using either "e" or "E" to separate the mantissa from the exponent, as in 3.14E5, which means 3.14×10^5. To force a literal to be a float, add the suffix "f" or "F," as in 2.0f or 1.234e-3F.

1.1.3 Pointers, Arrays, and Structures

We next discuss how to combine fundamental types to form more complex ones.

Pointers

Each variable is stored in the computer's memory at some location, or ***address***. A ***pointer*** holds the value of such an address. Given a type T, the type T* denotes a pointer to a variable of type T. For example, int* is a pointer to an integer. The ***address-of*** operator, &, returns the address of a variable. Accessing the object addressed by a pointer is called ***dereferencing***, and is done using the * operator.

For example, in the code fragment below, the variable p is declared to be a pointer to a char, and is initialized to point to variable ch. Thus, *p is another way of referring to ch. Observe that when the value of ch is changed, the value of *p changes as well.

```
char ch = 'Q';
char* p = &ch;              // p holds the address of ch
cout << *p;                 // outputs the character 'Q'
ch = 'Z';                   // ch now holds 'Z'
cout << *p;                 // outputs the character 'Z'
```

Programmers often find it convenient to have a ***null pointer*** value, which points to nothing. By convention, such a pointer is assigned the value zero. An attempt to dereference a null pointer results in a run-time error. All C++ implementations define a special symbol NULL, which is equal to zero. This definition is activated by inserting the statement "#include <cstdlib>" in the beginning of a program file.

We mentioned earlier that the special type void is used to indicate no type information at all. Although we cannot declare a variable to be of type void, we can declare a pointer to be of type void*. Such a pointer can point to a variable of ***any*** type. Since the compiler is unable to check the correctness of such references, the use of void* pointers is discouraged.

Caution

Beware when declaring two or more pointers on the same line. The * operator binds with the variable name, not with the type name. Consider the following misleading declaration.

    int* x, y, z;   // same as: int* x; int y; int z;

This declares one pointer variable x, but the other two variables are plain integers. The simplest way to avoid this confusion is to declare one variable per statement.

We will see that pointers are fundamental to the implementation of many data structures. Pointers need not point to only fundamental types, such as char and int, they may also point to complex types and even to functions.

Arrays

An ***array*** is a collection of elements of the same type. Given any type T and a constant N, a variable of type T[N] holds an array of N elements, each of type T. Each element of the array is referenced by its ***index***, that is, a number from 0 to $N - 1$. The following statements declare two arrays; one holds three doubles and the other holds 10 double pointers.

    double f[3];   // array of 3 doubles: f[0], f[1], f[2]
    double* p[10];   // array of 10 double pointers: p[0] ... p[9]
    f[2]   = 25.3;
    p[4]   = &f[2];   // p[4] points to f[2]
    cout << *p[4];   // outputs "25.3"

C++ provides no built-in runtime checking for array subscripting out of bounds. This decision is consistent with C++'s general philosophy of not introducing any feature that would slow the execution of a program. Indexing an array outside of its declared bounds is a common programming error. Such an error often occurs "silently," and only much later are its effects noticed. In Section 1.5.5, we will see that the vector type of the C++ Standard Template Library (STL) provides many of the capabilities of a more complete array type, including run-time index checking.

A two-dimensional array is implemented as an "array of arrays." For example "int A[15][30]" declares A to be an array of 30 objects, each of which is an array of 15 integers. An element in such an array is be indexed as A[i][j], where i is in the range 0 to 14 and j is in the range 0 to 29.

When declaring an array, we can initialize its values by enclosing the elements in curly braces ({...}). When doing so, we do not have to specify the size of the array, since the compiler can figure this out.

    int a[]   = {10, 11, 12, 13};   // declares and initializes a[4]
    bool b[] = {false, true};   // declares and initializes b[2]
    char c[] = {'c', 'a', 't'};   // declares and initializes c[3]

Pointers and Arrays

There is an interesting connection between arrays and pointers, which C++ inherited from the C programming language—the name of an array can be used as a pointer to the array's initial element and vice versa. In the example below, c is an array of characters, and p and q are pointers to the first element of c. They all behave essentially the same, however.

```cpp
char c[] = {'c', 'a', 't'};
char *p = c;                    // p points to c[0]
char *q = &c[0];                // q also points to c[0]
cout << c[2] << p[2] << q[2];   // outputs "ttt"
```

This implicit conversion between array names and pointers can be confusing, but it helps to explain many of C++'s apparent mysteries. For example, given two arrays c and d, the comparison c==d does not test whether the contents of the two arrays are equal. Rather it compares the addresses of their initial elements, which is probably not what the programmer had in mind.

Strings

A string literal, such as "Hello World", is represented as a fixed-length array of characters that ends with the null character. Character strings represented in this way are called *C-style strings*, since they were inherited from C. Unfortunately, this representation alone does not provide many string operations, such as concatenation and comparison. It also possesses all the peculiarities of C++ arrays, as mentioned earlier.

For this reason, C++ provides a string type as part of its Standard Template Library (STL). When we need to distinguish, we will call these *STL strings*. In order to use STL strings it is necessary to include the header file <string>. Since STL strings are part of the standard namespace (see Section 1.1.4), their full name is std::string. By using the statement "using std::string" we can omit the "std::" prefix. STL strings may be concatenated using the + operator, they may be compared with each other using lexicographic (or dictionary) order, and they may be input and output using the >> and << operators, respectively. For example:

```cpp
#include <string>
using std::string;
// ...
string s = "to be";
string t = "not " + s;          // t = "not to be"
string u = s + " or " + t;      // u = "to be or not to be"
if (s > t)                      // true: "to be" > "not to be"
    cout << u;                  // outputs "to be or not to be"
```

There are other STL string operations, as well. For example, we can append one string to another using the += operator. Also, strings may be indexed like arrays and the number of characters in a string s is given by s.size(). Since some library functions require the old C-style strings, there is a conversion function s.c_str(), which returns a pointer to a C-style string. Here are some examples:

```
s = "John";                    // s = "John"
int i = s.size();              // i = 4
char c = s[3];                 // c = 'n'
s += " Smith";                 // s = "John Smith"
char *p = s.c_str();           // p is a C-style string
```

The C++ STL provides many other string operators including operators for extracting, searching for, and replacing substrings. We will not discuss these here. In Chapter 11, we present algorithms for text and string processing.

C-Style Structures

A **structure** is useful for storing an aggregation of elements. Unlike an array, the elements of a structure may be of different types. Each **member**, or **field**, of a structure is referred to by a given name. For example, consider the following structure for storing information about an airline passenger. The structure includes the passenger's name, meal preference, and information as to whether this passenger is in the frequent flyer program. We create an enumerated type to handle meal preferences.

```
enum MealType { NO_PREF, REGULAR, LOW_FAT, VEGETARIAN };

struct Passenger {
    string    name;            // possible value: "John Smith"
    MealType  mealPref;        // VEGETARIAN
    bool      isFreqFlyer;     // true
    string    freqFlyerNo;     // "293145"
};
```

This defines a new type called Passenger. Let us declare and initialize a variable named "pass" of this type.

```
Passenger pass = { "John Smith", VEGETARIAN, true, "293145" };
```

The individual members of the structure are accessed using the **member selection operator**, which has the form struct_name.member. For example, we could change some of the above fields as follows.

```
pass.name = "Pocahontas";      // change name
pass.mealPref = REGULAR;       // change meal preference
```

What we have discussed so far might be called a **C-style structure**. In general, structures and classes in C++ provide a much wider range of capabilities than what is possible in C-style structures. In addition to having member data, classes and structures in C++ can be associated with functions, called **member functions**. They also provide **access control**, which restricts access to member variables and functions. We will discuss these issues later in Section 1.5. Until then, whatever we say about structures applies to classes as well. Structures of the same type may be assigned to one another. By default, such an assignment involves copying the members of one structure to the other.

Pointers, Dynamic Memory, and the "new" Operator

We often find it useful in data structures to create objects dynamically as the need arises. The C++ runtime system reserves a large block of memory called the **free store**, for this reason. (This memory is also sometimes called **heap memory**, but this should not be confused with the heap data structure, which will be discussed in Chapter 7.) The operator new dynamically allocates the correct amount of storage for an object of a given type from the free store and returns a pointer to this object. That is, the value of this pointer is the address where this object resides in memory. Indeed, C++ allows for pointer variables to any data type, even to other pointers or to individual cells in an array.

For example, suppose that in our airline system we encounter a new passenger. We would like to dynamically create a new instance using the new operator. Let p be a pointer to a Passenger structure. This implies that *p refers to the actual structure; hence, we could access one of its members, say the mealPref field, using the expression (*p).mealPref. Because complex objects like structures are often allocated dynamically, C++ provides a shorter way to access members using the "->" operator.

  pointer_name->member   is equivalent to   (*pointer_name).member

For example, we could allocate a new passenger object and initialize its members as follows.

```
Passenger *p;
// ...
p = new Passenger;                    // p points to the new Passenger
p->name = "Pocahontas";               // set the structure members
p->mealPref = REGULAR;
p->isFreqFlyer = false;
p->freqFlyerNo = "NONE";
```

It would be natural to wonder whether we can initialize the members using the curly brace ({...}) notation used above. The answer is no, but we will see another more convenient way of initializing members when we discuss classes and constructors in Section 1.5.2.

This new passenger object continues to exist in the free store until it is explicitly deleted—a process that is done using the delete operator, which destroys the object and returns its space to the free store.

     delete p;   // destroy the object p points to

The delete operator should only be applied to objects that have been allocated through new. Since the object at p's address was allocated using the new operator, then the C++ runtime system knows how much memory to deallocate for this delete statement. Unlike some programming languages such as Java, C++ does not provide automatic *garbage collection*. This means that C++ programmers have the responsibility of explicitly deleting all dynamically allocated objects.

Memory Leaks

Failure to delete dynamically allocated objects can cause problems. If we were to change the (address) value of p without first deleting the structure to which it points, there would be no way for us to access this object. It would continue to exist for the lifetime of the program, using up space that could otherwise be used for other allocated objects. Having such inaccessible objects in dynamic memory is called a *memory leak*. We should strongly avoid memory leaks, especially in programs that do a great deal of memory allocation and deallocation. A program with memory leaks can run out of usable memory even when there is a sufficient amount of memory present. An important rule for a disciplined C++ programmer is the following:

Remember

If an object is allocated with new, it should eventually be deallocated with delete.

Arrays can also be allocated with new. When this is done, it is not possible to delete the array using the standard delete operator. Instead, the operator delete[ ] must be used. Here is an example that allocates a character buffer of 500 elements, and then later deallocates it.

```
char *buffer = new char[500];        // allocate array of 500 chars
// ...                                // use the array
delete [] buffer;                    // delete the array
```

References

Pointers provide one way to refer indirectly to an object. Another way is through references. A *reference* is simply an alternative name for an object. Given a type T, the notation T& indicates a reference to an object of type T. Unlike pointers, which can be NULL, a reference in C++ must refer to an actual variable. When a reference is declared, its value must be initialized. Afterwards, any access to the reference is treated exactly as if it is an access to the underlying object.

```
string author = "Samuel Clemens";
string &penName = author;            // penName is an alias for author
penName = "Mark Twain";              // now author = "Mark Twain"
cout << author;                      // outputs "Mark Twain"
```

What good are references? References are most often used for passing function arguments and are also often used for returning results from functions. These uses will be discussed later.

1.1.4   Scope and Namespaces

We can easily name variables without concern for naming conflicts in small problems. It is much harder for us to avoid conflicts in large software systems, which may consist of hundreds of files written by many different programmers. C++ has a number of mechanisms that aid in providing names and limiting their scope.

Constants and Typedef

Good programmers commonly like to associate names with constant quantities. By adding the keyword const to a declaration, we indicate that the value of the associated object cannot be changed. Constants may be used virtually anywhere that literals would be used, for example, in an array declaration. As a hint to the reader, we will use all capital letters when naming constants.

```
const double PI         = 3.14159265;
const int    CUT_OFF[]  = {90, 80, 70, 60};
const int    N_DAYS     = 7;
const int    N_HOURS    = 24*N_DAYS; // using a constant expression
int counter[N_HOURS];                // constant used for array size
```

Note that enumerations (see Section 1.1.2) provide another convenient way to define integer-valued constants, especially within structures and classes.

In addition to associating names with constants, it is often useful to associate a name with a type. This association can be done with a typedef declaration. Rather than declaring a variable, a typedef defines a new type name.

```
typedef char* BufferPtr;        // type BufferPtr is a pointer to char
typedef double Coordinate;      // type Coordinate is a double

BufferPtr p;                    // p is a pointer to char
Coordinate x, y;                // x and y are of type double
```

By using typedef we can provide shorter or more meaningful synonyms for various types. The type name Coordinate provides more of a hint to the reader of the meaning of variables x and y than does double. Also, if later we decide to change our coordinate representation to int, we need only change the typedef statement. We will indicate user-defined types by capitalizing the first character of their names.

Local and Global Scopes

When a group of C++ statements are enclosed in curly braces ({...}), they define a **block**. Variables and types that are declared within a block are only accessible from within the block. They are said to be **local** to the block. Blocks can be nested within other blocks. In C++, a variable may be declared outside of any block. Such a variable is **global**, in the sense that it is accessible from everywhere in the program. The portions of a program from which a given name is accessible are called its **scope**.

Two variables of the same name may be defined within nested blocks. When this happens, the variable of the inner block becomes active until leaving the block. Thus a local variable "hides" any global variables of the same name, as shown in the following example.

```
const int cat = 1;              // global cat

int main() {
    const int cat = 2;          // this cat is local to main
    cout << cat;                // outputs 2 (local cat)
    return EXIT_SUCCESS;
}

int dog = cat;                  // dog = 1 (from the global cat)
```

Namespaces

Global variables present many problems in large software systems, because they can be accessed and possibly modified anywhere in the program. They also can lead to programming errors, because an important global variable may be hidden by a local variable of the same name. As a result, it is best to avoid global variables. We may not be able to avoid globals entirely, however. For example, when we perform output, we actually use the system's global standard output stream object, cout. If we were to define a variable with the same name, then the system's cout stream would be inaccessible.

A *namespace* is a mechanism that allows a group of related names to be defined in one place. This helps organize global objects into natural groups and so minimize the problems of globals. For example, the following declares a namespace myglobals containing two variables, cat and dog.

```
namespace myglobals {
    int cat;
    string dog = "bow wow";
}
```

Namespaces may generally contain definitions of more complex objects, including types, classes, and functions. We can access an object x in namespace group, using the notation group::x, which is called its *fully qualified name*. For example, myglobals::cat refers to the copy of variable cat in the myglobals namespace.

We have already seen an example of a namespace. Many standard system objects, such as the standard input and output streams cin and cout, are defined in a system namespace called std. Their fully qualified names are std::cin and std::cout, respectively. Since namespaces are a relatively recent addition to C++, on some older C++ systems it is not necessary to include the std:: specifier.

The Using Statement

If we are repeatedly using variables from the same namespace, it is possible to avoid entering namespace specifiers by telling the system that we want to "use" a particular specifier. We communicate this desire by utilizing the using statement, which makes some or all of the names from the namespace accessible, without explicitly providing the specifier. This statement has two forms that allow us to list individual names or to make every name in the namespace accessible, as shown below.

```
using std::string;          // makes just std::string accessible
using std::cout;            // makes just std::cout accessible

using namespace myglobals;  // makes all of myglobals accessible
```

1.2   Expressions

An *expression* combines variables and literals with operators to create new values. In the discussion below, we group operators according to the types of objects they may be applied to. Throughout, we use var to denote a variable or anything to which a value may be assigned. In official C++ jargon, this is called an *lvalue*. We use exp to denote an expression and type to denote a type.

Member Selection and Indexing

Some operators access a member of a structure, class, or array. We let class_name denote the name of a structure or class; pointer denotes a pointer to a structure or class and array denotes an array or a pointer to the first element of an array.

class_name . member	class/structure member selection
pointer −> member	class/structure member selection
array [exp]	array subscripting

Arithmetic Operators

The following are the binary arithmetic operators:

exp + exp	addition
exp − exp	subtraction
exp * exp	multiplication
exp / exp	division
exp % exp	modulo (remainder)

There are also unary minus (−x) and unary plus (+x) operations. Division between two integer operands results in an integer result by truncation, even if the result is being assigned to a floating point variable. The modulo operator n%m yields the remainder that would result from the integer division i/j.

Increment and Decrement Operators

The *post-increment* operator returns a variable's value and then increments it by 1. The post-decrement operator is analogous but decreases the value by 1. The *pre-increment* operator first increments the variables and then returns the value.

var ++	post increment
var −−	post decrement
++ var	pre increment
−− var	pre decrement

The following code fragment illustrates the increment and decrement operators.

```
int a[] = {0, 1, 2, 3};
int i = 2;
int j = i++;                    // j = 2 and now i = 3
int k = --i;                    // i = 2 and k = 2
cout << a[k++];                 // a[2] (= 2) is output; now k = 3
```

Relational and Logical Operators

C++ provides the usual comparison operators.

exp < exp	less than
exp > exp	greater than
exp <= exp	less than or equal
exp >= exp	greater than or equal
exp == exp	equal to
exp != exp	not equal to

These return a Boolean result—either true or false. Comparisons can be made between numbers, characters, and STL strings (but not C-style strings). Pointers can be compared as well, but it is usually only meaningful to test whether pointers are equal or not equal (since their values are memory addresses).

The following logical operators are also provided.

! exp	logical not
exp && exp	logical and
exp || exp	logical or

The operators && and || evaluate sequentially from left to right. If the left operand of && is false, the entire result is false, and the right operand is not evaluated. The || operator is analogous, but evaluation stops if the left operand is true.

This "short circuiting" is quite useful, in evaluating a chain of conditional expressions, where the left condition guards against an error committed by the right condition. For example, the following code first tests that a Passenger pointer p is non-null before accessing it. It would result in an error if the execution were not stopped if the first condition is not satisfied.

```
if ((p != NULL) && p->isFreqFlyer) ...
```

Bitwise Operators

The following operators act on the representations of numbers as binary bit strings. They can be applied to any integer type, and the result is an integer type.

˜ exp	bitwise complement
exp & exp	bitwise and
exp ^ exp	bitwise exclusive-or
exp | exp	bitwise or
exp1 << exp2	shift exp1 left by exp2 bits
exp1 >> exp2	shift exp1 right by exp2 bits

The left shift operator always fills with zeros. How the right shift fills depends on a variable's type. In C++ integer variables are "signed" quantities by default, but they may be declared as being "unsigned," as in "unsigned int x." If the left operand of a right shift is unsigned, the shift fills with zeros and otherwise the right shift fills with the number's sign bit. Note that the input (>>) and output (<<) operators are not in this group. They will be discussed later.

Assignment Operators

In addition to the familiar assignment operator (=), C++ includes a special form, for each of the arithmetic binary operators (+, −, *, /, %) and each of the bitwise binary operators (&, |, ^, <<, >>), that combines a binary operation with assignment. For example, the statement "n += 2" means "n = n + 2." Some examples are shown below.

```
int     i = 10;
int     j = 5;
int     k = 1;
string  s = "yes";
i    -=    4;              // i = i - 4 = 6
j    *=   -2;              // j = j * (-2) = -10
k    <<=   1;              // k = k << 1 = 2
s    +=    " or no";       // s = s + " or no" = "yes or no"
```

These assignment operators not only provide notational convenience, but they can be more efficient to execute as well. For example, in the string concatenation example above, the new text can just be appended to s without the need to generate a temporary string to hold the intermediate result.

Remember that the name of an array in C++ is the same as a pointer to its first member. Thus, C++ does not allow the contents of one array A to be copied to another array B by a simple assignment of the form "B = A." Instead, the elements of A should be copied one by one to B, for example, using a loop. Better still, we can use an STL vector rather than standard C++ arrays to implement A and B. The STL vector provides all the capabilities of C++ arrays, but vectors can be copied using the assignment operator. See Section 1.5.5.

Other Operators

Here are some other useful operators.

class_name :: member	class scope resolution
namespace_name :: member	namespace resolution
bool_exp ? true_exp : false_exp	conditional expression

We have seen the namespace resolution operator in Section 1.1.4. The conditional expression is a variant of "if-then-else" for expressions. If bool_exp evaluates to true, the value of true_exp is returned, and otherwise the value of false_exp is returned.

The following example shows how to use this to return the minimum of two numbers, x and y.

smaller = (x < y ? x : y)   // smaller = min(x,y)

We also have the following operations on input/output streams.

stream >> var	stream input
stream << exp	stream output

Although they look like the bitwise shift operators, the input (>>) and output (<<) stream operators are quite different. They are examples of C++'s powerful capability to overload operators to work on different types. These operators are not an intrinsic part of C++, but are provided by including the file <iostream>. We refer the reader to the references given in the chapter notes for more information on input and output in C++.

The above discussion provides a somewhat incomplete list of all the C++ operators, but it nevertheless covers the most common ones. Later we will introduce others, including casting operators.

Operator Precedence

Operators in C++ are assigned a **_precedence_**, which determines the order in which operations are performed in the absence of parentheses. We show the precedence of the operators in C++ in Table 1.1. Operators in C++ are evaluated according to this ordering, from highest to lowest, unless parentheses are used to determine the order of evaluation. Except for && and ||, which guarantee left-to-right evaluation, the order of evaluation of subexpressions is dependent on the implementation. Thus, a program that critically depends on evaluation occurring from left to right may function correctly with one compiler and incorrectly with another.

Operator Precedence

Type	Operators
scope resolution	namespace_name :: member
selection/subscripting	class_name.member pointer−>member array[exp]
postfix operators	var++ var−−
prefix operators	++var −−var +exp −exp ˜exp !exp
multiplication/division	* / %
addition/subtraction	+ −
shift	<< >>
comparison	< <= > >=
equality	== !=
bitwise and	&
bitwise exclusive-or	ˆ
bitwise or		
logical and	&&
logical or	||
conditional	bool_exp ? true_exp : false_exp
assignment	= += −= *= /= %= >>= <<= &= ˆ= |=

Table 1.1: The C++ precedence rules. The notation "exp" denotes any expression.

1.2.1 Casting in Expressions

Casting is an operation that allows us to change the type of a variable. In essence, we can take a variable of one type and **_cast_** it into an equivalent variable of another type. Casting is useful in many situations. There are two fundamental types of casting that can be done in C++. We can either cast with respect to the fundamental types or we can cast with respect to class objects and pointers. We discuss casting with fundamental types here, and we consider casting with objects in Section 2.2.4. We will begin by introducing the traditional way of casting in C++, and later we will present C++'s newer casting operators.

Traditional C-Style Casting

Let exp be some expression, and let T be a type. To cast the value of the expression to type T we can use the notation "(T)exp." We call this a *C-style cast*. If the desired type is a type name (as opposed to a type expression), there is an alternate *functional-style cast*. This has the form "T(exp)." Some examples are shown below. In both cases the integer value 14 is cast to a double value 14.0.

```
int      cat = 14;
double  dog = (double) cat;            // traditional C-style cast
double  pig = double(cat);             // C++ functional cast
```

Both forms of casting are legal, but some authors prefer the functional-style cast.

Casting to a type of higher precision or size is often needed in forming expressions. The results of certain binary operators depend on the variable types involved. For example, division between integers always produces an integer result by truncating the fractional part. If a floating-point result is desired, we must cast the operands *before* performing the operation, as shown below.

```
int      i1  = 18;
int      i2  = 16;
double  dv1 = i1 / i2;                 // dv1 has value 1.0
double  dv2 = double(i1) / double(i2); // dv2 has value 1.125
double  dv3 = double( i1 / i2 );       // dv3 has value 1.0
```

When i1 and i2 are cast to doubles, double-precision division is performed. When i1 and i2 are not cast, truncated integer division is performed. In the case of dv3, the cast is performed after the integer division, and so precision is still lost.

Explicit Cast Operators

Casting operations can vary from harmless to dangerous, depending on how similar the two types are and whether information is lost. For example, casting a short to an int is harmless, because no information is lost. Casting from a double to an int is more dangerous because the fractional part of the number is lost. Casting from a double* to char* is dangerous because the meaning of converting such a pointer will likely vary from machine to machine. One important element of good software design is that programs be *portable*, meaning that they behave the same on different machines.

For this reason, newer versions of C++ have introduced a number of new casting operators, which make the safety of the cast much more explicit. These are called the static_cast, dynamic_cast, const_cast and reinterpret_cast. We will discuss only the static_cast here and will consider the others as the need arises.

Static Casting

Static casting is used whenever a conversion is made between two related types, for example numbers to numbers or pointers to pointers. Its syntax is given below.

static_cast ⟨ ⟨desired_type⟩ ⟩ (⟨expression⟩);

The most common use is for conversions between numeric types. Some of these conversions may involve the loss of information, for example a conversion from a double to an int. This conversion is done by truncating the fractional part (not rounding). For example, consider the following:

```
double  d1 = 3.2;
double  d2 = 3.9999;
int     i1 = static_cast<int>(d1);      // i1 has value 3
int     i2 = static_cast<int>(d2);      // i2 has value 3
```

This type of casting is much uglier than the C-style and functional-style casts shown earlier. But this form is appropriate, because it serves as a visible warning to the programmer that a potentially unsafe operation is taking place. In our examples in this book, we will use the functional style for safe casts (such as integer to double) and these newer cast operators for all other casts. Some older C++ compilers may not support the newer cast operators, but then the traditional C-style and functional-style casts can be used instead.

Implicit Casting

There are many instances where the programmer has not requested an *explicit cast*, but a change of types is required. In many of these cases, C++ will perform an *implicit cast*. That is, the compiler will automatically insert a cast into the machine-generated code. For example, when numbers of different types are involved in an operation, the compiler automatically casts to the stronger type. C++ will allow an assignment that implicitly loses information, but the compiler will usually issue a warning message.

```
int    i  = 3;
double d  = 4.8;
double d3 = i / d;      // d3 = 0.625 = double(i)/d
int    i3 = d3;         // i3 = 0      = int(d3)
                        // Warning! Assignment may lose information
```

A general rule with casting is to "play it safe." If a compiler's behavior regarding the implicit casting of a value is uncertain, then we are safest in using an explicit cast. Doing so makes our intentions clear.

1.3　Control Flow

Control flow in C++ is similar to that of other high-level languages. We review the basic structure and syntax of control flow in C++ in this section, including method returns, if statements, switch statements, loops, and restricted forms of "jumps" (the break and continue statements).

If Statement

Every programming language includes a way of making choices, and C++ is no exception. The most common method of making choices in a C++ program is through the use of an *if statement*. The syntax of an *if statement* in C++ is as follows:

```
if (⟨boolean_exp⟩)
    ⟨true_statement⟩
[else if (⟨boolean_exp⟩)
    ⟨else_if_statement⟩]
[else
    ⟨else_statement⟩]
```

where each statement can be a block of statements enclosed in braces ({...}). In addition, the "else if" and "else" parts are optional; either or both may be omitted from a valid if statement (we indicated these optional parts by enclosing them in brackets, "[" and "]").

The boolean_exp is typically of type bool, but in general the if statement accepts an arithmetic or pointer value. The true_statement will be executed if the value is nonzero (or non-null for pointers). Nevertheless, using an arithmetic or pointer value is a holdover from the C programming language and is discouraged, as it tends to lead to more programming errors.

Switch Statement

A *switch statement* provides an efficient way to distinguish between many different options, according to the value of an integral type. In the following example, a single character is input, and based on the character's value, an appropriate editing function is called. The comments explain the equivalent if-then-else structure, but the compiler is free to select the most efficient way to execute the statement.

```
char command;
cin >> command;                          // input command character
switch (command) {                       // switch based on command value
  case 'I' :                             // if (command == 'I')
    editInsert();
    break;
  case 'D' :                             // else if (command == 'D')
    editDelete();
    break;
  case 'R' :                             // else if (command == 'R')
    editReplace();
    break;
  default :                              // else
    cout << "Unrecognized command\n";
    break;
}
```

The argument of the switch can be any integral type or enumeration. The "default" case is executed if none of the cases equals the switch argument.

Each case in a switch statement should be terminated with a break statement, which causes execution to exit the switch statement. Otherwise, the flow of control "falls through" to the next case.

While and Do-While Loops

C++ has two kinds of conditional loops for iterating over a set of statements as long as some specified condition holds. These two loops are the standard *while loop* and the *do-while loop*. One loop tests a Boolean condition before performing an iteration of the loop body and the other tests a condition after. Let us consider the while loop first.

```
while (⟨boolean_expression⟩)
    ⟨loop_body_statement⟩
```

At the beginning of each iteration, the loop tests the Boolean expression and then executes the loop body only if this expression evaluates to true. The loop body statement can also be a block of statements.

Consider, for example, the following fragment, which prints elements of an array until finding the first element that is not strictly positive.

```
const int NUM_ELEMENTS = 100;
float a[NUM_ELEMENTS];
// ...
int i = 0;
while (a[i] > 0) {
  cout << a[i] << '\n';
  i++;
}
```

The do-while loop is similar to the while loop in that the condition is tested at the end of the loop execution, rather than before. It has the following syntax.

> **do**
> ⟨loop_body_statement⟩
> **while** (⟨boolean_expression⟩)

For Loop

In its simplest form, a *for loop* provides for repeated code based on an integer index. The functionality of a for loop is significantly more flexible. In particular, the usage of a for loop is split into three optional sections—the initialization, the condition, and the increment—and the body statement.

> **for** ([⟨initialization⟩]; [⟨condition⟩]; [⟨increment⟩])
> ⟨body_statement⟩

In the ⟨initialization⟩ section, we can specify the code to be performed before starting the loop. Typically this involves declaring and initializing a loop-control variable or counter.

In the ⟨condition⟩ section, we specify the repeat condition of the loop. This condition is a Boolean expression. The body of the for loop will be executed each time the condition is true when evaluated at the beginning of a potential iteration. When the condition evaluates to false, execution leaves the loop and jumps to the next statement after the for loop.

In the ⟨increment⟩ section we declare the incrementing statement for the loop, which is performed after the body during each iteration. The incrementing statement may be any legal statement, allowing for significant flexibility in coding. In fact, we can view a for loop as being equivalent to a while loop structured as ⟨initialization⟩ **while** (⟨condition⟩) { ⟨body_statement⟩ ⟨increment⟩ }.

The following example shows a simple for loop, which prints the positive elements of an array, one per line. Recall that '\n' generates a newline character.

```
const int NUM_ELEMENTS = 100;
float a[NUM_ELEMENTS];
// ...
for (int i = 0; i < NUM_ELEMENTS; i++) {
  if (a[i] > 0) { cout << a[i] << '\n'; }
}
```

In this example, the loop variable i was declared as int i = 0. Before each iteration, the loop tests the condition "i < NUM_ELEMENTS" and executes the loop body only if this is true. Finally, at the end of each iteration the loop uses the statement i++ to increment the loop variable i before again testing the condition.

There is an interesting scoping issue that arises with for loops like the one above, in which a counter variable is declared in the initialization. Is the variable i local to just the for loop or to the surrounding scope? The official C++ standard says that the variable is local to the for loop. Not all C++ compilers implement this rule correctly, however, so beware.

Break and Continue Statements

C++ provides statements to change control flow, including the break, continue, and return statements. We will discuss the first two here, and leave the return statement for later. A break statement is used to "break" out of a loop or switch statement. When it is executed, it causes the flow of control to immediately exit the innermost switch statement or loop (for loop, while loop, or do-while loop). The break statement is useful when the condition for terminating the loop is determined inside the loop. For example, in an input loop, termination often depends on a specific value that has been input. The following code fragment inputs integers and outputs their sum. It terminates as soon as a negative number is input.

```
int sum = 0;                        // holds the sum
while (true) {                       // this would loop forever
  int x;
  cin >> x;                          // input x
  if (x < 0) break;                  // exit loop if x is negative
  sum += x;                          // otherwise add x to sum
}
cout << "Sum is " << x << '\n';
```

The other statement that is often useful for altering loop behavior is the continue statement. The continue statement can only be used inside loops (for, while, and do-while). The continue statement causes the execution to skip to the end of the loop, ready to start a new iteration.

1.4   Functions

A *function* is a chunk of code that can be called to perform some task. Functions accept *arguments*, that is, variables through which information is passed into (or possibly out of) the function. A function may also *return* a value. A function *declaration* specifies the function's name, its arguments and their types, and the type of value that the function returns. A function *definition* specifies the C++ statements that are executed when the function is *called*, that is, *invoked*. A function must be declared before it is invoked. A function may be declared many times but may only be defined once. As an example, consider the following program, which first declares and then later defines a function evenSum(). This function is given two arguments, an integer array a and its length n. It determines whether the sum of array values is even and returns a Boolean result. We have provided a main program, which shows how the function is called.

```cpp
bool evenSum(int a[], int n);                    // function declaration
int main() {
  const int listLength = 6;
  int list[listLength] = {4, 2, 7, 8, 5, 6};
  bool result = evenSum(list, listLength);       // call the function
  if (result)    cout << "even sum.\n";
  else           cout << "odd sum.\n";
  return EXIT_SUCCESS;
}
bool evenSum(int a[], int n) {                    // function definition
  int sum = 0;
  for (int i = 0; i < n; i++) sum += a[i];
  return (sum % 2) == 0;
}
```

Let us consider this example in more detail. We see from the function definition that it takes two arguments, the first is an integer array of unspecified length and the second is an integer. In general, function arguments are given as a comma-separated list, each consisting of an argument type followed by an argument name. If a function has no arguments, an empty pair of parentheses is used. In front of the function name we give its type, bool in this case. If the function returns no value, the special type void is used—such functions are often called *procedures*.

The names a and n in the function definition are *formal arguments* and the variables list and listLength in the call are the *actual arguments*. When the function is called in the main program, the types of the actual arguments must agree with the corresponding formal arguments. Exact type agreement is not always necessary, however, for the compiler may perform implicit type conversions in some cases, such as casting a short actual argument to match an int formal argument.

A function's name, formal argument types, and return type constitute its ***signature***. A function's declaration and its definition must have the same signatures. By the way, it was not necessary to separate the function's declaration from its definition in this case. We could have just as easily placed the entire definition before the function main(). A function may be defined in one file but called from other files. In such cases, it is necessary to provide a declaration of the function in each file that calls the function. This requirement is often satisfied using header files, as we will discuss in Section 1.6.

1.4.1 Argument Passing

By default, arguments in C++ programs are passed ***by value***. When arguments are passed by value, the system makes a copy of the variable to be passed to the function. This means that modifications made to the formal arguments in the function do not alter the actual argument. Going against this default, we can explicitly define a formal argument to be a reference type, which has the effect of passing the argument ***by reference***. That is, modifications to the arguments in the function would modify the actual argument. An example is shown below.

```cpp
void f(int value, int &ref) {        // one value and one reference
  value++;                            // no effect on the actual argument
  ref++;                             // modifies the actual argument
  cout << value << '\n';             // outputs 2
  cout << ref << '\n';              // outputs 6
}

int main() {
  int cat = 1;
  int dog = 5;
  f(cat, dog);                       // pass cat by value, dog by ref
  cout << cat << '\n';               // outputs 1
  cout << dog << '\n';               // outputs 6
  return EXIT_SUCCESS;
}
```

Modifying function arguments is felt to be a rather sneaky way of passing information back from a function, and it is best avoided if there is a convenient alternative. Another way to modify an argument is to pass the address of the argument, rather than the argument itself. Even though a pointer is passed by value (and, hence, the address of where it is pointing cannot be changed), we can access the pointer and modify the variables to which it points. Reference arguments achieve essentially the same result with less notational burden (since a reference is implemented as an address).

Constant References as Arguments

There is a good reason for choosing to pass structure and class arguments by reference. In particular, passing a large structure or class by value results in a copy being made of the entire structure. All this copying may be quite inefficient for large structures and classes. Passing such an argument by reference is much more efficient, since only the address of the structure need be passed.

Since most function arguments are not modified, an even better practice is to pass an argument as a "constant reference." Such a declaration informs the compiler that, even though the argument is being passed by reference, the function cannot alter its value. Furthermore, the function is not allowed to pass the argument to another function that might modify its value. Here is an example using the Passenger structure, which we defined earlier. The attempt to modify the argument would result in a compiler error message.

```
void someFunction(const Passenger &pass) {
  pass.name = "new name";          // ILLEGAL!
}
```

When writing small programs, we can easily avoid modifying the arguments that are passed by reference for the sake of efficiency. But in large programs, which may be distributed over many files, enforcing this rule is much harder. Fortunately, passing class and structure arguments as a constant reference allows the compiler to do the checking for us. Henceforth, whenever we pass a class or structure as an argument, we will typically pass it as a reference, usually a constant reference.

Array Arguments

We have discussed passing large structures and classes by reference, but what about large arrays? Would passing an array by value result in making a copy of the entire array? The answer is no. When an array is passed to a function, it is converted to a pointer to its initial element. That is, an object of type T[ ] is converted to type T*. Thus, an assignment to an element of an array within a function does modify the actual array contents. In short, arrays are not passed by value.

By the same token, it is not meaningful to pass an array back as the result of a function call. Essentially, an attempt to do so will only pass a pointer to the array's initial element. If returning an array is our goal, then we should either explicitly return a pointer or consider returning an object of type vector from the C++ Standard Template Library.

1.4.2 Overloading

Overloading means defining functions or operators that have the same name, but whose effect depends on the types of their actual arguments.

Function Overloading

Function overloading occurs when two or more functions are defined with the same name but with different argument lists. Such definitions are useful in situations where we desire two functions that achieve essentially the same purpose, but do it with different types of arguments. A natural use of function overloading is in procedures that print their arguments. In particular, a function that prints an integer would be different from a function that prints a Passenger structure, but both could use the same name, print(), as shown in the following example.

```
void print(int x)                    // print an integer
  { cout << x; }
void print(const Passenger &pass) {  // print a Passenger
  cout << pass.name << " " << pass.mealPref;
  if (pass.isFreqFlyer) {
    cout << " " << pass.freqFlyerNo;
  }
}
```

When the print() function is used, the compiler considers the types of the actual argument and invokes the appropriate function, that is, the one with signature closest to the actual arguments.

Operator Overloading

C++ also allows overloading of operators, such as +, *, +=, and <<. Not surprisingly, such a definition is called ***operator overloading***. Suppose we would like to write an equality test for two Passenger objects. We can denote this in a natural way by overloading the == operator, as shown below.

```
bool operator==(const Passenger &x, const Passenger &y) {
  return     x.name        == y.name
          && x.mealPref    == y.mealPref
          && x.isFreqFlyer == y.isFreqFlyer
          && x.FreqFlyerNo == y.FreqFlyerNo;
}
```

This definition is similar to a function definition, but in place of a function name we use "operator==." In general, the == is replaced by whatever operator is being defined. For binary operators we have two arguments, and for unary operators we have just one.

Using Overloading

There are several useful applications of function and operator overloading. For example, overloading the $==$ operator allows us to naturally test for the equality of two objects, p1 and p2, with the expression "p1$==$p2."

Another useful application of operator overloading is for defining input and output operators for classes and structures. Here is how to define an output operator for our Passenger structure. The type ostream is the system's output stream type. The standard output, cout is of this type.

```
ostream& operator<<(ostream &out, const Passenger &pass) {
  out << pass.name << " " << pass.mealPref;
  if (pass.isFreqFlyer) {
    out << " " << pass.freqFlyerNo;
  }
  return out;
}
```

In order for this operator to work properly, we should also define an output operator for MealType (which is the type of pass.mealPref), since it is also a user-defined type. Notice that the operator returns the output stream. This practice is not strictly required, but it is good practice in defining output operators because it allows us to perform multiple outputs with a single statement, as shown below.

```
Passenger pass1 = // ...              // details omitted
Passenger pass2 = // ...

cout << pass1 << pass2 << '\n';
```

The output in this case will not be very pretty, but we could easily modify our output operator to produce nicer formatting.

There is much more that could be said about function and operator overloading, and indeed C++ functions in general. We refer the reader to a more complete reference on C++ for this information. One additional thing we will note, however, is that operator overloading is a powerful mechanism, and it is easy to abuse. Specifically, we do not want to define operators that perform in a way that is counter-intuitive or confusing. In general, we should use operator and function overloading sparingly and only when the meaning of the overloaded operator or function is obvious.

1.5 Classes

The concept of a **class** is fundamental to C++, since it provides a way to define new user-defined types, complete with associated functions and operators. By restricting access to certain class members, it is possible to separate out the properties that are essential to a class's correct use from the details needed for its implementation. Classes are fundamental to programming using an object-oriented approach, which is a programming paradigm we discuss in the next chapter.

1.5.1 Class Structure

A class consists of **members**. Members that are variables or constants are **data members** (also called **member variables**) and members that are functions are called **member functions** (also called **methods**). Data members may be of any type, and may even be classes themselves, or pointers or references to classes. Member functions typically act on the member variables, and so define the behavior of the class.

Access Control

One important feature of classes is the notion of **access control**. Members may be declared to be **public**, which means that they are accessible from outside the class, or **private**, which means that they are accessible only from within the class. (We will discuss two exceptions to this later: protected access and friend functions.)

Classes are often used to implement data structures. Class member variables are typically made private, because they deal with the details of how the data structure is implemented. Users of the data structure do not need to know this information. Since the data structure designer may want to change the implementation at some time in the future, we do not want to allow users to access this information. All external access to class objects takes place through the public members, or the **public interface** as it is called. The general syntax for a class is as follows.

```
class ⟨class_name⟩ {
private:
    // ... private members
public:
    // ... public members
};
```

There is no required order between the private and public sections. In fact, we can alternate between sections of different types. Many programmers prefer to list the public members first, since this is usually of most interest to someone using

the class. Since our focus throughout this book will be on how data structures
are implemented, we will usually list the private members first. If no such *access
specifier* is given, the default is private for classes and public for structures. In fact,
this is the only real difference between data contained in classes and structures in
C++.

Member Functions

Let us return to our passenger example, but this time we will define a class to hold
passenger objects. Our class structure begins with the same member variables that
we used in our earlier Passenger structure (see Section 1.1.3). To this we will add a
few member function declarations. The first member function has the same name as
the class itself. Such a function is called a *constructor*, since its job is to initialize,
or construct, the class's member data. Notice that the constructor does not have a
return type. The member function isFrequentFlyer() in our example tests whether
the passenger is a frequent flyer and the function makeFrequentFlyer() makes a
passenger a frequent flyer and assigns a frequent flyer number. Note that this is
only a partial definition, since we will be adding more member functions later. As
usual we use " //..." to indicate omitted code.

```
enum MealType { NO_PREF, REGULAR, LOW_FAT, VEGETARIAN };

class Passenger {                        // Passenger (as a class)
private:
   string     name;                      // passenger name
   MealType   mealPref;                  // meal preference
   bool       isFreqFlyer;               // is a frequent flyer?
   string     freqFlyerNo;               // frequent flyer number
public:
   // ...
   Passenger();                          // default constructor
   bool isFrequentFlyer() const;         // is this a frequent flyer?
                                         // make this a frequent flyer
   void makeFrequentFlyer(const string &newFreqFlyerNo);
   // ...
};
```

Class member functions can be placed in two major categories: *accessor functions*, which only read class data and *update functions*, which may alter class data.
The keyword "const" indicates that the member function isFrequentFlyer() is an
accessor. This informs the user of the class that this function will not change the
object contents. It also allows the compiler to catch a potential error should we
inadvertently attempt to modify any class member variables.

We have declared two member functions, but we still need to define them. Member functions may either be defined within the class body or outside. When a member function is defined outside the class body, it is necessary to specify both the name of the class as well as the name of the function, so the compiler knows which class is involved. This definition is done using the same scope resolution operator (::) that we introduced for namespaces. The form is class_name::member.

```
bool Passenger::isFrequentFlyer() const
  { return isFreqFlyer; }
void Passenger::makeFrequentFlyer(const string &newFreqFlyerNo) {
  isFreqFlyer = true;
  freqFlyerNo = newFreqFlyerNo;
}
```

These function definitions appear after the class definition. Notice that member names, such as isFreqFlyer and freqFlyerNo, are used without reference to a particular object. These functions will be invoked on a particular Passenger object. For example, let pass be a variable of type Passenger. We may invoke these public member functions on pass using the same member selection operator we introduced with structures, as shown below. Only public members may be accessed in this way.

```
Passenger pass;                          // pass is a Passenger
// ...
if (!pass.isFrequentFlyer()) {           // not already a frequent flyer?
  pass.makeFrequentFlyer("392953");      // set pass's freq flyer number
}
pass.name = "Joe Blow";                  // ERROR! name is a private member
```

In-Class Function Definition

In the above examples, we have shown member functions being defined outside of the class body. We can also define members within the class body, which can be useful for information hiding. In addition, when we define a member function within a class, we are giving a hint to the compiler that this function should be expanded *in line*. With an "in-line expansion," the compiler simply expands the contents of the function body each time it is encountered, rather than using the usual call-return mechanism.

An in-line function can be executed more efficiently than a regular function. In-line functions are especially useful for frequently used, short member functions, for example. If used excessively, in-line functions can result in much larger executable files, however. Thus, a rule of thumb is that in-line functions are best used for member functions consisting of only a few lines, with no loops and no recursive function calls.

Let us rewrite the above class definition, but this time using in-class function definitions for these two functions:

```
class Passenger {                              // Passenger (using in-line functions)
private:
  string     name;                             // passenger name
  MealType   mealPref;                         // meal preference
  bool       isFreqFlyer;                      // is a frequent flyer?
  string     freqFlyerNo;                      // frequent flyer number
public:
  // ...
  bool isFrequentFlyer() const
    { return isFreqFlyer; }
  void makeFrequentFlyer(const string& newFreqFlyerNo) {
    isFreqFlyer = true;
    freqFlyerNo = newFreqFlyerNo;
  }
};
```

C++ allows the combination of both in-class and out-of-class function definitions within the same class.

1.5.2   Constructors and Destructors

The above declaration of the class variable pass suffers from the shortcoming that we have not initialized any of its classes members. An important aspect of classes is the capability to initialize a class's member data. A ***constructor*** is a special member function whose task is to perform such an initialization. It is invoked whenever a new class object comes into existence. There is an analogous ***destructor*** member function, which is called whenever a class object goes out of existence.

Constructors

A constructor member function's name is the same as the class, and it has no return type. Because objects may be initialized in different ways, it is natural to define different constructors, and rely on function overloading to determine which one is to be called.

Returning to our Passenger class, let us define three constructors. The first constructor has no arguments. Such a constructor is called a ***default constructor***, since it is used in the absence of any initialization information. The second constructor is given a name, meal preference, and a frequent flyer number. The third constructor is given a passenger from which to copy information. This is called a ***copy constructor***. In the first case, we can only select reasonable default values for the members, but this is superior to providing no initialization at all.

We show below the relevant portions of constructors in a class definition.

```
class Passenger {
private:
  // ...
public:
  Passenger();                           // default constructor
  Passenger(const string &nm, MealType mPref, string ffn = "NONE");
  Passenger(const Passenger &pass);  // copy constructor
  // ...
};
```

Look carefully at the second constructor. The notation ffn="NONE" indicates that this argument for ffn is a ***default argument***. That is, an actual argument need not be given, and if so, the value "NONE" will be used instead. If a newly created passenger is not a frequent flyer, we simply omit this parameter. The constructor tests for this special value, and sets things up accordingly. Default arguments can be assigned any legal value and can be used for more than one argument. It is often useful to define default values for all the arguments of a constructor. Such a constructor is the default constructor, because it will be called if no arguments are given. Default arguments can be used with any function (not just constructors). The associated constructor definitions are shown in Code Fragment 1.1. Note that the default argument is not repeated in the function definition.

```
Passenger::Passenger() {               // default constructor
  name = "--NO NAME--";
  mealPref = NO_PREF;
  isFreqFlyer = false;
  freqFlyerNo = "NONE";
}
                                       // constructor given member values
Passenger::Passenger(const string& nm, MealType mp, string ffn) {
  name = nm;
  mealPref = mp;
  isFreqFlyer = (ffn != "NONE");       // true only if ffn given
  freqFlyerNo = ffn;
}
                                       // copy constructor
Passenger::Passenger(const Passenger& pass) {
  name = pass.name;
  mealPref = pass.mealPref;
  isFreqFlyer = pass.isFreqFlyer;
  freqFlyerNo = pass.freqFlyerNo;
}
```

Code Fragment 1.1: Constructors for the Passenger class.

Here are some examples of how the constructors above can be invoked to define Passenger objects. Note that in the cases of p3 and pp2 we have omitted the frequent flyer number.

```
Passenger p1;                           // default constructor
Passenger p2("John Smith", VEGETARIAN, 293145); // 2nd constructor
Passenger p3("Pocahontas", REGULAR); // not a frequent flyer
Passenger p4(p3);                       // copied from p3
Passenger p5 = p2;                      // copied from p2
Passenger* pp1 = new Passenger;         // default constructor
Passenger* pp2 = new Passenger("Joe Blow", NO_PREF); // 2nd constr.
Passenger pa[20];                       // default constructor for each pa[i]
```

Although they look different, the declarations for p4 and p5 both call the copy constructor. These declarations take advantage of a bit of notational magic, which C++ provides to make copy constructors look more like the type definitions we have seen so far. The declarations for pp1 and pp2 create new passenger objects from the free store, and return a pointer to each. The declaration of pa declares an array of Passenger. The individual members of the array are always initialized from the default constructor.

Initializing Class Members with Initializer Lists

There is a subtlety that we glossed over in our presentations of the constructors. Recall that a string is a class in the standard template library. Our initialization using "name=nm" above relied on the fact that the string class has an assignment operator defined for it. If the type of name is a class without an assignment operator, this type of initialization might not be possible.

In order to deal with difficult class member initializations, C++ provides an alternate method of initialization, called an ***initializer list***. This list is placed between the constructor's argument list and its body. It consists of a colon (:) followed by a comma-separated list of the form member_name(initial_value).

In our example, only the name member is a class, and so it is the only one that might require initialization using an initializer list. To illustrate the feature, let us initialize the first three members using an initializer list and initialize the last member in the body of the constructor. The initializer list will be executed before the body of the constructor.

```
                // constructor using an initializer list
Passenger::Passenger(const string &nm, MealType mp, string ffn)
  : name(nm), mealPref(mp), isFreqFlyer(ffn != "NONE") {
  freqFlyerNo = ffn;
}
```

Destructors

A constructor is called whenever a class object comes into existence. A ***destructor*** is a member function that is automatically called when a class object ceases to exist. If a class object comes into existence dynamically using the new operator, the destructor will be called when this object is destroyed using the delete operator. If a class object comes into existence because it is a local variable in a function that has been called, the destructor will be called when the function returns.

Destructors are needed in certain circumstances. If, during its lifetime, an object acquires any resources—for example, it opens files or allocates memory—then these resources should to be returned when the object is destroyed. It is the destructor's job to do this cleaning up. For us, the most common use of destructors will be for deallocating any memory that has been allocated by the class. The destructor for a class T is denoted ~T(). It takes no arguments and has no return type.

Let us consider a class Vect, which allocates a fixed-sized vector of integers using an array, shown in Code Fragment 1.2. The constructor is provided an argument size indicating the size of the vector, and allocates an array of this size. (Recall that an array may be represented as a pointer to its initial element.) The destructor returns this space to the free store. Remember that when arrays are deleted we must use "delete[ ]" rather than "delete."

We are not strictly required by C++ to provide our own destructor. Nonetheless, if our class allocates memory, we should write a destructor to free this memory. If we did not provide the above destructor, the deletion of an object of type Vect would cause a memory leak, that is, an inaccessible block of memory that cannot be removed. The job of explicitly deallocating objects that were allocated is one of the chores that C++ programmers must endure.

```cpp
class Vect {
private:
    int*        theVect;        // the array holding the vector
    int         vectSize;       // size of the vector
public:
    Vect(int size = 10) {       // constructor, given size
        vectSize = size;
        theVect = new int[size];    // allocate the array
    }
    // ...                      (other functions omitted)
    ~Vect()                     // destructor
        { delete [] theVect; }  // free the allocated array
};
```

Code Fragment 1.2: The class Vect, which implements a simple fixed-sized vector of integers.

1.5.3   Classes and Memory Allocation

When a class performs memory allocation using new, care must be taken to avoid a number of common programming errors. We have shown above that failure to deallocate storage in a class's destructor can result in memory leaks. A somewhat more insidious problem occurs when classes that allocate memory fail to provide a copy constructor or an assignment operator. Consider the following example, using our Vect class.

```
Vect a(100);                    // a is a vector of size 100
Vect b = a;                     // initialize b from a (DANGER!)
Vect c;                         // c is a vector (default size 10)

c = a;                          // assign a to c (DANGER!)
```

It would seem that we have just created three separate vectors, all of size 100, but have we? In reality all three of these vectors share the same 100-element array. Let us see why this has occurred.

The declaration of object a invokes the vector constructor, which allocates an array of 100 integers, and a.theVect points to this array. The declaration "Vect b=a" initializes b from a using a copy constructor. Since we provided no such constructor in Vect, the system uses its default, which simply copies each member of a to b. In particular it sets "b.theVect=a.theVect." Notice that this does not copy the contents of the array; rather it copies the pointer to the array's initial element. This default action is sometimes called a ***shallow copy***, because only the pointers are copied, not the underlying array contents.

The declaration of c invokes the constructor with a default argument value of 10, and hence allocates an array of 10 elements in the free store. Because we have not provided an assignment operator, the statement "c=a," does the same shallow-copy of a to c. Only pointers are copied, not array contents. Note that in the process we have lost the pointer to c's 10-element array. We have just created a memory leak.

Now a, b, and c all have members that point to the same array in the free store. If one of the three, say b, were to change the contents of its array, both a and c would be changed implicitly as well, without any warning. Worse yet, if one of the three were to be deleted before the others (for example, if this variable was declared in a nested block), the destructor would delete the shared array. When either of the other two attempts to access the now deleted array, the results would be disastrous. In short, there are many problems here.

Fortunately, there is a simple fix for all of these problems. The problems arose because we allocated memory and we used the system's copy constructor and assignment operator. To fix this we implement our own copy constructor and assignment operator. The copy constructor allocates memory for the newly created array and copies the contents. It is shown in Code Fragment 1.3.

```
Vect::Vect(const Vect &a) {          // copy constructor from a
  vectSize = a.vectSize;             // copy sizes
  theVect = new int[vectSize];       // allocate new array
  for (int i = 0; i < vectSize; i++) {  // copy the vector contents
    theVect[i] = a.theVect[i];
  }
}

Vect& Vect::operator=(const Vect &a) {  // assignment operator from a
  if (this != &a) {                     // avoid self-assignment
    delete [] theVect;                  // delete old array
    vectSize = a.vectSize;              // set new size
    theVect = new int[vectSize];        // allocate new array
    for (int i=0; i < vectSize; i++) {  // copy the vector contents
      theVect[i] = a.theVect[i];
    }
  }
  return *this;
}
```

Code Fragment 1.3: Copy constructor and assignment operator for the class Vect.

The assignment operator is also shown in Code Fragment 1.3. The argument is the object on the right side of the assignment operator. The assignment operator deletes the existing array storage, allocates a new array of the proper size, and copies elements into this new array. The if statement checks against the possibility of self assignment (a=a). We perform this check using the this keyword. For any class object, this is a pointer which is automatically defined to be the address of this object. If this equals the address of a, then a and the current object are the same objects. This means that we have a self assignment, which we simply ignore.

The self-assignment test may seem superfluous. After all, what programmer would ever write "a=a"? Nonetheless, self assignments may arise in subtler ways. For example, consider the array assignment "A[i] = A[2*i]" in the case $i = 0$.

Notice that we return a reference to the current object at the end of the assignment. Such an approach is useful for assignment operators, since it allows us to chain together assignments, as in "a=b=c." The assignment "b=c" invokes the assignment operator, copying variable c to b and then returns a reference to b. This result is then assigned to variable a.

The only other changes needed to complete the job would be to add the appropriate function declarations to the Vect class. By using the copy constructor and assignment operator, we avoid the above memory leak and the dangerous shared array. The lessons of the last two sections can be summarized in the following rule.

Remember

> Every class that allocates its own objects using new should:
> - Define a **destructor** to free any allocated objects.
> - Define a **copy constructor**, which allocates its own new member storage and copies the contents of member variables.
> - Define an **assignment operator**, which deallocates old storage, allocates new storage, and copies all member variables.

Some programmers recommend that these functions be included for every class, even if memory is not allocated, but we will not be so fastidious. In rare instances, we may want to forbid users from using one or more of these operations. For example, we may not want a huge data structure to be copied inadvertently. In this case, we can define empty copy constructors and assignment functions and make them private members of the class.

1.5.4   Class Friends and Class Members

Complex data structures typically involve the interaction of many different classes. In such cases, there are often issues coordinating the actions of these classes to allow sharing of information. We discuss some of these issues in this section.

We said private members of a class may only be accessed from within the class, but there is an exception to this. Specifically, we can declare a function as a *friend*, which means that this function may access the class's private data. There are a number of reasons for defining friend functions. One is that syntax requirements may forbid us from defining a member function. For example, consider a class SomeClass. Suppose that we want to define an overloaded output operator for this class, and this output operator needs access to private member data. To handle this, the class declares that the output operator is a friend of the class, as shown below.

```cpp
class SomeClass {
private:
  int secret;
public:
  // ...                                // give << operator access to secret
  friend ostream& operator<<(ostream &out, const SomeClass &x);
};

ostream& operator<<(ostream &out, const SomeClass &x)
  { cout << x.secret; }
```

Another time when it is appropriate to use friends is when two different classes are closely related. For example, Code Fragment 1.4 shows an example of two classes Vector and Matrix, that use friendship in order to define a member function that multiplies a vector times a matrix.

```
class Matrix;                              // Matrix definition comes later

class Vector {                             // a 3-element vector
private:
  double coord[3];
public:
  // ...
  friend class Matrix;                     // allow Matrix access to coord
};

class Matrix {                             // a 3x3 array
private:
  double a[3][3];
public:
  // ...
  Vector multiplyBy(const Vector& v) {     // multiply (a * v)
    Vector w(0, 0, 0);
    for (int i = 0; i < 3; i++)
      for (int j = 0; j < 3; j++)
        w.coord[i] += a[i][j] * v.coord[j];
    return w;
  }
};
```

Code Fragment 1.4: An example of using friendship in related class definitions. Class Vector stores a vector and class Matrix stores a matrix. We define a member function multiplyBy() for Matrix that multiplies a vector times this matrix. We can make Matrix class a friend of the Vector class. This allows all the member functions of Matrix to have access to the private members of Vector. Some details have been omitted.

The ability to declare friendship relationships between classes is useful, but the extensive use of friends often indicates a poor class structure design. For example, in the above case, a better solution would be to have class Vector define a public subscripting operator. Then the multiplyBy() function could use this public member to access the vector class, rather than access private member data.

Note that "friendship" is not transitive. For example, if a new class Tensor was made a friend of Matrix, Tensor would not be a friend of Vector, unless class Vector were to explicitly declare it to be so.

Nesting Classes and Types within Classes

We have seen that classes may contain member variables and member functions. Classes may define new types as well. For example, we can nest a class definition within another class. Such nesting is often convenient in the design of data structures. For example, suppose that we want to design a complex data structure, called Complex. Suppose further that this structure will be composed of many node objects, given by a class Node. Since only the Complex class will access the Node class, we can define the Node class as a private *type member* of Complex.

```
class Complex {
private:
  class Node {
    // ... (Node definition here)
  };
  // ... (Remainder of Complex definition)
}
```

In this way, only the Complex class can use the Node type. In addition to declaring new user-defined classes, such as Node, we can embed other sorts of user-defined entities inside the class definition, such as enumerations, structures, and typedefs. These other kinds of entities may be private to the class or may be made publicly available to users of the class.

1.5.5   The Standard Template Library

The *Standard Template Library* (*STL*) is a collection of useful classes for common data structures. In addition to the string class, which we have seen many times, it also provides data structures for the following *standard containers*. We will be discussing many of these data structures later in this book, so don't worry if their names seem unfamiliar.

stack	Container with last-in, first-out access
queue	Container with first-in, first-out access
deque	Double-ended queue
vector	Resizeable array
list	Doubly linked list
priority_queue	Queue ordered by value
set	Set
map	Associative array (dictionary)

Templates and the STL Vector Class

One of the important features of the STL is that each such object can store objects of any one type. Contrast this with the Vect class of Section 1.5.2, which can only hold integers. Such a class whose definition depends on a user-specified type is called a *template*. We will discuss templates in greater detail in Chapter 2, but we briefly mention how they are used with container objects here.

We specify the type of the object being stored in the container in angled brackets (<...>). For example, we could define vectors to hold 100 integers, 500 characters, and 20 passengers as follows:

```
#include <vector>

vector<int> scores(100);              // 100 integer scores
vector<char> buffer(500);             // buffer of 500 characters
vector<Passenger> passenList(20);     // list of 20 Passengers
```

As usual, the include statement provides the necessary declarations for using the vector class. Each instance of an STL vector can only hold objects of one type.

Vectors can be indexed using either the usual index operator ([ ]) or the at() member function. The advantage of the latter is that it performs range checking and generates an error exception if the index is out of bounds. (We will discuss exceptions in Section 2.4.) Recall that standard arrays in C++ do not even know their size, and hence range checking is not even possible. In contrast, a vector object's size is given by its size() member function. Unlike standard arrays, one vector object can be assigned to another. A vector can be resized by calling the resize() member function. We show several examples of uses of the STL vector class below.

```
int i = // ...

cout << scores[i];                    // index range unchecked
buffer.at(i) = buffer.at(2 * i);      // index range checked
vector<int> newScores = scores;       // assign scores to newScores
scores.resize(scores.size() + 10);    // add 10 more scores
```

There is much about vector and other STL containers that we do not have space to explore. We refer the interested reader to a more complete C++ reference for more information about the Standard Template Library.

1.6   C++ Program and File Organization

Let us now consider the broader issue of how to organize an entire C++ program. A typical large C++ program consists of many files, with related pieces of code residing within each file. For example, C++ programmers commonly place each major class in its own file.

Source Files

There are two common files types, source files and header files. *Source files* typically contain most of the executable statements and data definitions. This includes the bodies of functions and definitions of any global variables.

Different compilers use different file naming conventions. Source file names typically have distinctive suffixes, such as ".cc", ".cpp", and ".C". Source files may be compiled separately by the compiler, and then these files are combined into one program by a system program called a *linker*.

Each nonconstant global variable and function may be defined only once. Other source files may share such a global variable or function provided they have a matching declaration. To indicate that a global variable is defined in another file, the type specifier "extern" is added. This keyword is not needed for functions. For example, consider the declarations extracted from two files below. The file Source1.cpp defines a global variable cat and function foo(). The file Source2.cpp can access these objects by including the appropriate matching declarations and adding "extern" for variables.

File: Source1.cpp

```
    int cat = 1;                         // definition of cat
    int foo(int x) { return x+1; }       // definition of foo
```

File: Source2.cpp

```
    extern int cat;                      // cat is defined elsewhere
    int foo(int x);                      // foo is defined elsewhere
```

Header Files

Since source files using shared objects must provide identical declarations, we commonly store these shared declarations in a *header file*, which is then read into each such source file using an #include statement. Statements beginning with # are handled by a special program, called the *preprocessor*, which is invoked automatically by the compiler. A header file typically contains many declarations, including classes, structures, constants, enumerations, and typedefs. Header files generally do not contain the definition (body) of a function. In-line functions are an exception, however, as their bodies are given in a header file.

Except for some standard library headers, the convention is that header file names end with a ".h" suffix. Standard library header files are indicated with angled brackets, as in <iostream>, while other local header files are indicated using quotes, as in "myIncludes.h".

As a general rule, we should avoid including namespace using directives in header files, because any source file that includes such a header file will have its namespace expanded as a result. We will make one exception to this in our examples, however. Some of our header files will include a using directive for the STL string class, because it is so useful.

1.6.1 An Example Program

To make this description more concrete, let us consider an example of a simple yet complete C++ program. Our example consists of one class, called CreditCard, which defines a credit card object, and a procedure that uses this class.

The CreditCard Class

The credit card object defined by CreditCard is a simplified version of a traditional credit card. It has an identifying number, identifying information about the owner, and information about the credit limit and the current balance. It does not charge interest or late payments, but it does restrict charges that would cause a card's balance to go over its spending limit.

The main class structure is presented in the header file CreditCard.h and is shown in Code Fragment 1.5.

Before discussing the class, let us say a bit about the general file structure. The first two lines (containing #ifndef and #define) and the last line (containing #endif) are used to keep the same header file from being expanded twice. We will discuss this later. The next lines include the header files for strings and standard input and output.

This class has four private data members. We provide a simple constructor to initialize these members. There are four *accessor functions*, which provide access to read the current values of these member variables. Of course, we could have alternately defined the member variables as being public and saved the work of providing these accessor functions. But this would allow users to modify any of these member variables directly. We usually prefer to restrict the modification of member variables to special *update functions*. We include two such update functions, chargeIt() and makePayment(). We have also defined a stream output operator for the class.

```
#ifndef CREDIT_CARD_H                          // avoid repeated expansion
#define CREDIT_CARD_H

#include <string>                              // provides string
#include <iostream>                            // provides ostream

using std::string;                             // make string accessible

class CreditCard {
private:                                        // private member data
    string    number;                          // credit card number
    string    name;                            // card owner's name
    int       limit;                           // credit limit
    double    balance;                         // credit card balance
public:
                                                // standard constructor
    CreditCard(string no, string nm, int lim, double bal=0);
                                                // accessors functions
    string    getNumber()   const   { return number; }
    string    getName()     const   { return name; }
    double    getBalance()  const   { return balance; }
    int       getLimit()    const   { return limit; }
                                                // update functions
    bool chargeIt(double price);               // make a charge

    void makePayment(double payment)           // make a payment
       { balance -= payment; }
};
                                                // print card information
std::ostream& operator<<(std::ostream& out, const CreditCard& c);
#endif
```

Code Fragment 1.5: The header file CreditCard.h, which contains the definition of class CreditCard.

The accessor functions and makePayment() are short; so we define them within the class body. The other member functions and the output operator is defined outside the class in the file CreditCard.cpp, shown in Code Fragment 1.6. This approach of defining a header file with the class definition and an associated source file with the longer member function definitions is common in C++.

```cpp
#include "CreditCard.h"                    // provides CreditCard
                                           // standard constructor
CreditCard::CreditCard(string no, string nm, int lim, double bal) {
  number = no;
  name = nm;
  balance = bal;
  limit = lim;
}
                                           // make a charge
bool CreditCard::chargeIt(double price) {
  if (price + balance > double(limit))
    return false;                          // over limit
  balance += price;
  return true;                             // the charge goes through
}
                                           // print card information
std::ostream& operator<<(std::ostream& out, const CreditCard& c) {
  out << "Number = "    << c.getNumber()   << "\n"
      << "Name = "      << c.getName()     << "\n"
      << "Balance = "   << c.getBalance()  << "\n"
      << "Limit = "     << c.getLimit()    << "\n";
  return out;
}
```

Code Fragment 1.6: The file CreditCard.cpp, which contains the definition of the out-of-class member functions for class CreditCard.

The Main Test Program

Our main program is in the file TestCard.cpp. It consists of a main function, but this function does little more than call the function testCard(), which does all the work. We include CreditCard.h to provide the CreditCard declaration. We do not need to include iostream and string, since CreditCard.h does this for us, but it would not have hurt to do so.

The testCard() function declares an array of pointers to CreditCard. We allocate three such objects and initialize them. We then perform a number of payments and print the associated information. We show the complete code for the Test class in Code Fragment 1.7.

```cpp
#include <vector>                           // provides STL vector
#include "CreditCard.h"                     // provides CreditCard, cout, string

using namespace std;                        // make std accessible

void testCard() {                           // CreditCard test function
  vector<CreditCard*> wallet(10);           // vector of 10 CreditCard pointers
                                            // allocate 3 new cards
  wallet[0] = new CreditCard("5391 0375 9387 5309", "John Bowman", 2500);
  wallet[1] = new CreditCard("3485 0399 3395 1954", "John Bowman", 3500);
  wallet[2] = new CreditCard("6011 4902 3294 2994", "John Bowman", 5000);

  for (int j=1; j <= 16; j++) {             // make some charges
    wallet[0]->chargeIt(double(j));         // explicitly cast to double
    wallet[1]->chargeIt(2 * j);             // implicitly cast to double
    wallet[2]->chargeIt(double(3 * j));
  }

  cout << "Card payments:\n";
  for (int i=0; i < 3; i++) {               // make more charges
    cout << *wallet[i];
    while (wallet[i]->getBalance() > 100.0) {
      wallet[i]->makePayment(100.0);
      cout << "New balance = " << wallet[i]->getBalance() << "\n";
    }
    cout << "\n";
    delete wallet[i];                       // deallocate storage
  }
}

int main() {                                // main function
  testCard();
  return EXIT_SUCCESS;                       // successful execution
}
```

Code Fragment 1.7: The file TestCard.cpp.

The output of the Test class is sent to the standard output stream. We show this output in Code Fragment 1.8.

Avoiding Multiple Header Expansions

A typical C++ program includes many different header files, which often include other header files. As a result, the same header file may be expanded many times. Such repeated header expansion is wasteful and can result in compilation errors,

```
Card payments:
Number = 5391 0375 9387 5309
Name = John Bowman
Balance = 136
Limit = 2500
New balance = 36

Number = 3485 0399 3395 1954
Name = John Bowman
Balance = 272
Limit = 3500
New balance = 172
New balance = 72

Number = 6011 4902 3294 2994
Name = John Bowman
Balance = 408
Limit = 5000
New balance = 308
New balance = 208
New balance = 108
New balance = 8
```

Code Fragment 1.8: Sample Program Output.

because of repeated definitions. To avoid this repeated expansion, most header files use a combination of preprocessor commands. Let us explain the process, illustrated in Code Fragment 1.5.

Let us start with the second line. The #define statement defines a preprocessor variable CREDIT_CARD_H. This variable's name is typically based on the header file name, and by convention, it is written in all capitals. The name itself is not important as long as different header files use different names. The entire file is enclosed in a preprocessor "if" block starting with #ifndef on top and ending with #endif at the bottom. The "ifndef" is read "if not defined," meaning that the header file contents will be expanded only if the preprocessor variable CREDIT_CARD_H is *not* defined.

Here is how it works. The first time the header file is encountered, the variable CREDIT_CARD_H has not yet been seen, and so the header file is expanded by the preprocessor. In the process of doing this expansion, the second line defines the variable CREDIT_CARD_H. Hence, any attempt to include the header file will find that CREDIT_CARD_H is defined, and so the file will not be expanded.

Throughout this book we will omit these preprocessor commands from our examples, but they should be included in each header file we write.

1.7   Writing a C++ Program

As with any programming language, writing a program in C++ involves three fundamental steps:

1. Design
2. Coding
3. Testing and Debugging.

We briefly discuss each of these steps in this section.

1.7.1   Design

The design step is perhaps the most important in the process of writing a program. In this step, we decide how to divide the workings of our program into classes, we decide how these classes will interact, what data each will store, and what actions each will perform. Indeed, one of the main challenges that beginning C++ programmers face is deciding what classes to define to do the work of their program. While general prescriptions are hard to come by, there are some general rules of thumb that we can apply when determining how to define our classes.

- *Responsibilities*: Divide the work into different *actors*, each with a different responsibility. Try to describe responsibilities using action verbs. These actors will form the classes for the program.
- *Independence*: Define the work for each class to be as independent from other classes as possible. Subdivide responsibilities between classes so that each class has autonomy over some aspect of the program. Give data (as member variables) to the class that has jurisdiction over the actions that require access to this data.
- *Behaviors*: Define the behaviors for each class carefully and precisely, so that the consequences of each action performed by a class will be well understood by other classes with which it interacts. These behaviors will define the member functions that this class performs. The set of behaviors for a class is sometimes referred to as a *protocol*, for we expect the behaviors for a class to hold together as a cohesive unit.

Defining the classes, together with their member variables and member functions, determines the design of a C++ program. A good programmer will naturally develop greater skill in performing these tasks over time, as experience teaches him or her to notice patterns in the requirements of a program that match patterns that he or she has seen before.

In order to accelerate the development of this skill, throughout this text we discuss various ***design patterns*** for designing object-oriented programs. These patterns provide a framework for defining classes and the interactions between these classes.

Many programmers do their initial designs using ***CRC cards***. Component-responsibility-collaborator, or CRC cards are simple index cards that subdivide the work required of a program. The use of such cards allows a programmer to iteratively refine his or her organizational structure so as to ultimately arrive at a coherent set of classes. The main idea behind this tool is to have each card represent a component, which will ultimately become a class in our program. We write the name of each component on the top of its index card. On the left-hand side of its card we begin writing the responsibilities for this component. On the right-hand side, we list the collaborators for this component, that is, the other components that this component will have to interact with to perform its duties. The design process iterates through an action/actor cycle, where we first identify an action (that is, a responsibility), and we then determine an actor (that is, a component) that is best suited to perform that action. The design is complete when we have assigned all actions to actors.

By the way, in using index cards to perform our design, we are of course assuming that each component will have a small set of responsibilities and collaborators. This assumption is no accident, for it helps keep our programs manageable, even when they must necessarily be large.

An alternative to CRC cards is the use of UML (Unified Modeling Language) diagrams to express the design of a program. UML diagrams are a standard visual notation to express object-oriented software designs. Several computer-aided tools are available to build UML diagrams.

1.7.2 Coding

Once we have decided on the classes and their respective responsibilities for our programs, we are ready to begin coding. We create the actual code for the classes in our program by using either an independent text editor (such as emacs, notepad, or vi), or the editor embedded in an ***integrated development environment*** (IDE), such as Microsoft's Visual C++ or Borland's C-Builder.

Once we have completed coding for a program (or file), we then compile this file into working code by invoking a compiler. If our program contains syntax errors, they will be identified, and we will have to go back into our editor to fix the offending lines of code. Once we have eliminated all syntax errors and created the appropriate compiled code, we then run our program.

Readability and Style

Programs should be made easy to read and understand. Good programmers should therefore be mindful of their coding style and develop a style that communicates the important aspects of a program's design for both humans and computers. Much has been written about good coding style. Here are some of the main principles.

- Use meaningful names for identifiers. Try to choose names that can be read aloud and reflect the action, responsibility, or data each identifier is naming. The tradition in most C++ circles is to capitalize the first letter of each word in an identifier, except for the first word in an identifier for a variable or method. So, in this tradition, "Date," "Vector," "DeviceManager" would identify classes, and "isFull()," "insertItem()," "studentName," and "studentHeight" would respectively identify member functions and variables.
- Use named constants and enumerations instead of embedded values. Readability, robustness, and modifiability are enhanced if we include a series of definitions of named constant values in a class definition. These can then be used within this class and others to refer to special values for this class. Our convention will be to fully capitalize such constants, as shown below:

```cpp
const int MIN_CREDITS = 12;      // min. credits in a term
const int MAX_CREDITS = 24;      // max. credits in a term
                                 // enumeration for year
enum Year { FRESHMAN, SOPHOMORE, JUNIOR, SENIOR };
```

- Indent statement blocks. Typically programmers indent each statement block by four spaces; in this book we typically use two spaces to avoid having our code overrun the book's margins.
- Organize each class in a consistent order. In the examples in this book we will usually use the following order:
    1. private member data
    2. private/protected member functions (internal utilities)
    3. public member functions.

  Of course, consistency is no substitute for clarity. We note that some C++ programmers prefer to put private member variables last. We put them first so we can read each class sequentially and understand the data each function is working with.

- Use comments that add meaning to a program and explain ambiguous or confusing constructs. In-line comments are good for quick explanations and do not need to be sentences. Block comments are good for explaining the purpose of a method and complex code sections.

1.7.3 Testing and Debugging

Testing is the process of verifying the correctness of a program, while debugging is the process of tracking the execution of a program and discovering the errors in it. Testing and debugging are often the most time-consuming activity in the development of a program.

Testing

A careful testing plan is an essential part of writing a program. While verifying the correctness of a program over all possible inputs is usually not feasible, we should aim at executing the program on a representative subset of inputs. At the very minimum, we should make sure that every method in the program is tested at least once (method coverage). Even better, each code statement in the program should be executed at least once (statement coverage).

Programs often tend to fail on *special cases* of the input. Such cases need to be carefully identified and tested. For example, when testing a method that sorts an array of integers (that is, arranges them in ascending order), we should consider the following inputs:

- The array has zero length (no elements)
- The array has one element
- All the elements of the array are the same
- The array is already sorted
- The array is reverse sorted.

In addition to special inputs to the program, we should also consider special conditions for the structures used by the program. For example, if we use an array to store data, we should make sure that boundary cases, such as inserting/removing at the beginning or end of the subarray holding data, are properly handled. While it is essential to use hand-crafted test suites, it is also advantageous to run the program on a large collection of randomly generated inputs.

There is a hierarchy among the classes and functions of a program induced by the "caller-callee" relationship. Namely, a function *A* is above a function *B* in the hierarchy if *A* calls *B*. There are two main testing strategies, ***top-down*** and ***bottom-up***, which differ in the order in which functions are tested.

Bottom-up testing proceeds from lower-level functions to higher-level functions. Namely, bottom-level functions, which do not invoke other functions, are tested first, followed by functions that call only bottom-level functions, and so on. This strategy ensures that errors found in a method are not likely to be caused by lower-level functions nested within it.

Top-down testing proceeds from the top to the bottom of the method hierarchy. It is typically used in conjunction with **stubbing**, a boot-strapping technique that replaces a lower-level method with a **stub**, a replacement for the method that simulates the output of the original method. For example, if function A calls function B to get the first line of a file, we can replace B with a stub that returns a fixed string when testing A.

Debugging

The simplest debugging technique consists of using **print statements** (typically using the stream output operator, "<<") to track the values of variables during the execution of the program. A problem with this approach is that the print statements need to be removed or commented out before the program can be executed as part of a "production" software system.

A better approach is to run the program within a **debugger**, which is a specialized environment for controlling and monitoring the execution of a program. The basic functionality provided by a debugger is the insertion of **breakpoints** within the code. When the program is executed within the debugger, it stops at each breakpoint. While the program is stopped, the current value of variables can be inspected. In addition to fixed breakpoints, advanced debuggers allow for specification of **conditional breakpoints**, which are triggered only if a given expression is satisfied.

Many IDEs, such as Visual C++ and C-Builder provide built-in debuggers.

1.8 Exercises

Reinforcement

R-1.1 What are the contents of string s after executing the following statements.

```
string s = "abc";
string t = "cde";
s += s + t[1] + s;
```

R-1.2 Consider the following attempt to allocate a 10-element array of pointers to doubles and initialize the associated double values to 0.0. Rewrite the following (*incorrect*) code to do this correctly. (Hint: Storage for the doubles needs to be allocated.)

```
double* dp[10]
for (int i = 0; i < 10; i++) dp[i] = 0.0;
```

R-1.3 Write a C++ function printArray(A, m, n) that prints an $m \times n$ two-dimensional array A of integers, declared to be "int** A," to the standard output. Each of the m rows should appear on a separate line.

R-1.4 What (if anything) is different about the behavior of the following two functions f() and g() which increment a variable and print its value?

```
void f(int x)
  { std::cout << ++x; }
void g(int& x)
  { std::cout << ++x; }
```

R-1.5 Modify the CreditCard class from Code Fragment 1.6 to check that the price argument passed to function chargeIt() and the payment argument passed to function makePayment() are positive.

R-1.6 Modify the CreditCard class from Code Fragment 1.5 to charge interest on each payment.

R-1.7 Modify the CreditCard class from Code Fragment 1.5 to charge a late fee for any payment that is past its due date.

R-1.8 Modify the CreditCard class from Code Fragment 1.5 to include *modifier functions*, which allow a user to modify internal variables in a CreditCard class in a controlled manner.

R-1.9   Modify the declaration of the first for loop in the Test class in Code Fragment 1.7 so that its charges will eventually cause exactly one of the three credit cards to go over its credit limit. Which credit card is it?

R-1.10   Write a C++ class, AllKinds, that has three member variables of type int, long, and float, respectively. Each class must include a constructor function that initializes each variable to a nonzero value, and each class should include functions for setting the value of each type, getting the value of each type, and computing and returning the sum of each possible combination of types.

R-1.11   Write a short C++ function, isMultiple(), that takes two long values, n and m, and returns true if and only if n is a multiple of m, that is, $n = m \cdot i$ for some integer i.

R-1.12   Write a short C++ function, isTwoPower(), that takes an int i and returns true if and only if i is a power of 2. Do not use multiplication or division, however.

R-1.13   Write a short C++ function that takes an integer n and returns the sum of all the integers smaller than n.

R-1.14   Write a short C++ function that takes an integer n and returns the sum of all the odd integers smaller than n.

R-1.15   Write a short C++ function that takes a positive double value x and returns the number of times we can divide x by 2 before we get a number less than 2.

Creativity

C-1.1   Write a short C++ program that prints its own source code when executed, but does not perform any input or file reading.

C-1.2   Write a C++ function that takes an STL vector of int values and prints all the odd values in the vector.

C-1.3   Write a C++ function that takes an array containing the set of all integers in the range 1 to 52 and shuffles it into random order. Use the built-in function rand(), which returns a pseudo-random integer each time it is called. Your function should output each possible order with equal probability.

C-1.4 Write a short C++ program that outputs all possible strings formed by using each the characters 'a', 'b', 'c', 'd', 'e', and 'f' exactly once.

C-1.5 Write a short C++ program that takes all the lines input to standard input
and writes them to standard output in reverse order. That is, each line is
output in the correct order, but the ordering of the lines is reversed.

C-1.6 Write a short C++ program that takes two arguments of type STL vec-
tor<double>, a and b, and returns the element-by-element product of a
and b. That is, it returns a vector c of the same length such that $c[i] =
a[i] \cdot b[i]$.

C-1.7 Write an efficient C++ function that takes any integer value i and returns
2^i, as a long value. Your function should **not** multiply 2 by itself i times;
there are much faster ways of computing 2^i.

C-1.8 The **greatest common divisor**, or GCD, of two positive integers n and m is
the largest number j, such that n and m are both multiples of j. Euclid proposed a simple algorithm for computing GCD(n,m), where $n > m$, which
is based on a concept known as the Chinese Remainder Theorem. The
main idea of the algorithm is to repeatedly perform modulo computations
of consecutive pairs of the sequence that starts $(n, m, \ldots)$, until reaching
zero. The last nonzero number in this sequence is the GCD of n and m.
For example, for $n = 80,844$ and $m = 25,320$, the sequence is as follows:

$$
\begin{aligned}
80,844 \bmod 25,320 &= 4,884 \\
25,320 \bmod 4,884 &= 900 \\
4,884 \bmod 900 &= 384 \\
900 \bmod 384 &= 132 \\
384 \bmod 132 &= 120 \\
132 \bmod 120 &= 12 \\
120 \bmod 12 &= 0
\end{aligned}
$$

So, GCD of 80,844 and 25,320 is 12. Write a short C++ function to
compute GCD(n,m) for two integers n and m.

Projects

P-1.1 A common punishment for school children is to write out the same sentence multiple times. Write a C++ stand-alone program that will write out the following sentence one hundred times: "I will always use object-oriented design." Your program should number each of the sentences and it should "accidentally" make eight different random-looking typos at various points in the listing, so that it looks like a human typed it all by hand.

P-1.2 Write a C++ program, which given a starting day (Sunday through Saturday) as a string, and a four-digit year, prints a calendar for that year. Each month should contain the name of the month, centered over the dates for that month and a line containing the names of the days of the week, running from Sunday to Saturday. Each week should be printed on a separate line. Be careful to check for a leap year.

P-1.3 The ***birthday paradox*** says that the probability that two people in a room will have the same birthday is more than half as long as n, the number of people in the room, is more than 23. This property is not really a paradox, but many people find it surprising. Design a C++ program that can test this paradox by a series of experiments on randomly generated birthdays, which test this paradox for $n = 5, 10, 15, 20, \ldots, 100$. You should run at least 10 experiments for each value of n and it should output, for each n, the number of experiments for that n, such that two people in that test have the same birthday.

Chapter Notes

For more detailed information about the C++ programming language and the Standard Template Library, we refer the reader to books by Stroustrup [93], Lippmann and Lajoie [67], Musser and Saini [83], and Horstmann [49]. Lippmann also wrote a short introduction to C++ [66]. For more advanced information of how to use C++'s features in the most effective manner, consult the books by Meyers [79, 78]. For an introduction to C++ assuming a background of C see the book by Pohl [86]. For an explanation of the differences between C++ and Java see the book by Budd [19].

Chapter

2

Object-Oriented Design

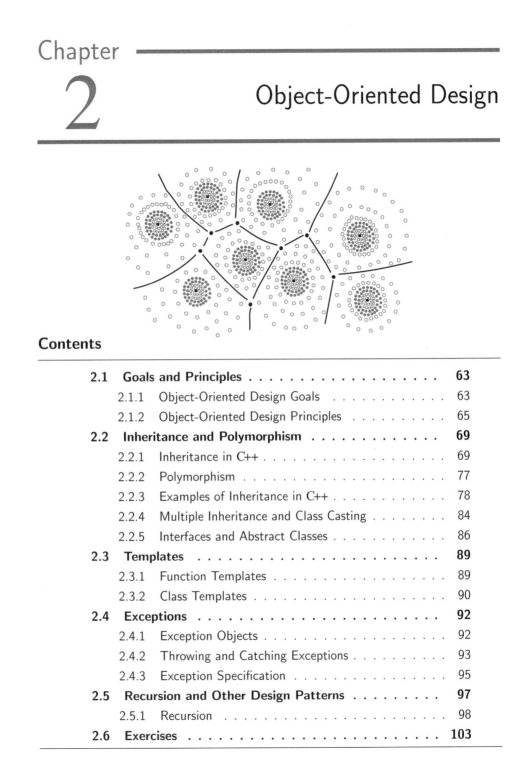

Contents

In the early days of the information age, computers were expensive and large, but had slow processors and small memories. It should come as no surprise then, that early computers had a limited number of applications, most of which dealt with numeric processing, not information management. Modern computers, on the other hand, are continually becoming cheaper and smaller, while also coming equipped with faster processors and larger memories. Consequently, modern computers are used for myriad different applications. Indeed, many modern toys, such as singing dolls and talking action figures, have embedded processors with more speed and memory than the first digital computer, ENIAC, which was the size of a large room. In addition, computing researchers of a couple decades ago used the term "supercomputers" to refer to computing devices that were slower and had smaller memories than today's personal computers. Thus, modern computers are significantly smaller, cheaper, faster, and higher capacity than their predecessors. Yet these advances bring higher expectations for software.

Creating software has become a complex enterprise. Designing and implementing a new software application typically involves the interaction of pieces of software written by many different people in several different organizations. These people may not know each other and may not even be willing to share the source code for their respective software pieces. In addition, over time there is a natural tendency to want to upgrade old software, adding new features for applications in new environments. The challenge for software engineers is to create software that is itself complex, but nevertheless appears conceptually simple, so as to easily integrate with other software and allow for future modifications.

Motivated by the need for software to evolve and have many authors, a driving force in research in software engineering and programming languages has been the development of methodologies that can produce designs that are conceptually *simple* enough to be understandable while being *powerful* enough to solve hard problems efficiently. Achieving such a balance is not easy, but a methodology that is showing considerable promise is *object-oriented design*.

As the name implies, the main "actors" in object-oriented design are *objects*. An object in C++ comes from a *class*, which is a specification of the data *members* that the object contains, as well as the *member functions* (also called *methods* or operations) that the object can execute. Each class presents to the outside world a concise and consistent view of the objects that are instances of this class, without going into too much unnecessary detail or giving others access to the inner workings of the objects. This view of computing is intended to fulfill several goals and incorporate several design principles, which we discuss in this chapter, as well as the mechanisms in C++ that help us implement these principles.

2.1 Goals and Principles

The fundamental goal of dealing with the complexity of building modern software naturally gives rise to several subgoals. These subgoals are directed at the production of quality software, including good implementations of data structures and algorithms.

2.1.1 Object-Oriented Design Goals

When discussing important design goals for software, researchers and software engineers typically agree that software implementations should achieve ***robustness***, ***adaptability***, and ***reusability***. (See Figure 2.1.) We discuss each of these important issues in this section.

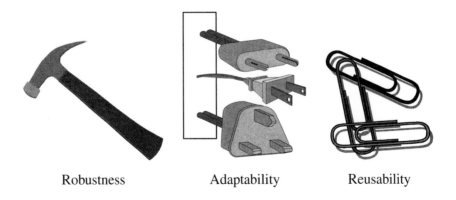

Robustness   Adaptability   Reusability

Figure 2.1: Goals of object-oriented design.

Robustness

Every good programmer wants to produce software that is correct, which means that a program produces the right output for all the anticipated inputs in the program's application. In addition, we want software to be ***robust***, that is, capable of handling unexpected inputs that are not explicitly defined for its application. For example, if a program is expecting a positive integer (say, representing the price of an item) and instead is given a negative integer, then the program should be able to recover gracefully from this error. A program that does not gracefully handle such unexpected-input errors can be embarrassing for the programmer.

More importantly, in ***life-critical applications***, where a software error can lead to injury or loss of life, software that is not robust is deadly. This importance was driven home in the late 1980s in accidents involving Therac-25, a radiation-therapy machine, which severely overdosed six patients between 1985 and 1987, some of whom died from complications resulting from their radiation overdoses. All six accidents were traced to software errors, with one of the most troubling being a user-interface error involving unexpected inputs (a fast-typing radiologist could backspace over a radiation dosage on the screen without the previous characters actually being deleted from the input).

The goal of robustness goes beyond the need to handle unexpected inputs, however. Software should produce correct solutions, even given the well-known limitations of computers. For example, if a user wishes to store more elements in a data structure than originally expected, then the software should expand the capacity of this structure to handle more elements. This philosophy of robustness is present, for example, in the vector class in C++'s Standard Template Library, which defines an expandable array. In addition, if an application calls for numerical computations, those numbers should be represented fully and should not overflow or underflow. Indeed, software should achieve ***correctness*** for its full range of possible inputs, including boundary cases, such as when an integer value is 0 or 1 or the maximum or minimum possible values. Robustness and correctness do not come automatically, however, they must be designed in from the start.

Adaptability

Modern software projects, such as word processors, Web browsers, and Internet search engines, typically involve large programs that are expected to last for many years. Therefore, software needs to evolve over time in response to changing conditions in its environment. These changes can be expected, such as the need to adapt to an increase in CPU or network speed, or they can be unexpected, such as the need to add new functionality because of new market demands. Software should also be able to adapt to unexpected events that, in hindsight, really should have been expected, such as the coming of a new millennium and its effects on date calculations (the "year 2000" problem). Thus, another important goal of quality software is that it achieve ***adaptability*** (also called ***evolvability***). Related to this concept is ***portability***, which is the ability of software to run with minimal change on different hardware and operating system platforms. The fact that different implementations of C++ are allowed to implement some language features differently, such as the number of bits in a long integer, make portability difficult to achieve.

Reusability

Going hand in hand with adaptability is the desire that software be reusable, that is, code should be usable as a component of different systems in various applications. Developing quality software can be an expensive enterprise, and its cost can be offset somewhat if the software is designed in a way that makes it easily reusable in future applications. Such reuse should be done with care, however. One of the major sources of software errors in the Therac-25 arose from inappropriate reuse of software from the Therac-20 (which was not designed for the hardware platform used with the Therac-25). So, for software to be truly reusable, we must be clear about what it does and does not do. Given this clarity, however, software reuse can be a significant cost-saving and time-saving technique.

2.1.2 Object-Oriented Design Principles

Chief among the principles of the object-oriented approach, which are intended to facilitate the goals outlined above, are the following (see Figure 2.2):

- Abstraction
- Encapsulation
- Modularity.

We briefly discuss these principles in this section.

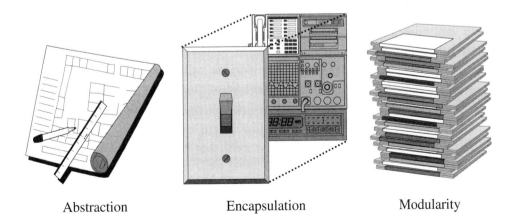

Abstraction   Encapsulation   Modularity

Figure 2.2: Principles of object-oriented design.

Abstraction

The notion of ***abstraction*** is to distill a complicated system down to its most fundamental parts and describe these parts in a simple, precise language. Typically, describing the parts of a system involves naming them and describing their functionality. For example, a typical text-editor graphical user interface (GUI) provides an abstraction of an ***edit menu*** that offers several text-editing operations, including cutting and pasting portions of text or other graphical objects. Without going into details about the ways a GUI represents and displays text and graphical objects, the concepts of cutting and pasting are simple and precise. The ***cut*** operation deletes the selected text and graphics and places them into an external storage buffer. The ***paste*** operation inserts the contents of the external storage buffer at a specific location in the text. Thus, the abstract functionality of an edit menu and its cutting and pasting operations is specified in a language precise enough to be clear, but simple enough to "abstract away" unnecessary details. This combination of clarity and simplicity benefits robustness, since it leads to understandable and correct implementations.

Applying this paradigm to the design of data structures gives rise to ***abstract data types*** (ADTs). An ADT is a mathematical model of a data structure that specifies the type of data stored, the operations supported on them, and the types of parameters of the operations. An ADT specifies an ***interface***, which means that it specifies ***what*** each operation does, but not ***how*** it does it.

An ADT is realized by a concrete data structure, which is modeled in C++ by a ***class***. A class defines the data being stored and the operations supported by the objects that are instances of the class. Also, unlike interfaces, classes specify ***how*** the operations are performed. A C++ class is said to ***implement an interface*** if its functions give life to all of those of the interface.

Encapsulation

Another important principle of object-oriented design is ***encapsulation***, which is also known as ***information hiding***. This principle states that different components of a software system should not reveal the internal details of their respective implementations. Consider again our example of an edit menu with cutting and pasting functionality in a text-editor graphical user interface (GUI). One of the main reasons an edit menu is so useful is that we can completely understand how to use it without understanding exactly how it is implemented. For example, we do not need to know how the menu is drawn, how selected text to be cut or pasted is represented, how selected portions of text are stored in an external buffer, or how various graphical objects, such as graphs, images, or drawings, are identified, stored, and copied in and out of the external buffer. Indeed, the code associated with the edit menu should not depend on all of these details to work correctly. Instead, the edit menu should provide an interface that is sufficiently specified for other software components to use its methods effectively, while also requiring well-defined interfaces from other software components that it needs. In general terms, the principle of encapsulation states that all the different components of a large software system should operate on a strictly need-to-know basis.

One of the main advantages of encapsulation is that it gives the programmer freedom in implementing the details of a system. The only constraint on the programmer is to maintain the abstract interface that outsiders see. For example, the programmer of the edit menu code in a text-editor GUI might at first implement the cut and paste operations by copying actual screen images in and out of an external buffer. Later, he or she may be dissatisfied with this implementation, since it does not allow compact storage of the selection, and it does not distinguish text and graphic objects. If the programmer has designed the cut-and-paste interface with encapsulation in mind, switching the underlying implementation to one that stores text as text and graphic objects in an appropriate compact format should not cause any problems to functions that need to interface with this GUI. Thus, encapsulation yields adaptability, for it allows the implementation details of parts of a program to change without adversely affecting other parts.

Modularity

In addition to abstraction and encapsulation, a principle fundamental to object-oriented design is *modularity*. Modern software systems typically consist of several different components that must interact correctly in order for the entire system to work properly. Keeping these interactions straight requires that these different components be well organized. In the object-oriented approach, this structure centers around the concept of modularity. Modularity refers to an organizing structure in which different components of a software system are divided into separate functional units. For example, a house or apartment can be viewed as consisting of several interacting units: electrical, heating and cooling, plumbing, and structural. Rather than viewing these systems as one giant jumble of wires, vents, pipes, and boards, the organized architect designing a house or apartment will view them as separate modules that interact in well-defined ways. In so doing, he or she is using modularity to bring a clarity of thought that provides a natural way of organizing functions into distinct manageable units. In like manner, using modularity in a software system can also provide a powerful organizing framework that brings clarity to an implementation.

The structure imposed by modularity helps to enable software reusability. If software modules are written in an abstract way to solve general problems, then modules can be reused when instances of these same general problems may arise in other contexts.

For example, the structural definition of a wall is the same from house to house, typically being defined in terms of 2- by 4-inch studs, spaced a certain distance apart, etc. Thus, an organized architect can reuse his or her wall definitions from one house to another. In reusing such a definition, some parts may require redefinition, for example, a wall in a commercial building may be similar to that of a house, but the electrical system might be different. Thus, our architect may wish to organize the various structural components, such as electrical and structural, in a *hierarchical* fashion, which groups similar abstract definitions together in a level-by-level manner that goes from specific to more general as one traverses up the hierarchy.

A common use of such hierarchies is in an organizational chart, where each link going up can be read as "is a," as in "a ranch is a house is a building." (See Figure 2.3.) Likewise, this kind of hierarchy is useful in software design, for it groups together common functionality at the most general level, and views specialized behavior as an extension of the general one.

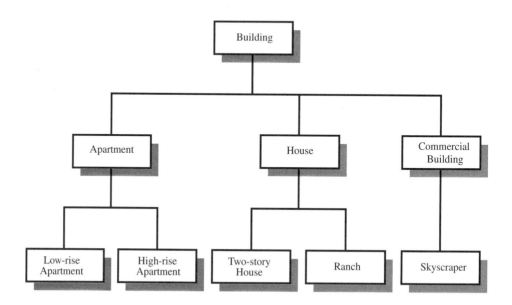

Figure 2.3: An example of an "is a" hierarchy involving architectural buildings.

2.2   Inheritance and Polymorphism

To take advantage of hierarchical relationships common in software projects, the object-oriented design approach provides ways of reusing code in a software system. Reusing software saves programming time and reduces errors. Indeed, once a software component is completely debugged, we are better off reusing it than copying it and slightly modifying it at several different locations, for all this copying and modifying can introduce new errors into a program.

2.2.1   Inheritance in C++

The object-oriented paradigm provides a modular and hierarchical organizing structure for reusing code, through a technique called ***inheritance***. This technique allows the design of generic classes that can be specialized to more particular classes, with the specialized classes reusing the code from the generic class. For example, suppose that we are designing a set of classes to represent people at a university. We might have a generic class Person, which defines elements common to all people. We could then define specialized classes such as Student, Administrator, and Instructor, each of which provides specific information about a particular type of person.

A generic class is also known as a ***base class***, ***parent class***, or ***superclass***. It defines "generic" members that apply in a multitude of situations. Any class that ***specializes*** or ***extends*** a base class need not give new implementations for the general functions, for it ***inherits*** them. It should only define those functions that are specialized for this particular class. Such a class is called a ***derived class***, ***child class***, or ***subclass***.

Let us consider an example to illustrate these concepts. Suppose that we are writing a program to deal with people at a university. Below we show a partial implementation of a generic class for a Person. We use "// ..." to indicate code that is irrelevant to the example and so has been omitted.

```
class Person {                        // Person (base class)
private:
    string      name;                 // name
    string      ssn;                  // social security number
public:
    // ...
    void print();                     // print information
    string getName();                 // retrieve name
};
```

Suppose we next wish to define a student object. We can derive our class Student from class Person, as shown below.

```
class Student : public Person {          // Student (derived from Person)
private:
   string        major;                  // major subject
   int           gradYear;               // graduation year
public:
   // ...
   void print();                         // print information
   void changeMajor(string newMajor);    // change major
};
```

The "public Person" phrase indicates that the Student is derived from the Person class. (The keyword "public" specifies *public inheritance*. We will discuss other types of inheritance later.) When we derive classes in this way, we think of there being an implied "is a" relationship between them. In this case, a Student "is a" Person. In particular, a Student object inherits all the member data and member functions of class Person in addition to providing its own members. The relationship between these two classes is shown graphically in a *class inheritance diagram* in Figure 2.4.

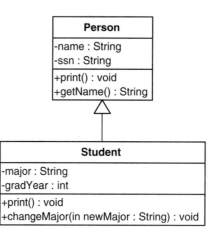

Figure 2.4: A class inheritance diagram, showing a base class Person and derived class Student. Entries tagged with "–" are private and entries tagged with "+" are public. Each block of the diagram consists of three parts: the class name, the class member variables, and the class member functions. The type (or return type) of each member is indicated after the colon (":"). The arrow indicates that Student is derived from Person.

Member Functions

An object of type Person can access the public members of Person. An object of type Student can access the public members of both classes. If a Student object invokes the shared print() function, it will use its own version by default. We use the ***class scope operator*** (::) to specify which class's function is used, as in Person::print() and Student::print().

```
Person person(...);                 // declare a Person (details omitted)
Student student(...);               // declare a Student (details omitted)

cout << student.getName() << '\n'; // invokes Person::getName()
person.print();                     // invokes Person::print()
student.print();                    // invokes Student::print()
person.changeMajor("Physics");      // ERROR!
student.changeMajor("English");     // okay
```

C++ programmers often find it useful for a derived class to explicitly invoke a member function of a base class. For example, in the process of printing information for a student, it is natural to first print the information of the Person base class, and then print information particular to the student. Performing this task is done using the class scope operator.

```
void Person::print() {              // definition of Person print
   cout << "Name "   << name    << '\n';
   cout << "SSN "    << ssn     << '\n';
}

void Student::print() {             // definition of Student print
   Person::print();                 // first print Person information
   cout << "Major "  << major    << '\n';
   cout << "Year "   << gradYear << '\n';
}
```

Without the "Person::" specifier used above, the Student::print() function would call itself recursively (which is a concept we discuss in Section 2.5.1).

Protected Members

Even though class Student is inherited from class Person, member functions of Student do not have access to private members of Person. For example, it would not be possible to add the following member function to Student.

```
void Student::printName() {
    cout << name << '\n';          // ERROR! name is private to Person
}
```

Special access privileges for derived classes can be provided by declaring members to be "protected." A protected member is "public" to all classes derived from this one, but "private" to all other functions. From a syntactic perspective, the keyword protected behaves in the same way as the keyword private and public. In the class example above, had we declared name to be protected rather than private, the above function printName() would work fine.

Although C++ makes no requirements on the order in which the various sections of a class appear, there are two common ways of doing it. The first is to declare public members first and private members last. This way is probably the more popular method, because it emphasizes the elements that are important to a user of the class. The other way is to present private members first and public members last. This tends to be easier to read for an implementor, because elements are introduced before they are used. Since our focus in this book will largely be on how to implement data structures, we will prefer this latter approach, as shown below.

```
class ⟨class_name⟩ {

private:
        // ... private members

protected:
        // ... protected members

public:
        // ... public members

};
```

As always, clarity is a more important consideration than adherence to an arbitrary standard, and so we will deviate from this model at times.

Illustrating Class Protection

Consider for example, three classes: a base class Base, a derived class Derived, and an unrelated class Unrelated. The base class defines three integer members, one of each access type.

```
class Base {
  private:
    int priv;

  protected:
    int prot;

  public:
    int publ;
};

class Derived: public Base {

  void someMemberFunction() {
    cout << priv;              // ERROR: private member
    cout << prot;              // okay
    cout << publ;              // okay
  }
};

class Unrelated {
  Base X;

  void anotherMemberFunction() {
    cout << X.priv;            // ERROR: private member
    cout << X.prot;            // ERROR: protected member
    cout << X.publ;            // okay
  }
};
```

When designing a class, we should give careful thought to the access privileges we give each member variable or function. Member variables are almost always declared to be private or at least protected, since they determine the details of the class's implementation. A user of the class can access only the public class members, which consist of the principal member functions for accessing and manipulating class objects. Finally, protected members are commonly used for utility functions, which may be useful to derived classes. We will see many examples of these three access types in the examples appearing in later chapters.

Constructors and Destructors

We saw in Section 1.5.2, that when a class object is created, the class's constructor is called. When a derived class is constructed, it is the responsibility of this class's constructor to take care that the appropriate constructor is called for its base class. Class hierarchies in C++ are constructed bottom-up: base class first, then its members, then the derived class itself. For this reason, the constructor for a base class needs to be called in the initializer list (see Section 1.5.2) of the derived class. The example below shows how constructors might be implemented for the Person and Student classes.

```
Person::Person(const string &nm, const string &ss)
   : name(nm),                        // initialize name
     ssn(ss) { }                      // initialize ssn

Student::Student(const string &nm, const string &ss,
                 const string &maj, int year)
   : Person(nm, ss),                  // initialize Person members
     major(maj),                      // initialize member
     gradYear(year) { }               // initialize graduation year
```

Only the Person(nm,ss) call has to be in the initializer list. The other initializations could be placed in the constructor function body ({...}), but putting class initializations in the initialization list is generally more efficient. Suppose that we create a new student object.

```
Student* s = new Student("John Smith","123-45-6789","Physics",2010);
```

Note that the constructor for the Student class first makes a function call to Person("John Smith", "123-45-6789") to initialize the Person base class, and then it initializes the major to "Physics" and the year to 2010.

Classes are destroyed in the opposite order from their construction. For example, suppose that we write destructors for these two classes. (Such a destructor is not really needed in this case, because neither class allocates storage or other resources.)

```
Person::~Person()                     // Person destructor
   { ... }
Student::~Student()                   // Student destructor
   { ... }
```

If we were to destroy our student object, the Student destructor would be called first, followed by the Person destructor. Unlike constructors, the Student destructor does not need to (and in fact cannot) call the Person destructor.

```
delete s;                             // calls ~Student() then ~Person()
```

Static Binding

When a class is derived from a base class, as with Student and Person, the derived class becomes a ***subtype*** of the base class, which means that we can use the derived class wherever the base class is acceptable. For example, suppose that we create an array of pointers to university people.

```
Person* pp[100];              // array of 100 Person pointers
pp[0] = new Person(...);      // add a Person (details omitted)
pp[1] = new Student(...);     // add a Student (details omitted)
```

Since getName() is common to both classes, it can be invoked on either elements of the array. A more interesting issue arises if we attempt to invoke print(). Since pp[1] holds the address of a Student object, we might think that the function Student::print() would be called. Surprisingly, the function Person::print() is called in both cases, in spite of the apparent difference in the two objects. Furthermore, pp[i] is not even allowed to access Student member functions.

```
cout << pp[1]->getName() << '\n'; // okay
pp[0]->print();                   // calls Person::print()
pp[1]->print();                   // also calls Person::print() (!)
pp[1]->changeMajor("English");    // ERROR!
```

The reason for apparently anomalous behavior is called ***static binding***—when determining which member function to call, C++ default action is to consider an object's declared type, not its actual contents. Since pp[1] is declared to be a pointer to a Person, the members for that class are used. Nonetheless, C++ provides a way to achieve the desired dynamic effect, using the technique we describe next.

Dynamic Binding and Virtual Functions

As we saw above, C++ uses ***static binding*** by default to determine which member function to call for a derived class. Alternatively, in ***dynamic binding***, an object's contents determine which member function is called. To specify that a member function should use dynamic binding, the keyword "virtual" is added to the function's declaration. Let us redefine our Person and Student, but this time we will declare the print() function to be virtual.

```
class Person {                       // Person (base class)
  virtual void print() { ... }       // print (details omitted)
  // ...
};
class Student : public Person {      // Student (derived from Person)
  virtual void print() { ... }       // print (details omitted)
  // ...
};
```

Let us consider the effect of this change on our array example, thereby illustrating the usefulness of dynamic binding.

```
Person* pp[100];                    // array of 100 Person pointers
pp[0] = new Person(...);            // add a Person (details omitted)
pp[1] = new Student(...);           // add a Student (details omitted)
pp[0]->print();                     // calls Person::print()
pp[1]->print();                     // calls Student::print()
```

In this case pp[1] contains a pointer to an object of type Student, and by the power of dynamic binding with virtual functions, the function Student::print() will be called. The decision as to which function to call is made at run-time, hence the name *dynamic binding*.

Virtual Destructors

There is no such thing as a virtual constructor. Such a concept does not make any sense. Virtual destructors, however, are very important. In our array example, since we store objects of both types Person and Student in the array, it is important that the appropriate destructor be called for each object. However, if the destructor is nonvirtual, then only the Person destructor will be called in each case. In our example, this choice is not a problem. But if the Student class had allocated memory dynamically, the fact that the wrong destructor is called would result in memory leaks (see Section 1.5.3).

When writing a base class, we cannot know, in general, whether a derived class may need to implement a destructor. So, to be safe, whenever defining any virtual functions, we strongly recommend that a virtual destructor be defined as well. This destructor may do nothing at all, and that is fine. It is provided just in case derived classes need to define their own destructors. This principle is encapsulated in the following rule of thumb, which is important enough that many compilers will issue a warning message if it is ignored.

Remember

> If a class defines any virtual functions, it should define a *virtual destructor*, even if it is empty.

Dynamic binding is a powerful technique, since it allows us to create an object, such as the array pp above, whose behavior varies depending on its contents. This technique is fundamental to the concept of polymorphism, which we discuss in the next section.

2.2.2   Polymorphism

Literally, "polymorphism" means "many forms." In the context of object-oriented design, it refers to the ability of a variable to take different types. Polymorphism is typically applied in C++ using pointer variables. In particular, a variable p declared to be a pointer to some class S implies that p can point to any object belonging to any derived class T of S.

Now consider what happens if both of these classes define a virtual member function a(), and let us consider which of these functions is called when we invoke p->a(). Since dynamic binding is used, if p points to an object of type T, then it will invoke T::a(). In this case, T is said to *override* function a() from S. Alternatively, if p points to an object of type S, it will invoke S::a().

Polymorphism such as this is useful because the caller of p->a() does not have to know whether the pointer p refers to an instance of T or S in order to get the a() function to execute correctly. A pointer variable p that points to a class object that has at least one virtual function is said to be *polymorphic*. That is, p can take many forms, depending on the specific class of the object it is referring to. This kind of functionality allows a specialized class T to extend a class S, inherit the "generic" functions from class S, and redefine other functions from class S to account for specific properties of objects of class T.

Inheritance, polymorphism, and function overloading support reusable software. We can define classes that inherit generic member variables and functions and can then define new, more specific variables and functions that deal with special aspects of objects of the new class. For example, suppose that we defined a generic class Person and then derived three classes Student, Administrator, and Instructor. We could store pointers to all these objects in a list of type Person*. When we invoke a virtual member function, such as print(), to any element of the list, it will call the function appropriate to the individual element's type.

Specialization

There are two primary ways of using inheritance, one of which is *specialization*. In using specialization, we are specializing a general class to a particular derived class. Such derived classes typically possess an "is a" relationship to their base class. The derived classes inherit all the members of the base class. For each inherited function, if that function operates correctly, independent of whether it is operating for a specialization, no additional work is needed. If, on the other hand, a general function of the base class would not work correctly on the derived class, then we should override the function to have the correct functionality for the derived class.

For example, we could have a general class, Dog, which has a function drink() and a function sniff(). Specializing this class to a Bloodhound class would probably not require that we override the drink() function, as all dogs drink pretty much the same way. But it could require that we override the sniff() function, as a Bloodhound has a much more sensitive sense of smell than a "generic" dog. In this way, the Bloodhound class specializes the functions of its base class, Dog.

Extension

Another way of using inheritance is **extension**. In using extension, we reuse the code written for functions of the base class, but we then add new functions that are not present in the base class, so as to extend its functionality. For example, returning to our Dog class, we might wish to create a derived class, BorderCollie, which inherits all the generic functions of the Dog class, but then adds a new function, herd(), since Border Collies have a herding instinct that is not present in generic dogs, thereby extending the functionality of a generic dog.

2.2.3   Examples of Inheritance in C++

To make some of the above notions about inheritance and polymorphism more concrete, let us consider a simple example in C++. We consider an example of several classes that print numeric progressions. A **numeric progression** is a sequence of numbers, where the value of each number depends on one or more of the previous values. For example, an **arithmetic progression** determines a next number by addition of a fixed increment. A **geometric progression** determines a next number by multiplication by a fixed base value. In any case, a progression requires a way of defining its first value and it needs a way of identifying the current value as well.

Arithmetic progression (increment 1)	$0, 1, 2, 3, 4, 5, \ldots$
Arithmetic progression (increment 3)	$0, 3, 6, 9, 12, \ldots$
Geometric progression (base 2)	$1, 2, 4, 8, 16, 32, \ldots$
Geometric progression (base 3)	$1, 3, 9, 27, 81, \ldots$

We begin by defining a class, Progression, shown in Code Fragment 2.1, which defines the "generic" members and functions of a numeric progression. Specifically, it defines the following two long-integer variable members:

- first: first value of the progression
- cur: current value of the progression.

We also define the following three member functions of Progressions.

firstValue(): Reset the progression to the first value, and return it.
Input: None; *Output:* Long Integer.

nextValue(): Step the progression to the next value and return it.
Input: None; *Output:* Long Integer.

printProgression(*n*): Reset the progression, and print the first *n* values of the progression.
Input: Integer; *Output:* None.

We say that the function printProgression() has no output in the sense that it does not return any value, whereas the functions firstValue() and nextValue() both return long-integer values. That is, firstValue() and nextValue() are functions, and printProgression() is a procedure. There is also a constructor, Progression(), which initializes all the member variables whenever such an object is created.

```
class Progression {
protected:                              // member data
    long first;                         // first value of the progression
    long cur;                           // current value of the progression

    virtual long firstValue() {         // reset and return first value
        cur = first;
        return cur;
    }
    virtual long nextValue()            // advance and return next value
        { return ++cur; }
public:
    Progression(long f = 0)             // constructor given first value
        { cur = first = f; }
    void printProgression(int n);       // print the first n values
    virtual ~Progression() { }          // virtual destructor
};

void Progression::printProgression(int n) {
    std::cout << firstValue();          // print the first value
    for (int i = 2; i <= n; i++) {
        std::cout << ' ' << nextValue(); // print values 2 through n
    }
    std::cout << '\n';                  // print end of line
}
```

Code Fragment 2.1: Generic numeric progression class.

Arithmetic and Geometric Progression Classes

Let us consider a class ArithProgression, shown in Code Fragment 2.2, where we add a fixed increment, inc, to each value to determine the next.

```
class ArithProgression : public Progression {
protected:                                    // member data
  long inc;                                   // increment amount
  virtual long nextValue() {                  // advance by adding increment
    cur += inc;
    return cur;
  }
public:
  ArithProgression(long i = 1)                // constructor (default increment = 1)
    : Progression() { inc = i; }              // initializes base class and inc
};
```
Code Fragment 2.2: Class for arithmetic progressions.

Polymorphism is at work here. When a Progression reference is pointing to an ArithProgression object, it will use the ArithProgression functions firstValue() and nextValue(). Even though the function printProgression() is not virtual, it makes use of polymorphism. Its calls to the firstValue() and nextValue() functions are implicitly for the "current" object, which will be of the ArithProgression class. In the definition of the ArithProgression class, we have added a constructor, which uses an initializer list to initialize the base class, Progression.

Let us next define GeomProgression, shown in Code Fragment 2.3, which implements a geometric progression, where we start with 1 (instead of 0) and multiply each value by a base value to determine the next value. As with the ArithProgression class, this new class inherits the member variables first and cur, and the member functions firstValue() and printProgression() from Progression. Observe that in our constructor, we invoked the Progression constructor with a value of 1.

```
class GeomProgression : public Progression {
protected:                                    // member data
  long base;                                  // base amount
  virtual long nextValue() {                  // advance by multiplying
    cur *= base;
    return cur;
  }
public:
  GeomProgression(long b = 2)                 // constructor (default base = 2)
    : Progression(1)                          // progression starts at 1
    { base = b; }
};
```
Code Fragment 2.3: Class for geometric progressions.

A Fibonacci Progression Class

As a further example, we define a FibonacciProgression class that represents another kind of progression, the ***Fibonacci progression***, where the next value is defined as the sum of the current and previous values. We show the FibonacciProgression class in Code Fragment 2.4. Recall that each element of a Fibonacci series is the sum of the previous two elements:

$$\text{Fibonacci progression (first} = 0, \text{second} = 1\text{):} \quad 0, 1, 1, 2, 3, 5, 8, \ldots$$

In addition to the current value cur, we also store the value of the previous element, denoted prev, in the Progression base class. The constructor is given the first two elements of the sequence. The variable first is inherited from the base class. We add a member variable second, to store this second element. The default values for the first and second elements are 0 and 1, respectively. The initialization process is a bit tricky, because we need to create a "fictitious" element that precedes the first element. Note that setting this element to the value *second* − *first* achieves the desired result.

```
class FibonacciProgression : public Progression {
protected:                           // member data
  long second;                       // second value
  long prev;                         // previous value

  virtual long firstValue() {        // reset and return first value
    cur = first;
    prev = second − first;           // create fictitious previous
    return cur;
  }
  virtual long nextValue() {         // advance by (current + previous)
    long temp = prev;
    prev = cur;
    cur += temp;
    return cur;
  }
public:
                                     // constructor from first and second
  FibonacciProgression(long f = 0, long s = 1)
    : Progression(f) {               // initialize base with first
    second = s;
    prev = second − first;           // create fictitious previous
  }
};
```

Code Fragment 2.4: Class for the Fibonacci progression.

Combining the Progression Classes

In order to visualize how the three different progression classes are derived from
the generic Progression class, we give their inheritance diagram in Figure 2.5.

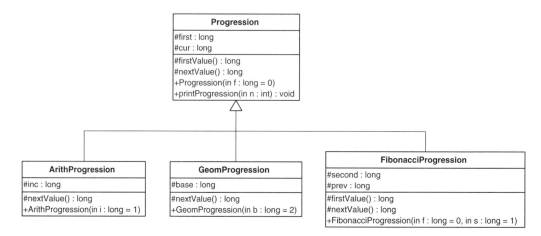

Figure 2.5: Inheritance diagram for class Progression and its derived classes. We
tag entries with "#" that are protected; entries tagged with "+" are public.

To complete our example, we define the main function shown in Code Fragment 2.5, which performs a simple test of each of the three classes. In this class,
variable prog is a polymorphic array of pointers to class Progression. Since each of
its members points to an object of class ArithProgression, GeomProgression, or FibonacciProgression, the functions appropriate to the given progression are invoked
in each case. The output is shown in Code Fragment 2.6. Notice that this program
has a (unimportant) memory leak because we never deleted the allocated object.

The example presented in this section provides a simple illustration of inheritance and polymorphism in C++. The Progression class, its derived classes, and the
tester program have a number of shortcomings, however, which might not be immediately apparent. One problem is that the geometric and Fibonacci progressions
grow quickly, and there is no provision for handling the inevitable overflow of the
long integers involved. For example, since $3^{40} > 2^{63}$, a geometric progression with
base $b = 3$ will overflow a 64-bit long integer after 40 iterations. Likewise, the
94th Fibonacci number is greater than 2^{63}; hence, the Fibonacci progression will
overflow a 64-bit long integer after 94 iterations. Another problem is that we may
not allow arbitrary starting values for a Fibonacci progression. For example, do we
allow a Fibonacci progression starting with 0 and -1? Dealing with input errors or
error conditions that occur during the running of a C++ program requires that we
have some mechanism for handling them. We discuss this topic later in Section 2.4.

```
/** Test program for the progression classes */
int main() {
  Progression* prog[6];
                                        // test ArithProgression
  cout << "Arithmetic progression with default increment:\n";
  prog[0] = new ArithProgression();
  prog[0]->printProgression(10);
  cout << "Arithmetic progression with increment 5:\n";
  prog[1] = new ArithProgression(5);
  prog[1]->printProgression(10);
                                        // test GeomProgression
  cout << "Geometric progression with default base:\n";
  prog[2] = new GeomProgression();
  prog[2]->printProgression(10);
  cout << "Geometric progression with base 3:\n";
  prog[3] = new GeomProgression(3);
  prog[3]->printProgression(10);
                                        // test FibonacciProgression
  cout << "Fibonacci progression with default start values:\n";
  prog[4] = new FibonacciProgression();
  prog[4]->printProgression(10);
  cout << "Fibonacci progression with start values 4 and 6:\n";
  prog[5] = new FibonacciProgression(4, 6);
  prog[5]->printProgression(10);
  return EXIT_SUCCESS;                  // successful execution
}
```

Code Fragment 2.5: Program for testing the progression classes.

```
Arithmetic progression with default increment:
0 1 2 3 4 5 6 7 8 9
Arithmetic progression with increment 5:
0 5 10 15 20 25 30 35 40 45
Geometric progression with default base:
1 2 4 8 16 32 64 128 256 512
Geometric progression with base 3:
1 3 9 27 81 243 729 2187 6561 19683
Fibonacci progression with default start values:
0 1 1 2 3 5 8 13 21 34
Fibonacci progression with start values 4 and 6:
4 6 10 16 26 42 68 110 178 288
```

Code Fragment 2.6: Output of TestProgression program from Code Fragment 2.5.

2.2.4   Multiple Inheritance and Class Casting

In the examples we have shown so far, a subclass has been derived from a single base class and we didn't have to deal with the problem of viewing an object of a specific declared class as also being of an inherited type. We discuss some related, more-advanced C++ programming issues in this section.

Multiple and Restricted Inheritance

In C++, we are allowed to derive a class from a number of base classes, that is, C++ allows *multiple inheritance*. Although multiple inheritance can be useful, especially in defining interfaces, it introduces a number of complexities. For example, if both base classes provide a member variable with the same name or a member function with the same declaration, the derived class must specify from which base class the member should be used (which is complicated). For this reason, we will use single inheritance almost exclusively.

We have been using public inheritance in our previous examples, indicated by the keyword public in specifying the base class. Remember that private base class members are not accessible in a derived class. Protected and public members of the base class become protected and public members of the derived class, respectively. C++ supports two other types of inheritance. These different types of inheritance diminish the access rights for base class members. In *protected inheritance*, fields declared to be public in the base class become protected in the child class. In *private inheritance*, fields declared to be public and protected in the base class become private in the derived class. An example is shown below.

```
class Base {                                  // base class
protected: int foo;
public:     int bar;
};
class Derive1 : public Base {                 // public inheritance
  //  foo is protected and bar is public
};
class Derive2 : protected Base {              // protected inheritance
  //  both foo and bar are protected
};
class Derive3 : private Base {                // public inheritance
  //  both foo and bar are private
};
```

Protected and private inheritance are not used as often as public inheritance. We will only use public inheritance in this book.

Casting in an Inheritance Hierarchy

An object variable can be viewed as being of various types, but it can be declared as only one type. Thus, a variable's declared type determines how it is used, and even determines how certain methods will act on it. Enforcing that all variables be typed and that operations declare the types they expect is called ***strong typing***, which helps prevent bugs. Nonetheless, we sometimes need to explicitly change, or ***cast***, a variable from one type to another. We have already introduced type casting in Section 1.2.1. We now discuss how it works for classes.

To illustrate an example where we may want to perform a cast, recall our class hierarchy consisting of a base class Person and derived class Student. Suppose that we are storing pointers to objects of both types in an array pp. The following attempt to change a student's major would be flagged as an error by the compiler.

```
Person* pp[100];                    // array of 100 Person pointers
pp[0] = new Person(...);            // add a Person (details omitted)
pp[1] = new Student(...);           // add a Student (details omitted)
// ...
pp[1]->changeMajor("English");      // ERROR!
```

The problem is that the base class Person does not have a function changeMajor(). Notice that this is different from the case of the function print(), because the print function was provided in both classes. Nonetheless, we "know" that pp[1] points to an object of class Student, and so this operation should be legal.

To access the changeMajor() function, we need to cast the pp[1] pointer from type Person* to type Student*. Because the contents of a variable are dynamic, we need to use the C++ run-time system to determine whether this cast is legal, which is what a ***dynamic cast*** does. The syntax of a dynamic cast is shown below.

$$\textbf{dynamic\_cast} < \langle \text{desired\_type} \rangle > (\langle \text{expression} \rangle);$$

Dynamic casting can only be applied to polymorphic objects, that is, objects that come from a class with at least one virtual function. Below we show how to use dynamic casting to change the major of pp[1].

```
Student* sp = dynamic_cast<Student*>(pp[1]); // cast pp[1] to Student*
sp->changeMajor("Chemistry");                // now changeMajor is legal
```

Dynamic casting is most often applied for casting pointers within the class hierarchy. If an illegal pointer cast is attempted, then the result is a null pointer. For example, we would get a null pointer from an attempt to cast pp[0] as above, since it points to a Person object.

As an example of a dynamic cast, suppose we want to access all the elements of the pp array. If an element points to an object of type Student, we may want to change its major to "Undecided," and otherwise we do nothing:

```
for (int i = 0; i < 100; i++) {
  Student *sp = dynamic_cast<Student*>(pp[i]);
  if (sp != NULL)                          // cast succeeded?
    sp->changeMajor("Undecided");
}
```

The casting we have discussed here could also have been done using the traditional C-style cast or through a static cast (recall Section 1.2.1). Unfortunately, no error checking would be performed in that case. An attempt to cast a Person object pointer to a Student pointer would succeed "silently," but any attempt to use such a pointer would have disastrous consequences.

2.2.5 Interfaces and Abstract Classes

For two objects to interact, they must "know" about each other's member functions. To enforce this "knowledge," the object-oriented design paradigm asks that classes specify the *application programming interface* (API), or simply *interface*, that their objects present to other objects. In the *ADT-based* approach (see Section 2.1.2) to data structures followed in this book, an interface defining an ADT is specified as a type definition and a collection of member functions for this type, with the arguments for each method being of specified types.

Some programming languages provide a mechanism for defining ADTs. One example is Java's *interface*. An interface is a collection of function declarations with no data and no bodies. That is, the member functions of an interface are always empty. When a class implements an interface, it must implement all of the member functions declared in the interface.

C++ does not provide a direct mechanism for specifying interfaces. Nonetheless, throughout this book we will often provide *informal interfaces*, even though they are not legal C++ structures. For example, a *stack* data structure (see Chapter 4) is a container that supports various operations such as, inserting (or *pushing*) an element onto the top of the stack, removing (or *popping*) an element from the top of the stack, and testing whether the stack is empty. Below we provide an example of a minimal interface for a stack of integers.

```
class Stack {                    // informal interface - not a class
public:
  bool isEmpty() const;          // is the stack empty?
  void push(int x);              // push x onto the stack
  int pop();                     // pop the stack and return result
};
```

Abstract Classes

The above informal interface is **not** a valid construct in C++; it is just a documentation aid. In particular, it does not contain any data members or definitions of member functions. Nonetheless, it is useful, since it provides important information about a stack's public member functions and how they are called.

An **abstract class** in C++ is a class that is used only as a base class for inheritance; it cannot be used to create instances directly. At first the idea of creating a class that cannot be instantiated seems to be nonsense, but it is often very important. For example, suppose that we want to define a set of geometric shape classes, say, Circle, Rectangle, and Triangle. It is natural to derive these related classes from a single generic base class, say, Shape. Each of the derived classes will have a virtual member function draw(), which draws the associated object. The rules of inheritance require that we define such a function for the base class, but it is unclear what such a function means for a generic shape.

One way to handle this would be to define Shape::draw() with an empty function body ({ }), which would be a rather unnatural solution. What is really desired here is some way to inform the compiler that the class Shape is **abstract**; it is not possible to create objects of type Shape, only its subclasses. In C++, we define a class as being abstract by specifying that one or more members of its functions are **abstract**, or **pure virtual**. A function is declared pure virtual by giving "=0" in place of its body. C++ does not allow the creation of an object that has one or more pure virtual functions. Thus, any derived class must provide concrete definitions for all pure virtual functions of the base class.

As an example, recall our Progression class and consider the member function nextValue(), which computes the next value in the progression. The meaning of this function is clear for each of the derived classes: ArithProgression, GeomProgression, and FibonacciProgression. However, in the base class Progression we invented a rather arbitrary default for the nextValue() function. (Go back and check it. What progression does it compute?) It would be more natural to leave this function undefined. We show below how to make it a **pure virtual** member function.

```
class Progression {                  // abstract base class
    // ...
    virtual long nextValue() = 0;    // pure virtual function
    // ...
};
```

As a result, the compiler will not allow the creation of objects of type Progression, since the function nextValue() is "pure virtual." However, its derived classes, ArithProgression for example, can be defined because they provide a definition for this member function.

Interfaces and Abstract Base Classes

We said above that C++ does not provide a direct mechanism for defining interfaces for abstract data types. Nevertheless, we can use abstract base classes to achieve much of the same purpose.

In particular, we may construct a class for an interface in which all the functions are pure virtual, as shown below for the example of a simple stack ADT.

```cpp
class Stack {                              // stack interface as an abstract class

public:
    virtual bool isEmpty() const = 0;   // is the stack empty?
    virtual void push(int x) = 0;       // push x onto the stack
    virtual int pop() = 0;              // pop the stack and return result
};
```

A class that implements this stack interface can be derived from this abstract base class, and then provide concrete definitions for all of these virtual functions, as shown below.

```cpp
class ConcreteStack : public Stack {  // implements Stack

private:
    // ...                               // member data for the implementation

public:
    virtual bool isEmpty() { ... }      // implementation of members
    virtual void push(int x) { ... }    // ... (details omitted)
    virtual int pop() { ... }
};
```

The implementation must provide definitions for all pure virtual functions in order to be used. In this way, the compiler can check that all the public members promised by the interface are provided by the implementation.

There are limitations to this method of defining interfaces, however. In particular, complications arise when two or more classes are defined, where one class needs to return a copy of an element of another class. This often happens in the design of complex data structures, as we shall see throughout later chapters. For this reason we will use only informal interfaces for defining our ADT interfaces.

2.3   Templates

Inheritance is only one mechanism that C++ provides in support of polymorphism. In this section, we consider another way—using **templates**.

2.3.1   Function Templates

Let us consider the following function, which returns the minimum of two integers.

```
int min(int a, int b)              // returns the minimum of a and b
   { return (a < b ? a : b); }
```

Such a function is very handy, so we might like to define a similar function for computing the minimum of two variables of other types, such as long, short, float, double. Each such function would require a different declaration and definition, however, and making many copies of the same function is an error-prone solution, especially for longer functions.

C++ provides an automatic mechanism, called the **function template**, to produce a generic function for an arbitrary type T. A function template provides a well-defined pattern from which a concrete function may later be formally defined, or **instantiated**. The example below defines a min() function template.

```
template <typename T>
T min(T a, T b)                    // returns the minimum of a and b
   { return (a < b ? a : b); }
```

The declaration takes the form of the keyword "template" followed by the notation <typename T>, which is the parameter list for the template. In this case, there is just one parameter T. The keyword "typename" indicates that T is the name of some type. (Older versions of C++ do not support this keyword, and instead the keyword "class" must be used.) We can have other types of template parameters, integers for example, but type names are the most common. Observe that the type parameter T takes the place of "int" in the original definition of the min() function.

We can now invoke our templated function to compute the minimum of objects of many different types. The compiler looks at the argument types, and determines which form of the function to **instantiate**.

```
cout << min(3, 4)       << '\n';   // invokes min<int>(3, 4)
cout << min(6.9, 3.5)   << '\n';   // invokes min<double>(6.9, 3.5)
cout << min('t', 'g')   << '\n';   // invokes min<char>('t', 'g')
```

The template type does not need to be a fundamental type. We could use any type in this example, provided that the less than operator (<) is defined for this type.

2.3.2   Class Templates

In addition to function templates, C++ allows classes to be templated, which is a powerful mechanism, for it allows us to provide one data structure declaration that can be applied to many different types. In fact, the Standard Template Library uses class templates extensively.

Let us consider an example of a template for a restricted class BasicVector that stores a vector of elements, which is a simplified version of a structure discussed in greater detail in Chapter 5. This class has a constructor, which is given the size of the array to allocate. It also has a member function elemAtRank(i), which returns a reference to the element at index i.

We present a partial implementation of a class template for class BasicVector below. We will omit many of the other member functions, such as the copy constructor, assignment operator, and destructor. In this case, the template parameter Object takes the place of the actual type that will be used.

```
template <typename Object>
class BasicVector {
    Object* a;                          // array storing the elements
    int capacity;                       // length of array a
  public:
    BasicVector(int capac = 10) {       // constructor
      capacity = capac;
      a = new Object[capacity];         // allocate array storage
    }
    Object& elemAtRank(int r)           // access element at index r
      { return a[r]; }
    // ...
};
```

To *instantiate* a concrete instance of the class BasicVector, we provide the class name followed by the actual type parameter enclosed in angled brackets (<...>). For example,

```
BasicVector<int>     iv(5);        // vector of 5 integers
BasicVector<double>  dv(20);       // vector of 20 doubles
BasicVector<string>  sv(10);       // vector of 10 strings
// ...
iv.elemAtRank(3)   = 8;            // iv[3]  = 8
dv.elemAtRank(14)  = 2.5;          // dv[14] = 2.5
sv.elemAtRank(7)   = "hello";      // sv[7]  = "hello"
```

Templated Arguments

The actual argument in the instantiation of a class template can itself be a templated type. For example, we could create a BasicVector whose individual elements are themselves of type BasicVector<int>.

```
BasicVector<BasicVector<int> > xv(5); // vector of 5 BasicVectors

// ...

xv.elemAtRank(2).elemAtRank(8) = 15; // xv[2][8] = 15
```

In this case, because no capacity argument could be provided to the constructor, each element of the vector is constructed using the default capacity of 10. Thus the above definition declares a BasicVector consisting of five elements, each of which is a BasicVector consisting of 10 integers. Such a structure therefore behaves much like a two-dimensional array of integers. Note that in the declaration of xv we intentionally left a space after "<int>." The reason is that without the space, the character combination ">>" would be interpreted as a right-shift operator by the compiler.

Template Members

When member functions are defined outside the class they must be defined using the notation of function templates. In this case, the class name itself must be listed with the template parameter. For example, suppose that we had given the definition of the elemAtRank() function outside the class. It would be done as follows.

```
template <typename Object>          // definition outside of class

Object& BasicVector<Object>::elemAtRank(int r) {
    return a[r];
}
```

When templates are involved, function signatures can become quite complicated and cumbersome. Even error messages printed by the compiler can be quite hard to understand when using templates. Thus, we recommend that programmers implement and debug each class using a concrete type before turning it into a template.

2.4   Exceptions

Exceptions are unexpected events that occur during the execution of a program. An exception can be the result of an error condition or simply an unanticipated input. In C++, exceptions can be thought of as being objects themselves.

2.4.1   Exception Objects

In C++, an exception is *"**thrown**"* by code that encounters some unexpected condition. Exceptions can also be thrown by the C++ run-time environment should it encounter an unexpected condition, like running out of memory. A thrown exception is *"**caught**"* by other code that "handles" the exception somehow, or the program is terminated unexpectedly. (We will say more about catching exceptions shortly.)

Exceptions are a relatively recent addition to C++. Prior to having exceptions, errors were typically handled by having the program abort at the source of the error or by having the involved function return some special value. Exceptions provide a much cleaner mechanism for handling errors. Nevertheless, for historical reasons, many of the functions in the C++ standard library do not throw exceptions. Typically they return some sort of special error status, or set an error flag, which can be tested.

Exceptions are thrown when a piece of code finds some sort of problem during execution. Since there are many types of possible errors, when an exception is thrown, it is identified by a type. Typically this type is a class whose members provide information as to the exact nature of the error, for example a string containing a descriptive error message.

Exception types often form hierarchies. For example, a special-purpose library may generate many different types of errors. We might begin by defining one generic exception, MathException, representing all types of mathematical errors. The errMsg member class holds an error message for this generic exception, which provides further information. The constructor is given the error message.

```
class MathException {                          // generic math exception
private:
   string errMsg;                              // error message
public:
   MathException(const string& err)            // constructor
      { errMsg = err; }
};
```

Using Inheritance to Define New Exception Types

The above MathException class would likely have other member functions, for example, for accessing the error message. We may then add more specific exceptions, such as ZeroDivideException, to handle division by zero, and NegativeRootException, to handle attempts to compute the square root of a negative number. We could use class inheritance to represent this hierarchical relationship, as follows.

```
class ZeroDivideException : public MathException {
public:
  ZeroDivideException(const string& err) // divide by zero
  : MathException(err) { }
};
class NegativeRootException : public MathException {
public:
  NegativeRootException(const string& err) // negative square root
  : MathException(err) { }
};
```

2.4.2 Throwing and Catching Exceptions

Exceptions are typically processed in the context of "try" and "catch" blocks. A *try block* is a block of statements proceeded by the keyword try. After a try block, there are one or more *catch blocks*. Each catch block specifies the type of exception that it catches. Execution begins with the statements of the try block. If all goes smoothly, then execution leaves the try block and skips over its associated catch blocks. If an exception is thrown, then the control immediately jumps into the appropriate catch block for this exception.

For example, suppose that we were to use our mathematical library as part of the implementation of a numerical application. We would enclose the computations of the application within a try block. After the try block, we would catch and deal with any exceptions that arose in the computation.

```
try {
  // ... application computations
  if (divisor == 0)                        // attempt to divide by 0?
    throw ZeroDivideException("Divide by zero in Module X");
}
catch (ZeroDivideException& zde) {
  // handle division by zero
}
catch (MathException& me) {
  // handle any math exception other than division by zero
}
```

Processing the above try block is done as follows. The computations of the try block are executed. When an attempt is discovered to divide by zero, ZeroDivideException is thrown, and execution jumps immediately to the associated catch statement, where corrective recovery and clean up should be performed.

Let us study the entire process in somewhat greater detail. The throw statement is typically written as follows:

throw ⟨exception_constructor⟩([⟨param⟩,⟨param⟩,...]);

where the parameters are arguments to the exception's constructor.

Exceptions may also be thrown by the C++ run-time system itself. For example, if an attempt to allocate space in the free store using the new operator fails due to lack of space, then a bad_alloc exception is thrown by the system.

When an exception is thrown, it must be *caught* or the program will abort. In any particular function, an exception in that function can be passed through to the calling function or it can be caught in that function. When an exception is caught, it can be analyzed and dealt with. The general syntax for a *try-catch block* in C++ is as follows:

```
try
    ⟨try_statements⟩
catch ( ⟨exception_type⟩ ⟨identifier⟩ )
    ⟨catch_statements1⟩
[ catch ( ⟨exception_type⟩ ⟨identifier⟩ )
    ⟨catch_statements2⟩ ]
    . . .
[ catch ( ... )
    ⟨catch_statements3⟩ ]
```

Execution begins in the ⟨try_statements⟩. If this execution generates no exceptions, then the flow of control continues with the first statement after the last line of the entire try-catch block. If, on the other hand, an exception is generated, execution in the try block terminates at that point and execution jumps to the first catch block matching the exception thrown. Thus, an exception thrown for a derived class will be caught by its base class. For example, if we had thrown NegativeRootException in the example above, it would be caught by catch block for MathException. Note that because the system executes the first matching catch block, exceptions should be listed in order of most specific to least specific. The special form "catch(...)" catches *all* exceptions.

The ⟨identifier⟩ for the catch statement identifies the exception object itself. As we said before, this object usually contains additional information about the exception, and this information may be accessed from within the catch block. As is common in passing class arguments, the exception is typically passed as a reference or a constant reference. Once execution of the catch block completes, control flow continues with the first statement after the last catch block.

The recovery action taken in a catch block depends very much on the particular application. It may be as simple as printing an error message and terminating the program. It may require complex clean-up operations, such as deallocating dynamically allocated storage and restoring the program's internal state. There are also some interesting cases in which the best way to handle an exception is to ignore it (which can be specified by having an empty catch block). Ignoring an exception is usually done, for example, when the programmer does not care whether there was an exception or not. Another legitimate way of handling exceptions is to throw another exception, possibly one that specifies the exceptional condition more precisely.

2.4.3 Exception Specification

When we declare a function, we should also specify the exceptions it might throw. This convention has both a functional and courteous purpose. For one, it lets users know what to expect. It also lets the compiler know which exceptions to prepare for. The following is an example of such a function definition:

```
void calculator() throw(ZeroDivideException, NegativeRootException) {
    // function body ...
}
```

This definition indicates that the function calculator() (and any other functions it calls) can throw these two exceptions or exceptions derived from these types, but no others.

By specifying all the exceptions that might be thrown by a function, we prepare others to be able to handle all of the exceptional cases that might arise from using this function. Another benefit of declaring exceptions is that we do not need to catch those exceptions in our function, which is appropriate, for example, in the case where other code is responsible for causing the circumstances leading up to the exception.

The following illustrates an exception that is "passed through:"

```
void getReadyForClass() throw(ShoppingListTooSmallException,
                             OutOfMoneyException) {
    goShopping();  // I don't have to try or catch the exceptions
                   // which goShopping() might throw because
                   // getReadyForClass() will just pass these along.
    makeCookiesForTA();
}
```

A function can declare that it throws as many exceptions as it likes. Such a listing can be simplified somewhat if all exceptions that can be thrown are derived classes of the same exception. In this case, we only have to declare that a function throws the appropriate base class.

Suppose that a function does not contain a throw specification. It would be natural to assume that such a function does not throw any exceptions. In fact, it has quite a different meaning. If a function does not provide a throw specification, then it may throw *any* exception. Although this is confusing, it was necessary to maintain compatibility with older versions of C++. To indicate that a function throws no exceptions, provide the throw specifier with an empty list of exceptions.

```
void func1();                         // can throw any exception
void func2() throw();                 // can throw no exceptions
```

Generic Exception Class

We will be declaring many different exceptions in this book. In order to structure these exceptions hierarchically, we need to have one generic exception class, which will serve as the "mother of all exceptions." C++ does not provide such a generic exception, so we will create one of our own. This class, called RuntimeException, is shown in Code Fragment 2.7. It has an error message as its only member. It provides a constructor, which is given the error message and provides a friend function that prints the message.

```
class RuntimeException {              // generic run-time exception
private:
  string errorMsg;
public:
  RuntimeException(const string& err) { errorMsg = err; }
  string getMessage() const { return errorMsg; }
};

inline std::ostream& operator<<(std::ostream& out, const RuntimeException& e)
  { return out << e.getMessage(); }
```

Code Fragment 2.7: Class for geometric progressions.

By deriving all of our exceptions from this base class, for any exception e, we can output e's error message by using this inherited output operator.

2.5   Recursion and Other Design Patterns

One of the main advantages of object-oriented design is that it facilitates software that is reusable, robust, and adaptable. Designing quality object-oriented code takes more than simply understanding the object-oriented design methodologies, however. It requires the effective use of these and other object-oriented techniques. Computing researchers and practitioners have developed a variety of organizational concepts and methodologies for designing quality object-oriented software that is concise, correct, and reusable. Of special relevance to this book is the concept of a ***design pattern***, which describes a solution to a "typical" software design problem. A pattern provides a general template for a solution that can be applied in many different situations. It describes the main elements of a solution in an abstract way that can be specialized for the specific problem at hand. It consists of a name, which identifies the pattern, a context, which describes the scenarios to which this pattern applies, a template, which describes how the pattern is applied, and a result, which describes and analyzes what the pattern produces. Design patterns are important but sometimes neglected in the discussion of data structures and algorithms.

We present several design patterns in this book, and we show how they can be applied to design quality implementations of data structures and algorithms. These design patterns fall into two groups—patterns for solving algorithm design problems and patterns for solving software design problems. Some of the algorithm design patterns we discuss include the following:

- Recursion (Sections 2.5.1 and 4.1)
- Amortization (Section 5.1.3)
- Divide-and-conquer (Section 10.1.1)
- Prune-and-search, also known as decrease-and-conquer (Section 10.7.1)
- Brute force (Section 11.2.1)
- The greedy method (Section 11.4.2)
- Dynamic programming (Section 11.5.2).

Likewise, some of the software design patterns we discuss include:

- Position (Section 5.2.1)
- Iterator (Section 5.5)
- Template method (Section 6.3.5)
- Compositions and Comparators (Section 7.1.4)
- Locator (Section 7.4)
- Decorator (Section 12.3.1).

Next, we discuss one of the above design patterns, namely, recursion. Rather than describe each of the other concepts here, however, we introduce them throughout the text as noted above.

2.5.1   Recursion

We have seen that repetition can be achieved by writing loops, such as for loops and while loops. Another way to achieve repetition is through ***recursion***, which means a function that calls itself. We have seen examples of functions calling other functions, so it should come as no surprise that most modern programming languages, including C++, allow a function to call itself. In this section, we will see why this capability provides an elegant and powerful alternative for performing repetitive tasks.

The Factorial Function

To illustrate recursion, let us begin with a simple example of computing the value of the ***factorial function***. The factorial of a positive integer n, denoted $n!$, is defined to be the product of the integers from 1 to n. If $n = 0$, then $n!$ is defined to be 1 by convention. More formally, for any integer $n \geq 0$,

$$n! = \begin{cases} 1 & \text{if } n = 0 \\ n \cdot (n-1) \cdot (n-2) \cdots 3 \cdot 2 \cdot 1 & \text{if } n \geq 1. \end{cases}$$

For example, $5! = 5 \cdot 4 \cdot 3 \cdot 2 \cdot 1 = 120$. To make the connection with functions clearer, we use the notation $\mathsf{factorial}(n)$ to denote $n!$.

The factorial function can be defined in a manner that suggests a recursive formulation. Observe that

$$\mathsf{factorial}(5) = 5 \cdot (4 \cdot 3 \cdot 2 \cdot 1) = 5 \cdot \mathsf{factorial}(4).$$

Thus, we can define $\mathsf{factorial}(5)$ in terms of $\mathsf{factorial}(4)$. In general, for a positive integer n, we can define $\mathsf{factorial}(n)$ to be $n \cdot \mathsf{factorial}(n-1)$. This leads to the following ***recursive definition***.

$$\mathsf{factorial}(n) = \begin{cases} 1 & \text{if } n = 0 \\ n \cdot \mathsf{factorial}(n-1) & \text{if } n \geq 1. \end{cases}$$

This definition is typical of many recursive definitions. First, it contains one or more ***base cases***, which are defined nonrecursively in terms of fixed quantities. In this case, $n = 0$ is the base case. It also contains one or more ***recursive cases***, which are defined by appealing to the definition of the function being defined. Observe that there is no circularity in this definition, because each time the function is invoked its argument is smaller by one.

A Recursive Implementation of the Factorial Function

Let us consider a C++ implementation of the factorial function shown in Code Fragment 2.8 under the name recursiveFactorial(). Notice that no looping was needed here. The repeated recursive invocations of the function takes the place of looping.

```
int recursiveFactorial(int n) {            // recursive factorial function
    if (n == 0) return 1;                  // basis case
    else return n * recursiveFactorial(n−1);   // recursive case
}
```

Code Fragment 2.8: A recursive implementation of the factorial function.

We can illustrate the execution of a recursive function definition by means of a ***recursion trace***. Each entry of the trace corresponds to a recursive call. Each new recursive function call is indicated by an arrow to the newly called function. When the function returns, an arrow showing this return is drawn and the return value may be indicated with this arrow. An example of a trace is shown in Figure 2.6.

What is the advantage of using recursion? Although the recursive implementation of the factorial function is somewhat simpler than an iterative version, in this case there is no compelling reason for preferring recursion over iteration. For some problems, however, a recursive implementation can be significantly simpler and easier to understand than an iterative implementation. We shall see such an example next.

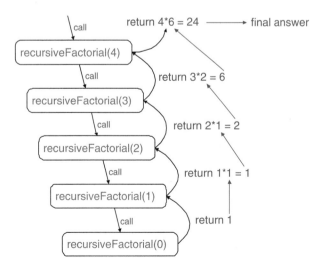

Figure 2.6: A recursion trace for the call recursiveFactorial(4).

Drawing an English Ruler

As a more complex example of the use of recursion, consider how to draw the markings of a typical English ruler. A ruler is broken up into 1-inch intervals, and each interval consists of a set of *ticks* placed at intervals of 1/2 inch, 1/4 inch, and so on. As the size of the interval decreases by half, the tick length decreases by one. (See Figure 2.7.)

```
    ---- 0              ----- 0             --- 0
    -                   -                   -
    --                  --                  --
    -                   -                   -
    ---                 ---                 --- 1
    -                   -                   -
    --                  --                  --
    -                   -                   -
    ---- 1              ----                --- 2
    -                   -                   -
    --                  --                  --
    -                   -                   -
    ---                 ---                 --- 3
    -                   -
    --                  --
    -                   -
    ---- 2              ----- 1

     (a)                 (b)                 (c)
```

Figure 2.7: Three sample outputs of the ruler-drawing function: (a) a 2-inch ruler with major tick length 4, (b) a 1-inch ruler with major tick length 5, and (c) a 3-inch ruler with major tick length 3.

Each multiple of 1 inch also has a numeric label. The longest tick length is called the *major tick length*. We will not worry about actual distances, however, and just print one tick per line.

A Recursive Approach to Ruler Drawing

Our approach to drawing such a ruler consists of three functions. The main function drawRuler() draws the entire ruler. Its arguments are the total number of inches in the ruler, nInches, and the major tick length, majorLength. The utility function drawOneTick() draws a single tick of the given length. It can also be given an optional integer label, which is printed if it is nonnegative.

The interesting work is done by the recursive function drawTicks(), which draws the sequence of ticks within some interval. Its only argument is the tick length associated with the interval's central tick. Consider the 1-inch ruler with major tick length 5 shown in Figure 2.7(b). Ignoring the lines containing 0 and 1, let us consider how to draw the sequence of ticks lying between these lines. The central tick (at 1/2 inch) has length 4. Observe that the two patterns of ticks above and below this central tick are identical, and each has a central tick of length 3. In general, an interval with a central tick length $L \geq 1$ is composed of the following:

- An interval with a central tick length $L - 1$
- A single tick of length L
- An interval with a central tick length $L - 1$.

With each recursive call, the length decreases by one. When the length drops to zero, we simply return. As a result, this recursive process will always terminate. This suggests a recursive process, in which the first and last steps are performed by calling the drawTicks$(L - 1)$ recursively. The middle step is performed by calling the function drawOneTick(L). This recursive formulation is shown in Code Fragment 2.9. As in the factorial example, the code has a base case (when $L = 0$). In this instance we make two recursive calls to the function.

```
                                            // one tick with optional label
void drawOneTick(int tickLength, int tickLabel = −1) {
  for (int i = 0; i < tickLength; i++)
    cout << "-";
  if (tickLabel >= 0) cout << " " << tickLabel;
  cout << "\n";
}
void drawTicks(int tickLength) {            // draw ticks of given length
  if (tickLength > 0) {                     // stop when length drops to 0
    drawTicks(tickLength−1);                // recursively draw left ticks
    drawOneTick(tickLength);                // draw center tick
    drawTicks(tickLength−1);                // recursively draw right ticks
  }
}
void drawRuler(int nInches, int majorLength) { // draw the entire ruler
  drawOneTick(majorLength, 0);              // draw tick 0 and its label
  for (int i = 1; i <= nInches; i++) {
    drawTicks(majorLength−1);              // draw ticks for this inch
    drawOneTick(majorLength, i);           // draw tick i and its label
  }
}
```

Code Fragment 2.9: A recursive implementation of a function that draws a ruler.

Illustrating Ruler Drawing using a Recursion Trace

The recursive execution of the recursive drawTicks function, defined above, can be visualized using a recursion trace.

The trace for drawTicks is more complicated than in the factorial example, however, because each instance makes two recursive calls. To illustrate this, we will show the recursion trace in a form that is reminiscent of an outline for a document. See Figure 2.8.

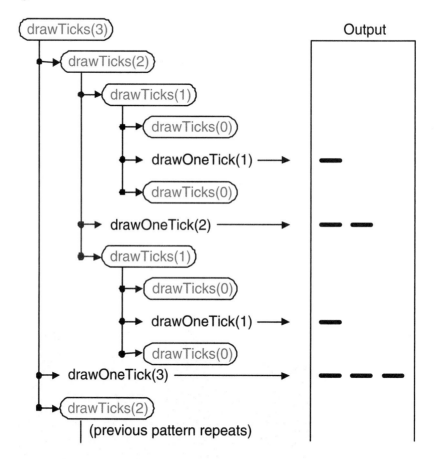

Figure 2.8: A partial recursion trace for the call drawTicks(3). The second pattern of calls for drawTicks(2) is not shown, but it is identical to the first.

Throughout this book we shall see many other examples of how recursion can be used in the design of data structures and algorithms. Section 4.1 contains more examples and a more detailed investigation of issues arising in recursion.

2.6 Exercises

Reinforcement

R-2.1 Give three examples of life-critical software applications.

R-2.2 Give an example of a software application where adaptability can mean the difference between a prolonged sales lifetime and bankruptcy.

R-2.3 Describe a component from a text-editor GUI (other than an "edit" menu) and the member functions that it encapsulates.

R-2.4 A derived class's constructor explicitly invokes its base class's constructor, but a derived class's destructor cannot invoke its base class's destructor. Why does this apparent asymmetry make sense?

R-2.5 Draw a class inheritance diagram for the following set of classes:

- Class Dog is derived from Object and adds a member variable tail and member functions bark() and jump().
- Class Cat is derived from Object and adds a member variable nose and member functions purr() and jump().
- Class Sheep is derived from Object and adds member variables color and length, and member functions clip() and clone() (which overrides the Object clone() function).
- Class Poodle is derived from Dog and adds a function groom().
- Class Puppy is derived from Dog and adds a member variable weight and member functions sleep() and isTrained().

R-2.6 Give a short fragment of C++ code that uses the progression classes from Section 2.2.3 to find the 7th value of a Fibonacci progression that starts with 3 and 4 as its first two values.

R-2.7 If we choose inc = 128, how many calls to the nextValue() function from the ArithProgression class of Section 2.2.3 can we make before we cause a long-integer overflow, assuming a 64-bit long integer?

R-2.8 Suppose we have a member variable p that is declared of type Progression, using the classes of Section 2.2.3. Suppose further that p actually refers to an instance of the class GeomProgression that was created with the default constructor. If we cast p to type Progression and call p.firstValue(), what will be returned? Why?

R-2.9 Consider the inheritance of classes from Exercise R-2.5, and let *d* be an object variable of type Dog. If *d* refers to an actual object of type Poodle, can it be cast to the class Puppy? Why or why not?

R-2.10 Generalize the Person-Student class hierarchy to include classes Faculty, UndergraduateStudent, GraduateStudent, Professor, Instructor. Explain the inheritance structure of these classes, and derive some appropriate member variables for each class.

R-2.11 Consider the following code fragment:

```
class Object
  { public: virtual void printMe() = 0; };
class Place : public Object
  { public: virtual void printMe() { cout << "Buy it.\n"; } };
class Region : public Place
  { public: virtual void printMe() { cout << "Box it.\n"; } };
class State : public Region
  { public: virtual void printMe() { cout << "Ship it.\n"; } };
class Maryland : public State
  { public: virtual void printMe() { cout << "Read it.\n"; } };

int main() {
  Region*   mid = new State;
  State*    md = new Maryland;
  Object*   obj = new Place;
  Place*    usa = new Region;
  md->printMe();
  mid->printMe();
  (dynamic_cast<Place*>(obj))->printMe();
  obj = md;
  (dynamic_cast<Maryland*>(obj))->printMe();
  obj = usa;
  (dynamic_cast<Place*>(obj))->printMe();
  usa = md;
  (dynamic_cast<Place*>(usa))->printMe();
  return EXIT_SUCCESS;
          }
```

What is the output from calling the main() function of the Maryland class?

R-2.12 Show the complete recursion trace and output for the call drawTicks(4), generalizing the results shown in Figure 2.8.

Creativity

C-2.1 Design a class Line that implements a line, which is represented by the formula $y = ax + b$. Your class should store a and b as double member variables. Write a member function intersect(ℓ) that returns the x coordinate at which this line intersects line ℓ. If the two lines are parallel, then your function should throw an exception Parallel. Write a C++ program that creates a number of Line objects and tests each pair for intersection. Your program should print an appropriate error message for parallel lines.

C-2.2 Write a C++ class that is derived from the Progression class to produce a progression where each value is the absolute value of the difference between the previous two values. You should include a default constructor that starts with 2 and 200 as the first two values and a parametric constructor that starts with a specified pair of numbers as the first two values.

C-2.3 Write a C++ class that is derived from the Progression class to produce a progression where each value is the square root of the previous value. (Note that you can no longer represent each value with an integer.) You should include a default constructor that starts with $65,536$ as the first value and a parametric constructor that starts with a specified (double) number as the first value.

C-2.4 Rewrite all the classes in the Progression hierarchy so that all values are from the BigInteger class, in order to avoid overflows all together.

C-2.5 As a function of L, how many lines of output are generated by the call drawTicks(L), including all of the recursive calls it generates.

Projects

P-2.1 Write a C++ program that can take a positive integer greater than 2 as input and write out the number of times one must repeatedly divide this number by 2 before getting a value less than 2.

P-2.2 Write a C++ program that "makes change." Your program should input two numbers, one that is a monetary amount charged and the other that is a monetary amount given. It should return the number of each kind of bill and coin to give back as change for the difference between the amounts given and charged. The values assigned to the bills and coins can be based on the monetary system of any government. Try to design your program so that it returns the fewest number of bills and coins as possible.

P-2.3 Implement a templated C++ class Vector that manipulates a numeric vector. Your class should be templated with any numerical scalar type T, which supports the operations $+$ (addition), $-$ (subtraction), and $*$ (multiplication). In addition, type T should have constructors $T(0)$, which produces the additive identity element (typically 0) and $T(1)$, which produces the multiplicative identity (typically 1). Your class should provide a constructor, which is given the size of the vector as an argument. It should provide member functions (or operators) for vector addition, vector subtraction, multiplication of a scalar and a vector, and vector dot product. Write a class Complex that implements a complex number by overloading the operators for addition, subtraction, and multiplication. Implement three concrete instances of your class Vector with the scalar types int, double, and Complex, respectively.

Chapter Notes

The reader interested in learning more about the contribution to computing that was made by ENIAC and other historical computing devices is referred to the book by Williams [104] or the Web site (http://ftp.arl.mil/~mike/comphist/) for the Army Research Laboratory's "History of Computing Information." For a broad overview of recent developments in computer science and engineering, we refer the reader to *The Computer Science and Engineering Handbook* [98].

The reader interested in further studying object-oriented programming is referred to the books by Booch [14], Budd [18], and Liskov and Guttag [68]. Liskov and Guttag [68] also provide a nice discussion of abstract data types, as does the survey paper by Cardelli and Wegner [20] and the book chapter by Demurjian [27] in the *The Computer Science and Engineering Handbook* [98]. Design patterns are described in the book by Gamma, *et al.* [37]. The class inheritance diagram notation we use is derived from the book by Gamma, *et al.*

More information about the Therac-25 incident can be found in [63].

Chapter

3

Analysis Tools

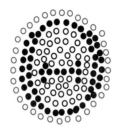

Contents

In a classic story, the famous mathematician Archimedes was asked to deter-mine if a golden crown commissioned by the king was indeed pure gold, and not part silver, as an informant had claimed. As the story goes, Archimedes discovered a way to determine this while stepping into a (Greek) bath. He noted that water spilled out of the bath in proportion to the amount of him that went in. Realiz-ing the implications of this fact, he immediately got out of the bath and ran naked through the city shouting, "Eureka, eureka!," celebrating his discovery. For he had discovered an analysis tool (displacement), which, when combined with a simple scale, could determine if the king's new crown was "good" or not. This discovery was unfortunate for the goldsmith, however, for when Archimedes did his analysis, the crown displaced more water than an equal-weight lump of pure gold, indicating that the crown was not, in fact, pure gold.

In this book, we are interested in the design of "good" data structures and algo-rithms. Simply put, a ***data structure*** is a systematic way of organizing and access-ing data, and an ***algorithm*** is a step-by-step procedure for performing some task in a finite amount of time (so we would not consider a procedure that goes into an infinite loop as an algorithm). These concepts are central to computing, but to be able to classify some data structures and algorithms as "good," we must have precise ways of analyzing them.

The primary analysis tool used in this book involves characterizing the running times of algorithms and data structure operations, with space usage also being of interest. Running time is a natural measure of "goodness," since time is a precious resource. We can always buy more storage space; we cannot buy more time. But focusing on running time as a primary measure of goodness raises the issue of how best to measure an algorithm's running time.

In general, the running time of an algorithm or C++ function increases with the input size, although it may also vary for distinct inputs of the same size. Also, run-ning time is affected by the hardware environment (processor, clock rate, memory, disk, etc.) and software environment (operating system, programming language, compiler, interpreter, etc.) in which the algorithm is implemented, compiled, and executed. All other factors being equal, the running time of the same algorithm on the same input data will be smaller if the computer has, say, a much faster processor or if the implementation is done in a program compiled into native machine code (which C++ produces) instead of an interpreted implementation run on a virtual machine (which is the environment typically used by the programming languages Java and Python).

In this chapter, we present one of the main tools used to analyze data structures and algorithms—asymptotic analysis. We describe how to specify algorithms using pseudo-code and how to characterize their running time as a function of their input size. We also include brief reviews of important mathematical concepts.

3.1 Running Time and Pseudo-Code

In this section, we discuss proper ways of defining running times and specifying algorithms.

3.1.1 How Should Running Time be Measured?

The running time of an algorithm or data structure operation typically depends on a number of factors in addition to the input size. So what is the proper way of measuring an algorithm's running time? If an algorithm has been implemented, we can study its running time by executing it on various test inputs and recording the actual time spent in each execution. Such measurements can be taken in an accurate manner by using system calls that are built into the language or operating system for which the algorithm is written (for example, by using the system clock() function or profiling tools). In general, we are interested in determining the dependency of the running time on the size of the input. In order to determine this, we can perform several experiments on many different test inputs of various sizes. We can then visualize the results of such experiments by plotting the performance of each run of the algorithm as a point with x-coordinate equal to the input size, n, and y-coordinate equal to the running time, t. (See Figure 3.1.) To be meaningful, this analysis requires that we choose good sample inputs and test enough of them to be able to make sound statistical claims about the algorithm.

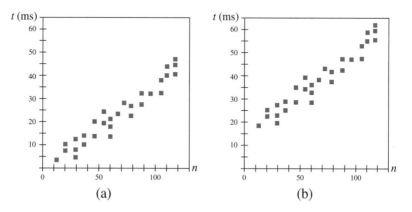

(a) (b)

Figure 3.1: Results of an experimental study on the running time of an algorithm. A dot with coordinates (n, t) indicates that on an input of size n, the running time of the algorithm is t milliseconds (ms). (a) The algorithm executed on a fast computer; (b) the algorithm executed on a slow computer.

Requirements for a General Analysis Methodology

While experimental studies on running times are useful, they have some limitations.

- Experiments can be done only on a limited set of test inputs, and may not be indicative of the running time on other inputs that were not included in the experiment.
- It is difficult to compare the efficiency of two algorithms unless experiments on their running times have been performed in the same hardware and software environments.
- It is necessary to implement and execute an algorithm in order to study its running time experimentally.

We would like a general methodology for analyzing the running time of algorithms that:

- Takes into account all possible inputs
- Allows us to evaluate the relative efficiency of any two algorithms in a way that is independent from the hardware and software environment
- Can be performed by studying a high-level description of the algorithm without actually implementing it or running experiments on it.

This methodology aims at associating, with each algorithm, a function $f(n)$ that characterizes the running time of the algorithm as a function of the input size n. Typical functions that will be encountered include n and n^2. For example, we will write statements of the type "Algorithm A runs in time proportional to n," meaning that if we were to perform experiments, we would find that the actual running time of algorithm A on **any** input of size n is approximately cn, where c is a constant that depends on the hardware and software environment used in the experiment. Given two algorithms A and B, where A runs in time proportional to n and B runs in time proportional to n^2, we will prefer A to B, since function n grows at a smaller rate than function n^2. These, of course, are intuitive notions of the growth of two familiar functions, but our methodology will make such notions precise.

3.1.2   Pseudo-Code

Programmers are often asked to describe algorithms in a way that is intended for human eyes only. Such descriptions are not computer programs, but are more structured than usual prose. In particular, these "high-level" descriptions combine natural language and familiar structures from a programming language, in a way that is both clear and informative. Such descriptions also facilitate the high-level analysis of a data structure or algorithm. We call these descriptions *pseudo-code*.

A Pseudo-Code Example

The array-maximum problem is the simple problem of finding the maximum element in an array *A* storing *n* integers. To solve this problem, we can use an algorithm called arrayMax, which is shown in pseudo-code in Code Fragment 3.1, while a complete C++ implementation is shown in Code Fragment 3.2. Variable *currentMax* starts out being equal to the first element of *A*, and at the beginning of the *i*th iteration of the loop, *currentMax* is equal to the maximum of the first *i* elements in *A*. Since we compare *currentMax* to $A[i]$ in iteration *i*, this claim is also true after iteration *i*, for each $i = 0, 1, \ldots, n-1$. Thus, after $n-1$ iterations *currentMax* will equal the maximum element in *A*.

Algorithm arrayMax(A, n):

    Input: An array *A* storing $n \geq 1$ integers.

    Output: The maximum element in *A*.

    $currentMax \leftarrow A[0]$

    for $i \leftarrow 1$ **to** $n-1$ **do**

      if $currentMax < A[i]$ **then**

        $currentMax \leftarrow A[i]$

    return *currentMax*

Code Fragment 3.1: Algorithm arrayMax.

```cpp
// Finds the maximum element in array A of n integers
int arrayMax(int A[], int n) {
  int currentMax = A[0];          // executed once
  for (int i=1; i < n; i++)       // executed once; n times; n-1 times, resp.
    if (currentMax < A[i])        // executed n-1 times
        currentMax = A[i];        // executed at most n-1 times
  return currentMax;              // executed once
}
```

```cpp
// Testing method called when the program is executed
int main() {
  const int n = 9;
  int num[n] = { 10, 15, 3, 5, 56, 107, 22, 16, 85 };
  cout << "Array:";
  for (int i=0; i < n; i++)
    cout << " " << num[i];        // prints one element of the array
  cout << ".\n";
  cout << "The maximum element is " << arrayMax(num,n) << ".\n";
  return EXIT_SUCCESS;
}
```

Code Fragment 3.2: Algorithm arrayMax within a complete C++ program.

What Is Pseudo-Code?

Note that, in the above example, the pseudo-code is more compact than the C++ code and is easier to read and understand. Pseudo-code is a mixture of natural language and high-level programming constructs used to describe the main ideas behind a generic implementation of a data structure or algorithm. There really is no precise definition of the ***pseudo-code*** language, however, because of its reliance on natural language. At the same time, to help achieve clarity, pseudo-code mixes natural language with standard programming language constructs, such as:

- *Expressions:* We use standard mathematical symbols to express numeric and Boolean expressions. We use the left arrow sign ($\leftarrow$) as the assignment operator in assignment statements (equivalent to the C++ "=" operator) and we use the equal sign (=) as the equality relation in Boolean expressions (which is equivalent to the "==" relation in C++).

- *Function declarations:* **Algorithm** name(*param*1, *param*2, ...) declares a new function "name" and its parameters.

- *Decision structures:* **if** condition **then** true-actions [**else** false-actions]. We use indentation to indicate what actions should be included in the true-actions and false-actions.

- *While-loops:* **while** condition **do** actions. We use indentation to indicate what actions should be included in the loop actions.

- *Repeat-loops:* **repeat** actions **until** condition. We use indentation to indicate what actions should be included in the loop actions.

- *For-loops:* **for** variable-increment-definition **do** actions. We use indentation to indicate what actions should be included among the loop actions.

- *Array indexing:* $A[i]$ represents the ith cell in the array A. The cells of an n-celled array A are indexed from $A[0]$ to $A[n-1]$ (consistent with C++).

- *Function calls:* This includes both class member functions and "plain" functions.

- *Function returns:* **return** value. This operation returns the value specified to the function that called this one.

When we write pseudo-code, we must keep in mind that we are writing for a human reader, not a computer. Thus, we should strive to communicate high-level ideas, not low-level implementation details. At the same time, we should not gloss over important steps. Like many forms of human communication, finding the right balance is an important skill that is refined through practice. We provide several opportunities for such practice in the exercises included in this book.

3.2 A Quick Mathematical Review

In this section, we briefly review some of the fundamental concepts from discrete mathematics that will arise in several of our discussions. In addition to these fundamental concepts, we include a list of other useful mathematical facts that apply in the context of data structure and algorithm analysis in Appendix A.

3.2.1 Summations

Another notation that appears again and again in the analysis of data structures and algorithms is the **summation**, which is defined as follows:

$$\sum_{i=a}^{b} f(i) = f(a) + f(a+1) + f(a+2) + \cdots + f(b).$$

Summations arise in data structure and algorithm analysis because the running times of loops naturally give rise to summations. For example, a summation that often arises in data structure and algorithm analysis is the geometric summation.

Proposition 3.1: *For any integer $n \geq 0$ and any real number $0 < a \neq 1$, consider*

$$\sum_{i=0}^{n} a^i = 1 + a + a^2 + \cdots + a^n$$

(remembering that $a^0 = 1$ if $a > 0$). This summation is equal to

$$\frac{1 - a^{n+1}}{1 - a}.$$

Moreover, if $a < 1$, then

$$\sum_{i=0}^{\infty} a^i = \frac{1}{1 - a}.$$

Summations as shown in Proposition 3.1 are called **geometric** summations, because each term is geometrically larger than the previous one if $a > 1$. That is, the terms in such a geometric summation exhibit exponential growth. For example, everyone working in computing should know that

$$1 + 2 + 4 + 8 + \cdots + 2^{n-1} = 2^n - 1,$$

for this is the largest integer that can be represented in binary notation using n bits.

Another summation that arises in several contexts is

$$\sum_{i=1}^{n} i = 1 + 2 + 3 + \cdots + (n-2) + (n-1) + n.$$

This summation often arises in the analysis of loops. This summation also has an interesting history. In 1787, a German elementary school teacher decided to keep his 9- and 10-year old pupils occupied with the task of adding up all the numbers from 1 to 100. But almost immediately after giving this assignment, one of the children claimed to have the answer! The teacher was suspicious, for the student had only the answer on his slate, with no calculations. But the answer was correct—5,050. That student was none other than Carl Gauss, who would grow up to be one of the greatest mathematicians of all times. It is widely suspected that young Gauss derived the answer to his teacher's assignment using the following identity.

Proposition 3.2: *For any integer $n \geq 1$,*

$$\sum_{i=1}^{n} i = \frac{n(n+1)}{2}.$$

We give two "visual" justifications of Proposition 3.2 in Figure 3.2.

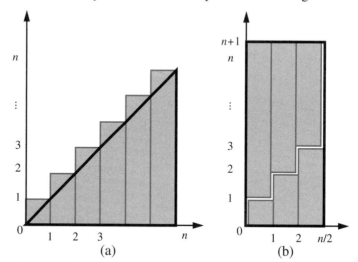

(a)   (b)

Figure 3.2: Visual justifications of Proposition 3.2. Both illustrations visualize the identity in terms of the total area covered by n unit-width rectangles with heights $1, 2, \ldots, n$. In (a), the rectangles are shown to cover a big triangle of area $n^2/2$ (base n and height n) plus n small triangles of area $1/2$ each (base 1 and height 1). In (b), which applies only when n is even, the rectangles are shown to cover a big rectangle of base $n/2$ and height $n+1$.

3.2.2 Logarithms and Exponents

One of the interesting and sometimes even surprising aspects of the analysis of data structures and algorithms is the ubiquitous presence of logarithms and exponents, where we say

$$\log_b a = c \qquad \text{if} \qquad a = b^c.$$

As is the custom in the computing literature, we omit writing the base b of the logarithm when $b = 2$. For example, $\log 1024 = 10$.

There are a number of important rules for logarithms and exponents, including:

Proposition 3.3: *Let a, b, and c be positive real numbers.*

1. $\log_b ac = \log_b a + \log_b c$
2. $\log_b a/c = \log_b a - \log_b c$
3. $\log_b a^c = c \log_b a$
4. $\log_b a = (\log_c a)/\log_c b$
5. $b^{\log_c a} = a^{\log_c b}$
6. $(b^a)^c = b^{ac}$
7. $b^a b^c = b^{a+c}$
8. $b^a/b^c = b^{a-c}$.

Also, as a notational shorthand, we use $\log^c n$ to denote the function $(\log n)^c$ and we use $\log \log n$ to denote $\log(\log n)$. Rather than show how we could derive each of the above identities, which all follow from the definition of logarithms and exponents, let us instead illustrate these identities with a few examples of their usefulness.

Example 3.4: *We illustrate some interesting cases when the base of a logarithm or exponent is 2. The rules cited refer to Proposition 3.3.*

- $\log(2n \log n) = 1 + \log n + \log \log n$, *by rule 1 (twice)*
- $\log(n/2) = \log n - \log 2 = \log n - 1$, *by rule 2*
- $\log \sqrt{n} = \log(n)^{1/2} = (\log n)/2$, *by rule 3*
- $\log \log \sqrt{n} = \log(\log n)/2 = \log \log n - 1$, *by rules 2 and 3*
- $\log_4 n = (\log n)/\log 4 = (\log n)/2$, *by rule 4*
- $\log 2^n = n$, *by rule 3*
- $2^{\log n} = n$, *by rule 5*
- $2^{2 \log n} = (2^{\log n})^2 = n^2$, *by rules 5 and 6*
- $4^n = (2^2)^n = 2^{2n}$, *by rule 6*
- $n^2 2^{3 \log n} = n^2 \cdot n^3 = n^5$, *by rules 5, 6, and 7*
- $4^n/2^n = 2^{2n}/2^n = 2^{2n-n} = 2^n$, *by rules 6 and 8*

3.3   Justification Techniques⋆

Sometimes, we will want to make strong claims about a certain data structure or algorithm. We may, for example, wish to show that our algorithm is correct or that it runs fast. In order to rigorously make such claims, we must use mathematical language, and in order to back up such claims, we must justify or **prove** our statements. Fortunately, there are several simple ways to do this.

3.3.1   By Example

Some claims are of the generic form, "There is an element x in a set S that has property P." To justify such a claim, we need only produce a particular $x \in S$ that has property P. Likewise, some hard-to-believe claims are of the generic form, "Every element x in a set S has property P." To justify that such a claim is false, we only need to produce a particular x from S that does not have property P. Such an instance is called a **counterexample**.

Example 3.5: *A certain Professor Amongus claims that every number of the form $2^i - 1$ is a prime, when i is an integer greater than 1. Professor Amongus is wrong.*

Justification: *To prove Professor Amongus is wrong, we need to find a counterexample. Fortunately, we need not look too far, for $2^4 - 1 = 15 = 3 \cdot 5$.*   ■

3.3.2   The "Contra" Attack

Another set of justification techniques involves the use of the negative. The two primary such methods are the use of the **contrapositive** and the **contradiction**. The use of the contrapositive method is like looking through a negative mirror. To justify the statement "if p is true, then q is true" we instead establish that "if q is not true, then p is not true." Logically, these two statements are the same, but the latter, which is called the **contrapositive** of the first, may be easier to think about.

Example 3.6: *If ab is odd, then a is odd or b is even.*

Justification: *To justify this claim, consider the contrapositive, "If a is even and b is odd, then ab is even." So, suppose $a = 2i$, for some integer i. Then $ab = (2i)b = 2(ib)$; hence, ab is even.*   ■

⋆We use a star ($\star$) to indicate sections containing material more advanced than the material in the rest of the chapter; this material can be considered optional in a first reading.

Besides showing a use of the contrapositive justification technique, the previous example also contains an application of **DeMorgan's Law**. This law helps us deal with negations, for it states that the negation of a statement of the form "*p* or *q*" is "not *p* and not *q*." Likewise, it states that the negation of a statement of the form "*p* and *q*" is "not *p* or not *q*."

Another negative justification technique is justification by **contradiction**, which also often involves using DeMorgan's Law. In applying the justification by contradiction technique, we establish that a statement *q* is true by first supposing that *q* is false and then showing that this assumption leads to a contradiction (such as $2 \neq 2$ or $1 > 3$). By reaching such a contradiction, we show that no consistent situation exists with *q* being false, so *q* must be true. Of course, in order to reach this conclusion, we must be sure our situation is consistent before we assume *q* is false.

Example 3.7: *If ab is odd, then a is odd or b is even.*

Justification: *Let ab be odd. We wish to show that a is odd or b is even. So, with the hope of leading to a contradiction, let us assume the opposite, namely, suppose a is even and b is odd. Then $a = 2i$ for some integer i. Hence, $ab = (2i)b = 2(ib)$, that is, ab is even. But this is a contradiction: ab cannot simultaneously be odd and even. Therefore a is odd or b is even.*   ■

3.3.3   Induction and Loop Invariants

Most of the claims we make about a running time or a space bound involve an integer parameter *n* (usually denoting an intuitive notion of the "size" of the problem). Moreover, most of these claims are equivalent to saying some statement $q(n)$ is true "for all $n \geq 1$." Since this is making a claim about an infinite set of numbers, we cannot justify this exhaustively in a direct fashion.

Induction

We can often justify claims such as those above as true, however, by using the technique of **induction**. This technique amounts to showing that, for any particular $n \geq 1$, there is a finite sequence of implications that starts with something known to be true and ultimately leads to showing that $q(n)$ is true. Specifically, we begin a justification by induction by showing that $q(n)$ is true for $n = 1$ (and possibly some other values $n = 2, 3, \ldots, k$, for some constant k). Then we justify that the inductive "step" is true for $n > k$, namely, we show "if $q(i)$ is true for $i < n$, then $q(n)$ is true." The combination of these two pieces completes the justification by induction.

Example 3.8: *Consider the Fibonacci sequence, where $F(1) = 1$, $F(2) = 2$, and $F(n) = F(n-1) + F(n-2)$ for $n > 2$. We claim that $F(n) < 2^n$.*

Justification: We will show our claim is right by induction.
Base cases: *($n \leq 2$). $F(1) = 1 < 2 = 2^1$ and $F(2) = 2 < 4 = 2^2$.*
Induction step: *($n > 2$). Suppose our claim is true for $n' < n$. Consider $F(n)$. Since $n > 2$, $F(n) = F(n-1) + F(n-2)$. Moreover, since $n - 1 < n$ and $n - 2 < n$, we can apply the inductive assumption (sometimes called the "inductive hypothesis") to imply that $F(n) < 2^{n-1} + 2^{n-2}$. But*

$$2^{n-1} + 2^{n-2} < 2^{n-1} + 2^{n-1} = 2 \cdot 2^{n-1} = 2^n. \qquad \blacksquare$$

Let us do another inductive argument, this time for a fact we have seen before.

Proposition 3.9: *(which is the same as Proposition 3.2)*

$$\sum_{i=1}^{n} i = \frac{n(n+1)}{2}.$$

Justification: We will justify this equality by induction.
Base case: $n = 1$. Trivial, for $1 = n(n+1)/2$, if $n = 1$.
Induction step: $n \geq 2$. Assume the claim is true for $n' < n$. Consider n.

$$\sum_{i=1}^{n} i = n + \sum_{i=1}^{n-1} i.$$

By the induction hypothesis, then

$$\sum_{i=1}^{n} i = n + \frac{(n-1)n}{2},$$

which we can simplify as

$$n + \frac{(n-1)n}{2} = \frac{2n + n^2 - n}{2} = \frac{n^2 + n}{2} = \frac{n(n+1)}{2}.$$

This completes the justification. $\qquad \blacksquare$

We may sometimes feel overwhelmed by the task of justifying something true for *all $n \geq 1$*. We should remember, however, the concreteness of the inductive technique. It shows that, for any particular n, there is a finite step-by-step sequence of implications that starts with something true and leads to the truth about n. In short, the inductive argument is a formula for building a sequence of direct justifications.

Loop Invariants

The final justification technique we discuss in this section is the ***loop invariant***, which is used to analyze and prove the correctness of loops:

> To prove some statement S about a loop is correct, define S in terms of a series of smaller statements $S_0, S_1, \ldots, S_k$, where:
>
> 1. The ***initial*** claim, S_0, is true before the loop begins.
> 2. If S_{i-1} is true before iteration i begins, then we can show that S_i will be true after iteration i is over.
> 3. The final statement, S_k, implies the statement S that we wish to justify as being true.

We have, in fact, already seen the loop-invariant justification technique at work in Section 3.1.2 (for arguing the correctness of arrayMax), but let us nevertheless give one more example of its usage, to justify the correctness of algorithm arrayFind, shown in Code Fragment 3.3, for finding an element x in an array A.

Algorithm arrayFind(x, A):

    Input: An element x and an n-element array, A.
    Output: The index i such that $x = A[i]$ or -1 if no element of A is equal to x.

    for $i \leftarrow 0$ to $n-1$ **do**
      if $x = A[i]$ **then**
        return i
    return -1

Code Fragment 3.3: Algorithm arrayFind.

To show that arrayFind is correct, we use a loop invariant argument. That is, we inductively define a series of statements, S_i, that lead to the correctness of our algorithm. Specifically, we claim the following at the beginning of iteration i:

$$S_i: x \text{ is not equal to any of the first } i \text{ elements of } A.$$

This claim is true at the beginning of the first iteration of the loop, since there are no elements among the first 0 in A (this kind of a trivially true claim is said to hold ***vacuously***). In iteration i, we compare element x to element $A[i]$ and return the index i if these two elements are equal, which is clearly correct and completes the algorithm in this case. If the two elements x and $A[i]$ are not equal, then we have found one more element not equal to x and we increment the index i. Thus, the claim S_i will be true for this new value of i; hence, it is true at the beginning of the next iteration. If the for-loop terminates without ever returning an index in A, then it must be true that $i = n$. That is, S_n is true—there are no elements of A equal to x. Therefore, the algorithm correctly returns the nonindex value -1.

3.4   Analysis of Algorithms

As we noted above, experimental analysis is valuable, but it has its limitations. If we wish to analyze a particular algorithm without performing experiments on its running time, we can take the following more analytical approach:

1. Code up the algorithm in some high-level computer language (like C++).
2. Determine, for each instruction i of the compiled and linked low-level program, the time t_i needed to execute the instruction.
3. Determine, for each instruction i of the low-level language, the number of times n_i that instruction i gets executed when the algorithm is run.
4. Sum up the products $n_i \cdot t_i$ over all the instructions, which yields the running time of the algorithm.

This approach can often give us an accurate estimate of the running time, but it is complicated to pursue since it requires a detailed understanding of the low-level language generated by a program's compilation and its run-time environment.

3.4.1   Primitive Operations

So, instead, we perform our analysis directly on the high-level code or pseudo-code. We define a set of high-level ***primitive operations*** that are largely independent from the programming language used and can be identified also in the pseudo-code. Primitive operations include the following:

- Assigning a value to a variable
- Calling a function
- Performing an arithmetic operation (for example, adding two numbers)
- Comparing two numbers
- Indexing into an array or following a pointer reference
- Returning from a function.

Specifically, a primitive operation corresponds to a low-level instruction whose execution time depends on the hardware and software environment but is nevertheless constant. Instead of analyzing the specific execution time of each primitive operation, we will simply ***count*** how many primitive operations are executed, and use this number t as a high-level estimate of the running-time of the algorithm. This operation count will correlate to an actual running time in a specific hardware and software environment, for each primitive operation corresponds to a constant-time instruction, and there are only a fixed number of primitive operations. The implicit assumption in this approach is that the running times of different primitive operations will be fairly similar. Thus, the number, t, of primitive operations an algorithm performs will be proportional to the actual running time of that algorithm.

Counting Primitive Operations

We now show how to count the number of primitive operations executed by an algorithm, using as an example algorithm arrayMax, whose pseudo-code and C++ implementation are given in Code Fragments 3.1 and 3.2, respectively. The following analysis can be carried out looking either at the pseudo-code or at the C++ implementation.

- Initializing variable *currentMax* to $A[0]$ corresponds to two primitive operations (indexing into an array and assigning a value to a variable) and is executed only once at the beginning of the algorithm. Thus, it contributes two units to the count.
- At the beginning of the for loop, counter i is initialized to 1. This action corresponds to executing one primitive operation (assigning a value to a variable).
- Before entering the body of the for loop, condition $i < n$ is verified. This action corresponds to executing one primitive instruction (comparing two numbers). Since counter i starts at 1 and is incremented by 1 at the end of each iteration of the loop, the comparison $i < n$ is performed n times. Thus, this comparison contributes n units to the count.
- The body of the for loop is executed $n - 1$ times (for values $1, 2, \ldots, n - 1$ of the counter). At each iteration, $A[i]$ is compared with *currentMax* (two primitive operations, indexing and comparing), $A[currentMax]$ is possibly assigned to *currentMax* (two primitive operations, indexing and assigning), and the counter i is incremented (two primitive operations, summing and assigning). Hence, at each iteration of the loop, either four or six primitive operations are performed, depending on whether $A[i] \leq currentMax$ or $A[i] > currentMax$. Therefore, the body of the loop contributes between $4(n - 1)$ and $6(n - 1)$ units to the count.
- Returning the value of variable *currentMax* corresponds to one primitive operation, and is executed only once.

To summarize, the number of primitive operations $t(n)$ executed by algorithm arrayMax is at least

$$2 + 1 + n + 4(n - 1) + 1 = 5n$$

and at most

$$2 + 1 + n + 6(n - 1) + 1 = 7n - 2.$$

The best case ($t(n) = 5n$) occurs when $A[0]$ is the maximum element, so that variable *currentMax* is never reassigned. The worst case ($t(n) = 7n - 2$) occurs when the elements are sorted in increasing order, so that variable *currentMax* is reassigned at each iteration of the for loop.

3.4.2 Average-Case and Worst-Case Analysis

Like the arrayMax function, an algorithm may run faster on some inputs than it does on others. In such cases, we may wish to express the running time of such an algorithm as an average taken over all possible inputs. Unfortunately, such an *average case* analysis is typically quite challenging. It requires us to define a probability distribution on the set of inputs, which is typically a difficult task. Figure 3.3 schematically shows how, depending on the input distribution, the running time of an algorithm can be anywhere between the worst-case time and the best-case time. For example, what if inputs are really only of types "A" or "D?"

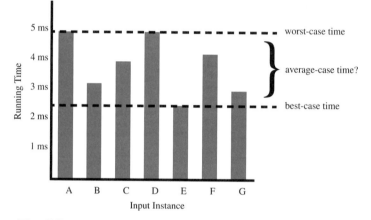

Figure 3.3: The difference between best-case and worst-case time. Each bar represents the running time of some algorithm on a different possible input.

An average-case analysis also typically requires that we calculate expected running times based on a given input distribution. Such an analysis often requires heavy mathematics and probability theory.

Therefore, for the remainder of this book, unless we specify otherwise, we will characterize running times in terms of the *worst case*. We shall say that algorithm arrayMax executes $t(n) = 7n - 2$ primitive operations *in the worst case*, meaning that the maximum number of primitive operations executed by the algorithm, taken over all inputs of size n, is $7n - 2$.

This type of analysis is much easier than an average case analysis, as it does not require probability theory; it just requires the ability to identify the worst-case input, which is often straightforward. In addition, taking a worst-case approach can actually lead to better algorithms. Making the standard of success that of having an algorithm perform well in the worst case necessarily requires that it perform well on *every* input. That is, designing for the worst case leads to stronger algorithmic "muscles," much like a track star who always practices by running up hill.

3.5 Asymptotic Notation

We have clearly gone into laborious detail for evaluating the running time of such a simple algorithm as the arrayMax algorithm. There are a number of questions that this analysis raises:

- Is this level of detail really needed?
- How important is it to figure out the exact number of primitive operations performed by an algorithm?
- How carefully must we define the set of primitive operations? For example, how many primitive operations are used in the statement y = a∗x + b? (We may argue that two arithmetic operations and one assignment are executed, but we may be disregarding the additional "hidden" assignment of the result of a∗x to a temporary variable before performing the sum.)

In general, each step in a pseudo-code description and each statement in a high-level language implementation corresponds to a small number of primitive operations that does not depend on the input size. Thus, we can perform a simplified analysis that estimates the number of primitive operations executed up to a constant factor, by counting the steps of the pseudo-code or the statements of the high-level language executed. Going back to algorithm arrayMax, our simplified analysis indicates that between $5n$ and $7n - 2$ steps are executed on an input of size n.

Simplifying the Analysis Further

It is useful in algorithm analysis to focus on the growth rate of the running time as a function of the input size n, taking a "big-picture" approach, rather than being bogged down with small details. It is often enough just to know that the running time of an algorithm, such as arrayMax, **grows proportionally to** n, with its true running time being n times a small constant factor that depends on the hardware and software environment and varies in a certain range depending on the specific input.

We formalize our method for analyzing data structures and algorithms using a mathematical notation for functions that disregards constant factors. Namely, we characterize the running time and memory requirements of an algorithm by using functions that map integers to real numbers in a way that focuses attention on the primary "big-picture" aspects in a running time or space requirement function.

3.5.1 The "Big-Oh" Notation

Let $f(n)$ and $g(n)$ be functions mapping nonnegative integers to real numbers. We say that $f(n)$ is $O(g(n))$ if there is a real constant $c > 0$ and an integer constant $n_0 \geq 1$, such that $f(n) \leq cg(n)$ for every integer $n \geq n_0$. This definition is often referred to as the "big-Oh" notation, for it is sometimes pronounced as "$f(n)$ is **big-Oh** of $g(n)$." Alternatively, we can also say "$f(n)$ is **order** $g(n)$." (This definition is illustrated in Figure 3.4.)

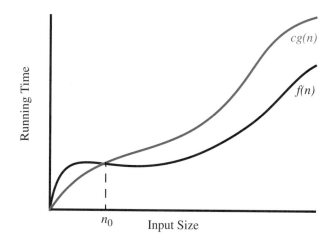

Figure 3.4: Illustrating the "big-Oh" notation. The function $f(n)$ is $O(g(n))$, for $f(n) \leq c \cdot g(n)$ when $n \geq n_0$.

Example 3.10: $7n - 2$ is $O(n)$.

Justification: *By the big-Oh definition, we need to find a real constant $c > 0$ and an integer constant $n_0 \geq 1$, such that $7n - 2 \leq cn$ for every integer $n \geq n_0$. It is easy to see that a possible choice is $c = 7$ and $n_0 = 1$. Indeed, this is one of infinitely many choices available because any real number greater than or equal to 7 will work for c, and any integer greater than or equal to 1 will work for n_0.*   ■

The big-Oh notation allows us to say that a function of n is "less than or equal to" another function (by the inequality "$\leq$" in the definition), up to a constant factor (by the constant c in the definition) and in the **asymptotic** sense as n grows toward infinity (by the statement "$n \geq n_0$" in the definition).

The big-Oh notation is used widely to characterize running times and space bounds in terms of some parameter n, which varies from problem to problem, but is usually defined as an intuitive notion of the "size" of the problem. For example, if we are interested in finding the largest element in an array of integers (see arrayMax given in Code Fragments 3.1 and 3.2), it would be most natural to let n denote the number of elements of the array. The big-Oh notation allows us to ignore constant factors and lower order terms and focus on the main components of a function that affect its growth.

Using the big-Oh notation, we can write the following mathematically precise statement on the running time of algorithm arrayMax (see Code Fragment 3.1 and Code Fragment 3.2) in **any** hardware and software environment.

Proposition 3.11: *The running time of algorithm* arrayMax *for computing the maximum element in an array of n integers is $O(n)$.*

Justification: As shown in Section 3.4.1, the number of primitive operations executed by algorithm arrayMax is at most $7n - 2$. Hence, there is a positive constant a that depends on the time unit and on the hardware and software environment where the algorithm is implemented, compiled, and executed, such that the running time of algorithm arrayMax on an input of size n is at most $a(7n - 2)$. We apply the big-Oh definition with $c = 7a$ and $n_0 = 1$ and conclude that the running time of algorithm arrayMax is $O(n)$. ∎

Let us consider a few additional examples that illustrate the big-Oh notation.

Example 3.12: $20n^3 + 10n\log n + 5$ *is $O(n^3)$.*

Justification: $20n^3 + 10n\log n + 5 \le 35n^3$, for $n \ge 1$. ∎

In fact, any polynomial $a_k n^k + a_{k-1} n^{k-1} + \cdots + a_0$ will always be $O(n^k)$.

Example 3.13: $3\log n + \log\log n$ *is $O(\log n)$.*

Justification: $3\log n + \log\log n \le 4\log n$, for $n \ge 2$. *Note that $\log\log n$ is not even defined for $n = 1$. That is why we use $n \ge 2$.* ∎

Example 3.14: 2^{100} *is $O(1)$.*

Justification: $2^{100} \le 2^{100} \cdot 1$, for $n \ge 1$. *Note that variable n does not appear in the inequality, since we are dealing with constant-valued functions.* ∎

Example 3.15: $5/n$ *is $O(1/n)$.*

Justification: $5/n \le 5(1/n)$, for $n \ge 1$ *(even though this is actually a **decreasing** function).* ∎

In general, we should use the big-Oh notation to characterize a function as closely as possible. While it is true that the function $f(n) = 4n^3 + 3n^{4/3}$ is $O(n^5)$ or even $O(n^3 \log n)$, it is more accurate to say that $f(n)$ is $O(n^3)$. Consider, by way of analogy, a scenario where a hungry traveler driving along a long country road happens upon a local farmer walking home from a market. If the traveler asks the farmer how much longer he must drive before he can find some food, it may be truthful for the farmer to say, "certainly no longer than 12 hours," but it is much more accurate (and helpful) for him to say, "you can find a market just a few minutes drive up this road." Thus, even with the big-Oh notation, we should strive as much as possible to tell the **whole** truth.

Instead of always applying the big-Oh definition directly to obtain a big-Oh characterization, we can use the following rules to simplify notation.

Proposition 3.16: *Let $d(n)$, $e(n)$, $f(n)$ and $g(n)$ be functions mapping nonnegative integers to nonnegative reals. Then*

1. *If $d(n)$ is $O(f(n))$, then $ad(n)$ is $O(f(n))$, for any constant $a > 0$.*
2. *If $d(n)$ is $O(f(n))$ and $e(n)$ is $O(g(n))$, then $d(n) + e(n)$ is $O(f(n) + g(n))$.*
3. *If $d(n)$ is $O(f(n))$ and $e(n)$ is $O(g(n))$, then $d(n)e(n)$ is $O(f(n)g(n))$.*
4. *If $d(n)$ is $O(f(n))$ and $f(n)$ is $O(g(n))$, then $d(n)$ is $O(g(n))$.*
5. *If $f(n)$ is a polynomial of degree d (that is, $f(n) = a_0 + a_1 n + \cdots + a_d n^d$), then $f(n)$ is $O(n^d)$.*
6. *n^x is $O(a^n)$ for any fixed $x > 0$ and $a > 1$.*
7. *$\log n^x$ is $O(\log n)$ for any fixed $x > 0$.*
8. *$\log^x n$ is $O(n^y)$ for any fixed constants $x > 0$ and $y > 0$.*

It is considered poor taste to include constant factors and lower order terms in the big-Oh notation. For example, it is not fashionable to say that the function $2n^2$ is $O(4n^2 + 6n \log n)$, although this is completely correct. We should strive instead to describe the function in the big-Oh in **simplest terms**.

Example 3.17: $2n^3 + 4n^2 \log n$ is $O(n^3)$.

Justification: *We apply the rules of Proposition 3.16 as follows:*

- *$\log n$ is $O(n)$ (Rule 8).*
- *$4n^2 \log n$ is $O(4n^3)$ (Rule 3).*
- *$2n^3 + 4n^2 \log n$ is $O(2n^3 + 4n^3)$ (Rule 2).*
- *$2n^3 + 4n^3$ is $O(n^3)$ (Rule 5 or Rule 1).*
- *$2n^3 + 4n^2 \log n$ is $O(n^3)$ (Rule 4).*

Some functions appear often in the analysis of algorithms and data structures, and we often use special terms to refer to them. The term *linear* is often used, for example, to refer to the class of functions that are $O(n)$. Table 3.1 shows this and other related terms commonly used in algorithm analysis.

logarithmic	linear	quadratic	polynomial	exponential
$O(\log n)$	$O(n)$	$O(n^2)$	$O(n^k)\ (k \geq 1)$	$O(a^n)\ (a > 1)$

Table 3.1: Terminology for classes of functions.

3.5.2 "Relatives" of the Big-Oh

Just as the big-Oh notation provides an asymptotic way of saying that a function is "less than or equal to" another function, the following notations provide asymptotic ways of making other types of comparisons.

Let $f(n)$ and $g(n)$ be functions mapping integers to real numbers. We say that $f(n)$ is $\Omega(g(n))$ (pronounced "$f(n)$ is big-Omega of $g(n)$") if $g(n)$ is $O(f(n))$; that is, there is a real constant $c > 0$ and an integer constant $n_0 \geq 1$, such that $f(n) \geq cg(n)$, for $n \geq n_0$. This definition allows us to say asymptotically that one function is greater than or equal to another, up to a constant factor. Likewise, we say that $f(n)$ is $\Theta(g(n))$ (pronounced "$f(n)$ is big-Theta of $g(n)$") if $f(n)$ is $O(g(n))$ and $f(n)$ is $\Omega(g(n))$; that is, there are real constants $c' > 0$ and $c'' > 0$, and an integer constant $n_0 \geq 1$, such that $c'g(n) \leq f(n) \leq c''g(n)$, for $n \geq n_0$.

The big-Theta allows us to say that two functions are asymptotically equal, up to a constant factor. We consider some examples of these notations below.

Example 3.18: $3\log n + \log\log n$ *is* $\Omega(\log n)$.

Justification: $3\log n + \log\log n \geq 3\log n$, *for* $n \geq 2$. ■

This example shows that lower order terms are not dominant in establishing lower bounds, with the big-Omega notation. Thus, as the next example sums up, lower order terms are not dominant in the big-Theta notation either.

Example 3.19: $3\log n + \log\log n$ *is* $\Theta(\log n)$.

Justification: *This follows from Examples 3.13 and 3.18.* ■

"Distant Cousins" of the Big-Oh

There are also some ways of saying that one function is strictly less than or strictly greater than another asymptotically, but these are not used as often as the big-Oh, big-Omega, and big-Theta. Nevertheless, for the sake of completeness, we give their definitions as well.

Let $f(n)$ and $g(n)$ be functions mapping integers to real numbers. We say that $f(n)$ is $o(g(n))$ (pronounced "$f(n)$ is little-oh of $g(n)$") if, for any constant $c > 0$, there is a constant $n_0 > 0$, such that $f(n) \leq cg(n)$ for $n \geq n_0$. Likewise, we say that $f(n)$ is $\omega(g(n))$ (pronounced "$f(n)$ is little-omega of $g(n)$") if $g(n)$ is $o(f(n))$, that is, if, for any constant $c > 0$, there is a constant $n_0 > 0$, such that $g(n) \leq cf(n)$ for $n \geq n_0$. Intuitively, $o(\cdot)$ is analogous to "less than" in an asymptotic sense, and $\omega(\cdot)$ is analogous to "greater than" in an asymptotic sense.

Example 3.20: *The function $f(n) = 12n^2 + 6n$ is $o(n^3)$ and $\omega(n)$.*

Justification: *Let us first show that $f(n)$ is $o(n^3)$. Let $c > 0$ be any constant. If we take $n_0 = (12 + 6)/c$, then, for $n \geq n_0$,*

$$cn^3 \geq 12n^2 + 6n^2 \geq 12n^2 + 6n.$$

Thus, $f(n)$ is $o(n^3)$.

To show that $f(n)$ is $\omega(n)$, let $c > 0$ again be any constant. If we take $n_0 = c/12$, then, for $n \geq n_0$,

$$12n^2 + 6n \geq 12n^2 \geq cn.$$

Thus, $f(n)$ is $\omega(n)$. ◼

For the reader familiar with limits, we note that $f(n)$ is $o(g(n))$ if and only if

$$\lim_{n \to \infty} \frac{f(n)}{g(n)} = 0,$$

provided this limit exists. The main difference between the little-oh and big-Oh notions is that $f(n)$ is $O(g(n))$ if *there exist* constants $c > 0$ and $n_0 \geq 1$, such that $f(n) \leq cg(n)$, for $n \geq n_0$; whereas $f(n)$ is $o(g(n))$, if *for all* constants $c > 0$, there is a constant n_0, such that $f(n) \leq cg(n)$, for $n \geq n_0$. Intuitively, $f(n)$ is $o(g(n))$ if $f(n)$ becomes insignificant compared to $g(n)$ as n grows toward infinity. As previously mentioned, asymptotic notation is useful because it allows us to concentrate on the main factor determining a function's growth.

3.6 Asymptotic Analysis

Suppose we have two algorithms solving the same problem: an algorithm A, which has a running time of $O(n)$, and an algorithm B, which has a running time of $O(n^2)$. Which one is better? We know that algorithm A is ***asymptotically better*** than algorithm B, although for a given (small) value of n, it is possible for algorithm B to have lower running time than algorithm A.

We can use the asymptotic notation to order functions by asymptotic growth rate. The following list of functions is ordered by increasing growth rate, that is, if a function $f(n)$ precedes a function $g(n)$ in the list, then $f(n)$ is $O(g(n))$:

$$\log n \quad \log^2 n \quad \sqrt{n} \quad n \quad n\log n \quad n^2 \quad n^3 \quad 2^n.$$

We illustrate the difference in the growth rate of the above functions in Table 3.2.

n	$\log n$	$\sqrt{n}$	n	$n\log n$	n^2	n^3	2^n
4	2	2	4	8	16	64	16
16	4	4	16	64	256	4,096	65,536
64	6	8	64	384	4,096	262,144	1.84×10^{19}
256	8	16	256	2,048	65,536	16,777,216	1.15×10^{77}
1,024	10	32	1,024	10,240	1,048,576	1,073,741,824	1.79×10^{308}

Table 3.2: Growth of several functions.

The Floor and Ceiling Functions

One additional comment concerning asymptotic analysis is in order. The value of a logarithm or square root is typically not an integer, yet the running time of an algorithm is typically expressed by means of an expression involving functions such as these. Thus, an algorithm analysis may sometimes involve the use of the so-called "floor" and "ceiling" functions, which are defined respectively as follows:

- $\lfloor x \rfloor$ = the largest integer less than or equal to x.
- $\lceil x \rceil$ = the smallest integer greater than or equal to x.

These functions give us a way to convert real-valued functions into integer-valued functions. Even so, functions used to analyze data structures and algorithms are often expressed simply as real-valued functions (for example, $n\log n$ or $n^{3/2}$). We should read such a running time as having a "big" ceiling function surrounding it. Fortunately, this assumption is made without loss of rigor, for the constant factor implicitly in the big-oh notation saves us from needlessly over-using these functions. (See Exercise R-3.18.)

The Importance of Asymptotics

We further illustrate the importance of the asymptotic viewpoint in Table 3.3. This table explores the maximum size allowed for an input instance for various running times to be solved in 1 second, 1 minute, and 1 hour, assuming each operation can be processed in 1 microsecond (1 μs). It also shows the importance of good algorithm design, because an algorithm with an asymptotically slow running time (for example, one that is $O(n^2)$) is easily beaten in the long run by an algorithm with an asymptotically faster running time (for example, one that is $O(n \log n)$), even if the constant factor for the asymptotically faster algorithm is worse.

Running Time	Maximum Problem Size (n)		
	1 second	1 minute	1 hour
$400n$	2,500	150,000	9,000,000
$20n \lceil \log n \rceil$	4,096	166,666	7,826,087
$2n^2$	707	5,477	42,426
n^4	31	88	244
2^n	19	25	31

Table 3.3: Maximum size of a problem that can be solved in one second, one minute, and one hour, for various running times measured in microseconds.

The importance of good algorithm design goes beyond just what can be solved effectively on a given computer, however. As shown in Table 3.4, even if we achieve a dramatic speed-up in hardware, we still cannot overcome the handicap of an asymptotically slow algorithm. This table shows the new maximum problem size achievable for any fixed amount of time, assuming algorithms with the given running times are now run on a computer 256 times faster than the previous one.

Running Time	New Maximum Problem Size
$400n$	$256m$
$20n \lceil \log n \rceil$	approx. $256((\log m)/(7 + \log m))m$
$2n^2$	$16m$
n^4	$4m$
2^n	$m + 8$

Table 3.4: Increase in the maximum size of a problem that can be solved in a certain fixed amount of time, by using a computer that is 256 times faster than the previous one, for various running times of the algorithm. Each entry is given as a function of m, the previous maximum problem size.

3.6.1 Using the Big-Oh Notation

It is considered poor taste, in general, to say "$f(n) \le O(g(n))$," since the big-Oh already denotes the "less-than-or-equal-to" concept. Likewise, although common, it is not completely correct to say "$f(n) = O(g(n))$" (with the usual understanding of the "=" relation), and it is actually wrong to say "$f(n) \ge O(g(n))$" or "$f(n) > O(g(n))$." It is best to say "$f(n)$ *is* $O(g(n))$." For the more mathematically inclined, it is also correct to say,

$$\text{"}f(n) \in O(g(n)),\text{"}$$

for the big-Oh notation is, technically speaking, denoting a whole collection of functions.

Even with this interpretation, there is considerable freedom in how we can use arithmetic operations with the big-Oh notation, provided the connection to the definition of the big-Oh is clear. For example, we can say,

$$\text{"}f(n) \text{ is } g(n) + O(h(n)),\text{"}$$

which would mean that there are constants $c > 0$ and $n_0 \ge 1$, such that $f(n) \le g(n) + ch(n)$ for $n \ge n_0$. In fact, we may sometimes wish to give the exact leading term in an asymptotic characterization, in which case we would say that "$f(n)$ is $g(n) + O(h(n))$," where $h(n)$ grows slower than $g(n)$. For example, we could say that $2n \log n + 4n + 10\sqrt{n}$ is $2n \log n + O(n)$.

Some Words of Caution

A few words of caution about asymptotic notation are in order at this point. First, note that the use of the big-Oh and related notations can be somewhat misleading should the constant factors they "hide" be very large. For example, while it is true that the function $10^{100} n$ is $\Theta(n)$, if this is the running time of an algorithm being compared to one whose running time is $10 n \log n$, we should prefer the $\Theta(n \log n)$ time algorithm, even though the linear-time algorithm is asymptotically faster. This preference is because the constant factor, 10^{100}, which is called "one googol," is believed by many astronomers to be an upper bound on the number of atoms in the observable universe. So we are unlikely to ever have a real-world problem that has this number as its input size. Thus, even when using the big-Oh notation, we should at least be somewhat mindful of the constant factors and lower order terms we are "hiding."

The above observation raises the issue of what constitutes a "fast" algorithm. Generally speaking, any algorithm running in $O(n \log n)$ time (with a reasonable constant factor) should be considered efficient. Even an $O(n^2)$ time function may

Caution

be fast enough in some contexts, that is, when n is small. But an algorithm running in $\Theta(2^n)$ time should never be considered efficient.

There is a famous story about the inventor of the game of chess. He asked only that his king pay him 1 grain of rice for the first square on the board, 2 grains for the second, 4 grains for the third, 8 for the fourth, and so on. It is an interesting test of programming skills to write a program to exactly compute the number of grains of rice the king would have to pay. In fact, a C++ program written to compute this number in a single integer value will probably cause an integer overflow to occur (although the run-time system will not complain).

If we must draw a line between efficient and inefficient algorithms, it is natural to make this distinction be between algorithms running in polynomial time and those requiring exponential time. That is, make the distinction between algorithms with a running time that is $O(n^k)$, for some constant $k \geq 1$, and those with a running time that is $\Theta(c^n)$, for some constant $c > 1$. Like so many notions we have discussed in this section, this too should be taken with a "grain of salt," for an algorithm running in $\Theta(n^{100})$ time should probably not be considered "efficient." Even so, the distinction between polynomial-time and exponential-time algorithms is considered a robust measure of tractability.

To summarize, the asymptotic notations of big-Oh, big-Omega, and big-Theta provide a convenient language for us to analyze data structures and algorithms. As mentioned earlier, these notations provide convenience because they let us concentrate on the "big picture" rather than low-level details.

3.6.2 Examples of Asymptotic Algorithm Analysis

We conclude this chapter by analyzing two algorithms that solve the same problem but have rather different running times. The problem we are interested in is the one of computing the so-called *prefix averages* of a sequence of numbers. Namely, given an array X storing n numbers, we want to compute an array A, such that $A[i]$ is the average of elements $X[0], \ldots, X[i]$, for $i = 0, \ldots, n-1$, that is,

$$A[i] = \frac{\sum_{j=0}^{i} X[j]}{i+1}.$$

Computing prefix averages has many applications in economics and statistics. For example, given the year-by-year returns of a mutual fund, an investor will typically want to see the fund's average annual returns for the last year, the last three years, the last five years, and the last ten years.

A Quadratic-Time Algorithm

Our first algorithm for the prefix averages problem, called prefixAverages1, is shown in Code Fragment 3.4. It computes every element of A separately, following the definition.

Algorithm prefixAverages1(X):

    Input: An n-element array X of numbers.

    Output: An n-element array A of numbers such that $A[i]$ is
       the average of elements $X[0], \ldots, X[i]$.

Let A be an array of n numbers.
for $i \leftarrow 0$ **to** $n-1$ **do**
    $a \leftarrow 0$
    for $j \leftarrow 0$ **to** i **do**
        $a \leftarrow a + X[j]$
    $A[i] \leftarrow a/(i+1)$
return array A

Code Fragment 3.4: Algorithm prefixAverages1.

Let us analyze the prefixAverages1 algorithm.

- Initializing and returning array A at the beginning and end can be done with a constant number of primitive operations per element, and takes $O(n)$ time.
- There are two nested **for** loops, which are controlled by counters i and j, respectively. The body of the outer loop, controlled by counter i, is executed n times, for $i = 0, \ldots, n-1$. Thus, statements $a = 0$ and $A[i] = a/(i+1)$ are executed n times each. This implies that these two statements, plus the incrementing and testing of counter i, contribute a number of primitive operations proportional to n, that is, $O(n)$ time.
- The body of the inner loop, which is controlled by counter j, is executed $i+1$ times, depending on the current value of the outer loop counter i. Thus, statement $a = a + X[j]$ in the inner loop is executed $1+2+3+\cdots+n$ times. By recalling Proposition 3.2, we know that $1+2+3+\cdots+n = n(n+1)/2$, which implies that the statement in the inner loop contributes $O(n^2)$ time. A similar argument can be done for the primitive operations associated with incrementing and testing counter j, which also take $O(n^2)$ time.

The running time of algorithm prefixAverages1 is given by the sum of three terms. The first and the second term are $O(n)$, and the third term is $O(n^2)$. By a simple application of Proposition 3.16, the running time of prefixAverages1 is $O(n^2)$.

A Linear-Time Algorithm

In order to compute prefix averages more efficiently, we can observe that two consecutive averages $A[i-1]$ and $A[i]$ are similar:

$$
\begin{aligned}
A[i-1] &= (X[0]+X[1]+\cdots+X[i-1])/i \\
A[i] &= (X[0]+X[1]+\cdots+X[i-1]+X[i])/(i+1).
\end{aligned}
$$

If we denote the **prefix sum** $X[0]+X[1]+\cdots+X[i]$ with S_i, we can compute the prefix averages as $A[i] = S_i/(i+1)$. It is easy to keep track of the current prefix sum while scanning array X with a loop. We are now ready to present Algorithm prefixAverages2 in Code Fragment 3.5.

Algorithm prefixAverages2(X):

    Input: An n-element array X of numbers.

    Output: An n-element array A of numbers such that $A[i]$ is
        the average of elements $X[0],\ldots,X[i]$.

Let A be an array of n numbers.
$s \leftarrow 0$
for $i \leftarrow 0$ **to** $n-1$ **do**
  $s \leftarrow s + X[i]$
  $A[i] \leftarrow s/(i+1)$
return array A

Code Fragment 3.5: Algorithm prefixAverages2.

The analysis of the running time of algorithm prefixAverages2 follows:

- Initializing and returning array A at the beginning and end can be done with a constant number of primitive operations per element, and takes $O(n)$ time.
- Initializing variable s at the beginning takes $O(1)$ time.
- There is a single **for** loop, which is controlled by counter i. The body of the loop is executed n times, for $i = 0,\ldots,n-1$. Thus, statements $s = s + X[i]$ and $A[i] = s/(i+1)$ are executed n times each. This implies that these two statements plus the incrementing and testing of counter i contribute a number of primitive operations proportional to n, that is, $O(n)$ time.

The running time of algorithm prefixAverages2 is given by the sum of three terms. The first and the third term are $O(n)$, and the second term is $O(1)$. By a simple application of Proposition 3.16, the running time of prefixAverages2 is $O(n)$, which is much better than the quadratic-time algorithm prefixAverages1.

3.7 Exercises

Most of the following exercises are designed to build the reader's comfort with using asymptotic notation and the other analysis tools developed in this chapter. For some additional mathematical tools, refer to Appendix A.

Reinforcement

R-3.1 Graph the functions $12n$, $6n \log n$, n^2, n^3, and 2^n using a logarithmic scale for the x- and y-axes; that is, if the function value $f(n)$ is y, plot this as a point with x-coordinate at $\log n$ and y-coordinate at $\log y$.

R-3.2 Algorithm A uses $10n \log n$ operations, while algorithm B uses n^2 operations. Determine the value n_0, such that A is better than B for $n \geq n_0$.

R-3.3 Repeat the previous problem assuming B uses $n\sqrt{n}$ operations.

R-3.4 Show that $\log^3 n$ is $o(n^{1/3})$.

R-3.5 Show that the following two statements are equivalent:

(a) The running time of algorithm A is $O(f(n))$.

(b) In the worst case, the running time of algorithm A is $O(f(n))$.

R-3.6 Order the following list of functions by the big-Oh notation. Group together (for example, by underlining) those functions that are big-Theta of one another.

$$
\begin{array}{ccccc}
6n \log n & 2^{100} & \log \log n & \log^2 n & 2^{\log n} \\
2^{2^n} & \lceil \sqrt{n} \rceil & n^{0.01} & 1/n & 4n^{3/2} \\
3n^{0.5} & 5n & \lfloor 2n \log^2 n \rfloor & 2^n & n \log_4 n \\
4^n & n^3 & n^2 \log n & 4^{\log n} & \sqrt{\log n}
\end{array}
$$

(Hint: When in doubt about two functions $f(n)$ and $g(n)$, consider $\log f(n)$ and $\log g(n)$ or $2^{f(n)}$ and $2^{g(n)}$.)

R-3.7 Bill has an algorithm, find2D, to find an element x in an $n \times n$ array A. The algorithm find2D iterates over the rows of A, and calls the algorithm arrayFind, of Code Fragment 3.3, on each one, until x is found or it has searched all rows of A. What is the worst-case running time of find2D in terms of n? Is this a linear-time algorithm? Why or why not?

R-3.8 For each function $f(n)$ and time t in the following table, determine the largest size n of a problem that can be solved in time t assuming that the algorithm to solve the problem takes $f(n)$ microseconds. Recall that $\log n$ denotes the logarithm in base 2 of n. Some entries have already been completed to get you started.

	1 Second	1 Hour	1 Month	1 Century
$\log n$	$\approx 10^{300000}$			
$\sqrt{n}$				
n				
$n \log n$				
n^2				
n^3				
2^n				
$n!$		12		

R-3.9 Show that if $f(n)$ is $O(g(n))$ and $d(n)$ is $O(h(n))$, then $f(n) + d(n)$ is $O(g(n) + h(n))$.

R-3.10 Show that $O(\max\{f(n), g(n)\}) = O(f(n) + g(n))$.

R-3.11 Show that $f(n)$ is $O(g(n))$ if and only if $g(n)$ is $\Omega(f(n))$.

R-3.12 Show that if $p(n)$ is a polynomial in n, then $\log p(n)$ is $O(\log n)$.

R-3.13 Show that $(n+1)^5$ is $O(n^5)$.

R-3.14 Show that 2^{n+1} is $O(2^n)$.

R-3.15 Show that n is $o(n \log n)$.

R-3.16 Show that n^2 is $\omega(n)$.

R-3.17 Show that $n^3 \log n$ is $\Omega(n^3)$.

R-3.18 Show that $\lceil f(n) \rceil$ is $O(f(n))$ if $f(n)$ is a positive nondecreasing function that is always greater than 1.

R-3.19 Justify the fact that if $d(n)$ is $O(f(n))$ and $e(n)$ is $O(g(n))$, then $d(n)e(n)$ is $O(f(n)g(n))$.

R-3.20 Give a big-Oh characterization, in terms of n, of the running time of the Ex1 function shown in Code Fragment 3.6.

R-3.21 Perform a similar analysis for function Ex2 shown in Code Fragment 3.6.

R-3.22 Perform a similar analysis for function Ex3 shown in Code Fragment 3.6.

R-3.23 Perform a similar analysis for function Ex4 shown in Code Fragment 3.6.

R-3.24 Perform a similar analysis for function Ex5 shown in Code Fragment 3.6.

```cpp
void Ex1(int n) {
  int a;
  for (int i=0; i < n; i++) a = i;
}
void Ex2(int n) {
  int a;
  for (int i=0; i < n; i+=2) a = i;
}
void Ex3(int n) {
  int a;
  for (int i=0; i < n*n; i++) a = i;
}
void Ex4(int n) {
  int a;
  for (int i=0; i < n; i++)
    for (int j=0; j <= i; j++) a = i;
}
void Ex5(int n) {
  int a;
  for (int i=0; i < n*n; i++)
    for (int j=0; j <= i; j++) a = i;
}
```

Code Fragment 3.6: A collection of C++ functions.

Creativity

C-3.1 Al and Bill are arguing about the performance of their sorting algorithms. Al claims that his $O(n \log n)$-time algorithm is *always* faster than Bill's $O(n^2)$-time algorithm. To settle the issue, they implement and run the two algorithms on many randomly generated data sets. To Al's dismay, they find that if $n < 100$, the $O(n^2)$-time algorithm actually runs faster, and only when $n \geq 100$ is the $O(n \log n)$-time one better. Explain why this scenario is possible. You may give numerical examples.

C-3.2 Communication security is extremely important in computer networks, and one way many network protocols achieve security is to encrypt messages. Typical *cryptographic* schemes for the secure transmission of messages over such networks are based on the fact that no efficient algorithms are known for factoring large integers. Hence, if we can represent a secret message by a large prime number p, we can transmit over the network the number $r = p \cdot q$, where $q > p$ is another large prime number that acts as the *encryption key*. An eavesdropper who obtains the transmitted number r on the network would have to factor r in order to figure out the secret message p.

Using factoring to figure out a message is very difficult without knowing the encryption key q. To understand why, consider the following naive factoring algorithm:

> For every integer p, such that $1 < p < r$, check if p divides r. If so, print "The secret message is p!" and stop; if not, continue.

a. Suppose that the eavesdropper uses the above algorithm and has a computer that can carry out a division between two integers of up to 100 bits each, in 1 microsecond (1 millionth of a second). Give an estimate of the time that it will take, in the worst case, to decipher the secret message if r has 100 bits.

b. What is the worst-case time complexity of the above algorithm? Since the input to the algorithm is just one large number r, assume that the input size n is the number of bytes needed to store r, that is, $n = (\log_2 r)/8$, and that each division takes time $O(n)$.

C-3.3 Give an example of a positive function $f(n)$, such that $f(n)$ is neither $O(n)$ nor $\Omega(n)$.

C-3.4 Show that $\sum_{i=1}^{n} i^2$ is $O(n^3)$.

C-3.5 Show that $\sum_{i=1}^{n} i/2^i < 2$. (Hint: Try to bound this sum term by term with a geometric progression.)

C-3.6 Show that $\log_b f(n)$ is $\Theta(\log f(n))$ if $b > 1$ is a constant.

C-3.7 Describe an algorithm for finding both the minimum and maximum of n numbers using fewer than $3n/2$ comparisons. (Hint: First construct a group of candidate minimums and a group of candidate maximums.)

C-3.8 Given a set $A = \{a_1, a_2, \ldots, a_n\}$ of n integers, describe, in pseudo-code, an efficient algorithm for computing each of partial sums

$$s_k = \sum_{i=1}^{k} a_i,$$

for $k = 1, 2, \ldots, n$. (Note: Remember that we are assuming that arrays begin indexing from 0.) What is the running time of this algorithm?

C-3.9 A degree-n **polynomial** $p(x)$ is a function of the form

$$p(x) = \sum_{i=0}^{n} a_i x^i,$$

where x is a real number, each a_i is a constant, and $a_n \neq 0$.

a. Describe a simple $O(n^2)$ time algorithm for computing $p(x)$ for a particular value of x.

b. Consider now a rewriting of $p(x)$ as

$$p(x) = a_0 + x(a_1 + x(a_2 + x(a_3 + \cdots + x(a_{n-1} + xa_n) \cdots))),$$

which is known as **Horner's method**. Characterize, using the big-Oh notation, the number of multiplications and additions this method of evaluation uses.

C-3.10 Consider the following induction "justification" that all sheep in a flock are the same color:

Base case: One sheep. It is clearly the same color as itself.

Induction step: A flock of n sheep. Take a sheep, a, out of the flock. The remaining $n-1$ are all the same color by induction. Now put sheep a back in the flock, and take out a different sheep, b. By induction, the $n-1$ sheep (now with a in their group) are all the same color. Therefore, a is the same color as all the other sheep; hence, all the sheep in the flock are the same color.

What is wrong with this "justification?"

C-3.11 Consider the following "justification" that the Fibonacci function, $F(n)$, defined as $F(1) = 1$, $F(2) = 2$, $F(n) = F(n-1) + F(n-2)$, is $O(n)$.
Base case $(n \le 2)$: $F(1) = 1$, which is $O(1)$, and $F(2) = 2$, which is $O(2)$.
Induction step $(n > 2)$: Assume the claim is true for $n' < n$. Consider n. $F(n) = F(n-1) + F(n-2)$. By induction, $F(n-1)$ is $O(n-1)$ and $F(n-2)$ is $O(n-2)$. Then, $F(n)$ is $O((n-1)+(n-2))$, by the identity presented in Exercise R-3.9. Therefore, $F(n)$ is $O(n)$, since $O((n-1)+(n-2))$ is $O(n)$.
What is wrong with this "justification?"

C-3.12 Consider the Fibonacci function, $F(n)$, from the previous exercise. Show by induction that $F(n)$ is $\Omega((3/2)^n)$.

C-3.13 Draw a visual justification of Proposition 3.2 analogous to that of Figure 3.2(b) for the case when n is odd.

C-3.14 An array A contains $n-1$ unique integers in the range $[0, n-1]$; that is, there is one number from this range that is not in A. Design an $O(n)$-time algorithm for finding that number. You are allowed to use only $O(1)$ additional space besides the array A itself.

C-3.15 An evil king has a cellar containing n bottles of expensive wine, and his guards have just caught a spy trying to poison the king's wine. Fortunately, the guards caught the spy after he succeeded in poisoning only one bottle. Unfortunately, they don't know which one. To make matters worse, the poison the spy used was very deadly; just one drop diluted even a billion to one will still kill someone. Even so, the poison works slowly; it takes a full month for the person to die. Design a scheme that allows the evil king to determine exactly which one of his wine bottles was poisoned in just one month's time while using at most $O(\log n)$ of his taste testers.

C-3.16 Show that the summation $\sum_{i=1}^{n} \lceil \log_2 i \rceil$ is $O(n \log n)$.

C-3.17 Show that the summation $\sum_{i=1}^{n} \lceil \log_2 i \rceil$ is $\Omega(n \log n)$.

C-3.18★ Show that the summation $\sum_{i=1}^{n} \lceil \log_2(n/i) \rceil$ is $O(n)$. You may assume that n is a power of 2.   (Hint: Use induction to reduce the problem to that for $n/2$.)

C-3.19 Let S be a set of n lines, such that no two are parallel and no three meet in the same point. Show by induction that the lines in S determine $\Theta(n^2)$ intersection points.

C-3.20 Suppose that each row of an $n \times n$ array A consists of 1's and 0's such that, in any row of A, all the 1's come before any 0's in that row. Assuming A is already in memory, describe an algorithm running in $O(n)$ time (not $O(n^2)$ time) for finding the row of A that contains the most 1's.

C-3.21 Suppose that each row of an $n \times n$ array A consists of 1's and 0's such that, in any row i of A, all the 1's come before any 0's in that row. Suppose further that the number of 1's in row i is at least the number in row $i+1$, for $i = 0, 1, \ldots, n-2$. Assuming A is already in memory, describe an algorithm running in $O(n)$ time (not $O(n^2)$ time) for counting the number of 1's in the array A.

C-3.22 Describe, in pseudo-code, an algorithm for multiplying an $n \times m$ matrix A and an $m \times p$ matrix B. Recall that the product $C = AB$ is defined so that $C[i][j] = \sum_{k=1}^{m} A[i][k] \cdot B[k][j]$. What is the running time of your algorithm?

Projects

P-3.1 Program the two algorithms, prefixAverages1 and prefixAverages2 from Section 3.6.2, and perform a careful experimental analysis of their running times. Plot their running times as a function of their input sizes as scatter plots on both a linear-linear scale and a linear-log scale. Choose representative values of the size n, and run at least 5 tests for each size value n in your tests.

P-3.2 Perform a careful experimental analysis that compares the relative running times of the functions shown in Code Fragment 3.6.

Chapter Notes

The methodology for analyzing algorithms is traditionally within a model of computation called the **RAM**, or **random access machine** (not to be confused with "random access memory"). Within this model, a computer consists of a **central processing unit** (or **CPU**) and a **memory**. The CPU performs elementary operations, such as loads, stores, additions, and comparisons, and the memory stores the program and data in **cells** that have integer addresses. The term "random access" refers to the ability of the CPU to access an arbitrary memory cell with one primitive operation. Each primitive operation executed by an algorithm corresponds to a constant number of elementary computations of the RAM. Our approach of counting primitive operations is equivalent to this approach theoretically, but does not require the conceptual burden of an abstract model like the RAM.

Our use of the big-Oh notation is consistent with most authors' usage, but we have taken a slightly more conservative approach than some. The big-Oh notation has prompted several discussions in the algorithms and computation theory community over its proper use [17, 46, 60]. Knuth [58, 60], for example, defines it using the notation $f(n) = O(g(n))$, but he refers to this "equality" as being only "one way," even though he mentions that the big-Oh is actually defining a set of functions. We have chosen to take a more standard view of equality and view the big-Oh notation truly as a set, following the suggestions of Brassard [17]. The reader interested in studying average-case analysis is referred to the book chapter by Vitter and Flajolet [101]. Likewise, the reader interested in further study on the experimental analysis of algorithms is referred to the book chapter by McGeoch [71] or the survey book by Fleischer *et al.* [33].

We include a number of useful mathematical facts in Appendix A. The reader interested in further study into the analysis of algorithms is referred to the books by Graham, Knuth, and Patashnik [44], and Sedgewick and Flajolet [91]. The reader interested in learning more about the history of mathematics is referred to the book by Boyer and Merzbach [15]. Our version of the famous story about Archimedes is taken from [80].

Chapter

4

Stacks, Queues, and Recursion

Contents

Stacks and queues are among the simplest of all data structures, but they are also among the most important. Stacks and queues are used in a host of different applications that include many more sophisticated data structures. In addition, stacks and queues are among the few kinds of data structures that are often implemented in the hardware microinstructions inside a CPU. In fact, there are some CPUs that have their entire assembly language based on the concept of performing operations on registers that are stored in a stack. Also, as we discuss in this chapter, the stack structure is used in the C++ run-time system, and the queue structure is used in most operating systems. Thus, the stack and queue structures are central to many important features of modern computing environments.

As another indication of the importance of stacks and queues, we note that the C++ Standard Template Library (STL) provides stacks and queues as fundamental types. The STL containers are well understood by other programmers, and they are convenient, general, and efficient. If an STL container provides the desired functionality, it is almost always preferable to use the STL container, rather than defining our own. However, our focus here is not in learning how to use the STL data structures, such as stacks and queues, but instead in learning how to write our own data structures. For this reason, we use stacks and queues as examples in how to design simple data structures "from scratch." The principles that we learn here will be applicable to more complex data structures, which are not provided by the STL.

In this chapter, we define the stack and queue abstract data types in a general way, and we give two alternative implementations for them: arrays and linked lists. To illustrate the usefulness of stacks and queues, we present several examples of their application. We also present a generalization of stacks and queues, called the double-ended queue, and show how it can be implemented using a doubly linked list.

In addition, this chapter includes discussions of several programming concepts, including recursion, interfaces, casting, sentinels, and the adapter pattern. Indeed, we begin this chapter with a general discussion of how to use recursion and we explain in the subsequent section how recursion can be implemented with the stack data structure. We discuss linear recursion, higher-order recursion, and how to analyze recursive algorithms using recursion traces.

We conclude this chapter with a case study that uses a stack to build a simple stock analysis application. This case study also illustrates how good use of efficient data structures can make the difference between a fast algorithm and a slow one, as we provide two algorithms for the stock analysis problem, one running in quadratic time and the other running in linear time.

4.1   Using Recursion

As we discussed in Section 2.5.1, **recursion** is the concept of defining a function so that it calls itself as a subroutine. Whenever a function calls itself, we refer to this as a **recursive** call. We also consider a function f to be recursive if it calls a function that ultimately leads to a call back to f. In this section, we discuss how to use recursion to define efficient algorithms. The main benefit of this approach to algorithm design is that it allows us to take advantage of the repeated structure present in many problems. By making our algorithm description exploit this repeated structure in a recursive way, we can often avoid complex case analyses and nested loops. This approach can therefore lead to more readable algorithm descriptions, while still being quite efficient. In addition, recursion is a useful way for defining objects that have a repeated similar structural form, such as in the following examples.

Example 4.1: *Modern operating systems define file-system directories (which are also sometimes called "folders") in a recursive way. Namely, a file system consists of a top-level directory, and the contents of this directory consists of files and other directories, which in turn can contain files and other directories, and so on. The base directories in the file system contain only files, but by using this recursive definition, the operating system allows for directories to be nested arbitrarily deep (as long as there is enough space in memory).*

Example 4.2: *Much of the syntax in modern programming languages is defined in a recursive way. For example, C++ defines an expression list using the following notation:*

> *expression-list:*
>> *assignment-expression*
>> *expression-list , assignment-expression*

In other words, an expression list consists of an assignment expression or a expression list followed by a comma and an assignment expression. That is, an expression list consists of a comma-separated list of assignment expressions. Similarly, arithmetic expressions are defined recursively in terms of primitives (like variables and constants) and arithmetic expressions. In fact, declarators in C++ are also defined recursively.

Example 4.3: *There are also many examples of recursion in art and nature. One of the most classic examples of recursion used in art is in the Russian Matryoshka dolls. Each doll is made of solid wood or is hollow and contains another Matryoshka doll inside it.*

4.1.1 Linear Recursion

The simplest form of recursion is *linear recursion*, where a function is defined so that it makes, at most, one recursive call each time it is invoked. This type of recursion is useful whenever we can view an algorithmic problem in terms of a first or last element, plus a remaining set that has the same structure as the original set.

Summing the Elements of an Array Recursively

Suppose, for example, we are given an array, A, of n integers that we wish to sum together. We can solve this summation problem using linear recursion by observing that the sum of all n integers in A is equal to $A[0]$, if $n = 1$, or the sum of the first $n - 1$ integers in A plus the last element in A. In particular, we can solve this summation problem using the recursive algorithm described in Code Fragment 4.1.

Algorithm LinearSum(A, n):

    Input: An integer array A and an integer n

    Output: The sum of the first n integers in A

    if $n = 1$ **then**

        return $A[0]$

    else

        return LinearSum($A, n - 1$) $+ A[n - 1]$

Code Fragment 4.1: Summing the elements in an array using linear recursion.

This example also illustrates an important property that a recursive function should always possess—the function terminates. We ensure this by writing nonrecursive statements for the case $n = 1$. In addition, we always perform the recursive call on a smaller value of the parameter ($n - 1$) than that which we were given (n), so that, at some point (at the "bottom" of the recursion) we will perform the nonrecursive part of the computation (returning $A[0]$). In general, an algorithm that uses linear recursion almost always has the following form:

- *Test for base cases.* We begin by testing for a set of base cases (and there better be at least one). These base cases should be defined so that every possible chain of recursive calls will eventually reach a base case, and the handling of each base case should not use recursion.
- *Recurse.* After testing for base cases, we then perform a single recursive call. This recursive step may involve a test that decides which of several possible recursive calls to make, but it should ultimately choose to make just one of these each time we perform this step. Moreover, we should define each possible recursive call so that it makes progress towards a base case.

Analyzing Recursive Algorithms using Recursion Traces

We can analyze the running of a recursive algorithm by using a visual tool known as a ***recursion trace***. We used recursion traces, for example, to analyze and visualize the recursive Fibonacci function of Section 2.5.1, and we will similarly use recursion traces for the recursive sorting algorithms of Sections 10.1 and 10.3.

To draw a recursion trace, we create a box for each recursive call, labeling that box with the important parameters that lead to the base case(s). Whenever an instance x of our function makes a recursive call, we visualize this by drawing a line from x's box to the box of the call. For example, we illustrate the recursion trace of the LinearSum algorithm of Code Fragment 4.1 in Figure 4.1. We label each box in this trace with the parameters used to make this call. Each time we make a recursive call, we draw a line to the box representing the recursive call. We can also use this diagram to visualize our stepping through the algorithm, since it proceeds by going from the call for n to the call for $n-1$, to the call for $n-2$, and so on, all the way down to the call for 1. When the final call finishes, it returns its value back to the call for 2, which adds in its value, and returns this partial sum to the call for 3, and so on, until the call for $n-1$ returns its partial sum to the call for n.

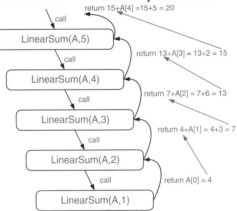

Figure 4.1: An example recursion trace for the LinearSum algorithm, for the input array $A = \{4,3,6,2,5\}$.

From the figure, it should be clear that the running time of the algorithm is $O(n)$ to sum the integers in an n-element array, since we spend a constant amount of time performing the nonrecursive part of each call. Moreover, we can also immediately see that the memory space used by the algorithm (in addition to the array A) is also $O(n)$, since we will need a constant amount of memory space for each box in the trace at the point we make the final recursive call (for $n = 1$). Incidentally, another technique that can be used to analyze the running time of a recursive algorithm is to use a ***recurrence relation***, which is a topic discussed in Section 10.1.3.

Reversing an Array by Recursion

Let us consider another example of linear recursion. Namely, let us consider the problem of reversing the n elements of an array, A, so that the first element becomes the last, the second element becomes second to the last, and so on. We can solve this problem using linear recursion, by observing that the reversal of an array can be achieved by swapping the first and last elements and then recursively reversing the remaining elements in the array. We describe the details of this algorithm in Code Fragment 4.2, using the convention that the first time we call this algorithm we do so as ReverseArray$(A, 0, n)$.

Algorithm ReverseArray(A, i, n):

    Input: An integer array A and integers i and n

    Output: The reversal of the n integers in A starting at index i

    if $n > 1$ **then**

        Swap $A[i]$ and $A[i+n-1]$

        Call ReverseArray$(A, i+1, n-2)$

    return

Code Fragment 4.2: Reversing the elements of an array using linear recursion.

Note that, in this algorithm, we actually have two base cases, namely, when $n = 0$ and when $n = 1$. Moreover, in either case, we simply return, since an array with zero elements or one element is trivially equal to its reversal. Furthermore, note that in our recursive step we are guaranteed to make progress towards one of these two base cases. If n is odd, we will eventually reach the $n = 1$ case, and if n is even, we will eventually reach the $n = 0$ case.

The above argument immediately implies that the recursive algorithm of Code Fragment 4.2 is guaranteed to terminate. Even if we had designed an "infinitely recursive" function, however, it will not actually run forever. Each active recursive call in a recursive algorithm requires that we keep some information in memory about this call (we give the details of how this is done in Section 4.2.3). Thus, if we ever design an infinitely recursive algorithm, it will, in practice, use up all the memory available and abort at some point.

In general, to design a recursive algorithm for a given problem, it is useful to think of the different ways we can subdivide this problem so as to define problems that have the same general structure as the original problem. For example, with the ReverseArray procedure, we added the parameters i and n, so that a recursive call to reverse the inner part of the array A would have the same structure (and be called using the same syntax) as the call to reverse all of A. If one has difficulty finding the repeated structure needed to design a recursive algorithm, it is sometimes useful to work out the problem on a few concrete examples.

Computing Powers via Linear Recursion

As a more interesting example of using linear recursion, let us consider the problem of raising a number x to an arbitrary positive integer, n. That is, we wish to compute the function

$$\text{power}(x, n) = x^n.$$

This function has an immediate recursive definition based on linear recursion:

$$\text{power}(x, n) = \begin{cases} 1 & \text{if } n = 0 \\ x \cdot \text{power}(x, n - 1) & \text{otherwise.} \end{cases}$$

This definition leads immediately to a linearly recursive algorithm that uses $O(n)$ function calls to compute $\text{power}(x, n)$. We can compute the power function much faster than this, however, by using the following linearly recursive definition:

$$\text{power}(x, n) = \begin{cases} 1 & \text{if } n = 0 \\ x \cdot \text{power}(x, (n-1)/2)^2 & \text{if } n > 0 \text{ is odd} \\ \text{power}(x, n/2)^2 & \text{if } n > 0 \text{ is even.} \end{cases}$$

To illustrate how this definition works, consider the following examples:

$$\begin{aligned} 2^4 &= 2^{(4/2)2} = (2^{4/2})^2 = (2^2)^2 = 4^2 = 16 \\ 2^5 &= 2^{1+(4/2)2} = 2(2^{4/2})^2 = 2(2^2)^2 = 2(4^2) = 32 \\ 2^6 &= 2^{(6/2)2} = (2^{6/2})^2 = (2^3)^2 = 8^2 = 64 \\ 2^7 &= 2^{1+(6/2)2} = 2(2^{6/2})^2 = 2(2^3)^2 = 2(8^2) = 128. \end{aligned}$$

This definition suggests the algorithm of Code Fragment 4.3. To analyze this algorithm, we observe that each recursive call of the Power algorithm divides the exponent, n, by two. Thus, there are only $O(\log n)$ recursive calls, not $O(n)$. That is, by using linear recursion and the squaring function, we improve the running time for the power function from $O(n)$ to $O(\log n)$, which is a big improvement.

Algorithm Power(x, n):

    Input: A number x and integer $n \geq 0$
    Output: The value x^n

    if $n = 0$ **then**
        return 1
    if n is odd **then**
        $y \leftarrow \text{Power}(x, (n-1)/2)$
        return $x \cdot y \cdot y$
    else
        $y \leftarrow \text{Power}(x, n/2)$
        return $y \cdot y$

Code Fragment 4.3: Computing the power function using linear recursion.

Tail Recursion

Using recursion can often be a useful tool for designing algorithms that have elegant, short definitions. But this usefulness does come at a modest cost. Namely, whenever we use a recursion function to solve a problem, we have to use some of the memory locations in our computer to keep track of the state of each active recursive call. When computer memory is at a premium, then it is useful in some cases to be able to derive nonrecursive algorithms from recursive ones.

We can use the stack data structure, discussed in Section 4.2, to convert a recursive algorithm into a nonrecursive algorithm, but there are some instances when we can do this conversion more easily and efficiently. Specifically, we can easily convert algorithms that use *tail recursion*. An algorithm uses tail recursion if it uses linear recursion and the algorithm only makes a recursive call as its last operation. For example, the algorithm of Code Fragment 4.2 uses tail recursion to reverse the elements of an array. It is not enough that the last statement in the function definition includes a recursive call, however. In order for a function to use tail recursion, the recursive call must be the very last thing the function does (unless we are in a base case, of course). For example, the algorithm of Code Fragment 4.1 does not use tail recursion, even though its last statement includes a recursive call. This recursive call is not actually the last thing the function does, for after it gets the value returned from the recursive call, it adds this value to $A[n-1]$ and returns this sum.

When an algorithm uses tail recursion, we can convert the recursive algorithm into a nonrecursive one, by iterating through the recursive calls rather than calling them explicitly. We illustrate this type of conversion by revisiting the problem of reversing an array, giving a nonrecursive algorithm in Code Fragment 4.4 that performs this task by iterating the recursive calls from the algorithm of Code Fragment 4.2. We initially call this algorithm as IterativeReverseArray$(A,0,n)$.

Algorithm IterativeReverseArray(A,i,n):
    Input: An integer array A and integers i and n
    Output: The reversal of the n integers in A starting at index i
    while $n > 1$ **do**
        Swap $A[i]$ and $A[i+n-1]$
        $i \leftarrow i+1$
        $n \leftarrow n-2$
    return

Code Fragment 4.4: Reversing the elements of an array using iteration.

4.1.2 Higher-Order Recursion

When an instance of a recursive algorithm makes more than a single recursive call, we say that the algorithm uses ***higher-order recursion***.

Binary Recursion

One of the most common forms of higher-order recursion is ***binary recursion***. In an algorithm that uses binary recursion, we can make two recursive calls. These calls can be used to solve two similar halves of some problem, as we did, for instance, in Section 2.5.1 for drawing an English ruler. As another example, let us revisit the problem of summing the n elements of an integer array A, but let us now use binary recursion to solve this problem. In this case, we can sum the elements in A by recursively summing the elements in the first half of A and recursively summing the elements in the second half of A, and then adding these two values together. We give the details in Code Fragment 4.5, which we initially call as BinarySum$(A, 0, n)$.

Algorithm BinarySum(A, i, n):
    Input: An integer array A and integers i and n
    Output: The sum of the n integers in A starting at index i
    if $n = 1$ **then**
        return $A[i]$
    return BinarySum$(A, i, \lceil n/2 \rceil)$ + BinarySum$(A, i + \lceil n/2 \rceil, \lfloor n/2 \rfloor)$

Code Fragment 4.5: Summing the elements in an array using binary recursion.

To analyze this algorithm, we visualize its running using a recursion trace, which we show in Figure 4.2. Notice that the edges in our trace go from a box to another box labeled with half its size. Thus, the depth of our recursion is $O(\log n)$ instead of the $O(n)$ depth used by the LinearSum algorithm. The running time of our algorithm is still $O(n)$, however, since we have to visit each box in stepping through our algorithm and there are $O(n)$ boxes. Nevertheless, since the depth of the recursion is $O(\log n)$ in this case, we need only use $O(\log n)$ additional space besides the array A in order to sum up the n elements.

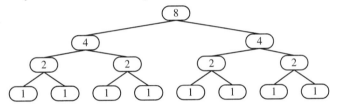

Figure 4.2: A recursion trace for the BinarySum algorithm, for the case when $n = 8$.

Computing Fibonacci Numbers via Binary Recursion

Let us consider the problem of computing kth Fibonacci number. Recall from Section 2.2.3, that the Fibonacci numbers are defined so that $F_0 = 0$, $F_1 = 1$, and

$$F_i = F_{i-1} + F_{i-2},$$

for $i > 1$. Given this definition, we can easily create an algorithm based on the use of binary recursion to compute the kth Fibonacci number, by calling BinaryFib(k) for the algorithm given in Code Fragment 4.6.

Algorithm BinaryFib(k):

    Input: An integer k

    Output: The kth Fibonacci number

    if $k \leq 1$ **then**

        return k

    else

        return BinaryFib($k-1$) + BinaryFib($k-2$)

Code Fragment 4.6: Computing the kth Fibonacci number using binary recursion.

Unfortunately, in spite of the Fibonacci definition looking like a binary recursion, using this technique is inefficient in this case. In fact, it takes an exponential number of calls to compute the kth Fibonacci number in this way. Specifically, let n_k denote the number of calls needed to compute BinaryFib(k). Then, we have the following values for the n_k's:

$$
\begin{aligned}
n_0 &= 1 \\
n_1 &= 1 \\
n_2 &= n_1 + n_0 + 1 = 1 + 1 + 1 = 3 \\
n_3 &= n_2 + n_1 + 1 = 3 + 1 + 1 = 5 \\
n_4 &= n_3 + n_2 + 1 = 5 + 3 + 1 = 9 \\
n_5 &= n_4 + n_3 + 1 = 9 + 5 + 1 = 15 \\
n_6 &= n_5 + n_4 + 1 = 15 + 9 + 1 = 25 \\
n_7 &= n_6 + n_5 + 1 = 25 + 15 + 1 = 41 \\
n_8 &= n_7 + n_6 + 1 = 41 + 25 + 1 = 67.
\end{aligned}
$$

If we follow the pattern forward, we see that the number of calls more than doubles for each two consecutive indices. That is, n_4 is more than twice n_2, n_5 is more than twice n_3, n_6 is more than twice n_4, and so on. Thus, $n_k > 2^{k/2}$, which means that the BinaryFib(k) makes a number of calls that are exponential in k. In other words, using binary recursion to compute Fibonacci numbers is very inefficient.

Computing Fibonacci Numbers via Linear Recursion

The main problem with the above approach, based on binary recursion, is that the computation of the kth Fibonacci number is really a linearly recursive problem. It is not a good candidate for using binary recursion. We simply got tempted into using binary recursion because of the way the kth Fibonacci number depends on two previous values. But we can compute the kth Fibonacci number much more efficiently using linear recursion.

In order to use linear recursion, however, we need to slightly redefine the problem so that the main problem will have the same form as any recursive call it would make. One way to accomplish this conversion is to define the recursive function so that it returns a pair (F_k, F_{k-1}), where F_k is the kth Fibonacci number and F_{k-1} is the $(k-1)$st Fibonacci number (using the convention that $F_{-1} = 0$). Then we can use the linearly recursive algorithm of Code Fragment 4.7.

Algorithm LinearFibonacci(k):

> *Input:* An integer k
>
> *Output:* A pair (F_k, F_{k-1}) such that F_k is the kth Fibonacci number and F_{k-1} is the $(k-1)$st Fibonacci number
>
> **if** $k \leq 1$ **then**
> > **return** $(k, 0)$
> **else**
> > $(i, j) \leftarrow$ LinearFibonacci($k-1$)
> > **return** $(i + j, i)$

Code Fragment 4.7: Computing the kth Fibonacci number using linear recursion.

The description given in Code Fragment 4.7 shows that using linear recursion to compute Fibonacci numbers is much more efficient than using binary recursion. Since each recursive call to LinearFibonacci decreases the argument k by 1, the original call LinearFibonacci(k) results in a sequence of $k-1$ additional calls. That is, computing the kth Fibonacci number via linear recursion requires only $O(k)$ function calls. This performance is significantly faster than the exponential time needed for the algorithm based on binary recursion, which was given in Code Fragment 4.6. Therefore, when using binary recursion we should first try to fully partition the problem in two (as we did for summing the elements of an array) or we should be sure that overlapping recursive calls are really necessary.

Usually, we can eliminate overlapping recursive calls by using more memory to keep track of previous values. In fact, this approach is a central part of a technique called ***dynamic programming***, which is related to recursion and is discussed in Section 11.5.2.

Multiple Recursion

Another type of higher order recursion is ***multiple recursion***, where a procedure may make multiple recursive calls, with that number potentially being more than two. One of the most common applications of this type of recursion is when we wish to enumerate various configurations in order to solve a combinatorial puzzle. For example, the following are all instances of summation puzzles.

$$
\begin{aligned}
POT + PAN &= BIB \\
DOG + CAT &= PIG \\
BOY + GIRL &= BABY
\end{aligned}
$$

To solve such a puzzle, we need to assign a unique digit (that is, $0, 1, \ldots, 9$) to each letter in the equation in order to make the equation true. Typically, we solve such a puzzle by using our human observations of the particular puzzle we are trying to solve to eliminate configurations (that is, possible partial assignments of digits to numbers) until we can work through the feasible configurations left, testing for the correctness of each one. If the number of possible configurations is not too large, however, we can use a computer to simply enumerate all the possibilities and test each one, without employing any human observations. In addition, such an algorithm can use multiple recursion to work through the configurations in a systematic way.

We show pseudo-code for such an algorithm in Code Fragment 4.8. To keep the description general enough to be used with any addition puzzle, we will describe the algorithm to enumerate and test all k-length sequences of the digits 0 through 9 without repetitions. Each position in the current sequence S will correspond to an assignment of a digit to a letter. For example, the first position could stand for B, the second for O, the third for Y, and so on. To keep track of the digits that have already been chosen, we will use a set U, of unused digits, so that a digit i will be unused up to this point if and only if i is in U. Initially, S is an empty sequence, and $U = \{0, 1, \ldots, 9\}$.

Another way to view the algorithm of Code Fragment 4.8 is that it is enumerating every possible k-length ***permutation*** of elements in U (without repetition), and testing each permutation for being a possible solution to our puzzle. Alternatively, we could use a similar method to simply enumerate all such permutations. In either case, the running time involves a function call for every possible permutation.

Algorithm PuzzleSolve(k, S, U):

> *Input:* An integer k, sequence S, and set U
>
> *Output:* An enumeration of all k-length extensions to S using elements in U

> **for** each i in U **do**
>
>> {Define a new set T that contains all the elements in U but i}
>>
>> Let $T \leftarrow U - \{i\}$ {i is now being used}
>>
>> Add i to the end of S
>>
>> **if** $k = 1$ **then**
>>
>>> Test if S represents a satisfying configuration
>>>
>>> **if** S represents a satisfying configuration **then**
>>>
>>>> **return** "Solution found: " S
>>
>> **else**
>>
>>> Call PuzzleSolve($k - 1, S, T$)
>>
>> Remove i from the end of S {i is now unused}

Code Fragment 4.8: Enumerating all possible configurations of digits.

In Figure 4.3, we show an example recursion trace of the PuzzleSolve algorithm applied to the problem of enumerating all the permutations of the characters "a," "b," and "c." That is, we use $U = \{a, b, c\}$ and $k = 3$. Note that the initial call spawns three recursive calls, which each in turn spawn two more. Thus, our recursion trace ultimately leads to $3! = 6$ base-case calls. If we had asked for all permutations of four characters, the initial call would have spawned four recursive calls, each of which would look like Figure 4.3.

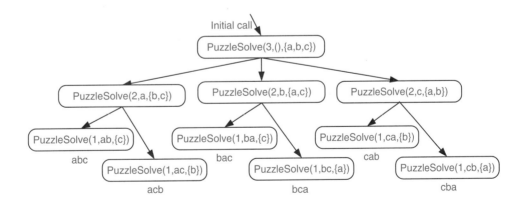

Figure 4.3: An example recursion trace for the PuzzleSolve algorithm, for enumerating all permutations of the characters "a," "b," and "c." We show the output of the final calls directly below their respective boxes.

4.2   Stacks

A *stack* is a container of objects that are inserted and removed according to the ***last-in first-out*** (***LIFO***) principle. Objects can be inserted into a stack at any time, but only the most recently inserted (that is, "last") object can be removed at any time. The name "stack" is derived from the metaphor of a stack of plates in a spring-loaded, cafeteria plate dispenser. In this case, the fundamental operations involve the "pushing" and "popping" of plates on the stack. When we need a new plate from the dispenser, we "pop" the top plate off the stack, and when we add a plate, we "push" it down on the stack to become the new top plate. Perhaps an even more amusing metaphor would be a PEZ® candy dispenser, which stores mint candies in a spring-loaded container that "pops" out the top-most candy in the stack when the top of the dispenser is lifted. (See Figure 4.4.) Stacks are a fundamental data structure. They are used in many applications, including the following.

Example 4.4: *Internet Web browsers store the addresses of recently visited sites on a stack. Each time a user visits a new site, that site's address is "pushed" onto the stack of addresses. The browser then allows the user to "pop" back to previously visited sites using the "back" button.*

Example 4.5: *Text editors usually provide an "undo" mechanism that cancels recent editing operations and reverts to former states of a document. This undo operation can be accomplished by keeping text changes in a stack.*

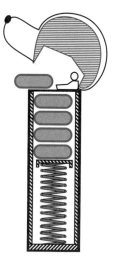

Figure 4.4: A schematic drawing of a PEZ® dispenser; a physical implementation of the stack ADT. (PEZ® is a registered trademark of PEZ Candy, Inc.)

4.2.1   The Stack Abstract Data Type

A stack S is an abstract data type (ADT) that supports the following two functions:

push(o): Insert object o at the top of the stack.
Input: Object; **Output:** None.

pop(): Remove from the stack and return the top object on the stack; an error occurs if the stack is empty.
Input: None; **Output:** Object.

Additionally, let us also define the following supporting functions:

size(): Return the number of objects in the stack.
Input: None; **Output:** Integer.

isEmpty(): Return a Boolean indicating if the stack is empty.
Input: None; **Output:** Boolean.

top(): Return the top object on the stack, without removing it; an error occurs if the stack is empty.
Input: None; **Output:** Object.

Example 4.6: *The following table shows a series of stack operations and their effects on an initially empty stack of integers.*

Operation	Output	Stack Contents
push(5)	–	(5)
push(3)	–	(5,3)
pop()	3	(5)
push(7)	–	(5,7)
pop()	7	(5)
top()	5	(5)
pop()	5	()
pop()	"error"	()
isEmpty()	true	()
push(9)	–	(9)
push(7)	–	(9,7)
push(3)	–	(9,7,3)
push(5)	–	(9,7,3,5)
size()	4	(9,7,3,5)
pop()	5	(9,7,3)
push(8)	–	(9,7,3,8)
pop()	8	(9,7,3)
pop()	3	(9,7)

A Stack Interface

When implementing an abstract data type, our principal concern is specifying the **Application Programming Interface** (API), or simply *interface*, which describes the names of the public members that the ADT must support and how they are to be declared and used. An interface is not a complete description of all the public members, but rather a list of members that any implementation must provide.

The informal interface for our stack ADT is given in Code Fragment 4.9. This interface defines a class template. Recall from Section 2.3 that such a definition implies that the actual type of object being stored in the stack will be provided by the user as type Object. Type Object may be any type that can be copied. This includes fundamental types, (such as int or double), a built-in or user-defined classes (such as string), and pointers and references.

```
/**
 * Interface for a stack: A collection of objects that are inserted
 * and removed according to the last-in first-out principle.
 */
template <typename Object>
class Stack {
public:
  /**
   * Returns number of objects in the stack.
   */
  int size() const;
  /**
   * Returns true if the stack is empty, false otherwise.
   */
  bool isEmpty() const;
  /**
   * Returns the top object in the stack.
   * Throws StackEmptyException if the stack is empty.
   */
  Object& top() throw(StackEmptyException);
  /**
   * Inserts an object at the top of the stack.
   */
  void push(const Object& obj);
  /**
   * Removes and returns the top object from the stack.
   * Throws StackEmptyException if the stack is empty.
   */
  Object pop() throw(StackEmptyException);
};
```

Code Fragment 4.9: An informal Stack interface (not a complete C++ class).

Recall from Section 1.1.3 that arrays in C++ are treated as a pointer to their initial element. Hence, pushing an array on our stack would be equivalent to pushing a pointer to the array.

The error condition that occurs when calling function pop() or top() on an empty stack is signaled by throwing an exception of type StackEmptyException, which is defined in Code Fragment 4.10.

```
/**
 * Exception thrown on performing top or pop of an empty stack.
 */
class StackEmptyException : public RuntimeException {
public:
  StackEmptyException(const string& err) : RuntimeException(err) {}
};
```

Code Fragment 4.10: Exception thrown by functions pop() and top() of the Stack interface when called on an empty stack. This class is derived from RuntimeException from Section 2.4.

As we mentioned above, stacks are provided as one of the "built-in" classes in C++'s Standard Template Library (STL). As a templated type it can be used for storing almost any type of object. It includes the member functions push(), pop(), top(), size(), and empty() (equivalent to our isEmpty()). There are a few differences between the STL stack interface and ours. The STL pop() member function only performs the pop operation and does not return a value. Also, an attempt to invoke top() or pop() on an empty STL stack is undefined. In our implementation an exception is thrown.

We still need to provide a concrete class that implements the functions of the interface associated with this ADT. We give a simple implementation of the Stack interface later.

Access to Elements

Notice that in our stack interface in Code Fragment 4.9, the member function top() returns a reference to the object at the top of the stack, whereas the function pop() returns an actual copy of an object. Why did we make this distinction?

When designing an abstract data type, it is important to consider exactly what type of access we would like to provide to users of the data type. C++ provides many choices for how these elements may be accessed. It is possible to return a copy of the element (as pop() does), a reference to the element (as top() does), a constant reference to the element, or a pointer to the element. Depending on how we intend the data structure to be used, all of these may be reasonable choices.

One of the advantages of returning a reference to an element is that it allows the user to modify this element, as in "st.top() = 5." Had top() returned a copy of this object, such an assignment would not be possible. Another advantage becomes evident if the type Object is a large class. Returning a copy would involve invoking a copy constructor for the object and possibly allocating new memory. Accessing such a structure through a reference can be much more efficient.

In many cases, it is not desirable to allow a user to modify the contents of an object. For example, a data structure may store objects in ascending order. Allowing the user to modify elements could destroy the data structure's integrity. Nonetheless, it may still be desirable to avoid the cost of making a copy of the object. In this case, returning a ***constant reference*** is an excellent choice. It provides access for reading the object, but not for modifying it, and no object copying is required. Code Fragment 4.11 shows how a constant reference function is declared. Notice that this function returns a constant reference (indicated by the first "const"), and it is declared to be a constant member function (indicated by the second "const"). By declaring this to be a constant member function, we inform the compiler that this function does not modify the Stack object, which is often important. For example, suppose that a Stack object is passed to a function as a constant reference argument (const Stack&). In such a case, the compiler would not allow the use of a "nonconst" version of function top().

```
template <typename Object>
class Stack {
public:
  // ...
  const Object& top() const throw(StackEmptyException);
```

Code Fragment 4.11: Declaration of a constant reference version of top() for the Stack interface.

It is possible to provide both constant and nonconstant reference accessors simultaneously. The compiler simply uses the one that it appropriate for the particular occasion. Unless there is a reason to deny class users the ability to modify elements, it is a good idea to provide both types. In our code examples, we will usually show only one, but this is just to save space.

After discussing the value of using references, it is natural to wonder why we declared the function pop() to return a copy of the object that was removed, rather than a reference. In this case, it would not make sense to return a reference because the object is no longer in the stack, and there is nothing for the reference to refer to. Thus copying is unavoidable. As we mentioned above, the STL avoids this by defining pop() so that it does not return any value.

4.2.2   A Simple Array-Based Implementation

We can implement a stack by storing its elements in an array. Specifically, the stack in this implementation consists of an N-element array S plus an integer variable t that gives the index of the top element in array S. (See Figure 4.5.)

S 0   1   2 t N–1

Figure 4.5: Realization of a stack by means of an array S. The top element in the stack is stored in the cell $S[t]$.

Recalling that arrays start at index 0 in C++, we initialize t to -1, and use this value for t to identify when the stack is empty. Likewise, we can use this variable to determine the number of elements in a stack ($t+1$). We also introduce a new type of exception, called StackFullException, to signal the error condition that arises if we try to insert a new element and the array S is full. Exception StackFullException is specific to our implementation of a stack and is not defined in the stack ADT. Given this new exception, we can then implement the stack ADT functions as described in Code Fragment 4.12.

Algorithm size():
>   **return** $t+1$

Algorithm isEmpty():
>   **return** ($t < 0$)

Algorithm top():
>   **if** isEmpty() **then**
>>   throw a StackEmptyException
>
>   **return** $S[t]$

Algorithm push(o):
>   **if** size() $= N$ **then**
>>   throw a StackFullException
>
> $t \leftarrow t + 1$
> $S[t] \leftarrow o$

Algorithm pop():
>   **if** isEmpty() **then**
>>   throw a StackEmptyException
>
> $o \leftarrow S[t]$.
> $t \leftarrow t - 1$
>   **return** o

>   **Code Fragment 4.12:** Implementation of a stack by means of an array.

A C++ Implementation of a Stack

A concrete C++ implementation of the above pseudo-code specification, by means of class ArrayStack implementing the Stack interface, is given in Code Fragments 4.13 and 4.14.

In Code Fragment 4.13, we show the private member data and principal stack member functions. We use an enumeration to define the constant capacity value. This is the simplest and most reliable way of defining integer member constants in C++.

Recall that an array can be represented as a pointer to its first element in C++. Thus the stack contents array S is declared as a pointer to type Object.

We have supplied a constructor to initialize the member data based on a given capacity value. This constructor initializes the capacity, allocates storage for the stack's array, and initializes the top pointer. The remaining stack functions are just straightforward implementations of the pseudo-code specification in Code Fragment 4.12.

Since ArrayStack allocates memory, we should provide a copy constructor, assignment operator, and a destructor (recall Section 1.5.2). These are presented in Code Fragment 4.14. The copy constructor copies the associated data members and then allocates and copies the contents of the stack array. The assignment operator first checks against self-assignment, then deletes the existing stack and allocates and copies the stack contents. The destructor simply deallocates the stack array.

In our implementation, we dynamically allocate storage for the stack array. An alternative method would be to use the STL's vector class for storing this array. One advantage of using the STL vector is that it automatically provides its own storage allocation and housekeeping functions, and therefore, it would not be necessary for us to provide them. The vector class also allows for automatic extensibility of the array, so there is no need to throw a StackFullException. Nonetheless, it is important to see how to implement these basic data structures from scratch, without the use of any STL objects.

Other than the housekeeping functions, Code Fragments 4.13 and 4.14 form a nearly complete include file, which might be called ArrayStack.h. We have not shown the #include statements, which include the header file containing declarations for the various exceptions that are used here. We have also not shown some of the other elements that are common to include files (see Section 1.6.1), and instead concentrate on just the class structure.

```
template <typename Object>
class ArrayStack {
private:                              // member data
  enum { CAPACITY = 1000 };          // default capacity of stack
  int      capacity;                 // actual length of stack array
  Object*  S;                        // the stack array
  int      t;                        // index of the top of the stack
public:
                                     // constructor given max capacity
  ArrayStack(int cap = CAPACITY) {
    capacity = cap;
    S        = new Object[capacity];
    t        = -1;
  }
  int size() const                   // number of elements in the stack
    { return (t + 1); }
  bool isEmpty() const               // is the stack empty?
    { return (t < 0); }
                                     // return the top of the stack
  Object& top() throw(StackEmptyException) {
    if (isEmpty())
      throw StackEmptyException("Access to empty stack");
    return S[t];
  }
                                     // push object onto the stack
  void push(const Object& elem) throw(StackFullException) {
    if (size() == capacity)
      throw StackFullException("Stack overflow");
    S[++t] = elem;
  }
                                     // pop the stack
  Object pop() throw(StackEmptyException) {
    if (isEmpty())
      throw StackEmptyException("Access to empty stack");
    return S[t--];
  }
  // ...
```

Code Fragment 4.13: Start of the array-based implementation of the Stack interface, showing the private member variables and the principal stack member functions. (Continues in Code Fragment 4.14.)

```
// ... (continuation of ArrayStack)
ArrayStack(const ArrayStack& st);   // copy constructor
                                    // assignment operator constructor
ArrayStack& operator=(const ArrayStack& st);
~ArrayStack()                       // destructor
    { delete [] S; }
};

template <typename Object>          // copy constructor
ArrayStack<Object>::
ArrayStack(const ArrayStack& st) {
  capacity  = st.capacity;
  t         = st.t;
  S         = new Object[capacity];
  for (int i = 0; i <= t; i++) {    // copy contents
    S[i] = st.S[i];
  }
}

template <typename Object>          // assignment operator
ArrayStack<Object>& ArrayStack<Object>::
operator=(const ArrayStack& st) {
  if (this != &st) {                // avoid self copy (x = x)
    delete [] S;                    // delete old contents
    capacity  = st.capacity;
    t         = st.t;
    S         = new Object[capacity];
    for (int i = 0; i <= t; i++) {  // copy contents
      S[i] = st.S[i];
    }
  }
  return *this;
}
```

Code Fragment 4.14: Continuation of class ArrayStack, showing housekeeping functions. (Continued from Code Fragment 4.13.)

Running Time

Table 4.1 shows the running times for member functions in a realization of a stack by an array.

Method	Time
size	$O(1)$
isEmpty	$O(1)$
top	$O(1)$
push	$O(1)$
pop	$O(1)$

Table 4.1: Performance of a stack realized by an array. The space usage is $O(N)$, where N is the size of the array, determined at the time the stack is instantiated. Note that the space usage is independent from the number $n \leq N$ of elements that are actually in the stack.

Each of the stack functions in the array realization executes a constant number of statements involving arithmetic operations, comparisons, and assignments. Thus, in this implementation of the Stack ADT, each function runs in constant time, that is, they each run in $O(1)$ time.

The array implementation of a stack is both simple and efficient, and is widely used in a variety of computing applications. Nevertheless, this implementation has one negative aspect—it must assume a fixed upper bound N on the ultimate size of the stack. In Code Fragment 4.13, we chose the default capacity value $N = 1,000$ more or less arbitrarily. An application may actually need much less space than this, in which case we would be wasting memory.

Alternatively, an application may need more space than this, in which case our stack implementation may "crash" the application with an error as soon as it tries to push its $(N+1)$st object on the stack. Thus, even with its simplicity and efficiency, the array-based stack implementation is not necessarily ideal.

Fortunately, there are other implementations, discussed later in this chapter, that do not have a size limitation and use space proportional to the actual number of elements stored in the stack. In cases where we have a good estimate on the number of items needing to go in the stack, however, the array-based implementation is hard to beat. Stacks serve a vital role in a number of computing applications, so it is helpful to have a fast stack ADT implementation, such as the simple array-based implementation.

4.2.3   Implementing Recursion and Function Calls

Stacks are important elements in the run-time environment of virtually all programming languages, including C++.

The C++ Run-time Stack

A running C++ program has a private stack, called the ***run-time stack*** or simply ***stack***, which is used to keep track of local variables and other important information on functions, as they are invoked during execution. (See Figure 4.6.) Moreover, the existence of this stack is what enables a programming language like C++ to implement recursion.

More specifically, during the execution of a program, the run-time system uses a stack whose elements are ***descriptors***, of the currently active (that is, nonterminated) invocations of functions. These descriptors are called ***frames***. A frame for some invocation of function cool() stores the current values of the local variables and parameters of function cool(), as well as information on the function that called cool() and on what needs to be returned.

How Functions are Called

Skipping a few details, we can provide a somewhat simplified explanation of how functions are called.

As a program is executing, a register, called the ***program counter***, keeps track of which machine instruction is currently being executed. When the function cool() invokes another function fool(), the current value of the program counter is recorded in the frame of the current invocation of cool() (so the system will know where to return to when function fool() is done). At the top of the stack is the frame of the ***running function***, that is, the function that is currently executing.

The remaining elements of the stack are frames of the ***suspended functions***. A function is suspended when it calls another function, and it remains suspended until the function it has called finally returns. Together the running and suspended functions constitute the current set of ***active functions***. When a new function is invoked, a frame for this function is pushed onto the stack. As one function calls another and then another, the frames for these functions are successively pushed onto the stack. As functions terminate, these stack frames are popped off the run-time stack.

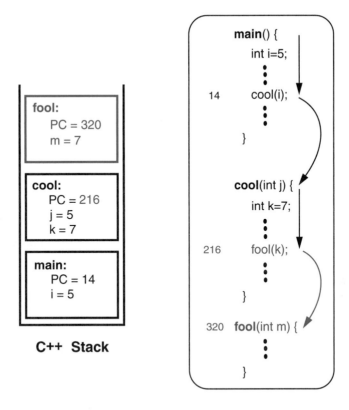

C++ Stack

C++ Program

Figure 4.6: An example of a run-time stack: Method fool() has just been called by function cool(), which itself was previously called by function main(). Note the values of the program counter (PC), parameters, and local variables stored in the stack frames. When the invocation of function fool() terminates, the invocation of function cool() will resume its execution at instruction 217, which is obtained by incrementing the value of the program counter stored in the stack frame.

Implementing Call by Value

Among other things, the stack performs parameter passing to functions. Assume that we are passing function arguments *by value*. This means that the current *value* of a variable (or expression) is passed as an argument to a called function. In the case of a variable *x* of a primitive type, such as an int or float, the variable's current value is copied onto the stack frame of the newly called function. (This simple assignment is also illustrated in Figure 4.6.) Note that if the called function changes the value of this local variable, it will *not* change the value of the variable in the calling function.

Implementing Call by Reference

In contrast, when an argument is passed *by reference*, the system copies the address of the argument to the stack frame. The system knows that this is a reference argument, and hence any use of the argument within the called function is redirected through this pointer so that it is applied to the original argument in the calling function.

Implementing Recursion with a Stack

One of the benefits of using a stack to implement function invocation is that it allows programs to use *recursion*. That is, it allows a function to call itself as a subroutine. Interestingly, early programming languages, such as Cobol and Fortran, did not originally use run-time stacks to implement function and procedure calls. But because of the elegance and efficiency that recursion allows, all modern programming languages, including the modern versions of classic languages like Cobol and Fortran, utilize a run-time stack for function and procedure calls.

To illustrate better how a run-time stack allows for recursive functions, let us consider a C++ implementation of the classic recursive definition of the factorial function, $n! = n(n-1)(n-2)\cdots 1$, as shown in Code Fragment 4.15.

```
long factorial(long n) {          // returns n!
  if (n <= 1)
    return 1;                      // 0! = 1! = 1
  else
    return n * factorial(n−1);     // n! = n * (n-1)!
}
```

Code Fragment 4.15: Recursive function factorial().

The first time we call the function factorial, its stack frame includes a local variable storing the value n. The function factorial() recursively calls itself to compute the factorial of $n-1$, which pushes a new frame on the run-time stack (this frame is for the call with value $n-1$). In turn, this recursive invocation calls itself to compute the factorial of $n-2$, etc. The chain of recursive invocations, and thus the run-time stack, grows only up to size n, because calling factorial(1) returns 1 immediately without invoking itself recursively. The run-time stack allows for the function factorial() to exist simultaneously in several active frames (as many as n at some point). Each frame stores the value of its parameter n as well as the value to be returned. Eventually, when the first recursive call terminates, it returns $(n-1)!$, which is then multiplied by n to compute $n!$ for the original call of the factorial function.

4.3 Queues

Another fundamental data structure is the *queue*, which is a close "cousin" of the stack. A queue is a container of objects that are inserted and removed according to the *first-in first-out* (*FIFO*) principle. Elements can be inserted in a queue at any time, but only the element that has been in the queue the longest can be removed at any time. We usually say that elements enter the queue at the *rear* and are removed from the *front*. The metaphor for this terminology is a line of people waiting to get on an amusement park ride. People enter at the rear of the line and get on the ride from the front of the line.

4.3.1 The Queue Abstract Data Type

Formally, the queue abstract data type defines a container that keeps objects in a sequence, where element access and deletion are restricted to the first element in the sequence, which is called the *front* of the queue, and element insertion is restricted to the end of the sequence, which is called the *rear* of the queue. This restriction enforces the rule that items are inserted and deleted in a queue according to the first-in first-out (FIFO) principle.

The *queue* abstract data type (ADT) supports the following two functions:

enqueue(o): Insert object o at the rear of the queue.
Input: Object; **Output:** None.

dequeue(): Remove and return from the queue the object at the front; an error occurs if the queue is empty.
Input: None; **Output:** Object.

Notice that, as with the stack pop() operation, the dequeue() operation returns the object that was removed (an alternative to avoid unnecessary copying by defining dequeue() so that no value is returned). The queue ADT also includes the following supporting member functions:

size(): Return the number of objects in the queue.
Input: None; **Output:** Integer.

isEmpty(): Return a Boolean value indicating if the queue is empty.
Input: None; **Output:** Boolean.

first(): Return, but do not remove, a reference to the front element in the queue; an error occurs if the queue is empty.
Input: None; **Output:** Object.

We illustrate the operations in the queue ADT in the following example.

Example 4.7: *The following table shows a series of queue operations and their effects on an initially empty queue Q of integers.*

Operation	Output	front $\leftarrow$ Q $\leftarrow$ rear
enqueue(5)	–	(5)
enqueue(3)	–	(5,3)
dequeue()	5	(3)
enqueue(7)	–	(3,7)
dequeue()	3	(7)
front()	7	(7)
dequeue()	7	()
dequeue()	"error"	()
isEmpty()	true	()
enqueue(9)	–	(9)
enqueue(7)	–	(9,7)
size()	2	(9,7)
enqueue(3)	–	(9,7,3)
enqueue(5)	–	(9,7,3,5)
dequeue()	9	(7,3,5)

A Queue Interface

Our interface for the queue ADT is given in Code Fragment 4.16. As with the stack ADT, the class is templated, which implies that the type Object will be provided by the user.

Note that the size() and isEmpty() functions have the same meaning as their counterparts in the Stack ADT. These two functions, as well as the front() function, are known as *accessor* functions, for they return a value and do not change the contents of the data structure. Also note the use of the QueueEmptyException to indicate the error state of an empty queue.

Example Applications

There are several possible applications for queues. Stores, theaters, public offices, reservation centers, and other similar service organizations typically serve customers according to the FIFO principle. A queue would therefore be a logical choice for a data structure to handle transaction processing for such applications. For example, it would be a natural choice for handling incoming calls to an automated airline reservation center, where callers are requesting seats on flights for a particular airline.

```
/**
 * Interface for a queue: A collection of objects that are inserted
 * and removed according to the first-in first-out principle.
 */
template <typename Object>
class Queue {
public:
  /**
   * Returns the number of objects in the queue.
   */
  int size() const;
  /**
   * Returns true if the queue is empty, false otherwise.
   */
  bool isEmpty() const;
  /**
   * Returns the front object of the queue.
   * Throws QueueEmptyException if the queue is empty.
   */
  Object& front() throw(QueueEmptyException);
  /**
   * Inserts an object at the rear of the queue.
   */
  void enqueue (const Object& obj);
  /**
   * Remove and returns the object at the front of the queue.
   * Throws QueueEmptyException if the queue is empty.
   */
  Object dequeue() throw(QueueEmptyException);
};
```

Code Fragment 4.16: An informal Queue interface (not a complete C++ class).

4.3.2 A Simple Array-Based Implementation

We present a simple realization of a queue by means of an array, Q, with capacity N, for storing its elements, say, with $N = 1,000$. The main issue with this implementation is deciding how to keep track of the front and rear of the queue.

One possibility is to adapt the approach we used for the stack implementation, letting $Q[0]$ be the front of the queue, and then letting the queue grow from there. This is not an efficient solution, however, for it requires that we move all the elements forward one array cell each time we perform a dequeue() operation. Such an implementation would therefore require $\Theta(n)$ time to perform the dequeue() function, where n is the current number of objects in the queue. If we want to achieve constant time for each queue function, we need a different approach.

Using an Array in a Circular Way

To avoid moving objects once they are placed in Q, we define two variables, f and r, which have the following meanings:

- f is an index to the cell of Q storing the first element of the queue (which is the next candidate to be removed by a dequeue() operation), unless the queue is empty (in which case $f = r$).

- r is an index to the next available array cell in Q.

Initially, we assign $f = r = 0$, which indicates that the queue is empty. Now, when we remove an element from the front of the queue, we can simply increment f to index the next cell. Likewise, when we add an element, we can simply increment r to index the next available cell in Q. This scheme allows us to implement the enqueue() and dequeue() functions in constant time, that is, $O(1)$ time. Nonetheless, there is still a problem with this approach.

Consider, for example, what happens if we repeatedly enqueue and dequeue a single element N different times. We would have $f = r = N$. If we were then to try to insert the element just one more time, we would get an array-out-of-bounds error (since the N valid locations in Q are from $Q[0]$ to $Q[N-1]$), even though there is plenty of room in the queue in this case. To avoid this problem and be able to utilize all of the array Q, we let the f and r indices "wrap around" the end of Q. That is, we now view Q as a "circular array" that goes from $Q[0]$ to $Q[N-1]$ and then immediately back to $Q[0]$ again. (See Figure 4.7.)

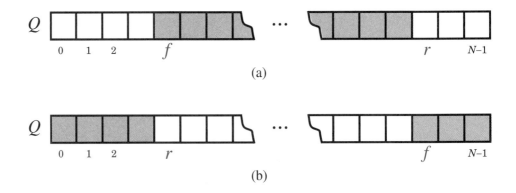

Figure 4.7: Using array Q in a circular fashion: (a) the "normal" configuration with $f \leq r$; (b) the "wrapped around" configuration with $r < f$. The cells storing queue elements are highlighted.

Using the Modulo Operator to Implement a Circular Array

Implementing this circular view of Q is actually pretty easy. Each time we increment f or r, we simply need to compute this increment as "$(f+1)$ mod N" or "$(r+1)$ mod N," respectively, where the operator "mod" is the *modulo* operator. This operator is computed for a positive number by taking the remainder after an integral division, so that, if x is non-negative and y is positive, then x mod $y = x - \lfloor x/y \rfloor y$. That is, if $r = x$ mod y, then there is a non-negative integer q, such that $x = qy + r$. C++ uses "%" to denote the modulo operator. By using the modulo operator, we can view Q as a circular array and implement each queue function to run in a constant amount of time (that is, $O(1)$ time). Thus, we can solve the array-overflow problem by using the modulo operator, but one small problem yet remains with this approach. We describe how to use this approach to implement a queue in Code Fragment 4.17.

Algorithm size():
    return $(N - f + r)$ mod N

Algorithm isEmpty():
    return $(f = r)$

Algorithm front():
    if isEmpty() **then**
        throw a QueueEmptyException
    return $Q[f]$

Algorithm dequeue():
    if isEmpty() **then**
        throw a QueueEmptyException
    $temp \leftarrow Q[f]$
    $f \leftarrow (f+1)$ mod N
    return $temp$

Algorithm enqueue(o):
    if size() $= N - 1$ **then**
        throw a QueueFullException
    $Q[r] \leftarrow o$
    $r \leftarrow (r+1)$ mod N

Code Fragment 4.17: Implementation of a queue using a circular array. The implementation uses the modulo operator to "wrap" indices around the end of the array and it also includes two member variables, f and r, which index the front of the queue and first empty cell after the rear of the queue respectively.

The above implementation contains an important detail, which might at first be missed. Namely, consider the situation that occurs if we enqueue N objects into Q without dequeuing any of them. We would have $f = r$, which is the same condition that occurs when the queue is empty. Hence, we would not be able to tell the difference between a full queue and an empty one in this case. Fortunately, this is not a big problem, and a number of ways for dealing with it exist. The solution we describe is to insist that Q can never hold more than $N - 1$ objects. (We explore another solution in an exercise.)

Note that we introduced a new exception, called QueueFullException, to signal that no more elements can be inserted in the queue. Also note the way we compute the size of the queue by means of the expression $(N - f + r)$ mod N, which gives the correct result both in the "normal" configuration (when $f \leq r$) and in the "wrapped around" configuration (when $r < f$). Our implementation of a queue by means of an array is similar to that of a stack, and is left as an exercise.

Table 4.2 shows the running times of functions in a realization of a queue by an array. As with our array-based stack implementation, each of the queue functions in the array realization executes a constant number of statements involving arithmetic operations, comparisons, and assignments. Thus each function in this implementation runs in $O(1)$ time.

Method	Time
size	$O(1)$
isEmpty	$O(1)$
front	$O(1)$
enqueue	$O(1)$
dequeue	$O(1)$

Table 4.2: Performance of a queue realized by an array. The space usage is $O(N)$, where N is the size of the array, determined at the time the queue is created. Note that the space usage is independent from the number $n < N$ of elements that are actually in the queue.

As with the array-based stack implementation, the only real disadvantage of the array-based queue implementation is that we artificially set the capacity of the queue to be some number N. In a real application, we may actually need more or less queue capacity than this, but if we have a good estimate of the number of elements that will be in the queue at the same time, then the array-based implementation is quite efficient. One such possible application of a queue is dynamic memory allocation in C++, which we discuss next.

4.3.3 Memory Allocation in C++

We have already discussed (in Section 4.2.3) how the C++ run-time system allocates a function's local variables in that function's frame on the run-time stack. The stack is not the only kind of memory available for program data in C++, however. Memory can also be allocated dynamically by using the new operator, which is built into C++. For example, in Chapter 1, we learned that we can allocate an array of 100 integers as follows:

int* items = new int[100];

Memory allocated in this manner can be deallocated with "delete [ ] items."

Instead of using the run-time stack for this object's memory, C++ uses memory from another area of storage—the **memory heap** (which should not be confused with the "heap" data structure we will discuss in Chapter 7). We illustrate this memory area, together with the other memory areas, in Figure 4.8. The storage available in the memory heap is divided into **blocks**, which are contiguous array-like "chunks" of memory that may be of variable or fixed sizes.

To simplify the discussion, let us assume that blocks in the memory heap are of a fixed size, say, 1,024 bytes, and that one block is big enough for any object we might want to create. (Efficiently handling the more general case is actually an interesting research problem.)

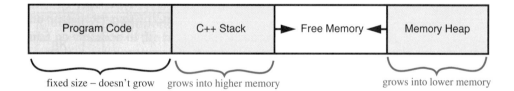

Figure 4.8: A schematic view of the layout of memory addresses in a C++ program.

The memory heap must be able to allocate memory blocks quickly for new objects. Different run-time systems use different approaches. We therefore exercise this freedom and choose to use a queue to manage the unused blocks in the memory heap. When a function uses the new operator to request a block of memory for some new object, the run-time system can perform a dequeue() operation on the queue of unused blocks to provide a free block of memory in the memory heap. Likewise, when the user deallocates a block of memory using delete, then the run-time system can perform an enqueue() operation to return this block to the queue of available blocks.

4.4   Linked Lists

In previous sections, we presented stack and queue ADTs, and discussed some of their important applications. We also showed how to implement these abstract data types with concrete data structures based on arrays. While these implementations are quite simple, they have the drawback of not being very adaptable, since the size N of the array must be fixed in advance. There are other ways to implement these data structures, however, that do not have this drawback. In this section, we explore an important alternate implementation, which is known as the singly linked list.

4.4.1   Singly Linked Lists

A *linked list* in its simplest form is a collection of *nodes* that together form a linear ordering. The ordering is determined as in the children's game "Follow the Leader," in that each node is a compound object that stores a data member, called its *element*, and a pointer, called *next*, to the next node in the list. Figure 4.9 shows an example of a list containing 3-character strings of common airport abbreviations.

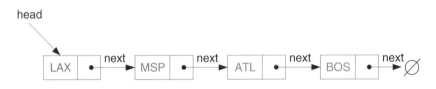

Figure 4.9: A singly linked list. Elements are indicated in blue, and the next pointers are shown with black arrows. The NULL object is denoted as ∅. The head pointer is a single variable.

Moving from one node to another by following a *next* pointer is known as *link hopping* or *pointer hopping*. The first and last node of a linked list are called the *head* and *tail* of the list, respectively. We can identify the tail as the node having a null *next* pointer, which indicates the end of the list. A linked list defined in this way is known as a *singly linked list*.

Like an array, a singly linked list keeps the elements in a certain linear order, which is determined by the chain of *next* pointers between the nodes. Unlike an array, a singly linked list does not have a predetermined fixed size and uses space proportional to the number of its elements.

More precisely, the space usage of a singly linked list with n elements is $O(n)$, since it has n nodes and each node uses $O(1)$ space to store a copy of the associated element and a link to the next node. That is, each node of a singly linked list consists of two fields: the element value associated with the node and a pointer to the next node in the linked list. In addition, the linked list class itself maintains a pointer to the head of the list. Other information may also be stored, such as a pointer to the tail of the list and the number of elements in the list.

With a singly linked list, we can easily insert or delete an element at the head of the list in $O(1)$ time, as shown in Figure 4.10. We create a new node, set its *next* pointer to refer to the same object as the head, and then set the head to point to the new node. Note that this simple procedure works even when the linked list is empty and the head is equal to the null pointer.

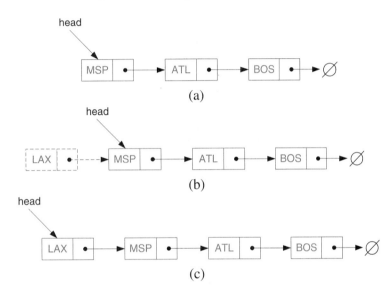

Figure 4.10: Insertion of an element at the head of a singly linked list: (a) before the insertion; (b) creation of a new node; (c) after the insertion. Deleting an element from the head of the list is a symmetric operation, which can be visualized by looking first at (c), then (b), and finally (a).

We can also insert an element at the tail of the list in $O(1)$ time, provided we keep a pointer to the tail node, as shown in Figure 4.11. In this case, we create a new node, assign its next pointer to null, set the next pointer of the tail to point to this new object, and then assign the tail pointer itself to this new node.

We cannot delete the tail node of a singly linked list in $O(1)$ time, however. Even if we have a tail pointer directly to the last node of the list, we must be able to access the node *before* the last node, in order to remove the last node. This is one time when it is appropriate to say, "you can't get there from here," for we cannot reach the node before a node v by following next links from v. The only way to

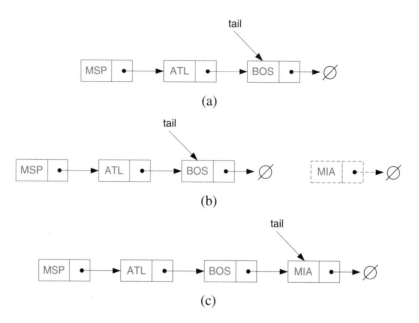

Figure 4.11: Insertion of an element at the tail of a singly linked list: (a) before the insertion; (b) creation of a new node; (c) after the insertion. Note that it is crucial that we set the next pointer for the tail in (b) before we assign the tail variable to point to the new node in (c).

access the node before v is to start from the head of the list and search all the way through the list until coming to a node whose **next** pointer points to v. But if v is the last node, such link hopping takes an amount of time proportional to the number of elements in the list, that is, $\Theta(n)$ time.

4.4.2 Implementing a Stack with a Singly Linked List

Let us explore using a singly linked list to implement the stack ADT. In principle, the top of the stack could be either at the head or at the tail of the list. Since we can insert and delete elements in $O(1)$ time only at the head, it is more efficient to have the top of the stack at the head.

Let us consider a class called LinkedStack. First we need to define an object for the nodes of the list. We define a Node structure, as shown in Code Fragment 4.18. This small object is not sufficiently complex to merit being a class. It consists of two members, the node's element, elem, and the pointer to the next node, next. We define the type NodePtr to be a pointer to such a node. Since this structure is only used by our stack, we embed its definition within LinkedStack. Because derived classes may want to access nodes, we will insert this definition in the protected portion of LinkedStack.

```
struct Node {                                // a node in the stack
    Object element;                          // element
    Node* next;                              // next pointer
    Node(const Object& e = Object(), Node* n = NULL)
        : element(e), next(n) { }            // constructor
};
typedef Node* NodePtr;                       // pointer type to node
```

Code Fragment 4.18: The structure Node, which will be used to represent a node in class LinkedStack. (See Code Fragment 4.19.)

The principal elements of class LinkedStack appear in Code Fragment 4.19. The private data members of our class LinkedStack consist of a pointer to the head of the linked list as our top of stack pointer, denoted tp. Also, in order to perform operation size() in $O(1)$ time, we keep track of the current number of elements in the data member sz.

Housekeeping Functions

Because our LinkedClass class allocates memory, we must be careful with our memory management by defining a copy constructor, assignment operator, and a destructor. Throughout most of this book, we will usually omit these functions. Since this is the first linked structure we have seen, however, let us take a moment to see how they are defined.

We first define two utility member functions, which will be useful for copying and deleting. The member function removeAll() removes all the elements from the queue by repeated popping. The member function copyFrom() creates a copy of the contents of an existing linked stack. This function is only called when the current object is empty. Since these functions are only for internal use, we declare them to be protected. Using these two functions, we can define a copy constructor, assignment operator, and destructor, which we present in Code Fragment 4.20. We present copyFrom() in Code Fragment 4.21.

The functions copyFrom() and removeAll() require $O(n)$ time, where n is the number of elements in the list, but they are not part of the stack ADT. All of the stack ADT operations can be done in $O(1)$ time. In addition to being time efficient, this linked list implementation has some significant advantages over the fixed-size array stack. There is no artificial limit to its size, and it uses $O(n)$ space, where n is the current number of elements in the stack.

```
template <typename Object>
class LinkedStack {
protected:                                          // local node structure
  // ... (insert Node here)
private:                                             // member data
  NodePtr tp;                                        // pointer to stack top
  int sz;                                            // number of items in stack
public:
  LinkedStack() {                                    // default constructor
    tp = NULL;
    sz = 0;
  }
  int size() const { return sz; }                    // number of elements in stack
  bool isEmpty() const { return sz == 0; }           // is the stack empty?
                                                     // return stack top
  Object& top() throw(StackEmptyException) {
    if (isEmpty())
      throw StackEmptyException("Top of empty stack");
    return tp->element;
  }
  void push(const Object& e) {                       // push element onto stack
    NodePtr v = new Node(e, tp);
    tp = v;                                          // v is now the top
    sz++;
  }
  Object pop() throw(StackEmptyException) {          // pop top element
    if (isEmpty())
      throw StackEmptyException("Pop of empty stack");
    NodePtr old = tp;                                // node to remove
    tp = tp->next;
    sz--;
    Object result = old->element;                    // element to return
    delete old;
    return result;
  }
// ... (insert housekeeping functions here)
};
```

Code Fragment 4.19: Class LinkedStack, which implements the Stack ADT using a linked list. Function push() allocates a new node containing the new element and pointing to the current top of stack. The function pop() deletes the storage for the node that has been removed and updates to top pointer. (Continues in Code Fragment 4.20.)

```
// ... (continuation of LinkedStack)
protected:                                      // protected utilities
  void removeAll()                              // remove entire stack contents
    { while (!isEmpty()) pop(); }
  void copyFrom(const LinkedStack& ls);         // copy from ls

public:
  LinkedStack(const LinkedStack& ls)            // copy constructor
    { copyFrom(ls); }                           // copy new contents
                                                // assignment operator
  LinkedStack& operator=(const LinkedStack& ls) {
    if (this != &ls) {                          // avoid self copy (x = x)
      removeAll();                              // remove old contents
      copyFrom(ls);                             // copy new contents
    }
    return *this;
  }
  ~LinkedStack()                                // destructor
    { removeAll(); }                            // destroy old contents
```

Code Fragment 4.20: Implementation of the copy constructor, assignment operator, and destructor for the LinkedStack. The code for the utility function copyFrom() is shown in Code Fragment 4.21.

```
template <typename Object>                      // copy from stack ls
void LinkedStack<Object>::copyFrom(const LinkedStack& ls) {
  tp = NULL;
  NodePtr p    = ls.tp;                         // p is current node in ls
  NodePtr prev = NULL;
  while (p != NULL) {
    NodePtr v = new Node(p->element, NULL);     // create copy of p
    if (tp == NULL) tp = v;                     // if first node
    else prev->next = v;                        // else link after prev
    prev = v;
    p    = p->next;
  }
  sz = ls.sz;
}
```

Code Fragment 4.21: Implementation of the copyFrom() functions.

4.4.3   Implementing a Queue with a Singly Linked List

As with the stack, we can provide an efficient implementation of the queue ADT using a singly linked list. Recall that we delete from the head of the queue and insert at the rear. For efficiency reasons, we choose the front of the queue to be at the head of the linked list, and the rear of the queue to be at the tail of the list. (Why would it be bad to insert at the head of the linked list and remove from the tail?) The class structure for the resulting LinkedQueue class is similar to the structure of LinkedStack, with the exception that we need to maintain pointers to both the head and tail of the linked list. The implementations of the main functions are shown in Code Fragment 4.22. Each of the functions of this implementation runs in $O(1)$ time. We avoid the need to specify a maximum size for the queue, as was done in the array-based queue implementation, but this benefit comes at the expense of increasing the amount of space used per element. Still, the functions in the implementation of the singly linked list queue are more complicated than we might like, for we must take extra care in how we deal with special cases where the queue is empty before an enqueue() or where the queue becomes empty after a dequeue().

```
// ... (part of class LinkedQueue)
void enqueue(const Object& e) {              // enqueue element
  NodePtr v = new Node(e, NULL);
  if (sz == 0) head = v;                      // if empty, this is new head
  else tail->next = v;                        // else link after tail
  tail = v;                                   // v is now the tail
  sz++;
}
Object dequeue() throw(QueueEmptyException) { // dequeue
  if (isEmpty())
    throw QueueEmptyException("Dequeue of empty queue");
  NodePtr old = head;                         // node to remove
  head = head->next;
  if ((--sz) == 0) tail = NULL;               // deletion causes empty queue
  Object result = old->element;
  delete old;
  return result;
}
// ...
```

Code Fragment 4.22: The functions enqueue() and dequeue() in the implementation of the Queue ADT by means of a singly linked list. Notice that when we enqueue to an empty queue, the new element is not only the new tail, but also becomes the new head. Similarly, when we remove the last element by dequeuing, we need to update the tail as well as the head.

4.5 Double-Ended Queues

Consider now a queue-like data structure that supports insertion and deletion at both the front and the rear of the queue. Such an extension of a queue is called a ***double-ended queue***, or ***deque***, which is usually pronounced "deck" to avoid confusion with the dequeue() function of the regular queue ADT, which is pronounced like the abbreviation "D.Q." An easy way to remember the "deck" pronunciation is to observe that a deque is like deck of cards in the hands of a crooked card dealer—it is possible to deal off both the top and the bottom.

4.5.1 The Deque Abstract Data Type

The deque abstract data type is richer than both the stack and the queue ADTs. The fundamental functions of the deque ADT are as follows (where we use D to denote the deque):

insertFirst(o): Insert a new object o at the beginning of D.
Input: Object; *Output:* None.

insertLast(o): Insert a new object o at the end of D.
Input: Object; *Output:* None.

removeFirst(): Remove the first object of D; an error occurs if D is empty.
Input: None; *Output:* None.

removeLast(): Remove the last object of D; an error occurs if D is empty.
Input: None; *Output:* None.

Additionally, the deque includes the following support functions:

first(): Return the first object of D; an error occurs if D is empty.
Input: None; *Output:* Object.

last(): Return the last object of D; an error occurs if D is empty.
Input: None; *Output:* Object.

size(): Return the number of objects of D.
Input: None; *Output:* Integer.

isEmpty(): Determine if D is empty.
Input: None; *Output:* Boolean.

| Caution |

Notice that in contrast to the stack pop() and queue and dequeue operations, we have defined the deque removal operations so that they do not return any value. It would be easy to achieve the same effect by performing two calls, say, to first() and removeFirst(). Henceforth, we will usually define removal functions in this manner. When complex classes and structures are stored in data structures, it is desirable to avoid unnecessary copying and the constructor and destructor calls that would result.

Example 4.8: *The following table shows a series of operations and their effects on an initially empty deque D of integers.*

Operation	Output	D
insertFirst(3)	–	(3)
insertFirst(5)	–	(5,3)
first()	5	(5,3)
removeFirst()	–	(3)
insertLast(7)	–	(3,7)
last()	7	(3,7)
removeFirst()	–	(7)
removeLast()	–	()

4.5.2 Implementing a Deque with a Doubly Linked List

Since the deque requires insertion and removal at both ends of a list, using a singly linked list would be inefficient. Recall that when we use a singly linked list as described in the previous section, deletions at the tail of the list cannot be done in constant time, even if we keep a pointer to the tail node. There is a type of linked list, however, that allows for a great variety of operations, including insertion and removal at both ends, to run in $O(1)$ time—the **doubly linked** list. A node in a doubly linked list stores two pointers—a **next** link, which points to the next node in the list, and a **prev** link, which points to the previous node in the list.

For the sake of variety, we will add a twist to our implementation of doubly linked lists. In contrast to our implementation of the singly linked list, we will add two **sentinel** nodes at the beginning and end of the list. These are called the **header** and **trailer** respectively. These nodes do not store any element, and they are not counted in the size() operation. A doubly linked list with these sentinels is shown in Figure 4.12. The doubly linked list class object stores three entities—pointers to the header and trailer nodes and a count of the number of elements in the list (not counting the sentinels).

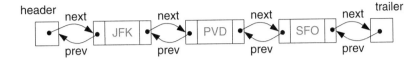

Figure 4.12: A doubly linked list with sentinels, header and trailer, marking the ends of the list. An empty list would have these sentinels pointing to each other. We do not show the null prev pointer for the header nor do we show the null next pointer for the trailer.

The primary advantage of these sentinels is that they simplify the code for insertion and removal operations. This is because the head and tail of the list no longer need to be treated as special cases. Of course, we pay a small price by requiring additional space of the sentinel nodes and the extra work needed in construction and destruction. Since construction and destruction are performed only once in the lifetime of a data structure, it usually is of greater importance to simplify the code for commonly performed operations, such as insertion and removal.

Inserting or removing elements at either end of a doubly linked list is straightforward to do in $O(1)$ time. (See Figure 4.13.) Indeed, the *prev* links eliminate the need to traverse the list to get to the node just before the tail.

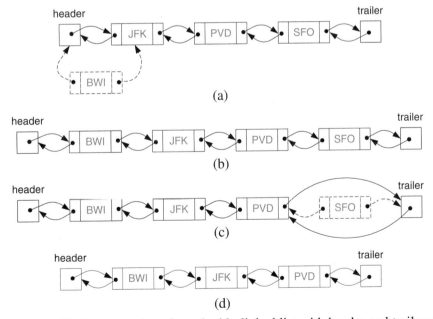

Figure 4.13: Update operations for a doubly linked list with header and trailer sentinels: (a) inserting at the head; (b) after the insertion and before deleting at the tail; (c) deleting at the tail; (d) after the deletion.

Because of our sentinels, for any insertion of a new element e, we can assume we have access to the node p before the place e should go and the node q after the place e should go. To insert a new element between the two nodes p and q (either or both of which could be sentinels), we create a new node t. We then have t's *prev* and *next* pointers refer to p and q respectively, and then have p's *next* pointer refer to t, and have q's *prev* pointer refer to t. Likewise, if we wish to remove an element stored at a node t, we can again assume we have access to the nodes p and q on either side of t. To remove a node t between two nodes p and q, we simply have p and q point to each other instead of t. We then delete the node t to avoid any memory leaks.

A C++ Deque Implementation

We define a class LinkedDeque, which implements a deque as a doubly linked list using a structure similar to LinkedList. Rather than presenting the whole class, we just present the principal differences in Code Fragment 4.23 and 4.24. Observe that the node structure contains both a previous and next link. The private class variables of Code Fragment 4.24 have pointers to both the header and trailer sentinel nodes. The constructor allocates these nodes and has them point to each other.

```
struct Node {                                    // a node in the deque
    Object  element;                             // element
    Node*  prev;                                 // previous node
    Node*  next;                                 // next node
    Node(const Object& e = Object(), Node* p = NULL, Node* n = NULL)
        : element(e), prev(p), next(n) { }       // constructor
};
typedef Node* NodePtr;                           // pointer to node
```

Code Fragment 4.23: The node structure for class LinkedDeque.

Table 4.3 shows the running times of functions in a realization of a deque by a doubly linked list. Note that every function of the deque ADT runs in $O(1)$ time.

Method	Time
size	$O(1)$
isEmpty	$O(1)$
first, last	$O(1)$
insertFirst, insertLast	$O(1)$
removeFirst, removeLast	$O(1)$

Table 4.3: Performance of a deque realized by a doubly linked list. The space usage is $O(n)$, where n is number of elements in the deque.

4.5.3   The Adapter Design Pattern

There is a simple mapping that takes the member functions of the stack and queue ADTs and implements them using deque operations.

Specifically, there are the simple correspondences for the stack ADT shown in Table 4.4.

Stack Method	Deque Implementation
size()	size()
isEmpty()	isEmpty()
top()	first()
push(*o*)	insertFirst(*o*)
pop()	removeFirst()

Table 4.4: Implementing a Stack with a Deque.

Observe that because the deque's symmetry, performing insertions and removals from the rear of the deque would be equally efficient. Likewise, we have the simple correspondences for the queue ADT shown in Table 4.5.

Queue Method	Deque Implementation
size()	size()
isEmpty()	isEmpty()
front()	first()
enqueue(*o*)	insertLast(*o*)
dequeue()	removeFirst()

Table 4.5: Implementing a Queue with a Deque.

Let us consider the implementation of a stack in greater detail. Such an implementation of a class DequeStack is shown in Code Fragment 4.25.

This class has a deque as its only data member. Each stack operation is implemented by invoking the appropriate deque operations. Notice that many of the operations of DequeStack are implemented as one-line calls to Deque operations.

In cases where the deque might throw an exception, we catch this exception and map it to the corresponding stack exception.

```
template <typename Object>
class LinkedDeque {
protected:                                  // local node structure
  // ... (insert Node here)
private:                                     // member data
  NodePtr header;                            // pointer to header sentinel
  NodePtr trailer;                           // pointer to trailer sentinel
  int sz;                                    // number of elements
public:
  LinkedDeque() {                            // default constructor
    header = new Node;
    trailer = new Node;
    header->next = trailer;                  // trailer follows header
    trailer->prev = header;                  // header precedes trailer
    sz = 0;
  }
  // ...                                      // return first element
  Object& first() throw(DequeEmptyException) {
    if (isEmpty())
      throw DequeEmptyException("First of empty deque");
    return header->next->element;
  }
  void insertFirst(const Object& e) {        // insert new node at head
    NodePtr oldFirst = header->next;         // old first node
    NodePtr t = new Node(e, header, oldFirst); // new node to insert
    oldFirst->prev = t;
    header->next = t;
    sz++;
  }
  void removeLast() {                        // remove node at tail
    if (isEmpty())
      throw DequeEmptyException("Remove on empty deque");
    NodePtr old = trailer->prev;             // node to remove
    NodePtr newLast = old->prev;             // new last node
    trailer->prev = newLast;
    newLast->next = trailer;
    sz--;
    delete old;
  }
  // ... (many functions omitted)
};
```

Code Fragment 4.24: Some of the important member functions of the implementation of the deque ADT by means of a doubly linked list. Note that thanks to the use of sentinels, we do not need to check for special cases when inserting into an empty deque or a deletion that results in an empty deque.

```
template <typename Object>
class DequeStack {
private:                                  // member data
  LinkedDeque<Object> D;                  // the deque
public:
  DequeStack() : D() { }                  // default constructor
  int size() const { return D.size(); }          // number of elements in stack
  bool isEmpty() const { return D.isEmpty(); } // is the stack empty?
                                          // return the top of the stack
  const Object& top() const throw(StackEmptyException) {
    try {
      return D.first();
    } catch (const DequeEmptyException& e) {
      throw StackEmptyException("Top of empty stack");
    }
  }
  void push(const Object& elem)           // push onto stack
    { D.insertFirst(elem); }
  Object pop() throw(StackEmptyException) { // pop the stack
    try {
      Object result = D.first();
      D.removeFirst();
      return result;
    } catch (const DequeEmptyException& e) {
      throw StackEmptyException("Pop of empty stack");
    }
  }
};
```

Code Fragment 4.25: Implementation of the Stack interface by means of a deque.

Defining the Adapter Design Pattern

The DequeStack functions shown in Code Fragment 4.25 illustrate an important design pattern—the *adapter* pattern. This pattern adjusts functions from one class so they can be used to implement member functions of another class.

There are several situations for which the adapter pattern comes in handy. One is the situation illustrated in the DequeStack class, where we want to specialize a general class and simplify its usage by changing the names of some of its functions. In the case of the DequeStack class, we adapt class LinkedDeque, which implements the more powerful Deque interface, so that it can be used to implement the simpler Stack interface.

4.6   Sample Case Study Application

In this section, we describe a stack application used to solve a simple financial analysis problem.

Given a series of n daily price quotes for a stock, we call the **span** of the stock's price on a certain day the maximum number of consecutive days up to the current day that the price of the stock has been less than or equal to its price on that day. (See Figure 4.14.)

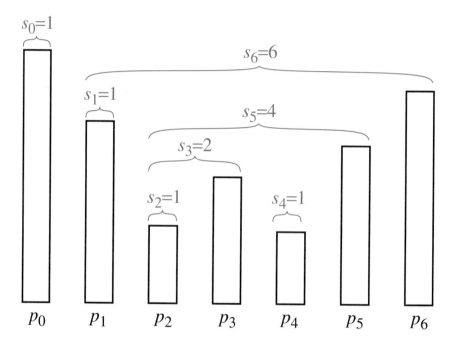

Figure 4.14: Daily prices for a stock and span on each day.

The Stock Span Problem

More formally, assume that price quotes begin with day 0 and that p_i denotes the price on day i. The span s_i on day i is equal to the maximum integer k, such that $k \leq i+1$ and $p_j \leq p_i$ for $j = i-k+1,\ldots,i$. Given the prices $p_0, p_1, \ldots, p_{n-1}$, the **stock span** problem is to compute all the spans $s_0, s_1, \ldots, s_{n-1}$.

4.6.1 A Quadratic-Time Algorithm

We show a straightforward solution to our problem in Code Fragment 4.26.

Algorithm computeSpans1(P):

Input: An n-element array P of numbers
Output: An n-element array S of numbers such that $S[i]$ is the largest integer k such that $k \leq i+1$ and $P[j] \leq P[i]$ for $j = i-k+1, \ldots, i$

for $i = 0$ **to** $n-1$ **do**
    $k \leftarrow 0$
    done $\leftarrow$ **false**
    repeat
        if $P[i-k] \leq P[i]$ **then**
            $k \leftarrow k+1$
        else
            done$\leftarrow$**true**
    until $(k > i)$ **or** *done*
    $S[i] \leftarrow k$
return array S

Code Fragment 4.26: Algorithm computeSpans1.

We analyze the running time of algorithm computeSpans1() as follows.

- Initializing the array S at the beginning and returning it at the end requires a constant number of primitive operations per element; hence, takes $O(n)$ time.
- There is a **repeat** loop nested within a **for** loop. The **for** loop, controlled by counter i, is executed n times, for $i = 0, \ldots, n-1$. The statements inside the **for** loop but outside the **repeat** loop are executed n times. That is, these statements, plus the incrementing and testing of counter i, contribute $O(n)$ primitive operations to the total running time.
- In iteration i of the outer **for** loop, the body of the inner **repeat** loop is executed at most $i+1$ times. Indeed, in the worst case, element $S[i]$ is larger than all the preceding elements. Thus, testing for the **if** condition ($S[i-k] \leq S[i]$), executing one of the ensuing statements, and testing for the **until** condition is performed $i+1$ times during iteration i of the outer loop ($i = 0, \ldots, n-1$). Therefore, the worst-case running time is proportional to $1 + 2 + 3 + \cdots + n$. Recalling Proposition 3.2, the total time contributed by the statements in the inner loop is $O(n(n+1)/2)$, which is $O(n^2)$.

The running time of computeSpans1() is therefore given by the sum of three terms. The first and the second terms are $O(n)$, and the third term is $O(n^2)$. Thus, the running time of algorithm computeSpans1() is $O(n^2)$.

4.6.2   A Linear-Time Algorithm

To compute spans more efficiently, we observe that the span s_i on a certain day i can be easily computed if we know the closest day preceding i, such that the price on that day is higher than the price on day i. (See Figure 4.15.) If such a preceding day exists for a day i, let us denote it with $h(i)$, and otherwise let us define $h(i) = -1$. The span on day i is given by $s_i = i - h(i)$.

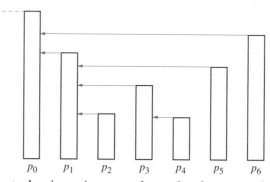

$p_0 \qquad p_1 \qquad p_2 \qquad p_3 \qquad p_4 \qquad p_5 \qquad p_6$

Figure 4.15: Daily stock prices. Arrows point to the closest previous higher price.

Our second algorithm, computeSpans2(), shown in Code Fragment 4.27, uses a stack as an auxiliary data structure to store days $i, h(i), h(h(i))$, etc. When going from day $i - 1$ to day i, we repeatedly pop days with prices less than or equal to p_i, and then push day i.

An example run of algorithm computeSpans2() is shown in Figure 4.16.

We assume that stack D is implemented so that each stack ADT operation takes $O(1)$ time. With this assumption, our analysis of the running time of algorithm computeSpans2() is as follows.

- Initializing the array S at the beginning and returning it at the end can be done with $O(1)$ primitive operations per element, and takes $O(n)$ time.

- There is a **while** loop nested within a **for** loop. The **for** loop, controlled by counter i, is executed n times, for $i = 0, \ldots, n - 1$. Thus, the statements in the **for** loop outside the **while** loop are executed at most n times, that is, such statements (plus the incrementing and testing of counter i) take $O(n)$ time.

- Consider now the execution of the inner **while** loop during iteration i of the **for** loop. Statement *done*←**true** is executed at most once, since this causes a subsequent exit from the loop. Let t_i be the number of times statement D.pop() is executed. Conditions (**not** (D.isEmpty() **or** *done*)) and ($P[i] \geq P[D.\text{top}()]$) are each tested at most $t_i + 1$ times.

Algorithm computeSpans2(*P*):

> *Input:* An *n*-element array *P* of numbers, and an empty stack *D*
>
> *Output:* An *n*-element array *S* of numbers such that $S[i]$ is the largest integer k such that $k \le i+1$ and $P[j] \le P[i]$ for $j = i-k+1, \ldots, i$

> **for** $i = 0$ **to** $n-1$ **do**
> > *done* ← **false**
> > **while not** (D.isEmpty() **or** *done*) **do**
> > > **if** $P[i] \ge P[D.\text{top}()]$ **then**
> > > > D.pop()
> > >
> > > **else**
> > > > *done*←**true**
> >
> > **if** D.isEmpty() **then**
> > > $h \leftarrow -1$
> >
> > **else**
> > > $h \leftarrow D$.top()
> >
> > $S[i] \leftarrow i - h$
> > D.push(i)
>
> **return** array S

Code Fragment 4.27: Algorithm computeSpans2.

Summarizing the Running Time

Summing up the total running time contribution of the statements in the **while** loop, we get the following:

$$O\left(\sum_{i=0}^{n-1}(t_i+1)\right).$$

Once an element is popped out from stack D, it is never pushed in again by the algorithm. Hence,

$$\sum_{i=0}^{n-1} t_i \le n.$$

In other words, the total time spent performing all the statements in the **while** loop is $O(n)$. Note that the running time of algorithm computeSpans2() is given by the sum of three terms, each of which is $O(n)$. Therefore, the running time of computeSpans2() is $O(n)$.

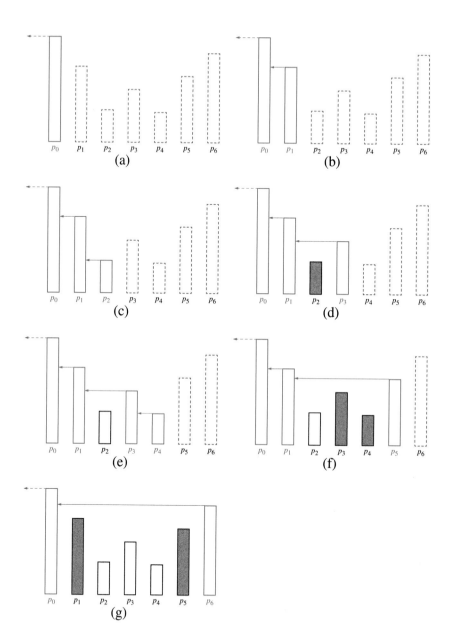

Figure 4.16: A sample run of algorithm computeSpans2(). The contents of the stack D at the end of each iteration of the **for** loop are visualized by highlighting and connecting with arrows the bars associated with the days stored in D. The dashed bars denote days not yet examined by the algorithm. The shaded bars denote days popped from D in the current iteration.

4.6.3 C++ Implementation

Function computeDailyHighSpan(), shown in Code Fragment 4.28, is an implementation of algorithm computeSpans2(). An array of objects of class Quote, is used by function computeDailyHighSpan() to access the price information and to store the computed spans. Since class Quote is small and has no significant internal structure, we will not worry about developing a complete class structure.

```cpp
#include <iostream>
#include <vector>
#include "LinkedStack.h"

using namespace std;                          // make std stuff available

/**
 * A stock-quote class, which contains a day's stock price and span.
 */
class Quote {
public:
  int day;                                    // which day
  int price;                                  // this day's price
  int span;                                   // this day's span
  Quote(int d = 0, int p = 0)                 // constructor
    {  day = d; price = p;  }
};
/**
 * Compute the span of the stock price on each day by means of a
 * stack, and store the information in the Quote array Q.
 */
void computeDailyHighSpan(vector<Quote>& Q) {
  int prevHigh;                               // previous higher day
  LinkedStack<Quote> D;
  for (int i = 0 ; i < Q.size(); i++) {       // process the current day i
    while ( !D.isEmpty() &&                   // if stack not empty and
            Q[i].price >= D.top().price ) {    // ... today's price is higher
      D.pop();
    }
    if (D.isEmpty()) prevHigh = −1;           // day i is a new high
    else prevHigh = D.top().day;              // else stack top is high

    Q[i].span = i − prevHigh;                 // compute and store the span
    D.push(Q[i]);                             // add current to the stack
  }
}
```

Code Fragment 4.28: Implementation of algorithm computeDailyHighSpan().

4.7   Exercises

Reinforcement

R-4.1 Give three examples of recursion in everyday life.

R-4.2 Describe a linearly recursive algorithm for finding the minimum element in an n-element array.

R-4.3 Give an algorithm that uses tail recursion to convert every element in an integer array A into its absolute value.

R-4.4 Draw a recursion trace for the Power function given in Code Fragment 4.3, showing the value of the parameter n inside each box.

R-4.5 Describe a binary recursive method for searching for an element x in an n-element unsorted array A. What is the running time of your method? How much space does it use in addition to the array A (including the space needed for the run-time stack)?

R-4.6 Draw a recursion trace for solving the addition puzzle, $HE + SHE = WOW$, using the algorithm of Code Fragment 4.8 for the set of digits $U = \{0,1,2,3,4,5\}$. Show the tentative values of the letters, O, E, S, H, and W, in each box of the recursion trace. (Recall that every letter must be assigned a unique digit, but the algorithm can stop at the point the first solution is found.)

R-4.7 Describe a recursive algorithm for printing all of the permutations of the sequence $(1,2,\ldots,n)$. What is the running time of your algorithm?

R-4.8 Describe the output of the following series of stack operations:

push(8), push(3), pop(), push(2), push(5), pop(), pop(), push(9), push(1), pop(), push(7), push(6), pop(), pop(), push(4), pop(), pop().

R-4.9 Describe the output for the following sequence of queue operations:

enqueue(5), enqueue(3), dequeue(), enqueue(2), enqueue(8), dequeue(), dequeue(), enqueue(9), enqueue(1), dequeue(), enqueue(7), enqueue(6), dequeue(), dequeue(), enqueue(4), dequeue(), dequeue().

R-4.10 Describe the output for the following sequence of deque operations:

insertFirst(3), insertLast(8), insertLast(9), insertFirst(5), removeFirst(), removeLast(), first(), insertLast(7), removeFirst(), last(), removeLast().

R-4.11 Describe, in pseudo-code, how to insert an element at the beginning of a singly linked list, assuming that the list does *not* have a sentinel header node, and instead uses a pointer variable head to point to the first node in the list.

R-4.12 Give an algorithm for finding the penultimate node in a singly linked list where the last element is indicated by a null *next* pointer.

R-4.13 Give an algorithm for determining, just by link hopping, whether a doubly linked list with header and trailer sentinels is empty (that is, do not make use of a *size* member variable).

R-4.14 Describe a recursive algorithm for finding the maximum element in an array A of n elements. What is the running time and space usage of your algorithm?

Creativity

C-4.1 Consider the alternate definition of the Power method given in Code Fragment 4.29. Show that this algorithm is correct. How many calls will this function make to compute $\text{Power}(x,n)$? You may assume that n is a power of 2, for the sake of analysis.

Algorithm Power(x,n):
   Input: A number x and integer $n \geq 0$
   Output: The value x^n
    if $n = 0$ **then**
       return 1
    if n is odd **then**
       return $x \cdot \text{Power}(x, \lfloor n/2 \rfloor) \cdot \text{Power}(x, \lfloor n/2 \rfloor)$
    else
       return $\text{Power}(x, \lfloor n/2 \rfloor) \cdot \text{Power}(x, \lfloor n/2 \rfloor)$

Code Fragment 4.29: An alternate algorithm for the power function.

C-4.2 Suppose we are given an n-element array A whose elements are taken from the set $\{1, 2, \ldots, n-1\}$. Describe a recursive algorithm for finding a repeated element in A. What is the running time of your algorithm?

C-4.3 Suppose you are given an n-element array A containing distinct integers that are listed in increasing order. Given a number k, describe a recursive algorithm to find two integers in A that sum to k, if such a pair exists. What is the running time of your algorithm?

C-4.4 Given an n-element unsorted array A of n integers and an integer k, describe a recursive algorithm for finding the largest element in A smaller than k. Your algorithm cannot use any global variables, that is, it can only use local variables and values passed as parameters.

C-4.5 Given an n-element unsorted array A of n integers and an integer k, describe a recursive algorithm for rearranging the elements in A so that all elements less than or equal to k come before any elements larger than k. What is the running time of your algorithm?

C-4.6 In the ***Towers of Hanoi*** puzzle, we are given a platform with three pegs, a, b, and c, sticking out of it. On peg a is a stack of n disks, each larger than the next, so that the smallest is on the top and the largest is on the bottom. The puzzle is to move all the disks from peg a to peg c, moving one disk at a time, so that we never place a larger disk on top of a smaller one. See Figure 4.17 for an example of the case $n = 4$. Describe a recursive algorithm for solving the Towers of Hanoi puzzle for arbitrary n. (Hint: Consider first the subproblem of moving all but the nth disk from peg a to another peg using the third as "temporary storage.")

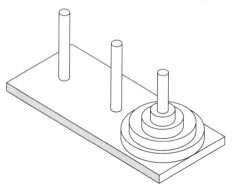

Figure 4.17: An illustration of the Towers of Hanoi puzzle.

C-4.7 A second-order ***Davenport-Schinzel*** sequence S is a sequence of symbols such that no symbol is ever immediately next to a copy of itself and, for any pair of symbols, x and y, we can have a subsequence in S that alternates two times between x and y, but it cannot alternate three times in this way. That is, we can have $S = \ldots x \ldots y \ldots x \ldots$, but we cannot have $S = \ldots x \ldots y \ldots x \ldots y \ldots$. For example, abcdcb and abcdbefe are second-order Davenport-Schinzel sequences, whereas abcabc and abba are not. Describe a recursive algorithm for building a longest second-order Davenport-Schinzel sequence using n symbols, which incidentally will have length $2n - 1$.

C-4.8 Describe, in pseudo-code, a nonrecursive method for finding, by link hopping, the middle node of a doubly linked list with header and trailer sentinels, and an odd number of real nodes between them. (Note: This method must only use link hopping; it cannot use a counter.) What is the running time of this method?

C-4.9 Describe how to implement the queue ADT using two stacks. What is the running time of the enqueue() and dequeue() functions in this case?

C-4.10 Give an algorithm for concatenating two singly linked lists L and M, with header sentinel nodes, into a single list L' that contains all the nodes of L (in their original order) followed by all the nodes of M (also in their original order). What is the running time of this method, if we let n denote the number of nodes in L and we let m denote the number of nodes in M?

C-4.11 Give an algorithm for concatenating two doubly linked lists L and M, with header and trailer sentinel nodes, into a single list L', as in the previous exercise. What is the running time of this method?

C-4.12 Describe, in pseudo-code, how to swap two nodes x and y in a singly linked list L given pointers only to x and y. Repeat this exercise for the case when L is a doubly linked list. What are the running times of each of these functions in terms of n, the number of nodes in L?

C-4.13 In most programming languages, parenthetic symbols (), [], and {} must be balanced and properly nested. We define a ***parenthetically correct*** string of characters as a string that matches one of the following patterns, where S denotes a (possibly empty) string without any parenthetic symbols, and P, P', and P'' recursively denote parenthetically correct strings:

- S
- $P'(P)P''$
- $P'[P]P''$
- $P'\{P\}$.

Design an algorithm that checks whether a string is parenthetically correct in time proportional to the size of the string using a stack as an auxiliary data structure.

C-4.14 Describe, in pseudo-code, a linear-time algorithm for reversing a queue Q. To access the queue, you are only allowed to use the functions of the queue ADT.

C-4.15 Describe, in pseudo-code, a linear-time algorithm for reversing a singly linked list L, so that the ordering of the nodes becomes exactly opposite of what it was before.

C-4.16★ Describe, in pseudo-code, an algorithm for reversing a singly linked list L using only a constant amount of additional space and not using any recursion. What is the running time of this method?

C-4.17 Give a pseudo-code description for an array-based implementation of the double-ended queue ADT. What is the running time for each operation?

C-4.18 Describe how to implement the stack ADT using two queues. What is the running time of the push() and pop() functions in this case?

C-4.19 Describe a recursive algorithm for enumerating all permutations of the numbers $\{1, 2, \ldots, n\}$. What is the running time of your method?

C-4.20 Describe a recursive algorithm that counts the number of nodes in a singly linked list.

C-4.21 Give a recursive algorithm to compute the product of two positive integers m and n using only addition.

Projects

P-4.1 Design an ADT for a two-color, double-stack ADT that consists of two stacks—one "red" and one "blue"—and has as its operations color-coded versions of the regular stack ADT operations. For example, this ADT should allow for both a red push() operation and a blue push() operation. Give an efficient implementation of this ADT using a single array whose capacity is set at some value N that is assumed to always be larger than the sizes of the red and blue stacks combined.

P-4.2 Implement the stack ADT with a singly linked list (without using the any classes from the Standard Template Library).

P-4.3 Implement the stack ADT using the STL vector class.

P-4.4 Implement the queue ADT using an array.

P-4.5 Implement the queue ADT using a singly linked list.

P-4.6 Complete the implementation of class LinkedDeque.

P-4.7 Implement the deque ADT with an array used in a circular fashion.

P-4.8 Implement the Stack and Queue interfaces with a unique class that is derived from class LinkedDeque (Code Fragment 4.24).

P-4.9 When a share of common stock of some company is sold, the **capital gain** (or, sometimes, loss) is the difference between the share's selling price and the price originally paid to buy it. This rule is easy to understand for a single share, but if we sell multiple shares of stock bought over a long period of time, then we must identify the shares actually being sold. A standard accounting principle for identifying which shares of a stock were sold in such a case is to use a FIFO protocol—the shares sold are the ones that have been held the longest (indeed, this is the default method built into several personal finance software packages). For example, suppose we buy 100 shares at $20 each on day 1, 20 shares at $24 on day 2, 200 shares at $36 on day 3, and then sell 150 shares on day 4 at $30 each. Then applying the FIFO protocol means that of the 150 shares sold, 100 were bought on day 1, 20 were bought on day 2, and 30 were bought on day 3. The capital gain in this case would therefore be $100 \cdot 10 + 20 \cdot 6 + 30 \cdot (-6)$, or $940. Write a program that takes as input a sequence of transactions of the form

$$\text{buy } x \text{ share(s) at \$} y \text{ each}$$

or

$$\text{sell } x \text{ share(s) at \$} y \text{ each,}$$

assuming that the transactions occur on consecutive days and the values x and y are integers. Given this input sequence, the output should be the total capital gain (or loss) for the entire sequence, using the FIFO protocol to identify shares.

Chapter Notes

The fundamental data structures of stacks, queues, and linked lists discussed in this chapter belong to the folklore of computer science. They were first chronicled by Knuth in his seminal book on *Fundamental Algorithms* [57]. In this chapter, we have taken the approach of defining the fundamental data structures of stacks, queues, and deques, first in terms of their ADTs and then in terms of concrete implementations. This approach to data structure specification and implementation is an outgrowth of software engineering advances brought on by the object-oriented design approach, and is now considered a standard approach for teaching data structures. We were introduced to this approach to data structure design by the classic books by Aho, Hopcroft, and Ullman on data structures and algorithms [4, 5]. For further study of abstract data types, please see the book by Liskov and Guttag [68], the survey paper by Cardelli and Wegner [20], or the book chapter by Demurjian [27]. The naming conventions we use for the member functions of the stack, queue, and deque ADTs are taken from JDSL [42]. JDSL is a data structures library in Java that builds on approaches taken for C++ in the libraries STL [83] and LEDA [76]. Some changes in the ADTs have been made because of differences in C++ and Java.

Chapter

5

Vectors, Lists, and Sequences

Contents

The concept of a sequence, where each object comes before or after another, is fundamental. We see it in a line-by-line listing of the code of a computer program, where the order of instructions determines the computation that the program represents. We also see it in the sequence of network packets that together comprise an e-mail message, which, if it is to make sense, requires that the packets be assembled in the same order in which they are sent. Sequences are interesting, then, for they represent the important relationships of "next" and "previous" between related objects. In addition, sequences are widely used to realize and implement other data structures; hence, they are foundational building blocks for data structure design.

In this chapter, we present the **vector**, **list**, and **sequence** ADTs, each of which represents a collection of linearly arranged elements and provides functions for accessing, inserting, and removing arbitrary elements. The different types of sequences are distinguished from one another by the specific ways in which these operations are defined. Stacks, queues, and deques, studied in Chapter 4, can be viewed as restricted types of sequences that access only the first and/or last elements. An important property of a sequence is that, just as with stacks, queues, and deques, the order of the elements in a sequence is determined by the operations in the abstract data type specification, and not by the values of the elements.

The vector ADT is an extension of the concrete array data structure. It provides accessor functions that can index into the middle of a sequence and it also provides update functions for adding and removing elements by their indices. To avoid confusion with the way items are accessed in the concrete array data structure, we typically use the term **rank** to refer to the index of an element in a vector.

The list ADT, on the other hand, is an object-oriented extension of the concrete linked list data structure. It provides accessor and update functions based on an object-oriented encapsulation of the node objects used by linked lists. We call these abstract node objects **positions**, for they provide an object-oriented way of referring to "places" where elements are stored, independent of the specific implementation of the list.

Finally, the full sequence ADT is a unification of the vector and list concepts. Therefore, it is useful in contexts where we desire a generic data structure that can be implemented naturally using either an array or a linked list. We show, however, that this generality comes at a cost, for we give two basic ways of implementing a sequence, with an array and with a doubly linked list, and we point out performance trade-offs between these two implementations.

We illustrate the use of the sequence ADT through the implementation of a well-known (but very inefficient) sorting algorithm known as **bubble-sort**. We also discuss the **iterator** (or **enumeration**) design pattern and mention its realization by means of a vector or list.

5.1 Vectors

Suppose we are given a linear sequence S that contains n elements. We can uniquely refer to each element e of S using an integer in the range $[0, n-1]$ that is equal to the number of elements of S that precede e in S. We define the **rank** of an element e in S to be the number of elements that are before e in S. Hence, the first element in a sequence has rank 0 and the last element has rank $n-1$. This definition is consistent with the way arrays are indexed in C++ and other programming languages (including C and Java).

Caution

Note that we do **not** imply that an array should be used to implement a sequence in such a way that the element at rank 0 is stored at index 0 in the array, although that is one possibility. The rank definition offers us a way to refer to the "index" of an element in a sequence without having to worry about the exact implementation of that list. So, in general, if an element is the rth element in a sequence, then it has rank $r-1$. Also, if an element of the sequence has rank r, its previous element (if it exists) has rank $r-1$, and its next element (if it exists) has rank $r+1$. The rank of an element may change whenever the sequence is updated, however. For example, if we insert a new element at the beginning of the sequence, the rank of each of the other elements increases by one.

A linear sequence that supports access to its elements by their ranks is called a **vector**. Rank is a simple yet powerful notion, since it can be used to specify where to insert a new element into a vector or where to remove an old element. For example, we can give the rank that a new element will have after it is inserted (for example, insert at rank 2). We could also use rank to specify an element to be removed (for example, remove the element at rank 2).

Example 5.1: *In the following, we show a series of rank-based operations on an initially empty vector S.*

Operation	Output	S
insert 7 at rank 0	–	(7)
insert 4 at rank 0	–	$(4,7)$
return the element at rank 1	7	$(4,7)$
insert 2 at rank 2	–	$(4,7,2)$
return the element at rank 3	"error"	$(4,7,2)$
remove the element at rank 1	–	$(4,2)$
insert 5 at rank 1	–	$(4,5,2)$
insert 3 at rank 1	–	$(4,3,5,2)$
insert 9 at rank 4	–	$(4,3,5,2,9)$
return the element at rank 2	5	$(4,3,5,2,9)$

5.1.1 The Vector Abstract Data Type

A *vector S* is an ADT that supports the following fundamental functions.

elemAtRank(r): Return the element of S at rank r; an error condition occurs if $r < 0$ or $r > n - 1$, where n is the current number of elements.
Input: Integer; *Output:* Object.

replaceAtRank(r, e): Replace with e the element at rank r; an error condition occurs if $r < 0$ or $r > n - 1$, where n is the current number of elements.
Input: Integer r and object e; *Output:* None.

insertAtRank(r, e): Insert a new element e into S to have rank r; an error condition occurs if $r < 0$ or $r > n$, where n is the number of elements before the insertion.
Input: Integer r and object e; *Output:* None.

removeAtRank(r): Remove from S the element at rank r; an error condition occurs if $r < 0$ or $r > n - 1$, where n is the current number of elements.
Input: Integer; *Output:* None.

In addition, a vector supports the functions size() and isEmpty(). Note that removeAtRank() does not return the element that it is removing; if we wish to use that element as well as remove it, we should call elemAtRank() first. The repertory of functions we have given for the vector is small, but it is sufficient for us to define an adapter class (see Section 4.5.3) that realizes the deque ADT. One possible adaptation is given in Table 5.1. (See Exercise C-5.13.)

Deque Function	*Realization with Vector Functions*
size()	size()
isEmpty()	isEmpty()
first()	elemAtRank(0)
last()	elemAtRank(size() $- 1$)
insertFirst(e)	insertAtRank(0, e)
insertLast(e)	insertAtRank(size(), e)
removeFirst()	removeAtRank(0)
removeLast()	removeAtRank(size() $- 1$)

Table 5.1: Realization of a deque by means of a vector.

5.1.2 A Simple Array-Based Implementation

An obvious choice for implementing the vector ADT is to use an array A, where $A[i]$ stores the element at rank i. In this case, we choose the size N of array A sufficiently large, and we maintain in a member variable the number $n < N$ of elements in the vector. The details of the implementation of the functions of the vector ADT are reasonably simple. To implement the elemAtRank(r) operation, for example, we just return $A[r]$. Implementations of functions insertAtRank(r, e) and removeAtRank(r) are given in Code Fragment 5.1. An important (and time-consuming) part of this implementation involves the shifting of elements up or down to keep the occupied cells in the array contiguous. These shifting operations are required to maintain our rule of always storing an element of rank i at index i in A. (See Figure 5.1 and also Exercise R-5.11.)

Algorithm insertAtRank(r, e):

    for $i = n-1, n-2, \ldots, r$ **do**

        $A[i+1] \leftarrow A[i]$ {make room for the new element}

    $A[r] \leftarrow e$

    $n \leftarrow n+1$

Algorithm removeAtRank(r):

    for $i = r, r+1, \ldots, n-2$ **do**

        $A[i] \leftarrow A[i+1]$ {fill in for the removed element}

    $n \leftarrow n-1$

Code Fragment 5.1: Functions in an array implementation of the vector ADT.

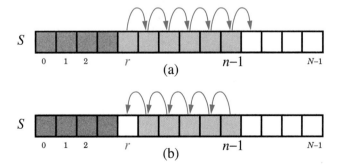

Figure 5.1: Array-based implementation of a vector S storing n elements: (a) shifting up for an insertion at rank r; (b) shifting down for a removal at rank r.

Table 5.2 shows the running times of the functions of a vector realized by means of an array. The functions isEmpty(), size(), and elemAtRank(r) clearly run in $O(1)$ time, but the insertion and removal functions can take much longer than this. In particular, insertAtRank(r, e) runs in time $O(n)$ in the worst case. Indeed, the worst case for this operation occurs when $r = 0$, since all the existing n elements have to be shifted forward. A similar argument applies to the function removeAtRank(r), which runs in $O(n)$ time, because we have to shift backward $n - 1$ elements in the worst case ($r = 0$). In fact, assuming that each possible rank is equally likely to be passed as an argument to these operations, their average running time is $O(n)$, for we will have to shift $n/2$ elements on average.

Function	Time
size	$O(1)$
isEmpty	$O(1)$
elemAtRank	$O(1)$
replaceAtRank	$O(1)$
insertAtRank	$O(n)$
removeAtRank	$O(n)$

Table 5.2: Performance of a vector with n elements realized by an array. The space usage is $O(N)$, where N is the size of the array.

Looking more closely at insertAtRank(r, e) and removeAtRank(r), we note that they each run in time $O(n - r + 1)$, for only those elements at rank r and higher have to be shifted up or down. Thus, inserting or removing an item at the end of a vector, using the functions insertAtRank(n, e) and removeAtRank($n - 1$), respectively take $O(1)$ time each. Moreover, this observation has an interesting consequence for the adaptation of the vector ADT to the deque ADT given in Section 5.1.1. If the vector ADT in this case is implemented by means of an array as described above, then functions insertLast and removeLast of the deque each run in $O(1)$ time. However, functions insertFirst and removeFirst of the deque each run in $O(n)$ time.

Actually, with a little effort, we can produce an array-based implementation of the vector ADT that achieves $O(1)$ time for insertions and removals at rank 0, as well as insertions and removals at the end of the vector. Achieving this requires that we give up on our rule that an element at rank i is stored in the array at index i, however, we would have to use a circular-array approach like the one we used in Section 4.3 to implement a queue. We leave the details of this implementation for an exercise (C-5.14).

5.1.3 An Extendable Array Implementation

A major weakness of the simple array implementation for the vector ADT given in Section 5.1.2 is that it requires advance specification of a fixed capacity, N, for the total number of elements that may be stored in the vector. If the actual number of elements, n, of the vector is much smaller than N, then this implementation will waste space. Worse, if n increases past N, then this implementation will crash. Fortunately, there is a simple way to fix this major drawback.

Let us provide a means to grow the array A that stores the elements of a vector S. Of course, in C++ (and most other programming languages) we cannot actually grow the array A; its capacity is fixed at some number N, as we have already observed. Instead, when an **overflow** occurs, that is, when $n = N$ and function insertAtRank() is called, we perform the following steps:

(a) Allocate a new array B of capacity $2N$.
(b) Copy $A[i]$ to $B[i]$, for $i = 0, \dots, N-1$.
(c) Deallocate A, and let $A = B$, that is, we use B as the array supporting S.

This array replacement strategy is known as an **extendable array**, for it can be viewed as extending the end of the underlying array to make room for more elements. (See Figure 5.2.) Intuitively, this strategy is much like that of the hermit crab, which moves into a larger shell when it outgrows its previous one.

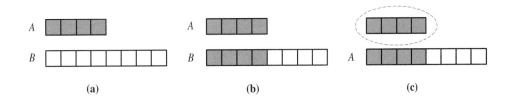

(a) (b) (c)

Figure 5.2: An illustration of the three steps for "growing" an extendable array: (a) create new array B; (b) copy elements from A to B; (c) reassign A to refer to the new array and delete the old array.

We give an implementation of the vector ADT using an extendable array in Code Fragment 5.2 and 5.3. Even though we do not show them, the class also provides **housekeeping functions** consisting of a copy constructor, assignment operator, and a destructor.

```
template <typename Object>
class ArrayVector {
private:
    int         capacity;              // length of array
    int         sz;                    // number of elements in vector
    Object*     a;                     // array storing the elements
protected:
    void overflow();                   // handle overflow by resizing
public:
    ArrayVector(int initCap = 16) {    // constructor
        capacity   = initCap;
        sz         = 0;
        a          = new Object[capacity];
    }
    int size() const                   // number of elements
        { return sz; }
    bool isEmpty() const               // is vector empty?
        { return size() == 0; }
    Object& elemAtRank(int r)          // access element at rank r
        { return a[r]; }
    void replaceAtRank(int r, const Object& e) // replace element at given rank
        { a[r] = e; }
    void removeAtRank(int r);          // remove element at given rank
    void insertAtRank(int r, const Object& e); // insert element at given rank
    // ... (housekeeping functions omitted)
};
```

Code Fragment 5.2: Class ArrayVector realizing the vector ADT by means of an extendable array. For simplicity, we have omitted checks for error conditions and the housekeeping functions, copy constructor, assignment operator, and destructor. (Continued in Code Fragment 5.3.)

```
// ...                                   // out-of-class definitions
template <typename Object>
void ArrayVector<Object>::
removeAtRank(int r) {                     // remove element at given rank
  for (int i = r; i < sz−1; i++)
    a[i] = a[i+1];                        // shift elements down
  sz−−;
}

template <typename Object>
void ArrayVector<Object>::
insertAtRank(int r, const Object& e) {    // insert element at given rank
  if (sz == capacity) overflow();         // handle overflow
  for (int i = sz−1; i >= r; i−−)
    a[i+1] = a[i];                        // shift elements up
  a[r] = e;
  sz++;
}

template <typename Object>
void ArrayVector<Object>::
overflow() {                              // handle overflow by resizing
  capacity *= 2;                          // double capacity
  Object* b = new Object[capacity];
  for (int i = 0; i < sz; i++) {          // copy contents to new array
    b[i] = a[i];
  }
  delete [] a;                            // discard old array
  a = b;                                  // make b the new array
}
```

Code Fragment 5.3: Class ArrayVector, providing function definitions for removeAtRank() and insertAtRank() and overflow(). This code only provides means for the array to grow; there is no corresponding means to shrink the array. We leave the details for dealing with these weaknesses as exercises (C-5.1 and C-5.3). (Continued from Code Fragment 5.2.)

In terms of efficiency, this array replacement strategy might at first seem slow. Performing just one array replacement required by an element insertion takes $O(n)$ time, which is not very good. Still, notice that after we perform an array replacement, our new array allows us to add n new elements to the vector before the array must be replaced again. This simple fact allows us to show that the running time of a series of operations performed on an initially empty vector is actually quite efficient. As a shorthand notation, let us refer to the insertion of an element meant to be the last element in a vector as a "push" operation. Using a design pattern called ***amortization***, we can show that performing a sequence of such push operations on a vector implemented with an extendable array is actually quite efficient.

Proposition 5.2: *Let S be a vector implemented by means of an extendable array A, as described above. The total time to perform a series of n push operations in S, starting from S being empty and A having size $N = 1$, is $O(n)$.*

Justification: We justify this proposition using a simple accounting trick known as ***amortization***. To perform this analysis, we view the computer as a coin-operated appliance that requires the payment of one ***cyber-dollar*** for a constant amount of computing time. When an operation is executed, we should have enough cyber-dollars available in our current "bank account" to pay for that operation's running time. Thus, the total amount of cyber-dollars spent for any computation will be proportional to the total time spent on that computation. The beauty of using this analysis method is that we can overcharge some operations in order to save up cyber-dollars to pay for others.

Let us assume that one cyber-dollar is enough to pay for the execution of each push operation in S, excluding the time spent for growing the array. Also, let us assume that growing the array from size k to size $2k$ requires k cyber-dollars for the time spent copying the elements. We shall charge each push operation three cyber-dollars. Thus, we overcharge each push operation that does not cause an overflow by two cyber-dollars. Think of the two cyber-dollars profited in an insertion that does not grow the array as being "stored" at the element inserted.

An overflow occurs when the vector S has 2^i elements, for some $i \geq 0$, and the size of the array used by S is 2^i. Thus, doubling the size of the array will require 2^i cyber-dollars. Fortunately, these cyber-dollars can be found at the elements stored in cells 2^{i-1} through $2^i - 1$. (See Figure 5.3.) Note that the previous overflow occurred when the number of elements became larger than 2^{i-1} for the first time, and thus the cyber-dollars stored in cells 2^{i-1} through $2^i - 1$ were not previously spent. Therefore, we have a valid amortization scheme in which each operation is charged three cyber-dollars and all the computing time is paid for. That is, we can pay for the execution of n push operations using $3n$ cyber-dollars.   ■

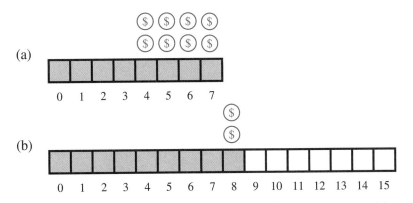

Figure 5.3: Illustration of a series of push operations on a vector: (a) an 8-cell array is full, with two cyber-dollars "stored" at cells 4 through 7; (b) a push operation causes an overflow and a doubling of capacity. Copying the eight old elements to the new array is paid for by the cyber-dollars already stored in the table; inserting the new element is paid for by one of the cyber-dollars charged to the push operation; and two cyber-dollars profited are stored at cell 8.

Fixed Length Capacity Increment

When an overflow occurs, our ArrayVector class doubles the capacity of the current array storage. An alternative to this approach would be to increment the capacity by some fixed quantity c. Does it matter which approach we use? In fact it does. The next proposition shows that by using a fixed increment, then the time to perform a series of n push operations increases from linear time to at least quadratic time.

Proposition 5.3: *If we create an initially empty vector, and expand this vector by a fixed value c, then performing a series of n push operations on this vector takes $\Omega(n^2)$ time.*

Justification: Let $c_0 > 0$ denote the initial size of the array. An overflow will be caused by a push operation when the current number of elements in the table is $c_0 + ic$, for $i = 0, \ldots, m - 1$, where $m = \lfloor (n - c_0)/c \rfloor$. Hence, by Proposition 3.2, the total time for handling the overflows is proportional to

$$\sum_{i=0}^{m-1}(c_0 + ci) = c_0 m + c \sum_{i=0}^{m-1} i = c_0 m + c\frac{m(m-1)}{2}.$$

This is $\Omega(m^2)$, and since m is proportional to n, the total time to perform n push operations is $\Omega(n^2)$. ∎

Figure 5.4 compares the running times of a series of push operations.

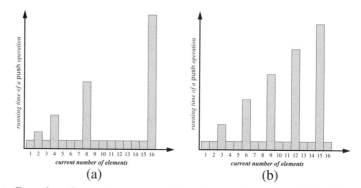

(a)   (b)

Figure 5.4: Running times of a series of push operations by (a) doubling capacity, which gives $O(n)$ time, or (b) using a fixed increment of 3, which gives $O(n^2)$ time.

5.1.4 The STL vector Class

There are some similarities and differences between our vector ADT and the vector STL class, which are highlighted in Table 5.3.

As with our ArrayVector class, an attempt to insert (using push_back()) more elements than the current capacity causes the vector's capacity to expand.

Notice that an STL vector object v can be indexed in two ways, v[i] and v.at(i). The first does no index bounds error checking, while the second throws an exception of type out_of_range if the value of the index is not between 0 and v.size()-1. Our Vector ADT function v.replaceAtRank(r,e) is equivalent to the STL assignment "v[r]=e." There are no direct STL counterparts to the Vector ADT functions of insertAtRank() and removeAtRank(), but the STL vector class supports more general functions for insertion and removal. We will discuss these in Section 5.5.

Function	Description	
size()	Returns the size of the vector	
empty()	Returns a Boolean indicating whether the vector is empty	
capacity()	Returns the current capacity of the vector	
operator[r]	Returns a reference to the element at rank r	(no index check)
at(r)	Returns a reference to the element at rank r	(index checked)
front()	Returns a reference to the first element	
back()	Returns a reference to the last element	
push_back(e)	Inserts e at the end of the vector	
pop_back()	Removes the last element	
vector(n)	Creates a vector of size n (default 0)	

Table 5.3: Some of the functions supported by the STL class vector.

5.2 Lists

Using a rank is not the only means of referring to the place where an element appears in a list. If we have a list S implemented with a (singly or doubly) linked list, then it could possibly be more natural and efficient to use a **node** instead of a rank as a means of identifying where to access and update a list. In this section, we explore a way of abstracting the node concept of "place" in a list without revealing the details of how the list is implemented.

5.2.1 Node-Based Operations and Positions

Let S be a linear list implemented using a doubly linked list. We would like to define functions for S that take nodes of the list as parameters and provide nodes as return types. Such functions could provide significant speedups over rank-based functions, for finding the rank of an element in a linked list requires searching through the list incrementally from its beginning or end, counting elements as we go.

For instance, we could define a hypothetical function removeAtNode(v) that removes the element of S stored at node v of the list. Using a node as a parameter allows us to remove an element in $O(1)$ time by simply going directly to the place where that node is stored and then "linking out" this node through an update of the *next* and *prev* links of its neighbors. Similarly, we could insert, in $O(1)$ time, a new element e into S with an operation such as insertAfterNode(v, e), which specifies the node v after which the node of the new element should be inserted. In this case, we simply "link in" the new node.

Defining functions of a list ADT by adding such node-based operations raises the issue of how much information we should be exposing about the implementation of our list. Certainly, it is desirable for us to be able to use either a singly or doubly linked list without revealing this detail to a user. Likewise, we do not wish to allow a user to modify the internal structure of a list without our knowledge. Such modification would be possible, however, if we provide a pointer to a node in our list in a form that allows the user to access internal data in that node (such as a *next* or *prev* field).

To abstract and unify the different ways of storing elements in the various implementations of a list, we introduce the concept of **position** in a list, which formalizes the intuitive notion of "place" of an element relative to others in the list.

Positions

So as to safely expand the set of operations for lists, we abstract a notion of "position" that allows us to enjoy the efficiency of doubly or singly linked list implementations without violating object-oriented design principles. In this framework, we view a list as a container of elements that stores each element at a position, and that keeps these positions arranged in a linear order. As with pointers, it is convenient to have a position that refers to nothing, called a ***null position***. A ***position*** is itself an abstract data type that supports the following functions.

element(): Return a reference to the element stored at this position; an error occurs if this is a null position.
Input: None; ***Output:*** Object.

isNull(): Test whether this is a null position.
Input: None; ***Output:*** Boolean.

A position is always defined ***relatively***, that is, in terms of its neighbors. In a list, a position p will always be "after" some position q and "before" some position s (unless p is the first or last position). (See Figure 5.5.)

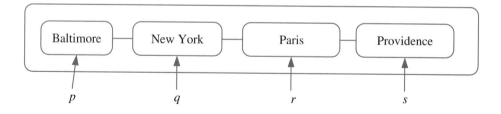

Figure 5.5: An illustration of positions in a list. The positions in the current order are p, q, r, and s. For example, q is defined as the position after position p and before position r.

A position p, which is associated with some element e in a list S, does not change, even if the rank of e changes in S, unless we explicitly remove e (and, hence, destroy position p). Moreover, the position p does not change even if we replace or swap the element e stored at p with another element. These facts about positions allow us to define a rich set of position-based list functions that take position objects as parameters and also provide position objects as return values. For instance, in the array implementation, a position corresponds to a cell of the array, which is identified by an integer index, and in the doubly linked list implementation, a position corresponds to a node of the list, which is identified by a node pointer.

5.2.2 The List Abstract Data Type

Using the concept of position to encapsulate the idea of "node" in a list, we can define another type of sequence ADT, called simply the **list** ADT. This ADT supports the following functions for a list S:

first(): Return the position of the first element of S; an error occurs if S is empty.
Input: None; *Output:* Position.

last(): Return the position of the last element of S; an error occurs if S is empty.
Input: None; *Output:* Position.

isFirst(p): Return a Boolean value indicating whether the given position is the first one in the list.
Input: Position; *Output:* Boolean.

isLast(p): Return a Boolean value indicating whether the given position is the last one in the list.
Input: Position; *Output:* Boolean.

before(p): Return the position of the element of S preceding the one at position p; an error occurs if p is either null or the first position.
Input: Position; *Output:* Position.

after(p): Return the position of the element of S following the one at position p; an error occurs if p is either null or the last position.
Input: Position; *Output:* Position.

The above functions allow us to refer to relative positions in a list, starting at the beginning or end, and to move incrementally up or down the list. These positions can intuitively be thought of as nodes in the list, but note that there are no specific references to node objects and their *prev* and *next* links in these functions. In addition to the above functions, we include the generic functions size() and isEmpty(), with the usual meanings.

We also include the following update functions for the list ADT. In all cases, position arguments are assumed to be non-null, and otherwise an error occurs.

replaceElement(p, e): Replace the element at position p with e.
> *Input:* Position p and object e; *Output:* None.

swapElements(p, q): Swap the elements stored at positions p and q, so that the element that is at position p moves to position q and the element that is at position q moves to position p.
> *Input:* Two positions; *Output:* None.

insertFirst(e): Insert a new element e into S as the first element.
> *Input:* Object e; *Output:* Position of the newly inserted element e.

insertLast(e): Insert a new element e into S as the last element.
> *Input:* Object e; *Output:* Position of the newly inserted element e.

insertBefore(p, e): Insert a new element e into S before position p in S.
> *Input:* Position p and Object e; *Output:* Position of the newly inserted element e.

insertAfter(p, e): Insert a new element e into S after position p in S.
> *Input:* Position p and Object e; *Output:* Position of the newly inserted element e.

remove(p): Remove from S the element at position p.
> *Input:* Position; *Output:* None.

The list ADT allows us to view an ordered collection of objects in terms of their places, without worrying about the exact way those places are represented. Also, note that there is some redundancy in the above repertory of operations for the list ADT. For example, we can perform operation insertFirst(e) by performing the operation insertBefore(first(), e), and operation insertLast(e) can be replaced with insertAfter(last(), e). The redundant functions can be viewed as shortcuts for common operations that help code readability.

Note that an error condition occurs if a position passed as argument to one of the list operations is invalid. Reasons for a position p to be invalid include:

- p is a null position
- p refers to an element that was previously deleted from the list
- p is a position of a different list.

We will usually only check for the first such error in our implementations, since the others are much harder to detect. When any of these errors are detected, an InvalidPositionException will be thrown. We illustrate the operations of the list ADT in the following example.

Example 5.4: *We show a series of operations for an initially empty list S below. We use variables p_1, p_2, and so on, to denote different positions, and we show the object currently stored at such a position in parentheses.*

Operation	Output	S
insertFirst(8)	$p_1(8)$	(8)
insertAfter($p_1,5$)	$p_2(5)$	(8,5)
insertBefore($p_2,3$)	$p_3(3)$	(8,3,5)
insertFirst(9)	$p_4(9)$	(9,8,3,5)
before(p_3)	$p_1(8)$	(9,8,3,5)
last()	$p_2(5)$	(9,8,3,5)
remove(p_4)	–	(8,3,5)
swapElements(p_1,p_2)	–	(5,3,8)
replaceElement($p_3,7$)	3	(5,7,8)
insertAfter(first(),2)	$p_5(2)$	(5,2,7,8)

The list ADT, with its built-in notion of position, is useful in a number of settings. For example, a program that models several people playing a game of cards could model each person's hand as a list. Since most people like to keep cards of the same suit together, inserting and removing cards from a person's hand could be implemented using the functions of the list ADT, with the positions being determined by a natural ordering of the suits. Likewise, a simple text editor embeds the notion of positional insertion and removal, since such editors typically perform all updates relative to a **cursor**, which represents the current position in the list of characters of text being edited.

The specific List interface implemented is given in Code Fragment 5.4. Error conditions are signaled by the following exceptions:

EmptyContainerException: thrown if the list is empty and an attempt is made at accessing an element of it (for example, by the first() function).

BoundaryViolationException: thrown if an attempt is made at accessing an element whose position is outside the range of positions of the list (for example, calling function after() on the last position of the sequence).

InvalidPositionException: thrown if a position provided as argument is not valid (for example, it is a null pointer or it has no associated list).

```
template <typename Object>
class List {                                    // List interface
public:
  class Position;                               // node position type
                                                // query functions
  int size() const;
  bool isEmpty() const;
  bool isFirst(const Position& p) const         throw(InvalidPositionException);
  bool isLast(const Position& p) const          throw(InvalidPositionException);
                                                // accessor functions
  Position first() const                        throw(EmptyContainerException);
  Position last() const                         throw(EmptyContainerException);
  Position before(const Position& p) const      throw(InvalidPositionException,
                                                      BoundaryViolationException);
  Position after(const Position& p) const       throw(InvalidPositionException,
                                                      BoundaryViolationException);
                                                // update functions
  Position insertBefore(const Position& p, const Object& element)
                                                throw(InvalidPositionException);
  Position insertAfter(const Position& p, const Object& element)
                                                throw(InvalidPositionException);
  Position insertFirst(const Object& element);
  Position insertLast(const Object& element);
  void remove(const Position& p)                throw(InvalidPositionException);
  void replaceElement(const Position& p, const Object& element)
                                                throw(InvalidPositionException);
  void swapElements(const Position& a, const Position& b)
                                                throw(InvalidPositionException);
};
```

Code Fragment 5.4: An informal List interface. (This is not a complete C++ class.)

5.2.3   Doubly Linked List Implementation

Suppose we wish to implement the list ADT using a doubly linked list, which we will call NodeList. We see that we can implement all the operations of the list ADT in $O(1)$ time.

First we define a structure Node to store the list's nodes. The definition is given in Code Fragment 5.5. This structure is essentially the same as the node structure presented in Code Fragment 4.24. We will nest this definition within the protected section of class NodeList. We have chosen to use a structure rather than a class because this simple object possesses no internal structure. Furthermore, since its definition is protected within NodeList, only NodeList and its derived classes will be able to access its members. Thus, we will achieve encapsulation.

```
struct Node {                                    // node in the NodeList
  Object element;                                // element
  Node* prev;                                    // previous node
  Node* next;                                    // next node
  Node(const Object& e = Object(), Node* p = NULL, Node* n = NULL)
     : element(e), prev(p), next(n) { }          // constructor
};
typedef Node* NodePtr;                           // pointer to a Node
```

Code Fragment 5.5: Class Node realizing a node of a doubly linked list. Its definition will be nested within the protected section of class NodeList, whose definition is given in Code Fragment 5.10.

We implement the position ADT by a class Position, whose only member variable is a pointer, node, to a node in the linked list. Its definition is given in Code Fragment 5.6. This class definition will also be nested within class NodeList, but it will be placed in the public section because Position objects can be accessed from outside the class. Since member functions of class NodeList will need to access the contents of the private member variable of node, we make the NodeList class a friend of Position. Recall that this means that member functions of NodeList may access the private members of Position.

```
class Position {                                 // position in NodeList
private:
  NodePtr node;                                  // pointer to the node
public:
  Position(NodePtr n = NULL)                     // constructor
     { node = n; }
  Object& element() const                        // return element
       throw(InvalidPositionException) {
    if (node == NULL) throw InvalidPositionException("Null position");
    return node->element;
  }
  bool isNull() const                            // a null position?
     { return node == NULL; }
  friend class NodeList<Object>;                 // allow access
};
```

Code Fragment 5.6: Class Position realizing a node of a doubly linked list. The function element() returns the element contained within the associated node. The constructor creates a position given a pointer to a Node object. This definition will be nested within the public section of class NodeList, whose definition is given in Code Fragment 5.10.

Why did we bother to define the Position as a class, rather than just using a pointer to a node in the linked list? Remember that there are many ways to implement a list. By defining a Position to be a pointer, we would restrict ourselves to pointer-based representations, such as linked lists. If we had chosen to implement the list as an array instead, then rather than using a pointer, it would be more natural to use an integer index to represent a position. By hiding this information as a private member of the class Position, we maintain the flexibility to chose whichever representation is most appropriate for our implementation. Because of C++'s ability to expand short member functions in-line, we do not suffer any loss in efficiency by encapsulating information in this way.

Function element(), of the Position class, throws an InvalidPositionException when its node value is NULL. Its code is shown in Code Fragment 5.7.

```
                                                // use invalid position
class InvalidPositionException : public RuntimeException {
public:
   InvalidPositionException(const string& err) : RuntimeException(err) {}
};
```

Code Fragment 5.7: Class InvalidPositionException for positions used incorrectly at run time. This class is derived from the RuntimeException class from Section 2.4.

Consider how we might implement the insertAfter(p,e) function, for inserting an element e after position p. We create a new node v to hold the element e, link v into its place in the list, and then update the next and prev pointers of v's two new neighbors. This function is given in pseudo-code in Code Fragment 5.8.

Algorithm insertAfter(p,e):
    Create a new node v
    v.element $\leftarrow e$
    v.prev $\leftarrow p$ {link v to its predecessor}
    v.next $\leftarrow p$.next   {link v to its successor}
    p.next.prev $\leftarrow v$ {link p's old successor to v}
    p.next $\leftarrow v$ {link p to its new successor, v}
    return Position(v)   {the position for the element e}

Code Fragment 5.8: Inserting an element e after a position p in a linked list.

We illustrate insertAfter(p,e) in Figure 5.6. Recalling our use of sentinels (Section 4.5.2), note that this algorithm works even if p is the last real position. The algorithms for functions insertBefore(), insertFirst(), and insertLast() are similar to that for function insertAfter(). We leave their details as an exercise (R-5.5).

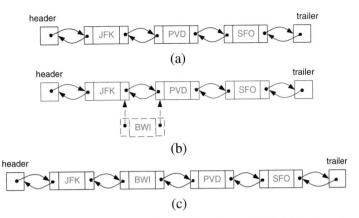

Figure 5.6: Adding a new node after the position for "JFK": (a) before the insertion; (b) creating node v with element "BWI" and linking it in; (c) after the insertion.

Next, consider the remove(p) function, which removes the element e stored at position p. To perform this operation we link the two neighbors of v to refer to one another as new neighbors—linking out v. After v is linked out, we delete this node. This algorithm is given in Code Fragment 5.9 and is illustrated in Figure 5.7. Recalling our use of sentinels, notice that this algorithm requires no special cases.

Algorithm remove(p):
    $v \leftarrow$ nodePtr(p)   {convert position to a node pointer}
    v.prev.next $\leftarrow v$.next   {linking out v}
    v.next.prev $\leftarrow v$.prev
    delete v

Code Fragment 5.9: Removing an element e stored at a position p in a linked list.

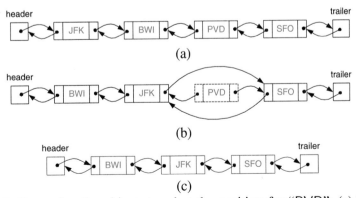

Figure 5.7: Removing the object stored at the position for "PVD": (a) before the removal; (b) linking out the old node; (c) after the removal.

Portions of the class NodeList, which implements the list ADT using a doubly linked list, are shown in Code Fragments 5.10 and 5.11. Code Fragment 5.10 shows basic NodeList class structure. The utility function nodePtr(p) checks the validity of position p and returns a pointer to the associated node. We also present the data members, consisting of the size of the list (not counting the sentinels) and the sentinel nodes.

Code Fragment 5.11 shows additional accessor and update functions. In function insertAfter(), observe that the node constructor initializes the node's prev and next pointers. All the list ADT functions run in $O(1)$ time.

Using Positions

In order to use the NodeList class, we will need to declare variables of type Position. Because the class Position is nested within class NodeList, the scope-resolution operator is needed to specify which class's Position is desired. If Node-List had not been templated, the position type would be "NodeList::Position." Types defined within templated classes require a more complex syntax, however, because the type name itself is affected by the template argument. The general way to refer to Position from outside the NodeList class is:

template<typename Object> NodeSequence<Object>::Position

The "template<typename Object>" indicates that the rest of the line is a templated definition, and the "NodeSequence<Object>::Position" is the templated type name.

Fortunately, when such a type is used in a program, this long declaration is often not needed. Once a templated type has been instantiated with a concrete object type, the resulting class is a simple (nontemplated) class. Thus, the simpler syntax can be used. For example, we could declare a NodeList L holding objects of type int and a Position p for such a list as follows.

```
typedef NodeList<int>    IntList;        // a list of integers
typedef IntList::Position    IntPosition;  // a position in IntList
IntList L;                                // L is a NodeList of ints
IntPosition p = L.insertFirst(8);         // p points to 8
L.insertAfter(p, 5);                      // now L=(8,5)
L.insertBefore(p, 9);                     // now L=(9,8,5)
```

```
template <typename Object>
class NodeList {
protected:
  // ... (insert Node class definition here)
public:
  // ... (insert Position class definition here)
protected:                               // utility to convert Position to node pointer
  NodePtr nodePtr(const Position& p) const throw(InvalidPositionException) {
    if (p.node == NULL)
      throw InvalidPositionException("Attempt to use null position");
    else return p.node;
  }
protected:                                    // data members
  int      sz;                                // number of items
  NodePtr  header;                            // head of list sentinel
  NodePtr  trailer;                           // tail of list sentinel
public:
  NodeList() {                                // default constructor
    sz = 0;
    header  = new Node;                       // create sentinels
    trailer = new Node;
    header->next = trailer;                   // head points to trailer
    trailer->prev = header;                   // trailer points to head
  }
  int size() const                           // list size
    { return sz; }
  bool isEmpty() const                        // is the list empty?
    { return (sz == 0); }
  bool isFirst(const Position& p) const       // is this the first?
      throw(InvalidPositionException) {
    NodePtr v = nodePtr(p);
    return v->prev == header;
  }
  bool isLast(const Position& p) const        // is this the last?
      throw(InvalidPositionException) {
    NodePtr v = nodePtr(p);
    return v->next == trailer;
  }
  // ...
```

Code Fragment 5.10: The class NodeList, which implements the list ADT using a doubly linked list. Note that the definitions of Node and Position from Code Fragments 5.5 and 5.6 are inserted here. (Continued in Code Fragment 5.11.)

```
// ... (continuation of NodeList)
Position first() const                                       // return first element
    throw(EmptyContainerException) {
  if (isEmpty()) throw EmptyContainerException("List is empty");
  return Position(header−>next);
}
Position before(const Position& p) const                     // return item before p
    throw(BoundaryViolationException, InvalidPositionException) {
  NodePtr v = nodePtr(p);
  NodePtr prev = v−>prev;
  if (prev == header)
    throw BoundaryViolationException("Advance past beginning of list");
  return Position(prev);
}
Position insertAfter(const Position& p, const Object& element)
    throw(InvalidPositionException) {                         // insert after p
  NodePtr v = nodePtr(p);
  sz++;
  NodePtr newNode = new Node(element, v, v−>next);
  v−>next−>prev = newNode;                                    // link node into list
  v−>next       = newNode;
  return Position(newNode);
}
void remove(const Position& p)                               // remove a given node
    throw(InvalidPositionException) {
  sz−−;
  NodePtr v = nodePtr(p);
  v−>prev−>next = v−>next;                                    // unlink from the list
  v−>next−>prev = v−>prev;
  delete v;
}
void replaceElement(const Position& p, const Object& element)
    throw(InvalidPositionException) {                         // replace element
  NodePtr v = nodePtr(p);
  v−>element = element;
}
// ... (some functions omitted)
};
```

Code Fragment 5.11: Additional functions of the NodeList class. (Continued from Code Fragment 5.10.)

5.2.4 The STL list Class

The C++ Standard Template Library (STL) provides a built-in class for doubly linked lists, called list, which supports similar functionality to the list ADT defined above.

Table 5.4 presents some of the functions provided by the built-in list class from STL.

Function	Description
size()	Returns the size of the list
empty()	Returns a Boolean indicating whether the list is empty
front()	Returns a reference to the first element
back()	Returns a reference to the last element
push_front(e)	Inserts e at the beginning of the list
push_back(e)	Inserts e at the end of the list
pop_front()	Removes the first element
pop_back()	Removes the last element
list()	Creates an empty list

Table 5.4: Some of the functions supported by the STL class vector.

Similarities and Differences with Our List ADT

The STL functions front() and back() correspond to our List ADT functions first() and last(), except that the STL functions return the element rather than its position.

The STL push and pop functions are essentially equivalent to our List ADT insert and remove functions, respectively, when applied to the beginning and end of the list.

The STL also provides functions for inserting and removing nodes from arbitrary positions in the list. We will discuss these functions later in Section 5.5 when we discuss iterators.

5.3   Sequences

In this section, we define an abstract data type that generalizes the vector and list ADTs. This ADT therefore provides access to its elements using both ranks and positions, and is a versatile data structure for a wide variety of applications.

5.3.1   The Sequence Abstract Data Type

A *sequence* is an ADT that supports all the functions of both the vector ADT (discussed in Section 5.1) and the list ADT (discussed in Section 5.2), plus the following two "bridging" functions that provide connections between ranks and positions:

atRank(r): Return the position of the element at rank r.
Input: Integer; *Output:* Position.

rankOf(p): Return the rank of the element at position p.
Input: Position; *Output:* Integer.

Multiple Inheritance in the Sequence ADT

The definition of the sequence ADT is an example of *multiple inheritance*, since the sequence inherits functions from two other "super" ADTs. Therefore, its functions include the union of the functions of its super ADTs. See Code Fragment 5.12 for a description of the interface.

```
template <typename Object>                        // Sequence interface
class Sequence : public List<Object>, public Vector<Object> {
public:                                           // "bridging" methods
    Position atRank(int rank) const               throw(BoundaryViolationException);
    int rankOf(Position position) const           throw(InvalidPositionException);
};
```

Code Fragment 5.12: An informal Sequence interface. (This is not a complete C++ class definition.) The bridging functions are used to convert ranks to positions and vice versa.

5.3.2 Implementing a Sequence with a Doubly Linked List

One possible implementation of a sequence, of course, is with a doubly linked list. Then, all of the functions of the list ADT can be easily implemented to run in $O(1)$ time each. But the functions from the vector ADT can also be implemented with a doubly linked list, though in a less efficient manner. In particular, if we want the functions from the list ADT to run efficiently (using position objects to indicate where accesses and updates should occur), then we can no longer explicitly store the ranks of elements in the sequence. Hence, to perform the operation elemAtRank(r), we must perform link "hopping" from one of the ends of the list until we locate the node storing the element at rank r. As a slight optimization, we can start hopping from the closest end of the sequence, achieving a running time that is

$$O(\min(r+1, n-r)),$$

which is $O(n)$. The worst case occurs when $r = \lfloor n/2 \rfloor$.

Operations insertAtRank(r, e) and removeAtRank(r) also perform link hopping to locate the node storing the element with rank r, and then insert or delete a node, as shown in Figures 5.6. and 5.7. The running time of this implementation of insertAtRank(r, e) and removeAtRank(r) is

$$O(\min(r+1, n-r+1)),$$

which is $O(n)$. One advantage of this approach is that, if $r = 0$ or $r = n-1$, as is the case in the adaptation of the vector ADT to the deque ADT given in Section 5.1.1, then insertAtRank() and removeAtRank() run in $O(1)$ time.

In Code Fragments 5.13 and 5.14, we show selected portions of an implementation of the Sequence interface by means of a doubly linked list. The implementation is based on a class NodeSequence, which is derived (through class inheritance) from the implementation of a list given in Section 5.3.2. Like its parent class, NodeList, the class NodeSequence uses the class Node to implement the nodes of the linked list. It defines an internal utility function, checkRank(r), which throws a BoundaryViolationException if its argument r is an invalid rank, that is, if

$$r < 0 \ \textbf{or} \ r > n-1.$$

```
template <typename Object>
class NodeSequence : public NodeList<Object> {
protected:                                          // utilities
  void checkRank(int rank) const                    // check for valid rank
     throw(BoundaryViolationException) {
    if (rank < 0 || rank >= sz)
      throw BoundaryViolationException("Invalid rank");
  }
public:
  typedef NodeList<Object>::Position Position;
  Position atRank(int rank) const                   // position of rank
     throw(BoundaryViolationException);
  int rankOf(const Position& p) const               // get rank of element
     throw(InvalidPositionException);
  Object elemAtRank (int rank) const                // element at this rank
     throw(BoundaryViolationException) {
    checkRank(rank);
    return atRank(rank).element();
  }
  void insertAtRank (int rank, const Object& element) // insert at given rank
     throw(BoundaryViolationException) {
    if (rank == size())                             // no checkRank if last
      insertLast(element);
    else {
      checkRank(rank);
      insertBefore( atRank(rank), element );
    }
  }
  void removeAtRank (int rank)                       // remove from rank
     throw(BoundaryViolationException) {
    checkRank(rank);
    Position p = atRank(rank);                       // position to remove
    remove(p);
  }
  void replaceAtRank (int rank, const Object& element) // replace at rank
     throw(BoundaryViolationException) {
    checkRank(rank);
    replaceElement( atRank(rank), element );
  }
};
```

Code Fragment 5.13: An implementation of a NodeSequence, which implements the sequence ADT using a doubly linked list. The member functions atRank() and rankOf() are defined in Code Fragment 5.11. Note that all the functions defined here run in $O(n)$ time.

```
template <typename Object>
NodeSequence<Object>::Position NodeSequence<Object>::
atRank(int rank) const                         // position of rank
    throw(BoundaryViolationException) {
  NodePtr v;
  checkRank(rank);
  if (rank <= size()/2) {                       // scan forward from head
    v = header->next;
    for (int i = 0; i < rank; i++)
      v = v->next;
  }
  else {                                        // scan back from tail
    v = trailer->prev;
    for (int i = 1; i < size()-rank; i++)
      v = v->prev;
  }
  return Position(v);
}


template <typename Object>
int NodeSequence<Object>::
rankOf(const Position &p) const                 // get rank of position
    throw(InvalidPositionException) {
  NodePtr v = first();
  int i = 0;
  while (v != trailer) {                         // search for p.node
    if (p.node == v) return i;                   // found it here
    v = v->next;                                 // else advance
    i++;
  }                                              // did not find it?
  throw InvalidPositionException("Position not found");
}
```

Code Fragment 5.14: Definition of the "bridging" functions atRank() and rankOf() of class NodeSequence, continued from Code Fragment 5.10. In chechRank(), we scan through the list from either the head or tail, whichever is shorter. Note that both functions run in $O(n)$ time.

The out-of-class function definitions atRank() and rankOf(), which are presented in Code Fragment 5.14, are each preceded by a lengthy preamble of declarations. Such preambles are necessary when member functions are defined outside of a templated class. Let us take a close look at one of them.

```
template <typename Object>
NodeSequence<Object>::Position
NodeSequence<Object>::atRank(int rank) const
    throw(BoundaryViolationException) { ... }
```

The initial "template <typename Object>" indicates that this is a templated definition. Next, "NodeSequence<Object>::Position" is the fully qualified return type, that is, a Position object as declared within class NodeSequence. Finally, "NodeSequence<Object>::atRank" is the fully qualified name of the function.

These complex preambles can be quite intimidating at first. It is helpful when first reading them to ignore the nonessential elements: the references to templates and template parameters, the scoping operator (::), and the exceptions. With these elements removed, the declaration is much easier to understand, as shown below.

```
Position atRank(int rank) const { ... }
```

When writing complex templated code like this, it is a good idea to first implement and test the class structure without the templates, using typedef type definitions to specify generic types, such as Object. Once the code is debugged, we can then add all the template declarations.

The worst-case running times of the functions of a vector implemented by means of a doubly linked list are the same as those of the implementation with an array (see Table 5.2), except for the function elemAtRank(). The doubly linked list implementation has the advantage that it requires space $O(n)$, proportional to the number of elements effectively present in the sequence, whereas the array implementation needs space proportional to the size of the array. The trade-off is that operation elemAtRank() is more efficient in the array implementation, since this operation requires $O(n)$ time in the worst case when we use a doubly linked list. Still, implementing a sequence with a doubly linked list allows other kinds of insertion and deletion operations to be performed very quickly; namely, the functions of the list ADT.

5.3.3 Implementing a Sequence with an Array

Suppose we want to implement a sequence S by storing each element e of S in a cell $A[i]$ of an array A. We can define a position object p to hold an index i and a reference to array A, as member variables. We can then implement function element(p) by simply returning $A[i]$. A major drawback with this approach, however, is that the cells in A have no way to reference their corresponding positions. Thus, after performing an insertFirst() operation, we have no way of informing the existing positions in S that their ranks each went up by 1 (remember that positions in a sequence are always defined relative to their neighboring positions, not their ranks). Hence, if we are going to implement a general sequence with an array, we need a different approach.

Consider an alternate solution in which, instead of storing the elements of S in array A, we store a pointer to a new kind of position object in each cell of A, and we store a sequence element in each position. The new position object p holds the index i and the element e associated with p. With this data structure, illustrated in Figure 5.8, we can easily scan through the array to update the i variable for each position whose rank changes because of an insertion or deletion.

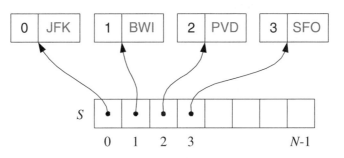

Figure 5.8: An array-based implementation of the sequence ADT.

In this array-based implementation of a sequence, the functions insertFirst(), insertBefore(), insertAfter(), and remove() take $O(n)$ time because we have to shift position objects to make room for the new position or to fill in the hole created by the removal of the old position (just as in the insert and remove functions based on rank). All the other position-based functions take $O(1)$ time.

Note that we can use an array in a circular fashion like we used for implementing a queue (see Section 4.3.2). With a little work, we can then perform functions insertFirst() in $O(1)$ time. Note that functions insertBefore(), insertAfter(), and remove() still take $O(n)$ time. Now, the worst case occurs when the element to be inserted or removed has rank $\lfloor n/2 \rfloor$.

5.3.4   Comparing Sequence Implementations

Table 5.5 compares the running times of the implementations of the general sequence ADT, by means of an array (used in a circular fashion) and by means of a doubly linked list.

Operations	Array	List
size, isEmpty	$O(1)$	$O(1)$
atRank, rankOf, elemAtRank	$O(1)$	$O(n)$
first, last, before, after	$O(1)$	$O(1)$
replaceElement, swapElements	$O(1)$	$O(1)$
replaceAtRank	$O(1)$	$O(n)$
insertAtRank, removeAtRank	$O(n)$	$O(n)$
insertFirst, insertLast	$O(1)$	$O(1)$
insertAfter, insertBefore	$O(n)$	$O(1)$
remove	$O(n)$	$O(1)$

Table 5.5: Comparison of the running times of the functions of a sequence implemented with either an array (used in a circular fashion) or a doubly linked list. We denote with n the number of elements in the sequence at the time the operation is performed. The space usage is $O(n)$ for the doubly linked list implementation, and $O(N)$ for the array implementation, where N is the size of the array.

Summarizing this table, we see that the array-based implementation is superior to the linked-list implementation on the rank-based access operations, atRank(), rankOf(), and elemAtRank(). It is equal in performance to the linked-list implementation on all the other access operations. Regarding update operations, the linked-list implementation beats the array-based implementation in the position-based update operations, insertAfter(), insertBefore(), and remove(). Even so, the array-based and linked-list implementations have the same worst-case performance on the rank-based update functions, insertAtRank() and removeAtRank(), though for different reasons. In update operations insertFirst() and insertLast(), the two implementations have comparable performance.

Considering space usage, note that an array requires $O(N)$ space, where N is the size of the array (unless we utilize an extendable array), while a doubly linked list uses $O(n)$ space, where n is the number of elements in the sequence. Since n is less than or equal to N, this implies that the asymptotic space usage of a linked-list implementation is superior to that of a fixed-size array, although there is a small constant factor overhead that is larger for linked lists, since arrays do not need links to maintain the ordering of their cells.

5.4 Case Study: Bubble-Sort on a Sequence

In this section, we illustrate the use of the sequence ADT and its implementation trade-offs with sample C++ functions, using the well-known *bubble-sort* algorithm.

5.4.1 The Bubble-Sort Algorithm

Consider a sequence of n elements such that any two elements in the sequence can be compared according to an order relation (for example, companies compared by revenue, states compared by population, or words compared lexicographically). The *sorting* problem is to reorder the sequence so that the elements are in non-decreasing order. The *bubble-sort* algorithm (see Figure 5.9) solves this problem by performing a series of *passes* over the sequence. In each pass, the elements are scanned by increasing rank, from rank 0 to the end of the sequence. At each position in a pass, an element is compared with its neighbor, and if these two consecutive elements are found to be in the wrong relative order (that is, the preceding element is larger than the succeeding one), then the two elements are swapped. The sequence is sorted by completing n such passes.

pass	swaps	sequence
		$(5,7,2,6,9,3)$
1st	$7 \leftrightarrow 2\ 7 \leftrightarrow 6\ 9 \leftrightarrow 3$	$(5,2,6,7,3,9)$
2nd	$5 \leftrightarrow 2\ 7 \leftrightarrow 3$	$(2,5,6,3,7,9)$
3rd	$6 \leftrightarrow 3$	$(2,5,3,6,7,9)$
4th	$5 \leftrightarrow 3$	$(2,3,5,6,7,9)$

Figure 5.9: The bubble-sort algorithm on a sequence of integers. For each pass, the swaps performed and the sequence after the pass are shown.

The bubble-sort algorithm has the following properties:

- In the first pass, once the largest element is reached, it will keep on being swapped until it gets to the last position of the sequence.
- In the second pass, once the second largest element is reached, it will keep on being swapped until it gets to the second-to-last position of the sequence.
- In general, at the end of the ith pass, the right-most i elements of the sequence (that is, those at ranks from $n-1$ down to $n-i$) are in final position.

The last property implies that it is correct to limit the number of passes made by a bubble-sort on an n-element sequence to n. Moreover, it allows the ith pass to be limited to the first $n-i+1$ elements of the sequence.

5.4.2 A Sequence-Based Analysis of Bubble-Sort

Assume that the implementation of the sequence is such that the accesses to elements and the swaps of elements performed by bubble-sort take $O(1)$ time each. That is, the running time of the ith pass is $O(n-i+1)$. We have that the overall running time of bubble-sort is

$$O\left(\sum_{i=1}^{n}(n-i+1)\right).$$

We can rewrite the above sum as

$$O(n+(n-1)+\cdots+2+1).$$

That is, it is

$$O\left(\sum_{i=1}^{n}i\right).$$

By Proposition 3.2, we have

$$\sum_{i=1}^{n}i = \frac{n(n+1)}{2}.$$

Thus, bubble-sort runs in $O(n^2)$ time provided that accesses and swaps can each be implemented in $O(1)$ time. As we will see in future chapters, this performance for sorting is quite inefficient. We discuss the bubble-sort algorithm here only to show how sequences can be used in an algorithm, not as an example of a good sorting algorithm.

Code Fragment 5.15 contains two implementations of bubble-sort on a sequence of integers. The two implementations differ in the preferred choice of functions to access and modify the sequence. Note the use of a "typedef typename" in bubbleSort2(). This is used to provide a shorter and more convenient name for Sequence::Position. We have seen the use of typedef before, but why was the additional typename needed? The reason is that Sequence is not a concrete type but rather a template argument. The notation Sequence::X could be used to access either a static member function X or a member type X. Since the compiler does not know which, the keyword typename is provided to instruct the compiler that we are accessing a member type.

Note that function bubbleSort1() accesses the elements only through the rank-based interface functions atRank() and elemAtRank(). It is a rank-based implementation of the bubble-sort algorithm, and it is suitable only for the array implementation of the sequence, where atRank() and elemAtRank() take $O(1)$ time.

```
template <typename Sequence>
void bubbleSort1(Sequence& S) {                 // bubble-sort using ranks
  int n = S.size();
  for (int i = 0; i < n; i++)                    // i-th pass
    for (int j = 1; j < n−i; j++)
      if ( S.elemAtRank(j−1) > S.elemAtRank(j) )
        S.swapElements(S.atRank(j−1), S.atRank(j));
}

template <typename Sequence>
void bubbleSort2(Sequence& S) {                 // bubble-sort using positions
  typedef typename Sequence::Position Position;
  int n = S.size();
  for (int i = 0; i < n; i++) {                  // i-th pass
    Position prec = S.first();
    for (int j = 1; j < n−i; j++) {
      Position succ = S.after(prec);
      if ( prec.element() > succ.element() )
        S.swapElements(prec, succ);
      prec = succ;
    }
  }
}
```

Code Fragment 5.15: Two C++ implementations of bubble-sort.

Given such an array-based implementation, this function will run in $O(n^2)$ time. On the other hand, if we implement the sequence used by this algorithm using a doubly linked list, then each atRank() call takes $O(n)$ time in the worst case; hence, the entire algorithm would actually run in $O(n^3)$ worst-case time with a linked-list implementation.

Function bubbleSort2() accesses the elements only through the position-based interface functions first() and after(). It is a position-based implementation of the bubble-sort algorithm, and it is suitable for both the array and the linked-list implementation of the sequence. Indeed, both implementations support constant-time performance for the first() and after() functions. Thus, bubbleSort2() runs in $O(n^2)$ time, no matter which implementation is used for the sequence.

The two bubble-sort implementations given above show the importance of providing efficient implementations of ADTs. Nevertheless, in spite of its implementation simplicity, computing researchers generally feel that the bubble-sort algorithm is not a good sorting method, because, even if implemented in the best possible way, it still takes quadratic time. Indeed, there are sorting algorithms that run in $O(n \log n)$ time, and are thus much more efficient than bubble-sort. We explore some of them in Chapters 7 and 10.

5.5   Iterators

A typical computation on a vector, list, or sequence is to march through its elements in order, one at a time, for example, to look for a specific element.

An **iterator** is a software design pattern that abstracts the process of scanning through a collection of elements one element at a time. An iterator consists of a sequence S, a current position in S, and a way of stepping to the next position in S and making it the current position. Thus, an iterator extends the concept of the position ADT, which we introduced in Section 5.2. In fact, a position can be thought of as an iterator that does not go anywhere. An iterator encapsulates the concepts of "place" and "next" in a collection of objects.

5.5.1   Iterator Functions

We define the ObjectIterator ADT as supporting the following two functions:

> hasNext(): Test whether there are elements left in the iterator.
> **Input:** None; **Output:** Boolean.

> next(): Return the next element in the iterator and step to the next position.
> **Input:** None; **Output:** Object.

Note that this ADT has the notion of the "current" element in a traversal through a sequence. The first element in an iterator is returned by the first call to the function next(), assuming of course that the iterator contains at least one element. An iterator provides a unified scheme to access all the elements of a container (a collection of objects) in a way that is independent from the specific organization of the collection. An iterator for a sequence should return the elements according to their linear ordering.

For example, we can define a class ObjectIterator within the NodeList class. This iterator is accessed by NodeList<T>::ObjectIterator, where T is the element type of the list. In order to create a new iterator for a list, we add a member function elements() to NodeList, which returns such an iterator for the entire sequence. Code Fragment 5.16 shows how such an iterator could be used to print the elements of a NodeList object. This function assumes that the stream output operator (<<) is defined for type Object.

```
template <typename Object>
void print(NodeList<Object>& L) {                    // print a NodeList
  NodeList<Object>::ObjectIterator iter = L.elements(); // element iterator
  while (iter.hasNext()) {                            // while more remain
    cout << iter.next() << " ";                       // print next/advance
  }
}
```

Code Fragment 5.16: Example of the use of an iterator object to print the elements of a NodeList object. The function *L*.elements() returns an iterator for the list *L*, and each call to iter.next() returns the next element of the list.

STL Iterators

The iterator design pattern is a central concept that runs throughout the C++ Standard Template Library (STL). Indeed, STL provides iterators for all its standard containers, including vector, list, and deque. In particular, given a container X, the corresponding STL container type is X::iterator.

Each STL container provides two functions for generating iterators. Function begin() returns an iterator that is positioned at the beginning of the container. Function end() returns an iterator that is positioned just beyond the end of the container. The begin() function is analogous to our elements() function. The end() function is used primarily to determine when we have reached the end of the container. To test that an iteration has exhausted all of its elements, we test whether it is equal to end(). Thus end() is used to achieve the same purpose as our hasNext() function.

The STL iterator interface is quite different from ours. Notationally, an STL iterator behaves much like a pointer in C++. Given an iterator iter, we can access the current element using the pointer dereference operator (*), as in *iter. Such a reference may be used for reading and writing, depending on the type of iterator. The prefix and postfix increment operators (++) may be used to advance to the next position in the container. Our function iter.next() is essentially equivalent to the STL operation *(iter++). Here is an example of how an STL iterator would be used to print the elements of an STL list object. Code Fragment 5.17 presents an equivalent function to Code Fragment 5.16, but using an STL iterator.

```
using namespace std;                                 // make std available
template <typename Object>
void print(list<Object>& L) {                        // print an STL list
  list<Object>::iterator iter = L.begin();            // vector iterator
  while (iter != L.end()) {                            // while more remain
    cout << *iter << " ";                             // print next
    ++iter;                                           // advance
  }
}
```

Code Fragment 5.17: Using an STL iterator to print the elements of an STL list.

5.5.2   More About Iterators

There are several additional issues regarding iterators, which we explore in this subsection.

When Iterators Become Invalid

Note that, depending on the implementation of the container, the operations of insertion and removal may result in elements being moved in the container. As a result an iterator may become **invalid**, meaning that it may no longer refer to a valid element, or it may skip or repeat some element. For example, removing an element from a list will almost certainly render any iterator invalid that points to the deleted element. Inserting into an array may cause elements to be moved around to make room for the new element. This will invalidate an iterator that points to such an element. Inserting into a doubly linked list, however, does not cause nodes to be moved, and hence need not invalidate any iterators. It is usually the responsibility of the user of the container to make sure that no invalid iterators are used.

Iterators and Positions

STL iterators serve the same role as positions do in our containers. In fact, positions can be viewed as iterators that don't move. Rather than use positions explicitly, however, STL uses iterators to specify the positions at which to apply insertions and deletions. Table 5.6 presents some of the iterator functions of the STL containers vector and list.

Function	Description
begin()	Returns an iterator positioned at the beginning of the container
end()	Returns an iterator positioned just beyond the end of the container
insert(i, e)	Inserts e just prior to the position indicated by iterator i
erase(i)	Removes the element at the position indicated by iterator i

Table 5.6: Some of the functions supported by STL containers that involve iterators.

Thus, the STL function insert() is analogous to our function insertBefore() and the STL function erase() is analogous to our function remove().

Using Iterators

For ADTs that support the notion of position, such as list and sequence ADTs, we can also provide a function positions() that returns an iterator of the positions in the container. We define the class PositionIterator. It supports the same interface as ObjectIterator, but each call to next() returns the Position pointing to the current node, rather than the element stored in this node. Thus, we can use iterators to extend the ADTs of some of our standard data structures to give them more versatility.

Implementing Iterators

There are many ways to implement the iterator ADT. For simple containers, such as NodeList, it is sufficient to store a single pointer to the current element. Thus, like class Position, an iterator need not use any more space than a simple pointer, while providing a uniform interface for accessing different containers.

For more sophisticated structures, it may not be as easy to navigate the entire structure based on a single pointer. In these cases, an iterator can be implemented by copying all of the object's elements into some other structure, from which the iterator may then draw them.

We can use many of the data structures presented in this and the previous chapter to implement such iterators. For example, we can implement an iterator by inserting all the elements of the collection into a stack. Function hasNext() corresponds to isEmpty(), while function next() corresponds to pop(). In case there is a given order in which the elements should be returned by the iterator, we should insert the elements into the stack in reverse order. Alternatively, we can realize an iterator with a queue, which allows us to insert the elements in order.

Forward and Backward Iterators

The iterator functions given above define a restricted type of iterator that allows only one pass through the elements. More powerful iterators can also be defined, which allow movement forward and backward over a certain ordering of the elements, and that provide repeated access to the current element. An important application of a sequence is to realize such iterators: namely, an iterator can be implemented with a sequence S and a position *cur* that keeps track of the current element.

5.6   A Hierarchy of Sequence ADTs

In this chapter, we have presented three ADTs for sequences: vector, list, and sequence. These ADTs can be further refined, by grouping functions with similar purpose, and can be organized in a coherent inheritance hierarchy.

5.6.1   Functions of a Container

A *container* is a data structure that stores and organizes a collection of objects, called the elements of the container, and provides access to them through the functions of an abstract data type. Some people use the term *collection* instead of container with essentially the same meaning.

Stacks, queues, deques, vectors, lists, and sequences, which we studied in this chapter and the previous one, are all examples of containers. However, a position is not a container, since it stores a single element and not a collection of elements.

The Container ADT

The functions of a container, specified by its ADT, can be grouped in four main categories.

- *Query functions*, which return information on the container or specific elements of it (for example, function size()). These functions typically have a Boolean or integer return type.
- *Accessor functions*, which return elements or positions of the container (for example, function first() in a sequence).
- *Update functions*, which change the container by adding elements (for example, the insertAtRank() function of a vector), removing elements (for example, the dequeue() function of a queue), or altering the relation between elements (for example, the swapElements() function of a list).

In addition, a concrete implementation of a container must also provide:

- *Constructor functions*, which generate an instance of the container. For example, the NodeList class has a constructor returning an empty list (see Code Fragment 5.10).

5.6.2   Inspectable Containers

Containers that do not provide update functions are called ***inspectable containers***. Once instantiated via a constructor, these containers support "read-only" access and cannot be modified. Thus, they protect their elements from erroneous or malicious update attempts by other objects. Note that some authors use the term "immutable" instead of "inspectable" for inspectable containers.

An obvious limitation of inspectable containers is that they cannot be used when their elements are subject to updates during the life of the container. However, by exploiting inheritance, we can actually get all the protection provided by inspectable containers while at the same time retaining the flexibility of update functions. Consider, for example, the vector ADT defined in Section 5.1.1. We can restructure this ADT as follows (see Figure 5.10):

- We introduce a new ADT, the ***inspectable vector***, that contains only query functions size() and isEmpty(), and accessor function elemAtRank().
- We redefine the vector ADT as ***extending*** the inspectable vector and ***adding*** update functions replaceAtRank(), insertAtRank(), and removeAtRank().

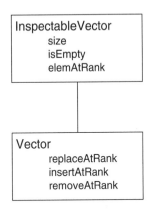

Figure 5.10:   Inheritance hierarchy where interface Vector inherits from InspectableVector.

The revised vector ADT is functionally equivalent to the original one, that is, it provides the same functions. However, we now have a simple and powerful way to protect instances of the vector ADT. Namely, we can reference a vector instance vect with a variable of type inspectable vector, thus allowing only the query and accessor functions to be executed on vect. Likewise, we can restructure the list and sequence ADTs by introducing inspectable versions of them.

5.6.3   Inheritance Structure of Sequence ADTs

After separating the update functions from the other functions, we need to restructure the simple hierarchical organization of the vector, list, and sequence ADTs given in Section 5.3.1. For this purpose, we introduce a super-interface, Inspectable-Container, that provides the generic functions size(), isEmpty(), and elements(). By exploiting the power of multiple inheritance, we finally obtain the organization shown in Figure 5.11. In Exercise C-5.16, we explore how to extend the ADT hierarchy to include the stack, queue, and deque ADTs given in Chapter 4.

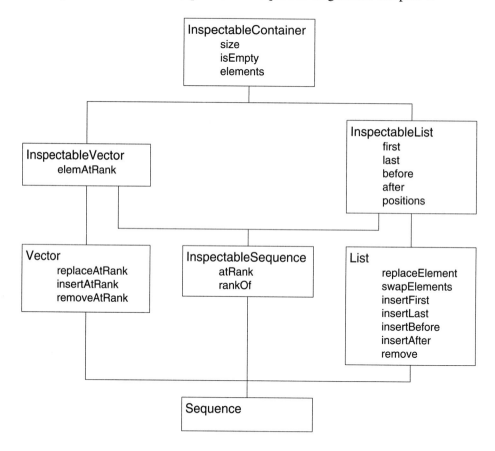

Figure 5.11: Inheritance hierarchy for ADTs representing sequences.

5.7   Exercises

Reinforcement

R-5.1 Give a detailed justification of the running times shown in Table 5.2 for the functions of a vector implemented with an array that does not expand in size.

R-5.2 Give an adapter class to support the Stack interface using the functions of the vector ADT.

R-5.3 Give a templated C++ function sum(v) that returns the sum of elements in an STL vector v. Use an STL iterator to enumerate the elements of v. Assume that the element type of v is any numeric type that supports the $+$ operator.

R-5.4 Rewrite the justification of Proposition 5.2 under the assumption that the the cost of growing the array from size k to size $2k$ is $3k$ cyber-dollars. How much should each push operation be charged to make the amortization work?

R-5.5 Give pseudo-code descriptions of algorithms for performing the functions insertBefore(p,e), insertFirst(e), and insertLast(e) of the list ADT, assuming the list is implemented using a doubly linked list.

R-5.6 Draw pictures illustrating each of the major steps in the algorithms given in the previous exercise.

R-5.7 Draw a picture illustrating the final state of a doubly linked list after performing the algorithm for insertAfter(p,e), but with the order of the last two assignment statements in Code Fragment 5.8 reversed, so the pseudo-code (which is now incorrect) would become:

> Create a new node v
> v.setElement(e)
> v.setPrev(p)
> v.setNext(p.getNext())
> p.setNext(v)
> (p.getNext()).setPrev(v)
> **return** v

R-5.8 Provide the details of an array implementation of the list ADT. In particular, describe how the index fields of the position objects are updated after an insertion or deletion of an element.

R-5.9 Provide C++ code fragments for the functions of the List interface of Code Fragment 5.4 that are not included in Code Fragments 5.10 and 5.11.

R-5.10 Let MySequence be a sequence of 99 Dalmatian puppies, and let Boiler be a Dalmatian puppy. Give the value returned or the exception thrown by each of the following statements that make calls to functions of the MySequence object.

    a. size()
    b. isEmpty()
    c. rankOf(first())
    d. rankOf(last())
    e. rankOf(atRank(0))
    f. rankOf(atRank(99))
    g. rankOf(atRank(100))
    h. rankOf(atRank(size()))
    i. rankOf(before(last()))
    j. rankOf(after(before(first())))
    k. rankOf(insertFirst(Boiler))
    l. rankOf(insertBefore(first(), Boiler))
    m. remove(first())
    n. remove(insertAtRank(1, Boiler))

R-5.11 Give pseudo-code describing how to implement all the operations in the sequence ADT using an array used in a circular fashion. What is the running time for each of these functions?

R-5.12 Using the Sequence interface functions, describe a recursive function for determining if a sequence S of n integer objects contains a given integer k. Your function should not contain any loops. How much space does your function use in addition to the space used for S?

R-5.13 Give a short fragment of pseudo-code describing a new Sequence function makeFirst(p) that moves the element of a sequence S at position p to be the first element in S while keeping the relative ordering of the remaining elements in S unchanged. Your function should run in $O(1)$ time if S is implemented with a doubly linked list.

R-5.14 Describe how to use a list and a position in that list to implement an iterator. Include pseudo-code fragments describing the functions hasNext() and next().

R-5.15 Describe how to use a vector and an integer rank index to implement an iterator. Include pseudo-code fragments describing the functions hasNext() and next().

Creativity

C-5.1 Describe what changes need to be made to the extendable array implementation given in Code Fragment 5.2 in order to avoid unexpected termination due to an error. Specify the new types of exceptions you would add, and when and where they should be thrown.

C-5.2 Give complete C++ code for a new class, ShrinkingVector, that extends the ArrayVector class shown in Code Fragment 5.2 and adds a function, shrinkToFit(), which replaces the underlying array with an array whose capacity is exactly equal to the number of elements currently in the vector.

C-5.3 Describe what changes need to be made to the extendable array implementation given in Code Fragment 5.2 in order to shrink the size N of the array by half any time the number of elements in the vector goes below $N/4$.

C-5.4★ Show that using an extendable array that grows and shrinks as described in the previous exercise implies that a sequence of n insertions and removals at the end of a vector with initial capacity $N = 1$ takes $O(n)$ time.

C-5.5 Show how to improve the implementation of function insertAtRank() in Code Fragment 5.2 so that, in case of an overflow, the elements are copied into their final place in the new array.

C-5.6★ Consider an implementation of the vector ADT using an extendable array, but instead of copying the elements of the vector into an array of double the size (that is, from N to $2N$) when its capacity is reached, we copy the elements into an array with $\lceil\sqrt{N}\rceil$ additional cells, going from capacity N to $N + \lceil\sqrt{N}\rceil$. Show that performing a sequence of n push operations (that is, insertions at the end) runs in $\Theta(n^{3/2})$ time in this case.

C-5.7 The NodeList implementation given in Code Fragments 5.10 and 5.11 does not do any error checks to test if a given position p is actually a member of this particular list. For example, if p is a position in list S and we call T.insertAfter(p, e) on a different list T, then we will add the element to S just after p. Describe how to change the NodeList implementation in an efficient manner to disallow such misuses.

C-5.8 Give a C++ function shuffle(*L*) that shuffles the elements of an STL list *L*, and returns the shuffled list. This works like a perfect shuffling of a deck of cards, that is, the list is split into two sublists of equal size and elements are taken in alternating order from each sublist.

C-5.9 Describe an implementation of the functions insertLast() and insertBefore() realized by using combinations of only the functions isEmpty(), checkPosition(), insertAfter(), and insertFirst().

C-5.10 Suppose we want to extend the Sequence abstract data type with functions rankOfElement(*e*) and positionOfElement(*e*), which respectively return the rank and the position of the (first occurrence of) element *e* in the sequence. Show how to implement these functions by expressing them in terms of other functions of the Sequence interface.

C-5.11 Consider the following fragment of C++ code, assuming that the constructor MySequence() creates an empty sequence of integer objects. Recall that division between integers performs truncation (for example, $7/2 = 3$).

```
Sequence<int> seq;
for (int i = 0; i < n; i++)
    seq.insertAtRank(i/2, i);
```

a. Assume that the **for** loop is executed 10 times, that is, n=10, and show the sequence after each iteration of the loop.
b. Draw a schematic illustration of the sequence at the end of the **for** loop, for a generic number n of iterations.

(Hint: Consider separately the cases of n being even and n being odd.)

C-5.12 Design algorithms for reversing a sequence that access the sequence only through a restricted set of functions, as indicated below. Each algorithm should rearrange the elements of the sequence. Returning a new sequence is not allowed, although other sequences may be used for auxiliary storage.

a. Reverse a sequence using only the functions size(), first(), last(), remove(), and insertFirst().
b. Reverse a sequence using only the functions size(), first(), remove(), and insertFirst().

C-5.13 Give an adaptation of the vector ADT to the deque ADT that is different from that given in Table 5.1.

C-5.14 Describe the structure and pseudo-code for an array-based implementation of the vector ADT that achieves $O(1)$ time for insertions and removals at rank 0, as well as insertions and removals at the end of the vector. Your implementation should also provide for a constant time elemAtRank() function. (Hint: Think about how to extend the circular array implementation of the queue ADT given in the previous chapter.)

C-5.15 Give a C++ code fragment for the function rankOf(p), which is missing from the implementation given in Code Fragment 5.13.

C-5.16 Extend the inheritance hierarchy shown in Figure 5.10 to include the stack, queue, and deque ADTs.

C-5.17 In the children's game "hot potato," a group of n children sit in a circle passing an object, called the "potato," around the circle (say in a clockwise direction). The children continue passing the potato until a leader rings a bell, at which point the child holding the potato must leave the game, and the other children close up the circle. This process is then continued until there is only one child remaining, who is declared the winner. Using the sequence ADT, describe an efficient method for implementing this game. Suppose the leader always rings the bell immediately after the potato has been passed k times. (Determining the last child remaining in this variation of hot potato is known as the ***Josephus problem***.) What is the running time of your method, in terms of n and k, assuming the sequence is implemented with a doubly linked list? What if the sequence is implemented with an array?

C-5.18★ Using the Sequence ADT, describe an efficient way of putting a sequence representing a deck of n cards into random order. You may assume a function, randomInteger(n), which returns a random number between 0 and $n - 1$, inclusive. Your method should guarantee that every possible ordering is equally likely. What is the running time of your method, if the sequence is implemented with an array? What if it is implemented with a linked list?

C-5.19 Using the Enumeration ADT, describe an algorithm for finding the minimum and maximum of a sequence of integer elements using, at most, $3n/2$ comparisons between elements. (Hint: Consider the elements in pairs.)

C-5.20 Show that only $n-1$ passes are needed in the execution of bubble-sort on a sequence with n elements.

C-5.21 Give a pseudo-code description of an implementation of the bubble-sort algorithm that uses only two stacks and, at most, five additional variables to sort a collection of objects stored initially in one of the stacks. You may operate on the stacks using only functions of the stack ADT. The final output should be one of the stacks containing all the elements so that a sequence of pop operations would list the elements in order.

C-5.22 Give a pseudo-code description of an implementation of the bubble-sort algorithm that uses only one queue and, at most, five additional variables to sort a collection of objects stored initially in the queue. You may operate on the queue using only functions of the queue ADT. The final output should be the queue containing all the elements so that a sequence of dequeue operations would list the elements in order.

Projects

P-5.1 Implement the vector ADT by means of an extendable array used in a circular fashion, so that insertions and deletions at the beginning and end of the vector run in constant time.

P-5.2 Write a simple text editor, which stores a string of characters using the list ADT, together with a cursor object that highlights the position of some character in the string (or possibly the position before the first character). Your editor should support the following operations and redisplay the current text (that is, the list) after performing any one of them.

- left: move cursor left one character (or do nothing if at end of the text).
- right: move cursor right one character (or do nothing if at end of the text).
- delete: delete the character to the right of the cursor (or do nothing if at end of the text).
- insert c: insert the character c just after the cursor.

P-5.3 Implement the sequence ADT by means of an extendable array used in a circular fashion, so that insertions and deletions at the beginning and end of the sequence run in constant time.

P-5.4 Implement the sequence ADT by means of a singly linked list.

P-5.5 Write a complete adapter class that implements the sequence ADT using an STL vector object.

P-5.6 Write a simulator for a person arranging a group of cards in his or her hand. The simulator should represent the sequence of cards using the list ADT so that cards of the same suit are kept together. Implement this strategy by means of four "fingers" into the hand, one for each of the suits of hearts, clubs, spades, and diamonds, so that adding a new card to the person's hand or playing a correct card from the hand can be done in constant time. Your simulator should have a graphical or ASCII output that shows the person's hand of cards and the "finger" positions in the hand after each play. The possible plays should include the following:

- newCard(c, s): add the new card c of suit s to the hand.
- playDown(s): remove a card of suit s from the player's hand; if there is no card of suit s, then remove an arbitrary card from the hand.

Chapter Notes

Sequences and iterators are pervasive concepts in the C++ Standard Template Library (STL) [83], and they play fundamental roles in JDSL, the data structures library in Java. For further information on STL vector and list classes, see books by Stroustrup [93], Lippmann and Lajoie [67], and Musser and Saini [83]. With minor exceptions, the sequence ADT is a generalization and extension of the Java java.util.Vector API (for example, see the book by Arnold and Gosling [7]) and the list ADTs proposed by several authors, including Aho, Hopcroft, and Ullman [5], who introduce the "position" abstraction, and Wood [105], who defines a list ADT similar to ours. Implementations of sequences via arrays and linked lists are discussed in Knuth's seminal book, *Fundamental Algorithms* [58]. Knuth's companion volume, *Sorting and Searching* [59], describes the bubble-sort method and the history of this and other sorting algorithms.

Chapter

6

Trees

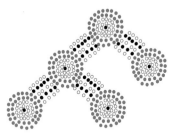

Contents

Productivity experts say that breakthroughs come by thinking "nonlinearly." In this chapter, we discuss one of the most important nonlinear data structures in computing—*trees*. Tree structures are indeed a breakthrough in data organization, for they allow us to implement a host of algorithms much faster than when using linear data structures, such as list, vectors, and sequences. Trees also provide a natural organization for data, and consequently have become ubiquitous structures in file systems, graphical user interfaces, databases, Web sites, and other computer systems.

It is not always clear what productivity experts mean by "nonlinear" thinking, but when we say that trees are "nonlinear," we are referring to an organizational relationship that is richer than the simple "before" and "after" relationships between objects in sequences. The relationships in a tree are *hierarchical*, with some objects being "above" and some "below" others. Actually, the main terminology for tree data structures comes from family trees, with the terms "parent," "child," "ancestor," and "descendent" being the most common words used to describe relationships. We show an example of a family tree in Figure 6.1.

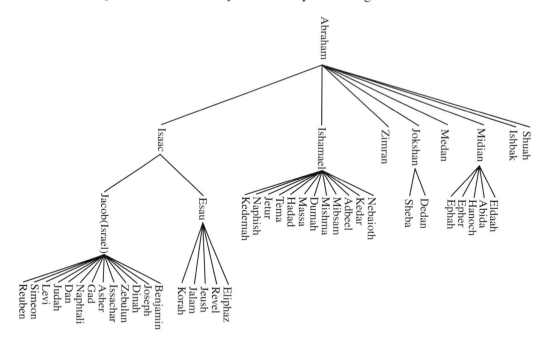

Figure 6.1: A family tree showing some descendents of Abraham, as recorded in Genesis, chapters 25–36.

6.1 The Tree Abstract Data Type

A *tree* is an abstract data type that stores elements hierarchically. With the exception of the top element, each element in a tree has a *parent* element and zero or more *children* elements. A tree is usually visualized by placing elements inside ovals or rectangles, and by drawing the connections between parents and children with straight lines. (See Figure 6.2.) We typically call the top element the *root* of the tree, but it is drawn as the highest element, with the other elements being connected below (just the opposite of a botanical tree).

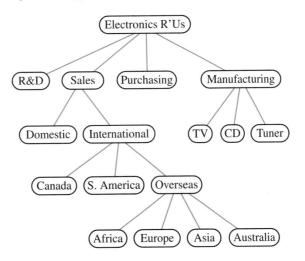

Figure 6.2: A tree with 17 nodes representing the organizational structure of a fictitious corporation. *Electronics R'Us* is stored at the root. The children of the root store *R&D*, *Sales*, *Purchasing*, and *Manufacturing*. The internal nodes store *Sales*, *International*, *Overseas*, *Electronics R'Us*, and *Manufacturing*. The other nodes are external nodes.

6.1.1 Terminology and Basic Properties

A *tree* T is a set of *nodes* storing elements in a *parent-child* relationship with the following properties:

- T has a special node r, called the *root* of T, with no parent node.
- Each node v of T different from r has a unique *parent* node u.

Note that, according to the above definition, a tree cannot be empty, since it must have at least one node, the root.

One could also allow the definition to include empty trees, but we adopt the convention that a tree always has a root so as to keep our presentation simple and to avoid having to always deal with the special case of an empty tree in our algorithms.

If node *u* is the parent of node *v*, we say that *v* is a ***child*** of *u*. Two nodes that are children of the same parent are ***siblings***. A node is ***external*** if it has no children, and it is ***internal*** if it has one or more children. External nodes are also known as ***leaves***. The ***subtree*** of *T* ***rooted*** at a node *v* is the tree consisting of all the descendents of *v* in *T* (including *v* itself). An ***ancestor*** of a node is either the node itself or an ancestor of the parent of the node. Conversely, we say that a node *v* is a ***descendent*** of a node *u* if *u* is an ancestor of *v*. For example, in Figure 6.2, *Sales* is an ancestor of *Europe*, and *Europe* is a descendent of *Sales*.

Example 6.1: *When using single inheritance, the inheritance relation between classes in a C++ program forms a tree. The base class is the root of the tree.*

Example 6.2: *In most operating systems, files are organized hierarchically into nested directories (also called folders), which are presented to the user in the form of a tree. (See Figure 6.3.) More specifically, the internal nodes of the tree are associated with directories and the external nodes are associated with regular files. In the UNIX and Linux operating systems, the root of the tree is appropriately called the "root directory," and is represented by the symbol "/." It is the ancestor of all directories and files in such a file system.*

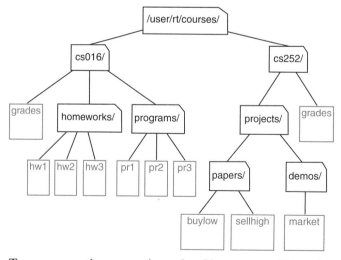

Figure 6.3: Tree representing a portion of a file system. The subtree rooted at cs016/ contains 10 nodes.

Ordered Trees

A tree is ***ordered*** if there is a linear ordering defined for the children of each node; that is, we can identify children of a node as being the first, second, third, and so on. Such an ordering is determined by the use we wish to make for the tree, and it is usually indicated in a drawing of a tree by arranging siblings left to right, corresponding to their linear relationship. Ordered trees typically indicate the linear order relationship existing between siblings by listing them in a sequence or iterator in the correct order.

Example 6.3: *A structured document, such as a book, is hierarchically organized as a tree whose internal nodes are chapters, sections, and subsections, and whose external nodes are paragraphs, tables, figures, the bibliography, and so on. (See Figure 6.4.) The root of the tree corresponds to the book itself. We could in fact consider expanding the tree further to show paragraphs consisting of sentences, sentences consisting of words, and words consisting of characters. In any case, such a tree is an example of an ordered tree, because there is a well-defined ordering among the children of each node.*

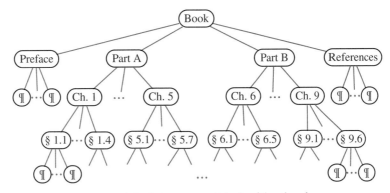

Figure 6.4: A tree associated with a book.

A ***binary tree*** is an ordered tree in which every node has at most two children. A binary tree is ***proper*** if each node has either zero or two children. Thus, in a proper binary tree, every internal node has exactly two children. For each internal node in a binary tree, we label each child as either being a ***left child*** or a ***right child***. These children are ordered so that a left child comes before a right child. The subtree rooted at a left or right child of an internal node v is called a ***left subtree*** or ***right subtree***, of v, respectively. The convention in this book is that, unless otherwise stated, every binary tree is a proper binary tree. Of course, even an improper binary tree is still a general tree, with the property that each internal node has two children at most.

Caution

Binary trees have a number of useful applications. We discuss two common uses in the examples below.

Example 6.4: An important class of binary trees arises in contexts where we wish to represent a number of different outcomes that can result from answering a collection of yes-or-no questions. Each internal node is associated with a question. Starting at the root, we go to the left or right child of the current node, depending on whether the answer to the question is "Yes" or "No." Such trees are known as **decision** *trees, because each external node v in such a tree represents a decision of what to do if the questions associated with v's ancestors are answered in a way that leads to v. Figure 6.5 illustrates a binary decision tree that provides recommendations to a prospective investor. Each external node contains a recommended investment based on the answers provided.*

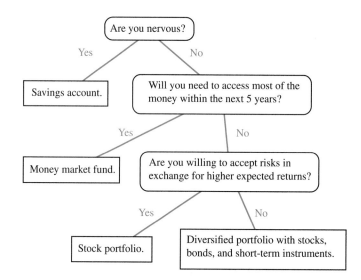

Figure 6.5: A binary decision tree providing investment advice.

Example 6.5: An arithmetic expression can be represented by a tree whose external nodes are associated with variables or constants, and whose internal nodes are associated with one of the operators +, −, ×, and /. (See Figure 6.6.) Each node in such a tree has a value associated with it.

- *If a node is external, then its value is that of its variable or constant.*
- *If a node is internal, then its value is defined by applying its operation to the values of its children.*

Such an arithmetic expression tree is a proper binary tree, since each of the oper-ators +, −, ×, and / take exactly two operands. Of course, if we were to allow for unary operators, like negation (−), as in "−x," then we could have an improper binary tree.

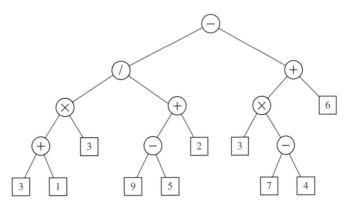

Figure 6.6: A binary tree representing an arithmetic expression. This tree represents the expression $((((3+1) \times 3)/((9-5)+2)) - ((3 \times (7-4))+6))$. The value associated with the internal node labeled "/" is 2.

6.1.2 Tree Functions

The tree ADT stores elements at positions, which, as with positions in a list, are defined relative to neighboring positions. The **positions** in a tree are its **nodes**, and neighboring positions satisfy the parent-child relationships that define a valid tree. Therefore we use the terms "position" and "node" interchangeably for trees. As with a list position, a position object for a tree supports the function:

element(): Return the object at this position.
Input: None; *Output:* Object.

However, the real power of node positions in a tree comes from the **accessor func-tions** of the tree ADT that return and accept positions, such as the following:

root(): Return the root of the tree.
Input: None; *Output:* Position.

parent(v): Return the parent of node v; an error occurs if v is root.
Input: Position; *Output:* Position.

children(v): Return an iterator of the children of node v.
Input: Position; *Output:* Iterator of positions.

If a tree T is ordered, then the iterator children(v) provides access to the children of v in order. If v is an external node, then children(v) is an empty iterator.

In addition to the above fundamental accessor functions, we also include the following *query functions*:

isInternal(v): Test whether node v is internal.
                Input: Position; *Output:* Boolean.

isExternal(v): Test whether node v is external.
                Input: Position; *Output:* Boolean.

isRoot(v): Test whether node v is the root.
                Input: Position; *Output:* Boolean.

These functions make programming with trees easier and more readable, since we can use them in the conditionals of if statements and while loops, rather than using a nonintuitive conditional or trying to catch an error condition. For instance, isInternal(v) and isExternal(v) can be performed by checking whether or not the iterator returned by function children(v) has any elements.

There are also a number of functions a tree should probably support that are not necessarily related to its tree structure. Such *generic functions* for a tree include the following:

size(): Return the number of nodes in the tree.
                Input: None; *Output:* Integer.

elements(): Return an iterator of all the elements stored at nodes of the tree.
                Input: None; *Output:* Iterator of objects.

positions(): Return an iterator of all the nodes of the tree.
                Input: None; *Output:* Iterator of positions.

swapElements(v, w): Swap the elements stored at the nodes v and w.
                Input: Two positions; *Output:* None.

replaceElement(v, e): Replace the element stored at node v with e.
                Input: A position and an object; *Output:* None.

We do not define any specialized update functions for a tree here. Instead, we prefer to describe different tree update functions in conjunction with specific applications of trees in subsequent chapters. In fact, we can imagine several kinds of tree update operations beyond those given in this book. Even though we are not including any update operations here, we nevertheless consider how we might organize this collection of tree ADT functions into a set of informal interfaces in the next section.

6.1.3 A Tree Interface

We can use the tree ADT to define an informal interface for trees. Rather than include all of the above tree functions directly, we divide the tree-specific functions from the generic functions, and further separate the query and accessor functions from the update functions. The resulting set of interfaces are shown in Code Fragment 6.1. Since we extend InspectableContainer (see Figure 5.11), the function isEmpty() is included, but according to our definition of a tree, it should always return false, since every tree has at least one node, the root.

```
template <typename Object>
class InspectablePositionalContainer
    : public InspectableContainer<Object> {
public:
    class Position;                                    // node position type
    class PositionIterator;                            // position iterator
    PositionIterator positions() const;                // get position iterator
};
template <typename Object>
class PositionalContainer :
    public InspectablePositionalContainer<Object> {
public:
    void swapElements(const Position& v, const Position& w);
    Object& replaceElement(const Position& v, const Object& e);
};
template <typename Object>
class InspectableTree
    : public InspectablePositionalContainer<Object> {
public:
    Position root() const;                             // get root of tree
    Position parent(const Position& v) const;          // get parent of v
    PositionIterator children(const Position& v) const; // iterator for children
    bool isInternal(const Position& v) const;          // internal node?
    bool isExternal(const Position& v) const;          // external node?
    bool isRoot(const Position& v) const;              // the root?
};
template <typename Object>
class Tree
    : public InspectableTree<Object>, PositionalContainer<Object> { };
```

Code Fragment 6.1: Informal interfaces InspectablePositionalContainer, PositionalContainer, InspectableTree, and Tree. Additional update functions may be added. (These are not complete classes.)

6.2   Basic Algorithms on Trees

In this section, we present algorithms for performing computations on a tree by accessing it through the tree ADT functions, which correspond to the functions of the InspectableTree interface.

6.2.1   Running-Time Assumptions

In order to analyze the running time of the algorithms presented throughout Section 6.2, we make the following reasonable assumptions on the running times of the functions of the tree ADT.

- The accessor functions root() and parent(v) take $O(1)$ time.

- The query functions isInternal(v), isExternal(v), and isRoot(v) take $O(1)$ time, as well.

- The accessor function children(v) takes $O(c_v)$ time, where c_v is the number of children of v.

- The functions swapElements(v, w) and replaceElement(v, e) take $O(1)$ time.

- The generic functions elements() and positions(), which return iterators, take $O(n)$ time, where n is the number of nodes in the tree.

- For the iterators returned by the functions elements(), positions(), and children(v), the functions hasNext() and next() take $O(1)$ time each.

In Section 6.4, we present data structures for trees that satisfy the above assumptions. Before we describe how to implement the tree ADT using a concrete data structure, however, let us describe how we can use the functions of the tree ADT to solve some interesting problems for trees.

For the remainder of this section, let us assume that we have access to a concrete implementation of a tree, called Tree. Let Position denote a position in this tree, and let PositionIterator denote a iterator of positions in the tree.

6.2.2 Depth and Height

Let v be a node of a tree T. The ***depth*** of v is the number of ancestors of v, excluding v itself. For example, in the tree of Figure 6.2, the node storing *International* has depth 2. Note that this definition implies that the depth of the root of T is 0.

The depth of a node v can also be recursively defined as follows:

- If v is the root, then the depth of v is 0.
- Otherwise, the depth of v is one plus the depth of the parent of v.

Based on the above definition, the recursive algorithm depth(T,v), shown in Code Fragment 6.2, computes the depth of a node v of T by calling itself recursively on the parent of v, and adding 1 to the value returned. Thus, each ancestor of v is visited by a recursive call, and contributes a value of 1 to the depth, as it should.

Algorithm depth(T,v):
  if T.isRoot(v) **then**
    return 0
  else
    return $1 +$ depth$(T, T$.parent$(v))$

Code Fragment 6.2: Algorithm depth(T,v) computes the depth of a node v in a tree T.

A simple C++ implementation of algorithm depth() is shown in Code Fragment 6.3.

```
int depth(const Tree& T, const Position& v) {
  if (T.isRoot(v))
    return 0;                            // root has depth 0
  else
    return 1 + depth(T, T.parent(v));    // 1 + (depth of parent)
}
```

Code Fragment 6.3: Function depth(v) implemented in C++.

The running time of algorithm depth(T,v) is $O(1+d_v)$, where d_v denotes the depth of the node v in the tree T, because the algorithm performs a constant-time recursive step for each ancestor of v. Thus, in the worst case, the depth algorithm runs in $O(n)$ time, where n is the total number of nodes in the tree T, since some nodes may have this depth in T. Although such a running time is a function of the input size, it is more accurate to characterize the running time in terms of the parameter d_v, since this will often be much smaller than n.

The *height* of a node v in a tree T is also defined recursively.

- If v is an external node, then the height of v is 0.
- Otherwise, the height of v is one plus the maximum height of a child of v.

The *height* of a tree T is the height of the root of T. For example, the tree of Figure 6.2 has height 4. In addition, height can also be viewed as follows.

Proposition 6.6: *The height of a tree T is equal to the maximum depth of an external node of T.*

We leave the justification of this fact to an exercise (R-6.4). We present here an algorithm, height1(), shown in Code Fragment 6.4 and implemented in C++ in Code Fragment 6.5, for computing the height of a tree T based on the above proposition. This algorithm utilizes an iterator of all the nodes in the tree to aid the computation of the depth of each external node by using algorithm depth() (Code Fragment 6.2) as a subroutine, keeping track of the maximum depth seen so far.

Algorithm height1(T):
    $h = 0$
    for each $v \in T$.positions() **do**
        if T.isExternal(v) **then**
            $h = \max(h, \text{depth}(T, v))$
    return h

Code Fragment 6.4: Algorithm height1(T) for computing the height of a tree T. Note that algorithm depth(), from Code Fragment 6.2, is used as a subroutine.

```
int height1(const Tree& T) {
    int h = 0;
    PositionIterator nodes = T.positions();
    while (nodes.hasNext()) {
        Position v = nodes.next();
        if (T.isExternal(v))                    // v is a leaf?
            h = max(h, depth(T, v));            // max depth among leaves
    }
    return h;
}
```

Code Fragment 6.5: Function height1() implemented in C++. We assume that a function max() is provided.

Unfortunately, algorithm height1() is not very efficient. Since height1() calls algorithm depth(v) on each external node v of T, the running time of height1() is given by $O(n + \sum_{v \in E}(1 + d_v))$, where n is the number of nodes of T, d_v is the depth of a node v, and E is the set of external nodes of T. Since $d_v \leq h \leq n - 1$ for each node v, and $|E| \leq n - 1$ (the upper bound is attained when the root has $n - 1$ children), algorithm height1() runs in time $O(n + \sum_{v \in E} n)$, which is $O(n^2)$ in the worst case. (See Exercise C-6.5.)

Algorithm height2(), shown in Code Fragment 6.6 and implemented in C++ in Code Fragment 6.7, computes the height of tree T in a more efficient manner by using the recursive definition of height. The algorithm is expressed by a recursive function height2(T,v) that computes the height of the subtree of T rooted at a node v. If the node v is external, then the algorithm returns 0. Otherwise, it gets an iterator of the children of v, recursively computes the height of each child, and returns 1 plus the maximum height returned from a recursive call. The height of tree T is obtained by calling height2(T, T.root()).

Algorithm height2(T, v):

  if T.isExternal(v) **then**

    return 0

  else

    $h = 0$

    for each $w \in T$.children(v) **do**

      $h = \max(h, \text{height2}(T, w))$

    return $1 + h$

Code Fragment 6.6: Algorithm height2() for computing the height of the subtree of tree T rooted at a node v.

```cpp
int height2(const Tree& T, const Position& v) {
  if (T.isExternal(v))
    return 0;                              // leaf has height 0
  else {
    int h = 0;
    PositionIterator children = T.children(v);
    while (children.hasNext())
      h = max(h, height2(T, children.next()));
    return 1 + h;                          // 1 + (max height)
  }
}
```

Code Fragment 6.7: Function height2() implemented in C++.

Algorithm height2() is much more efficient than Algorithm height1() (from Code Fragment 6.4). The algorithm is recursive, and if it is initially called on the root of T, it will eventually be called once on each node of T. Thus, we can determine the running time of this function by first determining the amount of time spent at each node (on the nonrecursive part), and then summing this time bound over all the nodes. The computation of an iterator children(v) takes $O(c_v)$ time, where c_v denotes the number of children of node v. Also, the while loop has c_v iterations, and each iteration of the loop takes $O(1)$ time plus the time for the recursive call on a child of v. Thus, algorithm height2() spends $O(1 + c_v)$ time at each node v, and its running time is $O(\sum_{v \in T}(1 + c_v))$. In order to complete the analysis, we make use of the following property.

Proposition 6.7: *Let T be a tree with n nodes, and let c_v denote the number of children of a node v of T. Then*

$$\sum_{v \in T} c_v = n - 1.$$

Justification: Each node of T, with the exception of the root, is a child of another node, and thus contributes one unit to the above sum.   ∎

By Proposition 6.7, the running time of algorithm height2(), when called on the root of T, is $O(n)$, where n is the number of nodes of T.

6.2.3 Preorder Traversal

A ***traversal*** of a tree T is a systematic way of accessing, or "visiting," all the nodes of T. In a ***preorder*** traversal of a tree T, the root of T is visited first and then the subtrees rooted at its children are traversed recursively. If the tree is ordered, then the subtrees are traversed according to the order of the children. The specific action associated with the "visit" of a node v depends on the application of this traversal, and could involve anything from incrementing a counter to performing some complex computation for v. The pseudo-code for the preorder traversal of the subtree rooted at a node v is shown in Code Fragment 6.8. We initially invoke this routine with the call preorder(T, T.root()).

Algorithm preorder(T, v):
    perform the "visit" action for node v
    for each child w of v **do**
        recursively traverse the subtree rooted at w by calling preorder(T, w)

Code Fragment 6.8: Algorithm preorder.

Tree Printing: An Application of Preorder Traversal

The preorder traversal of the tree associated with a document, as in Example 6.3, examines an entire document sequentially, from beginning to end. If the external nodes are removed before the traversal, then the traversal examines the table of contents of the document. (See Figure 6.7.)

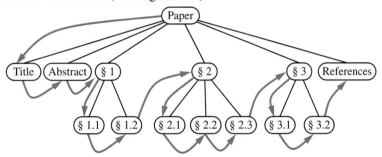

Figure 6.7: Preorder traversal of an ordered tree, where the children of each node are ordered from left to right.

The preorder traversal is also an efficient way to access all the nodes of a tree. To justify this, let us consider the running time of the preorder traversal of a tree T with n nodes under the assumption that visiting a node takes $O(1)$ time. The analysis of the preorder traversal algorithm is actually similar to that of algorithm height2() (Code Fragment 6.7), given in Section 6.2.2. At each node v, the nonrecursive part of the preorder traversal algorithm requires time $O(1+c_v)$, where c_v is the number of children of v. Thus, by Proposition 6.7, the overall running time of the preorder traversal of T is $O(n)$.

Algorithm preorderPrint(T, v), implemented in C++ in Code Fragment 6.9, performs a preorder printing of the subtree of a node v of T, that is, it performs the preorder traversal of the subtree rooted at v and prints the element stored at a node when the node is visited. Recall that, for an ordered tree T, method T.children(v) returns an iterator that accesses the children of v in order.

```
void preorderPrint(const Tree& T, const Position& v) {
    cout << v.element();                          // print element
    PositionIterator children = T.children(v);    // visit children
    while (children.hasNext()) {
        cout << " ";
        preorderPrint(T, children.next());
    }
}
```

Code Fragment 6.9: Function preorderPrint(T, v) that performs a preorder printing of the elements in the subtree of node v of T. We implicitly assume that an output operator (<<) is defined for the elements of the tree (see Section 1.4.2).

Using Preorder Traversal for Representing a Tree

There is an interesting variation of the preorderPrint() method that outputs a different representation of an entire tree. The ***parenthetic string representation*** $P(T)$ of tree T is recursively defined as follows. If T consists of a single node v, then

$$P(T) = v.\text{element}().$$

Otherwise,

$$P(T) = v.\text{element}() + \texttt{"("} + P(T_1) + P(T_2) + \cdots + P(T_k) + \texttt{")"},$$

where v is the root of T and $T_1, T_2, \ldots, T_k$ are the subtrees rooted at the children of v, which are given in order if T is an ordered tree. Note that the definition of $P(T)$ is recursive. Also, we are using "+" here to denote string concatenation. (Recall the string type from Section 1.1.3.) The parenthetic representation of the tree of Figure 6.2 is shown in Figure 6.8.

> *Electronics R'Us (*
>   *R&D*
>   *Sales (*
>   *Domestic*
>   *International (*
>   *Canada*
>   *S. America*
>   *Overseas (Africa   Europe   Asia   Australia)))*
>   *Purchasing*
>   *Manufacturing (TV   CD   Tuner))*

Figure 6.8: Parenthetic representation of the tree of Figure 6.2. Indentation, line breaks, and spaces have been added for clarity.

Note that, technically speaking, there are some computations that occur between and after the recursive calls at a node's children in the above algorithm. We still consider this algorithm to be a preorder traversal, however, since the primary action of printing a node's contents occurs prior to the recursive calls.

The C++ function parenPrint(), shown in Code Fragment 6.10, is a variation of function preorderPrint() (Code Fragment 6.9). It implements the definition given above to output a parenthetic string representation of a tree T.

We explore a modification of Code Fragment 6.10 in Exercise R-6.7, to display a tree in a fashion more closely matching that given in Figure 6.8.

```
void parenPrint(const Tree& T, const Position& v) {
  cout << v.element();                           // print node's element
  if (T.isInternal(v)) {
    PositionIterator children = T.children(v);
    cout << "( ";                                // open
    parenPrint(T, children.next());              // visit the first child
    while (children.hasNext()) {                  // for each other child
      cout << ", ";                              // print separator
      parenPrint(T, children.next());            // visit the next child
    }
    cout << " )";                                // close
  }
}
```

Code Fragment 6.10: Algorithm parenPrint().

6.2.4 Postorder Traversal

Whereas preorder traversal is useful for solving a tree problem where we must perform a computation for each node before performing any computations for its descendents, there is another traversal algorithm, called ***postorder*** traversal, for the opposite situation. This algorithm can be viewed as the opposite of the pre-order traversal, because it recursively traverses the subtrees rooted at the children of the root first, and then visits the root. Still, as with the preorder traversal, if the tree is ordered, we make recursive calls for the children of a node v according to their specified order. Pseudo-code for the postorder traversal is given in Code Fragment 6.11.

Algorithm postorder(T, v):

for each child w of v **do**
    recursively traverse the subtree rooted at w by calling postorder(T, w)
    perform the "visit" action for node v

Code Fragment 6.11: The function postorder().

The analysis of the running time of a postorder traversal is analogous to that of a preorder traversal. (See Section 6.2.3.) The total time spent in the nonrecursive portions of the algorithm is proportional to the time spent visiting the children of each node in the tree. Thus, a postorder traversal of a tree T with n nodes takes $O(n)$ time, assuming that visiting each node takes $O(1)$ time. That is, the postorder traversal runs in linear time.

An Illustrative Use of the Postorder Traversal

The name of the postorder traversal comes from the fact that this traversal method will visit a node *v* after it has visited all the other nodes in the subtree rooted at *v*. (See Figure 6.9.)

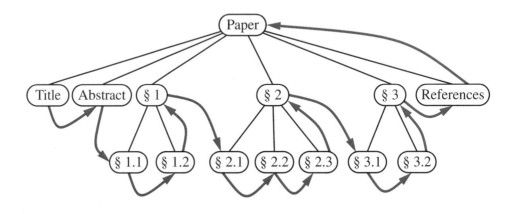

Figure 6.9: Postorder traversal of the ordered tree of Figure 6.7.

As an example of postorder traversal, we show a C++ function postorderPrint() in Code Fragment 6.12, which performs a postorder traversal of a tree *T*. This function prints the element stored at a node when it is visited.

```
void postorderPrint(const Tree& T, const Position& v) {
  PositionIterator children = T.children(v);
  while (children.hasNext()) {                          // visit children
    postorderPrint(T, children.next());
    cout << " ";
  }
  cout << v.element();                                  // print element
}
```

Code Fragment 6.12: The function postorderPrint(T, v), which prints the elements of the subtree of node *v* of *T*.

The postorder traversal method is useful for solving problems where we wish to compute some property for each node *v* in a tree, but computing that property for *v* requires that we have already computed that same property for *v*'s children. Such an application is illustrated in the following example.

Example 6.8: *Consider a file system tree T, where external nodes represent files and internal nodes represent directories (Example 6.2). Suppose we want to compute the disk space used by a directory, which is recursively given by the sum of:*

- *The size of the directory itself*
- *The sizes of the files in the directory*
- *The space used by the children directories.*

(See Figure 6.10.) This computation can be done with a postorder traversal of tree T. After the subtrees of an internal node v have been traversed, we compute the space used by v by adding the sizes of the directory v itself and of the files contained in v, to the space used by each internal child of v, which was computed by the recursive postorder traversals of the children of v.

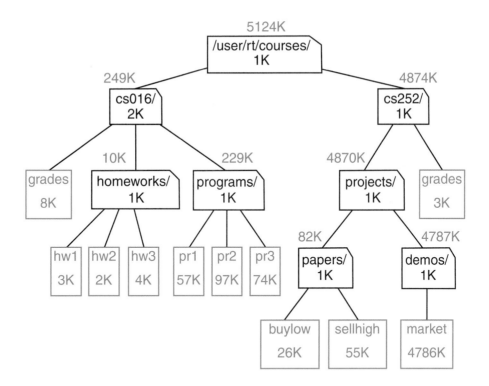

Figure 6.10: The tree of Figure 6.3 representing a file system, showing the name and size of the associated file/directory inside each node, and the disk space used by the associated directory above each internal node.

A Postorder Algorithm for Computing Disk Usage

Motivated by Example 6.8, algorithm diskSpace(), which is in Code Fragment 6.13, performs a postorder traversal of a file-system tree T, printing the name and disk space used by the directory associated with each internal node of T. When called on the root of tree T, diskSpace() runs in time $O(n)$, where n is the number of nodes of the tree, provided the auxiliary functions name(v) and size(v) take $O(1)$ time.

```
int diskSpace(const Tree& T, const Position& v) {
  int s = size(v);                               // start with size of v
  PositionIterator children = T.children(v);
  while (children.hasNext())
    s += diskSpace(T, children.next());          // add weights of subtrees
  if (T.isInternal(v))
    cout << name(v) << ": " << s << endl;        // print name and weight
  return s;
}
```

Code Fragment 6.13: The function diskSpace(), which prints the name and disk space used by the directory associated with v, for each internal node v of a file-system tree T. This function calls the auxiliary functions name() and size(), which should be defined to return the name and size of the file/directory associated with a node.

Other Kinds of Traversals

Preorder traversal is useful when we want to perform an action for a node and then recursively perform that action for its children, and postorder traversal is useful when we want to first perform an action on the descendents of a node and then perform that action on the node.

Although the preorder and postorder traversals are common ways of visiting the nodes of a tree, we can also imagine other traversals. For example, we could traverse a tree so that we visit all the nodes at depth d before we visit the nodes at depth $d + 1$. Such a traversal could be implemented, for example, using a queue, whereas the preorder and postorder traversals use a stack (this stack is implicit in our use of recursion to describe these functions, but we could make this use explicit, as well, to avoid recursion). In addition, binary trees, which we discuss next, support an additional traversal method, known as the inorder traversal.

6.3   Binary Trees

One kind of tree that is of particular interest is the binary tree. As we mentioned in Section 6.1.1, a proper *binary tree* is an ordered tree in which each internal node has two children. We make the convention that, unless otherwise stated, binary trees are assumed to be proper. Note that our convention for binary trees is made without loss of generality, for we can easily convert any improper binary tree into a proper one, as we explore in Exercise R-6.3. Even without such a conversion, we can consider an improper binary tree as proper, simply by viewing missing external nodes as "null nodes" or place holders that still count as nodes.

Binary trees arise naturally in many different applications. For example, an arithmetic expression tree (Example 6.5) is a binary tree, since each of the operators used to define this tree is a binary operator. Also, a decision tree (see Example 6.4) is a binary tree, since the outcome of a decision is always "yes" or "no." We discuss some of the specialized topics for binary trees below.

6.3.1   The Binary Tree ADT

As an abstract data type, a binary tree is a specialization of a tree that supports three additional accessor functions:

leftChild(v): Return the left child of v; an error condition occurs if v is an external node.
Input: Position; *Output:* Position.

rightChild(v): Return the right child of v; an error condition occurs if v is an external node.
Input: Position; *Output:* Position.

sibling(v): Return the sibling of node v; an error condition occurs if v is the root.
Input: Position; *Output:* Position.

Note that these functions would have additional error conditions if we are dealing with improper binary trees. For example, in an improper binary tree, an internal node may not have the left child or right child. Even so, as in Section 6.1.2 for the tree ADT, we do not define specialized update functions for binary trees here.

6.3.2   A Binary Tree Interface

We model a binary tree as an abstract data type with the informal interfaces In-spectableBinaryTree and BinaryTree, shown in Code Fragment 6.14. The relationships between these and related interfaces are shown in Figure 6.11. Since binary trees are ordered trees, the iterator returned by function children(v) (inherited from interface InspectableTree) accesses the left child of v before the right child of v.

```
template <typename Object>
class InspectableBinaryTree
  : public InspectableTree<Object> {
public:
  Position leftChild(const Position& v) const;      // left child of v
  Position rightChild(const Position& v) const;     // right child of v
  Position sibling(const Position& v) const;        // sibling of v
};
template <typename Object>
class BinaryTree
  : public InspectableBinaryTree<Object>, PositionalContainer<Object> { };
```

Code Fragment 6.14: Informal interfaces for InspectableBinaryTree, which is derived from InspectableTree (Code Fragment 6.1), and BinaryTree, which is derived from InspectableBinaryTree (Code Fragment 6.14) and PositionalContainer (Code Fragment 6.1). (These are not complete classes.)

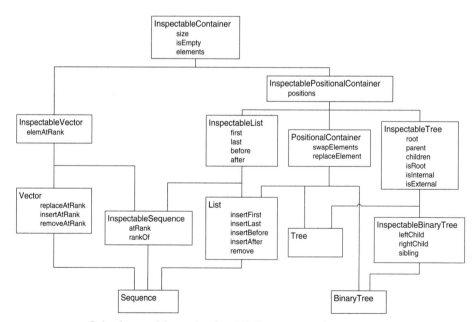

Figure 6.11: Inheritance hierarchy for ADTs representing sequences and trees.

6.3.3 Properties of Binary Trees

Binary trees have several interesting properties dealing with relationships between their heights and number of nodes. We denote the set of all nodes of a tree T, at the same depth d, as the **level** d of T. In a binary tree, level 0 has one node (the root), level 1 has, at most, two nodes (the children of the root), level 2 has, at most, four nodes, and so on. (See Figure 6.12.) In general, level d has, at most, 2^d nodes.

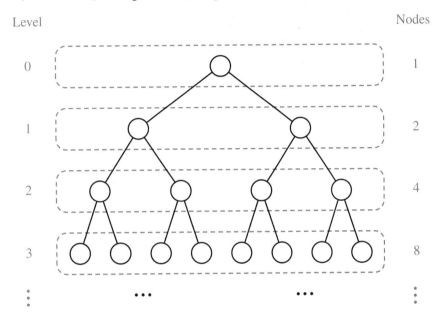

Figure 6.12: Maximum number of nodes in the levels of a binary tree.

We can see that the maximum number of nodes on the levels of a binary tree grows exponentially as we go down the tree. From this simple observation, we can derive the following properties relating the height of a binary T to its number of nodes. A detailed justification of these properties is left as an exercise (R-6.13).

Proposition 6.9: *Let T be a (proper) binary tree with n nodes, and let h denote the height of T. Then T has the following properties.*

1. *The number of external nodes in T is at least $h+1$ and at most 2^h.*
2. *The number of internal nodes in T is at least h and at most $2^h - 1$.*
3. *The total number of nodes in T is at least $2h+1$ and at most $2^{h+1} - 1$.*
4. *The height of T is at least $\log(n+1) - 1$ and at most $(n-1)/2$, that is, $\log(n+1) - 1 \leq h \leq (n-1)/2$.*

In addition, we also have the following relationship.

Proposition 6.10: *In a (proper) binary tree T, the number of external nodes is 1 more than the number of internal nodes.*

Justification: We justify this proposition by dividing up the nodes of a binary tree into two "piles:" an internal-node pile and an external-node pile, as if we were dividing pieces of candy between two preschoolers. If T itself has only one node v, then v is external, and the proposition clearly holds.

Otherwise, we remove from T an (arbitrary) external node w and its parent v, which is an internal node. We imagine placing w on the external-node pile and v on the internal-node pile. If v has a parent u, then we reconnect u with the former sibling z of w, as shown in Figure 6.13. This operation, which we call remove-AboveExternal(w), removes one internal node and one external node, and it leaves the tree being a proper binary tree.

Repeating this operation, we eventually are left with a single external node. Since the same number of external and internal nodes are removed and placed on their respective piles by the sequence of operations leading to this final tree, the number of external nodes of T is 1 more than the number of internal nodes.   ■

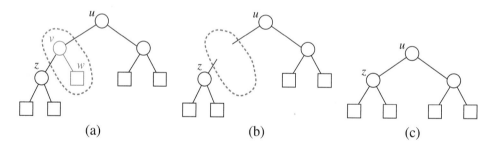

(a)   (b)   (c)

Figure 6.13: Operation removeAboveExternal(w), which removes an external node and its parent node, used in the justification of Proposition 6.10.

Note that the above relationship does not hold, in general, for nonbinary trees, although, as we explore in Exercise C-6.6, other interesting relationships can hold.

We make the following assumptions on the running time of the functions of any class that implements the BinaryTree interface.

- All the assumptions on the running time of the tree ADT functions made in Section 6.2 hold. In particular, for a binary tree, function children(v) takes $O(1)$ time, because each node has either zero or two children.
- Functions leftChild(v), rightChild(v), and sibling(v) each take $O(1)$ time.

6.3.4   Traversals of a Binary Tree

As with general trees, computations performed on binary trees often involve tree traversals. In this section, we present algorithms that perform traversal computations on binary trees. The algorithms will be expressed using the binary tree ADT functions, and will work even for improper binary trees, assuming the visit action for a null external node is to do nothing.

Preorder Traversal of a Binary Tree

Since any binary tree can also be viewed as a general tree, the preorder traversal for general trees (Code Fragment 6.8) can be applied to any binary tree. We can simplify the algorithm in the case of a binary tree traversal, however, as we show in Code Fragment 6.15.

Algorithm binaryPreorder(T, v):

  perform the "visit" action for node v
  if v is an internal node **then**
    binaryPreorder(T, T.leftChild(v))   {recursively traverse left subtree}
    binaryPreorder(T, T.rightChild(v))   {recursively traverse right subtree}

Code Fragment 6.15: Algorithm binaryPreorder(), which performs the preorder traversal of the subtree of a binary tree T rooted at node v.

As is the case for general trees, there are many applications of the preorder traversal for binary trees.

Postorder Traversal of a Binary Tree

Analogously, the postorder traversal for general trees (Code Fragment 6.11) can be specialized for binary trees, as shown in Code Fragment 6.16.

Algorithm binaryPostorder(T, v):

  if v is an internal node **then**
    binaryPostorder(T, T.leftChild(v))   {recursively traverse left subtree}
    binaryPostorder(T, T.rightChild(v))   {recursively traverse right subtree}
  perform the "visit" action for the node v

Code Fragment 6.16: Algorithm binaryPostorder() for performing the postorder traversal of the subtree of a binary tree T rooted at node v.

Evaluating an Arithmetic Expression

The postorder traversal of a binary tree can be used to solve the expression evaluation problem. In this problem, we are given an arithmetic expression tree, that is, a binary tree where each external node has a value associated with it and each internal node has an arithmetic operation associated with it (see Example 6.5), and we want to compute the value of the arithmetic expression represented by the tree.

Algorithm evaluateExpression(), given in Code Fragment 6.17, evaluates the expression associated with the subtree rooted at a node v of an arithmetic expression tree T by performing a postorder traversal of T starting at v. In this case, the "visit" action consists of performing a single arithmetic operation.

Algorithm evaluateExpression(T, v):
    if v is an internal node storing operator $\circ$ **then**
       $x \leftarrow$ evaluateExpression($T, T.$leftChild(v))
       $y \leftarrow$ evaluateExpression($T, T.$rightChild(v))
       return $x \circ y$
    else
       return the value stored at v

Code Fragment 6.17: Algorithm evaluateExpression() for evaluating the expression represented by the subtree of an arithmetic expression tree T rooted at node v. We assume that the operator $\circ$ takes two arguments and returns in constant time their combined value according to the definition of this operator.

The expression-tree evaluation application of the postorder traversal provides an $O(n)$-time algorithm for evaluating an arithmetic expression represented by a binary tree with n nodes. Indeed, like the general postorder traversal, the postorder traversal for binary trees can be applied to other "bottom-up" evaluation problems (such as the size computation given in Example 6.8) as well. The specialization of the postorder traversal for binary trees simplifies that for general trees, however, because we use the leftChild() and rightChild() functions to avoid a loop that iterates through the children of an internal node.

Interestingly, the specialization of the general preorder and postorder traversal methods to binary trees suggests a third traversal in a binary tree that is different from both the preorder and postorder traversals. We explore this third kind of traversal for binary trees in the next subsection.

Inorder Traversal of a Binary Tree

An additional traversal method for a binary tree is the ***inorder*** traversal. In this traversal, we visit a node between the recursive traversals of its left and right subtrees. The inorder traversal of the subtree rooted at a node v in a binary tree T is given in Code Fragment 6.18.

Algorithm inorder(T, v):
    if v is an internal node **then**
        inorder$(T, T.\text{leftChild}(v))$ {recursively traverse left subtree}
    perform the "visit" action for node v
    if v is an internal node **then**
        inorder$(T, T.\text{rightChild}(v))$ {recursively traverse right subtree}

Code Fragment 6.18: Algorithm inorder() for performing the inorder traversal of the subtree of a binary tree T rooted at a node v.

The inorder traversal of a binary tree T can be informally viewed as visiting the nodes of T "from left to right." Indeed, for every node v, the inorder traversal visits v after all the nodes in the left subtree of v and before all the nodes in the right subtree of v. (See Figure 6.14.)

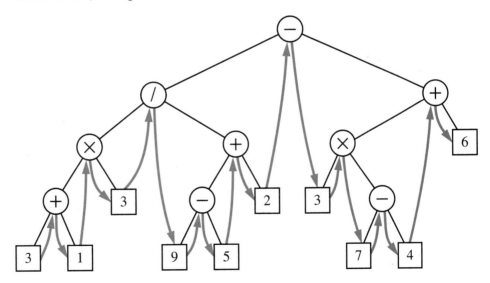

Figure 6.14: Inorder traversal of a binary tree.

Binary Search Trees

The inorder traversal algorithm also has several applications. One of the most important ones arises when we store an ordered sequence of elements in a binary tree, defining a structure we call a ***binary search tree***. Specifically, let us define a binary search tree so that each internal node v stores an element e, such that the elements stored in the left subtree of v are less than or equal to e, and the elements stored in the right subtree of v are greater than or equal to e. Furthermore, let us assume that the element fields of the external nodes are not used.

An inorder traversal of a binary search tree visits the elements stored in such a tree in nondecreasing order. A binary search tree can be viewed as a binary decision tree (recall Example 6.4) that supports searching, where the question asked at each internal node is whether the element at that node is less than, equal to, or larger than the element being searched for.

We can use a binary search tree T to locate an element with a certain value x by traversing down the tree T. At each internal node we compare the value of the current node to our search element x. If the answer to the question is "smaller," then the search continues in the left subtree. If the answer is "equal," then the search terminates successfully. If the answer is "greater," then the search continues in the right subtree. Finally, if we reach an external node (which is empty), then the search terminates unsuccessfully. (See Figure 6.15.)

Note that the time for searching in a binary search tree T is proportional to the height of T. Recall from Proposition 6.9 that the height of a tree with n nodes can be as small as $O(\log n)$ or as large as $\Omega(n)$. Thus, binary search trees are most efficient when they have small height. We illustrate an example search in a binary search tree in Figure 6.15; we study binary search trees in more detail in Section 9.1.

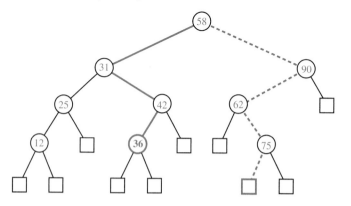

Figure 6.15: A binary search tree storing integers. The blue solid path is traversed when searching (successfully) for 36. The blue dashed path is traversed when searching (unsuccessfully) for 70.

Using Inorder Traversal for Tree Drawing

The inorder traversal can also be applied to the problem of computing a drawing of a binary tree. We can draw a binary tree T with an algorithm that assigns x- and y-coordinates to a node v of T using the following two rules (see Figure 6.16).

- $x(v)$ is equal to the number of nodes visited before v in the inorder traversal of T.
- $y(v)$ is equal to the depth of v in T.

In this application, we take the convention common in computer graphics that x-coordinates increase left to right and y-coordinates increase top to bottom. So the origin is in the upper left corner of the computer screen.

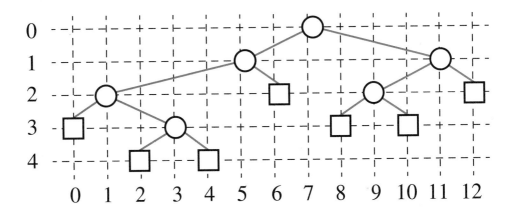

Figure 6.16: The inorder drawing algorithm for a binary tree.

A Unified Tree Traversal Framework

Viewed in an object-oriented framework, the tree-traversal algorithms we have discussed so far are all forms of iterators. Each traversal visits the nodes of a tree in a certain order, and is guaranteed to visit each node exactly once. We can unify the tree-traversal algorithms given above, into a single framework, however, by relaxing the requirement that each node be visited exactly once. The resulting traversal method is called the ***Euler tour traversal***, which we study next. The advantage of this traversal is that it allows for more general kinds of algorithms to be easily expressed.

The Euler Tour Traversal of a Binary Tree

The Euler tour traversal of a binary tree T can be informally defined as a "walk" around T, where we start by going from the root toward its left child, viewing the edges of T as being "walls" that we always keep to our left. (See Figure 6.17.) Each node v of T is encountered three times by the Euler tour:

- "On the left" (before the Euler tour of v's left subtree)
- "From below" (between the Euler tours of v's two subtrees)
- "On the right" (after the Euler tour of v's right subtree).

If v is external, then these three "visits" actually all happen at the same time.

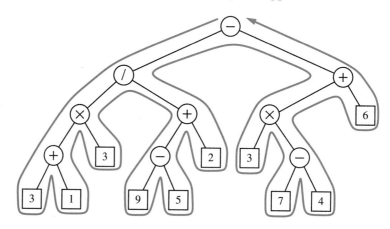

Figure 6.17: Euler tour traversal of a binary tree.

We give pseudo-code for the Euler tour of the subtree rooted at a node v in Code Fragment 6.19.

The preorder traversal of a binary tree is equivalent to an Euler tour traversal such that each node has an associated "visit" action occur only when it is encountered on the left. Likewise, the inorder and postorder traversals of a binary tree are equivalent to an Euler tour, where each node has an associated "visit" action occur only when it is encountered from below or on the right, respectively.

The Euler tour traversal extends the preorder, inorder, and postorder traversals, but it can also perform other kinds of traversals. For example, suppose we wish to compute the number of descendents of each node v in an n node binary tree T. We start an Euler tour by initializing a counter to 0, and then increment the counter each time we visit a node on the left. To determine the number of descendents of a node v, we compute the difference between the values of the counter when v is

Algorithm eulerTour(T, v):

   perform the action for visiting node v on the left

   if v is an internal node **then**

     recursively tour the left subtree of v by calling eulerTour(T, T.leftChild(v))

   perform the action for visiting node v from below

   if v is an internal node **then**

     recursively tour the right subtree of v by calling eulerTour(T, T.rightChild(v))

   perform the action for visiting node v on the right

Code Fragment 6.19: Algorithm eulerTour() for computing the Euler tour traversal of the subtree of a binary tree T rooted at a node v.

visited on the left and when it is visited on the right, and add 1. This simple rule gives us the number of descendents of v, because each node in the subtree rooted at v is counted between v's visit on the left and v's visit on the right. Therefore, we have an $O(n)$-time method for computing the number of descendents of each node in T.

The running time of the Euler tour traversal is easy to analyze, assuming that visiting a node takes $O(1)$ time. Namely, in each traversal, we spend a constant amount of time at each node of the tree during the traversal, so the overall running time is $O(n)$ for an n node tree.

Another application of the Euler tour traversal is to print a fully parenthesized arithmetic expression from its expression tree (Example 6.5). Algorithm printExpression, shown in Code Fragment 6.20, accomplishes this task by performing the following actions in an Euler tour:

- "On the left" action: if the node is internal, print "("
- "From below" action: print the value or operator stored at the node
- "On the right" action: if the node is internal, print ")".

Algorithm printExpression(T, v):

   if T.isExternal(v) **then**

     print the value stored at v

   else

     print "("

     printExpression(T, T.leftChild(v))

     print the operator stored at v

     printExpression(T, T.rightChild(v))

     print ")"

Code Fragment 6.20: An algorithm for printing the arithmetic expression associated with the subtree of an arithmetic expression tree T rooted at v.

6.3.5 The Template Function Pattern

The tree traversal functions described above are actually examples of an interesting object-oriented software design pattern, the **template function pattern**. This is not to be confused with templated classes or functions in C++, but the principal is similar. The template function pattern describes a generic computation mechanism that can be specialized for a particular application by redefining certain steps.

Euler Tour with the Template Function Pattern

Following the template function pattern, we can design an algorithm, template-EulerTour(), that implements a generic Euler tour traversal of a binary tree. When called on a node v, function templateEulerTour() calls several other auxiliary functions at different phases of the traversal. First of all, it creates a three-element structure r to store the result of the computation calling auxiliary function initResult(). Next, if v is an external node, templateEulerTour() calls auxiliary function visit-External(), else (v is an internal node) templateEulerTour() executes the following steps:

- Calls auxiliary function visitLeft(), which performs the computations associated with encountering the node on the left
- Recursively calls itself on the left child
- Calls auxiliary function visitBelow(), which performs the computations associated with encountering the node from below
- Recursively calls itself on the right subtree
- Calls auxiliary function visitRight(), which performs the computations associated with encountering the node on the right.

Finally, templateEulerTour() returns the result of the computation by calling auxiliary function returnResult(). Function templateEulerTour() can be viewed as a *template* or "skeleton" of an Euler tour. (See Code Fragment 6.21.)

In an object-oriented context, we can then write a class EulerTour that:

- Contains function templateEulerTour()
- Contains all the auxiliary functions called by templateEulerTour() as empty place holders (that is, with no instructions or returning null)
- Contains a function execute() that calls templateEulerTour(T, T.root()).

Class EulerTour itself does not perform any useful computation. However, we can extend it with the inheritance mechanism and override the empty functions to do useful tasks.

Algorithm templateEulerTour(T, v):

  $r \leftarrow$ initResult()

  if T.isExternal(v) **then**

    r.finalResult $\leftarrow$ visitExternal(T, v, r)

  else

    visitLeft(T, v, r)

    r.leftResult $\leftarrow$ templateEulerTour(T, T.leftChild(v))

    visitBelow(T, v, r)

    r.rightResult $\leftarrow$ templateEulerTour(T, T.rightChild(v))

    visitRight(T, v, r)

  return returnResult(r)

Code Fragment 6.21: Function templateEulerTour() for computing a generic Euler tour traversal of the subtree of a binary tree T rooted at a node v, following the template function pattern. This function calls the functions initResult(), visitExternal(), visitLeft(), visitBelow(), visitRight(), and returnResult().

Template Function Examples

As a first example, we can evaluate the expression associated with an arithmetic expression tree (see Example 6.5) by writing a new class EvaluateExpression that:

- Extends class EulerTour
- Overrides function initResult() by returning an array of three numbers
- Overrides visitExternal() by returning the value stored at the node
- Overrides visitRight() by combining r.leftResult and r.rightResult with the operator stored at the node, and setting r.finalResult equal to the result of the operation
- Overrides returnResult() by returning r.finalResult.

This approach should be compared with the direct implementation of the algorithm shown in Code Fragment 6.17.

As a second example, we can print the expression associated with an arithmetic expression tree (see Example 6.5) using a new class PrintExpression that:

- Extends class EulerTour
- Overrides visitExternal() by printing the value of the variable or constant associated with the node
- Overrides visitLeft() by printing "("
- Overrides visitBelow() by printing the operator associated with the node
- Overrides visitRight() by printing ")".

This approach should be compared with the direct implementation of the algorithm shown in Code Fragment 6.20.

C++ Implementation

A complete C++ implementation of the generic EulerTour class and of its specializations EvaluateExpressionTour and PrintExpressionTour are shown in Code Fragments 6.22 through 6.26. First we define a local structure TraversalResult with fields finalResult, leftResult, and rightResult, which stores the intermediate results. The main body of the generic class EulerTour is presented in Code Fragment 6.23, and the principal traversal function is defined in Code Fragment 6.24. Code Fragments 6.25 and 6.26 present two derived classes, the first of which evaluates an integer arithmetic expression tree and the second prints such an expression.

```
struct TraversalResult {
    int leftResult;                       // result from left subtree
    int rightResult;                      // result from right subtree
    int finalResult;                      // combined result
};
```

Code Fragment 6.22: Structure TraversalResult, where Euler tour results are stored.

```
template <typename BinaryTree>
class EulerTour {
protected:
    typedef typename BinaryTree::Position Position;   // position in the tree
    const BinaryTree* tree;                           // pointer to the tree
    // ... (insert TraversalResult here)
public:
    void initialize(const BinaryTree& T)              // initialize
        { tree = &T; }
protected:                                            // local utilities
    int eulerTour(const Position& v) const;           // perform the Euler tour
                                    // functions to be redefined by subclasses
    virtual void visitExternal   (const Position& v, TraversalResult& r) const {}
    virtual void visitLeft       (const Position& v, TraversalResult& r) const {}
    virtual void visitBelow      (const Position& v, TraversalResult& r) const {}
    virtual void visitRight      (const Position& v, TraversalResult& r) const {}
    TraversalResult initResult() const { return TraversalResult(); }
    int result(const TraversalResult& r) const { return r.finalResult; }
};
```

Code Fragment 6.23: Class EulerTour defining a generic Euler tour of a binary tree. This class realizes the template function pattern and must be specialized in order to get an interesting computation. (Continued in Code Fragment 6.24.)

```
template <typename BinaryTree>                          // do the tour
int EulerTour<BinaryTree>::eulerTour(const Position& v) const {
  TraversalResult r = initResult();
  if (tree->isExternal(v)) {                            // external node
    visitExternal(v, r);
  }
  else {                                                // internal node
    visitLeft(v, r);
    r.leftResult = eulerTour(tree->leftChild(v));       // recursive on left
    visitBelow(v, r);
    r.rightResult = eulerTour(tree->rightChild(v));     // recursive on right
    visitRight(v, r);
  }
  return result(r);
}
```

Code Fragment 6.24: The principal member function eulerTour(), which recursively traverses the tree and accumulates the results. (Continued from Code Fragment 6.23.)

```
template <typename BinaryTree>
class EvaluateExpressionTour : public EulerTour<BinaryTree> {
public:
  void execute(const BinaryTree& T) {                   // execute the tour
    initialize(T);
    std::cout << "The value is: " << eulerTour(tree->root()) << "\n";
  }
protected:                                              // leaf: return value
  typedef EulerTour<BinaryTree>::Position        Position;
  typedef EulerTour<BinaryTree>::TraversalResult TraversalResult;
  virtual void visitExternal(const Position& v, TraversalResult& r) const
    { r.finalResult = v.element().value(); }
                                                        // internal: do operation
  virtual void visitRight(const Position& v, TraversalResult& r) const
    { r.finalResult = v.element().operation(r.leftResult, r.rightResult); }
};
```

Code Fragment 6.25: Implementation of class EvaluateExpressionTour which specializes EulerTour to evaluate the expression associated with an arithmetic expression tree.

```
/**
 * This traversal specializes EulerTour to print out the arithmetic
 * expression stored in the tree.  The Traversal result is ignored.
 *
 * Note that Position is provided by in EulerTour.
 */
template <typename BinaryTree>
class PrintExpressionTour : public EulerTour<BinaryTree> {

public:
  void execute(const BinaryTree& T) {                      // execute the tour
    initialize(T);
    cout << "Expression: ";
    eulerTour(T.root());
    cout << endl;
  }

protected:
  typedef EulerTour<BinaryTree>::Position          Position;
  typedef EulerTour<BinaryTree>::TraversalResult TraversalResult;
  virtual void visitExternal(const Position& v, TraversalResult& r) const {
    v.element().print();                          // leaf: print value
  }
  virtual void visitLeft(const Position& v, TraversalResult& r) const {
    cout << "(";                                  // open new subexpression
  }
  virtual void visitBelow(const Position& v, TraversalResult& r) const {
    v.element().print();                          // internal: print operator
  }
  virtual void visitRight(const Position& v, TraversalResult& r) const {
    cout << ")";                                  // close subexpression
  }
};
```

Code Fragment 6.26: Implementation of class PrintExpressionTour, which specializes EulerTour to print the expression associated with an arithmetic expression tree.

Having presented these code fragments, we are now ready to describe in the next section a number of efficient ways of realizing the tree abstract data type using concrete data structures, such as sequences and linked structures.

6.4   Data Structures for Representing Trees

In this section, we describe concrete data structures for representing trees.

6.4.1   A Vector-Based Structure for Binary Trees

A simple structure for representing a binary tree T is based on a way of numbering the nodes of T. For every node v of T, let $p(v)$ be the integer defined as follows.

- If v is the root of T, then $p(v) = 1$.
- If v is the left child of node u, then $p(v) = 2p(u)$.
- If v is the right child of node u, then $p(v) = 2p(u) + 1$.

The numbering function p is known as a ***level numbering*** of the nodes in a binary tree T, for it numbers the nodes on each level of T in increasing order from left to right, although it may skip some numbers. (See Figure 6.18.)

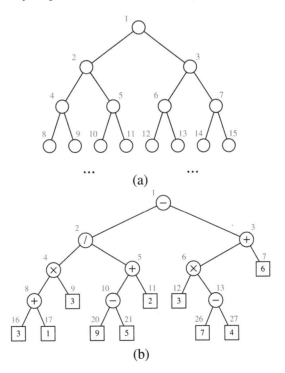

Figure 6.18: Binary tree level numbering: (a) general scheme; (b) an example.

The level numbering function p suggests a representation of a binary tree T by means of a vector S, such that node v of T is associated with the element of S at rank $p(v)$. (See Figure 6.19.) Typically, we realize the vector S by means of an extendable array. (See Section 5.1.3.) Such an implementation is simple and efficient, for we can use it to easily perform the functions root(), parent(), left-Child(), rightChild(), sibling(), isInternal(), isExternal(), and isRoot() by using simple arithmetic operations on the numbers $p(v)$ associated with each node v involved in the operation. That is, each position object v is simply a "wrapper" for the index $p(v)$ into the vector S. We leave the details of such implementations as a simple exercise (R-6.23).

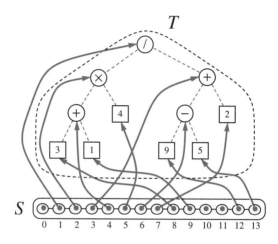

Figure 6.19: Representation of a binary tree T by means of a vector S.

Let n be the number of nodes of T, and let p_M be the maximum value of $p(v)$ over all the nodes of T. Vector S has size $N = p_M + 1$, since the element of S at rank 0 is not associated with any node of T. In general, vector S will also have a number of empty elements that do not refer to existing nodes of T. These empty slots could, for example, correspond to empty external nodes or even slots where descendents of such nodes would go. In fact, in the worst case, $N = 2^{(n+1)/2}$, the justification of which is left as an exercise (R-6.20). In Section 7.3, we will see a class of binary trees, called "heaps" for which $N = n + 1$. Moreover, if all external nodes are empty, as will be the case in our heap implementation, then we can save additional space by not even extending the size of the vector S to include external nodes whose index is past that of the last internal node in the tree. Thus, in spite of the worst-case space usage, there are applications for which the vector representation of a binary tree is space efficient. Still, for general binary trees, the exponential worst-case space requirement of this representation is prohibitive.

Table 6.1 summarizes the running times of the functions of a binary tree implemented with a vector. We do not include any functions for updating a binary tree in this table. Instead, we explore such operations in an exercise (C-6.18).

Operation	Time
positions, elements	$O(n)$
swapElements, replaceElement	$O(1)$
root, parent, children	$O(1)$
leftChild, rightChild, sibling	$O(1)$
isInternal, isExternal, isRoot	$O(1)$

Table 6.1: Running times of the functions of a binary tree T implemented with a vector S, where S is realized by means of an array. We denote the number of nodes of T with n, and the size of S with N. Functions hasNext(), and next() of the iterators elements(), positions(), and children(v) take $O(1)$ time. The space usage is $O(N)$, which is $O(2^{(n+1)/2})$ in the worst case.

The vector implementation of a binary tree is a fast and easy way of realizing the binary tree ADT, but it can be very space inefficient if the height of the tree is large. The next data structure we discuss for representing binary trees does not have this drawback.

6.4.2   A Linked Structure for Binary Trees

A natural way to realize a binary tree T is to use a ***linked structure***. In this approach, we represent each node v of T by an object which stores the associated element and pointers to the nodes for the children and parents of v. (See Figure 6.20.)

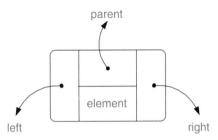

Figure 6.20: A node in a linked data structure for representing a binary tree.

We show a linked structure representation of a binary tree in Figure 6.21.

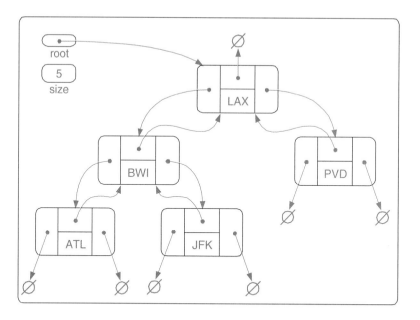

Figure 6.21: An example of a linked data structure for representing a binary tree.

If v is the root of T, then the pointer to the parent node is NULL, and if v is an external node, then the pointers to the children of v are NULL. If we wish to save space for cases when external nodes are empty, then we can have pointers to empty external nodes be NULL. That is, we can allow a pointer from an internal node to an external node child to be NULL. Even better, from an object-oriented viewpoint, we can use a specially created object, NULL_NODE, so that every missing external node pointer is a pointer to this object instead. Of course, if we use such place hold-

ers for external nodes, then we may have to be prepared for the parent() function throwing an exception should it be given such a place-holder external node.

Nodes and Positions in a Binary Tree

We define a structure Node (Code Fragment 6.27) to represent a node v object. It has a member variable element, which contains the associated element, and vari-ables left, right, and parent, which point to the associated relatives. As we have done before with other node types, this structure's declaration will be nested in the protected section of the binary tree class, and so it is only accessible to the binary tree and its derived classes.

```
struct Node {                                      // a node in the tree
  Object     element;                              // the element
  Node*      parent;                               // parent
  Node*      left;                                 // left child
  Node*      right;                                // right child
  Node() : element(Object())                       // default constructor
    { parent = left = right = NULL; }
  Node* sibling() const {                          // get our sibling
    return (this == parent->left ? parent->right : parent->left);
  }
};
typedef Node* NodePtr;                             // a node pointer
```

Code Fragment 6.27: Auxiliary structure Node for implementing a node in a binary tree. We define NodePtr to be a pointer to such a node. Its declaration is nested in the protected section of class LinkedBinaryTree, shown in Code Fragment 6.29.

The class Position (Code Fragment 6.28) represents a position in the binary tree. It supports the element() and isNull() member functions (see Section 5.2.1).

```
class Position {                                   // position in the tree
private:
  NodePtr node;                                    // pointer to the node
public:
  Position(NodePtr n = NULL)                       // constructor
    { node = n; }
  Object& element() const                          // get element
    { return node->element; }
  bool isNull() const                              // null position?
    { return node == NULL; }
  friend LinkedBinaryTree;                         // allow access
};
```

Code Fragment 6.28: Implementation of a Position class for binary tree nodes. In addition to the standard position functions, it provides a test for a null position. Its declaration is nested in the public section of class LinkedBinaryTree, shown in Code Fragment 6.29.

The class LinedBinaryTree implements the BinaryTree interface (Code Fragment 6.14) using a linked data structure. This class has two member variables, which store the size of the tree and a pointer to the Node object associated with the root of the tree.

Binary Tree Update Functions

In addition to the BinaryTree interface functions, LinkedBinaryTree also includes the following update functions.

expandExternal(v): Transform v from an external node into an internal node by creating two new external nodes and making them the left and right children of v, respectively; an error condition occurs if v is an internal node.
Input: Position; **Output:** None.

removeAboveExternal(w): Remove the external node w together with its parent v, replacing v with the sibling of w and return the position of this sibling (see Figure 6.13); an error condition occurs if w is an internal node or w is the root.
Input: Position; **Output:** Position (of sibling).

Class LinkedBinaryTree is shown in Code Fragment 6.29. Note that Node and Position declarations are to be inserted into this definition. It is much easier to manipulate the Node objects directly, rather than dealing with Position objects. For this reason, most of the public member functions of LinkedBinaryTree operate by first applying the utility function nodePtr() to extract the Node pointer associated with a given Position object, and then invoking a protected utility function, which does the actual work. These utility functions operate directly on Node pointers, which we have defined to be NodePtr. These utilities are shown in Code Fragment 6.30.

Class LinkedBinaryTree has a constructor with no arguments that returns a binary tree consisting of a single node. Starting from this single-node tree, we can build any binary tree by repeatedly applying the expandExternal() function. Likewise, we can dismantle any binary tree T using the removeAboveExternal() operation, ultimately reducing such a tree T to a single external node. We have not included any error checking in this implementation. In a complete implementation these two functions would throw an appropriate exception if the node to which they are applied is not of the proper type.

Note that the update functions expandExternal(v) and removeAboveExternal(v) work properly only when the external nodes are regular nodes, that is, they are not NULL nor the special NULL_NODE object. We explore alternate binary tree update functions in Exercise C-6.7.

```
template <typename Object>
class LinkedBinaryTree {
protected:
  // ... (insert Node definition here)
public:
  // ... (insert Position definition here)
private:                                       // member data
  NodePtr   theRoot;                           // pointer to the root
  int       sz;                                // number of nodes
protected:                                     // protected utilities
  // ... (insert LinkedBinaryTree utilities here)
public:
  LinkedBinaryTree()                           // constructor
    { theRoot = new Node; sz = 1; }
  int size() const                             // size of tree
    { return sz; }
  bool isEmpty() const                         // is tree empty?
    { return (sz == 0); }
  Position root() const                        // returns root
    { return Position(theRoot); }
  Position leftChild(const Position& v) const  // returns left child
    { return Position(nodePtr(v)->left); }
  // ... (rightChild(), parent(), and sibling() are omitted but similar)
  bool isRoot(const Position& v) const         // is v the root?
    { return isRoot(nodePtr(v)); }
  bool isInternal(const Position& v) const     // is v internal?
    { return isInternal(nodePtr(v)); }
  bool isExternal(const Position& v) const     // is v external?
    { return isExternal(nodePtr(v)); }
  void replaceElement(const Position& v, const Object& o)
    { replaceElement(nodePtr(v), o); }          // replace element
  void swapElements(const Position& v, const Position& w)
    { swapElements(nodePtr(v), nodePtr(w)); }   // swap elements
  void expandExternal(const Position& v)
    { expandExternal(nodePtr(v)); }             // expand external node
  Position removeAboveExternal(const Position& v)  // remove v and parent
    { return Position(removeAboveExternal(nodePtr(v))); }
  // ... (housekeeping and iterator functions omitted)
};
```

Code Fragment 6.29: The complete structure for LinkedBinaryTree. Most member functions are simple, or call the appropriate utility function (Also, see Code Fragments 6.27 through 6.30.)

```
// ... (utilities for LinkedBinaryTree)
NodePtr nodePtr(const Position& v) const          // convert to NodePtr
  { return v.node; }
bool isExternal(NodePtr n) const                  // is node external?
  { return (n->left == NULL && n->right == NULL); }
bool isInternal(NodePtr n) const                  // is node internal?
  { return ! isExternal(n); }
bool isRoot(NodePtr n) const                      // is node the root?
  { return (n == theRoot); }
void setRoot(NodePtr r)                           // make r the root
  { theRoot = r; r->parent = NULL; }
void replaceElement(NodePtr n, const Object& o)   // replace element
  { n->element = o; }
void swapElements(NodePtr n, NodePtr w) {         // swap elements
  Object temp = w->element;
  w->element = n->element;
  n->element = temp;
}
void expandExternal(NodePtr n) {                  // expand external node
  n->left  = new Node;    n->left->parent = n;
  n->right = new Node;    n->right->parent = n;
  sz += 2;
}
NodePtr removeAboveExternal(NodePtr n) {          // remove n and parent
  NodePtr p = n->parent;
  NodePtr s = n->sibling();
  if (isRoot(p)) setRoot(s);                      // p was root; now s is
  else {
    NodePtr g = p->parent;                        // the grandparent
    if (p == g->left)   g->left = s;              // replace parent by sibling
    else                g->right = s;
    s->parent = g;
  }
  delete n; delete p;                             // delete removed nodes
  sz -= 2;                                        // two fewer nodes
  return s;
}
```

Code Fragment 6.30: Utility functions for class LinkedBinaryTree. These functions do most of the work for the class by operating directly on pointers to Node objects. They are defined in the protected section of the LinkedBinaryTree. (See Code Fragment 6.29.)

Copying a Binary Tree

Another example use of the function expandExternal() is copying a binary tree T, to construct an exact copy T' of T. This construction is done recursively, starting with T' being a single external node v'. We call the recursive algorithm shown in Code Fragment 6.31 on the root v of T, which copies T using a preorder traversal. Such a function is useful as part of a copy constructor or assignment operator for binary trees.

Algorithm copy(T, T', v, v'):

    Input: A binary tree T containing a node v and a binary tree T' containing an external node v'

    Output: An augmentation of T' so that the subtree rooted at v' is an exact copy of the subtree of T rooted at v

  T'.replaceElement(v', v.element())

  if T.isInternal(v) **then**

    T'.expandExternal(v')

    copy(T, T', T.leftChild(v), T'.leftChild(v'))

    copy(T, T', T.rightChild(v), T'.rightChild(v'))

Code Fragment 6.31: Algorithm copy.

Let us now analyze the running times of the functions of class LinkedBinaryTree, which uses a linked structure representation.

- Functions size() and isEmpty() use a member variable storing the number of nodes of T, and each take $O(1)$ time.
- Function swapElements(v, w) swaps the elements of v and w in $O(1)$ time. Likewise, the function replaceElement(v, e) takes $O(1)$ time.
- Function positions() is implemented by performing an inorder traversal. Note any one of the three traversals discussed in Section 6.3.4 (preorder, inorder, and postorder) will serve the purpose. The nodes visited by the traversal are stored in an array and the output iterator is generated via an adapter class ArrayPositionIterator. Function elements() is similar. Thus, functions positions() and elements() take $O(n)$ time each.
- The adapter class ArrayPositionIterator supports hasNext(), and next() functions of iterators elements() and positions(), as well as the iterator children(v), in $O(1)$ time.

Considering the space required by this data structure, note that there is an object of class Node (Code Fragment 6.27) for every node of tree T. Thus, the overall space requirement is $O(n)$.

Table 6.2 summarizes the performance of this implementation of a binary tree.

Operation	Time
positions, elements	$O(n)$
swapElements, replaceElement	$O(1)$
root, parent, children	$O(1)$
leftChild, rightChild, sibling	$O(1)$
isInternal, isExternal, isRoot	$O(1)$
expandExternal, removeAboveExternal	$O(1)$

Table 6.2: Running times for the functions of an n-node binary tree implemented with a linked structure. The space usage is $O(n)$.

6.4.3   A Linked Structure for General Trees

We can extend the linked structure for binary trees to represent general trees. Since there is no limit to the number of children that a node v in a general tree can have, we use a container (for example, a list or vector) to store the children of v, instead of using member variables. This structure is schematically illustrated in Figure 6.22.

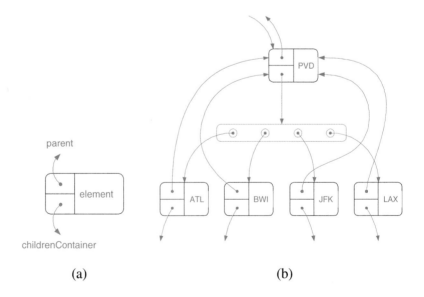

(a)   (b)

Figure 6.22: The linked structure for a tree: (a) the object associated with a node; (b) the portion of the data structure associated with a node and its children.

Table 6.3 summarizes the performance of the implementation of a tree by means of a linked structure. The analysis is left as an exercise (C-6.19), but we note that, by using a container to store the children of each node v, we can implement the children(v) method simply by calling the elements() function of the children container that v stores.

Operation	Time
size, isEmpty	$O(1)$
positions, elements	$O(n)$
swapElements, replaceElement	$O(1)$
root, parent	$O(1)$
children(v)	$O(c_v)$
isInternal, isExternal, isRoot	$O(1)$

Table 6.3: Running times of the functions of an n-node tree implemented with a linked structure. We let c_v denote the number of children of a node v. The space usage is $O(n)$.

6.4.4 Representing General Trees with Binary Trees

An alternative representation of a general tree T is obtained by transforming T into a binary tree T'. (See Figure 6.23.) We assume that either T is ordered or that it has been arbitrarily ordered. The transformation is as follows:

- For each node u of T, there is an internal node u' of T' associated with u.

- If u is an external node of T and does not have a sibling immediately following it, then the children of u' in T' are external nodes.

- If u is an internal node of T and v is the first child of u in T, then v' is the left child of u' in T.

- If node v has a sibling w immediately following it, then w' is the right child of v' in T'.

Note that the external nodes of T' are not associated with nodes of T, and serve only as place holders (hence, may even be null).

It is easy to maintain the correspondence between T and T', and to express operations in T in terms of corresponding operations in T'. Intuitively, we can think of the correspondence in terms of a conversion of T into T' that takes each set of siblings $\{v_1, v_2, \ldots, v_k\}$ in T with parent v and replaces it with a chain of right children rooted at v_1, which then becomes the left child of v.

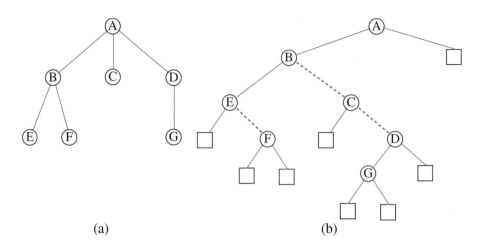

(a)   (b)

Figure 6.23: Representation of a tree by means of a binary tree: (a) tree T; (b) binary tree T' associated with T. The dashed edges connect nodes of T' associated with sibling nodes of T.

Table 6.4 summarizes the performance of the implementation of a tree by means of a binary tree. The analysis is left as an exercise (C-6.20).

Operation	Time
size, isEmpty	$O(1)$
positions, elements	$O(n)$
swapElements, replaceElement	$O(1)$
root	$O(1)$
parent(v)	$O(s_v)$
children(v)	$O(c_v)$
isInternal, isExternal, isRoot	$O(1)$

Table 6.4: Running times of the functions of a tree represented by means of a binary tree, which is, in turn, implemented with a linked structure. We denote with n the number of nodes of the tree, with c_v the number of children of a node v, and with s_v the number of siblings of v. The functions hasNext() and next() of the iterators returned by elements(), positions(), and children(v) take $O(1)$ time. The space usage is $O(n)$.

6.5   Exercises

Reinforcement

R-6.1 The following questions refer to the tree of Figure 6.3.

   a. Which node is the root?
   b. What are the internal nodes?
   c. How many descendents does node cs016/ have?
   d. How many ancestors does node cs016/ have?
   e. What are the siblings of node homeworks/?
   f. Which nodes are in the subtree rooted at node projects/?
   g. What is the depth of node papers/?
   h. What is the height of the tree?

R-6.2 Find the value of the arithmetic expression associated with each subtree of the binary tree of Figure 6.6.

R-6.3 Let T be an n-node improper binary tree (that is, each internal node has one or two children). Describe how to represent T by means of a ***proper*** binary tree T' with $O(n)$ nodes.

R-6.4 Give a justification of Proposition 6.6.

R-6.5 What is the running time of algorithm height2(T, v) (Code Fragment 6.6) when called on a node v distinct from the root of T?

R-6.6 Let T be the tree of Figure 6.3.

   a. Give the output of preorderPrint(T, T.root()) (Code Fragment 6.9).
   b. Give the output of parenPrint(T, T.root()) (which is shown in Code Fragment 6.10).

R-6.7 Describe a modification to the parenPrint() function given in Code Fragment 6.10, so that it uses the size() function for string objects to output the parenthetic representation of a tree with line breaks and spaces added to display the tree in a text window that is 80 characters wide.

R-6.8 Let T be an ordered tree with more than one node. Is it possible that the preorder traversal of T visits the nodes in the same order as the postorder traversal of T? If so, give an example; otherwise, argue why this cannot occur. Likewise, is it possible that the preorder traversal of T visits the nodes in the reverse order of the postorder traversal of T? If so, give an example; otherwise, argue why this cannot occur.

R-6.9★ Draw an expression tree that has four external nodes, storing the numbers 1, 5, 6, and 7 (with each number stored one per external node but not necessarily in this order), and has three internal nodes, each storing an operation from the set $\{+,-,\times,/\}$ of binary arithmetic operators, so that the value of the root is 21. The operators are assumed to return rational numbers (not integers), and an operator may be used more than once (but we only store one operator per internal node).

R-6.10 Answer the previous question for the case when T is a proper binary tree with more than one node.

R-6.11 Let T be a tree with n nodes. What is the running time of the function parenPrint$(T, T.\text{root}())$? (See Code Fragment 6.10.)

R-6.12 Draw a (single) binary tree T, such that

- Each internal node of T stores a single character
- A *preorder* traversal of T yields EXAMFUN
- An *inorder* traversal of T yields MAFXUEN.

R-6.13 Answer the following questions so as to justify Proposition 6.9.

   a. Draw a binary tree with height 7 and maximum number of external nodes.
   b. What is the minimum number of external nodes for a binary tree with height h? Justify your answer.
   c. What is the maximum number of external nodes for a binary tree with height h? Justify your answer.
   d. Let T be a binary tree with height h and n nodes. Show that

$$\log(n+1) - 1 \le h \le (n-1)/2.$$

   e. For which values of n and h can the above lower and upper bounds on h be attained with equality?

R-6.14 Modify the C++ function preorderPrint(), given in Code Fragment 6.9, so that it will print the strings associated with the nodes of a tree one per line, and indented proportionally to the depth of the node.

R-6.15 Let T be the tree of Figure 6.3. Draw, as best as you can, the output of the algorithm postorderPrint$(T, T.\text{root}())$. (See Code Fragment 6.12.)

R-6.16 Let T be the tree of Figure 6.10. Compute, in terms of the values given in this figure, the output of algorithm diskSpace$(T, T.\text{root}())$. (See Code Fragment 6.13.)

R-6.17 Let T be the binary tree of Figure 6.6.

    a. Give the output of algorithm preorderPrint(T, T.root()) (which is given in Code Fragment 6.9).

    b. Give the output of algorithm parenPrint(T, T.root()) (which is given in Code Fragment 6.10).

R-6.18 Let T be the binary tree of Figure 6.6.

    a. Give the output of algorithm postorderPrint(T, T.root()) (which is given in Code Fragment 6.12).

    b. Give the output of algorithm printExpression(T, T.root()) (which is given in Code Fragment 6.20).

R-6.19 Let T be a binary tree, such that all the external nodes have the same depth. Let D_e be the sum of the depths of all the external nodes of T, and let D_i be the sum of the depths of all the internal nodes of T. Find constants a and b, such that

$$D_e + 1 = aD_i + bn,$$

where n is the number of nodes of T. (Hint: Try to gain some intuition by drawing a few different binary trees, such that all the external nodes have the same depth.)

R-6.20 Let T be a binary tree with n nodes, and let p be the level numbering of the nodes of T, as given in Section 6.4.1.

    a. Show that, for every node v of T, $p(v) \leq 2^{(n+1)/2} - 1$.

    b. Show an example of a binary tree with at least five nodes that attains the above upper bound on the maximum value of $p(v)$ for some node v.

R-6.21 Show that the level numbering p of the nodes of a binary tree given in Section 6.4.1 assigns a unique integer to every node, that is, $p(u) \neq p(v)$ whenever $u \neq v$.

R-6.22 Draw the binary tree representation of the tree shown in Figure 6.2 using the binary-tree representation scheme described in Section 6.4.4.

R-6.23 Let T be a binary tree with n nodes that is realized with a vector, S, and let p be the level numbering of the nodes in T, as given in Section 6.4.1. Give pseudo-code descriptions of each of the functions root(), parent(), leftChild(), rightChild(), isInternal(), isExternal(), and isRoot().

R-6.24 Answer the following questions with reference to the following line of function isExternal() from class LinkedBinaryTree (Code Fragment 6.30):
return (v->left==**NULL** && v->right==**NULL**);

    a. Can we replace the above line with
        return v->left==**NULL**;
    and still get a correct behavior?
    b. Can we replace the above line with
        return v->right==**NULL**;
    and still get a correct behavior?
    c. Can we replace the above line with
        return v->parent==**NULL**;
    and still get a correct behavior?

Creativity

C-6.1 Let T be a tree whose nodes store strings. Give an algorithm that computes and prints, for every internal node v of T, the string stored at v and the height of the subtree rooted at v.

C-6.2★ Design an algorithm for drawing general trees.

C-6.3 Design algorithms for the following operations for a binary tree T.

- preorderNext(v): return the node visited after node v in a preorder traversal of T.
- inorderNext(v): return the node visited after node v in an inorder traversal of T.
- postorderNext(v): return the node visited after node v in a postorder traversal of T.

What are the worst-case running times of your algorithms?

C-6.4 Give an $O(n)$-time algorithm for computing the depth of all the nodes of a tree T, where n is the number of nodes of T.

C-6.5 Give an example of a tree T that causes Algorithm height1() (Code Fragment 6.5) to run in time $\Theta(n^2)$, where n is the number of nodes in T.

C-6.6 For a tree T, let $i(T)$ denote the number of its internal nodes, and let $e(T)$ denote the number of its external nodes. Show that, if every internal node in T has exactly three (3) children, then $e(T) = 2i(T) + 1$.

C-6.7 The update operations expandExternal() and removeAboveExternal() do not permit the creation of an improper binary tree. Give pseudo-code descriptions for alternate update operations suitable for improper binary trees. You may need to define new query operations as well.

C-6.8 The *balance factor* of an internal node v of a binary tree is the difference between the heights of the right and left subtrees of v. Show how to specialize the Euler tour traversal of Section 6.3.5 to print the balance factors of all the nodes of a binary tree.

C-6.9 Two ordered trees T' and T'' are said to be *isomorphic* if one of the following holds:

- Both T' and T'' consist of a single node
- Both T' and T'' have the same number k of subtrees, and the ith subtree of T' is isomorphic to the ith subtree of T'', for $i = 1, \ldots, k$.

Design an algorithm that tests whether two given ordered trees are isomorphic. What is the running time of your algorithm?

C-6.10 Extend the concept of an Euler tour to an ordered tree that is not necessarily a binary tree, and design a generic traversal of an ordered tree.

C-6.11 Let a visit action in the Euler tour traversal be denoted by a pair (v, a), where v is the visited node and a is one of *left*, *below*, or *right*. Design an algorithm for performing operation tourNext(v, a), which returns the visit action (w, b) following (v, a). What is the worst-case running time of your algorithm?

C-6.12 Algorithm preorderDraw() draws a binary tree T by assigning x- and y-coordinates to each node v as follows:

- Set $x(v)$ equal to the number of nodes preceding v in the preorder traversal of T.
- Set $y(v)$ equal to the depth of v in T.

a. Show that the drawing of T produced by algorithm preorderDraw() has no pairs of crossing edges.
b. Use algorithm preorderDraw() to redraw the binary tree shown in Figure 6.16.
c. Use algorithm postorderDraw(), which is similar to preorderDraw() but assigns x-coordinates using a postorder traversal, to redraw the binary tree of Figure 6.16.

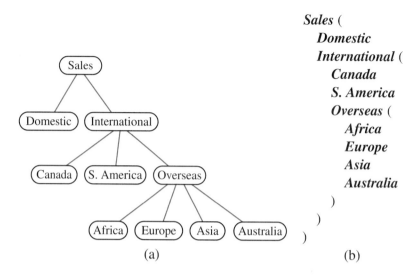

Sales (
   Domestic
   International (
      Canada
      S. America
      Overseas (
         Africa
         Europe
         Asia
         Australia
)
)
)

(a)   (b)

Figure 6.24: (a) Tree T; (b) indented parenthetic representation of T.

C-6.13 The ***indented parenthetic representation*** of a tree T is a variation of the parenthetic representation of T (see Figure 6.8) illustrated in Figure 6.24. Give an algorithm that prints the indented parenthetic representation of a tree.

C-6.14 Consider a variation of the linked data structure for binary trees where each node object has pointers to the node objects of the children but not to the node object of the parent. Describe an implementation of the functions of a binary tree with this data structure and analyze the time complexity for these functions.

C-6.15 Design an alternative implementation of the linked data structure for binary trees using a class for nodes that specializes into subclasses for an internal node, an external node, and the root node.

C-6.16 Justify the bounds in Table 6.1 by providing a detailed analysis of the running times of the functions of a binary tree T implemented with a vector S, where S is realized by means of an array.

C-6.17 Within the linked data structure for binary trees, explore an alternative design for implementing the iterators returned by functions elements(), nodes(), and children(v), such that each of these functions takes $O(1)$ time. Can you still achieve constant time implementations for the iterator functions hasNext(), nextObject(), and nextPosition() of the iterators returned?

C-6.18 Describe efficient implementations of the expandExternal() and remove-AboveExternal() binary tree update functions, described in Section 6.4.2, for the case when the binary tree is implemented using a vector S, where S is realized using an expandable array. Your functions should work even for null external nodes, assuming we represent such a node as a wrapper object storing an index to an empty or nonexistent cell in S. What are the worst-case running times of these functions? What is the running time of removeAboveExternal() if the internal node removed has only external node children?

C-6.19 Justify Table 6.3, summarizing the running time of the functions of a tree represented with a linked structure, by providing a description of each function's implementation and an analysis of its running time.

C-6.20 Justify the bounds in Table 6.4 for the running times of the functions of a tree represented by means of a binary tree, which is in turn implemented with a linked structure, by providing a description of each function's implementation and an analysis of its running time.

C-6.21 Let T be a binary tree with n nodes. Define a **Roman node** to be a node v in T, such that the number of descendents in v's left subtree differ from the number of descendents in v's right subtree by at most 5. Describe a linear-time method for finding each node v of T, such that v is not a Roman node, but all of v descendents are Roman nodes.

C-6.22 Let T' be the binary tree representing a tree T (see Section 6.4.4).

    a. Is a preorder traversal of T' equivalent to a preorder traversal of T?
    b. Is a postorder traversal of T' equivalent to a postorder traversal of T?
    c. Is an inorder traversal of T' equivalent to some well-structured traversal of T?

C-6.23 Describe, in pseudo-code, a nonrecursive method for performing an Euler tour traversal of a binary tree that runs in linear time and does not use a stack. (Hint: You can tell which visit action to perform at a node by taking note of where you are coming from.)

C-6.24 Describe, in pseudo-code, a nonrecursive method for performing an inorder traversal of a binary tree in linear time. (Hint: Use a stack.)

C-6.25 The **path length** of a tree T is the sum of the depths of all the nodes in T. Describe a linear-time method for computing the path length of a tree T (which is not necessarily binary).

C-6.26 Let T be a binary tree with n nodes (T may or may not be realized with a vector). Give a linear-time method that uses the functions of the Binary-Tree interface to traverse the nodes of T by increasing values of the level numbering function p given in Section 6.4.1. This traversal is known as the *level order traversal*.   (Hint: Use a queue.)

C-6.27 Define the *internal path length*, $I(T)$, of a tree T, to be the sum of the depths of all the internal nodes in T. Likewise, define the *external path length*, $E(T)$, of a tree T, to be the sum of the depths of all the external nodes in T. Show that if T is a binary tree with n internal nodes, then $E(T) = I(T) + 2n$.   (Hint: Use the fact that we can build T from a single root node via a series of n expandExternal operations.)

C-6.28 Let T be a tree with n nodes. Define the *lowest common ancestor* (LCA) between two nodes v and w as the lowest node in T that has both v and w as descendents (where we allow a node to be a descendent of itself). Given two nodes v and w, describe an efficient algorithm for finding the LCA of v and w. What is the running time of your method?

C-6.29 Let T be a tree with n nodes, and, for any node v in T, let d_v denote the depth of v in T. The *distance* between two nodes v and w in T is $d_v + d_w - 2d_u$, where u is the LCA u of v and w (as defined in the previous exercise). The *diameter* of T is the maximum distance between two nodes in T. Describe an efficient algorithm for finding the diameter of T. What is the running time of your method?

Projects

P-6.1 Complete the implementation of class LinkedBinaryTree taking into account error conditions.

P-6.2 Implement the binary tree ADT using a vector.

P-6.3 Implement the binary tree ADT using a linked structure.

P-6.4 Write a program that draws a binary tree.

P-6.5★ Write a program that draws a general tree.

P-6.6 Write a program that can input and display a person's family tree.

P-6.7 Implement the binary tree representation of the tree ADT. You may reuse the LinkedBinaryTree implementation of a binary tree.

P-6.8 A *slicing floorplan* is a decomposition of a rectangle with horizontal and vertical sides using horizontal and vertical *cuts*. (See Figure 6.25a.) A slicing floorplan can be represented by a binary tree, called a *slicing tree*, whose internal nodes represent the cuts, and whose external nodes represent the *basic rectangles* into which the floorplan is decomposed by the cuts. (See Figure 6.25b.) The *compaction problem* is defined as follows. Assume that each basic rectangle of a slicing floorplan is assigned a minimum width w and a minimum height h. The compaction problem is to find the smallest possible height and width for each rectangle of the slicing floorplan that is compatible with the minimum dimensions of the basic rectangles. Namely, this problem requires the assignment of values $h(v)$ and $w(v)$ to each node v of the slicing tree, such that

$$
w(v) = \begin{cases}
w & \text{if } v \text{ is an external node whose basic rectangle has minimum width } w \\[1em]
\max(w(w), w(z)) & \text{if } v \text{ is an internal node associated with a horizontal cut with left child } w \text{ and right child } z \\[1em]
w(w) + w(z) & \text{if } v \text{ is an internal node associated with a vertical cut with left child } w \text{ and right child } z
\end{cases}
$$

$$
h(v) = \begin{cases}
h & \text{if } v \text{ is an external node whose basic rectangle has minimum height } h \\[1em]
h(w) + h(z) & \text{if } v \text{ is an internal node associated with a horizontal cut with left child } w \text{ and right child } z \\[1em]
\max(h(w), h(z)) & \text{if } v \text{ is an internal node associated with a vertical cut with left child } w \text{ and right child } z
\end{cases}
$$

Design a data structure for slicing floorplans that supports the operations:
- Create a floorplan consisting of a single basic rectangle.
- Decompose a basic rectangle by means of a horizontal cut.
- Decompose a basic rectangle by means of a vertical cut.

- Assign minimum height and width to a basic rectangle.
- Draw the slicing tree associated with the floorplan.
- Compact the floorplan.
- Draw the compacted floorplan.

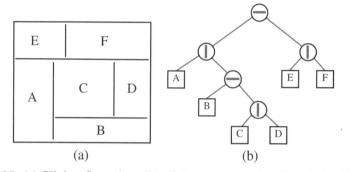

(a)   (b)

Figure 6.25: (a) Slicing floorplan; (b) slicing tree associated with the floorplan.

P-6.9 Write a program that takes, as input, a fully parenthesized, arithmetic expression and converts it to a binary expression tree. Your program should display the tree in some way and also print the value associated with the root. For an additional challenge, allow for the leaves to store variables of the form x_1, x_2, x_3, and so on, which are initially 0 and which can be updated interactively by your program, with the corresponding update in the printed value of the root of the expression tree.

Chapter Notes

The concept of viewing data structures as containers (and other principles of object-oriented design) can be found in object-oriented design books by Booch [14] and Budd [18]. The concept also exists under the name "collection class" in books by Golberg and Robson [39] and Liskov and Guttag [68]. Our use of the "position" abstraction derives from the "position" and "node" abstractions introduced by Aho, Hopcroft, and Ullman [5]. Discussions of the classic preorder, inorder, and postorder tree traversal methods can be found in Knuth's *Fundamental Algorithms* book [58]. The Euler tour traversal technique comes from the parallel algorithms community, as it is introduced by Tarjan and Vishkin [95] and is discussed by JáJá [51] and by Karp and Ramachandran [55]. The algorithm for drawing a tree is generally considered to be a part of the "folklore" of graph drawing algorithms. The reader interested in graph drawing is referred to works by Tamassia [94] and Di Battista *et al.* [28, 29]. The puzzler in Exercise R-6.9 was communicated by Micha Sharir.

Chapter

7

Priority Queues

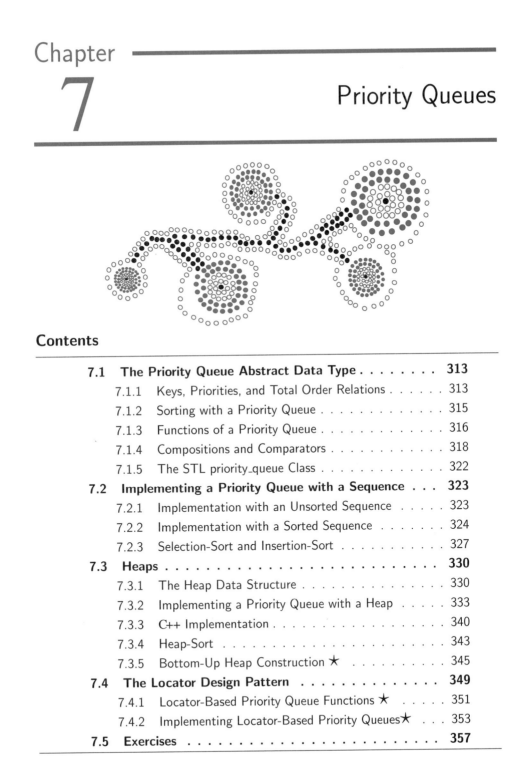

Contents

Having the right priorities is important to succeeding in life. On a quiet Saturday afternoon, presented with the opportunity of taking a nap, watching TV, playing soccer, or studying this chapter, the zealous student will certainly give first priority to the latter task. Outside of comfortable campus boundaries, priorities are an even more serious matter. Consider, for example, an air-traffic control center that has to decide which flight to clear for landing from among many approaching the airport. The priority of a flight may depend not only on the plane's distance from the runway, but also on the amount of fuel it has left. Choosing the next flight to land may be a life-critical decision. Another example is a standby passenger who, when she checks in, is told by the gate agent that she is "first" in line for a fully booked flight. Thus, she thinks she has top priority if seats become available. Little does she know that the airline will give first priority to a standby passenger who has arrived later, if such a passenger is given a better priority by the agent (priority here is measured in terms of the fare paid, frequent-flyer status, and check-in time).

In this chapter, we study data structures that store "prioritized elements," that is, elements that have priorities assigned to them. Such a priority is typically a numerical value, and we take the view that the smallest numerical value should have first priority. However, as we show in this chapter, we can support the opposite viewpoint just as easily. More generally, priorities can be viewed as arbitrary objects, so long as there is a consistent way of comparing pairs of such objects to see if one is less than or equal to the other. This general viewpoint allows us to define a fairly generic ADT for storing prioritized elements.

A *priority queue* is an abstract data type for storing a collection of prioritized elements that supports arbitrary element insertion but supports removal of elements in order of priority; that is, the element with first priority can be removed at any time. This ADT is fundamentally different from the position-based data structures such as stacks, queues, deques, sequences, and even trees, we discussed in previous chapters. These other data structures store elements at specific positions, which are often positions in a linear arrangement of the elements determined by the insertion and deletion operations performed. The priority queue ADT stores elements according to their priorities, and has no external notion of "position."

We present the priority queue ADT in Section 7.1. In Section 7.2, we present two implementations of a priority queue using sequences. These implementations are simple, but unfortunately not very efficient. Even so, they allow us to easily describe two well-known sorting algorithms, *insertion-sort* and *selection-sort*. In Section 7.3, we give a more efficient implementation of a priority queue, based on a concrete data structure known as a *heap*. A heap uses the hierarchical power of binary trees to support the priority queue operations in logarithmic time. This leads to a fast sorting algorithm known as *heap-sort*. We conclude this chapter with a discussion of a design pattern known as the *locator*.

7.1 The Priority Queue Abstract Data Type

In this section, we provide the framework for studying priority queues, based on the concepts of key and comparator, and we define the functions of a priority queue as an abstract data type (ADT).

7.1.1 Keys, Priorities, and Total Order Relations

Applications commonly require comparing and ranking objects according to parameters or properties, called "keys," that are assigned to each object in a collection. Formally, we define a *key* to be an object that is assigned to an element as a specific attribute for that element and that can be used to identify, rank, or weigh that element. Note that the key is assigned to an element, typically by a user or application; hence, a key might represent a property that an element did not originally possess.

The key an application assigns to an element is not necessarily unique, however, and an application may even change an element's key if it needs to. For example, we can compare companies by earnings or by number of employees; hence, either of these parameters can be used as a key for a company, depending on the information we wish to extract. Likewise, we can compare restaurants by a critic's food quality rating or by average entrée price. To achieve the most generality, then, we allow a key to be of any type that is appropriate for a particular application.

As in the standby passenger example, the key used for comparisons is often more than a single numerical value, such as price, length, weight, or speed. That is, a key can sometimes be a more complex property that cannot be quantified with a single number. For example, the priority of standby passengers is usually determined by taking into account a host of different factors, including frequent-flyer status, the fare paid, and check-in time. In some applications, the key for an object is data extracted from the object itself (for example, it might be a member variable storing the list price of a book, or the weight of a car). In other applications, the key is not part of the object but is externally generated by the application (for example, the quality rating given to a stock by a financial analyst, or the priority assigned to a standby passenger by a gate agent).

The concept of a key as an arbitrary object type is therefore quite general. But, in order to deal consistently with such a definition for keys and still be able to discuss when one key has priority over another, we need a way of robustly defining a rule for comparing keys.

Comparing Keys with Total Orders

A priority queue needs a comparison rule that will never contradict itself. In order for a comparison rule, which we denote by $\leq$, to be robust in this way, it must define a *total order* relation, which is to say that the comparison rule is defined for every pair of keys and it must satisfy the following properties:

- **Reflexive property**: $k \leq k$.
- **Antisymmetric property**: if $k_1 \leq k_2$ and $k_2 \leq k_1$, then $k_1 = k_2$.
- **Transitive property**: if $k_1 \leq k_2$ and $k_2 \leq k_3$, then $k_1 \leq k_3$.

Any comparison rule, $\leq$, that satisfies these three properties will never lead to a comparison contradiction. In fact, such a rule defines a linear ordering relationship among a set of keys. If a finite collection of keys has a total order defined for it, then the notion of the *smallest* key, $k_{\min}$, is well defined as the key, such that $k_{\min} \leq k$, for any other key k in our collection.

A *priority queue* is a container of elements, each having an associated key that is provided at the time the element is inserted. The name "priority queue" comes from the fact that keys determine the "priority" used to pick elements to be removed. The three fundamental functions of a priority queue P are as follows:

- insertItem(k, e): insert an element e with key k into P.
- minElement(): return an element of P with the smallest key, that is, an element whose key is less than or equal to that of every other element in P.
- removeMin(): remove from P an element with the smallest key.

Note that in a priority queue, more than one element can have the same key.

There are many applications where operations insertItem(), minElement(), and removeMin() play an important role. We consider one such application in the example that follows.

Example 7.1: *Suppose a certain flight is fully booked an hour prior to departure. Because of the possibility of cancellations, the airline maintains a priority queue of standby passengers hoping to get a seat. The priority of each passenger is determined by the fare paid, the frequent-flyer status, and the time when the passenger is inserted into the priority queue. When a passenger requests to fly standby, the associated passenger object is inserted into the priority queue with an* insertItem() *operation. Shortly before the flight departure, if seats become available (for example, due to last-minute cancellations), the airline repeatedly removes, from the priority queue, a standby passenger with first priority, using a combination of* minElement() *and* removeMin() *operations, and lets this person board.*

7.1.2 Sorting with a Priority Queue

Another important application of a priority queue is sorting, where we are given a collection S of n elements that can be compared according to a total order relation, and we want to rearrange them in increasing order (or at least in nondecreasing order if there are ties). The algorithm for sorting S with a priority queue Q, called PriorityQueueSort, is quite simple and consists of the following two phases:

1. In the first phase, we put the elements of S into an initially empty priority queue P through a series of n insertItem() operations, one for each element.
2. In the second phase, we extract the elements from P in nondecreasing order by means of a series of n combinations of minElement() and removeMin() operations, putting them back into S in order.

Pseudo-code for this algorithm is given in Code Fragment 7.1. It assumes that S is a sequence (pseudo-code for a different type, such as a list or vector, would be similar). The algorithm works correctly for any priority queue P, no matter how P is implemented. However, the running time of the algorithm is determined by the running times of operations insertItem(), minElement(), and removeMin(), which do depend on how P is implemented. Indeed, PriorityQueueSort() should be considered more a sorting "scheme" than a sorting "algorithm," because it does not specify how the priority queue P is implemented. The PriorityQueueSort() scheme is the paradigm of several popular sorting algorithms, including selection-sort, insertion-sort, and heap-sort, which we discuss in this chapter.

Algorithm PriorityQueueSort(S, P):

    Input: A sequence S storing n elements, on which a total order relation is defined, and a priority queue, P, that compares keys using the same total order relation

    Output: The sequence S sorted by the total order relation

      while !S.isEmpty() **do**

        $e \leftarrow S$.removeFirst()   {remove an element e from S}

        P.insertItem(e, e)   {the key is the element itself}

      while !S.isEmpty() **do**

        $e \leftarrow P$.minElement()   {get a smallest element from P}

        P.removeMin()   {remove this element from P}

        S.insertLast(e)   {add the element at the end of S}

Code Fragment 7.1: Algorithm PriorityQueueSort(). Note that the elements of the input sequence S serve both as keys and elements of the priority queue P.

7.1.3 Functions of a Priority Queue

Having described the priority queue abstract data type at an intuitive level, we now describe it in more detail. As an ADT, a priority queue P supports the following functions:

size(): Return the number of elements in P.
Input: None; *Output:* Integer.

isEmpty(): Test whether P is empty.
Input: None; *Output:* Boolean.

insertItem(k, e): Insert a new element e with key k into P.
Input: Objects k (key) and e (element); *Output:* None.

minElement(): Return a reference to the element with the smallest key of P (but do not remove the element); an error condition occurs if the priority queue is empty.
Input: None; *Output:* Object (element).

minKey(): Return a *constant reference* to the smallest key of P; an error condition occurs if the priority queue is empty.
Input: None; *Output:* Object (key).

removeMin(): Remove an element from P with the smallest key; an error condition occurs if the priority queue is empty.
Input: None; *Output:* None.

Simplicity of the Priority Queue ADT

As mentioned above, the primary functions of the priority queue ADT are just the insertItem(), minElement(), and removeMin() operations. The other operations are either secondary query functions (such as operation minKey()) or are generic functions that are included for all data structures (such as the operations size() and isEmpty()).

Note that the function minKey() returns a constant reference rather than a standard reference. This permits reading but not modification of the key. Providing the unrestricted ability to modify the key value would implicitly allow the user to change the priority of an item without informing the data structure of this change. This could undermine the data structure's integrity. If desired, the reference may be copied to a different variable, which then may be modified.

One of the interesting aspects of the priority queue ADT, which should now be obvious, is that the priority queue ADT is much simpler than the sequence ADT.

This simplicity is due to the fact that elements in a priority queue are inserted and removed based entirely on their keys, whereas elements are inserted and removed in a sequence based on their positions and ranks. Thus, only one insertion function and one deletion function are needed in the priority queue ADT, whereas the sequence ADT has many different functions for inserting and removing elements. We leave the writing of an informal C++ interface for the priority queue ADT as an exercise (R-7.1). The operations of the priority queue abstract data type are illustrated in the following example.

Example 7.2: *The following table shows a series of operations and their effects on an initially empty priority queue P, where an element e and its key k are indicated by the pair (k,e). The "Priority Queue" column is somewhat deceiving since it shows the items sorted by key. This view is more than is required of a priority queue. A priority queue need only have a way to retrieve a pair with minimum key. The way pairs are stored is implementation dependent.*

Operation	Output	Priority Queue
insertItem$(5,A)$	–	$\{(5,A)\}$
insertItem$(9,C)$	–	$\{(5,A),(9,C)\}$
insertItem$(3,B)$	–	$\{(3,B),(5,A),(9,C)\}$
insertItem$(7,D)$	–	$\{(3,B),(5,A),(7,D),(9,C)\}$
minElement$()$	B	$\{(3,B),(5,A),(7,D),(9,C)\}$
minKey$()$	3	$\{(3,B),(5,A),(7,D),(9,C)\}$
removeMin$()$	–	$\{(5,A),(7,D),(9,C)\}$
size$()$	3	$\{(5,A),(7,D),(9,C)\}$
minElement$()$	A	$\{(5,A),(7,D),(9,C)\}$
removeMin$()$	–	$\{(7,D),(9,C)\}$
removeMin$()$	–	$\{(9,C)\}$
removeMin$()$	–	$\{\}$
removeMin$()$	"error"	$\{\}$
isEmpty$()$	true	$\{\}$

There are still two important issues that we have left undetermined to this point:

- How do we keep track of the associations between elements and their keys?
- How do we compare keys so as to determine a smallest key?

Answering these questions involves the use of two interesting design patterns, which we describe in the next subsection.

7.1.4 Compositions and Comparators

The priority queue ADT implicitly makes use of two design patterns, composition and comparator, which we discuss in this subsection.

The Composition Pattern

The **composition pattern** defines a single object that is a composition of other objects. We use this pattern in the priority queue ADT when we define the objects being stored in the priority queue to actually be **pairs**. A pair (k,e) is the simplest composition, for it composes two objects, k and e, into a single **pair** object. To implement this concept, we define a class Item that stores these two objects as member variables and that provides functions to access and update these variables. In Code Fragment 7.2, we show an example C++ implementation of the composition pattern as applied to key-element pairs used in a priority queue. Other kinds of compositions include triples, which store three objects, quadruples, which store four objects, and general compositions, which can store an arbitrary number of objects (using, say, a sequence).

```
template <typename Key, typename Element>
class Item {                                    // a (key, element) pair
private:
  Key      _key;                                // key value
  Element  _elem;                               // element
public:
  Item(const Key& k = Key(), const Element& e = Element())
    : _key(k), _elem(e) { }                     // constructor
  const Key& key() const                        // gets the key (read only)
    { return _key; }
  Element& element()                            // gets the element
    { return _elem; }
  const Element& element() const                // gets the element (read only)
    { return _elem; }
  void setKey(const Key& k)                     // sets the key value
    { _key = k; }
  void setElement(const Element& e)             // sets the element
    { _elem = e; }
};
```

Code Fragment 7.2: Class Item for the key-element pairs stored in a priority queue.

We can also allow composition objects to store other composition objects, which would give rise to a hierarchical tree relationship defined on compositions, but we will not explore this usage in this book.

The Comparator Pattern

Another important issue in the priority queue ADT that we have so far left undefined is how to specify the total order relation for comparing keys. We have a number of design choices, concerning how to compare keys, that we can make at this point.

One possibility, and the one that is the most concrete, is to implement a different priority queue for each key type we want to use and each possible way of comparing keys of such types. The problem with this approach is that it is not very general, and it requires that we make many copies of essentially the same code.

A second, more general, approach is to assume that the priority queue is a templated class, where the types Key and Element that compose each Item object are both templates. We would then assume the type Key provides definitions of some or all of the relational operators: "<", "<=", "!=", and so on. If the key is a fundamental type, such as int or double, these operators are provided automatically. For user-defined types, these operators may be defined by operator overloading (see Section 1.4.2). Note that it is not necessary to explicitly define all of the operators. In fact, it is possible to define all the relational operators from "<" alone.

Let us consider a more concrete example. Suppose that class Point2D defines a two-dimensional point, that has two public member functions getX() and getY(), which access its x and y coordinates, respectively. We could define a lexicographical less-than operator as follows. If the x coordinates differ we use their relative values; otherwise, we use the relative values of the y coordinates.

```
bool operator<(const Point2D& p1, const Point2D& p2) {
    if (p1.getX() == p2.getX())  return p1.getY() < p2.getY();
    else                         return p1.getX() < p2.getX();
}
```

The approach of overloading the relational operators is general enough for many situations, but it relies on the assumption that objects of the same type are always compared in the same way. There are situations, however, where it is desirable to apply different comparisons to objects of the same type. Consider the following example.

Example 7.3: *Character string comparison may be sensitive or insensitive to the case of letters. Consider, for example, the two strings "cat" and "Cat." In the standard ASCII ordering of the characters, all upper-case letters come before lower-case letters. This implies that* "Cat" <"cat"*. On the other hand, when sorting names in the index of a book, the case of a character is typically ignored. For such a case-insensitive comparison,* "cat" = "Cat"*. It is desirable to be able to use both case-sensitive and case-insensitive comparisons on strings, depending on the application.*

Example 7.4: *A geometric algorithm may compare points p and q in a plane, by their x-coordinate (that is, $p \leq q$ if $x(p) \leq x(q)$), to sort them from left to right, while another algorithm may compare them by their y-coordinate (that is, $p \leq q$ if $y(p) \leq y(q)$), to sort them from bottom to top. In principle, there is nothing pertaining to the concept of a point that says whether points should be compared by x- or y-coordinates. Also, many other ways of comparing points can be defined (for example, we can compare the distances of p and q from the origin).*

One way of providing this flexibility is to use a special **comparison function**. In C++, a convenient way to provide such a function is to define a **comparator class**, which defines a comparison function as a member function. Typically such a class has no data members and no other member functions. There are many different ways to define a comparison member function. The approach that we will use is to overload the "()" operator. The resulting function takes two operands, a and b, and returns an integer, thus producing a "three-way" comparison. Assume that comp is a comparison class object. The comparison works as shown below.

> comp(a, b): Returns integer i, such that $i < 0$, $i = 0$, or $i > 0$, depending on whether $a < b$, $a = b$, or $a > b$, respectively.
> **Input:** Objects; **Output:** Integer.

Let us consider a more concrete example of a comparator class. We could define a lexicographical comparator class for Point2D as shown in Code Fragment 7.3.

```
class LexCompare {                                    // lex comparison
public:
  int operator()(const Point2D& p1, const Point2D& p2) const {
    if      (p1.getX() < p2.getX())                   // first compare x
      return −1;
    else if (p1.getX() > p2.getX())
      return +1;
    else if (p1.getY() < p2.getY())                   // x's equal; compare y
      return −1;
    else if (p1.getY() > p2.getY())
      return +1;
    else                                              // both x and y are equal
      return 0;
  }
};
```

Code Fragment 7.3: Example of a comparator class LexCompare for comparing coordinates in lexicographic order.

Using Comparator Objects

We can compare two objects p and q of class Point2D by defining a comparator object and invoking it with arguments p and q, as shown below.

```
Point2D p, q;
LexCompare lexCompare;
if (lexCompare(p, q) < 0) ...                    // if (p < q) ...
```

Note that overloading the "()" operator lets us use the lexCompare variable almost like it is a function, which is a notational convention also used in the STL. To use such a comparator object in the context of a more complex class, such as a priority queue, we would define our priority queue class to be templated with at least two types: the comparison key Key and the comparator class Comp. The comparator class is assumed to act on objects of type Key. The class stores a member variable comp of type Comp. To compare two keys p and q, we use comp(p,q), that is, we assume the Comp class has overloaded the "()" operator. Code Fragment 7.4 presents an example of this general structure. We show how to instantiate such a generic class on our Point2D class with the comparator LexCompare.

```
template <typename Key, typename Comp>
class GenericClass {                             // example class
  Comp comp;                                     // comparator object
  // ...
public:
  void memberFunction(Key p, Key q) {
    if (comp(p, q) > 0) { /* ... */ }            // compare keys using comp
  }
};
// ...
Point2D p, q;                                    // p and q are points
GenericClass<Point2D, LexCompare> concrete;
concrete.memberFunction(p, q);                   // compare p, q using LexCompare
// ...
```

Code Fragment 7.4: Example of the structure of a generic class that uses a comparator object Comp for performing comparisons. Observe that the key type and comparator class are specified as template arguments to the class.

Thus, for the most general and reusable form of a priority queue, we should not rely on the keys to provide their comparison rules. Instead, we use special *comparator* objects, external to the keys, to supply the comparison rules. In this way, a programmer can write a general priority queue implementation that works correctly in a wide variety of contexts.

7.1.5   The STL priority_queue Class

The C++ Standard Template Library (STL) defines a priority queue class, called priority_queue. There are some differences between our priority queue ADT and the interface given by STL.

Table 7.1 presents some of the functions provided by the STL priority_queue class.

Function	Description
size()	Returns the size of the priority queue
empty()	Returns a Boolean indicating whether the priority queue is empty
push(e)	Inserts e into the priority queue
top()	Returns a constant reference to an element with the largest value
pop()	Removes an element with the largest value

Table 7.1: Some of the functions supported by the STL class priority_queue.

One obvious difference between our priority queue and the STL's priority queue is that our access and removal functions act on the smallest element of the queue whereas the STL's functions act on the largest element. Of course, one could easily adapt our priority queue to one that acts on the largest element.

The other significant difference is that there is no distinction between keys and elements in the STL's priority queue. The distinction between keys and elements is handled entirely by the comparator class. For example, it is possible to define an STL priority queue whose underlying elements are of type Item. A programmer would provide a comparator that acts on Item objects, but this comparator would only consider the key field in making its comparisons. Thus, the two priority queues would behave in essentially the same way using this convention.

Comparator classes are defined differently in STL as well. As with our comparator functions, the STL comparator takes two arguments and works by overloading the "()" operator. However, rather than using the three-way comparison which returns a negative, zero, or positive integer, STL assumes a Boolean comparator that implements a "less-than" function. Given a comparator object comp, the invocation comp(a,b) returns true if $a < b$ and false otherwise. If no comparison argument is provided, then the standard less-than operator (<) is used by default.

7.2 Implementing a Priority Queue with a Sequence

In this section, we show how to implement a priority queue by storing the elements and keys in a sequence S. (See Chapter 5.) We provide two realizations, depending on whether or not we keep the keys in S sorted.

The performance of these realizations depends, in turn, on the implementation of the sequence S. We consider the cases when S is implemented with an array and with a doubly linked list. When analyzing the running time of the functions of a priority queue implemented with a sequence, we will assume that a comparison takes $O(1)$ time.

7.2.1 Implementation with an Unsorted Sequence

As our first implementation of a priority queue P, let us consider storing the elements of P and their keys in a sequence S. For the sake of generality, let us say that S is a general sequence implemented with either an array or a doubly linked list (the choice of specific implementation will not affect performance, as we will see). Thus, the elements of S are pairs (k, e), where e is an element of P and k is its key.

A simple way of implementing function insertItem(k, e) of P is to add the new pair object $p = (k, e)$ at the end of sequence S, by executing function insertLast(p) on S. This implementation of function insertItem() takes $O(1)$ time, independent of whether the sequence is implemented using an array or a linked list (see Section 5.3).

This choice means that S will be unsorted, for always inserting items at the end of S does not take into account the ordering of the keys. As a consequence, to perform operation minElement(), minKey(), or removeMin() on P, we must inspect all the elements of sequence S to find an element $p = (k, e)$ of S with minimum k.

Thus, no matter how the sequence S is implemented, the access and deletion functions on P all take $O(n)$ time, where n is the number of elements in P at the time the function is executed. Moreover, these functions run in $\Omega(n)$ time even in the best case, since they each require searching the entire sequence to find a minimum element. That is, these functions run in $\Theta(n)$ time. Therefore, by using an unsorted sequence to implement a priority queue, we achieve constant-time insertion, but linear-time access and deletion.

7.2.2   Implementation with a Sorted Sequence

An alternative implementation of a priority queue P also uses a sequence S, except that we store items sorted by keys. We can implement functions minElement() and minKey() in this case, simply by accessing the first element of the sequence with the first() function of S. Likewise, we can implement the removeMin() function of P as S.remove(S.first()). Assuming that S is implemented with a linked list or an array that supports constant-time, front-element removal (see Section 5.3), finding and removing the minimum in P takes $O(1)$ time. Thus, using a sorted sequence allows for simple and fast implementations of priority queue access and removal functions.

This benefit comes at a cost, however, for now the function insertItem() of P requires that we scan through the sequence S to find the appropriate position to insert the new element and key. Thus, implementing the insertItem() function of P now requires $O(n)$ time, where n is the number of elements in P at the time the function is executed. In summary, when using a sorted sequence to implement a priority queue, insertion runs in linear time whereas finding and removing the minimum can be done in constant time.

In Code Fragments 7.5 and 7.6, we show a priority queue implementation that uses a sorted sequence (and the key-element item of Code Fragment 7.2). The sequence is implemented using a NodeSequence object (see Section 5.3.2), but any implementation of the Sequence would suffice.

Comparing the Two Implementations

Table 7.2 compares the running times of the functions of a priority queue realized by means of a sorted and unsorted sequence, respectively. We see an interesting trade-off when we use a sequence to implement the priority queue ADT. An unsorted sequence allows for fast insertions but slow queries and deletions, while a sorted sequence allows for fast queries and deletions, but slow insertions.

Function	Unsorted Sequence	Sorted Sequence
size, isEmpty	$O(1)$	$O(1)$
insertItem	$O(1)$	$O(n)$
minElement, minKey, removeMin	$O(n)$	$O(1)$

Table 7.2: The running times of functions of a priority queue of size n, realized by means of an unsorted or sorted sequence, respectively. The bounds are independent of whether we use an array or a doubly linked list to implement the sequence.

```
template <typename Key, typename Element, typename Comp>
class SortedSeqPriorityQueue {
protected:                                     // typename shortcuts
  typedef Item<Key, Element>   Item;           // (key, element) pair
  typedef NodeSequence<Item>  Sequence;        // a sequence of items
public:
  typedef Sequence::Position       Position;   // position in sequence
protected:                                     // local utilities
  const Key& key(const Position& p) const      // position's key
    { return p.element().key(); }
  Element& element(const Position& p)          // position's element
    { Position t = p; return t.element().element(); }
private:                                        // member data
  Sequence S;                                   // sorted sequence
  Comp     comp;                                // comparator
public:
  SortedSeqPriorityQueue() : S(), comp() { }    // default constructor
  int size() const                              // number of items
    { return S.size(); }
  bool isEmpty() const                          // is the queue empty?
    { return S.isEmpty(); }
  // ...
```

Code Fragment 7.5: Portions of the C++ class SortedSeqPriorityQueue, which implements a priority queue by means of a sorted sequence. The definition begins with some type definitions for the types Item, Sequence, and Position. Two utility functions are provided: key(p) returns the key associated with position p and element(p) returns the element associated with position p. The element() function requires the use of a temporary variable t for technical reasons. The argument p is passed in as a constant reference, and so the compiler will not allow us to generate a nonconstant reference to the associated element directly. The data members are the sequence S and comparator comp. (Continued in Code Fragment 7.6.)

```
// ... (continuation of SortedSeqPriorityQueue)
void insertItem(const Key& k, const Element& e) { // insert into queue
  if (S.isEmpty())
    S.insertFirst(Item(k, e));                    // if empty insert first
  else if (comp(k, key(S.last())) > 0)            // greater than last?
    S.insertAfter(S.last(), Item(k,e));           // insert at end
  else {
    Position curr = S.first();                    // start search
    while (comp(k, key(curr)) > 0)                // skip over small keys
      curr = S.after(curr);
    S.insertBefore(curr, Item(k,e));              // insert here
  }
}
Element& minElement()                             // element with min key
    throw(EmptyContainerException) {
  if (S.isEmpty())
    throw EmptyContainerException("Minimum element of empty queue");
  else
    return element(S.first());
}
const Key& minKey() const                         // returns minimum key
    throw(EmptyContainerException) {
  if (S.isEmpty())
    throw EmptyContainerException("Minimum key of empty queue");
  else
    return key(S.first());
}
void removeMin()                                  // remove minimum
    throw(EmptyContainerException) {
  if (S.isEmpty())
    throw EmptyContainerException("Removal from empty queue");
  S.remove(S.first());
}
};
```

Code Fragment 7.6: Continuation from Code Fragment 7.5 of the C++ class Sort-edSeqPriorityQueue, which implements a priority queue by means of a sorted sequence.

7.2.3   Selection-Sort and Insertion-Sort

Recall the PriorityQueueSort() scheme introduced in Section 7.1.2. We are given an unsorted sequence S containing n elements, which we sort using a priority queue P in two phases. In phase one, we insert all the elements, and in phase two, we repeatedly remove elements using the minElement() and removeMin() operations. In this section, we consider two variations of the PriorityQueueSort() algorithm.

Selection-Sort

If we implement the priority queue P with an unsorted sequence, then the first phase of PriorityQueueSort() takes $O(n)$ time, for we can insert each element in constant time. In the second phase, assuming we can compare two keys in constant time, the running time of each minElement() and removeMin() operation is proportional to the number of elements currently in P. Thus, the bottleneck computation in this implementation is the repeated "selection" of the minimum element from an unsorted sequence in phase 2. For this reason, this algorithm is better known as *selection-sort*. (See Figure 7.1.)

		Sequence S	*Priority Queue P*
Input		$(7,4,8,2,5,3,9)$	$()$
Phase 1	(a)	$(4,8,2,5,3,9)$	(7)
	(b)	$(8,2,5,3,9)$	$(7,4)$
	⋮	⋮	⋮
	(g)	$()$	$(7,4,8,2,5,3,9)$
Phase 2	(a)	(2)	$(7,4,8,5,3,9)$
	(b)	$(2,3)$	$(7,4,8,5,9)$
	(c)	$(2,3,4)$	$(7,8,5,9)$
	(d)	$(2,3,4,5)$	$(7,8,9)$
	(e)	$(2,3,4,5,7)$	$(8,9)$
	(f)	$(2,3,4,5,7,8)$	(9)
	(g)	$(2,3,4,5,7,8,9)$	$()$

Figure 7.1: An illustration of selection-sort, on $S = (7,4,8,2,5,3,9)$. This algorithm follows the two-phase PriorityQueueSort() scheme, and uses a priority queue P implemented with an unsorted sequence. In the first phase, we repeatedly remove the first element from S and insert it into P (as the last element of the sequence implementing P). Note that at the end of the first phase, P is a copy of what was initially S. In the second phase, we repeatedly perform minElement() and removeMin() operations on P (each of which requires that we scan the entire sequence implementing P) and we add the elements removed from P to the end of S.

Let us analyze the selection-sort algorithm. As noted above, the bottleneck is the second phase, where we repeatedly remove an element with smallest key from the priority queue P. The size of P starts at n and incrementally decreases with each removeMin() until it becomes 0. Thus, the first removeMin() operation takes time $O(n)$, the second one takes time $O(n-1)$, and so on, until the last (nth) operation takes time $O(1)$. Therefore, the total time needed for the second phase is

$$O\left(n + (n-1) + \cdots + 2 + 1\right) = O\left(\sum_{i=1}^{n} i\right).$$

By Proposition 3.2

$$\sum_{i=1}^{n} i = \frac{n(n+1)}{2}.$$

Thus, phase two takes $O(n^2)$ time, as does the entire selection-sort algorithm.

Insertion-Sort

If we implement the priority queue P using a sorted sequence, then we improve the running time of the second phase to $O(n)$, for each operation minElement() and removeMin() on P now takes $O(1)$ time. Unfortunately, the first phase now becomes the bottleneck for the running time. Indeed, in the worst case, the running time of each insertItem() operation is proportional to the number of elements that are currently in the priority queue, which starts out having size zero and increases in size until it has size n. The first insertItem() operation takes $O(1)$ time, the second one takes $O(2)$ time, and so on, until the last (nth) operation takes $O(n)$ time. Thus, if we use a sorted sequence to implement P, then the first phase becomes the bottleneck phase. This sorting algorithm is therefore better known as *insertion-sort* (see Figure 7.2), for the bottleneck in this sorting algorithm involves the repeated "insertion" of a new element at the appropriate position in a sorted sequence.

Analyzing the running time of phase 1 of insertion-sort, we note that it is

$$O(1 + 2 + \ldots + (n-1) + n) = O\left(\sum_{i=1}^{n} i\right).$$

Again, by recalling Proposition 3.2, the first phase runs in $O(n^2)$ time; hence, so does the entire algorithm.

In other words, the running time of the PriorityQueueSort() implemented with a sorted sequence is $O(n^2)$. Therefore, both selection-sort and insertion-sort have running times that are $O(n^2)$. That is, their worst-case performance is similar to that of bubble-sort (Section 5.4), which also runs in $O(n^2)$ time.

		Sequence S	Priority Queue P
Input		$(7,4,8,2,5,3,9)$	$()$
Phase 1	(a)	$(4,8,2,5,3,9)$	(7)
	(b)	$(8,2,5,3,9)$	$(4,7)$
	(c)	$(2,5,3,9)$	$(4,7,8)$
	(d)	$(5,3,9)$	$(2,4,7,8)$
	(e)	$(3,9)$	$(2,4,5,7,8)$
	(f)	(9)	$(2,3,4,5,7,8)$
	(g)	$()$	$(2,3,4,5,7,8,9)$
Phase 2	(a)	(2)	$(3,4,5,7,8,9)$
	(b)	$(2,3)$	$(4,5,7,8,9)$
	$\vdots$	$\vdots$	$\vdots$
	(g)	$(2,3,4,5,7,8,9)$	$()$

Figure 7.2: Schematic visualization of the execution of insertion-sort on sequence $S = (7,4,8,2,5,3,9)$. This algorithm follows the two-phase PriorityQueueSort() scheme and uses a priority queue P, implemented by means of a sorted sequence. In the first phase, we repeatedly remove the first element of S and insert it into P, by scanning the sequence implementing P, until we find the correct position for the element. In the second phase, we repeatedly perform minElement() and remove-Min() operations on P, each of which returns the first element of the sequence implementing P, and we add the element at the end of S.

Although selection-sort and insertion-sort are similar, they actually have some interesting differences. For instance, selection-sort always takes $\Omega(n^2)$ time, because selecting the minimum in each step of the second phase requires scanning the entire priority-queue sequence. The running time of insertion-sort, on the other hand, varies depending on the input sequence. For example, if the input sequence S is in reverse order, then insertion-sort runs in $O(n)$ time, for we are always inserting the next element at the beginning of the priority-queue sequence in the first phase.

Alternately, we could change our definition of insertion-sort so that we insert elements starting from the end of the priority-queue sequence in the first phase, in which case performing insertion-sort on a sequence that is already sorted would run in $O(n)$ time. Indeed, the running time of insertion-sort is $O(n+I)$ in this case, where I is the number of *inversions* in the sequence, that is, the number of pairs of elements that start out in the input sequence in the wrong relative order. The number of inversions in a small sequence is relatively small; hence, insertion-sort is fairly efficient for small sequences. Its $O(n^2)$ worst-case performance makes insertion-sort inefficient for sorting large sequences, however.

7.3   Heaps

The two implementations of the PriorityQueueSort() scheme presented in the previous section suggest a possible way of improving the running time for priority-queue sorting. One algorithm (selection-sort) achieves a fast running time for the first phase, but has a slow second phase, whereas the other algorithm (insertion-sort) has a slow first phase, but achieves a fast running time for the second phase. If we can somehow balance the running times of the two phases, we might be able to significantly speed up the overall running time for sorting. This approach is, in fact, exactly what we can achieve using the priority-queue implementation discussed in this section.

In particular, an efficient realization of a priority queue uses a data structure called a **heap**. This data structure allows us to perform both insertions and removals in logarithmic time, which is a significant improvement over the sequence-based implementations discussed in Section 7.2. The fundamental way the heap achieves this improvement is to abandon the idea of storing elements and keys in a sequence and take the approach of storing elements and keys in a binary tree instead.

7.3.1   The Heap Data Structure

A heap (see Figure 7.3) is a binary tree T that stores a collection of keys at its internal nodes and that satisfies two additional properties: a relational property, defined in terms of the way keys are stored in T, and a structural property, defined in terms of the nodes of T itself. We assume that a total order relation on the keys is given, for example, by a comparator. Also, note that in our definition of a heap the external nodes of T do not store keys or elements and serve only as "place-holders."

The relational property of T, defined in terms of the way keys are stored, is the following:

Heap-Order Property: In a heap T, for every node v other than the root, the key stored at v is greater than or equal to the key stored at v's parent.

As a consequence of the heap-order property, the keys encountered on a path from the root to an external node of T are in nondecreasing order. Also, a minimum key is always stored at the root of T. This is the most important key and is informally said to be "at the top of the heap;" hence, the name "heap" for the data structure. By the way, the heap data structure defined here has nothing to do with the free-store memory heap (Section 4.3.3) used in the run-time environment supporting programming languages like C++.

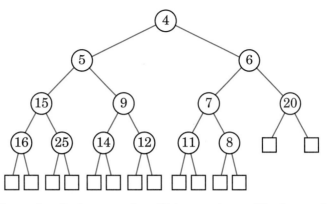

Figure 7.3: Example of a heap storing 13 integer keys. The last node is the one storing key 8, and external nodes are empty.

If we define our comparator to indicate the opposite of the standard total order relation between keys (so that compare(3,2) would, for example, return −1 rather than +1), then the root of the heap stores the largest key. This versatility comes essentially "for free" from our use of the comparator pattern. By defining the minimum key in terms of the comparator, the "minimum" key with a "reverse" comparator is in fact the largest. Thus, without loss of generality, we assume that we are always interested in the minimum key, which will always be at the root of the heap.

Caution

For the sake of efficiency, as will become clear later, we want the heap T to have as small a height as possible. We enforce this desire by insisting that the heap T satisfy an additional structural property: it must be *complete*. Recalling that level i of a binary tree T is the set of nodes of T that have depth i, we define this structural property as follows:

Complete Binary Tree Property: A heap T with height h is a *complete* binary tree, that is, levels $0, 1, 2, \ldots, h-1$ of T have the maximum number of nodes possible (namely, level i has 2^i nodes, for $0 \le i \le h-1$) and all the internal nodes are to the left of the external nodes in level $h-1$.

By saying that all the internal nodes on level $h-1$ are "to the left" of the external nodes, we mean that all the internal nodes on this level will be visited before any external nodes on this level in any standard tree traversal (for example, an inorder traversal). That is, in a standard drawing of a binary tree, all the internal nodes on level $h-1$ are drawn to the left of any of the external nodes on level $h-1$. (See Figure 7.3.) By insisting that a heap T be complete, we identify another important node in a heap T, other than the root, namely, the *last node* of T, which we define to be the right-most, deepest internal node of T (see Figure 7.3). Insisting that T be complete also has an important consequence, as shown in Proposition 7.5.

Proposition 7.5: *A heap T storing n keys has height*

$$h = \lceil \log(n+1) \rceil.$$

Justification: From the fact that T is complete, we know the number of internal nodes of T is at least

$$
\begin{aligned}
1 + 2 + 4 + \cdots + 2^{h-2} + 1 &= 2^{h-1} - 1 + 1 \\
&= 2^{h-1}.
\end{aligned}
$$

This lower bound is achieved when there is only one internal node on level $h-1$. Alternately, but also following from T being complete, we can say that the number of internal nodes of T is at most

$$1 + 2 + 4 + \cdots + 2^{h-1} = 2^h - 1.$$

This upper bound is achieved when all the 2^{h-1} nodes on level $h-1$ are internal. Since the number of internal nodes is equal to the number n of keys,

$$2^{h-1} \le n$$

and

$$n \le 2^h - 1.$$

Thus, by taking logarithms of both sides of these two inequalities, we see that

$$h \le \log n + 1$$

and

$$\log(n+1) \le h,$$

which implies that

$$h = \lceil \log(n+1) \rceil.$$

■

Proposition 7.5 has an important consequence, for it implies that if we can perform update operations on a heap in time proportional to its height, then those operations will run in logarithmic time. Therefore, let us turn to the problem of how to efficiently perform various priority queue functions using a heap.

7.3.2 Implementing a Priority Queue with a Heap

In this section, we show how to implement the priority queue ADT using a heap. Our heap-based data structure for a priority queue P consists of the following (see Figure 7.4):

- **heap**, a complete binary tree T whose elements are stored at internal nodes and have keys satisfying the heap-order property. We assume the binary tree T is implemented using a vector, as described in Section 6.4.1. For each internal node v of T, we denote the key of the element stored at v as $k(v)$.
- **last**, a pointer to the last node of T. Given the vector implementation of T, we assume that the member variable, last, is an integer index to the cell in the vector storing the last node of T.
- **comp**, a comparator that defines the total order relation among the keys.

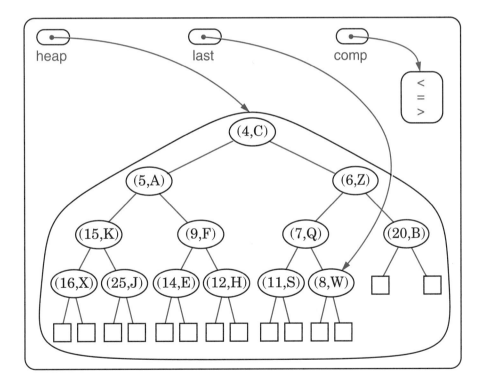

Figure 7.4: Heap-based implementation of a priority queue with integer keys and character elements. Each node of the heap stores a key-element pair. The heap-order property takes only the keys into account and ignores the elements.

The Vector Representation of a Heap

Note that when the heap T is implemented with a vector, the index of the last node w is always equal to n, and the first empty external node z has index equal to $n+1$. (See Figure 7.5.) Note that this index for z is valid even for the following cases.

- If the current last node w is the right-most node on its level, then z is the left-most node of the bottom-most level (see Figure 7.5b).
- If T has no internal nodes (that is, the priority queue is empty and the last node in T is not defined), then z is the root of T.

The simplifications that come from representing the heap T with a vector aid in our functions for implementing the priority queue ADT. For example, the update functions expandExternal(z) and removeAboveExternal(z) can also be performed in $O(1)$ time (assuming no vector expansion is necessary), for they simply involve allocating or deallocating a single cell in the vector. With this data structure, functions size() and isEmpty() take $O(1)$ time, as usual. In addition, functions minElement() and minKey() can also be performed in $O(1)$ time by accessing the element or key stored at the root of the heap (which is at rank 1 in the vector). Moreover, because T is a complete binary tree, the vector associated with heap T has $2n+1$ elements, $n+1$ of which are place-holder external nodes by our convention. Indeed, since all the external nodes have indices higher than any internal node, we don't even have to explicitly store all the external nodes. (See Figure 7.5.)

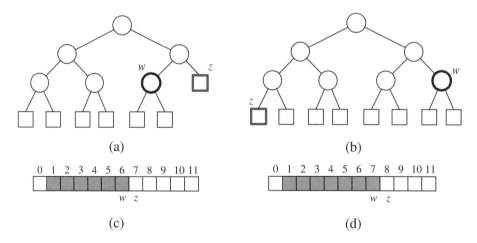

Figure 7.5: Last node w and first external node z in a heap: (a) regular case where z is right of w; (b) case where z is left-most on bottom level. The vector representation of (a) is shown in (c); similarly, the representation of (b) is shown in (d).

Insertion

Let us consider how to perform function insertItem() of the priority queue ADT using the heap T. In order to store a new key-element pair (k,e) into T, we need to add a new internal node to T. To keep T as a complete binary tree, we must add this new node so that it becomes the new last node of T. That is, we must identify the correct external node z where we can perform an expandExternal(z) operation and insert the new element at z while keeping T complete. (See Figure 7.6a and b.) Node z is called the *insertion position*.

Usually, node z is the external node immediately to the right of the last node w (see Figure 7.5a). In any case, by our vector implementation of T, the insertion position z is stored at index $n+1$, where n is the current size of the heap. Thus, we can identify the node z in constant time in the vector implementing T. Then, after performing expandExternal(z), node z becomes the last node, and we store the new key-element pair (k,e) in it, so that $k(z) = k$.

Up-Heap Bubbling after an Insertion

After this action, the tree T is complete, but it may violate the heap-order property. Hence, unless node z is the root of T (that is, the priority queue was empty before the insertion), we compare key $k(z)$ with the key $k(u)$ stored at the parent u of z. If $k(z) < k(u)$, then we need to restore the heap-order property, which can be locally achieved by swapping the key-element pairs stored at z and u. (See Figure 7.6c and d.) This swap causes the new key-element pair (k,e) to move up one level. Again, the heap-order property may be violated, and we continue swapping going up in T until no violation of the heap-order property occurs. (See Figure 7.6e through h.)

The upward movement by means of swaps is conventionally called *up-heap bubbling*. A swap either resolves the violation of the heap-order property or propagates it one level up in the heap. In the worst case, up-heap bubbling causes the new key-element pair to move all the way up to the root of heap T. (See Figure 7.6.) Thus, in the worst case, the running time of function insertItem() is proportional to the height of T, that is, it is $O(\log n)$ because T is complete.

If T is implemented with a vector, then we can find the new last node z in $O(1)$ time. For example, we could use inheritance to derive a vector-based implementation of a binary tree and add a function that returns the node with index $n+1$, that is, with level number $n+1$, as defined in Section 6.4.1. Alternately, we could even define an add() function, which adds a new element at the first external node z, at rank $n+1$ in the vector. In Code Fragment 7.9, shown later in this chapter, we show how to use this function to efficiently implement the function insertItem(). If, on the other hand, the heap T is implemented with a linked structure, then finding the insertion position z is a little more involved. (See Exercise C-7.9.)

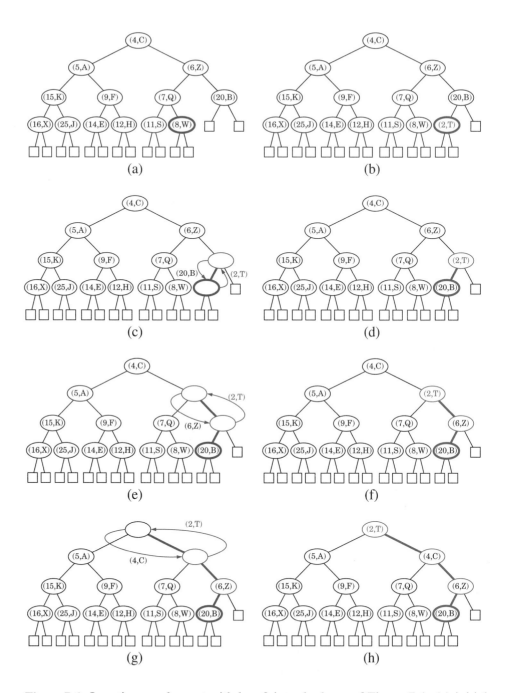

Figure 7.6: Inserting an element with key 2 into the heap of Figure 7.4: (a) initial heap; (b) adding a new last node to the right of the old one; (c and d) swap to locally restore the heap-order property; (e and f) another swap; (g and h) final swap.

Removal

Let us now turn to function removeMin() of the priority queue ADT. The algorithm for performing function removeMin() using heap T is illustrated in Figure 7.7.

We know that an element with the smallest key is stored at the root r of T (even if there is more than one smallest key). However, unless r is the only internal node of T, we cannot simply delete node r, because this action would disrupt the binary tree structure. Instead, we access the last node w of T, copy its key-element pair to the root r, and then delete the last node by performing operation removeAbove-External(T.rightChild(w)) of the binary tree ADT. This operation removes w and its right child, and replaces w with its left child. (See Figure 7.7a and b.) After this constant-time action, we need to update our pointer to the last node, which can be done simply by referencing the node at rank n (after the removal) in the vector implementing the tree T.

Down-Heap Bubbling after a Removal

We are not done, however, for, even though T is now complete, T may now violate the heap-order property. To determine whether we need to restore the heap-order property, we examine the root r of T. If both children of r are external nodes, then the heap-order property is trivially satisfied and we are done. Otherwise, we distinguish two cases:

- If the left child of r is internal and the right child is external, let s be the left child of r.
- Otherwise (both children of r are internal), let s be a child of r with the smallest key.

If the key $k(r)$ stored at r is greater than the key $k(s)$ stored at s, then we need to restore the heap-order property, which can be locally achieved by swapping the key-element pairs stored at r and s. (See Figure 7.7c and d.) (Note that we shouldn't swap r with s's sibling.) The swap we perform restores the heap-order property for node r and its children, but it may violate this property at s; hence, we may have to continue swapping down T until no violation of the heap-order property occurs. (See Figure 7.7e–h.) This downward swapping process is called ***down-heap bubbling***. A swap either resolves the violation of the heap-order property or propagates it one level down in the heap. In the worst case, a key-element pair moves all the way down to the level immediately above the bottom level. (See Figure 7.7.) Thus, the running time of function removeMin() is, in the worst case, proportional to the height of heap T, that is, it is $O(\log n)$.

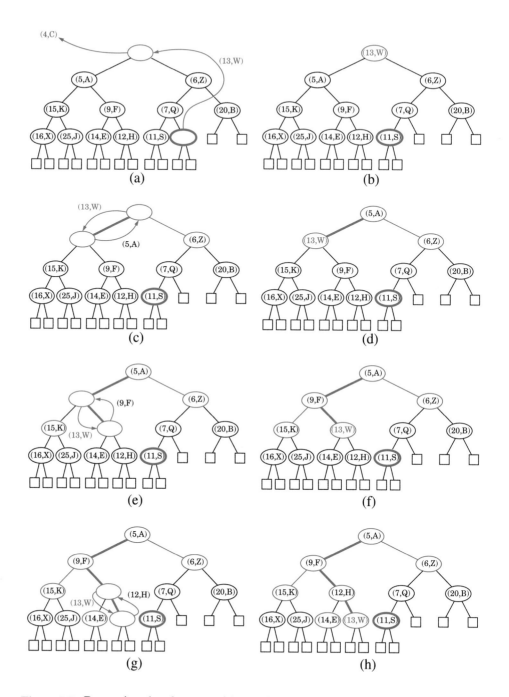

Figure 7.7: Removing the element with smallest key from a heap: (a and b) deletion of the last node, whose key-element pair is moved to the root; (c and d) swap to locally restore the heap-order property; (e and f) another swap; (g and h) final swap.

Analysis

Table 7.3 shows the running time of the priority queue ADT functions for the heap implementation of a priority queue, assuming that the heap T is realized by a data structure for binary trees that supports the binary tree ADT functions (except for elements()) in $O(1)$ time. The linked structure and vector-based structure from Section 6.4 easily satisfy this requirement.

Operation	Time
size, isEmpty	$O(1)$
minElement, minKey	$O(1)$
insertItem	$O(\log n)$
removeMin	$O(\log n)$

Table 7.3: Performance of a priority queue realized by means of a heap, which is, in turn, implemented with a vector-based structure for binary trees. We denote with n, the number of elements in the priority queue at the time a function is executed. The space requirement is $O(n)$ if the heap is realized with a linked structure, and is $O(N)$ if the heap is realized with a vector-based structure, where $N \geq n$ is the size of the array used to implement the vector.

In short, each of the priority queue ADT functions can be performed in $O(1)$ time or in $O(\log n)$ time, where n is the number of elements at the time the function is executed. This analysis is based on the following:

- The height of heap T is $O(\log n)$, since T is complete.
- In the worst case, up-heap and down-heap bubbling take time proportional to the height of T.
- Finding the insertion position in the execution of insertItem() and updating the last node position in the execution of removeMin() take constant time.
- The heap T has n internal nodes, each storing a copy of a key and an element, and $n + 1$ external nodes.

Thus, if heap T is implemented with the linked structure for binary trees, the space needed is $O(n)$. If we use a vector-based implementation for T instead, then the space is proportional to the size N of the array used for the vector representing T.

We conclude that the heap data structure is a very efficient realization of the priority queue ADT, independent of whether the heap is implemented with a linked structure or a vector. The heap-based implementation achieves fast running times for both insertion and removal, unlike the sequence-based priority queue implementations. Indeed, an important consequence of the efficiency of the heap-based implementation is that it can speed up priority-queue sorting to be much faster than the sequence-based insertion-sort and selection-sort algorithms.

7.3.3 C++ Implementation

A C++ implementation of a heap-based priority queue is shown in Code Fragments 7.7 and 7.9. To aid in modularity, we delegate the maintenance of the structure of the heap itself to a data structure, called **heap-tree**, that is derived from a binary tree and provides the following additional specialized update functions.

add(o): Expand the external node z immediately after the last node into an internal node, add o to this node, update the new last node to be z, and return z.
Input: Object o; **Output:** Position.

remove(): Remove and return the element stored in the last node w, reducing this node to an external node, and update the last node to be the node immediately before this one.
Input: None; **Output:** Object (element).

Using a vector-based implementation of a tree (see Section 6.4.1), operations add() and remove() take $O(1)$ time. In fact, remove() simply returns the last element and decrements the heap size. The heap-tree ADT is represented by the informal interface HeapTree shown in Code Fragment 7.7. We assume that a C++ class VectorHeapTree (not shown) implements the HeapTree interface with a vector and supports functions add() and remove() in $O(1)$ time.

Class HeapPriorityQueue implements the PriorityQueue interface using a heap tree. It is shown in Code Fragments 7.8 and 7.9. After defining some shortcuts for type names, we define utility functions key() and element() for accessing the key and element of a position, respectively. As was the case in Code Fragment 7.5, element() requires the use of a temporary variable t for technical reasons.

The data members consist of the heap tree T and the comparator comp. The constructor is given the capacity of the heap as an argument. The size() function uses the fact that we store the key-element items (see Code Fragment 7.2) in only the internal nodes of the heap tree (see Proposition 6.10).

```
template <class Object>                          // HeapTree interface
class HeapTree : public InspectableBinaryTree, PositionalContainer {
public:
    Position add(const Object &elem);            // add new last node
    Object remove();                             // remove last node
};
```

Code Fragment 7.7: Informal interface HeapTree for a heap-tree. It is derived from the interface InspectableBinaryTree with functions replaceElement() and swapElements(), inherited from the PositionalContainer interface, and adds the specialized update functions add() and remove(). (This is not a complete class.)

```
template <typename Key, typename Element, typename Comp>
class HeapPriorityQueue {                        // typename shortcuts
protected:
  typedef Item<Key, Element>   Item;             // (key, element) pair
  typedef VectorHeapTree<Item> HeapTree;         // a heap of items
  typedef HeapTree::Position    Position;        // a position in heap
protected:                                        // local utilities
  const Key& key(const Position& p) const        // position's key
    { return p.element().key(); }
  Element& element(const Position& p)            // position's element
    { return p.element().element(); }
private:                                          // member data
  HeapTree   T;                                  // heap tree
  Comp       comp;                               // comparator
public:
  HeapPriorityQueue(int capac = 100)             // constructor
    : T(capac), comp() { }
  int size() const                               // number of elements
    { return (T.size()-1)/2; }
  bool isEmpty() const                           // is the queue empty?
    { return size() == 0; }

  void insertItem(const Key& k, const Element& e); // insert (key, element)

  Element& minElement()                          // return min element
      throw(EmptyContainerException) {
    if (isEmpty())
      throw EmptyContainerException("Minimum element of empty queue");
    return element(T.root());
  }
  const Key& minKey() const                      // return minimum key
      throw(EmptyContainerException) {
    if (isEmpty())
      throw EmptyContainerException("Minimum key of empty queue");
    return key(T.root());
  }
  void removeMin() throw(EmptyContainerException); // remove minimum
};
```

Code Fragment 7.8: Class HeapPriorityQueue, which implements a priority queue by means of a heap. The definition begins with type definitions for the types Item, Sequence, and Position. Two utility functions are provided: $\text{key}(p)$ returns the key associated with position p and $\text{element}(p)$ returns the element associated with position p. (Continued in Code Fragment 7.9.)

The main work of the class is done in functions insertItem() and removeMin(), which are both defined outside the class in Code Fragment 7.9.

```
template <typename Key, typename Element, typename Comp>
void HeapPriorityQueue<Key, Element, Comp>::
insertItem(const Key& k, const Element& e) {          // insert key-element
  Position z = T.add(Item(k, e));
  while (!T.isRoot(z)) {                               // up-heap bubbling
    Position u = T.parent(z);
    if (comp(key(u), key(z)) <= 0) break;
    T.swapElements(u, z);
    z = u;
  }
}


template <typename Key, typename Element, typename Comp>
void HeapPriorityQueue<Key, Element, Comp>::
removeMin()                                            // remove minimum
    throw(EmptyContainerException) {
  if (isEmpty())
    throw EmptyContainerException("Removal from empty queue");
  if (size() == 1)
    T.remove();
  else {
    T.replaceElement(T.root(), T.remove());
    Position r = T.root();
    while (T.isInternal(T.leftChild(r))) {            // down-heap bubbling
      Position s = T.rightChild(r);
      if (T.isExternal(T.rightChild(r)) ||
          comp(key(T.leftChild(r)), key(T.rightChild(r))) <= 0)
        s = T.leftChild(r);
      if (comp(key(s), key(r)) < 0) {
        T.swapElements(r, s);
        r = s;
      }
      else break;
    }
  }
}
```

Code Fragment 7.9: Continuation from Code Fragment 7.8 of the class HeapPriorityQueue, showing the (out-of-class) definitions of functions insertItem() and removeMin(). Observe that comparisons between keys are made using the three-way comparator function, as defined in Section 7.1.4.

7.3.4 Heap-Sort

As we have previously observed, realizing a priority queue with a heap has the advantage that all the functions in the priority queue ADT run in logarithmic time or better. Hence, this realization is suitable for applications where fast running times are sought for all the priority queue functions. Therefore, let us again consider the PriorityQueueSort() sorting scheme from Section 7.1.2, which uses a priority queue P to sort a sequence S.

If we implement the priority queue P with a heap, then, during the first phase, each of the n insertItem() operations takes time $O(\log k)$, where k is the number of elements in the heap at the time. During the second phase, each of the n minElement() operations takes $O(1)$ time, and each of the removeMin() operations also runs in time $O(\log k)$, where k is the number of elements in the heap at the time. Since we always have $k \leq n$, each such operation runs in $O(\log n)$ time in the worst case. Thus, each phase takes $O(n \log n)$ time, so the entire priority-queue sorting algorithm runs in $O(n \log n)$ time when we use a heap to implement the priority queue. This sorting algorithm is better known as ***heap-sort***, and its performance is summarized in the following proposition.

Proposition 7.6: *The heap-sort algorithm sorts a sequence S of n comparable elements in $O(n \log n)$ time.*

Recalling Table 3.3, we stress that the $O(n \log n)$ running time of heap-sort is considerably better than the $O(n^2)$ running time shared by bubble-sort (Section 5.4), selection-sort, and insertion-sort (Section 7.2.3).

Implementing Heap-Sort In-Place

If the sequence S to be sorted is implemented by means of an array, we can speed up heap-sort and reduce its space requirement by a constant factor using a portion of the sequence S itself to store the heap, thus avoiding the use of an external heap data structure. This performance is accomplished by modifying the algorithm as follows:

1. We use a reverse comparator, which corresponds to a heap where the largest element is at the top. At any time during the execution of the algorithm, we use the left portion of S, up to a certain rank $i - 1$, to store the elements in the heap, and the right portion of S, from rank i to $n - 1$ to store the elements in the sequence. Thus, the first i elements of S (at ranks $0, \ldots, i - 1$) provide the vector representation of the heap (with modified level numbers starting at 0 instead of 1), that is, the element at rank k is greater than or equal to its "children" at ranks $2k + 1$ and $2k + 2$.

2. In the first phase of the algorithm, we start with an empty heap and move the boundary between the heap and the sequence from left to right, one step at a time. In step i ($i = 1, \ldots, n$), we expand the heap by adding the element at rank $i - 1$.

3. In the second phase of the algorithm, we start with an empty sequence and move the boundary between the heap and the sequence from right to left, one step at a time. At step i ($i = 1, \ldots, n$), we remove a maximum element from the heap and store it at rank $n - i$.

The above variation of heap-sort is said to be ***in-place***, since we use only a constant amount of space in addition to the sequence itself. Instead of transferring elements out of the sequence and then back in, we simply rearrange them. We illustrate in-place heap-sort in Figure 7.8. In general, we say that a sorting algorithm is in-place if it uses only a constant amount of memory in addition to the memory needed for the objects being sorted themselves. A sorting algorithm is considered space-efficient if it can be implemented in-place.

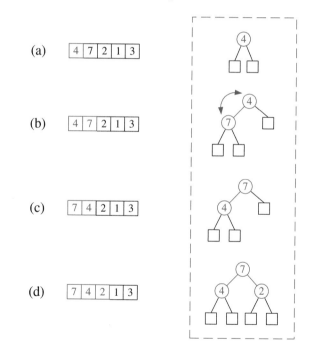

Figure 7.8: First three steps of the first phase of in-place heap-sort. The heap portion of the vector is highlighted in blue. We draw a binary tree view of the vector next to the heap, even though this tree is not actually constructed by the in-place algorithm.

7.3.5 Bottom-Up Heap Construction ⋆

The analysis of the heap-sort algorithm shows that we can construct a heap storing n key-element pairs in $O(n \log n)$ time, by means of n successive insertItem() operations, and then use that heap to extract the elements in order. However, if all the keys to be stored in the heap are given in advance, there is an alternative **bottom-up** construction function that runs in $O(n)$ time.

We describe this function in this section, observing that it can be included as one of the constructors in a Heap class, instead of filling a heap using a series of n insertItem() operations. For simplicity, we describe this bottom-up heap construction assuming the number n of keys is an integer of the type

$$n = 2^h - 1.$$

That is, the heap is a complete binary tree with every level being full, so the heap has height $h = \log(n+1)$.

Viewed nonrecursively, bottom-up heap construction consists of the following $h = \log(n+1)$ steps:

1. In the first step (see Figure 7.9a), we construct $(n+1)/2$ elementary heaps storing one key each.
2. In the second step (see Figure 7.9b and c), we form $(n+1)/4$ heaps, each storing three keys, by joining pairs of elementary heaps and adding a new key. The new key is placed at the root and may have to be swapped with the key stored at a child to preserve the heap-order property.
3. In the third step (see Figure 7.9d and e), we form $(n+1)/8$ heaps, each storing 7 keys, by joining pairs of three-way heaps (constructed in the previous step) and adding a new key. The new key is placed initially at the root, but may have to move down with a down-heap bubbling to preserve the heap-order property.

$$\vdots$$

i. In the generic ith step, $2 \le i \le h$ (see Figure 7.9f and g, where $i = 4$), we form $(n+1)/2^i$ heaps, each storing $2^i - 1$ keys, by joining pairs of heaps storing $(2^{i-1} - 1)$ keys (constructed in the previous step) and adding a new key. The new key is placed initially at the root, but may have to move down with a down-heap bubbling to preserve the heap-order property.

We illustrate bottom-up heap construction in Figure 7.9 for $h = 4$.

⋆We use a star (⋆) to indicate sections containing material more advanced than the material in the rest of the chapter; this material can be considered optional in a first reading.

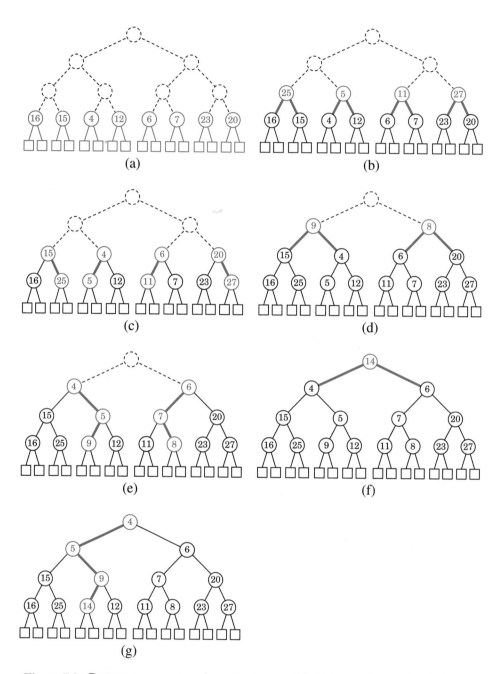

Figure 7.9: Bottom-up construction of a heap with 15 keys: (a) we begin by constructing one-key heaps on the bottom level; (b and c) we combine these heaps into three-key heaps and then (d and e) seven-key heaps, until (f and g) we create the final heap. The paths of the down-heap bubblings are highlighted in blue.

We can also describe bottom-up heap construction as a recursive algorithm, as shown in Code Fragment 7.10, which we call by passing a sequence storing the keys for which we wish to build a heap. We describe the construction algorithm as acting on keys, with the understanding that their elements accompany them.

Algorithm BottomUpHeap(S):

    Input: A sequence S storing $n = 2^h - 1$ keys

    Output: A heap T storing the keys in S.

    if S.isEmpty() **then**

        return an empty heap (consisting of a single external node).

    Remove the first key, k, from S.

    Split S into two sequences, S_1 and S_2, each of size $(n-1)/2$.

    $T_1 \leftarrow$ BottomUpHeap(S_1)

    $T_2 \leftarrow$ BottomUpHeap(S_2)

    Create binary tree T with root r storing k, left subtree T_1, and right subtree T_2.

    Perform a down-heap bubbling from the root r of T, if necessary.

    return T

Code Fragment 7.10: Recursive bottom-up heap construction.

Bottom-up heap construction is asymptotically faster than incrementally inserting n keys into an initially empty heap, as the following proposition shows.

Proposition 7.7: *Bottom-up construction of a heap with n keys takes $O(n)$ time.*

Justification: We analyze bottom-up heap construction using a "visual" approach, which is illustrated in Figure 7.10.

Let T be the final heap, let v be an internal node of T, and let $T(v)$ denote the subtree of T rooted at v. In the worst case, the time for forming $T(v)$ from the two recursively formed subtrees rooted at v's children is proportional to the height of $T(v)$. The worst case occurs when down-heap bubbling from v traverses a path from v all the way to a bottom-most external node of $T(v)$. Now consider the path $p(v)$ of T from node v to its inorder successor external node, that is, the path that starts at v, goes to the right child of v, and then goes down leftward until it reaches an external node. We say that path $p(v)$ is ***associated with*** node v. Note that $p(v)$ is not necessarily the path followed by down-heap bubbling when forming $T(v)$. Nevertheless, the length (number of edges) of $p(v)$ is equal to the height of $T(v)$. Hence, forming $T(v)$ takes time proportional to the length of $p(v)$, in the worst case. Thus, the total running time of bottom-up heap construction is proportional to the sum of the lengths of the paths associated with the internal nodes of T.

Note that for any two internal nodes u and v of T, paths $p(u)$ and $p(v)$ do not share edges, although they may share nodes. (See Figure 7.10.)

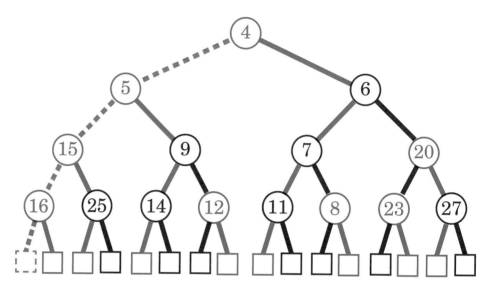

Figure 7.10: Visual justification of the linear running time of bottom-up heap construction, where the paths associated with the internal nodes have been highlighted with alternating colors. For example, the path associated with the root consists of the internal nodes storing keys 4, 6, 7, and 11, plus an external node.

Therefore, the sum of the lengths of the paths associated with the internal nodes of T is no more than the number of edges of heap T, that is, no more than $2n$. We conclude that the bottom-up construction of heap T takes $O(n)$ time.   ∎

To summarize, Proposition 7.7 states that the running time for the first phase of heap-sort can be reduced to be $O(n)$.

Unfortunately, the running time of the second phase of heap-sort cannot be made asymptotically better than $O(n \log n)$ (that is, it will always be $\Omega(n \log n)$ in the worst case). We will not justify this lower bound until Chapter 10, however.

Instead, we conclude this chapter by discussing a design pattern that allows us to extend the priority queue ADT to have additional functionality.

7.4 The Locator Design Pattern

As we saw with lists and binary trees, abstracting positional information in a container is a very powerful tool. The position ADT, described in Section 5.2.1, allows us to identify a specific "place" in a container that can store an element. A position can have its element changed, for example, as a consequence of a swapElements() operation, but the position stays the same. In Section 5.4, we gave applications of the position abstraction to implementations of the bubble-sort algorithm.

Tracking Elements as they Move

There are also applications where we need to keep track of elements as they are being moved around inside a positional container, however. For example, suppose we want to remove an element e from a sequence S. The deletion functions of the sequence ADT require that we specify either the position or the rank of e in S. If sequence S is modified by a series of swapElements() operations after the insertion of e, then element e is, in general, at a position and/or rank different from the one it had at the time it was inserted. Thus, in order to perform the deletion of element e, we would have to search for e inside S (spending time proportional to the size of S in the worst case), which is rather inefficient. Instead, we would like to have a mechanism for keeping track of the position of an element in a container.

Defining the Locator Pattern

A design pattern that fulfills this need is the ***locator***. A locator is a mechanism for maintaining the association between an element and its current position in a container. A locator "sticks" with a specific element, even if the element changes its position in the container. A locator is like a coat check; we can give our coat to a coat-room attendant, and we receive back a coat check, which is a "locator" for our coat. The position of our coat relative to the other coats can change, as other coats are added and removed, but our coat check can always be used to retrieve our coat. The important thing to remember about a locator is that it follows its item, even if it changes position.

Like a coat check, we can now imagine getting something back when we insert an element in a container—we can get back a locator for that element. For example, this locator can be used later to refer to the element within the container, to specify that this element should be removed from the container. Thus, we can conveniently extend the repertory of operations of a positional container, such as a sequence or a binary tree, with functions that support the locator design pattern.

Using Locators with Data Structures

Locators are useful in the context of data structures, for they allow us to define insertion operations that return a locator to the element inserted, and deletion operations that take a locator as an argument. These locators can therefore act like pointers, in the sense that they give our data structure quick access to its elements, but locators do not give data structure users access to the internal structure of how our data is stored.

Another important use of locators is to keep track of the items stored in a container whose operations do not refer to positions, but only to keys and elements, such as a priority queue. Indeed, the locator design pattern provides a generic mechanism for accessing an element, or key-element item, stored in a container in a way that abstracts from the concrete implementation of the container. As with positions, it is convenient to allow for a *null locator*, which refers to no item.

Locator Member Functions

As an abstract data type, a locator ℓ supports the following functions.

element(): Return a reference to the element of the item associated with ℓ.
Input: None; *Output:* Object (element).

key(): Return a *constant reference* to the key of the item associated with ℓ.
Input: None; *Output:* Object (key).

isNull(): Determine if this is a null locator.
Input: None; *Output:* Boolean.

Observe that we provide read-only access to the item's key. Because a container may organize nodes based on their key values, allowing the user unrestricted write access to the key value could undermine the integrity of the data structure. Functions for changing the key value must be provided by the container class, which can make any structural changes that might be needed.

Since the locator design pattern is a generalization of the position design pattern for key-based containers, it is natural to generalize the capabilities of positions to locators. For example, analogous to a PositionIterator object, which enumerates the positions of a position-based container, we can define a LocatorIterator object, which enumerates the locators of a key-based container.

For the sake of concreteness, we next discuss how we can use locators to extend the repertory of operations of the priority queue ADT to include functions that return locators and take locators as arguments.

7.4.1 Locator-Based Priority Queue Functions ⋆

We can use locators in a very natural way in the context of a priority queue. A locator in such a scenario stays attached to an item inserted in the priority queue, and allows us to access the item in a generic manner, independent of the specific implementation of the priority queue. This ability is important for a priority queue implementation, for there are no positions, *per se*, in a priority queue, since we do not refer to items by any notions of "rank," "index," or "node."

Although the implementations of the priority queue ADT that we have seen are based on underlying positional containers (sequences and trees), the position abstraction does not apply to the priority queue itself. Thus, we use locators to provide direct access to the items in a priority queue. A container class can give out locators when items are inserted, and accept them as parameters to fast update functions.

Extending the Priority Queue ADT

By using locators, we can extend the priority queue ADT with the following functions that access and modify a priority queue P.

min(): Return the locator to an item of P with smallest key.
    Input: None; *Output:* Locator.

insert(k,e): Insert a new item with element e and key k into P, and return a locator to the item.
    Input: Objects k (key) and e (element); *Output:* Locator.

remove(ℓ): Remove the item with locator ℓ from p.
    Input: Locator; *Output:* None.

replaceElement(ℓ,e): Replace e, the element of the item of P, with locator ℓ.
    Input: Locator, object; *Output:* None.

replaceKey(ℓ,k): Replace k, the key of the item of P, with locator ℓ.
    Input: Locator, object; *Output:* None.

We explore the use of these functions in the example that follows.

Example 7.8: *Consider the following series of locator-based operations and their effects on an initially empty priority queue P.*

Operation	Output	P
insert$(5,A)$	ℓ_1	$\{(5,A)\}$
insert$(3,B)$	ℓ_2	$\{(3,B),(5,A)\}$
insert$(7,C)$	ℓ_3	$\{(3,B),(5,A),(7,C)\}$
min$()$	ℓ_2	$\{(3,B),(5,A),(7,C)\}$
ℓ_2.key$()$	3	$\{(3,B),(5,A),(7,C)\}$
remove(ℓ_1)	–	$\{(3,B),(7,C)\}$
replaceKey$(\ell_2,9)$	–	$\{(7,C),(9,B)\}$
ℓ_2.key$()$	9	$\{(7,C),(9,B)\}$
replaceElement(ℓ_3,D)	–	$\{(7,D),(9,B)\}$

There are several applications in which the above locator-based functions are useful. For example, in a priority queue of standby airline passengers, a pessimistic passenger may decide to leave ahead of the boarding time (requiring us to perform operation remove()). At the same time, the priority of another passenger may have to be increased (requiring us to perform operation replaceKey()) after she pulls out her frequent-flyer gold card. If we are maintaining a database of standby passengers, we can implement these removal and replacement functions much faster if we access the items via their locators. The reason that such locator-based lookup functions are more efficient is that, as the implementers of the locators, we can encode information about our priority-queue that provides for fast lookup.

The locator-based lookups are often faster than lookups using a key value, because key values are provided by the user, whereas we provide the locators. For example, if we implement the priority queue with an unsorted sequence, then the locator for our priority queue can store the position of the item in the sequence. In this case, a locator-based access runs in $O(1)$ time, while a key-based access, which must look for the element in the sequence, runs in $O(n)$ time in the worst case.

Finally, we point out that locator-based functions can be used to implement nonlocator-based, container functions. Some of the functions of the priority queue ADT given in Section 7.1.3, for instance, can be expressed by simple combinations of the locator-based functions given above. For example, operation minElement() is equivalent to min().element(), and operation removeMin() is equivalent to a combination of remove() and min(). In addition, some applications call for us to restrict the operation replaceKey() so that it only increases or decreases the key. This restriction can be done by defining new functions increaseKey() or decreaseKey(), for example, which would take a locator as an argument. Further applications of priority queues extended with locator-based functions are given in Chapter 12.

7.4.2 Implementing Locator-Based Priority Queues⋆

We can extend the sequence-based and heap-based implementations of a priority queue to support locators. The existing implementations are not sufficient to support locators. For example, in the implementations of priority queues given in Code Fragments 7.5 and 7.8, each node of the data structure holds a key-element item, and each Position object points to a particular node. If it is necessary to move items around in the data structure, for example, when performing up-heap bubbling or down-heap bubbling, the original Position object no longer refers to the same object.

We present a class SortedSeqPriorityQueueLoc, which implements a locator-based priority queue, based on the SortedSeqPriorityQueue class given in Code Fragments 7.5. In order to implement locator-based functions, rather than storing a copy of the item in each node, we store a pointer to the item instead. A Locator object points directly to an item object. Rather than moving the items in the data structure around, we move the pointers instead. Since the items themselves never move, the pointer stored in each Locator object is always valid.

In order to implement this, each item needs to "know" its associated node of the data structure. We add an extra field of type Position to each Item object, which points to the associated node. The resulting "*locatable item*" structure is called a LocItem. It is derived from Item and therefore inherits the key and element attributes. It adds a node position, called pos. This structure is declared within the protected portion of SortedSeqPriorityQueueLoc, so we do not need to protect its members. This structure definition is presented in Code Fragment 7.11. We will also define a type definition LocItemPtr, which points to a LocItem object.

```
struct LocItem {                                    // a locatable item
    Item<Key,Element> item;                         // the item
    Position          pos;                          // its position
    //
    LocItem(const Key& k = Key(), const Element& e = Element())
        : item(k, e), pos() { }                     // constructor
    const Key& key() const                          // get key
        { return item.key(); }
    Element& element()                              // get element
        { return item.element(); }
};
```

Code Fragment 7.11: Structure LocItem, a "locatable item" in a priority queue. It will be placed in the protected section of class SortedSeqPriorityQueueLoc.

We define the Locator class in a manner analogous to the definition of class Position. Rather than pointing to a node in the data structure, its member variable, called locItem, points to an object of class LocItem. It provides all functions required by the Locator ADT. Since the functions of SortedSeqPriorityQueue need to access the private locItem member, we make this class a friend. The definition is presented in Code Fragment 7.12.

```
class Locator {                                    // a locator
private:
    LocItemPtr locItem;                            // pointer to the item
public:
    Locator(LocItemPtr ip = NULL)                  // constructor
        { locItem = ip; }
    bool isNull() const                            // is locator null?
        { return locItem == NULL; }
    const Key& key() const                         // get key (read-only)
        { return locItem->key(); }
    Element& element()                             // get element
        { return locItem->element(); }
    const Element& element() const                 // get element (read-only)
        { return locItem->element(); }
    friend class SortedSeqPriorityQueueLoc<Key, Element, Comp>;
};
```

Code Fragment 7.12: Class Locator, a locator for objects in a priority queue.

The principal parts of the class SortedSeqPriorityQueueLoc are presented in Code Fragments 7.13 and 7.14. Some functions, including the housekeeping functions, have been omitted. There are a number of subtle differences from the position-based class SortedSeqPriorityQueue, presented in Code Fragment 7.5, and this locator-based class. The sequence object S stores pointers to LocItem objects, rather than copies of Item objects. As a result, accessing the key or element value of a node requires that a pointer be dereferenced. The utility functions key(p) and element(p) assist in this by returning the key and element values of position p, respectively. Notice the differences between their implementations here and those given in Code Fragment 7.5.

Insertions are handled by the utility function locInsert(), which inserts a pointer to the new item in the appropriate spot in the sorted sequence. Notice the difference between functions replaceElement() and replaceKey(). In the first case, it sufficed simply to change the item's element, since this has no impact on the queue's structure. Changing a key, however, involves changing the node's location, which is done by removing the old node, changing the key, and then reinserting it.

The functions of the locator ADT are straightforward to implement, and each take $O(1)$ time.

```
template <typename Key, typename Element, typename Comp>
class SortedSeqPriorityQueueLoc {
protected:                                    // typename shortcuts
  struct LocItem;                             // a locatable item
  typedef LocItem*              LocItemPtr;   // a pointer to LocItem
  typedef NodeSequence<LocItemPtr> Sequence; // sequence
  typedef Sequence::Position    Position;     // position in sequence
  // ... (insert LocItem here)
public:
  // ... (insert Locator here)
protected:                                    // local utilities
  const Key& key(const Position& p) const     // position's key
    { return p.element()->key(); }
  Element& element(const Position& p)         // position's element
    { return p.element()->element(); }
  void locInsert(LocItemPtr locItem);         // insert utility
private:                                       // member data
  Sequence  S;                                // sorted sequence
  Comp      comp;                             // comparator
public:                                        // public functions
  SortedSeqPriorityQueueLoc() : S(), comp() { } // constructor
  Locator min() const                         // minimum item
      throw(EmptyContainerException) {
    if (S.isEmpty()) throw EmptyContainerException("Min of empty queue");
    else
      return Locator(S.first().element());
  }
  Locator insertItem(const Key& k, const Element& e) { // insert (key,element)
    LocItemPtr locItem = new LocItem(k, e);   // allocate new item
    locInsert(locItem);                       // insert it
    return Locator(locItem);                  // return its locator
  }
  void remove(Locator& loc)                   // remove item
      throw(InvalidPositionException) {
    if (loc.isNull()) throw InvalidPositionException("Removal of null locator");
    S.remove(loc.locItem->pos);               // remove from sequence
    delete loc.locItem;                       // delete the item
    loc.locItem = NULL;                        // invalidate pointer
  }
  // ...
```

Code Fragment 7.13: Class SortedSeqPriorityQueueLoc, which implements a locator-based priority queue by means of a sorted sequence. Continues in Code Fragment 7.14. (See also Code Fragments 7.11 and 7.12.)

```
// ... (continuation of SortedSeqPriorityQueueLoc)
void removeMin()                                        // remove minimum
    throw(EmptyContainerException) {
  Locator minLoc = min();                               // get locator to min
  remove(minLoc);                                       // remove it
}
void replaceElement(Locator& loc, const Element& newElement)
    throw(InvalidPositionException) {                   // replace an element
  if (loc.isNull())
    throw InvalidPositionException("Replacement using null locator");
  loc.locItem->item.setElement(newElement);            // modify the element
}
void replaceKey(Locator& loc, const Key& newKey)       // replace a key
    throw(InvalidPositionException) {
  if (loc.isNull())
    throw InvalidPositionException("Replacement using null locator");
  S.remove(loc.locItem->pos);                          // remove from sequence
  loc.locItem->item.setKey(newKey);                    // modify the key
  locInsert(loc.locItem);                              // reinsert in sequence
}
// ... (housekeeping and other functions omitted)
};
template <typename Key, typename Element, typename Comp>
void SortedSeqPriorityQueueLoc<Key, Element, Comp>::
locInsert(LocItemPtr locItem) {                        // insert utility
  Position& pos = locItem->pos;                         // insertion position
  Key k = locItem->key();                               // key to insert
  if (S.isEmpty())
    pos = S.insertFirst(locItem);                       // if empty insert first
  else if (comp(k, key(S.last())) > 0)                  // greater than last?
    pos = S.insertAfter(S.last(), locItem);             // insert at end
  else {
    Position curr = S.first();                          // start search
    while (comp(k, key(curr)) > 0)                      // skip over small keys
      curr = S.after(curr);
    pos = S.insertBefore(curr, locItem);                // insert here
  }
}
```

Code Fragment 7.14: Continuation of SortedSeqPriorityQueueLoc, which implements a priority queue supporting locator-based functions by means of a sorted sequence. (Continued from Code Fragment 7.13.)

7.5 Exercises

Reinforcement

R-7.1 Give a complete C++ informal interface for the Priority Queue ADT, including appropriate comments.

R-7.2 Although it is correct to use a "reverse" comparator with our priority queue ADT so that we retrieve and remove an element with the maximum key each time, it is confusing to have an element with maximum key returned by a function named "removeMin()." Write a short adapter class that can take any priority queue P and an associated comparator C and implement a priority queue that concentrates on the element with maximum key, using functions with names like removeMax(). (Hint: Define a new comparator C' in terms of C.)

R-7.3 The implementation of a priority queue using a sequence S that is, in turn, implemented as an array, only allows constant-time performance for the removeMin() function if S's array is implemented in a circular fashion, in order to support constant-time removal of the first element. Describe an alternative approach that involves having the removeMin() function always remove the last element in S, so that it runs in constant time, even if S's array is not circular.

R-7.4 Illustrate the performance of the selection-sort algorithm on the following input sequence: $(22, 15, 36, 44, 10, 3, 9, 13, 29, 25)$.

R-7.5 Illustrate the performance of the insertion-sort algorithm on the input sequence of the previous problem.

R-7.6 Give an example of a worst-case sequence with n elements for insertion-sort, and show that insertion-sort runs in $\Omega(n^2)$ time on such a sequence.

R-7.7 Where may an item with largest key be stored in a heap?

R-7.8 Illustrate the performance of the heap-sort algorithm on the following input sequence: $(2, 5, 16, 4, 10, 23, 39, 18, 26, 15)$.

R-7.9 Suppose a binary tree T is implemented using a vector S, as described in Section 6.4.1. If n items are stored in S in sorted order starting with index 1, is the tree T a heap?

R-7.10 Explain why the case where the right child of r is internal and the left child is external was not considered in the description of down-heap bubbling.

R-7.11 Is there a heap T storing seven distinct elements such that a preorder traversal of T yields the elements of T in sorted order? How about an inorder traversal? How about a postorder traversal?

R-7.12 Consider the numbering of the nodes of a binary tree defined in Section 6.4.1, and show that the insertion position in a heap with n keys is the node with number $n + 1$.

R-7.13 Show that the sum

$$\sum_{i=1}^{n} \log i,$$

which appears in the analysis of heap-sort, is $\Omega(n \log n)$.

R-7.14 An airport is developing a computer simulation of air-traffic control that handles events such as landings and takeoffs. Each event has a *time-stamp* that denotes the time when the event occurs. The simulation program needs to efficiently perform the following two fundamental operations:

- Insert a new event with a given time-stamp (that is, add a future event).
- Extract the event with smallest time-stamp (that is, determine the next event to process).

Which data structure would you use to support the above operations? Justify your answer.

R-7.15 A certain Professor Amongus claims that a preorder traversal of a heap will list out its keys in sorted order. Draw a small example of a heap that proves him wrong.

R-7.16 Show all the steps of the algorithm for removing key 16 from the heap of Figure 7.3.

R-7.17 Show all the steps of the algorithm for replacing 5 with 18 in the heap of Figure 7.3.

R-7.18 Draw an example of a heap whose keys are all the odd numbers from 1 to 59 (with no repeats), such that the insertion of an item with key 32 would cause up-heap bubbling to proceed all the way up to a child of the root (replacing that child's key with 32).

R-7.19 Complete Figure 7.8 by showing all the steps of the in-place heap-sort algorithm. Show both the sequence and the associated heap at the end of each step.

Creativity

C-7.1 Write a comparator for integer objects that determines order based on the number of 1s in each number's binary expansion, so that $i < j$ if the number of 1s in the binary representation of i is less than the number of 1s in the binary representation of j.

C-7.2 Show how to implement the stack ADT using only a priority queue and one additional member variable.

C-7.3 Show how to implement the (standard) queue ADT using only a priority queue and one additional member variable.

C-7.4 Assuming the input to the sorting problem is given in an array A, describe how to implement the selection-sort algorithm using only the array A and, at most, six additional (base-type) variables.

C-7.5 Assuming the input to the sorting problem is given in an array A, describe how to implement the insertion-sort algorithm using only the array A and, at most, six additional (base-type) variables.

C-7.6★ Assuming the input to the sorting problem is given in an array A, describe how to implement the heap-sort algorithm using only the array A and, at most, six additional (base-type) variables.

C-7.7 An alternative method for finding the last node during an insertion in a heap T is to store, in the last node and each external node of T, a pointer to the external node immediately to its right (wrapping to the first node in the next lower level for the right-most external node). Show how to maintain such a pointer in $O(1)$ time, per operation of the priority queue ADT, assuming T is implemented as a linked structure.

C-7.8 We can represent a path from the root to a given node of a binary tree by means of a binary string, where 0 means "go to the left child" and 1 means "go to the right child." For example, the path from the root to the node storing 8 in the heap of Figure 7.3 is represented by the binary string 101. Design a logarithmic-time algorithm for finding the last node of a heap holding n elements based on the above representation.

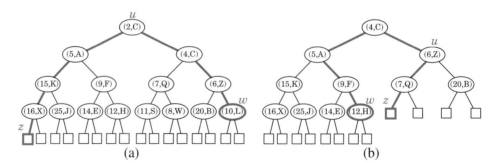

Figure 7.11: Finding the insertion position z in a heap: (a) the case when the current last node is the right-most node on its level; (b) an instance when this is not the case.

C-7.9 Suppose the binary tree T used to implement a heap can be accessed using only the functions of the binary tree ADT. That is, we cannot assume T is implemented as a vector. Given a pointer to the current last node, v, describe an efficient algorithm for finding the insertion point (that is, the new last node) using just the functions of the binary tree interface. Be sure and handle all possible cases, as illustrated in Figure 7.11. What is the running time of this function?

C-7.10 Show that, for any n, there is a sequence of insertions in a heap that requires $\Omega(n \log n)$ time to process.

C-7.11 Show that the problem of finding the kth smallest element in a heap takes at least $\Omega(k)$ time in the worst case.

C-7.12 Provide a justification of the time bounds in Table 7.2.

C-7.13 Tamarindo Airlines has the policy of giving generous rewards to their most loyal customers. In particular, at the end of each year, Tamarindo Airlines gives a booklet of first-class upgrade coupons to their top $\log n$ frequent flyers and a gift basket full of bananas and coconuts to the next $\sqrt{n}$ frequent flyers, based on the number of miles accumulated that year, where n is the total number of Tamarindo Airline's frequent flyers. Since Tamarindo Airlines cannot afford an expensive computer, they need the fastest possible algorithm to determine which customers will receive the rewards. The algorithm they currently use first sorts the flyers by the number of miles flown, and then scans the sorted list to pick the top $\log n$ and the next $\sqrt{n}$ flyers. This algorithm has time-complexity $O(n \log n)$. Can you suggest a more efficient algorithm that runs in $O(n)$ time? Describe your algorithm informally and justify its running time.

C-7.14 Develop an algorithm that computes the kth smallest element of a set of n distinct integers in $O(n + k \log n)$ time.

C-7.15 Let T be a heap storing n keys. Give an efficient algorithm for reporting all the keys in T that are smaller than or equal to a given query key x (which is not necessarily in T). For example, given the heap of Figure 7.3 and query key $x = 7$, the algorithm should report 4, 5, 6, 7. Note that the keys do not need to be reported in sorted order. Ideally, your algorithm should run in $O(k)$ time, where k is the number of keys reported.

C-7.16 Suppose the internal nodes of two binary trees, T_1 and T_2 respectively, hold items that satisfy the heap-order property. Describe a method for combining these two trees into a tree T, whose internal nodes hold the union of the items in T_1 and T_2 and also satisfy the heap-order property. Your algorithms should run in time $O(h_1 + h_2)$ where h_1 and h_2 are the respective heights of T_1 and T_2.

C-7.17 Show that the following summation, which arises in the analysis of bottom-up heap construction, is $O(1)$ for any positive integer h:

$$\sum_{i=1}^{h} \left(\frac{i}{2^i} \right).$$

Projects

P-7.1 Generalize the Heap data structure of Section 7.3 from a binary tree to a k-ary tree, for an arbitrary $k \geq 2$. Study the relative efficiencies of the resulting data structure for various values of k, by inserting and removing a large number of randomly generated keys into each data structure.

P-7.2 Give a C++ implementation of a priority queue based on an unsorted sequence.

P-7.3 Write a program that animates both the insertion-sort and selection-sort algorithms. Your animation should clearly show the migration of elements to their correct locations in the insertion-sort and the migration of the selection process in selection-sort.

P-7.4 Develop a C++ implementation of a priority queue that is based on a heap and supports the locator-based functions.

P-7.5 Write an applet or stand-alone graphical program that animates a heap. Your program should support all the priority queue operations and it should visualize the operations of the up-heap and down-heap bubbling procedures. (Extra: Visualize bottom-up heap construction as well.)

P-7.6 Implement the in-place heap-sort algorithm. Compare its running time with that of the standard heap-sort that uses an external heap.

Chapter Notes

Knuth's book on sorting and searching [59] describes the motivation and history for the selection-sort, insertion-sort, and heap-sort algorithms. The heap-sort algorithm is due to Williams [103], and the linear-time heap construction algorithm is due to Floyd [35]. Additional algorithms and analyses for heaps and heap-sort variations can be found in papers by Bentley [13], Carlsson [21], Gonnet and Munro [41], McDiarmid and Reed [70], and Schaffer and Sedgewick [90]. The locator pattern (also described in [42]), appears to be new.

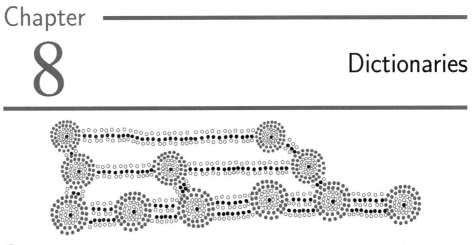

Contents

The familiar phrase, "Go look it up," might be heard when a lazy student asks for the definition of a word from an equally lazy teacher. This phrase is also the principle behind the ***dictionary*** abstract data type, which we discuss in this chapter.

As the name implies, the primary use of a dictionary is to store elements so that they can be located quickly using keys. The motivation for such searches is that each element in a dictionary typically stores additional useful information besides its search key, but the only way to get at that information is to use the search key. For example, a dictionary may hold bank accounts. Each account is an object that is identified by an account number and stores a wealth of additional information, including the current balance, the name and address of the account holder, and the history of deposits and withdrawals performed. An application wishing to operate on an account would have to provide the account number as a search key to get the account object from the dictionary.

As another example, a dictionary might hold a set of windows open in a graphical interface. The window objects are stored in the dictionary according to some identifier (like a process number), to determine a unique key value, but additional information is stored with each window object, including its dimensions, descriptions of its pull-down menus, its fonts, and its colors. A process wishing to send a message to a particular window object would need to be given a pointer to this object, which it could request from the dictionary using the window's ID as a key.

Like a priority queue, a dictionary is a container of key-element pairs. Nevertheless, although a total order relation on the keys is always required for a priority queue, it is optional for a dictionary. Indeed, the simplest form of a dictionary assumes only that we can determine whether two keys are equal. When a total order relation on the keys is defined, then we can talk about an ***ordered dictionary***, and we can specify additional ADT functions that refer to the ordering of the keys.

A computer dictionary is similar to a paper dictionary of words in the sense that both are used to look things up. The paper dictionary metaphor is not fully appropriate, however, for we typically desire a computer dictionary to be dynamic, so as to support element insertion and removal. Thus, the dictionary abstract data type has functions for the insertion, removal, and searching of elements with keys.

In this chapter, we describe several different techniques for realizing dictionaries. We show, for example, how to realize dictionaries using an unordered sequence. This implementation is simple, but not very efficient. So we introduce hash tables and skip lists, showing how these data structures can be used to realize dictionaries with fast query and update times. We conclude the chapter by discussing how the locator pattern presented in the previous chapter can be used to expand the collection of functions that are included in the dictionary ADT. Incidentally, in Chapter 9, we discuss other data structures that achieve fast dictionary-operation performance by using various kinds of balanced search trees.

8.1 The Dictionary Abstract Data Type

A dictionary stores key-element pairs (k, e), which we call **items**, where k is the key and e is the element. In order to achieve the highest level of generality, we allow both the keys and the elements stored in a dictionary to be of any object type. (See Figure 8.1.) For example, in a dictionary storing student records (such as the student's name, address, and course grades), the key might be the student's ID number. In some applications, the key may be the element itself. For example, if we had a dictionary storing prime numbers, we could use the numbers themselves as keys (and also as the elements).

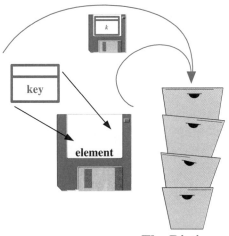

The Dictionary

Figure 8.1: A conceptual illustration of the dictionary ADT. Keys (labels) are assigned to elements (diskettes) by a user. The resulting items (labeled diskettes) are inserted into the dictionary (file cabinet). The keys can be used later to retrieve or remove the items.

We distinguish two types of dictionaries, **unordered dictionaries** and **ordered dictionaries**. In either case, we use a **key** as an identifier that is assigned by an application or user to an associated element. In the ordered dictionary, we assume that a total order relation is defined on the keys, and we provide additional functions that refer to this ordering. An ordered dictionary determines the relative order of two keys by means of a comparator (see Section 7.1.4), which is provided to the dictionary as a parameter of the ordered dictionary constructor's method. In an unordered (generic) dictionary, however, no order relation is assumed on the keys, and only equality testing between keys is used. Hence, in an unordered dictionary, we can use an *equality tester* object to test whether two keys, k_1 and k_2, are equal with function isEqualTo(k_1, k_2).

For the sake of generality, our definition allows a dictionary to store multiple items with the same key. Nevertheless, there are applications in which we want to disallow items with the same key (for example, in a dictionary storing student records, we would probably want to disallow two students having the same ID). In such cases when keys are unique, then the key associated with an object can be viewed as an "address" for that object in memory. Indeed, such dictionaries are sometimes referred to as "associative stores," for the key associated with an object determines its "location" in the dictionary.

8.1.1 The Dictionary ADT

As an ADT, a *dictionary* D supports the following functions.

size(): Return the number of items in D.
Input: None; *Output:* Integer.

isEmpty(): Test whether D is empty.
Input: None; *Output:* Boolean.

elements(): Return the elements stored in D.
Input: None; *Output:* Iterator of objects (elements).

keys(): Return the keys stored in D.
Input: None; *Output:* Iterator of objects (keys).

find(k): If D contains an item with key equal to k, then return the position of such an item. If not, a null position is returned.
Input: Object (key); *Output:* Position.

findAll(k): Return an iterator of positions for all items whose key equals k.
Input: Object (key); *Output:* Iterator (of Positions).

insertItem(k, e): Insert an item with element e and key k into D.
Input: Objects k (key) and e (element); *Output:* None.

removeElement(k): Remove an item with key equal to k from D. An error condition occurs if D has no such item.
Input: Object (key); *Output:* None.

removeAllElements(k): Remove the items with key equal to k from D.
Input: Object (key); *Output:* None.

When the operation find(k) is applied to a dictionary in which no item has key equal to k, the convention is to return a null position (Section 5.2.1). There are other possible ways to handle an attempt to find a nonexistent key. One possibility might be to throw an exception. This is not a very good choice, however, since the most common way to determine whether a key occurs in the dictionary is to attempt to "find" it, and test whether the operation succeeded.

The case of removal is different. We may assume that the user either knows that a key is in the dictionary, or has used find(k) to determine that a key is present prior to removing it. Thus, if the operation removeElement(k) is applied to a dictionary that has no key equal to k, an error condition results. In this case, we throw a NonexistentElementException. We do not impose this restriction on removeAllElements(k). By definition, it removes some number of elements. Removing zero elements is a legitimate possibility.

Example 8.1: *In the following, we show the effect of a series of operations on an initially empty dictionary storing integer keys and single-character elements. Even though the "Dictionary" column shows items in insertion order, this is not required. The way the items of a dictionary are stored is implementation dependent. The notation $p(x)$ indicates the position of the item storing element x.*

Operation	Output	Dictionary
insertItem($5,A$)		$\{(5,A)\}$
insertItem($7,B$)		$\{(5,A),(7,B)\}$
insertItem($2,C$)		$\{(5,A),(7,B),(2,C)\}$
insertItem($8,D$)		$\{(5,A),(7,B),(2,C),(8,D)\}$
insertItem($2,E$)		$\{(5,A),(7,B),(2,C),(8,D),(2,E)\}$
find(7)	$p(B)$	$\{(5,A),(7,B),(2,C),(8,D),(2,E)\}$
find(4)	"null"	$\{(5,A),(7,B),(2,C),(8,D),(2,E)\}$
find(2)	$p(C)$	$\{(5,A),(7,B),(2,C),(8,D),(2,E)\}$
findAll(2)	$p(C),p(E)$	$\{(5,A),(7,B),(2,C),(8,D),(2,E)\}$
size()	5	$\{(5,A),(7,B),(2,C),(8,D),(2,E)\}$
removeElement(5)		$\{(7,B),(2,C),(8,D),(2,E)\}$
removeElement(5)	"error"	$\{(7,B),(2,C),(8,D),(2,E)\}$
removeAllElements(2)		$\{(7,B),(8,D)\}$
find(2)	"null"	$\{(7,B),(8,D)\}$

Beware that the positions of elements within a dictionary may change after certain dictionary operations. This typically occurs with update operations, such as insertItem() and removeElement(), but depending on the implementation, this might even occur with access operations, such as find(). As a result, a position that refers to some element prior to such an operation may refer to an entirely different

element after the operation. In such cases, the Position object has become *invalid*.
Exactly which positions become invalid after an operation depends on the implementation of the dictionary and the elements involved. In an ideal implementation,
a position only becomes invalid if the object to which it refers is removed from the
dictionary. To achieve this best-case behavior, the positions need to "stick" to the
associated objects. We discuss such locator-based enhancements in Section 8.5.

There are other functions that could be included in the dictionary ADT. For
example, it is often the case that prior to using removeElement(k), operation find(k)
is used to determine whether the key is really in the dictionary. To avoid the need to
perform two separate searches for the same key, it would be reasonable to provide
an operation remove(p), which is given the position of the item to be deleted. As
with removeElement(), an exception would be thrown if a null position is given.
This will also be discussed later in Section 8.5.

As we have defined it, a dictionary may contain different items with equal keys.
In this case, operations find(k) and removeElement(k) are applied to an *arbitrary*
element whose associated key is equal to k. Also, if we wish to store an item e in
a dictionary so that the item is itself its own key, then we would insert e with the
function call insertItem(e,e).

Each of the dictionary operations given above requires that we have a mechanism for deciding whether two keys are equal. If the dictionary is ordered, then a
comparator class (Section 7.1.4) should be associated with the dictionary. To keep
our examples simple, we will not always explicitly provide a comparator class.
Instead, we will usually assume that keys can be compared using the standard relational operators, such as "==" and "<" (which of course can be overloaded in C++).

In order to provide access to both the key and element, we augment our Position
class from Section 5.2.1 to provide a function key(), which returns a reference to
the associated key. This is a constant reference, since allowing the user to modify
the key value could compromise the data structure's integrity. Thus, the functions
of our Position class for dictionaries are as follows:

> element(): Return a reference to the element of the associated item.
> **Input:** None; **Output:** Object (element).

> key(): Return a **constant reference** to the key of the associated
> item.
> **Input:** None; **Output:** Object (key).

> isNull(): Determine if this is a null position.
> **Input:** None; **Output:** Boolean.

The C++ Standard Template Library provides two dictionary classes, map and
multi_map. The multi_map class allows multiple entries with the same key value,

whereas map allows only a single instance of each key. We will discuss class map in Section 8.3.4.

8.1.2 Log Files

A simple way of realizing a dictionary is to use an unordered vector, list, or general sequence to store the key-element pairs. Such an implementation is often called a *log file* or *audit trail*. The primary applications of log files are situations where we wish to archive structured data. For example, many financial database systems store a dictionary of all their transactions in this way. Likewise, many operating systems programs, such as Web servers and remote login programs, store log files of all requests they process over the Internet. The typical scenario in such applications is that there are many insertions into the dictionary but few searches. For example, searching such an operating system log file typically occurs only after something goes wrong, such as a system crash. Thus, log files should support simple and fast insertions, possibly at the expense of search time. Formally, we say that a *log file* is an implementation of a dictionary D using a sequence S (for full generality) to store the items of D in arbitrary order. (See Figure 8.2.)

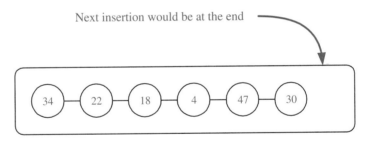

Figure 8.2: Realization of a dictionary D by means of a log file. We only show the keys in this dictionary, so as to highlight the way this dictionary is implemented with an unordered sequence.

Unordered Sequence Implementation

In using a log file to implement a dictionary, we assume that the sequence S used for a log file is implemented with either a vector or a doubly linked list (see Section 5.3). We also refer to the log file implementation of D as an *unordered sequence implementation*, since the keys have no influence on the linear arrangement of the items in S.

Analysis of the Log File Data Structure

The space required for a log file storing n items is $O(n)$, since both the vector and linked list data structures can maintain their memory usage to be proportional to their size. In addition, with a log file implementation of the dictionary ADT, we can realize operation insertItem(k, e) easily and efficiently, just by a single call to the insertLast() method on S, which simply adds the new item to the end of the sequence. Thus, we achieve $O(1)$ time for the insertItem(k, e) operation on D.

Unfortunately, this implementation does not allow for an efficient execution of the find() function. A find(k) operation must be performed by scanning through the entire sequence S, examining each of its items. For example, we can iteratively use the after() sequence operation until we either find an item with key equal to k or reach the end of the sequence. The worst case for the running time of this method clearly occurs when the search is unsuccessful, and we reach the end of the sequence having examined all of its n items. Thus, the find() function runs in $O(n)$ time.

Similarly, a linear amount of time is needed in the worst case to perform a removeElement(k) operation on D as well, for in order to remove an item with a given key, we must first find it by scanning through the entire sequence S. Thus the worst-case running time for performing removeElement(k) in a log file is $O(n)$.

The operations findAll() and removeAllElements() always require scanning through the entire sequence S, and hence their running time is $\Theta(n)$. That is, they run in linear time in both the best and worst case.

Applications for Log Files

Summarizing the above analysis, we see that implementing a dictionary with a log file provides for fast insertions, but at the expense of slow searches and removals. Thus, we should only use a log file where we either expect the dictionary to always be small or we expect the number of insertions to be large relative to the number of searches and removals. Of course, archiving database and operating system transactions are precisely situations such as this. Nevertheless, there are many other scenarios where the number of insertions in a dictionary will be roughly proportional to the number of searches and removals, and in these cases, the log file implementation is clearly inappropriate. The unordered dictionary implementation we discuss next can often be used, however, to achieve fast insertions, removals, and searches in many such cases.

8.2 Hash Tables

The keys associated with elements in a dictionary are often meant as "addresses" for those elements. Examples of such applications include a compiler's symbol table and a registry of environment variables in an operating system. Both of these structures consist of a collection of symbolic names, where each name serves as the "address" for properties about a variable's type and value. One of the most efficient ways to implement a dictionary in such circumstances is to use a *hash table*. Although hash tables have high worst-case running times for dictionary ADT operations, we will see that their expected-case running times are excellent. Letting n denote the number of items, the worst-case times are $O(n)$, but the expected-case times are only $O(1)$.

8.2.1 Bucket Arrays

A *bucket array* for a hash table is an array A of size N, where each cell of A is thought of as a "bucket" (that is, a container of key-element pairs) and the integer N defines the *capacity* of the array. If the keys are integers well distributed in the range $[0, N-1]$, this bucket array is all that is needed. An element e with key k is simply inserted into the bucket $A[k]$. Any bucket cells associated with keys not present in the dictionary are marked with a special value indicating that they are empty. (See Figure 8.3.)

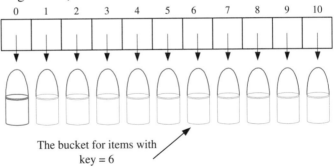

Figure 8.3: An illustration of a bucket array.

Of course, if keys are not unique, then two different elements may be mapped to the same bucket in A. In this case, we say that a *collision* has occurred. Clearly, if each bucket of A can store only a single element, then we cannot associate more than one element with a single bucket, which is a problem in the case of collisions. To be sure, there are ways of dealing with collisions, which we will discuss later, but the best strategy is to try to avoid them in the first place.

Analysis of the Bucket Array Structure

If keys are unique, then collisions are not a concern, and searches, insertions, and removals in the bucket array take worst-case time $O(1)$. This sounds like a great achievement, but it has two major drawbacks. The first is that it uses space $\Theta(N)$, which is not necessarily related to the number of items, n, actually present in the dictionary. Indeed, if N is large relative to n, then this implementation is wasteful of space. The second drawback is that the bucket array requires that keys be integers in the range $[0, N-1]$, which is often not the case. Since these two drawbacks are so common, we define the hash table data structure to consist of a bucket array together with a "good" mapping from our keys to integers in the range $[0, N-1]$.

8.2.2   Hash Functions

The second part of a hash table structure is a function, h, called a ***hash function***, that maps each key k in our dictionary to an integer in the range $[0, N-1]$, where N is the capacity of the bucket array for this table. Equipped with such a hash function, h, we can apply the bucket array method to arbitrary keys. The main idea of this approach is to use the hash function value, $h(k)$, as an index into our bucket array, A, instead of the key k (which is most likely inappropriate for use as a bucket array index). That is, we store the item (k, e) in the bucket $A[h(k)]$.

We say that a hash function is "good" if it maps the keys in our dictionary to minimize collisions as much as possible. For practical reasons, we would also like the evaluation of a given hash function to be fast and easy to compute. We view the evaluation of a hash function, $h(k)$, as consisting of two actions—mapping the key k to an integer, called the ***hash code***, and mapping the hash code to an integer within the range of indices $[0, N-1]$ of a bucket array, called the ***compression map***. (See Figure 8.4.)

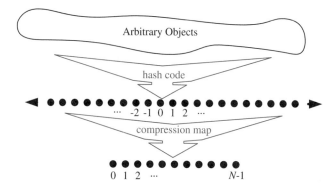

Figure 8.4: The two parts of a hash function: a hash code and a compression map.

8.2.3 Hash Codes

The first action that a hash function performs is to take an arbitrary key k in our dictionary and assign it an integer value. The integer assigned to a key k is called the **hash code** or **hash value** for k. This integer need not be in the range $[0, N-1]$, and may even be negative, but we want the set of hash codes assigned to our keys to avoid collisions as much as possible. In addition, to be consistent, the hash code we use for a key k should be the same as the hash code for any key that is equal to k (as determined by the equality tester for our dictionary).

Hash Codes in C++

The hash codes described below are based on the assumption that the number of bits of each type is known. This information is provided in the standard include file <limits>. This include file defines a templated class numeric_limits. Given a base type T (such as char, int, or float), the number of bits in a variable of type T is given by "numeric_limits<T>.digits."

Older C++ systems may not have this include file, however. For these systems, the include file <climits> defines a constant CHAR_BIT. Recall that sizeof(T) returns the length of type T as a function of the number of character bytes in T. Thus, the number of bits in type T can be computed using "sizeof(T)*CHAR_BIT."

Let us consider, then, several common data types and some example methods for assigning hash codes to objects of these types.

Casting to an Integer

To begin, we note that, for any data type X that is represented using at most as many bits as our integer hash codes, we can simply take an integer interpretation of its bits as a hash code for X. Thus, for the C++ fundamental types char, short, and int, we can achieve a good hash code simply by casting this type to int.

Summing Components

On many machines, the type long has a bit representation that is twice as long as type int. One possible hash code for a long object is to simply cast it down to an integer and then apply the integer hash code. The problem is that such a hash code ignores half of the information present in the original value. If many of the keys in our dictionary only differ in these bits, they will collide using this simple hash code. A better hash code, which takes all the original bits into consideration, is to sum an integer representation of the high-order bits with an integer representation of the low-order bits.

A Small C++ Example

For example, assuming that we have access to a function hashCode(x), which hashes a 32-bit integer, we could use this function to hash a 64-bit long integer by shifting the higher-order 32 bits to the right and adding the two 32-bit quantities. Recall from Section 1.2 that to perform a right shift that fills with zeros, we should first cast the variable to an unsigned quantity. Therefore, we define a type ulong to be an unsigned long, and cast the argument x to this type prior to shifting.

```
int hashCode(long x) {                                    // hash a 64-bit long
    typedef unsigned long ulong;
    return hashCode(int(ulong(x) >> 32) + int(x));  // merge two halves
}
```

Indeed, the approach of summing components can be extended to any object x whose binary representation can be viewed as a k-tuple $(x_0, x_1, \ldots, x_{k-1})$ of integers, for we can then form a hash code for x as $\sum_{i=0}^{k-1} x_i$. For example, given any floating-point number, we can sum its mantissa and exponent as long integers, and then apply a hash code for long integers to the result.

Polynomial Hash Codes

The summation hash code, described above, is not a good choice for character strings or other variable-length objects that can be viewed as tuples of the form $(x_0, x_1, \ldots, x_{k-1})$, where the order of the x_i's is significant. For example, consider a hash code for a character string s that sums the ASCII values of the characters in s. Unfortunately, this hash code produces lots of unwanted collisions for common groups of strings. In particular, "temp01" and "temp10" collide using this function, as do "stop", "tops", "pots", and "spot". A better hash code takes into consideration the positions of the x_i's. An alternative hash code, which does exactly this, chooses a nonzero constant, $a \neq 1$, and uses

$$x_0 a^{k-1} + x_1 a^{k-2} + \cdots + x_{k-2} a + x_{k-1}$$

as a hash code value. Mathematically speaking, this is simply a polynomial in a that takes the components $(x_0, x_1, \ldots, x_{k-1})$ of an object x as its coefficients. This hash code is therefore called a ***polynomial hash code***. By Horner's rule (see Exercise C-3.9), this polynomial can be rewritten as

$$x_{k-1} + a(x_{k-2} + a(x_{k-3} + \cdots + a(x_2 + a(x_1 + ax_0))\cdots)).$$

Intuitively, a polynomial hash code uses multiplication by the constant a as a way of "making room" for each component in a tuple of values, while also preserving a characterization of the previous components. Of course, on a typical computer, evaluating a polynomial will be done using the finite bit representation for a hash code; hence, the value will periodically overflow the bits used for an integer. Since we are more interested in a good spread of the object x with respect to other keys, we simply ignore such overflows. Still, we should be mindful that such overflows are occurring and choose the constant a so that it has some nonzero, low-order bits, which will serve to preserve some of the information content even if we are in an overflow situation.

We have done some experimental studies that suggest that 33, 37, 39, and 41 are good choices for a when working with character strings that are English words. In fact, in a list of over 50,000 English words formed as the union of the word lists provided in two variants of Unix, we found that taking a to be 33, 37, 39, or 41 produced less than seven collisions in each case! Many implementations of string hashing choose a polynomial hash function, using one of these constants for a, as a default hash code. For the sake of speed, however, some implementations only apply the polynomial hash function to a fraction of the characters in long strings.

Cyclic Shift Hash Codes

A variant of the polynomial hash code replaces multiplication by a with a cyclic shift of a partial sum by a certain number of bits. Such a function, applied to character strings in C++ could, for example, look like the following. We assume a 32-bit integer word length, and we assume access to a function hashCode(x) for integers. To achieve a 5-bit cyclic shift we form the "bitwise or" (see Section 1.2) of a 5-bit left shift and a 27-bit right shift. As before, we use an unsigned integer so that right shifts fill with zeros.

```
int hashCode(const char *p, int len) {      // hash a character array
    unsigned int h = 0;
    for (int i = 0; i < len; i++) {
        h = (h << 5) | (h >> 27);           // 5-bit cyclic shift
        h += (unsigned int) p[i];           // add in next character
    }
    return hashCode(int(h));
}
```

As with the traditional polynomial hash code, using the cyclic-shift hash code requires some fine-tuning. In this case, we must wisely choose the amount to shift by for each new character.

Experimental Results

In Table 8.1, we show the results of some experiments run on a list of just over 25,000 English words, which compare the number of collisions for various shift amounts.

	Collisions	
Shift	**Total**	**Max**
0	23739	86
1	10517	21
2	2254	6
3	448	3
4	89	2
5	4	2
6	6	2
7	14	2
8	105	2
9	18	2
10	277	3
11	453	4
12	43	2
13	13	2
14	135	3
15	1082	6
16	8760	9

Table 8.1: Comparison of collision behavior for the cyclic shift variant of the polynomial hash code as applied to a list of just over 25,000 English words. The "Total" column records the total number of collisions and the "Max" column records the maximum number of collisions for any one hash code. Note that, with a cyclic shift of 0, this hash code reverts to the one that simply sums all the characters.

These and our previous experiments show that if we choose our constant a or our shift value wisely, then either the polynomial hash code or its cyclic-shift variant are suitable for any object that can be written as a tuple $(x_0, x_1, \ldots, x_{k-1})$, where the order in tuples matters. In particular, note that using a shift of 5 or 6 is particularly good for English words. Also, note how poorly a simple addition of the values would be with no shifting (that is, for a shift of 0).

Hashing Floating-Point Quantities

On most machines, types int and float are both 32-bit quantities. Nonetheless, the approach of casting a float variable to type int would not produce a good hash function, since this would truncate the fractional part of the floating-point value. For the purposes of hashing, we do not really care about the number's value. It is sufficient to treat the number as a sequence of bits. Assuming that a char is stored as an 8-bit byte, we could interpret a 32-bit float as a 4-element character array, and a 64-bit double as an 8-element character array. C++ provides an operation called a *reinterpret cast*, to cast between such unrelated types. This cast treats quantities as a sequence of bits and makes no attempt to intelligently convert the meaning of one quantity to another.

For example, we could design a hash function for a float by first reinterpreting it as an array of characters and then applying the character-array hashCode() function defined above. We use the operator sizeof(), which returns the number of bytes in a type.

```
int hashCode(const float& x) {              // hash a float
  int len = sizeof(x);
  const char* p = reinterpret_cast<const char*>(&x);
  return hashCode(p, len);
}
```

Reinterpret casts are generally not portable operations, since the result depends on the particular machine's encoding of types as a pattern of bits. In our case, portability is not an issue since we are interested only in interpreting the floating point value as a sequence of bits. The only property that we require is that float variables with equal values must have the same bit sequence.

8.2.4 Compression Maps

The hash code for a key k will typically not be suitable for immediate use with a bucket array, because the range of possible hash codes for our keys will typically exceed the range of legal indices of our bucket array A. That is, incorrectly using a hash code as an index into our bucket array may result in an error condition, either because the index is negative or it exceeds the capacity of A. Thus, once we have determined an integer hash code for a key object k, there is still the issue of mapping that integer into the range $[0, N-1]$. This compression step is the second action that a hash function performs.

The Division Method

One simple *compression map* to use is

$$h(k) = |k| \bmod N,$$

which is called the *division method*. Additionally, if we take N to be a prime number, then this hash function helps "spread out" the distribution of hashed values. Indeed, if N is not prime, there is a higher likelihood that patterns in the distribution of keys will be repeated in the distribution of hash codes, thereby causing collisions. For example, if we hash the keys $\{200, 205, 210, 215, 220, \ldots, 600\}$ to a bucket array of size 100 using the division method, then each hash code will collide with three others. But if this same set of keys is similarly hashed to a bucket array of size 101, then there will be no collisions. If a hash function is chosen well, it should ensure that the probability of two different keys getting hashed to the same bucket is $1/N$. Choosing N to be a prime number is not always enough, however, for if there is a repeated pattern of key values of the form $iN + j$ for several different i's, then there will still be collisions.

The MAD Method

A more sophisticated compression function, which helps eliminate repeated patterns in a set of integer keys is the *multiply add and divide* (or "MAD") method. In using this method we define the compression function as

$$h(k) = |ak + b| \bmod N,$$

where N is a prime number, and a and b are nonnegative integers randomly chosen at the time the compression function is determined, so that $a \bmod N \neq 0$. This compression function is chosen in order to eliminate repeated patterns in the set of hash codes and to get us closer to having a "good" hash function, that is, one having the probability that any two different keys collide is $1/N$. This good behavior would be the same as if these keys were "thrown" into A uniformly at random.

With a compression function such as this, that spreads n integers fairly evenly in the range $[0, N - 1]$, and a mapping of the keys in our dictionary to integers, we have an effective hash function. Together, such a hash function and a bucket array define the key ingredients of the hash table implementation of the dictionary ADT.

But before we can give the details of how to perform such operations as find(), insertItem(), and removeElement(), we must first resolve the issue of how we will be handling collisions.

8.2.5   Collision-Handling Schemes

Recall that the main idea of a hash table is to take a bucket array, A, and a hash function, h, and use them to implement a dictionary by storing each item (k,e) in the "bucket" $A[h(k)]$. This simple idea is challenged, however, when we have two distinct keys, k_1 and k_2, such that $h(k_1) = h(k_2)$. The existence of such *collisions* prevents us from simply inserting a new item (k,e) directly in the bucket $A[h(k)]$. They also complicate our procedure for performing the find(k) operation. Thus, we must have a consistent strategy for resolving collisions.

Separate Chaining

A simple and efficient collision handling method is to have each bucket $A[i]$ store a pointer to a list, S_i, that stores all the items mapped to the bucket $A[i]$ by our hash function. The list S_i can be viewed as a miniature dictionary, implemented using the unordered sequence or *log file* method, but restricted to only hold items (k,e), such that $h(k) = i$. This *collision resolution* rule is known as *separate chaining*. Assuming that we implement each nonempty bucket in a miniature dictionary as a log file, we can perform the fundamental dictionary operations as follows:

- find(k):
  > $B \leftarrow A[h(k)]$
  > **if** B is empty **then**
  > > **return** Position(NULL)
  >
  > **else**
  > > {search for the key k in the sequence for this bucket}
  > > **return** B.find(k)

- insertItem(k,e):
  > **if** $A[h(k)]$ is empty **then**
  > > Create a new initially empty, sequence-based dictionary B
  > > $A[h(k)] \leftarrow B$
  >
  > **else**
  > > $B \leftarrow A[h(k)]$
  > B.insertItem(k,e)

- removeElement(k):
  > $B \leftarrow A[h(k)]$
  > **if** B is empty **then**
  > > throw a NonexistentElementException
  >
  > **else**
  > > B.removeElement(k)

In separate chaining, we handle each of the fundamental dictionary operations involving a key k with the miniature list-based dictionary stored at $A[h(k)]$. An insertion will put the new item at the end of this list, a search will go through this list until it reaches the end or finds an item with the desired key, and a deletion will remove an item in this list after it is found. We can "get away" with using the simple log-file dictionary implementation in these cases, because the spreading properties of the hash function help keep each miniature dictionary small. Indeed, a good hash function will try to minimize collisions as much as possible, which implies that most of our buckets are either empty or store just a single item. This observation allows us to make a slight change to our implementation so that, if a bucket $A[i]$ stores just a single item (k, e), we can simply have $A[i]$ point directly to the item (k, e) rather than to a list-based dictionary holding only the one item. We leave the details of this space optimization to an exercise (C-8.7). In Figure 8.5, we give an illustration of a simple hash table that uses the division compression function and separate chaining to resolve collisions.

Assuming that we are using a good hash function for holding the n items of our dictionary in a bucket array of capacity N, the expected size of each bucket would be n/N. This parameter, which is called the ***load factor*** of the hash table and is denoted with λ, should therefore be bounded by a small constant, preferably below 1. For, given a good hash function, the expected running time of operations find(), insertItem(), and removeElement() in a dictionary implemented with a hash table that uses this function is $O(\lceil n/N \rceil)$. Thus, we can implement the standard dictionary operations to run in $O(1)$ expected time, provided n is $O(N)$.

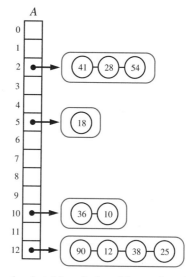

Figure 8.5: Example of a hash table of size 13, storing 10 integer keys, and using separate chaining for collisions, with compression map $h(k) = k \bmod 13$.

Open Addressing

The separate chaining rule has many nice properties, such as allowing for simple implementations of dictionary operations, but it nevertheless has one slight disadvantage: it requires the use of an auxiliary data structure—a list, vector, or sequence—to hold items with colliding keys as a log file. We can handle collisions in other ways besides using the separate chaining rule, however. In particular, if space is of a premium (for example, if we are writing a program for a small hand-held device), then we can use the alternative approach of always storing each item directly in a bucket, at most, one item per bucket. This approach saves space because no auxiliary structures are employed, but it requires a bit more complexity to deal with collisions. There are several methods for implementing this approach, which we discuss next. These methods are collectively referred to as ***open addressing*** schemes, which require that the load factor is always at most 1, that is, $n \leq N$, and that items are stored only in the bucket array itself.

Linear Probing

A simple open addressing strategy for collision handling is ***linear probing***. In this strategy, if we try to insert an item (k,e) into a bucket $A[i]$ that is already occupied, where $i = h(k)$, then we try next at $A[(i+1) \bmod N]$. If $A[(i+1) \bmod N]$ is also occupied, then we try $A[(i+2) \bmod N]$, and so on, until we find an empty bucket in A that is not occupied and can accept the new item. Once this bucket is located, we simply insert the item (k,e) there. Of course, using this collision resolution strategy requires that we change the implementation of the find(k) operation. In particular, to perform such a search we must examine consecutive buckets, starting from $A[h(k)]$, until we either find an item with key equal to k or we find an empty bucket (in which case the search is unsuccessful). (See Figure 8.6.)

The operation removeElement(k) is more complicated than this, however. Indeed, to fully implement this function, the contents of the bucket array are restored

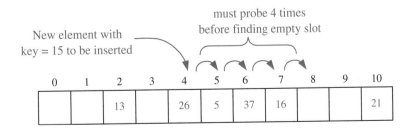

Figure 8.6: An insertion into a hash table using linear probing to resolve collisions. Here we use the compression map $h(k) = k \bmod 11$.

to look as though the item with key k was never inserted in its bucket $A[i]$ in the first place. Although performing such a restoration is certainly possible, it requires that we shift items down in buckets above $A[i]$, while not shifting others in this group (namely, the items that are already in their correct location). A typical way we can get around this difficulty is to replace the deleted item with a special "deactivated item" object. This object must be marked in some way so that we can immediately detect when it is occupying a given bucket. With this special marker possibly occupying buckets in our hash table, we modify our search algorithm for removeElement(k) or find(k), so that the search for a key k should skip over deactivated items and continue probing until reaching the desired item or an empty bucket. But our algorithm for the insertItem(k,e) should instead stop at a deactivated item and replace it with the new item to be inserted.

Linear probing saves space, but it complicates removals. Even with the use of the deactivated item object, the linear-probing collision-handling strategy suffers from an additional disadvantage. It tends to cluster the items of the dictionary into contiguous runs, which cause searches to slow down considerably.

Quadratic Probing

Another open addressing strategy, known as *quadratic probing*, involves iteratively trying buckets $A[(i + f(j)) \bmod N]$, for $j = 0, 1, 2, \ldots$, where $f(j) = j^2$, until an empty bucket is found. As with linear probing, the quadratic probing strategy complicates the removal operation, but it does avoid the kinds of clustering patterns that occur with linear probing. Nevertheless, it creates its own kind of clustering, called *secondary clustering*, where the set of filled array cells "bounces" around the array in a fixed pattern. If N is not chosen as a prime, then the quadratic probing strategy may not find an empty bucket in A even if one exists. In fact, even if N is prime, this strategy may not find an empty slot if the bucket array is at least half full. We explore the cause of this type of clustering in an exercise (C-8.10).

Double Hashing

Another open addressing strategy that does not cause clustering of the kind produced by linear probing or the kind produced by quadratic probing is the *double hashing* strategy. In this approach, we choose a secondary hash function h', and, if h maps some key k to a bucket $A[i]$, with $i = h(k)$, that is already occupied, then we iteratively try the buckets $A[(i + f(j)) \bmod N]$ next, for $j = 1, 2, 3, \ldots$, where $f(j) = j \cdot h'(k)$. In this scheme, the secondary hash function is not allowed to evaluate to zero. A common choice is $h'(k) = q - (k \bmod q)$, for some prime number $q < N$. Also, N should be a prime. Moreover, we should choose a secondary hash function that will attempt to minimize clustering as much as possible.

8.2.6   Load Factors and Rehashing

In all of the hash table schemes described above, the load factor, $\lambda = n/N$, should be kept below 1. Experiments and average-case analyses suggest that we should maintain $\lambda < 0.5$ for the open addressing schemes and we should maintain $\lambda < 0.9$ for separate chaining.

As we explore in Exercise C-8.10, some open addressing schemes can start to fail when $\lambda \geq 0.5$. Although the details of the average-case analysis of hashing are beyond the scope of this book, its probabilistic basis is quite intuitive. If our hash function is good, then we expect the hash function values to be uniformly distributed in the range $[0, N-1]$. Thus, to store n items in our dictionary, the expected number of keys in a bucket would be $\lceil n/N \rceil$ at most, which is $O(1)$ if n is $O(N)$.

With separate chaining, as λ gets close to 1, the probability of a collision also approaches 1, which adds overhead to our operations, since we must revert to linear-time, sequence-based methods in buckets that have collisions. Of course, in the worst case, a poor hash function could map every item to the same bucket, which would result in linear-time performance for all dictionary operations, but this is unlikely.

With open addressing, on the other hand, as the load factor λ grows beyond 0.5 and starts approaching 1, clusters of items in the bucket array start to grow as well. These clusters cause the probing strategies to "bounce around" the bucket array for a considerable amount of time before they can finish. At the limit, when λ is close to 1, all dictionary operations have linear expected running times, since, in this case, we expect to encounter a linear number of occupied buckets before finding one of the few remaining empty cells.

Rehashing into a New Table

Keeping the load factor below a certain threshold is vital for open addressing schemes and is also of concern to the separate chaining method. If the load factor of a hash table goes significantly above a specified threshold, then it is common to require that the table be resized (to regain the specified load factor) and all the objects inserted into this new resized table. Indeed, if we let our hash table become full, some implementations, including the example given in Code Fragment 8.3, may crash. When rehashing to a new table, it is a good requirement that the new array's size be at least double the previous size. Once we have allocated this new bucket array, we must define a new hash function to go with it (possibly computing new parameters, as in the MAD method). Given this new hash function, we then reinsert every item from the old array into the new array using this new hash function. This process is known as **rehashing**.

Even with periodic rehashing, a hash table is an efficient means of implementing an unordered dictionary. Indeed, if we always double the size of the table with each rehashing operation, then we can amortize the cost of rehashing all the elements in the table against the time used to insert them in the first place. The analysis of this rehashing process is similar to that used to analyze vector growth. (See Section 5.1.3.) Each rehashing will generally scatter the elements throughout the new bucket array. Thus, a hash table is a practical and effective implementation for an unordered dictionary

8.2.7 A C++ Hash Table Implementation

We present major portions of the LinearProbeHashTable class, which implements the dictionary ADT, using a hash table with linear probing to resolve collisions. This code fragment includes the main dictionary functions (we leave the rest to Exercise R-8.10).

The main data structure is a bucket array *A* of hash table entries. Each entry contains a key-element pair. A local structure called HashEntry is defined to hold this information. It is shown in Code Fragment 8.1. Since it is derived from class Item, it inherits the key() and element() functions. This class will be nested in the protected section of LinearProbeHashTable.

```
enum Status { EMPTY, USED, FREE };            // table entry status

struct HashEntry : public Item<Key, Element> {  // a hash table entry
    Status status;                              // entry status
    HashEntry(const Key& k = Key(),             // constructor
        const Element& e = Element(),
        Status st = EMPTY) : Item<Key,Element>(k, e), status(st) { }
};
typedef HashEntry* EntryPtr;                   // pointer to an entry
```

Code Fragment 8.1: The HashEntry structure, which makes up the elements of the bucket array for the class LinearProbeHashTable (see Code Fragment 8.3).

In order to know which entries hold items, we also store the *status* of each entry. We define an enumeration called Status, which has three possible values:

EMPTY: No item has ever been stored here.

USED: An item is currently being stored here.

FREE: This entry is "deactivated," that is, an element was stored here but has since been removed.

In order to specify the results of the find() operation, it is necessary to provide a Position class definition. Its only data member is a pointer to the corresponding entry in the bucket array A. It is shown in Code Fragment 8.2.

```
class Position {                          // a hash table position
private:
   EntryPtr node;                         // pointer to entry
public:
   Position(EntryPtr n = NULL)            // constructor
      { node = n; }
   Element& element()                     // get element
      { return node->element(); }
   const Key& key() const                 // get key
      { return node->key(); }
   bool isNull() const                    // a null position?
      { return node == NULL; }
   friend LinearProbeHashTable;           // give hash table access
};
```

Code Fragment 8.2: A Position class, which is used to refer to items in the hash table. This class is nested in the public section of LinearProbeHashTable (see Code Fragment 8.3).

The main portion of class LinearProveHashTable is presented in Code Fragment 8.3. The member variables consist of the size n of the dictionary, the capacity N of the bucket array, the bucket array A itself, and the hash comparator, hash. The capacity N is set based on a value given to the constructor. The hash comparator provides the hash function hashValue() and serves an as equality tester by supporting function isEqualTo().

The important work of the class is done by two utility functions, finder() and inserter(). They are responsible for searching the bucket array, and both return a pointer to an entry in the array. Their definitions are given in Code Fragment 8.4. Because they are out-of-class function definitions, all types must be fully qualified, and hence, each definition is preceded by an intimidating preamble of declarations.

Both functions start by invoking the hashValue() function of the hash comparator in order to compute the hash index of the key. The finder() function searches until finding the key (success), finding an empty entry (failure), or returning to the start (failure). If the key is found, a pointer to this table entry is returned, and otherwise a null pointer is returned. The function inserter() searches until finding an unused entry, and then stores the item here and returns a pointer to this entry. If no unused entry exists, it fails and returns a null pointer.

```
template <typename Key, typename Element, typename HashCmp>
class LinearProbeHashTable {
protected:                                              // local types
  // ... (insert HashEntry here)
public:                                                 // public types
  // ... (insert Position here)
private:                                                // member data
  int          n, N;                                    // size and capacity
  EntryPtr     A;                                       // array of entries
  HashCmp      hash;                                     // the hash comparator
protected:                                              // local utilities
  EntryPtr finder(const Key& key) const;                // search utility
  EntryPtr inserter(const Key& key, const Element& e);  // insert utility
public:
  LinearProbeHashTable(int capacity = 100)              // constructor
      : n(0), N(capacity), hash() { A = new HashEntry[N]; }
  int size() const        { return n; }                 // size of dictionary
  bool isEmpty() const    { return (n == 0); }          // empty dictionary?

  Position find(const Key& key) const                   // find a key
    { return Position(finder(key)); }

  void insertItem(const Key& key, const Element& element)
      throw(HashTableFullException) {                   // insert (key,element)
    EntryPtr e = inserter(key, element);                // attempt to insert
    if (e == NULL)                                       // failure
      throw HashTableFullException("Insertion into full hash table");
  }
  void removeElement(const Key& key)                    // remove using key
      throw(NonexistentElementException) {
    EntryPtr e = finder(key);                            // look up key
    if (e == NULL)                                       // not found?
      throw NonexistentElementException("Key not found");
    e->status = FREE;                                    // mark entry as free
    n--;                                                 // decrease size
  }
  // ... (some functions omitted)
};
```

Code Fragment 8.3: The principal portion of class LinearProbeHashTable, implementing the dictionary ADT using a hash table with linear probing to resolve collisions. (Also, see Code Fragments 8.1, 8.2, and 8.4.)

```
template <typename Key, typename Element, typename HashCmp>
LinearProbeHashTable<Key, Element, HashCmp>::EntryPtr
LinearProbeHashTable<Key, Element, HashCmp>::
finder(const Key& key) const {                      // search utility
    int i = hash.hashValue(key) % N;                // get hash index
    int start = i;                                  // starting point
    do {
        if (A[i].status == EMPTY) return NULL;      // item is not found
        if (A[i].status == USED &&
              hash.isEqualTo(A[i].key(), key))       // found it
            return &A[i];                           // return with success
        i = (i + 1) % N;                            // try next slot
    } while (i != start);                           // until back to start
    return NULL;                                    // return with failure
}

template <typename Key, typename Element, typename HashCmp>
LinearProbeHashTable<Key, Element, HashCmp>::EntryPtr
LinearProbeHashTable<Key, Element, HashCmp>::
inserter(const Key& key, const Element& element) { // insert utility
    int i = hash.hashValue(key) % N;                // get hash index
    int start = i;                                  // starting point
    do {
        if (A[i].status != USED) {                  // slot is available?
            A[i] = HashEntry(key, element, USED);   // store it here
            n++;                                    // increase size
            return &A[i];                           // return with success
        }
        i = (i + 1) % N;                            // try next slot
    } while (i != start);                           // until back to start
    return NULL;                                    // return with failure
}
```

Code Fragment 8.4: Definitions of the utility functions finder() and inserter(), which are used by class LinearProbeHashTable. (See Code Fragment 8.3.) The function finder(k) searches for an item with key k in the hash table. If found, it returns the index of the item in the hash table and otherwise returns a null pointer. The function inserter(k, e), attempts to insert the item (k, e) in the hash table. If successful, it returns a pointer to where the item was stored, and otherwise it returns a null pointer.

8.3 Ordered Dictionaries

In an ordered dictionary, we wish to perform the usual dictionary operations, but also maintain an order relation for the keys in our dictionary.

8.3.1 The Ordered Dictionary ADT

We can use a comparator to provide the order relation among keys, and, as we will see, use of such an ordering helps to efficiently implement the dictionary ADT. In addition, an ordered dictionary also supports the following functions beyond those included in the generic dictionary ADT:

closestBefore(k): Return the position of an item with the largest key less than or equal to k.
Input: Object (key); *Output:* Position.

closestAfter(k): Return the position of an item with smallest key greater than or equal to k.
Input: Object (key); *Output:* Position.

Each of these functions returns a null position if no item satisfies the query.

The ordered nature of the above operations makes the use of a log file or a hash table inappropriate for the dictionary, for neither of these data structures maintains any ordering of the keys in the dictionary. Indeed, hash tables achieve their best performance when their keys are distributed at random. Thus, we should consider new dictionary implementations when dealing with ordered dictionaries.

8.3.2 Look-Up Tables

If a dictionary D is ordered, we can store its items in a vector S by nondecreasing order of the keys. (See Figure 8.7.) We specify that S is a vector, rather than a general sequence, for the ordering of the keys in the vector S allows for faster searching than would be possible had S been, say, a linked list. We refer to this ordered vector implementation of a dictionary D as a ***look-up table***.

0	1	2	3	4	5	6	7	8	9	10
4	6	9	12	15	16	18	28	34		

Figure 8.7: Realization of a dictionary D by means of a look-up table. We show only the keys for this dictionary, so as to highlight its ordered vector implementation.

The space requirement of the look-up table is $O(n)$, which is similar to the log file, assuming we grow and shrink the array supporting the vector S to keep the size of this array proportional to the number of items in S. Unlike a log file, however, performing updates in a look-up table takes a considerable amount of time. In particular, performing the insertItem(k,e) operation in a look-up table requires $O(n)$ time in the worst case, since we need to shift up all the items in the vector with key greater than k to make room for the new item (k,e). Similar observations apply to operations removeElement(k) and removeAllElements(k), since it takes $O(n)$ time in the worst case to shift down all the items in the vector with key greater than k to close the "hole" left by the removed item (or items). The look-up table implementation is therefore inferior to the log file in terms of the worst-case running times of the dictionary update operations. Nevertheless, we can perform the operations find() and findAll() much faster in a look-up table.

8.3.3 Binary Search

A significant advantage of using an array-based vector S to implement an ordered dictionary D with n items is that accessing an element of S by its ***rank*** takes $O(1)$ time. We recall from Section 5.1 that the rank of an element in a vector is the number of elements preceding it. Thus, the first element in S has rank 0, and the last element has rank $n-1$.

The elements in S are the items of dictionary D, and since S is ordered, the item at rank i has a key no smaller than keys of the items at ranks $0,\ldots,i-1$, and no larger than keys of the items at ranks $i+1,\ldots,n-1$. This observation allows us to quickly "home in" on a search key k using a variant of the children's game "high-low." We call an item I of D a ***candidate*** if, at the current stage of the search, we cannot rule out that I has key equal to k. The algorithm maintains two parameters, low and high, such that all the candidate items have rank at least low and at most high in S. Initially, low $= 0$ and high $= n-1$, and we let key(i) denote the key at rank i, which has elem(i) as its element. We then compare k to the key of the median candidate, that is, the item with rank

$$\text{mid} = \lfloor(\text{low} + \text{high})/2\rfloor.$$

We consider three cases:

- If $k =$ key(mid), then we have found the item we were looking for, and the search terminates successfully returning Position(mid).
- If $k <$ key(mid), then we recurse on the first half of the vector, that is, on the range of ranks from low to mid -1.
- If $k >$ key(mid), we recurse on the range of ranks from mid $+1$ to high.

The above search method is called ***binary search***, and is given in pseudo-code in Code Fragment 8.5. Operation find(k), on an n-item dictionary implemented with vector S, consists of calling BinarySearch($S, k, 0, n-1$).

Algorithm BinarySearch(S, k, low, high):

   Input: An ordered vector S storing n items, whose keys are accessed with function key(i) and whose elements are accessed with function elem(i), a search key k, and integers low and high

   Output: The position of an element of S with key k and rank between low and high, if such an element exists, and otherwise a null position.

   if low $>$ high **then**
       return Position(NULL)
   else
       mid $\leftarrow \lfloor$(low $+$ high)$/2\rfloor$
       if $k =$ key(mid) **then**
           return Position(mid)
       else if $k <$ key(mid) **then**
           return BinarySearch(S, k, low, mid $- 1$)
       else
           return BinarySearch(S, k, mid $+ 1$, high)

        Code Fragment 8.5: Binary search in an ordered vector.

We illustrate the binary search algorithm in Figure 8.8.

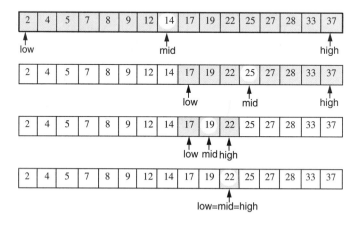

Figure 8.8: Example of a binary search to perform operation find(22), in a dictionary with integer keys, implemented with an array-based ordered vector. For simplicity, we show the keys stored in the dictionary but not the elements.

Analysis of Binary Search

Considering the running time of binary search, we observe that a constant number of primitive operations are executed at each recursive call of the BinarySearch() function. Hence, the running time is proportional to the number of recursive calls performed. A crucial fact is that, with each recursive call, the number of candidate items still to be searched in the sequence S is given by the value

$$\text{high} - \text{low} + 1.$$

Moreover, the number of remaining candidates is reduced by at least one half with each recursive call. Specifically, from the definition of mid, the number of remaining candidates is either

$$(\text{mid} - 1) - \text{low} + 1 \;=\; \left\lfloor \frac{\text{low} + \text{high}}{2} \right\rfloor - \text{low}$$
$$\leq \;\frac{\text{high} - \text{low} + 1}{2}$$

or

$$\text{high} - (\text{mid} + 1) + 1 \;=\; \text{high} - \left\lfloor \frac{\text{low} + \text{high}}{2} \right\rfloor$$
$$\leq \;\frac{\text{high} - \text{low} + 1}{2}.$$

Initially, the number of candidate items is n; after the first call to BinarySearch(), it is at most $n/2$; after the second call, it is at most $n/4$; and so on. In general, after the ith call to BinarySearch(), the number of candidate items remaining is at most $n/2^i$. In the worst case (unsuccessful search), the recursive calls stop when there are no more candidate items. Hence, the maximum number of recursive calls performed, is the smallest integer m, such that

$$n/2^m < 1.$$

In other words (recalling that we omit a logarithm's base when it is 2), $m \geq \log n$. Thus, we have

$$m = \lfloor \log n \rfloor + 1,$$

which implies that BinarySearch($S, k, 0, n - 1$), and hence function find() runs in $O(\log n)$ time.

Using Look-Up Tables as Ordered Dictionaries

There is a simple variation of binary search that performs findAll(k) in $O(\log n + s)$ time, where s is the number of elements in the iterator returned. The details are left as an exercise (C-8.4).

Thus, we can use a look-up table to perform fast dictionary searches, but using a look-up table for lots of dictionary updates would take a considerable amount of time. For this reason, the primary application for look-up tables is in situations where we expect few updates to the dictionary but many searches. Such a situation could arise, for example, in an ordered list of English words we use to order entries in an encyclopedia or help file.

Comparing Simple Ordered Dictionary Implementations

Table 8.2 compares the running times of the functions of a dictionary realized by either a log file or a look-up table. A log file allows for fast insertions but slow searches and removals, whereas a look-up table allows for fast searches but slow insertions and removals. Incidentally, although we do not explicitly discuss it, we note that a sorted sequence implemented with a doubly linked list would be slow in performing almost all the dictionary operations. (See Exercise R-8.1.)

Function	Log File	Look-Up Table
size, isEmpty	$O(1)$	$O(1)$
keys, elements	$O(n)$	$O(n)$
find	$O(n)$	$O(\log n)$
findAll	$\Theta(n)$	$O(\log n + s)$
insertItem	$O(1)$	$O(n)$
removeElement	$O(n)$	$O(n)$
removeAllElements	$\Theta(n)$	$O(n)$

Table 8.2: Comparison of the running times of the functions of a dictionary realized by means of a log file or a look-up table, which can also be viewed as implementations using an unsorted or sorted sequence, respectively. We denote the number of items in the dictionary at the time a function is executed with n, and the size of the iterator returned by operations findAll() and removeAllElements() with s.

8.3.4 The C++ Standard Template Library map Class

STL provides an ordered dictionary class, called map. The declaration map<K,E> defines a map whose keys are of type K and whose elements are of type E. In order to refer to its items, a map defines its own iterator type, map<K,E>::iterator. An iterator can be used to refer to an individual item or to an entire sequence of items; hence, it serves both the roles of a position and position iterator in our dictionary ADT. The key and element values of each item are given the rather uninformative names of "first" and "second," respectively. Thus, given an iterator p, the associated key is p->first, the associated element is accessed by p->second, and p++ advances the iterator to the item with the next higher key value.

The most obvious difference between our dictionary ADT and the STL map is that insertion is not typically performed by an insert() function (although such a function exists), but instead, through the subscript operator. This operator provides a single mechanism for inserting, replacing, and finding elements. A key-element pair (k, e) can be inserted (or replaced) in a map object M with the assignment "M[k]=e." The element associated with key k can be "found" by reading the value of M[k]. If the key k is not in the map, then it is automatically inserted, and the default value (typically 0) is used as the associated element value.

In addition to the subscript operator, the STL map class provides a number of member functions. Some of these are given in Table 8.3, and a short example is shown below, which creates a map with a few items and then prints these items.

```
map<string, int> Enroll;           // a (string,int) map
Enroll["ECON 101"]  = 324;         // insert("ECON 101", 324)
Enroll["ECON 101"]  = 330;         // replace "ECON 101" with 330
Enroll["CS 220"]    = 75;          // insert("CS 220", 75)
map<string, int>::iterator p;      // an iterator to the map
for (p = Enroll.begin(); p != Enroll.end(); p++) {
    cout << p->first << ' ' << p->second << '\n';
}
```

Function	Description
size()	Return the size of the map
empty()	Return a Boolean indicating whether the map is empty
erase(k)	Remove the element with key k
erase(p)	Remove the element pointed to by iterator p
find(k)	Find the element with key k and return an iterator to this item
begin()	Return an iterator pointing to the beginning of the map
end()	Return an iterator pointing just past the end of the map

Table 8.3: Some of the functions supported by the STL class map.

8.4 Skip Lists

An interesting data structure for efficiently realizing the ordered dictionary ADT is the ***skip list***. This data structure makes random choices in arranging the items in such a way that search and update times are $O(\log n)$ ***on average***, where n is the number of items in the dictionary. Interestingly, the notion of average time complexity used here does not depend on a probability distribution of the keys in the input. Instead, it depends on the use of a random-number generator in the implementation of the insertions to help decide where to place the new items. The running time is averaged over all possible outcomes of the random numbers used when inserting items.

Because they are used extensively in computer games, cryptography, and computer simulations, functions that generate numbers that can be viewed as random numbers are built into most modern computers. Some functions, called ***pseudo-random number generators***, generate random-like numbers deterministically, starting with an initial number called a ***seed***. Other methods use hardware devices to extract "true" random numbers from nature. In any case, we will assume that our computer has access to numbers that are sufficiently random for our analysis. For example, the C++ library function rand() generates a random integer in the range from 0 to RAND_MAX (which is defined in the standard include file <cstdlib>). A random number of type double in the range 0 to 1 can be generated as follows.

```
double r = double(rand()) / double(RAND_MAX);
```

The main advantage of using ***randomization*** in data structure and algorithm design is that the structures and functions that result are usually simple and efficient. We can devise a simple randomized data structure, called the skip list, which has the same logarithmic time bounds for searching as is achieved by the binary searching algorithm. Nevertheless, the bounds are ***expected*** for the skip list, while they are ***worst-case*** bounds for binary searching in a look-up table. On the other hand, skip lists are much faster than look-up tables for dictionary updates.

A ***skip list*** S for dictionary D consists of a series of lists $\{S_0, S_1, \ldots, S_h\}$. Each list S_i stores a subset of the items of D sorted by a nondecreasing key plus items with two special keys, denoted $-\infty$ and $+\infty$, where $-\infty$ is smaller than every possible key that can be inserted in D, and $+\infty$ is larger than every possible key that can be inserted in D. In addition, the lists in S satisfy the following:

- List S_0 contains every item of D (plus the items with keys $-\infty$ and $+\infty$).
- For $i = 1, \ldots, h-1$, list S_i contains (in addition to $-\infty$ and $+\infty$) a randomly generated subset of the items in list S_{i-1}.
- List S_h contains only $-\infty$ and $+\infty$.

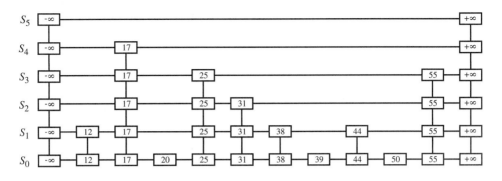

Figure 8.9: Example of a skip list.

An example skip list is shown in Figure 8.9. It is customary to visualize a skip list S with list S_0 at the bottom and lists $S_1, \ldots, S_h$ above it. Also, we refer to h as the **height** of skip list S.

Intuitively, the lists are set up so that S_{i+1} contains more or less every other item in S_i. As we shall see in the details of the insertion function, the items in S_{i+1} are chosen at random from the items in S_i by picking each item from S_i to also be in S_{i+1} with probability $1/2$. That is, in essence, we "flip a coin" for each item in S_i and place that item in S_{i+1} if the coin comes up "heads." Thus, we expect S_1 to have about $n/2$ items, S_2 to have about $n/4$ items, and, in general, S_i to have about $n/2^i$ items. In other words, we expect the height h of S to be about $\log n$. The halving of the number of items from one list to the next is not enforced as an explicit property of skip lists, however. Instead, randomization is used.

Using the position abstraction used for lists and trees, we view a skip list as a two-dimensional collection of positions arranged horizontally into **levels** and vertically into **towers**. Each level is a list S_i and each tower contains positions storing the same item across consecutive lists. The positions in a skip list can be traversed using the following operations:

after(p): Return the position following p on the same level.

before(p): Return the position preceding p on the same level.

below(p): Return the position below p in the same tower.

above(p): Return the position above p in the same tower.

We conventionally assume that the above operations return a null position if the position requested does not exist. Without going into the details, we note that we can easily implement a skip list by means of a linked structure, such that the above traversal functions each take $O(1)$ time, given a skip-list position p. Such a linked structure is essentially a collection of h doubly linked lists aligned at towers, which are also doubly linked lists.

8.4.1 Searching

The skip list structure allows for simple dictionary search algorithms. In fact, all of the skip list search algorithms are based on an elegant SkipSearch() function that takes a key k and finds the item in a skip list S with the largest key (which is possibly $-\infty$) that is less than or equal to k . Suppose we are given such a key k. We begin the SkipSearch function by setting a position variable p to the top-most, left position in the skip list S. That is, p is set to the position of the special item with key $-\infty$ in S_h. We then perform the following steps (see Figure 8.10):

1. If S.below(p) is null, then the search terminates—we are ***at the bottom*** and have located the largest item in S with key less than or equal to the search key k. Otherwise, we ***drop down*** to the next lower level in the present tower by setting $p \leftarrow S$.below(p).

2. Starting at position p, we move p forward until it is at the right-most position on the present level, such that key$(p) \leq k$. We call this the ***scan forward*** step. Note that such a position always exists, since each level contains the special keys $+\infty$ and $-\infty$. In fact, after we perform the scan forward for this level, p may remain where it started. In any case, we then repeat the previous step.

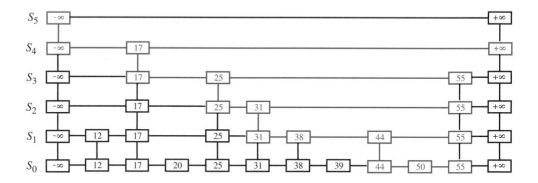

Figure 8.10: Example of a search in a skip list. The positions visited when searching for key 50 are highlighted in blue.

We give a pseudo-code description of the skip-list search algorithm, SkipSearch, in Code Fragment 8.6. Given this method, it is now easy to implement the operation find(k)—we simply perform $p \leftarrow$ SkipSearch(k) and test whether or not key$(p) = k$. If these two keys are equal, we return the position p; otherwise, we return a null position.

Algorithm SkipSearch(*k*):

    Input: A search key *k*

    Output: Position *p* in *S*, such that the item at *p* has the largest key less than or equal to *k*

    Let *p* be the top-most, left position of *S* (which should have at least 2 levels).

    while below(*p*) $\neq$ **null do**

        p $\leftarrow$ below(*p*)   {drop down}

        while key(after(*p*)) $\leq k$ **do**

            Let *p* $\leftarrow$ after(*p*)   {scan forward}

    return *p*

Code Fragment 8.6: Algorithm for searching in a skip list *S*.

As it turns out, the expected running time of algorithm SkipSearch() is $O(\log n)$. We postpone the justification of this fact, however, until Section 8.4.3.

8.4.2 Update Operations

Another feature of the skip list data structure is that, besides having an elegant search algorithm, it also provides simple algorithms for dictionary updates.

Insertion

The insertion algorithm for skip lists uses randomization to decide how many references to the new item (k, e) should be added to the skip list. We begin the insertion of a new item (k, e) into a skip list by performing a SkipSearch(*k*) operation. This gives us the position *p* of the bottom-level item with the largest key less than or equal to *k* (note that *p* may be the position of the special item with key $-\infty$). We then insert (k, e) in this bottom-level list immediately after position *p*. After inserting the new item at this level, we "flip" a coin. That is, we call a function rand(), which we assume returns a random number between 0 and 1, and if that number is less than $1/2$, then we consider the flip to have come up "heads"; otherwise, we consider the flip to have come up "tails." If the flip comes up tails, then we stop here. If the flip comes up heads, on the other hand, then we backtrack to the previous (next higher) level and insert (k, e) in this level at the appropriate position. We again flip a coin; if it comes up heads, we go to the next higher level and repeat. Thus, we continue to insert the new item (k, e) in lists until we finally get a flip that comes up tails. We link together all the references to the new item (k, e) created in this process to create the ***tower*** for (k, e). Finally, we return a position that points to the item at the bottom level.

We give the pseudo-code for this insertion algorithm for a skip list S in Code Fragment 8.7, and we illustrate this algorithm in Figure 8.11. Our insertion algorithm uses an operation insertAfterAbove$(p, q, (k, e))$ that inserts a position storing the item (k, e) after position p (on the same level as p) and above position q, returning the position r of the new item (and setting internal pointers so that after(), before(), above(), and below() functions will work correctly for p, q, and r).

Algorithm SkipInsert(k, e):
    Input: Item (k, e)
    Output: Position

    $p \leftarrow$ SkipSearch(k)
    $q \leftarrow$ insertAfterAbove$(p, \mathbf{null}, (k, e))$ {we are at the bottom level}
    $r =$ Position(q)
    while rand$() < 1/2$ **do**
        while above$(p) = \mathbf{null}$ **do**
            $p \leftarrow$ before(p) {scan backward}
        $p \leftarrow$ above(p) {jump up to higher level}
        $q \leftarrow$ insertAfterAbove$(p, q, (k, e))$ {insert new item}
    return r

Code Fragment 8.7: Insertion in a skip list, assuming rand() returns a random number between 0 and 1, and we never insert past the top level.

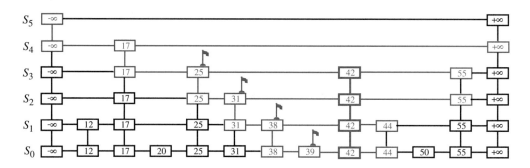

Figure 8.11: Insertion of an element with key 42 into the skip list of Figure 8.9. We assume that the random "coin flips" for the new item came up heads three times in a row, followed by tails. The positions visited are highlighted in blue. The positions inserted to hold the new item are drawn with thick lines, and the positions preceding them are flagged.

The expected running time of the insertion algorithm is $O(\log n)$, which we show in Section 8.4.3.

Removal

Like the search and insertion algorithms, the removal algorithm for a skip list S is quite simple. In fact, it is even easier than the insertion algorithm. Namely, to perform a removeElement(k) operation, we begin by performing a search for the given key k. If a position p with key k is not found, then a NonexistentElementException is thrown. Otherwise, if a position p with key k is found (on the bottom level), then we remove all the positions above p, which are easily accessed by using above() operations to climb up the tower of this item in S starting at position p. The removal algorithm is illustrated in Figure 8.12 and a detailed description of it is left as an exercise (R-8.17). As we show in the next subsection, the running time for removal in a skip list is expected to be $O(\log n)$.

Before we give this analysis, however, there are some minor improvements to the skip list data structure we would like to discuss. First, we do not actually need to store pointers to items at the levels of the skip list above 0, because all that is needed at these levels are pointers to keys. Second, we do not actually need the above() method. In fact, we do not need the before() function either. We can perform item insertion and removal in strictly a top-down, scan-forward fashion, thus saving space for "up" and "prev" pointers. We explore the details of this optimization in an exercise (C-8.11). Neither of these optimizations improve the asymptotic performance of skip lists by more than a constant factor, but these improvements can, nevertheless, be meaningful in practice. In fact, experimental evidence suggests that optimized skip lists can be faster in practice than AVL trees and other balanced search trees, which are discussed in Chapter 9.

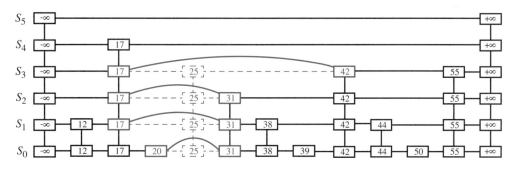

Figure 8.12: Removal of the item with key 25 from the skip list of Figure 8.11. The positions visited after the search for the position of S_0 holding the item are highlighted in blue. The positions removed are drawn with dashed lines.

The expected running time of the removal algorithm is $O(\log n)$, which we show in Section 8.4.3.

Maintaining the Top-most Level

A skip-list S must maintain a pointer to the top-most, left position in S as a member variable, and must have a policy for any insertion that wishes to continue inserting a new item past the top level of S. There are two possible courses of action we can take, both of which have their merits.

One possibility, called ***top-level capping***, is to restrict the top level, h, to be kept at some fixed value that is a function of n, the number of elements currently in the dictionary (from the analysis we will see that $h = \max\{10, 2\lceil \log n \rceil\}$ is a reasonable choice, and picking $h = 3\lceil \log n \rceil$ is even safer). Implementing this choice means that we must modify the insertion algorithm to stop inserting a new item once we reach the top-most level (unless $\lceil \log n \rceil < \lceil \log(n+1) \rceil$, in which case we can now go at least one more level, since the bound on the height is increasing).

Another possibility, called ***top-level freedom***, is to let an insertion continue inserting a new element as long as it keeps getting heads returned from the random number generator. As we show in the analysis of skip lists, the probability that an insertion will go to a level that is more than $O(\log n)$ is very low, so this design choice should also work.

Either choice will still result in our being able to perform element search, insertion, and removal in expected $O(\log n)$ time, however, which we show next.

8.4.3 A Probabilistic Analysis of Skip Lists ⋆

As we have shown above, skip lists provide a simple implementation of an ordered dictionary. In terms of worst-case performance, however, skip lists are not a superior data structure. In fact, if we allow top-level freedom, then the insertion algorithm can go into what is almost an infinite loop (it is not actually an infinite loop, however, since the probability of having a fair coin repeatedly come up heads forever is 0). Moreover, we cannot infinitely add elements to a list without eventually running out of memory. In any case, if we terminate item insertion at the highest level h, then the ***worst-case*** running time for performing the find(), insertItem(), and removeElement() operations in a skip list S with n items and height h is $O(n+h)$. This worst-case performance occurs when the tower of every item reaches level $h-1$, where h is the height of S. However, this event has very low probability. Judging from this worst case, we might conclude that the skip list structure is strictly inferior to the other dictionary implementations discussed earlier in this chapter. But this would not be a fair analysis, for this worst-case behavior is a gross overestimate.

⋆We use a star (⋆) to indicate sections containing material more advanced than the material in the rest of the chapter; this material can be considered optional in a first reading.

A Simplified Analysis

Because the insertion step involves randomization, an honest analysis of skip lists involves a bit of probability. At first, this might seem like a major undertaking, for a complete and thorough probabilistic analysis could require deep mathematics (and, indeed, there are several such deep analyses that have appeared in data structure and algorithm literature). Fortunately, such an analysis is not necessary to understand the expected asymptotic behavior of skip lists. The informal and intuitive probabilistic analysis we give here uses only basic concepts of probability theory.

Bounding the Height of a Skip List

Let us begin by determining the expected value of the height h of S (assuming that we do not terminate insertions early). The probability that a given item is stored in a position at level i is equal to the probability of getting i consecutive heads when flipping a coin, that is, this probability is $1/2^i$. Hence, the probability P_i that level i has at least one item is at most

$$P_i \le \frac{n}{2^i},$$

for the probability that any one of n different events occurs is, at most, the sum of the probabilities that each occurs.

The probability that the height h of S is larger than i is equal to the probability that level i has at least one item, that is, it is no more than P_i. This means that h is larger than, say, $3\log n$ with probability at most

$$
\begin{aligned}
P_{3\log n} &\le \frac{n}{2^{3\log n}} \\
&= \frac{n}{n^3} = \frac{1}{n^2}.
\end{aligned}
$$

More generally, given a constant $c > 1$, h is larger than $c\log n$ with probability at most $1/n^{c-1}$. That is, the probability that h is smaller than or equal to $c\log n$ is at least $1 - 1/n^{c-1}$. Thus, with high probability, the height h of S is $O(\log n)$.

Bounding the Search Time on Each Level

Consider the running time of a search in skip list S, and recall that such a search involves two nested **while** loops. The inner loop performs a scan forward on a level of S as long as the next key is no greater than the search key k, and the outer loop drops down to the next level and repeats the scan forward iteration. Since the height h of S is $O(\log n)$ with high probability, the number of drop-down steps is $O(\log n)$ with high probability.

So we have yet to bound the number of scan-forward steps we make. Let n_i be the number of keys examined while scanning forward at level i. Observe that, after the key at the starting position, each additional key examined in a scan-forward at level i cannot also belong to level $i+1$. If any of these items were on the previous level, we would have encountered them in the previous scan-forward step. Thus, the probability that any key is counted in n_i is $1/2$. Therefore, the expected value of n_i is exactly equal to the expected number of times we must flip a fair coin before it comes up heads. This expected value is 2. Hence, the expected amount of time spent scanning forward at any level i is $O(1)$. Since S has $O(\log n)$ levels with high probability, a search in S takes the expected time $O(\log n)$. By a similar analysis, we can show that the expected running time of an insertion or a removal is $O(\log n)$.

Space Usage

Finally, let us turn to the space requirement of a skip list S. As we observed above, the expected number of items at level i is $n/2^i$, which means that the expected total number of items in S is

$$\sum_{i=0}^{h} \frac{n}{2^i} = n \sum_{i=0}^{h} \frac{1}{2^i}$$

$$< 2n.$$

Hence, the expected space requirement of S is $O(n)$.

Performance Summary

Table 8.4 summarizes the performance of a dictionary realized by a skip list.

Operation	Time
size, isEmpty	$O(1)$
keys, elements	$O(n)$
find, insertItem, removeElement	$O(\log n)$ (expected)
findAll, removeAllElements	$O(\log n + s)$ (expected)

Table 8.4: Performance of a dictionary implemented with a skip list. We denote the number of items in the dictionary at the time the operation is performed with n, and the size of the iterator returned by operations findAll() and removeAllElements() with s. The expected space requirement is $O(n)$.

8.5　Locator-Based Dictionary Functions ⋆

As mentioned in Section 8.1.1, one disadvantage of our dictionary ADT is that, as elements are inserted or removed from the dictionary, objects may be moved, and as a result, a position that refers to some element prior to an insertion or removal operation may refer to an entirely different element after the operation. In order to avoid this problem, we need to define a dictionary ADT that is based on locators rather than positions. Recall from Section 7.4 that a Locator object is a generalization of a Position object for use in key-based containers. Unlike a position, which is associated with a particular node of the structure, a locator "sticks" to the associated key-element pair, even if it is moved around in the data structure. The operations of a locator-based dictionary ADT differ only in that operations that have returned an object of type Position, instead return an object of type Locator.

Dictionaries use keys as the primary means of accessing their elements, but we can define the following additional dictionary functions that make use of locators.

first(): Return a locator to an item with smallest key in D.
Input: None; *Output:* Locator.

last(): Return a locator to an item with largest key in D.
Input: None; *Output:* Locator.

locFind(k): If D contains an item with key equal to k, then return a locator to the position of such an item. If not, a null locator is returned.
Input: Object (key); *Output:* Locator.

locFindAll(k): Return an iterator of locators for all items whose key equals k.
Input: Object (key); *Output:* Iterator (of Locators).

locInsertItem(k, e): Insert an item with element e and key k into D, and return a locator to the inserted item.
Input: Objects k (key) and e (element); *Output:* Locator.

before(p): Return a locator to an item whose key is the largest key in D smaller than p.key(); return a null locator if p is the smallest key in D.
Input: Locator; *Output:* Locator.

after(p): Return a locator to an item whose key is the smallest key in D larger than p.key(); return a null locator if p is the largest key in D.
Input: Locator; *Output:* Locator.

In addition to the above operations, we can extend the set of operations for a dictionary D further with other functions that refer to locators. We can add functions akin to those defined for priority queues, such as remove(ℓ) and replaceKey(ℓ, k), with the same meanings as given in Section 7.4.1.

We will discuss implementation of a locator-based dictionary in Section 9.6.

Key-Based Containers

As abstract data types, priority queues and dictionaries share the notions of storing key-element items, support the locator pattern, and have several common functions. They are special cases of a more general ADT called ***key-based container***, which is a container of key-element items that are accessed through key-based functions.

Recalling the notion of an inspectable container (see Section 5.6), we define the following C++ interfaces for key-based containers, whose inheritance diagram is shown in Figure 8.13: InspectableContainer, InspectableKeyBasedContainer, KeyBasedContainer, InspectablePriorityQueue, PriorityQueue, InspectableDictionary, Dictionary, InspectableOrderedDictionary, and OrderedDictionary.

Because Dictionary is derived from InspectableDictionary and provides the ability to remove elements, the Dictionary class could be given the more cumbersome name of InspectableDictionaryWithRemoval. The shorter name Dictionary, however, is the standard name for this abstract data type. A similar remark applies to the PriorityQueue and OrderedDictionary classes.

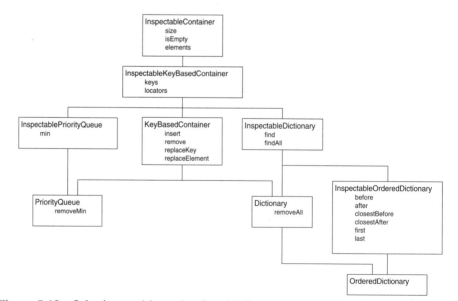

Figure 8.13: Inheritance hierarchy for ADTs representing key-based containers. Only locator-based access and update functions are shown.

8.6 Exercises

Reinforcement

R-8.1 Briefly describe how an ordered sequence implemented as a doubly linked list could be used to implement a dictionary D, and analyze the running time of the fundamental functions of the dictionary ADT.

R-8.2 Assuming that an ordered dictionary D is implemented with an ordered sequence, describe how to implement the following operations in $O(1)$ time:

minElement(): Return the element of an item of D with smallest key.
Input: None; **Output:** Object.

maxElement(): Return the element of an item of D with the largest key.
Input: None; **Output:** Object.

Argue why your implementation of these operations runs in $O(1)$ time, independent of whether the sequence is itself implemented with an array or a linked list.

R-8.3 What would be a good hash code for a vehicle identification that is a string of numbers and letters of the form "9X9XX99X9XX999999," where a "9" represents a digit and an "X" represents a letter?

R-8.4 Draw the 11-item hash table that results from using the hash function

$$h(i) = (2i+5) \bmod 11,$$

to hash the keys 12, 44, 13, 88, 23, 94, 11, 39, 20, 16, and 5, assuming collisions are handled by chaining.

R-8.5 What is the result of the previous exercise, assuming collisions are handled by linear probing?

R-8.6 Show the result of Exercise R-8.4, assuming collisions are handled by quadratic probing, up to the point where the method fails because no empty slot is found.

R-8.7 What is the result of Exercise R-8.4 assuming collisions are handled by double hashing using a secondary hash function $h'(k) = 7 - (k \bmod 7)$?

R-8.8 Give a pseudo-code description of an insertion into a hash table that uses quadratic probing to resolve collisions, assuming we also use the trick of replacing deleted items with a special "deactivated item" object.

R-8.9 Give a C++ code fragment describing the implementation of a function remove(p), which removes the item indicated by locator p from the hash table presented in Code Fragment 8.3.

R-8.10 Give C++ code fragments describing implementations of the findAll(k) and findRemoveAll(k) functions that could be included in the hash table implementation of Code Fragment 8.3.

R-8.11 Explain how to modify the C++ code fragment given in Code Fragment 8.3, so that the implementation uses rehashing instead of crashing when the table overflows. Do not worry about correctly handling locators that refer to entries in table. (See Exercise C-8.6.)

R-8.12 Explain how to modify the C++ code fragment given in Code Fragment 8.3, so that the implementation uses rehashing instead of crashing.

R-8.13 Show the result of rehashing the hash table shown in Figure 8.5, into a table of size 19, using the new hash function $h(k) = 2k \bmod 19$.

R-8.14 What is the worst-case running time for inserting n items into an initially empty hash table, where collisions are resolved by chaining? What if each sequence is stored in sorted order?

R-8.15 Explain why a hash table is not suited to implement the ordered dictionary ADT.

R-8.16 Draw an example skip list that results from performing the following sequence of operations on the skip list shown in Figure 8.12: removeElement(38), insertItem(48,x), insertItem(24,y), removeElement(55). Assume the coin flips for the first insertion yield two heads followed by tails, and those for the second insertion yield three heads followed by tails.

R-8.17 Give a pseudo-code description of the removeElement() dictionary operation, assuming the dictionary is implemented by a skip-list structure.

R-8.18 Give a good upper bound on the probability that there is a nonsentinel element at level $5 \log n$ in an n-element skip list (with top-level freedom).

Creativity

C-8.1 Suppose we are given two ordered dictionaries S and T, each with n items, and that S and T are implemented by means of array-based ordered sequences. Describe an $O(\log^2 n)$-time algorithm for finding the kth smallest key in the union of the keys from S and T (assuming no duplicates).

C-8.2⋆ Give an $O(\log n)$-time solution for the previous problem.

C-8.3 Suppose that the time to do a "probe" during a binary search is no longer constant. Instead, suppose it costs $O(\log m)$ time to probe in the middle of a subarray of size m. What is the running time for performing a binary search on an array of size n in this case?

C-8.4 Design a variation of binary search for performing findAll(k) in an ordered dictionary implemented with an ordered array, and show that it runs in time $O(\log n + s)$, where n is the number of elements in the dictionary and s is the size of the iterator returned.

C-8.5 Suppose that each row of an $n \times n$ array A consists of 1's and 0's, such that, in any row of A, all the 1's come before any 0's in that row. Assuming A is already in memory, describe a function running in $O(n \log n)$ time (not $O(n^2)$ time!) for counting the number of 1's in A.

C-8.6 Explain how to modify the C++ code fragment given in Code Fragment 8.3, so that the implementation uses rehashing instead of crashing when the table overflows. Locators referring to entries in the table should be valid after rehashing. (See Exercise R-8.11.)

C-8.7 Describe the changes that must be made in the pseudo-code descriptions of the fundamental dictionary functions when we implement a dictionary with a hash table, such that collisions are handled via separate chaining, but we add the space optimization that if a bucket stores just a single item, then we simply have the bucket reference that item directly.

C-8.8 The hash table dictionary implementation requires that we find a prime number between a number M and a number $2M$. Implement a function for finding such a prime by using the *sieve algorithm*. In this algorithm, we allocate a $2M$ cell Boolean array A, such that cell i is associated with the integer i. We then initialize the array cells to all be "true" and we "mark off" all the cells that are multiples of 2, 3, 5, 7, and so on. This process can stop after it reaches a number larger than $\sqrt{2M}$. (Hint: Consider a bootstrapping method for finding the primes up to $\sqrt{2M}$.)

C-8.9 Give the pseudo-code description for performing a removal from a hash table that uses linear probing to resolve collisions where we do not use a special marker to represent deleted elements. That is, we must rearrange the contents of the hash table so that it appears that the removed item was never inserted in the first place.

C-8.10 The quadratic probing strategy has a clustering problem that relates to the way it looks for open slots when a collision occurs. Namely, when a collision occurs at bucket $h(k)$, we check $A[(h(k) + f(j)) \bmod N]$, for $f(j) = j^2$, using $j = 1, 2, \ldots, N - 1$.

    a. Show that $f(j) \bmod N$ will assume at most $(N + 1)/2$ distinct values, for N prime, as j ranges from 1 to $N - 1$. As a part of this justification, note that $f(R) = f(N - R)$ for all R.

    b. A better strategy is to choose a prime N, such that N is congruent to 3 modulo 4 and then to check the buckets $A[(h(k) \pm j^2) \bmod N]$ as j ranges from 1 to $(N - 1)/2$, alternating between addition and subtraction. Show that this alternate type of quadratic probing is guaranteed to check every bucket in A.

C-8.11 Show that the functions above(p) and before(p) are not actually needed to efficiently implement a dictionary using a skip list. That is, we can implement item insertion and removal in a skip list using a strictly top-down, scan-forward approach, without ever using the above() or before() functions. (Hint: In the insertion algorithm, first repeatedly flip the coin to determine the level where you should start inserting the new item.)

C-8.12★ Assuming an ordered dictionary D is implemented as an unordered sequence, describe how to implement the following operation:

    locAtRank(r): Return a locator to an item (k, e) of D, such that D has exactly r items with key less than k.
    Input: Integer; *Output:* Locator.

What is the worst-case running time of this function?

C-8.13★ Describe how to implement the locator-based function before(p) as well as the locator-based function locClosestBefore(k) in a dictionary realized using an ordered sequence. Do the same using an unordered sequence implementation. What are the running times of these functions?

C-8.14★ Repeat the previous exercise using a skip list. What are the expected running times of the two locator-based functions in your implementation?

C-8.15 Describe an efficient ordered dictionary structure for storing n elements that have an associated set of $k < n$ keys that come from a total order. That is, the set of keys is smaller than the number of elements. Your structure should perform all the ordered dictionary operations in $O(\log k + s)$ expected time, where s is the number of elements returned.

C-8.16 Describe an efficient unordered dictionary structure for storing n elements that have an associated set of $k < n$ keys that have distinct hash codes. That is, the set of keys is smaller than the number of elements. Your structure should be able to perform all the ordered dictionary operations in $O(1 + s)$ expected time, where s is the number of elements returned.

C-8.17 Describe an efficient data structure for implementing the *bag* ADT, which supports a function add(e), for adding an element e to the bag, and a function remove(), which removes an arbitrary element in the bag. Show that both of these functions can be done in $O(1)$ time.

C-8.18⋆ Describe how to modify the skip list data structure to support the function atRank(i), which returns the position of the element in the "bottom" list S_0 at rank i, for $i \in [0, n-1]$. Show that your implementation of this function runs in $O(\log n)$ expected time.

Projects

P-8.1 Implement a class that realizes the comparator ADT, so as to be able to compare objects that are numeric strings (see Section 11.1). In this case, the character strings should be interpreted as numbers in some base, such as base 2 (binary strings) or base 10 (decimal numbers). In addition to the comparator operations, the StringNumberComparator should support a function setBase(b) that takes a positive integer less than or equal to 10 as the base for the numeric strings to be compared.

P-8.2 Implement the dictionary ADT with a hash table that handles collisions with separate chaining.

P-8.3 Implement the functions of the ordered dictionary ADT using an ordered sequence.

P-8.4 Implement a dictionary that supports locator-based functions by means of an ordered sequence.

P-8.5 Implement the functions of the ordered dictionary ADT using a skip list.

P-8.6 Extend the previous project by providing a graphical animation of the skip list operations. Visualize how items move up the skip list during insertions and are linked out of the skip list during removals. Also, in a search operation, visualize the scan-forward and drop-down

P-8.7 Perform a comparative analysis that studies the collision rates for various hash codes for character strings, such as various polynomial hash codes for different values of the parameter a. Use a hash table to determine collisions, but only count collisions where different strings map to the same hash code (not if they map to the same location in this hash table). Test these hash codes on text files found on the Internet.

P-8.8 Perform a comparative analysis as in the previous exercise but for 10-digit telephone numbers instead of character strings.

Chapter Notes

Interestingly, the binary search algorithm was first published in 1946, but was not published in a fully correct form until 1962. For further discussions on the lessons to be learned from this history, please see the discussions in Knuth's book [59] and the papers by Bentley [12] and Levisse [64].

Skip lists were introduced by Pugh [88]. Our analysis of skip lists is a simplification of a presentation given in the book by Motwani and Raghavan [82]. In addition, our discussion of universal hashing is also a simplification of a presentation given in that book. The reader interested in other probabilistic constructions for supporting the dictionary ADT (including more information about universal hashing) is referred to the text by Motwani and Raghavan [82]. For a more in-depth analysis of skip lists, the reader is referred to papers on skip lists that have appeared in the data structures literature [56, 84, 85]. Exercise C-8.10 was contributed by James Lee.

a tree T is the function that associates with each position p the balance factor of p, defined as the difference between the height of the left subtree of p and the height of the right subtree of p.

Suppose that a tree T satisfies the height-balance property, and so is an AVL tree. The insertion of a new node in T, as described in Section 9.1.2, causes the heights of some nodes of T to increase. In particular, the newly inserted node and some of its ancestors could increase their heights by one. Let us therefore analyze the situation where the height-balance property is violated after performing the simple insertion operation described for binary search trees. Let w be the newly inserted internal node, and let z be the first node we encounter in going up from w toward the root of T such that z is unbalanced (see Figure 9.11a). Also, let y denote the child of z with higher height (and note that y must be an ancestor of w). Finally, let x be the child of y with higher height (there cannot be a tie and node x must be an ancestor of w, or be w itself).

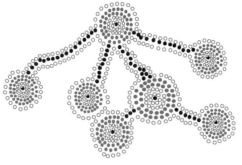

Figure 9.11: An example insertion of an element in an AVL tree that violates the height-balance property. Part (a) illustrates the tree before the insertion, while part (b) illustrates the tree after the insertion. (Continued in Figure 9.12.)

We rebalance the subtree rooted at z by calling the trinode restructuring method, restructure(x). A trinode restructuring temporarily renames the nodes x, y, and z as a, b, and c, so that a precedes b and b precedes c in an inorder traversal of T. There are four possible ways of mapping x, y, and z to a, b, and c, as shown in Figure 9.12, which are unified into one case by our relabeling. The trinode restructuring replaces z with the node called b, makes the children of this node be a and c, and makes the children of a and c be the four previous children of x, y, and z (other than x and y) while maintaining the inorder relationships of all the nodes in T.

People like choices. We like to have different ways of solving the same problem, so that we can explore different trade-offs and efficiencies. This chapter is devoted to the exploration of different ways of solving a problem we discussed in an earlier chapter—the implementation of an ordered dictionary (Chapter 8). Namely, we study several alternative data structures based on trees for realizing ordered dictionaries.

We begin this chapter by discussing binary search trees, in Section 9.1, and how they support a simple tree-based implementation of an ordered dictionary, but do not guarantee efficient worst-case performance. Nevertheless, they form the basis of many tree-based dictionary implementations, and we discuss several in this chapter. One of the classic implementations is the AVL tree, presented in Section 9.2, which is a binary search tree that achieves logarithmic-time search and update operations.

In Section 9.3, we introduce the concept of a multi-way search tree, which is an ordered tree where each internal node can store several items and have several children. A multi-way search tree is a generalization of the binary search tree studied in Section 9.1, and like the binary search tree, it can be specialized into an efficient data structure for dictionaries by imposing additional constraints. One of the advantages of using these multi-way trees is that they often require fewer internal nodes than binary search trees to store items. But, just as with binary search trees, multi-way trees require additional functions to make them efficient for all dictionary operations.

Section 9.4 is devoted to the discussion of $(2,4)$ trees, which are also known as 2-4 trees or 2-3-4 trees. These are multi-way search trees, such that all the external nodes have the same depth, and each node stores 1, 2, or 3 keys and has 2, 3, or 4 children, respectively. The advantage of these trees is that they have algorithms for inserting and removing keys that are simple and intuitive. Update operations rearrange a $(2,4)$ tree by means of natural operations that split and merge "nearby" nodes or transfer keys between them. A $(2,4)$ tree storing n items uses $O(n)$ space and supports searches, insertions, and removals in $O(\log n)$ worst-case time.

We present red-black trees in Section 9.5. These are binary search trees whose nodes are colored "red" and "black" in such a way that the coloring scheme guarantees logarithmic height. There is a simple, yet illuminating, correspondence between red-black and $(2,4)$ trees. Using this correspondence, we motivate and provide intuition for the somewhat more complex algorithms for insertion and removal in red-black trees, which are based on rotations and recolorings. Like an AVL tree, a red-black tree storing n items uses $O(n)$ space and supports searches, insertions, and removals in $O(\log n)$ worst-case time. The advantage that a red-black tree achieves over an AVL tree is that it can be restructured after an insertion or removal with only $O(1)$ rotations (although at the expense of more complex operations).

Finally, in Section 9.7, we discuss external searching, that is, searching in external memory (which will usually be a disk). We introduce a type of multi-way tree, called the B-tree, and we show how it can be used to store and search items so as to minimize the number of input-output (I/O) operations.

There are admittedly quite a few kinds of search trees discussed in this chapter, and we recognize that a reader or instructor with limited time might be interested in studying only selected topics. For this reason, in Figure 9.1, we show the conceptual dependencies between the sections in this chapter. Thus, for example, a reader can focus on binary search trees and then study AVL trees, (2,4) trees (possibly along with red-black trees as well), and/or external searching.

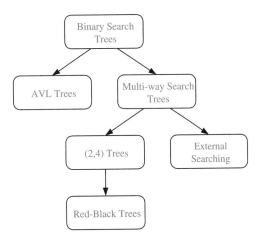

Figure 9.1: Dependencies between the sections in this chapter.

Since all of the data structures discussed in this chapter implement the ordered dictionary ADT, let us briefly review its fundamental operations before we begin.

- find(k): Return the position of an item with key k, and return a null position if no such item exists.
- findAll(k): Return an iterator of positions for all items whose key equals k.
- insertItem(k,e): Insert an item with element e and key k.
- removeElement(k): Remove an item with key equal to k. An error condition occurs if there is no such item.
- removeAllElements(k): Remove all items with key equal to k.

The ordered dictionary ADT also includes the search functions closestBefore(k) and closestAfter(k), which return a position of the nearest item before and after k, respectively. Their performance is similar to that of find().

9.1 Binary Search Trees

Binary trees are an excellent data structure for storing the items of an ordered dictionary. As we have seen in Section 6.3.4, a ***binary search tree*** is a binary tree T, such that each internal node v of T stores an item (k,e) of a dictionary D, and

- Keys stored at nodes in the left subtree of v are less than or equal to k.
- Keys stored at nodes in the right subtree of v are greater than or equal to k.

The external nodes of T do not store any key or element of D, and serve only as "placeholders." We can even allow these external nodes to be NULL or pointers to a special NULL_NODE object, so long as we have a positional wrapper for any external node that identifies the parent of such a node. Nevertheless, to simplify the discussions in this chapter, we assume that external nodes are actual nodes of the tree T; they just happen not to store anything.

No matter how we represent empty external nodes, the important property of a binary search tree is that it should represent an ordered dictionary. That is, a binary search tree should hierarchically represent an ordering of its keys, using relationships between parent and children. Specifically, it is easy to verify that an inorder traversal (Section 6.3.4) of a binary search tree T visits the keys of its dictionary in nondecreasing order. (See Figure 9.2a.)

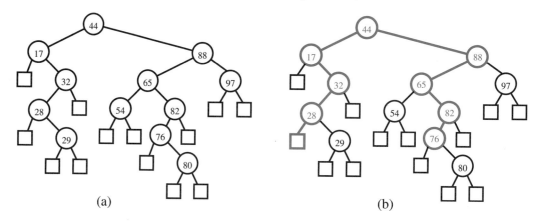

(a)   (b)

Figure 9.2: (a) A binary search tree T representing an ordered dictionary D with integer keys; (b) nodes of T visited when executing operations find(76) (successful) and find(25) (unsuccessful) on D. For simplicity, we show the keys but not the elements of D.

9.1.1   Searching

To perform operation find(k) in a dictionary D that is represented with a binary search tree T, we view the tree T as a decision tree (recall Figure 6.5). In this case, the question asked at each internal node v of T is whether the search key k is less than, equal to, or greater than the key stored at node v, denoted with key(v). If the answer is "less," the search continues in the left subtree. If the answer is "equal," the search terminates successfully. If the answer is "greater," the search continues in the right subtree. Finally, if we reach an external node, then the search terminates unsuccessfully. (See Figure 9.2b.)

In Code Fragment 9.1, we give a recursive function TreeSearch(), based on the above strategy for searching in a binary search tree T. Given a search key k and a node v of T, function TreeSearch() returns a node (position) w of the subtree $T(v)$ of T rooted at v, such that one of the following two cases occurs:

- w is an internal node of $T(v)$ that stores key k.
- w is an external node of $T(v)$, all the internal nodes of $T(v)$ that precede w in the inorder traversal have keys smaller than k, and all the internal nodes of $T(v)$ that follow w in the inorder traversal have keys greater than k.

Thus, function find(k) can be performed on dictionary D by calling the function TreeSearch(k, T.root()) on T. Let w be the node of T returned by this call of the TreeSearch() method. If node w is internal, we return a position pointing to this node, and otherwise, if w is external, then a null position is returned.

Algorithm TreeSearch(k, v):

    Input: A search key k, and a node v of a binary search tree T

    Output: A node w of the subtree $T(v)$ of T rooted at v, such that either w is an internal node storing key k or w is the external node where an item with key k would belong if it existed

    if v is an external node **then**

        return v

    if $k = $ key(v) **then**

        return v

    else if $k < $ key(v) **then**

        return TreeSearch(k, T.leftChild(v))

    else

        {we know $k > $ key(v)}

        return TreeSearch(k, T.rightChild(v))

            Code Fragment 9.1: Recursive search in a binary search tree.

Analysis of Binary Tree Searching

The analysis of the worst-case running time of searching in a binary search tree T is simple. Algorithm TreeSearch() is recursive and executes a constant number of primitive operations for each recursive call. Each recursive call of TreeSearch() is made on a child of the previous node. That is, TreeSearch() is called on the nodes of a path of T that starts from the root and goes down one level at a time. Thus, the number of such nodes is bounded by $h + 1$, where h is the height of T. In other words, since we spend $O(1)$ time per node encountered in the search, function find() on dictionary D runs in $O(h)$ time, where h is the height of the binary search tree T used to implement D. (See Figure 9.3.)

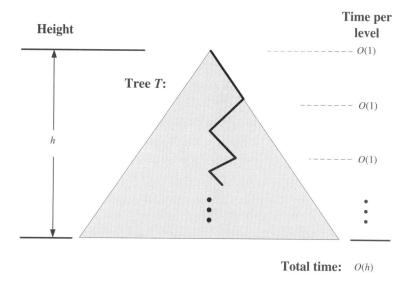

Figure 9.3: The running time of searching in a binary search tree. The figure uses standard visualization shortcuts of viewing a binary search tree as a big triangle and a path from the root as a zig-zag line.

    We can also show that a variation of the above algorithm performs operation findAll(k) in time $O(h + s)$, where s is the number of elements in the iterator returned. However, this method is slightly more complicated, and the details are left as an exercise (C-9.1).

    Admittedly, the height h of T can be as large as n, but we expect that it is usually much smaller. Indeed, we will show how to maintain an upper bound of $O(\log n)$ on the height of a search tree T in Section 9.2. Before we describe such a scheme, however, let us describe implementations for dictionary update functions.

9.1.2 Update Operations

Binary search trees allow implementations of the insertItem() and removeElement() operations using algorithms that are fairly straightforward, but not trivial.

Insertion

To perform the operation insertItem(k, e) on a dictionary D implemented with a binary search tree T, we start by calling the function TreeSearch(k, T.root()) on T. Let w be the node returned by TreeSearch().

- If w is an external node (no item with key k is stored in T), we replace w with a new internal node storing the item (k, e) and two external children, by means of operation expandExternal(w) on T (see Section 6.3.1). Note that w is the appropriate place to insert an item with key k.
- If w is an internal node (another item with key k is stored at w), we call TreeSearch(k, rightChild(w)) (or, equivalently, TreeSearch(k, leftChild(w))) and recursively apply the algorithm to the node returned by TreeSearch().

The above insertion algorithm eventually traces a path from the root of T down to an external node, which gets replaced with a new internal node accommodating the new item. Hence, an insertion adds the new item at the "bottom" of the search tree T. An example of insertion into a binary search tree is shown in Figure 9.4.

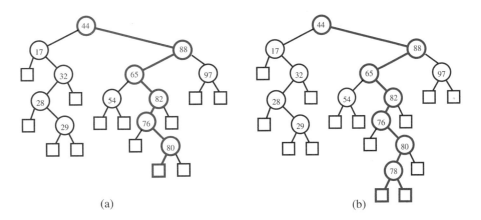

(a)　　　　　　　　　　　　　　　(b)

Figure 9.4: Insertion of an item with key 78 into the search tree of Figure 9.2. Finding the position to insert is shown in (a), and the resulting tree is shown in (b).

The analysis of the insertion algorithm is analogous to that for searching. The number of nodes visited is proportional to the height h of T in the worst case. Also, assuming a linked structure implementation for T (see Section 6.4.2), we spend $O(1)$ time at each node visited. Thus, function insertItem() runs in $O(h)$ time.

Removal

The implementation of the removeElement(k) operation on a dictionary D implemented with a binary search tree T is a bit more complex, since we do not wish to create any "holes" in the tree T. As with insertion, we begin by executing algorithm TreeSearch$(k, T.\text{root}())$ on T to find a node storing key k. If TreeSearch() returns an external node, then there is no element with key k in the dictionary, and an error exception is thrown. If TreeSearch() returns an internal node w instead, then w stores an item we wish to remove. We distinguish two cases (of increasing difficulty):

- If one of the children of node w is an external node, say node z, we simply remove w and z from T by means of operation removeAboveExternal(z) on T. This operation (see also Figure 6.13 and Section 6.4.2) restructures T by replacing w with the sibling of z, removing both w and z from T. This case is illustrated in Figure 9.5.

- If both children of node w are internal nodes, we cannot simply remove the node w from T, since this would create a "hole" in T. Instead, we proceed as follows (see Figure 9.6):

  ○ We find the first internal node y that follows w in an inorder traversal of T. Node y is the left-most internal node in the right subtree of w, and is found by going first to the right child of w and then down T from there, following left children. Also, the left child x of y is the external node that immediately follows node w in the inorder traversal of T.

  ○ We move the item of y into w. This action has the effect of removing the former item stored at w.

  ○ We remove nodes x and y from T by means of operation removeAboveExternal(x) on T. This action replaces y with x's sibling, and removes both x and y from T.

The analysis of the removal algorithm is analogous to that of the insertion and search algorithms. We spend $O(1)$ time at each node visited, and, in the worst case, the number of nodes visited is proportional to the height h of T. Thus, in a dictionary D implemented with a binary search tree T, the removeElement() function runs in $O(h)$ time, where h is the height of T.

We can also show that a variation of the above algorithm performs operation removeAllElements(k) in time $O(h + s)$, where s is the number of elements in the iterator returned. The details are left as an exercise (C-9.2).

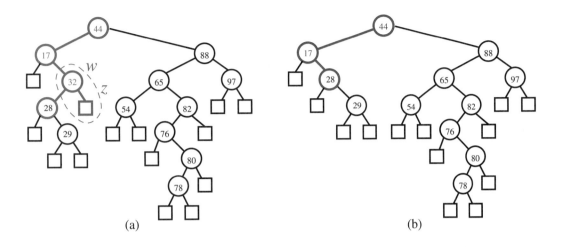

Figure 9.5: Removal from the binary search tree of Figure 9.4b, where the key to remove (32) is stored at a node (*w*) with an external child: (a) before the removal; (b) after the removal.

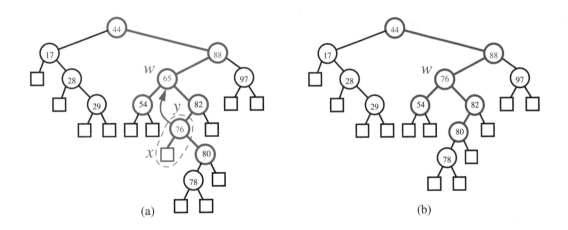

Figure 9.6: Removal from the binary search tree of Figure 9.4b, where the key to remove (65) is stored at a node whose children are both internal: (a) before the removal; (b) after the removal.

Best-case versus Worst-case

A binary search tree T is an efficient implementation of an ordered dictionary with n items but only if the height of T is small. In the best case, T has height h, such that $h = \lceil \log(n+1) \rceil$, which yields logarithmic-time performance for all the dictionary operations. In the worst case, however, T has height n; hence, it looks and feels like an ordered sequence. Such a worst-case configuration arises, for example, if we insert a set of keys in increasing or decreasing order. (See Figure 9.7.)

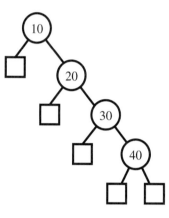

Figure 9.7: Example of a binary search tree with linear height, obtained by inserting keys in increasing order.

9.1.3 C++ Implementation

We present a C++ implementation of the binary search tree as a class Binary-SearchTree. This class is templated with three arguments (see Code Fragment 9.3). The first two are the key and element types, denoted Key and Element, respectively. The third template argument is the key-element item type, denoted BSTItem. By default, BSTItem is the same as the key-element Item class introduced in Chapter 7 (see Code Fragment 7.2). Recall that this class provides member functions key() and element() for accessing these objects.

The reason for making the key-element item a template is for further generalizations of binary search trees to AVL trees (Section 9.2) and red-black trees (Section 9.5). In order to reuse code, we will derive their key-element items from the base class BSTItem, and add additional member variables to store the information needed for maintaining these more advanced data structures. Note that because we have provided a default value for the BSTItem template parameter, a user of the BinarySearchTree class need only specify the key and element types.

A Binary Search Tree in C++

Our C++ binary search tree relies on any implementation of the BinaryTree ADT for storing the underlying tree (see Section 6.3.1). This ADT includes functions expandExternal() and removeAboveExternal() (see Section 6.4.2). Any concrete implementation of this ADT would suffice, for example, the LinkedBinaryTree class of Section 6.4.2. The nodes of this underlying binary tree are of type BSTItem. For convenience, we define a type name BTPosition to be a position in the underlying binary tree (see Code Fragment 9.3).

The BTPosition is a local type used internally for accessing the underlying binary tree. However, it does not provide the desired interface for a dictionary position. For example, the BTPosition::element() member function returns a reference to a key-element pair, and not a reference to the underlying element itself. For this reason, we define an adapter class, called Position. Its implementation is shown in Code Fragment 9.2. This declaration will be placed in the public section of class BinarySearchTree.

```
class Position {                                 // a Position
private:
    BTPosition btPos;                            // position of node
public:
    Position(const BTPosition &p) : btPos(p) { }  // constructor
    Element& element()                           // get element
        { return btPos.element().element(); }
    const Key& key() const                       // get key (read only)
        { return btPos.element().key(); }
    bool isNull() const                          // a null position?
        { return btPos.isNull(); }
};
```

Code Fragment 9.2: Class Position that stores a key-element pair in a binary search tree. This class will be included in the public section of class BinarySearchTree. (See Code Fragment 9.3).

The main portion of the BinarySearchTree class structure is shown in Code Fragment 9.3. The principal data member is the underlying binary tree T. It is declared to be a protected member of the class BinarySearchTree. This will make it possible for derived data structures, such as AVL trees and red-black trees, to access this underlying tree. We provide two utility functions. The first, key(p), returns the key associated with a node p of the underlying tree. The second, setItem(p, i), sets the key-element item of a node in the tree.

```
template <typename Key, typename Element,
                       typename BSTItem = Item<Key, Element> >
class BinarySearchTree {
protected:                                         // local types
   typedef BinaryTree<BSTItem>::Position BTPosition; // a tree position
public:                                            // public types
   // ... (insert Position here)
protected:                                         // member data
   BinaryTree<BSTItem> T;                          // the binary tree
protected:                                         // local utilities
   Key key(const BTPosition& p) const             // get position's key
     { return p.element().key(); }
                                                   // set a node's item
   void setItem(const BTPosition& p, const BSTItem& i) const {
     p.element().setKey(i.key());
     p.element().setElement(i.element());
   }
public:
   BinarySearchTree() : T() { }                    // constructor
   int size() const                               // size
     { return (T.size() − 1) / 2; }               // number of internals
   bool isEmpty() const
     { return size() == 0; }
   // ... (insert find, insert, and remove functions here)
};
```

Code Fragment 9.3: An implementation of the Dictionary ADT by a binary search tree. (Continued in Code Fragments 9.4 through 9.6.)

The implementations of find(), insertItem(), and removeElement() appear in Code Fragments 9.4 through 9.6. We define three protected utility functions finder(), inserter(), and remover() to handle the details of these respective operations. The advantage of defining these protected utility functions is that they contain common code that can be reused in the derived classes for AVL and red-black trees. These utility functions return the position of a node in the underlying tree. In the case of inserter(), this is the node that was inserted. In the case of remover(), this is the node that took the place of the deleted node in the tree. This additional information is used by the derived classes for AVL and red-black trees.

The utility functions are so long and complex that good C++ style requires that they be defined outside the class. We have presented them inside the class simply so that the code for related functions can all be presented in one place.

```
public:
  Position find(const Key& k) {                          // find a key
    BTPosition p = finder(k, T.root());                  // search for it
    if (T.isInternal(p))                                 // found it
      return Position(p);                                // return its position
    else                                                 // didn't find it
      return Position(NULL);                             // return null position
  }
protected:
  BTPosition finder(const Key& k, const BTPosition& p) {// find utility
    if (T.isExternal(p)) return p;                       // key not found
    Key curKey = key(p);                                 // key of current node
    if (k < curKey)
      return finder(k, T.leftChild(p));                  // search left subtree
    else if(k > curKey)
      return finder(k, T.rightChild(p));                 // search right subtree
    else                                                 // found it
      return p;                                          // return this position
  }
```

Code Fragment 9.4: The functions implementing the find() operation of class BinarySearchTree. The recursive utility function finder(), performs the actual search and returns a position of a tree node. (Continued from Code Fragment 9.3.)

```
public:
  void insertItem(const Key& k, const Element& e)   // insert (key,element)
    { inserter(k, e); }
protected:
  BTPosition inserter(const Key& k, const Element& e) {  // insert utility
    BTPosition p = finder(k, T.root());                  // find insertion spot
    while (T.isInternal(p))                              // key already exists?
      p = finder(k, T.rightChild(p));                    // look further
    T.expandExternal(p);                                 // add new node here
    setItem(p, BSTItem(k, e));                           // store (key,element)
    return p;                                            // return this position
  }
```

Code Fragment 9.5: The functions implementing the insertItem() operation of class BinarySearchTree. An item object is created, and then the utility function inserter() performs the actual insertion. (Continued from Code Fragment 9.3.)

```
public:
    void removeElement(const Key& k)                    // remove using key
        throw(NonexistentElementException) {
        BTPosition p = finder(k, T.root());             // find the node
        if (p.isNull())                                 // not found?
            throw NonexistentElementException("Remove nonexistent element");
        remover(p);                                     // remove it
    }
protected:
    BTPosition remover(const BTPosition& r) {           // remove utility
        BTPosition p;
        if (T.isExternal(T.leftChild(r)))               // left is external?
            p = T.leftChild(r);                         // remove from left
        else if (T.isExternal(T.rightChild(r)))         // right is external?
            p = T.rightChild(r);                        // remove from right
        else {                                          // both internal?
            p = T.rightChild(r);                        // p = replacement
            do                                          // find leftmost in
                p = T.leftChild(p);                     // ...right subtree
            while (T.isInternal(p));
            setItem(r, T.parent(p).element());          // copy parent(p) to r
        }
        return T.removeAboveExternal(p);                // remove p and parent
    }
```

Code Fragment 9.6: The functions implementing the removeElement() operation
of class BinarySearchTree. After finding the node r containing the item to be removed, the utility function remover() is called to perform the deletion. If node r
has an external child p, then function removeAboveExternal(p) is called. Otherwise, p is chosen to be the leftmost external node of the right subtree of r, the item
stored at p's parent is copied to node r (thus replacing the item previously stored at
r), and finally function removeAboveExternal(p) is called. (Continued from Code
Fragment 9.3.)

9.1.4 Performance

The performance of a dictionary implemented with a binary search is summarized in the following proposition and in Table 9.1.

Proposition 9.1: *A binary search tree T with height h for n key-element items uses $O(n)$ space and executes the dictionary ADT operations with the following running times. Operations* size() *and* isEmpty(), *each take $O(1)$ time. Operations* find(), insertItem(), *and* removeElement(), *each take time $O(h)$ time. Operation* findAll() *takes $O(h+s)$ time, where s is the size of the iterator returned, and operation* removeAllElements() *takes $O(h+r)$ time, where r is the number of removed elements.*

Method	Time
size, isEmpty	$O(1)$
find, insertItem, removeElement	$O(h)$
findAll, removeAllElements	$O(h+s)$

Table 9.1: Running times of the main functions of a dictionary realized by a binary search tree. We denote the current height of the tree with h and the size of the iterators returned by findAll() and removeAllElements() with s. The space usage is $O(n)$, where n is the number of items stored in the dictionary.

Note that the running time of search and update operations in a binary search tree varies dramatically depending on the tree's height. Nevertheless, we can take comfort that, on average, a binary search tree with n keys generated from a random series of insertions and removals of keys has expected height $O(\log n)$. Such a statement requires careful mathematical language to precisely define what we mean by a random series of insertions and removals, and sophisticated probability theory to prove. Its justification is beyond the scope of this book. Thus, we can be content knowing that random update sequences give rise to binary search trees that have logarithmic height on average, but, keeping in mind their poor worst-case performance, we should also take care in using standard binary search trees in applications where updates are not random.

Caution

The relative simplicity of their dictionary implementation, combined with good average-case performance, make binary search trees a rather attractive dictionary data structure in applications where the keys inserted and removed follow a random pattern and, occasionally, slow response time is acceptable. There are, however, applications where it is essential to have a dictionary with fast worst-case search and update time. The data structures presented in the next sections address this need.

9.2   AVL Trees

In the previous section, we discussed what should be an efficient dictionary data structure. However, the worst-case performance it achieves for the various operations is linear time, which is no better than the performance of sequence-based dictionary implementations (such as log files and look-up tables discussed in Chapter 8). In this section, we describe a simple way of correcting this problem so as to achieve logarithmic time for all the fundamental dictionary operations.

Definition

The simple correction is to add a rule to the binary search tree definition that will maintain a logarithmic height for the tree. The rule we consider in this section is the following ***height-balance property***, which characterizes the structure of a binary search tree T in terms of the heights of its internal nodes (recall from Section 6.2.2 that the height of a node v in a tree is the length of a longest path from v to an external node):

Height-Balance Property: For every internal node v of T, the heights of the children of v differ by at most 1.

Any binary search tree T that satisfies the height-balance property is said to be an ***AVL tree***, named after the initials of its inventors, Adel'son-Vel'skii and Landis. An example of an AVL tree is shown in Figure 9.8.

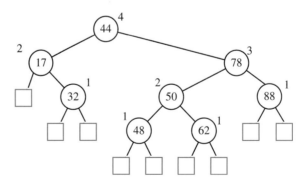

Figure 9.8: An example of an AVL tree. The keys are shown inside the nodes, and the heights are shown next to the nodes.

An immediate consequence of the height-balance property is that a subtree of an AVL tree is itself an AVL tree. The height-balance property has also the important consequence of keeping the height small, as shown in the following proposition.

Proposition 9.2: *The height of an AVL tree T storing n items is $O(\log n)$.*

Justification: Instead of trying to find an upper bound on the height of an AVL tree directly, it turns out to be easier to work on the "inverse problem" of finding a lower bound on the minimum number of internal nodes $n(h)$ of an AVL tree with height h. We will show that $n(h)$ grows at least exponentially, that is, $n(h)$ is $\Omega(c^h)$ for some constant $c > 1$. From this, it will be an easy step to derive that the height of an AVL tree storing n keys is $O(\log n)$.

To start with, notice that $n(1) = 1$ and $n(2) = 2$, because an AVL tree of height 1 must have at least one internal node and an AVL tree of height 2 must have at least two internal nodes. Now, for $h \geq 3$, an AVL tree with height h and the minimum number of nodes is such that both its subtrees are AVL trees with the minimum number of nodes: one with height $h - 1$ and the other with height $h - 2$. Taking the root into account, we obtain the following formula that relates $n(h)$ to $n(h-1)$ and $n(h-2)$, for $h \geq 3$:

$$n(h) = 1 + n(h-1) + n(h-2). \tag{9.1}$$

At this point, the reader familiar with the properties of Fibonacci progressions (Section 2.2.3 and Exercise C-3.12) will already see that $n(h)$ is a function exponential in h. For the rest of the readers, we will proceed with our reasoning.

Formula 9.1 implies that $n(h)$ is a strictly increasing function of h. Thus, we know that $n(h-1) > n(h-2)$. Replacing $n(h-1)$ with $n(h-2)$ in Formula 9.1 and dropping the 1, we get, for $h \geq 3$,

$$n(h) > 2 \cdot n(h-2). \tag{9.2}$$

Formula 9.2 indicates that $n(h)$ at least doubles each time h increases by 2, which intuitively means that $n(h)$ grows exponentially. To show this fact in a formal way, we apply Formula 9.2 repeatedly, yielding the following series of inequalities:

$$
\begin{aligned}
n(h) \;&>\; 2 \cdot n(h-2) \\
&>\; 4 \cdot n(h-4) \\
&>\; 8 \cdot n(h-6) \\
&\;\;\vdots \\
&>\; 2^i \cdot n(h-2i).
\end{aligned}
\tag{9.3}
$$

That is, $n(h) > 2^i \cdot n(h-2i)$, for any integer i, such that $h - 2i \geq 1$. Since we already know the values of $n(1)$ and $n(2)$, we pick i so that $h - 2i$ is equal to either 1 or 2. That is, we pick

$$i = \left\lceil \frac{h}{2} \right\rceil - 1.$$

By substituting the above value of i in formula 9.3, we obtain, for $h \geq 3$,

$$
\begin{aligned}
n(h) \ &> \ 2^{\lceil \frac{h}{2} \rceil - 1} \cdot n\left(h - 2\left\lceil \frac{h}{2} \right\rceil + 2\right) \\
&\geq \ 2^{\lceil \frac{h}{2} \rceil - 1} n(1) \\
&\geq \ 2^{\frac{h}{2} - 1}.
\end{aligned}
\tag{9.4}
$$

By taking logarithms of both sides of formula 9.4, we obtain

$$
\log n(h) \ > \ \frac{h}{2} - 1,
$$

from which we obtain

$$
h \ < \ 2\log n(h) + 2,
\tag{9.5}
$$

which implies that an AVL tree storing n keys has height at most $2\log n + 2$. ∎

By Proposition 9.2 and the analysis of binary search trees given in Section 9.1, the operations find() and findAll(), in a dictionary implemented with an AVL tree, run in time $O(\log n)$ and $O(\log n + s)$, respectively, where n is the number of items in the dictionary and s is the size of the iterator returned by findAll(). The important issue remaining is to show how to maintain the height-balance property of an AVL tree after an insertion or removal.

9.2.1 Update Operations

The insertion and removal operations for AVL trees are similar to those for binary search trees, but with AVL trees we must perform additional computations.

Insertion

An insertion in an AVL tree T begins as in an insertItem() operation described in Section 9.1.2 for a (simple) binary search tree. Recall that this operation always inserts the new item at a node w in T that was previously an external node, and it makes w become an internal node with operation expandExternal(). That is, it adds two external node children to w. This action may violate the height-balance property, however, for some nodes increase their heights by one. In particular, node w, and possibly some of its ancestors, increase their heights by one. Therefore, let us describe how to restructure T to restore its height balance.

Given a binary search tree T, we say that an internal node v of T is **balanced** if the absolute value of the difference between the heights of the children of v is at most 1, and we say that it is **unbalanced** otherwise. Thus, the height-balance property characterizing AVL trees is equivalent to saying that every internal node is balanced.

Suppose that T satisfies the height-balance property, and hence is an AVL tree, prior to our inserting the new item. As we have mentioned, after performing the operation expandExternal(w) on T, the heights of some nodes of T, including w, increase. All such nodes are on the path of T from w to the root of T, and these are the only nodes of T that may have just become unbalanced. (See Figure 9.9a.) Of course, if this happens, then T is no longer an AVL tree; hence, we need a mechanism to fix the "unbalance" that we have just caused.

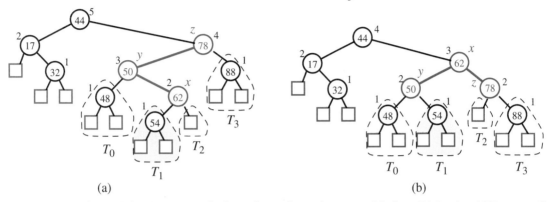

(a)   (b)

Figure 9.9: An example insertion of an element with key 54 in the AVL tree of Figure 9.8: (a) after adding a new node for key 54, the nodes storing keys 78 and 44 become unbalanced; (b) a trinode restructuring restores the height-balance property. We show the heights of nodes next to them, and we identify the nodes x, y, and z participating in the trinode restructuring.

We restore the balance of the nodes in the binary search tree T by a simple "search-and-repair" strategy. In particular, let z be the first node we encounter in going up from w toward the root of T, such that z is unbalanced. (See Figure 9.9a.) Also, let y denote the child of z with higher height (and note that y must be an ancestor of w). Finally, let x be the child of y with higher height (and if there is a tie, choose x to be an ancestor of w). Note that node x is a grandchild of z and could be equal to w. Since z becomes unbalanced because of an insertion in the subtree rooted at its child y, the height of y is 2 greater than its sibling.

We now rebalance the subtree rooted at z by calling the ***trinode restructuring*** function, restructure(x), described in Code Fragment 9.7 and illustrated in Figures 9.9 and 9.10. A trinode restructure temporarily renames the nodes x, y, and z as a, b, and c, so that a precedes b and b precedes c in an inorder traversal of T. There are four possible ways of mapping x, y, and z to a, b, and c, as shown in Figure 9.10, which are unified into one case by our relabeling. The trinode restructure then replaces z with the node called b, makes the children of this node be a and c, and makes the children of a and c be the four previous children of x, y, and z (other than x and y) while maintaining the inorder relationships of all the nodes in T.

Algorithm restructure(x):

> *Input:* A node x of a binary search tree T that has both a parent y and a grand-
> parent z
>
> *Output:* Tree T after a trinode restructuring (which corresponds to a single or
> double rotation) involving nodes x, y, and z

1: Let (a, b, c) be a left-to-right (inorder) listing of the nodes x, y, and z, and let
   (T_0, T_1, T_2, T_3) be a left-to-right (inorder) listing of the four subtrees of x, y, and
   z not rooted at x, y, or z.

2: Replace the subtree rooted at z with a new subtree rooted at b.

3: Let a be the left child of b and let T_0 and T_1 be the left and right subtrees of a,
   respectively.

4: Let c be the right child of b and let T_2 and T_3 be the left and right subtrees of c,
   respectively.

Code Fragment 9.7: The trinode restructure operation in a binary search tree.

The modification of a tree T caused by a trinode restructure operation is often
called a ***rotation***, because of the geometric way we can visualize the way it changes
T. If $b = y$, the trinode restructure method is called a ***single rotation***, for it can be
visualized as "rotating" y over z. (See Figure 9.10a and b.) Otherwise, if $b = x$, the
trinode restructure operation is called a ***double rotation***, for it can be visualized as
first "rotating" x over y and then over z. (See Figure 9.10c and d, and Figure 9.9.)
Some computer researchers treat these two kinds of rotations as separate functions,
each with two symmetric types. We have chosen, however, to unify these four
types of rotations into a single trinode restructure operation. No matter how we
view it, however, note that the trinode restructure function modifies parent-child
relationships of $O(1)$ nodes in T, while preserving the inorder traversal ordering of
all the nodes in T.

In addition to its order-preserving property, a trinode restructuring changes the
heights of several nodes in T, in order to restore balance. Recall that we execute the
function restructure(x) because z, the grandparent of x, is unbalanced. Moreover,
this unbalance is due to one of the children of x now having too large a height
relative to the height of z's other child. As a result of a rotation, we move the "tall"
child of x up while pushing the "short" child of z down. Thus, after performing
restructure(x), all the nodes in the subtree now rooted at the node we called b are
balanced. (See Figure 9.10.) Thus, we restore the height-balance property *locally*
at the nodes x, y, and z. In addition, since after performing the new item insertion
the subtree rooted at b replaces the one formerly rooted at z, which was taller by one
unit, all the ancestors of z that were formerly unbalanced become balanced. (See
Figure 9.9.) (The justification of this fact is left as Exercise C-9.13.) Therefore,
this one restructuring also restores the height-balance property *globally*.

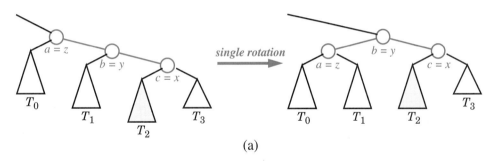

(a)

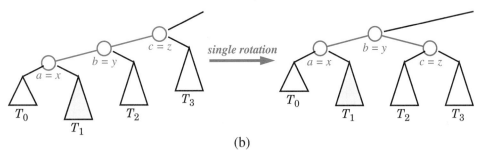

(b)

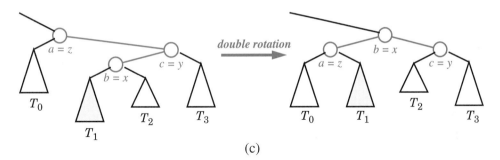

(c)

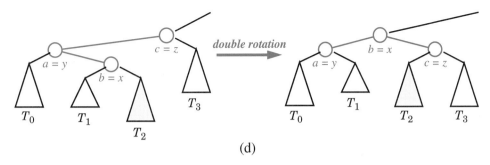

(d)

Figure 9.10: Schematic illustration of a trinode restructure operation (Code Fragment 9.7). Parts (a) and (b) show a single rotation, and parts (c) and (d) show a double rotation.

Removal

As was the case for insertItem(), we begin the implementation of the dictionary operation removeElement(k) on an AVL tree T by using the algorithm for performing this operation on a regular binary search tree (Section 9.1.2). The added difficulty in using this approach with an AVL tree is that it may violate the height-balance property. In particular, after removing an internal node with operation removeAboveExternal() and elevating one of its children into its place, there may be an unbalanced node in T on the path from the parent w of the previously removed node to the root of T. (See Figure 9.11a.) In fact, there can be at most one such unbalanced node. (The justification of this fact is left as Exercise C-9.10.)

As with insertion, we use trinode restructuring to restore balance in the tree T. In particular, let z be the first unbalanced node encountered going up from w toward the root of T. Also, let y be the child of z with larger height (note that node y is the child of z that is not an ancestor of w), and let x be a child of y with largest height. The choice of x may not be unique, since the subtrees of y may have the same height. If there is such a tie, x should be chosen to be on the same side relative to y as y is relative to z. In other words, both x and y are right children or both x and y are left children. (We leave the justification of this tie-breaking rule as Exercise C-9.11.) In any case, we then perform a restructure(x) operation, which restores the height-balance property *locally*, at the subtree that was formerly rooted at z and is now rooted at the node we temporarily called b. (See Figure 9.11b.)

Unfortunately, this trinode restructuring may reduce the height of the subtree rooted at b by 1, which may cause an ancestor of b to become unbalanced. Thus, a single trinode restructuring does not necessarily restore the height-balance property globally after a removal. So, after rebalancing z, we continue walking up T looking for unbalanced nodes. If we find another, we perform a restructure operation to restore its balance, and continue up T looking for more, all the way to the root. Since the height of T is $O(\log n)$, where n is the number of items, by Proposition 9.2, $O(\log n)$ trinode restructurings are sufficient to restore the height-balance property.

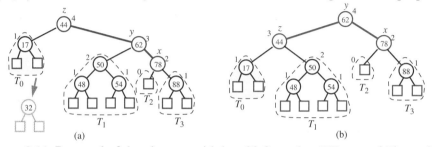

Figure 9.11: Removal of the element with key 32 from the AVL tree of Figure 9.8: (a) after removing the node storing key 32, the root becomes unbalanced; (b) a (single) rotation restores the height-balance property.

9.2.2 C++ Implementation

Let us now turn to the implementation details and analysis of using an AVL tree T with n internal nodes to implement an ordered dictionary with n items. The insertion and removal algorithms for T require that we are able to perform trinode restructurings and determine the difference between the heights of two sibling nodes. Regarding restructurings, we should extend the collection of operations of the binary tree ADT by adding the function restructure(). It is easy to see that a restructure() operation can be performed in $O(1)$ time if T is implemented with a linked structure (Section 6.4.2), which would not be the case with a vector (Section 6.4.1). Thus, we prefer a linked structure for representing an AVL tree.

Regarding height information, we can explicitly store the height of each internal node, v, in the associated item. This is the approach that we use here. Alternatively, we could store the *balance factor* of v, which is defined as the height of the left child of v minus the height of the right child of v. Thus, the balance factor of v is always equal to -1, 0, or 1, except during an insertion or removal, when it may become *temporarily* equal to -2 or $+2$.

In Code Fragment 9.8, we show the item class for the AVL tree, AVLItem. It is derived from class Item (see Code Fragments 7.2). It defines an additional member variable hgt, representing the height of the associated node, and it provides member functions for accessing and setting this value.

Class AVLTree is shown in Code Fragments 9.9 and 9.10. It is derived from class BinarySearchTree (see Code Fragment 9.3). Notice that unlike the class BinarySearchTree, we only use two template arguments in class AVLTree, since the key-element item is always AVLItem. The class AVLTree inherits the binary tree T from its parent class, as well as the functions size(), isEmpty(), find(), and findAll(). It overrides functions insertItem(), removeElement(), and removeAllElements(). We assume that the binary tree class supports the function restructure(), which performs a trinode restructuring. (Its implementation is left as Exercise P-9.5).

```
template <typename Key, typename Element>
class AVLItem : public Item<Key,Element> {          // an AVL item
private:
    int hgt;                                          // node height
public:
    AVLItem(const Key& k = Key(), const Element& e = Element(), int h = 0)
        : Item<Key, Element>(k, e), hgt(h) { }
    int height() const { return hgt; }               // get height
    void setHeight(int h) { hgt = h; }               // set height
};
```

Code Fragment 9.8: Class representing an item in an AVL tree.

The AVLTree class definition begins by defining a number of convenience type definitions for referring to AVLItem (under the simpler name of Item), the underlying binary search tree (as BST), the position in the underlying tree (BSTPosition), and the dictionary position (Position), which is used for return results.

The principal structural difference between class AVLTree and class Binary-SearchTree is that in the internal nodes of the tree we store AVLItem objects, each of which holds its height value, rather than plain Item objects. We also define a number of protected utility functions for manipulating heights and restoring the height-balance property. The function height() returns the height of a node of the tree, function setHeight() computes the height of a node by adding 1 to the height of the taller child, and isBalanced() tests whether a node satisfies the height-balance property. The function tallGrandchild() returns the tallest grandchild of a node. We leave its implementation as an exercise. The most important utility function is rebalance(), which is presented in Code Fragment 9.9.

```
void rebalance(BTPosition& z) {              // rebalancing utility
  while (!T.isRoot(z)) {                      // rebalance up to root
    z = T.parent(z);
    setHeight(z);                            // compute new height
    if (!isBalanced(z)) {                    // restructuring needed
      BTPosition x = tallGrandchild(z);
      z = T.restructure(x);                  // trinode restructure
      setHeight(T.leftChild(z));             // update heights
      setHeight(T.rightChild(z));
      setHeight(z);
    }
  }
}
```

Code Fragment 9.9: Local utility function rebalance(), which is used to restore balance in an AVL tree. It updates the height of the current node, and if needed, it performs a restructuring along the path to the root of the tree.

Method insertItem() (see Code Fragment 9.10) creates a new AVLItem object and then calls the parent class's utility function inserter() (Code Fragment 9.5), which inserts the new item and returns the inserted position. (This is the node storing key 54 in Figure 9.9(a).) The function rebalance() travels up to the root of the tree and along the way it updates the heights of all the nodes visited and performs a trinode restructuring, if necessary. Function removeElement() begins by calling the parent class's remover() utility (Code Fragment 9.6), which performs the removal of the item and returns the position of the replacing node. (This is the right child of the node labeled 17 in Figure 9.11(a).) The utility function rebalance() is then used to traverse the path from the removed position to the root.

```
template <typename Key, typename Element>
class AVLTree : public BinarySearchTree<Key, Element, AVLItem<Key, Element> > {
protected:                                            // local types
  typedef AVLItem<Key, Element>    Item;              // a tree node item
  typedef BinarySearchTree<Key, Element, Item> BST;   // base search tree
  typedef BST::BTPosition           BTPosition;       // a tree position
public:                                               // public types
  typedef BST::Position             Position;         // position
  // ... (insert AVLItem here)
protected:                                            // local utilities
  int height(const BTPosition& p) const {             // get height of p
    if(T.isExternal(p)) return 0;
    else return p.element().height();
  }
  void setHeight(BTPosition p) {                      // set height of p
    int leftHeight   = height(T.leftChild(p));
    int rightHeight  = height(T.rightChild(p));
    int maxHeight    = max(leftHeight, rightHeight);
    p.element().setHeight(1 + maxHeight);
  }
  bool isBalanced(const BTPosition& p) const {        // is p balanced?
    int bf = height(T.leftChild(p)) − height(T.rightChild(p));
    return ((−1 <= bf) && (bf <= 1));
  }
  BTPosition tallGrandchild(const BTPosition& p) const; // get tallest grandchild
  // ... (insert rebalance() here)
public:
  AVLTree() : BST() { }                               // constructor
  void insertItem(const Key& k, const Element& e) {   // insert (key,element)
    BTPosition p = inserter(k, e);                    // insert in base tree
    setHeight(p);                                     // compute its height
    rebalance(p);                                     // rebalance if needed
  }
  void removeElement(const Key& k)                    // remove using key
      throw(NonexistentElementException) {
    BTPosition p = finder(k, T.root());               // find in base tree
    if (p.isNull())                                   // not found?
      throw NonexistentElementException("Remove nonexistent element");
    BTPosition r = remover(p);                        // remove it
    rebalance(r);                                     // rebalance if needed
  }
};
```

Code Fragment 9.10: The class AVLTree, which implements an AVL tree.

9.2.3 Performance

We summarize the analysis of the performance of an AVL tree T as follows. Operations find(), insertItem(), and removeElement() visit the nodes along a root-to-leaf path of T, plus, possibly, their siblings, and spend $O(1)$ time per node. Thus, since the height of T is $O(\log n)$ by Proposition 9.2, each of the above operations takes $O(\log n)$ time. We leave the implementation and analysis of operations findAll() and removeAllElements() as interesting exercises. In Table 9.2, we summarize the performance of a dictionary implemented with an AVL tree. We illustrate this performance in Figure 9.12.

Operation	Time
size, isEmpty	$O(1)$
find, insertItem, removeElement	$O(\log n)$
findAll	$O(\log n + s)$
removeAllElements	$O(\log n + r)$

Table 9.2: Performance of an n-element dictionary realized by an AVL tree, where s denotes the size of the iterator returned by findAll() and r denotes the number of elements removed by removeAllElements(). The space usage is $O(n)$.

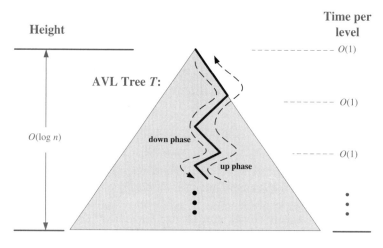

Figure 9.12: Illustrating the running time of searches and updates in an AVL tree. The time performance is $O(1)$ per level, broken into a down phase, which typically involves searching, and an up phase, which typically involves updating height values and performing local trinode restructurings (rotations).

9.3 Multi-Way Search Trees

Some of the data structures we discuss in this chapter are multi-way trees, that is, trees with internal nodes that have two or more children. In this section, we describe how multi-way trees can be used as search trees, including how multi-way trees store items and how to perform search operations in multi-way search trees. Recall that the *items* that we store in a search tree are pairs of the form (k, x), where k is the *key* and x is the element associated with the key. However, we do not discuss how to perform updates in multi-way search trees now, for the details for update functions depend on additional properties we might wish to maintain for multi-way trees, which we discuss in Sections 9.4 and 9.7.

Definition

Let v be a node of an ordered tree. We say that v is a *d-node* if v has d children. We define a *multi-way search tree* to be an ordered tree T, that has the following properties, which are illustrated in Figure 9.13a:

- Each internal node of T has at least two children. That is, each internal node is a d-node, such that $d \geq 2$.
- Each internal d-node v of T with children $v_1, \ldots, v_d$, stores an ordered set of $d-1$ key-element items $(k_1, x_1), \ldots, (k_{d-1}, x_{d-1})$, where $k_1 \leq \cdots \leq k_{d-1}$.
- Let us conventionally define $k_0 = -\infty$ and $k_d = +\infty$. For each item (k, x) stored at a node in the subtree of v rooted at v_i, $i = 1, \ldots, d$, and $k_{i-1} \leq k \leq k_i$.

That is, if we think of the set of keys stored at v as including the special fictitious keys $k_0 = -\infty$ and $k_d = +\infty$, then a key k stored in the subtree of T rooted at a child node v_i must be "in between" two keys stored at v. This simple viewpoint gives rise to the rule that a d-node stores $d-1$ regular keys, and it also forms the basis of the algorithm for searching in a multi-way search tree.

By the above definition, the external nodes of a multi-way search do not store any items and serve only as "placeholders." Thus, we view a binary search tree (Section 9.1) as a special case of a multi-way search tree, where each internal node stores one item and has two children. At the other extreme, a multi-way search tree may have only a single internal node storing all the items. In addition, while the external nodes could be NULL or pointers to a NULL_NODE object, we make the simplifying assumption that they are actual nodes that don't store anything.

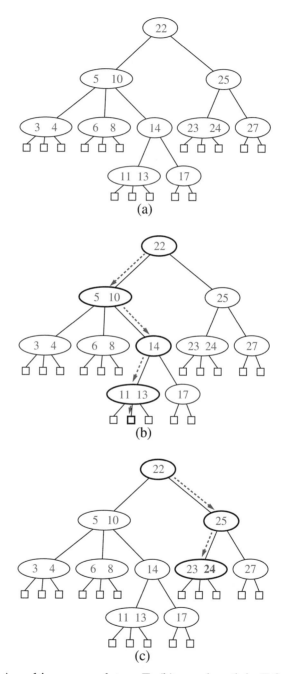

Figure 9.13: (a) A multi-way search tree T; (b) search path in T for key 12 (unsuccessful search); (c) search path in T for key 24 (successful search).

Whether internal nodes of a multi-way tree have two children or many, however, there is an interesting relationship between the number of items and the number of external nodes.

Proposition 9.3: *A multi-way search tree storing n items has n + 1 external nodes.*

We leave the justification of this proposition as an exercise (C-9.16).

Searching in a Multi-Way Tree

Given a multi-way search tree T, searching for an element with key k is simple. We perform such a search by tracing a path in T starting at the root. (See Figure 9.13b and c.) When we are at a d-node v during this search, we compare the key k with the keys $k_1, \ldots, k_{d-1}$ stored at v. If $k = k_i$ for some i, the search is successfully completed. Otherwise, we continue the search in the child v_i of v, such that $k_{i-1} < k < k_i$. (Recall that we conventionally define $k_0 = -\infty$ and $k_d = +\infty$.) If we reach an external node, then we know that there is no item with key k in T, and the search terminates unsuccessfully.

Data Structures

In Section 6.4, we discussed different ways of representing general trees. Each of these representations can also be used for multi-way search trees. In fact, in using a general tree to implement a multi-way search tree, the only additional information that we need to store at each node is the set of items (including keys) associated with that node. That is, we need to store, with v, a pointer to some container or collection object that stores the items for v.

Recall that when we use a binary search tree to represent an ordered dictionary D, we simply store a pointer to a single item at each internal node. In using a multi-way search tree T to represent D, we must store a pointer to the ordered set of items associated with v at each internal node v of T. This reasoning may at first seem like a circular argument, since we need a representation of an ordered dictionary to represent an ordered dictionary. We can avoid any circular arguments, however, by using the ***bootstrapping*** technique, where we use a previous (less advanced) solution to a problem to create a new (more advanced) solution. In this case, that consists of representing the ordered set associated with each internal node with a dictionary data structure that we have previously constructed (for example, a look-up table based on an ordered vector, as shown in Section 8.3.2). In particular, assuming we already have a way of implementing ordered dictionaries, we can realize a multi-way search tree by taking a tree T and storing such a dictionary at each d-node v of T.

The dictionary we store at each node v is known as a *secondary* data structure, for we are using it to support the bigger, *primary* data structure. We denote the dictionary stored at a node v of T as $D(v)$. The items we store in $D(v)$ will allow us to find which child node to move to the next during a search operation. Specifically, for each node v of T, with children $v_1, \ldots, v_d$ and items $(k_1, x_1), \ldots, (k_{d-1}, x_{d-1})$, we store in the dictionary $D(v)$ the items

$$(k_1, (x_1, v_1)), (k_2, (x_2, v_2)), \ldots, (k_{d-1}, (x_{d-1}, v_{d-1})), (+\infty, (\emptyset, v_d)).$$

That is, an item $(k_i, (x_i, v_i))$ of dictionary $D(v)$ has key k_i and element (x_i, v_i). Note that the last item stores the special key $+\infty$.

With the above realization of a multi-way search tree T, processing a d-node v while searching for an element of T with key k can be done by performing a search operation to find the item (k_i, x_i, v_i) in $D(v)$ with smallest key greater than or equal to k, such as in the closestAfter(k) operation (see Section 8.3.1). We distinguish two cases:

- If $k < k_i$, then we continue the search by processing child v_i. (Note that if the special key $k_d = +\infty$ is returned, then k is greater than all the keys stored at node v, and we continue the search processing child v_d).
- Otherwise ($k = k_i$), then the search terminates successfully.

Consider the space requirement for the above realization of a multi-way search tree T storing n items. By Proposition 9.3, using any of the common realizations of ordered dictionaries (Chapter 8) for the secondary structures of the nodes of T, the overall space requirement for T is $O(n)$.

Consider next the time spent answering a search in T. The time spent at a d-node v of T during a search depends on how we realize the secondary data structure $D(v)$. If $D(v)$ is realized with a vector-based sorted sequence (that is, a look-up table), then we can process v in $O(\log d)$ time. If $D(v)$ is realized using an unsorted sequence (that is, a log file) instead, then processing v takes $O(d)$ time. Let $d_{\max}$ denote the maximum number of children of any node of T, and let h denote the height of T. The search time in a multi-way search tree is either $O(hd_{\max})$ or $O(h \log d_{\max})$, depending on the specific implementation of the secondary structures at the nodes of T (the dictionaries $D(v)$). If $d_{\max}$ is a constant, the running time for performing a search is $O(h)$, irrespective of the implementation of the secondary structures.

Thus, the primary efficiency goal for a multi-way search tree is to keep the height as small as possible, that is, we want h to be a logarithmic function of n, the number of total items stored in the dictionary. A search tree with logarithmic height, such as this, is called a *balanced search tree*. In the next section, we discuss a balanced search tree that caps $d_{\max}$ at 4.

9.4 (2,4) Trees

A multi-way search tree that keeps the secondary data structures stored at each node small and also keeps the primary multi-way tree balanced is the $(2,4)$ tree, which is sometimes called 2-4 tree or 2-3-4 tree. This data structure achieves these goals by maintaining two simple properties (see Figure 9.14):

Size Property: Every internal node has at most four children.

Depth Property: All the external nodes have the same depth.

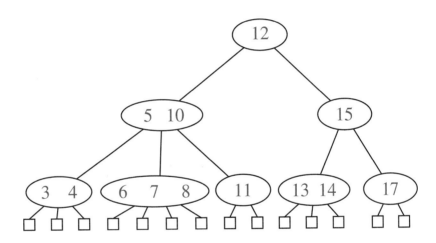

Figure 9.14: An example $(2,4)$ tree. Note that there are four 2-nodes, three 3-nodes, and one 4-node.

Again, we assume that external nodes are empty and, for the sake of simplicity, we describe our search and update functions assuming that external nodes are real nodes, although this latter requirement is not strictly needed.

Enforcing the size property for $(2,4)$ trees keeps the nodes in the multi-way search tree simple. It also gives rise to the alternative name "2-3-4 tree," since it implies that each internal node in the tree has 2, 3, or 4 children. Another implication of this rule is that we can represent the dictionary $D(v)$ stored at each internal node v using a vector, and still achieve $O(1)$-time performance for all operations (since $d_{\max} = 4$). The depth property, on the other hand, enforces an important bound on the height of a $(2,4)$ tree.

Proposition 9.4: *The height of a* $(2,4)$ *tree storing* n *items is* $\Theta(\log n)$.

Justification: Let h be the height of a $(2,4)$ tree T storing n items. We justify the proposition by showing that the claims

$$\frac{1}{2}\log(n+1) \leq h \tag{9.6}$$

and

$$h \leq \log(n+1) \tag{9.7}$$

are true.

To justify these claims note first that, by the size property, we can have at most 4 nodes at depth 1, at most 4^2 nodes at depth 2, and so on. Thus, the number of external nodes in T is at most 4^h. Likewise, by the depth property and the definition of a $(2,4)$ tree, we must have at least 2 nodes at depth 1, at least 2^2 nodes at depth 2, and so on. Thus, the number of external nodes in T is at least 2^h. In addition, by Proposition 9.3, the number of external nodes in T is $n+1$. Therefore, we obtain

$$2^h \leq n+1$$

and

$$n+1 \leq 4^h.$$

Taking the logarithm in base 2 of each of the above terms, we obtain

$$h \leq \log(n+1)$$

and

$$\log(n+1) \leq 2h,$$

which justifies our claims (9.6 and 9.7).   ■

Proposition 9.4 states that the size and depth properties are sufficient for keeping a multi-way tree balanced (Section 9.3). Moreover, this proposition implies that performing a search in a $(2,4)$ tree takes $O(\log n)$ time and that the specific realization of the secondary structures at the nodes is not a crucial design choice, since the maximum number of children d_{max} is a constant (4). We can, for example, use a simple ordered dictionary implementation, such a vector-based look-up table, for each secondary structure.

9.4.1 Update Operations

Maintaining the size and depth properties requires some effort after performing insertions and removals in a $(2,4)$ tree, however. We discuss these operations next.

Insertion

To insert a new item (k,x), with key k, into a $(2,4)$ tree T, we first perform a search for k. Assuming that T has no element with key k, this search terminates unsuccessfully at an external node z. Let v be the parent of z. We insert the new item into node v and add a new child w (an external node) to v on the left of z. That is, we add item (k,x,w) to the dictionary $D(v)$.

   Our insertion function preserves the depth property, since we add a new external node at the same level as existing external nodes. Nevertheless, it may violate the size property. Indeed, if a node v was previously a 4-node, then it may become a 5-node after the insertion. This causes the tree T to no longer be a $(2,4)$ tree. This type of violation of the size property is called an ***overflow*** at node v, and it must be resolved in order to restore the properties of a $(2,4)$ tree. Let $v_1,\ldots,v_5$ be the children of v, and let $k_1,\ldots,k_4$ be the keys stored at v. To remedy the overflow at node v, we perform a ***split*** operation on v as follows (see Figure 9.15).

- Replace v with two nodes v' and v'', where:
    - v' is a 3-node with children v_1,v_2,v_3 storing keys k_1 and k_2
    - v'' is a 2-node with children v_4,v_5 storing key k_4.

- If v was the root of T, create a new root node u; else, let u be the parent of v.
- Insert key k_3 into u and make v' and v'' children of u, so that if v was child i of u, then v' and v'' become children i and $i+1$ of u, respectively.

We show a sequence of insertions in a $(2,4)$ tree in Figure 9.16.

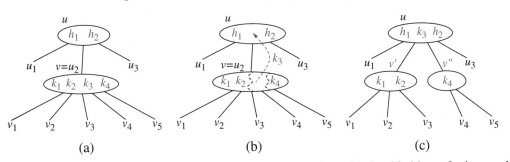

Figure 9.15: A node split: (a) overflow at a 5-node v; (b) the third key of v inserted into the parent u of v; (c) node v replaced with a 3-node v' and a 2-node v''.

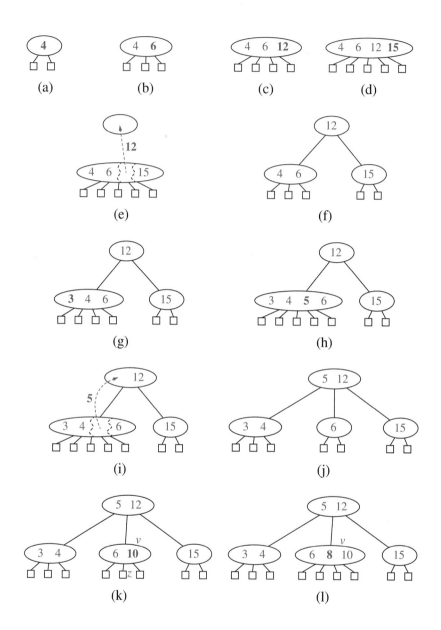

Figure 9.16: A sequence of insertions into a $(2,4)$ tree: (a) initial tree with one item; (b) insertion of 6; (c) insertion of 12; (d) insertion of 15, which causes an overflow; (e) split, which causes the creation of a new root node; (f) after the split; (g) insertion of 3; (h) insertion of 5, which causes an overflow; (i) split; (j) after the split; (k) insertion of 10; (l) insertion of 8.

Analysis of Insertion in a (2,4) Tree

A split operation affects a constant number of nodes of the tree and $O(1)$ items stored at such nodes. Thus, it can be implemented to run in $O(1)$ time.

As a consequence of a split operation on node v, a new overflow may occur at the parent u of v. If such an overflow occurs, it triggers in turn a split at node u. (See Figure 9.17.) A split operation either eliminates the overflow or propagates it into the parent of the current node. Hence, the number of split operations is bounded by the height of the tree, which is $O(\log n)$ by Proposition 9.4. Therefore, the total time to perform an insertion in a (2,4) tree is $O(\log n)$.

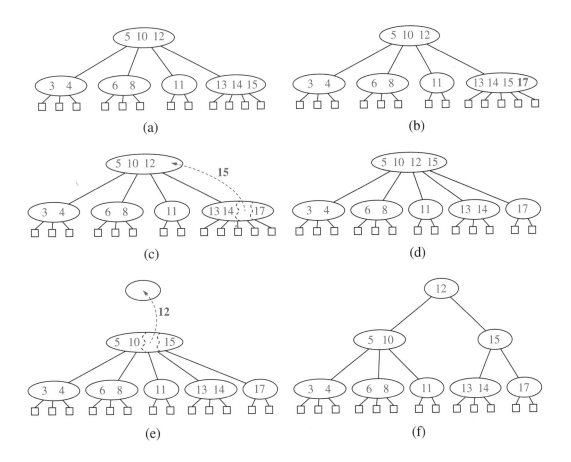

Figure 9.17: An insertion in a (2,4) tree that causes a cascading split: (a) before the insertion; (b) insertion of 17, causing an overflow; (c) a split; (d) after the split a new overflow occurs; (e) another split, creating a new root node; (f) final tree.

Removal

Let us now consider the removal of an item with key k from a $(2,4)$ tree T. We begin such an operation by performing a search in T for an item with key k. Removing such an item from a $(2,4)$ tree can always be reduced to the case where the item to be removed is stored at a node v whose children are external nodes. Suppose, for instance, that the item with key k that we wish to remove is stored in the ith item (k_i, x_i) at a node z that has only internal-node children. In this case, we swap the item (k_i, x_i) with an appropriate item that is stored at a node v with external-node children as follows (Figure 9.18d).

1. We find the right-most internal node v in the subtree rooted at the ith child of z, noting that the children of node v are all external nodes.

2. We swap the item (k_i, x_i) at z with the last item of v.

Once we ensure that the item to remove is stored at a node v with only external-node children (because either it was already at v or we swapped it into v), we simply remove the item from v (that is, from the dictionary $D(v)$) and remove the ith external node of v.

Removing an item (and a child) from a node v as described above preserves the depth property, for we always remove an external node child from a node v with only external-node children. However, in removing such an external node we may violate the size property at v. Indeed, if v was previously a 2-node, then it becomes a 1-node with no items after the removal (Figure 9.18d and e), which is not allowed in a $(2,4)$ tree. This type of violation of the size property is called an ***underflow*** at node v. To remedy an underflow, we check whether an immediate sibling of v is a 3-node or a 4-node. If we find such a sibling w, then we perform a ***transfer*** operation, in which we move a child of w to v, a key of w to the parent u of v and w, and a key of u to v. (See Figure 9.18b and c.) If v has only one sibling, or if both immediate siblings of v are 2-nodes, then we perform a ***fusion*** operation, in which we merge v with a sibling, creating a new node v', and move a key from the parent u of v to v'. (See Figure 9.19e and f.)

A fusion operation at node v may cause a new underflow to occur at the parent u of v, which in turn triggers a transfer or fusion at u. (See Figure 9.19.) Hence, the number of fusion operations is bounded by the height of the tree, which is $O(\log n)$ by Proposition 9.4. If an underflow propagates all the way up to the root, then the root is simply deleted. (See Figure 9.19c and d.) We show a sequence of removals from a $(2,4)$ tree in Figures 9.18 and 9.19.

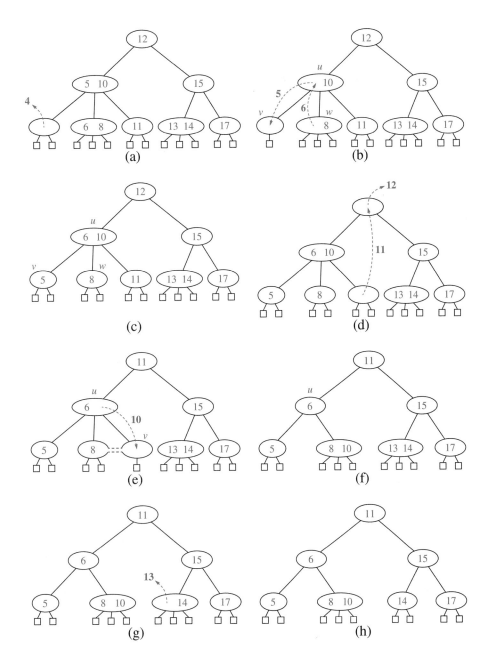

Figure 9.18: A sequence of removals from a (2,4) tree: (a) removal of 4, causing an underflow; (b) a transfer operation; (c) after the transfer operation; (d) removal of 12, causing an underflow; (e) a fusion operation; (f) after the fusion operation; (g) removal of 13; (h) after removing 13.

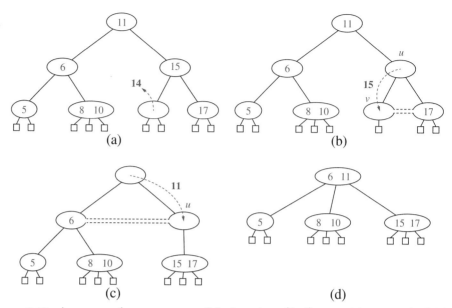

Figure 9.19: A propagating sequence of fusions in a $(2,4)$ tree: (a) removal of 14, which causes an underflow; (b) fusion, which causes another underflow; (c) second fusion operation, which causes the root to be removed; (d) final tree.

9.4.2   Performance

Table 9.3 summarizes the running times of the main operations of a dictionary realized with a $(2,4)$ tree. The time complexity analysis is based on the following:

- The height of a $(2,4)$ tree storing n items is $O(\log n)$, by Proposition 9.4.
- A split, transfer, or fusion operation takes $O(1)$ time.
- A search, insertion, or removal of an item visits $O(\log n)$ nodes.

Operation	Time
size, isEmpty	$O(1)$
find, insertItem, removeElement	$O(\log n)$
findAll	$O(\log n + s)$
removeAllElements	$O(\log n + r)$

Table 9.3: Performance of an n-element dictionary realized by a $(2,4)$ tree, where s denotes the size of the iterator returned by findAll() and r denotes the number of elements removed by removeAllElements(). The space usage is $O(n)$.

Thus, $(2,4)$ trees provide for fast dictionary search and update operations. $(2,4)$ trees also have an interesting relationship to the data structure we discuss next.

9.5 Red-Black Trees

Although AVL Trees and $(2,4)$ trees have a number of nice properties, there are some dictionary applications for which they are not well suited. For instance, AVL trees may require many restructure operations (rotations) to be performed after an element removal, and $(2,4)$ trees may require many fusing or split operations to be performed after either an insertion or removal. The data structure we discuss in this section, the red-black tree, does not have these drawbacks, however, as it requires that only $O(1)$ structural changes be made after an update in order to stay balanced.

A *red-black tree* is a binary search tree (see Section 9.1) with nodes colored red and black in a way that satisfies the following properties:

***Root Property*:** The root is black.

***External Property*:** Every external node is black.

***Internal Property*:** The children of a red node are black.

***Depth Property*:** All the external nodes have the same **black depth**, which is de-
fined as the number of black ancestors minus one.

An example of a red-black tree is shown in Figure 9.20.

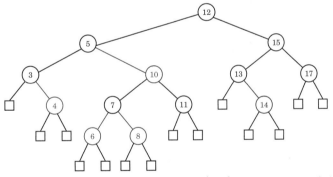

Figure 9.20: Red-black tree associated with the $(2,4)$ tree of Figure 9.14. Each external node of this red-black tree has 3 black ancestors; hence, it has black depth 3. We use the color blue instead of red. Also, we use the convention of giving an edge of the tree the same color as the child node.

As has been the convention in this chapter, we assume that items are stored in the internal nodes of a red-black tree, with the external nodes being empty placeholders. Also, we describe our algorithms assuming they are actual nodes, but we note in passing that at the expense of slightly more complicated search and update functions, external nodes could be NULL or pointers to a NULL_NODE object.

We can make the red-black tree definition more intuitive by noting an interesting correspondence between red-black and $(2,4)$ trees, as illustrated in Figure 9.21. Namely, given a red-black tree, we can construct a corresponding $(2,4)$ tree by merging every red node v into its parent, and storing the item from v at its parent. Conversely, we can transform any $(2,4)$ tree into a corresponding red-black tree by coloring each node black and performing the following transformation for each internal node v.

- If v is a 2-node, then keep the (black) children of v as is.

- If v is a 3-node, then create a new red node w, give v's first two (black) children to w, and make w and v's third child be the two children of v.

- If v is a 4-node, then create two new red nodes w and z, give v's first two (black) children to w, give v's last two (black) children to z, and make w and z be the two children of v.

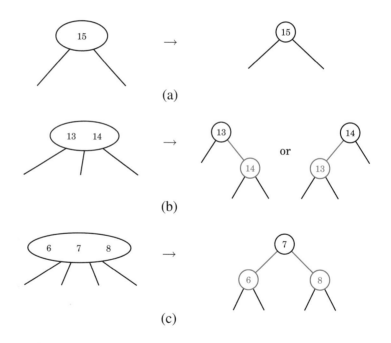

Figure 9.21: Correspondence between a $(2,4)$ tree and a red-black tree: (a) 2-node; (b) 3-node; (c) 4-node.

The correspondence between $(2,4)$ trees and red-black trees provides important intuition that we will use in our discussion of how to perform updates in red-black trees. In fact, the update algorithms for red-black trees are mysteriously complex without this intuition.

Proposition 9.5: *The height of a red-black tree storing n items is $O(\log n)$.*

Justification: Let T be a red-black tree storing n items, and let h be the height of T. We justify this proposition by establishing the following fact:

$$\log(n+1) \leq h \leq 2\log(n+1).$$

Let d be the common black depth of all the external nodes of T. Let T' be the $(2,4)$ tree associated with T, and let h' be the height of T'. We know that $h' = d$. Hence, by Proposition 9.4, $d = h' \leq \log(n+1)$. By the internal node property, $h \leq 2d$. Thus, we obtain $h \leq 2\log(n+1)$. The other inequality, $\log(n+1) \leq h$, follows from Proposition 6.9 and the fact that T has n internal nodes. ∎

We assume that a red-black tree is realized with a linked structure for binary trees (Section 6.4.2), in which we store a dictionary item and a color indicator at each node. Thus the space requirement for storing n keys is $O(n)$. The algorithm for searching in a red-black tree T is the same as that for a standard binary search tree (Section 9.1). Thus, searching in a red-black tree takes $O(\log n)$ time.

9.5.1 Update Operations

Performing the update operations in a red-black tree is similar to that of a binary search tree, except that we must additionally restore the color properties.

Insertion

Now consider the insertion of an element x with key k into a red-black tree T, keeping in mind the correspondence between T and its associated $(2,4)$ tree T' and the insertion algorithm for T'. The insertion algorithm initially proceeds as in a binary search tree (Section 9.1.2). Namely, we search for k in T until we reach an external node of T, and we replace this node with an internal node z, storing (k,x) and having two external-node children. If z is the root of T, we color z black; if not, we color z red. We also color the children of z black. This action corresponds to inserting (k,x) into a node of the $(2,4)$ tree T' with external children. In addition, this action preserves the root, external, and depth properties of T, but it may violate the internal property. Indeed, if z is not the root of T and the parent v of z is red, then we have a parent and a child (namely, v and z) that are both red. Note that by the root property, v cannot be the root of T, and by the internal property (which was previously satisfied), the parent u of v must be black. Since z and its parent are red, but z's grandparent u is black, we call this violation of the internal property a ***double red*** at node z.

To remedy a double red, we consider two cases.

Case 1: *The Sibling* w *of* v *is Black*. (See Figure 9.22.) In this case, the double red denotes the fact that we have created, in our red-black tree T, a malformed replacement for a corresponding 4-node of the $(2,4)$ tree T', which has as its children the four black children of u, v, and z. Our malformed replacement has one red node (v) that is the parent of another red node (z), while we want it to have the two red nodes as siblings instead. To fix this problem, we perform a ***trinode restructuring*** of T. The trinode restructuring is done by the operation restructure(z), which consists of the following steps (see again Figure 9.22; this operation is also discussed in Section 9.2).

- Take node z, its parent v, and grandparent u, and temporarily relabel them as a, b, and c, in left-to-right order, so that a, b, and c will be visited in this order by an inorder tree traversal.
- Replace the grandparent u with the node labeled b, and make nodes a and c the children of b, keeping inorder relationships unchanged.

After performing the restructure(z) operation, we color b black and we color a and c red. Thus, the restructuring eliminates the double red problem.

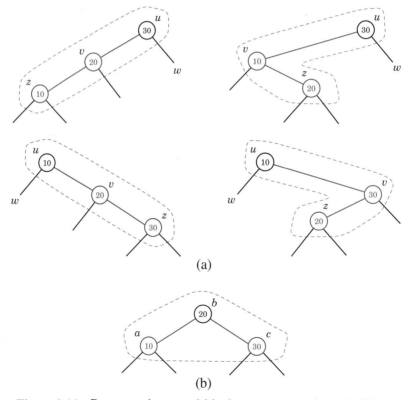

Figure 9.22: Restructuring a red-black tree to remedy a double red: (a) the four configurations for u, v, and z before restructuring; (b) after restructuring.

Case 2: *The Sibling* **w** *of* **v** *is Red.* (See Figure 9.23.) In this case, the double red denotes an overflow in the corresponding (2,4) tree T. To fix the problem, we perform the equivalent of a split operation. Namely, we do a ***recoloring***: we color v and w black and their parent u red (unless u is the root, in which case, it is colored black). It is possible that, after such a recoloring, the double red problem reappears, although higher up in the tree T, since u may have a red parent. If the double red problem reappears at u, then we repeat the consideration of the two cases at u. Thus, a recoloring either eliminates the double red problem at node z, or propagates it to the grandparent u of z. We continue going up T performing recolorings until we finally resolve the double red problem (with either a final recoloring or a trinode restructuring). Thus, the number of recolorings caused by an insertion is no more than half the height of tree T, that is, no more than $\log(n+1)$ by Proposition 9.5.

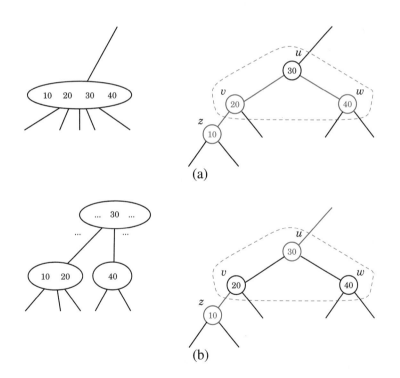

Figure 9.23: Recoloring to remedy the double red problem: (a) before recoloring and the corresponding 5-node in the associated (2,4) tree before the split; (b) after the recoloring (and corresponding nodes in the associated (2,4) tree after the split).

Figures 9.24 and 9.25 show a sequence of insertions in a red-black tree.

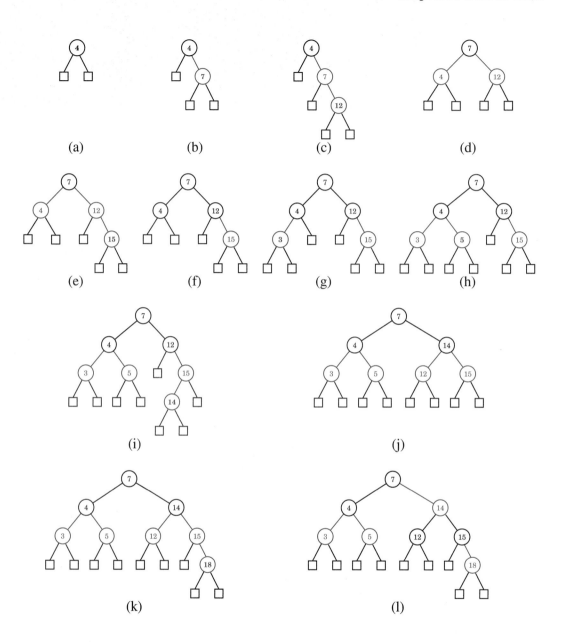

Figure 9.24: A sequence of insertions in a red-black tree: (a) initial tree; (b) insertion of 7; (c) insertion of 12, which causes a double red; (d) after restructuring; (e) insertion of 15, which causes a double red; (f) after recoloring (the root remains black); (g) insertion of 3; (h) insertion of 5; (i) insertion of 14, which causes a double red; (j) after restructuring; (k) insertion of 18, which causes a double red; (l) after recoloring. (Continued in Figure 9.25.)

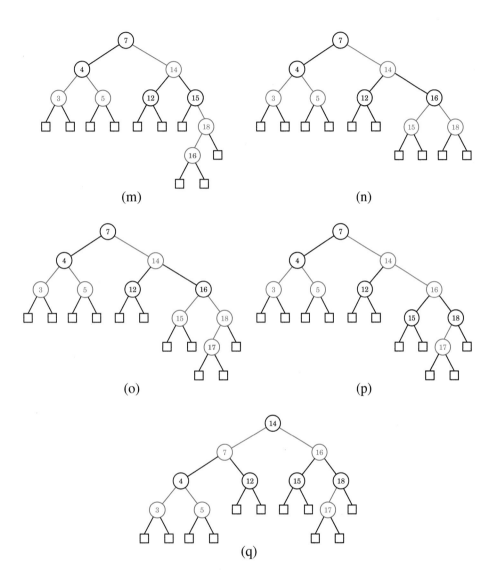

Figure 9.25: A sequence of insertions in a red-black tree : (m) insertion of 16, which causes a double red; (n) after restructuring; (o) insertion of 17, which causes a double red; (p) after recoloring there is again a double red, to be handled by a restructuring; (q) after restructuring. (Continued from Figure 9.24.)

The cases for insertion imply an interesting property for red-black trees. Namely, since the Case 1 action eliminates the double-red problem with a single trinode restructuring and the Case 2 action performs no restructuring operations, at most one restructuring is needed in a red-black tree insertion. By the above analysis and the fact that a restructuring or recoloring takes $O(1)$ time, we have the following:

Proposition 9.6: *The insertion of a key-element item in a red-black tree storing n items can be done in $O(\log n)$ time and requires at most $O(\log n)$ recolorings and one trinode restructuring (a* restructure() *operation).*

Removal

Suppose now that we are asked to remove an item with key k from a red-black tree T. Removing such an item initially proceeds as for a binary search tree (Section 9.1.2). First, we search for a node u storing such an item. If node u does not have an external child, we find the internal node v following u in the inorder traversal of T, move the item at v to u, and perform the removal at v. Thus, we may consider only the removal of an item with key k stored at a node v with an external child w. Also, as we did for insertions, we keep in mind the correspondence between red-black tree T and its associated $(2,4)$ tree T' (and the removal algorithm for T').

To remove the item with key k from a node v of T with an external child w we proceed as follows. Let r be the sibling of w, and x be the parent of v. We remove nodes v and w, and make r a child of x. If v was red (hence r is black) or r is red (hence v was black), we color r black and we are done. If, instead, r is black and v was black, then, to preserve the depth property, we give r a fictitious *double black* color. We now have a color violation, called the double black problem. A double black in T denotes an underflow in the corresponding $(2,4)$ tree T'. Recall that x is the parent of the double black node r. To remedy the double-black problem at r, we consider three cases.

Case 1: *The Sibling* **y** *of* **r** *is Black and has a Red Child* **z**. (See Figure 9.26.)
Resolving this case corresponds to a transfer operation in the $(2,4)$ tree T'. We perform a *trinode restructuring* by means of operation restructure(z). Recall that the operation restructure(z) takes the node z, its parent y, and grandparent x, labels them temporarily left to right as a, b, and c, and replaces x with the node labeled b, making it the parent of the other two. (See also the description of restructure() in Section 9.2.) We color a and c black, give b the former color of x, and color r black. This trinode restructuring eliminates the double black problem. Hence, at most one restructuring is performed in a removal operation in this case.

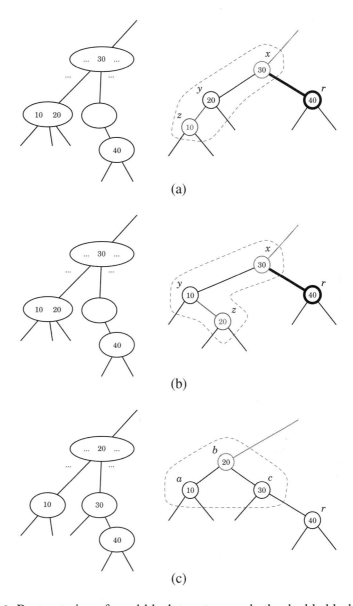

Figure 9.26: Restructuring of a red-black tree to remedy the double black problem: (a) and (b) configurations before the restructuring, where r is a right child and the associated nodes in the corresponding $(2,4)$ tree before the transfer (two other symmetric configurations where r is a left child are possible); (c) configuration after the restructuring and the associated nodes in the corresponding $(2,4)$ tree after the transfer. The grey color for node x in parts (a) and (b) and for node b in part (c) denotes the fact that this node may be colored either red or black.

Case 2: *The Sibling* **y** *of* **r** *is Black and Both Children of* **y** *are Black*. (See Figures 9.27 and 9.28.) Resolving this case corresponds to a fusion operation in the corresponding $(2,4)$ tree T'. We do a ***recoloring***; we color r black, we color y red, and, if x is red, we color it black (Figure 9.27); otherwise, we color x ***double black*** (Figure 9.28). Hence, after this recoloring, the double black problem may reappear at the parent x of r. (See Figure 9.28.) That is, this recoloring either eliminates the double black problem or propagates it into the parent of the current node. We then repeat a consideration of these three cases at the parent. Thus, since Case 1 performs a trinode restructuring operation and stops (and, as we will soon see, Case 3 is similar), the number of recolorings caused by a removal is no more than $\log(n+1)$.

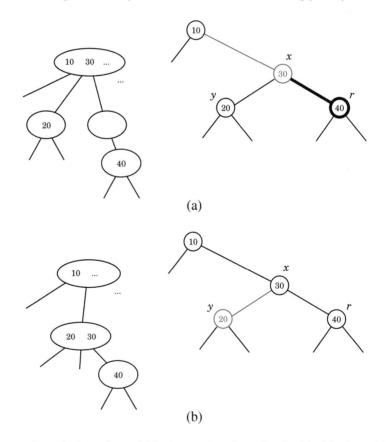

(a)

(b)

Figure 9.27: Recoloring of a red-black tree that fixes the double black problem: (a) before the recoloring and corresponding nodes in the associated $(2,4)$ tree before the fusion (other similar configurations are possible); (b) after the recoloring and corresponding nodes in the associated $(2,4)$ tree after the fusion.

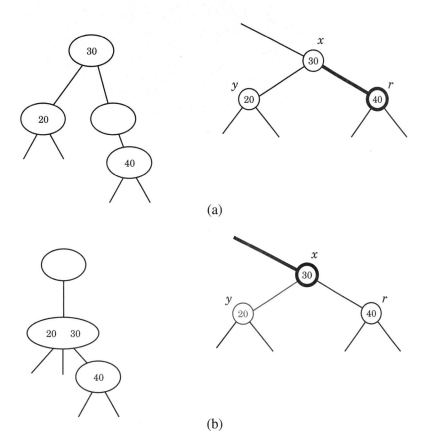

Figure 9.28: Recoloring of a red-black tree that propagates the double black problem: (a) configuration before the recoloring and corresponding nodes in the associated $(2,4)$ tree before the fusion (other similar configurations are possible); (b) configuration after the recoloring and corresponding nodes in the associated $(2,4)$ tree after the fusion.

Case 3: *The Sibling y of r is Red.* (See Figure 9.29.) In this case, we perform an
  adjustment operation, as follows. If y is the right child of x, let z be the right
  child of y; otherwise, let z be the left child of y. Execute the trinode restructure operation restructure(z), which makes y the parent of x. Color y black
  and x red. An adjustment corresponds to choosing a different representation
  of a 3-node in the $(2,4)$ tree T'. After the adjustment operation, the sibling of
  r is black, and either Case 1 or Case 2 applies, with a different meaning of x
  and y. Note that if Case 2 applies, the double-black problem cannot reappear.
  Thus, to complete Case 3 we make one more application of either Case 1 or
  Case 2 and we are done. Therefore, at most one adjustment is performed in
  a removal operation.

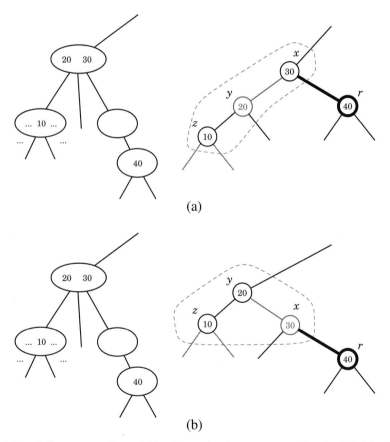

Figure 9.29: Adjustment of a red-black tree in the presence of a double black problem: (a) configuration before the adjustment and corresponding nodes in the associated $(2,4)$ tree (a symmetric configuration is possible); (b) configuration after the
adjustment with the same corresponding nodes in the associated $(2,4)$ tree.

From the above algorithm description, we see that the tree updating needed after a removal involves an upward march in the tree T, while performing, at most, a constant amount of work (in a restructuring, recoloring, or adjustment) per node. Thus, since any changes we make at a node in T during this upward march takes $O(1)$ time (because it affects a constant number of nodes), we have the following:

Proposition 9.7: *The algorithm for removing an item from a red-black tree with n items takes $O(\log n)$ time and performs $O(\log n)$ recolorings and at most one adjustment plus one additional trinode restructuring. Thus, it performs two* restructure() *operations at most.*

In Figures 9.30 and 9.31, we show a sequence of removal operations on a red-black tree. We illustrate Case 1 restructurings in Figure 9.30c and d. We illustrate Case 2 recolorings at several places in Figures 9.30 and 9.31. Finally, in Figure 9.31i and j, we show an example of a Case 3 adjustment.

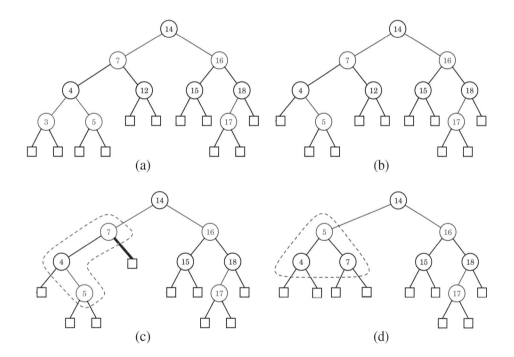

Figure 9.30: Sequence of removals from a red-black tree: (a) initial tree; (b) removal of 3; (c) removal of 12, causing a double black (handled by restructuring); (d) after restructuring. (Continued in Figure 9.31.)

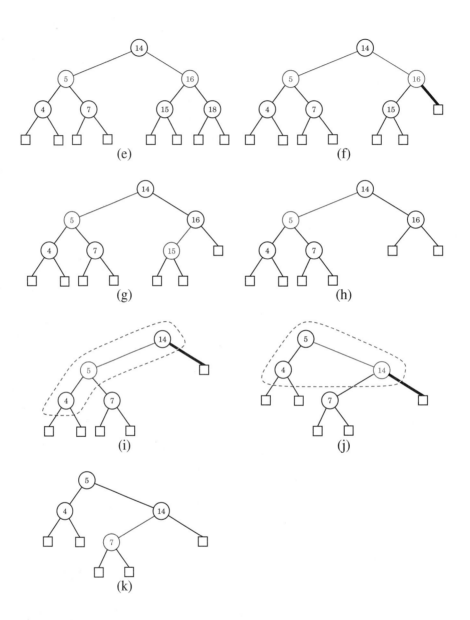

Figure 9.31: Sequence of removals in a red-black tree: (e) removal of 17; (f) removal of 18, causing a double black (handled by recoloring); (g) after recoloring; (h) removal of 15; (i) removal of 16, causing a double black (handled by an adjustment); (j) after the adjustment the double black needs to be handled by a recoloring; (k) after the recoloring (Continued from Figure 9.30.)

9.5.2 C++ Implementation

In Code Fragments 9.11 through 9.14, we show portions of a C++ implementation of a dictionary realized by means of a red-black tree. Class RBItem, shown in Code Fragment 9.11, is used to represent a key-element item for a node of the red-black tree. It is derived from class Item (see Code Fragments 7.2 and 9.3). It defines an additional member variable color, representing the color of the node. We also define an enumerated type Color, whose values are RED and BLACK.

```
enum Color {RED, BLACK};                        // item colors
template <typename Key, typename Element>
class RBItem : public Item<Key,Element> {        // a RBTree item
private:
  Color col;                                     // node color
public:
  RBItem(const Key& k = Key(),
         const Element& e = Element(), Color c = RED) // constructor
       : Item<Key,Element>(k, e), col(c) { }
  Color color() const { return col; }            // get color
  void setColor(Color c) { col = c; }            // set color
};
```

Code Fragment 9.11: Class implementing the item and node information of a red-black tree. The color of the node in the tree is stored as a member variable.

Class RBTree, partially shown in Code Fragments 9.12 through 9.14, is derived from BinarySearchTree (Code Fragments 9.3). As in the AVL tree, we assume that the base class's binary tree T implements the binary tree ADT, and, in addition, supports the function restructure() for performing trinode restructurings (rotations); its implementation is left as an exercise (P-9.5).

Class RBTree inherits functions size(), isEmpty(), find(), and findAll() from BinarySearchTree but overrides functions insertItem(), removeElement(), and removeAllElements(). The principal structural difference between class RBTree and class BinarySearchTree is that we refer to RBItem objects rather than Item objects in the internal nodes of the tree. We define a number of utility functions for accessing and manipulating node colors. Some of the utility functions of class RBTree are not shown.

The functions insertItem() and removeElement(), and the auxiliary rebalancing functions remedyDoubleRed() and remedyDoubleBlack() are shown in Code Fragments 9.13 and 9.14. The removal function begins by calling the parent class's finder() and remover() utilities (Code Fragment 9.6), which find and remove the item and return the position r of the replacing node. We then set the color of r and may call remedyDoubleBlack() to fix a double-black problem.

```
template <typename Key, typename Element>
class RBTree : public BinarySearchTree<Key, Element, RBItem<Key,Element> > {
protected:                                    // local types
  typedef RBItem<Key, Element>      Item;     // a tree node item
  typedef BinarySearchTree<Key, Element, Item> BST; // base search tree
  typedef BST::BTPosition          BTPosition;  // a tree position
public:                                       // public types
  typedef BST::Position            Position;  // a position
protected:                                    // local utilities
  Color color(const BTPosition& p) const {    // get position's color
    if (T.isExternal(p)) return BLACK;        // externals are black
    return p.element().color();
  }
  bool isRed(const BTPosition& p) const       // is p red?
    { return color(p) == RED; }
  bool isBlack(const BTPosition& p) const     // is p black?
    { return color(p) == BLACK; }
  void setRed(const BTPosition& p)            // make p red
    { if (T.isInternal(p)) p.element().setColor(RED); }
  void setBlack(const BTPosition& p)          // make p black
    { if (T.isInternal(p)) p.element().setColor(BLACK); }
  void setColor(const BTPosition& p, Color color)  // set p's color
    { if (T.isInternal(p)) p.element().setColor(color); }
  bool hasTwoExternalChildren(const BTPosition& p) const // 2 external children?
    { return (T.isExternal(T.leftChild(p)) &&
            T.isExternal(T.rightChild(p))); }
  bool hasRedChild(const BTPosition& p) const  // does p have red child?
    { return (isRed(T.leftChild(p)) || isRed(T.rightChild(p))); }
  // ... (other utilities omitted)
public:
  RBTree() : BST() { }                        // constructor
  // ... (insert insertItem() and removeElement() here)
};
```

Code Fragment 9.12: The class RBTree, which implements a red-black tree. Some of the local utility functions are not shown. (See also Code Fragments 9.13 and 9.14.)

```
public:
  void insertItem(const Key& k, const Element& e) {  // insert (key,element)
    BTPosition z = inserter(k, e);                     // insert in base tree
    if (T.isRoot(z))
      setBlack(z);                                     // root is always black
    else
      remedyDoubleRed(z);                              // rebalance if needed
  }
protected:
  void remedyDoubleRed(const BTPosition& z) {          // fix double-red z
    BTPosition v = T.parent(z);                        // v is z's parent
    if (T.isRoot(v) || isBlack(v)) return;             // v is black, all ok
                                                        // z, v are double-red
    if (isBlack(T.sibling(v)))    {                    // Case 1: restructuring
      v = T.restructure(z);
      setBlack(v);                                     // top vertex now black
      setRed(T.leftChild(v)); setRed(T.rightChild(v)); // children are red
    }
    else {                                             // Case 2: recoloring
      setBlack(v);                                     // make v black
      setBlack(T.sibling(v));                          // ..and its sibling
      BTPosition u = T.parent(v);                      // u is v's parent
      if (T.isRoot(u)) return;
      setRed(u);                                       // make u red
      remedyDoubleRed(u);                              // may need to fix u now
    }
  }
}
```

Code Fragment 9.13: Dictionary function insertItem() and utility function remedyDoubleRed() of class RBTree. It first creates a new RBItem object and then calls the parent class's utility function inserter() (Code Fragment 9.5), which inserts the new item and returns the inserted position. If the newly inserted node is the root, it is colored black. Otherwise, it is colored red, and remedyDoubleRed() is called to test for and fix any double-red problems. (See Code Fragment 9.12.)

```
public:
  void removeElement(const Key& k)                    // remove using key
      throw(NonexistentElementException) {
    BTPosition u = finder(k, T.root());               // find the node
    if (u.isNull())                                   // not found?
      throw NonexistentElementException("Remove nonexistent element");
    BTPosition r = remover(u);                        // remove u
    if (T.isRoot(r) || isRed(r) || wasParentRed(r))
      setBlack(r);                                    // fix by color change
    else                                              // r, parent both black
      remedyDoubleBlack(r);                           // fix double-black r
  }
protected:
  void remedyDoubleBlack(const BTPosition& r) {       // fix double-black r
    BTPosition x, y, z;
    x = T.parent(r);
    y = T.sibling(r);
    if (isBlack(y))  {
      if (hasRedChild(y)) {                           // Case 1: restructuring
        z = redChild(y);
        Color oldColor = color(x);                    // save top vertex color
        z = T.restructure(z);                         // restructure x,y,z
        setColor(z, oldColor);        setBlack(r);    // fix colors
        setBlack(T.leftChild(z));     setBlack(T.rightChild(z));
      }
      else {                                          // Case 2: recoloring
        setBlack(r); setRed(y);                       // r=black, y=red
        if (isBlack(x) && !T.isRoot(x))
        remedyDoubleBlack(x);                         // fix double-black x
        setBlack(x);
      }
    }
    else {                                            // Case 3: adjustment
      if (y == T.rightChild(x))  z = T.rightChild(y); // z is the grandchild
      else                       z = T.leftChild(y);  // ...on same side as y
      T.restructure(z);                               // restructure x,y,z
      setBlack(y); setRed(x);                         // y=black, x=red
      remedyDoubleBlack(r);                           // fix by Case 1 or 2
    }
  }
}
```

Code Fragment 9.14: Removal functions of RBTree. (See Code Fragment 9.12.)

9.5.3 Performance

Table 9.4 summarizes the running times of the main operations of a dictionary realized by means of a red-black tree. We illustrate the justification for these bounds in Figure 9.32.

Operation	Time
size, isEmpty	$O(1)$
find, insertItem, removeElement	$O(\log n)$
findAll	$O(\log n + s)$
removeAllElements	$O(\log n + r)$

Table 9.4: Performance of an n-element dictionary realized by a red-black tree, where s denotes the size of the iterator returned by findAll() and r denotes the number of elements removed by removeAllElements(). The space usage is $O(n)$.

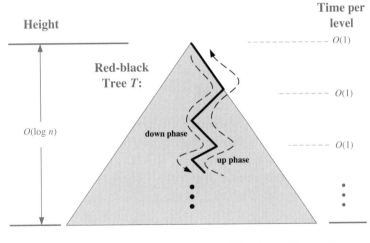

Figure 9.32: Illustrating the running time of searches and updates in a red-black tree. The time performance is $O(1)$ per level, broken into a down phase, which typically involves searching, and an up phase, which typically involves recolorings and performing local trinode restructurings (rotations).

Thus, a red-black tree achieves logarithmic worst-case running times for both searching and updating in a dictionary. The red-black tree data structure is slightly more complicated than its corresponding $(2,4)$ tree. Even so, a red-black tree has a conceptual advantage that only a constant number of trinode restructurings are ever needed to restore the balance in a red-black tree after an update.

9.6   Locator-Based Search Trees ⋆

As mentioned in Section 8.1.1, one disadvantage of our dictionary ADT is that as operations are performed on the dictionary, the dictionary Position objects may become invalid. This is because objects may be moved, and so a position that refers to some element prior to an operation may refer to an entirely different element after the operation. In order to avoid this problem, in Section 8.5 we defined a dictionary ADT that is based on locators rather than positions. Recall from Section 7.4 that a Locator object is a generalization of a Position object for use in key-based containers. Unlike a position, which is associated with a particular node of the structure, a locator "sticks" to the associated key-element pair, even if it is moved around in the data structure. The operations of the locator-based dictionary ADT differ only in that search and insertion operations return an object of type Locator and additional operations remove() and replaceKey() are supported.

In the case of binary search trees, the movement of a key-element pair may occur in a deletion operation. Indeed, when an item is removed from the tree, another item may need to be moved to fill the resulting hole, as shown in Figure 9.6. Our approach to supporting locator-based operations will be to avoid copying key-element pairs between nodes altogether. Instead, when we need to move information from one node to another, we will swap the entire nodes themselves, by unlinking each node from the tree and "relinking" each node into the location occupied by the other node. This operation will only be needed for internal nodes of the binary tree. Let us assume that the underlying binary tree class is augmented with a member function swapInternal(p,q), which swaps (by relinking) nodes p and q. We leave the implementation of this function as an exercise. (By the way, this is the same approach used in the implementation of the C++ STL map class.)

```
class Locator {                                    // a locator
  BTPosition btPos;                                // position of tree node
public:
  Locator(const BTPosition& p) : btPos(p) { }      // constructor
  Element& element() const                         // get element
    { return btPos.element().element(); }
  const Key& key() const                           // get key (read only)
    { return btPos.element().key(); }
  bool isNull() const                              // a null locator?
    { return btPos.isNull(); }
};
```

Code Fragment 9.15: Class Locator, which provides a locator to a key-element pair in a locator-based binary search tree. This will be included in the public section of class BinarySearchTreeLoc.

A Locator to a search-tree node is implemented like a Position in the position-based binary search tree (see Code Fragment 9.15). Each locator stores the position of the associated node in the underlying binary search tree. To see why this approach satisfies the requirements of a locator, observe that when two nodes are swapped through relinking, even though their conceptual position within the tree changes, the physical addresses of the nodes do not change. Thus, a pointer to a node remains valid from insertion to deletion.

The structural differences between the position-based and locator-based binary search trees are remarkably small. First, all occurrences of Position are replaced by Locator. Since these two objects provide the same public interface, this change is trivial. The locInsertItem() operation returns the Locator it receives from inserter() (rather than void). The only significant change occurs in the utility function remover(), and is shown in Code Fragment 9.16. The line of this function that invokes setItem() in the position-based code, is replaced with a call to swapInternal(). In this way, rather than copying the contents of nodes, and possibly invalidating positions pointing to these nodes, we relink the nodes and hence preserve the validity of these positions.

```
public:
    void removeElement(const Key& k)              // remove using key
        throw(NonexistentElementException) {
        BTPosition p = finder(k, T.root());        // find the node
        if (p.isNull())                            // not found?
            throw NonexistentElementException("Remove nonexistent element");
        remover(p);                                // remove it
    }
protected:
    BTPosition remover(const BTPosition& r) {      // remove utility
        BTPosition p;
        if (T.isExternal(T.leftChild(r)))          // left is external?
            p = T.leftChild(r);                    // remove from left
        else if (T.isExternal(T.rightChild(r)))    // right is external?
            p = T.rightChild(r);                   // remove from right
        else {                                     // both internal?
            p = T.rightChild(r);                   // p = replacement
            do                                     // find leftmost in
                p = T.leftChild(p);                // ...right subtree
            while (T.isInternal(p));
            T.swapInternal(T.parent(p), r);        // swap parent(p) and r
        }
        return T.removeAboveExternal(p);           // remove p and parent
    }
```

Code Fragment 9.16: The member functions for performing removal from a locator-based dictionary implemented with a binary search tree.

9.7   External Searching ⋆

In this section, we study the problem of implementing an ordered dictionary for a large collection of items that do not fit in main memory. One of the main applications of large dictionaries is database systems. When data cannot be held in main memory, it must be stored in **external memory**, which is usually a disk. The time to access information on a disk is so much slower than the time used to transfer that information, so data items on a disk are usually grouped into contiguous sections called **blocks**. We refer to these secondary-memory blocks as **disk blocks**. Likewise, we refer to the transfer of a block between secondary memory and main memory as a **disk transfer**. Even though we use this terminology, the search techniques we discuss in this section also apply when the main memory is the CPU cache and the secondary memory is the main (RAM) memory, for cache lines are also collected into blocks.

There is a great time difference that exists between main memory accesses and disk accesses, equal to several orders of magnitude for many systems. Thus, the main goal of maintaining a dictionary in external memory is to minimize the number of disk transfers needed to perform a query or update. In fact, the difference in speed between disk and internal memory is so great that we should be willing to perform a considerable number of internal-memory accesses if they allow us to avoid a few disk transfers. Let us, therefore, analyze the performance of dictionary implementations by counting the number of disk transfers each would require to perform the standard dictionary search and update operations. We refer to this count as the **I/O complexity** of the algorithms involved.

Let us consider first the simple dictionary realizations that use a sequence to store the items. If the sequence is implemented as an unsorted doubly linked list, that is, a list-based log file, then insertions can be performed with $O(1)$ transfers each, but removals and searching requires $\Theta(n)$ transfers in the worst case, where n is the number of items in the dictionary, since each link hop we perform could access a different block. This search time can be improved to $O(n/B)$ transfers (using a method we explore in Exercise C-9.21), where B denotes the number of nodes of the list that can fit into a block, but this is still poor performance. We could alternately implement the sequence using a sorted vector, that is, a look-up table. In this case, a search performs $O(\log_2 n)$ transfers, using the binary search algorithm, which is a nice improvement. But this solution requires $\Theta(n/B)$ transfers to implement an insert or remove operation in the worst case, for we may have to access all the blocks holding the array to move elements up or down. Thus, sequence-based implementations of a dictionary are not efficient from an external memory standpoint.

Since these simple implementations are I/O inefficient, we should consider the logarithmic-time strategies that use balanced binary trees (such as AVL trees or red-black trees) or other search structures with logarithmic average-case query and update times (such as skip lists). These methods store the dictionary items at the nodes of a binary tree or a graph (for skip lists). Typically, each node accessed for a query or update in one of these structures will be in a different block. Thus, these methods typically require $O(\log_2 n)$ transfers to perform a query or update operation. This is pretty good, but we can do much better. In particular, we describe, in the remainder of this section, how to perform dictionary query and update operations using only $O(\log_B n)$, that is, $O(\log n / \log B)$, transfers, where B is much larger than 2.

To improve the external-memory performance of the dictionary implementations discussed above, we should be willing to perform up to $O(B)$ internal-memory accesses to avoid a single disk transfer, where B denotes the size of a disk block. The hardware and software that drive the disk perform this many internal-memory accesses, just to bring a block into internal memory, and, even then, this is only a small part of the cost of a disk transfer. Thus, $O(B)$ high-speed, internal-memory accesses are a small price to pay to avoid a time-consuming disk transfer.

9.7.1　(a, b) Trees

To reduce the importance of the performance difference between internal-memory accesses and external-memory accesses for searching, we can represent our dictionary using a multi-way search tree (Section 9.3). This approach gives rise to a generalization of the $(2, 4)$ tree data structure known as the (a, b) tree.

An (a, b) tree is a multi-way search tree, such that each node has between a and b children and stores between $a - 1$ and $b - 1$ items. The algorithms for searching, inserting, and removing elements in an (a, b) tree are straightforward generalizations of the corresponding ones for $(2, 4)$ trees. The advantage of generalizing $(2, 4)$ trees to (a, b) trees is that a generalized class of trees provides a flexible search structure, where the size of the nodes and the running time of the various dictionary operations depends on the parameters a and b. By setting the parameters a and b appropriately with respect to the size of disk blocks, we can derive a data structure that achieves good external-memory performance.

An (a, b) **tree**, where a and b are integers, such that $2 \le a \le (b + 1)/2$, is a multi-way search tree T with the following additional restrictions:

Size Property: Each internal node has at least a children, unless it is the root, and has at most b children.

Depth Property: All the external nodes have the same depth.

Proposition 9.8: *The height of an* (a,b) *tree storing* n *items is* $\Omega(\log n/\log b)$ *and* $O(\log n/\log a)$.

Justification: Let T be an (a,b) tree storing n elements, and let h be the height of T. We justify the proposition by establishing the following bounds on h:

$$\frac{1}{\log b}\log(n+1) \leq h \leq \frac{1}{\log a}\log\frac{n+1}{2}+1.$$

By the size and depth properties, the number n'' of external nodes of T is at least $2a^{h-1}$ and at most b^h. By Proposition 9.3, $n'' = n+1$. Thus

$$2a^{h-1} \leq n+1 \leq b^h.$$

Taking the logarithm in base 2 of each term, we get

$$(h-1)\log a + 1 \leq \log(n+1) \leq h\log b.$$

∎

We recall that in a multi-way search tree T, each node v of T holds a secondary structure $D(v)$, which is itself a dictionary (Section 9.3). If T is an (a,b) tree, then $D(v)$ stores at most b items. Let $f(b)$ denote the time for performing a search in a $D(v)$ dictionary. The search algorithm in an (a,b) tree is exactly like the one for multi-way search trees given in Section 9.3. Hence, searching in an (a,b) tree T with n items takes $O(\frac{f(b)}{\log a}\log n)$ time. Note that if b is a constant (and thus a is also), then the search time is $O(\log n)$, independent of the specific implementation of the secondary structures.

The main application of (a,b) trees is for dictionaries stored in external memory (for example, on a disk or CD-ROM). Namely, to minimize disk accesses, we select the parameters a and b so that each tree node occupies a single disk block (so that $f(b) = 1$ if we wish to simply count block transfers). Providing the right a and b values in this context gives rise to a data structure known as the B-tree, which we will describe shortly. Before we describe this structure, however, let us discuss how insertions and removals are handled in (a,b) trees.

Update Operations

The insertion algorithm for an (a,b) tree is similar to that for a $(2,4)$ tree. An overflow occurs when an item is inserted into a b-node v, which becomes an illegal $(b+1)$-node. (Recall that a node in a multi-way tree is a d-node if it has d children.) To remedy an overflow, we split node v by moving the median item of v

into the parent of v and replacing v with a $\lceil (b+1)/2 \rceil$-node v' and a $\lfloor (b+1)/2 \rfloor$-node v''. We can now see the reason for requiring $a \le (b+1)/2$ in the definition of an (a,b) tree. Note that as a consequence of the split, we need to build the secondary structures $D(v')$ and $D(v'')$.

Removing an element from an (a,b) tree is also similar to removing elements from $(2,4)$ trees. An underflow occurs when a key is removed from an a-node v, distinct from the root, which causes v to become an illegal $(a-1)$-node. To remedy an underflow, we either perform a transfer with a sibling of v that is not an a-node or we perform a fusion of v with a sibling that is an a-node. The new node w resulting from the fusion is a $(2a-1)$-node. Here, we see another reason for requiring $a \le (b+1)/2$. Note that as a consequence of the fusion, we need to build the secondary structure $D(w)$.

Table 9.5 shows the performance of a dictionary realized with an (a,b) tree.

Method	Time
find()	$O\left(\frac{f(b)}{\log a} \log n \right)$
insertItem()	$O\left(\frac{g(b)}{\log a} \log n \right)$
removeElement()	$O\left(\frac{g(b)}{\log a} \log n \right)$

Table 9.5: Time bounds for functions of a dictionary realized by an (a,b) tree. Only the fundamental functions are shown. We let n denote the number of elements in the dictionary. The space usage is $O(n)$.

The time bounds in Table 9.5 are based on the following assumptions and facts.

- The (a,b) tree T is realized using the data structure described in Section 9.3, and the secondary structure of the nodes of T support search in $f(b)$ time, and split and fusion operations in $g(b)$ time, for some functions $f(b)$ and $g(b)$, which can be made to be $O(1)$ when we are only counting disk transfers.
- The height of an (a,b) tree storing n elements is $O((\log n)/(\log a))$, by Proposition 9.8.
- A search visits $O((\log n)/(\log a))$ nodes on a path between the root and an external node, and spends $f(b)$ time per node.
- A transfer operation takes $f(b)$ time.
- A split or fusion operation takes $g(b)$ time and builds a secondary structure of size $O(b)$ for the new node(s) created.
- An insertion or removal of an element visits $O((\log n)/(\log a))$ nodes on a path between the root and an external node, and spends $g(b)$ time per node.

9.7.2 B-Trees

A version of the (a,b) tree data structure, which is the best known method for maintaining a dictionary in external memory, is known as the "B-tree." (See Figure 9.33.) A **B-tree of order** d is an (a,b) tree with $a = \lceil d/2 \rceil$ and $b = d$. Since we discussed the standard dictionary query and update functions for (a,b) trees above, we restrict our discussion here to the I/O complexity of B-trees.

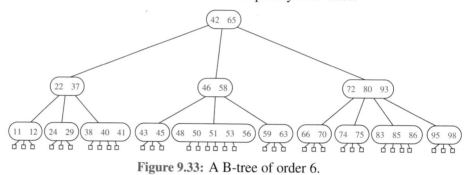

Figure 9.33: A B-tree of order 6.

An important property of B-trees is that we can choose d so that the d children pointers and the $d-1$ keys stored at a node can all fit into a single disk block, implying that d is $\Theta(B)$. This choice also allows us to assume that a and b are $\Theta(B)$ in the analysis of the search and update operations on (a,b) trees. Thus, $f(b)$ and $g(b)$ are both $O(1)$, because each time we access a node to perform a search or an update operation, we need only perform a single disk transfer.

As we have already observed above, each search or update requires that we examine at most $O(1)$ nodes for each level of the tree. Therefore, any dictionary search or update operation on a B-tree requires only $O(\log_{\lceil d/2 \rceil} n)$, that is, $O(\log n / \log B)$, disk transfers. For example, an insert operation proceeds down the B-tree to locate the node in which to insert the new item. If the node would **overflow** (to have $d+1$ children) because of this addition, then this node is **split** into two nodes that have $\lfloor (d+1)/2 \rfloor$ and $\lceil (d+1)/2 \rceil$ children, respectively. This process is then repeated at the next level up, and will continue for at most $O(\log_B n)$ levels.

Likewise, if a remove operation results in a node **underflow** (to have $\lceil d/2 \rceil - 1$ children), then we move pointers from a sibling node with at least $\lceil d/2 \rceil + 1$ children or we need to perform a **fusion** operation of this node with its sibling (and repeat this computation at the parent). As with the insert operation, this will continue up the B-tree for at most $O(\log_B n)$ levels. The requirement that each internal node have at least $\lceil d/2 \rceil$ children implies that each disk block used to support a B-tree is at least half full. Thus, we have the following:

Proposition 9.9: *A B-tree with n items has I/O complexity $O(\log_B n)$ for search or update operation, and uses $O(n/B)$ blocks, where B is the size of a block.*

9.8 Exercises

Reinforcement

R-9.1 Insert, into an initially empty binary search tree, items with the following keys (in this order): 30, 40, 24, 58, 48, 26, 11, 13. Draw the tree after each insertion.

R-9.2 Suppose that the functions of class BinarySearchTree, shown in Code Fragments 9.3 through 9.5, are used to perform the updates shown in Figures 9.4, 9.5, and 9.6. What is the node returned by the utility functions inserter() and remover() in each case?

R-9.3 A certain Professor Amongus claims that the order in which a fixed set of elements is inserted into a binary search tree does not matter—the same tree results every time. Give a small example that proves Professor Amongus wrong.

R-9.4 Professor Amongus claims he has a "patch" to his claim from the previous exercise, namely, that the order in which a fixed set of elements is inserted into an AVL tree does not matter—the same AVL tree results every time. Give a small example that proves that Professor Amongus is still wrong.

R-9.5 Is the rotation done in Figure 9.9 a single or a double rotation? What about the rotation in Figure 9.11?

R-9.6 Draw the AVL tree resulting from the insertion of an item with key 52 into the AVL tree of Figure 9.11b.

R-9.7 Draw the AVL tree resulting from the removal of the item with key 62 from the AVL tree of Figure 9.11b.

R-9.8 Explain why performing a rotation in an n-node binary tree represented using a sequence takes $\Omega(n)$ time.

R-9.9 Is the multi-way search tree of Figure 9.13a a $(2,4)$ tree? Justify your answer.

R-9.10 An alternative way of performing a split at a node v in a $(2,4)$ tree is to partition v into v' and v'', with v' being a 2-node and v'' being a 3-node. Which of the keys k_1, k_2, k_3, or k_4 do we store at v's parent in this case? Why?

R-9.11 Professor Amongus claims that a $(2,4)$ tree storing a set of items will always have the same structure, regardless of the order in which the items are inserted. Show that Professor Amongus is wrong.

R-9.12 Consider the following sequence of keys:

$$(5, 16, 22, 45, 2, 10, 18, 30, 50, 12, 1).$$

Consider the insertion of items with this set of keys in the order given into:

    a. An initially empty $(2,4)$ tree T'
    b. An initially empty red-black tree T''.

Draw T' and T'' after each insertion.

R-9.13 Draw four different red-black trees that correspond to the same $(2,4)$ tree using the correspondence rules described in the chapter.

R-9.14 For each of the following statements about red-black trees, determine whether it is true or false. If you think it is true, provide a justification. If you think it is false, give a counterexample.

    a. A subtree of a red-black tree is itself a red-black tree.
    b. The sibling of an external node is either external or it is red.
    c. Given a red-black tree T, there is an unique $(2,4)$ tree T' associated with T.
    d. Given a $(2,4)$ tree T, there is a unique red-black tree T' associated with T.

R-9.15 Draw an example red-black tree that is not an AVL tree. Your tree should have at least 6 nodes, but no more than 16.

R-9.16 Consider a tree T storing 100,000 items. What is the worst-case height of T in the following cases?

    a. T is an AVL tree.
    b. T is a $(2,4)$ tree.
    c. T is a red-black tree.
    d. T is a binary search tree.

R-9.17 Describe, in detail, the insertion and removal algorithms for an (a,b) tree.

R-9.18 Suppose T is a multi-way tree, such that each internal node has at least five and at most eight children. For what values of a and b is T a valid (a,b) tree?

R-9.19 For what values of d is the tree T of the previous exercise an order-d B-tree?

R-9.20 Draw the order-7 B-tree resulting from inserting the following keys (in this order) into an initially empty tree T:

$$(4,40,23,50,11,34,62,78,66,22,90,59,25,72,64,77,39,12).$$

R-9.21 Show each level of recursion in performing a four-way merge-sort of the sequence given in the previous exercise.

Creativity

C-9.1 Design a variation of algorithm TreeSearch() for performing the operation findAll(k) in an ordered dictionary implemented with a binary search tree T, and show that it runs in time $O(h+s)$, where h is the height of T and s is the size of the iterator returned.

C-9.2 Describe how to perform the operation removeAllElements(k) in an ordered dictionary implemented with a binary search tree T, and show that this function runs in time $O(h+s)$, where h is the height of T and s is the size of the iterator returned.

C-9.3 Draw an example of an AVL tree, such that a single removeElement() operation could require $\Theta(\log n)$ trinode restructurings (or rotations) from a leaf to the root in order to restore the height-balance property. (Use triangles to represent subtrees that are not affected by this operation.)

C-9.4 Show how to perform operation removeAllElements(k) in a dictionary implemented with an AVL tree in time $O(s \log n)$, where n is the number of elements in the dictionary at the time the operation is performed and s is the size of the iterator returned by the operation.

C-9.5 If we maintain a pointer to the position of the left-most internal node of an AVL tree, then operation first() can be performed in $O(1)$ time. Describe how the implementation of the other dictionary functions needs to be modified to maintain a pointer to the left-most position.

C-9.6★ Show that any n-node binary tree can be converted to any other n-node binary tree using $O(n)$ rotations. (Hint: Show that $O(n)$ rotations suffice to convert any binary tree into a *left chain*, where each internal node has an external right child.)

C-9.7 Let D be an ordered dictionary with n items implemented by means of an AVL tree. Show how to implement the following operation on D in time $O(\log n + s)$, where s is the size of the iterator returned:

findAllInRange(k_1, k_2): Return an iterator of all the elements in D with key k, such that $k_1 \le k \le k_2$.
Input: Objects; *Output:* Iterator.

C-9.8★ Let D be an ordered dictionary with n items implemented with an AVL tree. Show how to implement the following function for D in time $O(\log n)$:

countAllInRange(k_1, k_2): Compute and return the number of items in D with key k, such that $k_1 \le k \le k_2$.
Input: Objects; *Output:* Integer.

Note that this function returns a single integer.   (Hint: You will need to extend the AVL tree data structure, adding a new field to each internal node, and ways of maintaining this field during updates.)

C-9.9 Show that the nodes that become unbalanced in an AVL tree after operation expandExternal() is performed within the execution of an insertItem() operation, may be nonconsecutive on the path from the newly inserted node to the root.

C-9.10 Show that at most one node in an AVL tree becomes unbalanced after operation removeAboveExternal() is performed within the execution of a removeElement() dictionary operation.

C-9.11 Justify the correctness of the tie-breaking rule used in trinode restructuring for AVL-tree removal.

C-9.12 Give pseudo-code implementing the function tallGrandChild(p), which, given the position a node p, returns the position of the tallest grandchild of p. Your solution should use the tie-breaking rule described in our discussion of AVL-tree removal. You may assume that all four grandchildren of p exist, and the heights of all the nodes have been correctly computed.

C-9.13 Show that at most one trinode restructure operation (which corresponds to one single or double rotation) is needed to restore balance after any insertion in an AVL tree.

C-9.14 Let T and U be $(2,4)$ trees storing n and m items, respectively, such that all the items in T have keys less than the keys of all the items in U. Describe an $O(\log n + \log m)$ time method for *joining* T and U into a single tree that stores all the items in T and U (destroying the old versions of T and U).

C-9.15 Repeat the previous problem for red-black trees T and U.

C-9.16 Justify Proposition 9.3.

C-9.17 The Boolean indicator used to mark nodes in a red-black tree as being "red" or "black" is not strictly needed. Describe a scheme for implementing a red-black tree without adding any extra space to standard binary search tree nodes. How does your scheme affect the running times for searching and updating a red-black tree?

C-9.18 Let T be a red-black tree storing n items, and let k be the key of an item in T. Show how to construct from T, in $O(\log n)$ time, two red-black trees T' and T'', such that T' contains all the keys of T less than k, and T'' contains all the keys of T greater than k. This operation destroys T.

C-9.19 Show that the nodes of any AVL tree T can be colored "red" and "black" so that T becomes a red-black tree.

C-9.20 The *mergeable heap* ADT consists of operations insert(k,x), remove(k), unionWith(h), and minElement$()$, where the unionWith(h) operation performs a union of the mergeable heap h with the present one, destroying the old versions of both. Describe a concrete implementation of the mergeable heap ADT that achieves $O(\log n)$ performance for all its operations. For simplicity, you may assume that all keys in existing mergeable heaps are distinct, although this is not strictly necessary.

C-9.21 Show how to implement a dictionary in external memory using an unordered sequence, so that updates require only $O(1)$ transfers and $O(n/B)$ transfers in the worst case, where n is the number of elements and B is the number of list nodes that can fit into a disk block. (Hint: Consider an alternate linked list implementation that uses "fat" nodes.)

C-9.22 Change the rules that define red-black trees so that each red-black tree T has a corresponding $(4,8)$ tree, and vice versa.

C-9.23 Describe a modified version of the B-tree insertion algorithm so that each time we create an overflow because of a split of a node v, we redistribute keys among all of v's siblings, such that each sibling holds roughly the same number of keys (possibly cascading the split up to the parent of v).

What is the minimum fraction of each block that will always be filled using this scheme?

C-9.24 Suppose that instead of having the node-search function $f(d) = 1$ in an order-d B-tree T, we instead have $f(d) = \log d$. What does the asymptotic running time of performing a search in T now become?

C-9.25 Describe how to use a B-tree to implement the queue ADT so that the total number of disk transfers needed to process a sequence of n enqueue() and dequeue() operations is $O(n/B)$.

C-9.26 Another possible external-memory dictionary implementation is to use a skip list, but to collect, in individual blocks, consecutive groups of $O(B)$ nodes on any level in the skip list. In particular, we define an **order-d B-skip list** to be such a representation of a skip list structure, where each block contains at least $\lceil d/2 \rceil$ list nodes and at most d list nodes. In this case, let us also choose d to be the maximum number of list nodes from a level of a skip list that can fit into one block. Describe how we should modify the skip-list insertion and removal algorithms for a B-skip list so that the expected height of the structure is $O(\log n / \log B)$.

C-9.27 Suppose we are given a sequence S of n elements with integer keys, such that some items in S are colored "blue" and some elements in S are colored "red." In addition, say that a red element e **pairs** with a blue element f if they have the same key value. Describe an efficient external-memory algorithm for finding all the red-blue pairs in S. How many disk transfers does your algorithm perform?

Projects

P-9.1 Design a data structure for storing an email address book using the STL map class. Each entry of the address book should contain the full name, email address, and some descriptive information of the person. Each entry of the book should be accessible either by giving the person's name or their email address. Provide functions for inserting and deleting people from the address book. Also provide a function to print all the entries of the address book.

P-9.2 Implement a class that implements the dictionary ADT by adapting the STL map class.

P-9.3 Extend class BinarySearchTree, shown in Code Fragments 9.3 through 9.5, to support the functions of the ordered dictionary ADT (see Section 8.3.1).

P-9.4 Extend class BinarySearchTree, shown in Code Fragments 9.3 through 9.5, to support the locator-based functions of the ordered dictionary ADT (see Section 8.5).

P-9.5 Implement a class RestructurableNodeBinaryTree that supports the functions of the binary tree ADT, plus a function restructure() for performing a rotation operation. This class is a component of the implementation of an AVL tree given in Section 9.2.2.

P-9.6 Augment the class RestructurableNodeBinaryTree of the previous problem to include a function swapInternal(p,q), which, given the positions p and q of two internal nodes, swaps these nodes by unlinking each one and relinking it into the others position.

P-9.7 Implement the functions of the ordered dictionary ADT using an AVL tree.

P-9.8 Implement a dictionary that supports locator-based functions by means of an AVL tree.

P-9.9 Write a C++ class that implements all the functions of an ordered dictionary given in Chapter 8 using a $(2,4)$ tree.

P-9.10 Write a C++ class that can take any red-black tree and convert it into its corresponding $(2,4)$ tree and can take any $(2,4)$ tree and convert it into its corresponding red-black tree.

P-9.11 Write a C++ class that implements all the functions of a dictionary given in Chapter 8 by means of a red-black tree.

P-9.12 Form a three-programmer team and have each member implement a different one of the previous three projects. Perform extensive experimental studies to compare the speed of these three implementations. Try to design three sets of experiments, such that each favors a different implementation.

P-9.13 Write a C++ class that implements all the functions of a dictionary given in Chapter 8 by means of an (a,b) tree, where a and b are integer constants.

P-9.14 Implement the B-tree data structure, assuming a block size of $1,000$ and that keys are integers. Test the number of "disk transfers" needed to process a sequence of dictionary operations.

Chapter Notes

Some of the data structures discussed in this chapter are extensively covered by Knuth in his *Sorting and Searching* book [59], and by Mehlhorn in [74]. AVL trees are due to Adel'son-Vel'skii and Landis [1], who invented this class of balanced search trees in 1962. Binary search trees, AVL trees, and hashing are described in Knuth's *Sorting and Searching* [59] book. Average-height analyses for binary search trees can be found in the books by Aho, Hopcroft, and Ullman [5] and Cormen, Leiserson, and Rivest [25]. The handbook by Gonnet and Baeza-Yates [40] contains a number of theoretical and experimental comparisons among dictionary implementations. Aho, Hopcroft, and Ullman [4] discuss $(2,3)$ trees, which are similar to $(2,4)$ trees. Red-black trees were defined by Bayer [10]. Variations and interesting properties of red-black trees are presented in a paper by Guibas and Sedgewick [45]. The reader interested in learning more about different balanced tree data structures is referred to the books by Mehlhorn [74] and Tarjan [97], and the book chapter by Mehlhorn and Tsakalidis [77]. Knuth [59] is excellent additional reading that includes early approaches to balancing trees.

B-trees were invented by Bayer and McCreight [11], and Comer [24] provides a very nice overview of this data structure. The books by Mehlhorn [74] and Samet [89] also have nice discussions about B-trees and their variants. Aggarwal and Vitter [2] study the I/O complexity of sorting and related problems, establishing upper and lower bounds, including the lower bound for sorting given in this chapter. The reader interested in further study of I/O-efficient algorithms is encouraged to examine the survey paper of Vitter [100].

Chapter

10

Sorting, Sets, and Selection

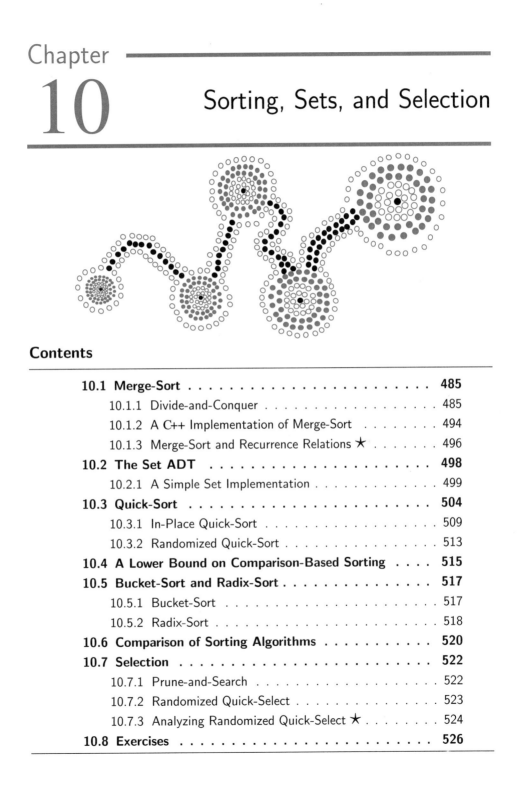

Contents

The Second Law of Thermodynamics suggests that Nature tends toward disorder. Humans, on the other hand, prefer order. Indeed, there are several advantages to keeping data in order. For example, the binary search algorithm, discussed in Section 8.1.2, works correctly only for an ordered vector. Since computers are intended to be tools for humans, we devote this chapter to the study of sorting algorithms and their applications. We recall that the sorting problem is defined as follows. Let S be a sequence of n elements that can be compared to each other according to a total order relation, that is, it is always possible to compare two elements of S to see which is larger or smaller, or if the two of them are equal. We want to rearrange S in such a way that the elements appear in increasing order (or in nondecreasing order if there are equal elements in S).

We have already presented several sorting algorithms in the previous chapters. In particular, in Section 7.1.2, we presented a simple sorting scheme, which is called PriorityQueueSort, that consists of inserting elements into a priority queue and then extracting them in nondecreasing order, by means of a series of remove-Min() operations. If the priority queue is implemented by means of a sequence, then PriorityQueueSort runs in $O(n^2)$ time and corresponds to the sorting method known as either insertion-sort or selection-sort, depending on whether the sequence realizing the priority queue is kept ordered or not (Section 7.2.3). If the priority queue is implemented by means of a heap (Section 7.3) instead, then PriorityQueueSort runs in $O(n\log n)$ time and corresponds to the sorting method known as heap-sort (Section 7.3.4).

In this chapter, we present four other sorting algorithms, called *merge-sort*, *quick-sort*, *bucket-sort*, and *radix-sort*. We also introduce the *set* abstract data type and show how the merge technique used in the merge-sort algorithm can be used in the implementation of its functions. Throughout this chapter, we assume that a total order relation is defined over the elements to be sorted. If this relation is induced by a comparator (Section 7.1.4), we assume that a comparison test takes $O(1)$ time.

This chapter also introduces some important design patterns. We have already seen the power of recursion to describe algorithms in an elegant manner. (See, for example, the tree traversal techniques presented in Chapter 6.) In this chapter, we show how recursion can be used in an algorithmic design pattern called *divide-and-conquer*, which is the main pattern used in the *merge-sort* and *quick-sort* algorithms. We also give another application (to the set ADT) of the software engineering design pattern known as the *template method* pattern. Finally, we introduce, the *prune-and-search* pattern, in the context of selection, which is also known as *decrease-and-conquer*.

10.1 Merge-Sort

In this section, we present the merge-sort algorithm, which, like some other sorting algorithms, is based on the ***divide-and-conquer*** algorithmic design pattern.

10.1.1 Divide-and-Conquer

The divide-and-conquer paradigm can be described in general terms as consisting of the following three steps:

1. ***Divide:*** If the input size is smaller than a certain threshold (say, one or two elements), solve the problem directly using a straightforward method and return the solution so obtained. Otherwise, divide the input data into two or more disjoint subsets.
2. ***Recur:*** Recursively solve the subproblems associated with the subsets.
3. ***Conquer:*** Take the solutions to the subproblems and "merge" them into a solution to the original problem.

The merge-sort algorithm applies this technique to the sorting problem.

Using Divide-and-Conquer for Sorting

Recall that in the sorting problem we are given a collection of n objects, typically stored in a vector, array, or sequence, together with a comparator defining a total order on these objects, and we are asked to produce an ordered representation of these objects. For the sake of generality, we focus on the version of the sorting problem that takes a sequence S of objects as input and returns S in sorted order. Specializations to other linear structures, such as lists, vectors, or arrays, are straightforward and left as exercises (R-10.3 and R-10.11). For the problem of sorting a sequence S with n elements, the three divide-and-conquer steps are as follows:

1. ***Divide:*** If S has zero or one element, return S immediately; it is already sorted. Otherwise (S has at least two elements), remove all the elements from S and put them into two sequences, S_1 and S_2, each containing about half of the elements of S; that is, S_1 contains the first $\lceil n/2 \rceil$ elements of S, and S_2 contains the remaining $\lfloor n/2 \rfloor$ elements.
2. ***Recur:*** Recursively sort sequences S_1 and S_2.
3. ***Conquer:*** Put back the elements into S by merging the sorted sequences S_1 and S_2 into a sorted sequence.

We can visualize an execution of the merge-sort algorithm by means of a binary tree T, called the **merge-sort tree**. Each node of T represents a recursive invocation (or call) of the merge-sort algorithm. With each node v of T, we associate the sequence S that is processed by the invocation associated with v. The children of node v are associated with the recursive calls that process the subsequences S_1 and S_2 of S. The external nodes of T are associated with individual elements of S, corresponding to instances of the algorithm that make no recursive calls.

Figure 10.1 summarizes an execution of the merge-sort algorithm by showing the input and output sequences processed at each node of the merge-sort tree. The step-by-step evolution of the merge-sort tree is shown in Figures 10.2 through 10.5.

This algorithm visualization in terms of the merge-sort tree, helps us analyze the running time of the merge-sort algorithm. In particular, since the size of the input sequence roughly halves at each recursive call of merge-sort, the height of the merge-sort tree is about $\log n$ (recall that the base of log is 2 if omitted).

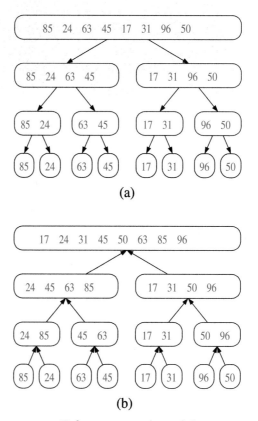

Figure 10.1: Merge-sort tree T for an execution of the merge-sort algorithm on a sequence with eight elements: (a) input sequences processed at each node of T; (b) output sequences generated at each node of T.

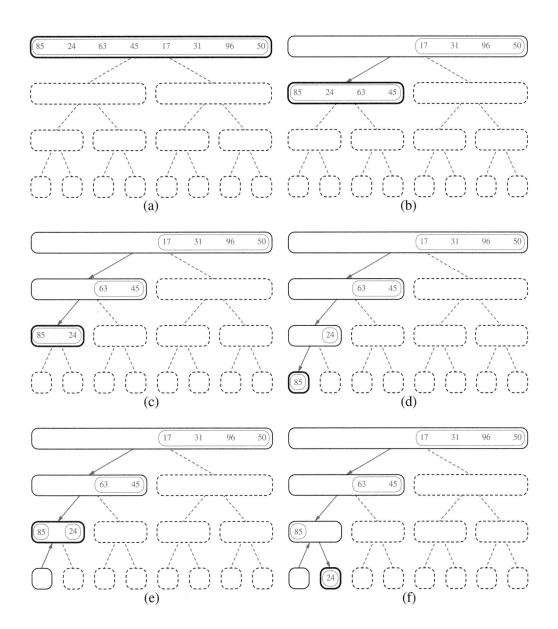

Figure 10.2: Visualization of an execution of merge-sort. Each node of the tree represents a recursive call of merge-sort. The nodes drawn with dashed lines represent calls that have not been made yet. The node drawn with thick lines represents the current call. The empty nodes drawn with thin lines represent completed calls. The remaining nodes (drawn with thin lines and not empty) represent calls that are waiting for a child invocation to return. (Continued in Figure 10.3.)

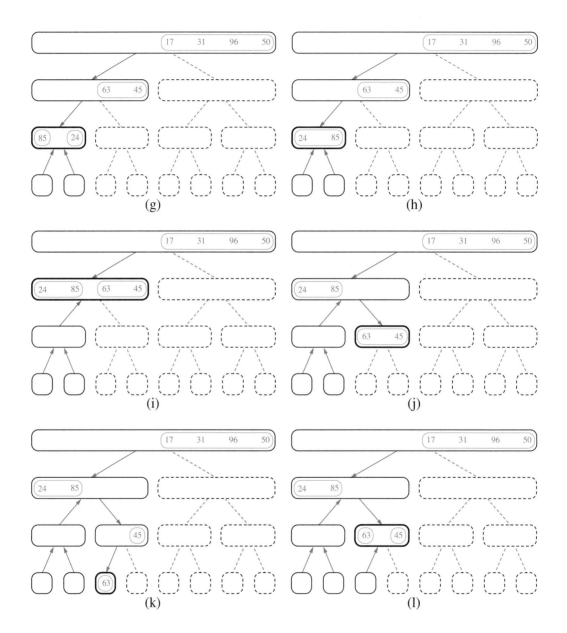

Figure 10.3: Visualization of an execution of merge-sort. Note the conquer step performed in (h). (Continued from Figure 10.2.)

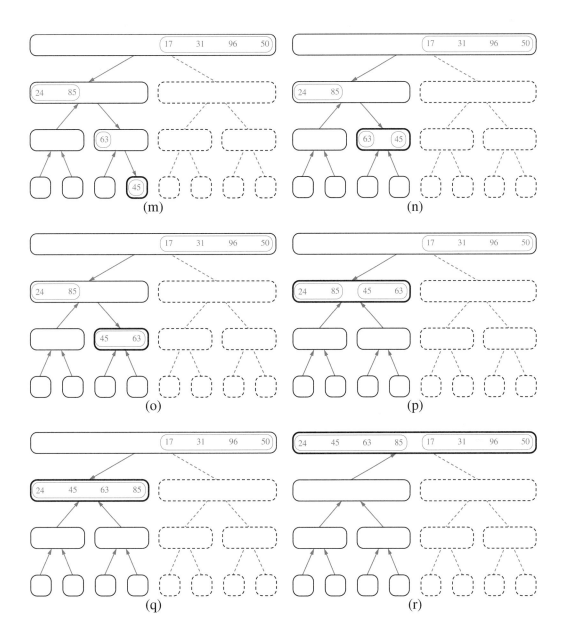

Figure 10.4: Visualization of an execution of merge-sort. Note the conquer steps performed in (o) and (q). (Continued from Figure 10.3.)

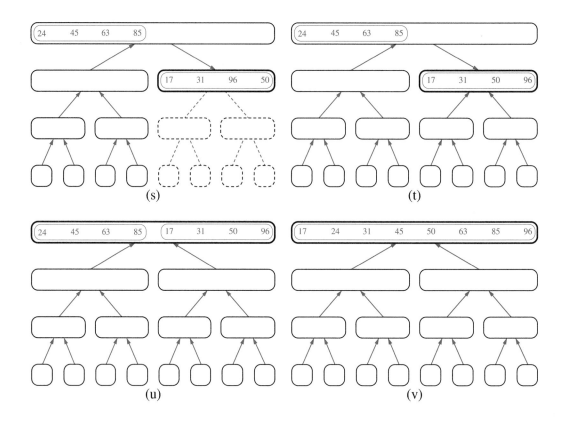

Figure 10.5: Visualization of an execution of merge-sort. Several invocations are omitted between (s) and (t). Note the conquer steps performed in (t) and (v). (Continued from Figure 10.4.)

Proposition 10.1: *The merge-sort tree associated with an execution of merge-sort on a sequence of size n has height $\lceil \log n \rceil$.*

We leave the justification of Proposition 10.1 as a simple exercise (R-10.1). We will use this proposition to analyze the running time of the merge-sort algorithm.

Having given an overview of merge-sort and an illustration of how it works, let us consider each of the steps of this divide-and-conquer algorithm in more detail. The divide and recur steps of the merge-sort algorithm are simple; dividing a sequence of size n involves separating it at the element with rank $\lceil n/2 \rceil$, and the recursive calls simply involve passing these smaller sequences as parameters. The difficult step is the conquer step, which merges two sorted sequences into a single sorted sequence. Thus, before we present our analysis of merge-sort, we need to say more about how this is done.

Merging Two Sorted Sequences

Algorithm merge(), in Code Fragment 10.1, merges two sorted sequences, S_1 and S_2, by iteratively removing a smallest element from one of these two and adding it to the end of the output sequence, S, until one of these two sequences is empty, at which point we copy the remainder of the other sequence to the output sequence.

We analyze the running time of the merge() algorithm by making some simple observations. Let n_1 and n_2 be the number of elements of S_1 and S_2, respectively. Also, let us assume that S_1, S_2, and S are implemented so that access to, insertion into, and deletion from their first and last positions take $O(1)$ time (see Section 5.3). Algorithm merge() has three while loops. Because of our assumptions, the operations performed inside each loop take $O(1)$ time each. The key observation is that, during each iteration of one of the loops, one element is removed from either S_1 or S_2. Since no insertions are made into S_1 or S_2, this observation implies that the running time of algorithm merge() is $O(n_1 + n_2)$. We show an example execution of algorithm merge() in Figure 10.6.

Algorithm merge(S_1, S_2, S):

    Input: Sequences S_1 and S_2 sorted in nondecreasing order, and an empty sequence S

    Output: Sequence S containing the elements from S_1 and S_2 sorted in nondecreasing order, with sequences S_1 and S_2 becoming empty

    while S_1 is not empty **and** S_2 is not empty **do**

      if S_1.first().element() $\leq$ S_2.first().element() **then**

        { move the first element of S_1 at the end of S }

        S.insertLast(S_1.first().element())

        S_1.remove(S_1.first())

      else

        { move the first element of S_2 at the end of S }

        S.insertLast(S_2.first().element())

        S_2.remove(S_2.first())

    { move the remaining elements of S_1 to S }

    while S_1 is not empty **do**

      S.insertLast(S_1.first().element())

      S_1.remove(S_1.first())

    { move the remaining elements of S_2 to S }

    while S_2 is not empty **do**

      S.insertLast(S_2.first().element())

      S_2.remove(S_2.first())

Code Fragment 10.1: Algorithm merge() for merging two sorted sequences.

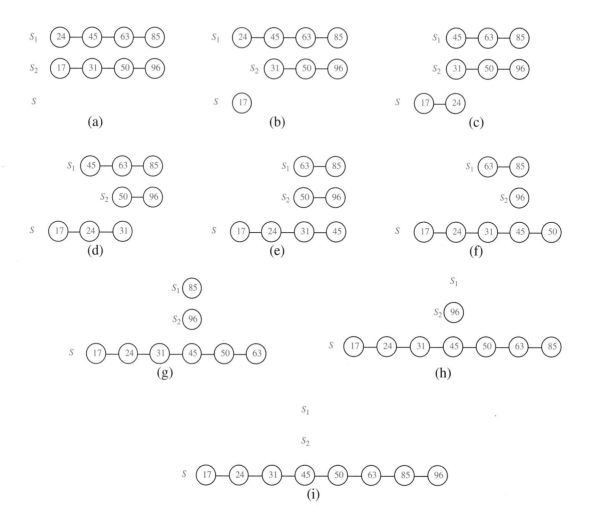

Figure 10.6: Example execution of merge() from Code Fragment 10.1.

The Running Time of Merge-Sort

To analyze the merge-sort algorithm, we begin by recalling the following fact:

Proposition 10.2: *Merging two sorted sequences S_1 and S_2 takes $O(n_1 + n_2)$ time, where n_1 is the size of S_1 and n_2 is the size of S_2.*

With this analysis of the crucial merge() algorithm used in the conquer step, let us analyze the running time of the entire merge-sort algorithm, assuming it is given an input sequence of n elements. For simplicity, we restrict our attention to the case where n is a power of 2. We leave it to an exercise (R-10.4) to show that the result of our analysis also holds when n is not a power of 2.

As we mentioned earlier, we analyze the merge-sort procedure by referring to the merge-sort tree T. (Recall Figures 10.2 through 10.5.) We call the ***time spent at a node*** v of T the running time of the recursive call associated with v, excluding the time taken waiting for the recursive calls associated with the children of v to terminate. In other words, the time spent at node v includes the running times of the divide and conquer steps, but excludes the running time of the recur step. We have already observed that the details of the divide step are straightforward; this step runs in time proportional to the size of the sequence for v. Also, as shown in Proposition 10.2, the conquer step, which consists of merging two sorted subsequences, also takes linear time. That is, letting i denote the depth of node v, the time spent at node v is $O(n/2^i)$, since the size of the sequence handled by the recursive call associated with v is equal to $n/2^i$.

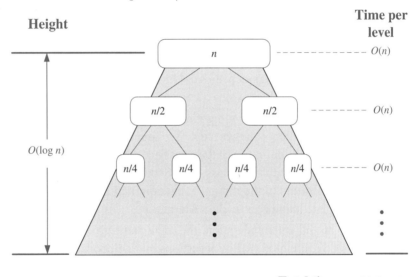

Figure 10.7: A visual time analysis of the merge-sort tree T. Each node is shown labeled with the size of its subproblem.

Looking at the tree T more globally, as shown in Figure 10.7, we see that, given our definition of "time spent at a node," the running time of merge-sort is equal to the sum of the times spent at the nodes of T. Observe that T has exactly 2^i nodes at depth i. This simple observation has an important consequence, for it implies that the overall time spent at all the nodes of T at depth i is $O(2^i \cdot n/2^i)$, which is $O(n)$. By Proposition 10.1, the height of T is $\lceil \log n \rceil$. Thus, since the time spent at each of the $\lceil \log n \rceil + 1$ levels of T is $O(n)$, we have the following result:

Proposition 10.3: *Algorithm merge-sort sorts a sequence of size n in $O(n \log n)$ time in the worst case.*

10.1.2 A C++ Implementation of Merge-Sort

The above algorithm description and analysis shows that the merge-sort algorithm runs in $O(n \log n)$ time, which asymptotically matches the fast running time of the heap-sort algorithm. In this section, we show how to implement the merge-sort algorithm in C++. Specifically, we present a C++ implementation of the merge-sort algorithm in Code Fragment 10.2.

Let us make a few observations about this implementation. The class Merge-Sort is templated with the object type Object and the sequence type Sequence that is used for storing the objects to be sorted.

The principal member of class MergeSort is the recursive function mergeSort(S), which sorts a sequence S of objects. It calls the utility function merge(S_1, S_2, S), which performs the conquer step by merging two sorted sequences S_1 and S_2 into the sorted sequence S. It also uses the utility function appendFirst(src, dst), which removes the first element of the source sequence src and appends it to the end of the destination sequence dst. Note that the class MergeSort does not contain any member data. It provides a convenient way to encapsulate these related functions.

Observe that the mergeSort() function is recursive and calls function merge() to perform the conquer step. We assume that the relational operators, such as < and <=, are defined for the sequence elements. Another possible approach is to define a comparator class (see Section 7.1.4) to determine the relative order of two elements in the merge() function, and then provide this comparator class as a template parameter to class MergeSort.

In this implementation, the input sequence, S, and the auxiliary sequences, S1 and S2, are modified by insertions and deletions only at the head and tail. Hence, each such update takes $O(1)$ time in a sequence implemented with a doubly linked list or with an array used in a circular fashion (see Table 5.5). For example, the class NodeSequence (see Code Fragment 5.13) satisfies these requirements.

Hence, for a sequence S of size n, the C++ function mergeSort(S) runs in time $O(n \log n)$, provided the following two conditions are satisfied:

1. S is implemented with a doubly linked list or with an array used in a circular fashion.

2. A comparison between two elements of S takes $O(1)$ time.

In general, when implementing an algorithm in C++, we should be sure to code the algorithm in a way that matches the assumptions present in the pseudo-code description of that algorithm.

```
template <typename Object, typename Sequence>
class MergeSort {
protected:                                           // utility functions
  void merge(Sequence& S1, Sequence& S2, Sequence& S); // merge utility
  void appendFirst(Sequence& src, Sequence& dst) {   // append utility
    Object obj = src.first().element();              // first of source
    src.remove(src.first());                         // remove it
    dst.insertLast(obj);                             // append to dest
  }
public:
  void mergeSort(Sequence& S);                       // merge sort S
};
template <typename Object, typename Sequence>
void MergeSort<Object, Sequence>::
merge(Sequence& S1, Sequence& S2, Sequence& S) {     // merge S1 and S2 to S
  while(!S1.isEmpty() && !S2.isEmpty())              // until either is empty
    if(S1.first().element() <= S2.first().element()) // copy smaller element
      appendFirst(S1, S);
    else
      appendFirst(S2, S);
  while(!S1.isEmpty())                               // copy remainder of S1
    appendFirst(S1, S);
  while(!S2.isEmpty())                               // copy remainder of S2
    appendFirst(S2, S);
}
template <typename Object, typename Sequence>
void MergeSort<Object, Sequence>::
mergeSort(Sequence& S) {                             // sort S
  Sequence S1, S2;
  int i;
  int n = S.size();
  if (n <= 1) return;                                // 0 or 1 elements
  for (i = n ; i > n/2 ; i--) appendFirst(S, S1);    // put half in S1
  for (       ; i > 0   ; i--) appendFirst(S, S2);   // put remainder in S2
  mergeSort(S1);                                     // sort S1
  mergeSort(S2);                                     // sort S2
  merge(S1, S2, S);                                  // merge S1 and S2 into S
}
```

Code Fragment 10.2: Class MergeSort, which implements the merge-sort algorithm. The public function mergeSort(S) sorts the sequence S using the utility functions merge() and appendFirst().

10.1.3 Merge-Sort and Recurrence Relations ⋆

There is another way to justify that the running time of the merge-sort algorithm is $O(n \log n)$ (Proposition 10.3). Namely, there is a justification that deals more directly with the recursive nature of the merge-sort algorithm. In this section, we present such an analysis of the running time of merge-sort, and introduce the mathematical concept of a ***recurrence relation***.

Let the function $t(n)$ denote the worst-case running time of merge-sort on an input sequence of size n. Since merge-sort is recursive, we can characterize function $t(n)$ by means of the following equalities, where function $t(n)$ is recursively expressed in terms of itself, as

$$t(n) = \begin{cases} b & \text{if } n = 1 \\ t(\lceil n/2 \rceil) + t(\lfloor n/2 \rfloor) + cn & \text{otherwise,} \end{cases}$$

where $b \geq 1$ and $c \geq 1$ are constants. A characterization of a function such as the one above is called a ***recurrence relation***, since the function appears on both the left- and right-hand sides of the equal sign. Although such a characterization is correct and accurate, what we really desire is a big-Oh type of characterization of $t(n)$ that does not involve the function $t(n)$ itself (that is, we want a ***closed-form*** characterization of $t(n)$).

In order to provide a closed-form characterization of $t(n)$, let us restrict our attention to the case where n is a power of 2 (we leave the problem of showing that our asymptotic characterization still holds in the general case as an exercise). In this case, we can simplify the definition of $t(n)$ to

$$t(n) = \begin{cases} b & \text{if } n = 1 \\ 2t(n/2) + cn & \text{otherwise.} \end{cases}$$

Even so, we must still try to characterize this recurrence equation in a closed-form way. One way to do this is to iteratively apply this equation, assuming n is relatively large. For example, after one more application of this equation, we can write a new recurrence for $t(n)$ as follows:

$$\begin{aligned} t(n) &= 2(2t(n/2^2) + (cn/2)) + cn \\ &= 2^2 t(n/2^2) + 2(cn/2) + cn \\ &= 2^2 t(n/2^2) + 2cn. \end{aligned}$$

If we apply the equation again, we get

$$t(n) = 2^3 t(n/2^3) + 3cn.$$

At this point, we see a pattern emerging, so that after applying this equation i times we get

$$t(n) \;=\; 2^i t(n/2^i) + icn.$$

The issue that remains, then, is to determine when to stop this process. To see when to stop, recall that we switch to the closed form $t(n) = b$ when $n \leq 1$, which will occur when $2^i = n$. In other words, this will occur when $i = \log n$. Making this substitution, then, yields

$$
\begin{aligned}
t(n) \;&=\; 2^{\log n} t(n/2^{\log n}) + (\log n)cn \\
&=\; nt(1) + cn\log n \\
&=\; nb + cn\log n.
\end{aligned}
$$

That is, we get a justification of the fact that $t(n)$ is $O(n\log n)$.

Confirming the Analysis via Induction

The above analysis that merge-sort runs in $O(n\log n)$ time made a few logical jumps, which may cast some doubts about its correctness. We can fully justify the outcome, however, using induction (see Section 3.3). Specifically, we can show the following:

Proposition 10.4: $t(n) \leq bn + cn\log n$.

Justification: Let us consider the two possibilities:

- **Base case**, $n = 1$. Then $t(n) = b = bn + cn\log n$.
- **General case**, $n > 1$. Let us assume that the claim is true for values less than n, and let us consider the case for n. Then $t(n) = 2t(n/2) + cn$. Since $n/2 < n$, we can apply our induction hypothesis that establishes the claim for $n/2$, as follows:

$$
\begin{aligned}
t(n) \;&\leq\; 2(b(n/2) + c(n/2)\log(n/2)) + cn \\
&=\; bn + cn(\log n - \log 2) + cn \\
&=\; bn + cn(\log n - 1) + cn \\
&=\; bn + cn\log n - cn + cn \\
&=\; bn + cn\log n.
\end{aligned}
$$

Thus, we have rigorously shown that $t(n)$ is $O(n\log n)$.   ■

In the next section, we show how sorting and the merge() algorithm can be used to implement an abstract data type for sets.

10.2   The Set ADT

In this section, we introduce the *set* ADT. A *set* is a container of distinct objects. That is, there are no duplicate elements in a set, and there is no explicit notion of keys or even an order. Even so, we include our discussion of sets here in a chapter on sorting, because sorting can play a vital role in efficient implementations of the set ADT, which is based on the well-known operations of *union*, *intersection*, and *subtraction* of two sets A and B:

$$A \cup B = \{x : x \in A \text{ or } x \in B\},$$
$$A \cap B = \{x : x \in A \text{ and } x \in B\},$$
$$A - B = \{x : x \in A \text{ and } x \notin B\}.$$

Example 10.5: *Most Internet search engines store, for each word x in their dictionary database, a set, $W(x)$, of Web pages that contain x, where each Web page is identified by a unique Internet address. When presented with a query for a word x, such a search engine need only return the Web pages in the set $W(x)$, sorted according to some proprietary priority ranking of page "importance." But when presented with a two-word query for words x and y, such a search engine must first compute the intersection $W(x) \cap W(y)$, and then return the Web pages in the resulting set sorted by priority. Many search engines use the algorithm described in this section to perform this intersection.*

The fundamental functions of the set ADT, acting on a set A, are as follows:

union(B): Replace A with the union of A and B, that is, execute $A \leftarrow A \cup B$.
Input: Set; *Output:* None.

intersect(B): Replace A with the intersection of A and B, that is, execute $A \leftarrow A \cap B$.
Input: Set; *Output:* None.

subtract(B): Replace A with the difference of A and B, that is, execute $A \leftarrow A - B$.
Input: Set; *Output:* None.

We have defined the operations union(), intersect(), and subtract() above so that they modify the contents of the set A involved. Alternatively, we could have defined these functions so that they not modify A but instead return a new set.

10.2.1 A Simple Set Implementation

In this section, we describe a way to implement the set ADT.

Sets in STL

The C++ Standard Template Library (STL) defines a primitive set class, called set, but this object does not support the set ADT operations of union, intersection, or subtraction. Its main set operations include insertion, deletion, and find. In other words, it behaves much like a dictionary in which there are keys but no associated elements.

Using a Sorted Sequence to Implement a Set

One of the simplest ways of implementing the set ADT is to store its elements in an ordered sequence. Even if a comparator is not provided, the elements themselves may have a natural order relation defined on them. In general, it should always be possible to impose an order on the elements. For example, we could use the memory addresses of the objects. Therefore, let us consider implementing the set ADT with an ordered sequence (we consider other implementations in several exercises).

We implement each of the three fundamental set operations using a generic version of the merge algorithm that takes, as input, two sorted sequences representing the input sets and constructs a sequence representing the output set, be it the union, intersection, or subtraction of the input sets. The ordering for the two sequences can be based on any consistent ordering rule (that is, a total order), provided the same ordering rule is used for the two sets on which we wish to perform a union, intersection, or subtraction. We describe the generic merge algorithm in detail in Code Fragment 10.3.

The generic merge function iteratively examines and compares the current elements a and b of sequences A and B, respectively, and finds out whether $a < b$, $a = b$, or $a > b$. Then, based on the outcome of this comparison, it determines whether it should copy one or none of the elements a and b to the end of the output sequence C. This determination is made based on the particular operation we are performing, be it a union, intersection, or subtraction.

For example, in a union operation, we copy the smaller of a and b to the output sequence, and, if they are equal, we copy just one (say a). This approach ensures that we will copy each element that is in one of the two sets, but we will not create duplicate entries. We specify the copy actions to perform using the auxiliary functions aIsLess(), bothEqual(), and bIsLess(), which we define depending on the operation we wish to perform.

Algorithm genericMerge(A, B):

  Input: Sets represented by sorted sequences A and B

  Output: Set represented by a sorted sequence C

   {We won't destroy A and B}

  let A' be a copy of A

  let B' be a copy of B

  while A' and B' are not empty **do**

   $a \leftarrow A'$.first()

   $b \leftarrow B'$.first()

   if $a < b$ **then**

    aIsLess(a, C)

    A'.removeFirst()

   else if $a = b$ **then**

    bothEqual(a, b, C)

    A'.removeFirst()

    B'.removeFirst()

   else

    bIsLess(b, C)

    B'.removeFirst()

  while A' is not empty **do**

   $a \leftarrow A'$.first()

   aIsLess(a, C)

   A'.removeFirst()

  while B' is not empty **do**

   $b \leftarrow B'$.first()

   bIsLess(b, C)

   B'.removeFirst()

Code Fragment 10.3: Generic merge algorithm, parametrized by functions aIsLess(), bothEqual(), and bIsLess(), which determine the composition of the set C. Note that this algorithm does not modify the input sequences.

Generic Merging as a Template Method Pattern

The generic merge algorithm is based on the ***template method pattern*** (see Section 6.3.5). The template method pattern is a software engineering design pattern describing a generic computation mechanism that can be specialized by redefining certain steps. In this case, we describe a method that merges two sequences into one and can be specialized by the behavior of three abstract functions.

Code Fragment 10.4 shows the class Merger providing a C++ implementation of the generic merge algorithm.

```
template <typename Object, typename Sequence>
class Merger {                                  // generic Merger
protected:                                      // local types
  typedef typename Sequence::ObjectIterator ObjectIterator;
private:                                         // member data
  ObjectIterator iterA, iterB;                   // iterators for A and B
  Object a, b;                                    // current objects
public:
  Merger() { }                                   // constructor
                                                 // generic merge function
  void merger(const Sequence& A, const Sequence& B, Sequence& C);
protected:                                       // overridden functions
  virtual void aIsLess(const Object& a, Sequence& C) = 0;
  virtual void bothEqual(const Object& a, const Object& b, Sequence& C) = 0;
  virtual void bIsLess(const Object& b, Sequence& C) = 0;
protected:                                       // local utilitites
  bool getFromA() {                              // get next from A
    if (iterA.hasNext()) { a = iterA.next(); return true; }
    return false;
  }
  bool getFromB() {                              // get next from B
    if (iterB.hasNext()) { b = iterB.next(); return true; }
    return false;
  }
};
template <typename Object, typename Sequence>
void Merger<Object, Sequence>::                  // generic merge function
merger(const Sequence& A, const Sequence& B, Sequence& C) {
  iterA = A.elements();                           // A's elements
  iterB = B.elements();                           // B's elements
  bool aExists = getFromA();                      // test for more in A
  bool bExists = getFromB();                      // test for more in B
  while (aExists && bExists) {                    // main merging loop
    if (a < b) { aIsLess(a, C); aExists = getFromA(); } // a is smaller
    else if (a == b) {                            // both are equal
      bothEqual(a, b, C);
      aExists = getFromA();
      bExists = getFromB();
    }
    else { bIsLess(b, C); bExists = getFromB(); }  // b is smaller
  }                                                // copy remainders
  while (aExists) { aIsLess(a, C); aExists = getFromA(); }
  while (bExists) { bIsLess(b, C); bExists = getFromB(); }
}
```

Code Fragment 10.4: Class Merger implementing the generic merge algorithm.

Using Inheritence to Derive Set Operations

To convert the generic Merger class into useful classes, we must extend it with classes that redefine the three auxiliary functions, aIsLess(), bothEqual(), and bIsLess().

In Code Fragment 10.5, we show how each of the operations of union, intersection, and subtraction can be described in terms of these methods. The auxiliary functions are redefined so that the template method merge() performs the following actions:

- In class UnionMerger, merge() copies every element from A and B into C, but does not duplicate any element.
- In class IntersectMerger, merge() copies every element that is in both A and B into C, but "throws away" any elements that are in one set but not in the other.
- In class SubtractMerger, merge() copies every element that is in A but not in B into C.

We could consider extending the set ADT, by adding functions insert() and remove(), for inserting and removing elements of a set. Such functions could be implemented in our sorted sequence approach by simple scans of the sequence representing a set, which can easily be done in $O(n)$ time, as we explore in an exercise (R-10.7).

Performance of Generic Merging

Let us analyze the running time of the generic merge algorithm. At each iteration of one of the loops, an element is removed from A, B, or both. Assuming that comparisons take $O(1)$ time, and that each call to an auxiliary function takes $O(1)$ time, the total running time of genericMerge(A,B) is $O(n_A + n_B)$, where n_A is the size of A and n_B is the size of B; that is, merging takes time proportional to the number of elements involved. Thus, we have the following:

Proposition 10.6: *The set ADT can be implemented with an ordered sequence and a generic merge scheme that supports operations* union(), intersect(), *and* subtract() *in $O(n)$ time, where n denotes the sum of sizes of the sets involved.*

```
template <typename Object, typename Sequence>   // set union
class UnionMerger : public Merger<Object, Sequence> {
protected:
  virtual void aIsLess(const Object& a, Sequence& C)
    { C.insertLast(a); }                        // add a
  virtual void bothEqual(const Object& a, const Object& b, Sequence& C)
    { C.insertLast(a); }                        // add a only
  virtual void bIsLess(const Object& b, Sequence& C)
    { C.insertLast(b); }                        // add b
public:
  UnionMerger() { }
};

template <typename Object, typename Sequence>   // set intersection
class IntersectMerger : public Merger<Object, Sequence> {
protected:
  virtual void aIsLess(const Object& a, Sequence& C)
    { }                                         // ignore
  virtual void bothEqual(const Object& a, const Object& b, Sequence& C)
    { C.insertLast(a); }                        // add a only
  virtual void bIsLess(const Object& b, Sequence& C)
    { }                                         // ignore
public:
  IntersectMerger() { }
};

template <typename Object, typename Sequence>   // set subtraction
class SubtractMerger : public Merger<Object, Sequence> {
protected:
  virtual void aIsLess(const Object& a, Sequence& C)
    { C.insertLast(a); }                        // add a
  virtual void bothEqual(const Object& a, const Object& b, Sequence& C)
    { }                                         // ignore
  virtual void bIsLess(const Object& b, Sequence& C)
    { }                                         // ignore
public:
  SubtractMerger() { }
};
```

Code Fragment 10.5: Classes derived from the Merger class by specializing the auxiliary functions to perform set union, intersection, and subtraction, respectively.

10.3 Quick-Sort

The next sorting algorithm we discuss is called *quick-sort*. Like merge-sort, this algorithm is also based on the *divide-and-conquer* paradigm, but it uses this technique in a somewhat opposite manner, as all the hard work is done *before* the recursive calls.

High-Level Description of Quick-Sort

The quick-sort algorithm sorts a sequence S using a simple recursive approach. The main idea is to apply the divide-and-conquer technique, whereby we divide S into subsequences, recur to sort each subsequence, and then combine the sorted subsequences by a simple concatenation. In particular, the quick-sort algorithm consists of the following three steps (see Figure 10.8):

1. **Divide:** If S has at least two elements (nothing needs to be done if S has zero or one element), select a specific element x from S, which is called the *pivot*. As is common practice, choose the pivot x to be the last element in S. Remove all the elements from S and put them into three sequences:
   - L, storing the elements in S less than x
   - E, storing the elements in S equal to x
   - G, storing the elements in S greater than x.

   Of course, if the elements of S are all distinct, then E holds just one element— the pivot itself.
2. **Recur:** Recursively sort sequences L and G.
3. **Conquer:** Put the elements back into S in order, by first inserting the elements of L, then those of E, and finally those of G.

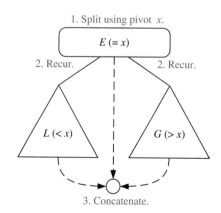

1. Split using pivot x.

$E\,(=x)$

2. Recur.   2. Recur.

$L\,(<x)$ $G\,(>x)$

3. Concatenate.

Figure 10.8: A visual schematic of the quick-sort algorithm.

Like merge-sort, the execution of quick-sort can be visualized by means of a binary recursion tree, called the ***quick-sort tree***. Figure 10.9 summarizes an execution of the quick-sort algorithm by showing the input and output sequences processed at each node of the quick-sort tree. The step-by-step evolution of the quick-sort tree is shown in Figures 10.10, 10.11, and 10.12.

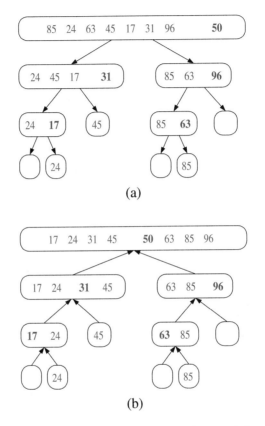

(a)

(b)

Figure 10.9: Quick-sort tree T for an execution of the quick-sort algorithm on a sequence with eight elements: (a) input sequences processed at each node of T; (b) output sequences generated at each node of T. The pivot used at each level of the recursion is shown in bold.

Unlike merge-sort, however, the height of the quick-sort tree associated with an execution of quick-sort is linear in the worst case. This happens, for example, if the sequence consists of n distinct elements and is already sorted. Indeed, in this case, the standard choice of the pivot as the largest element yields a subsequence L of size $n-1$, while subsequence E has size 1 and subsequence G has size 0. At each invocation of quick-sort on subsequence L, the size decreases by 1. Hence, the height of the quick-sort tree is $n-1$.

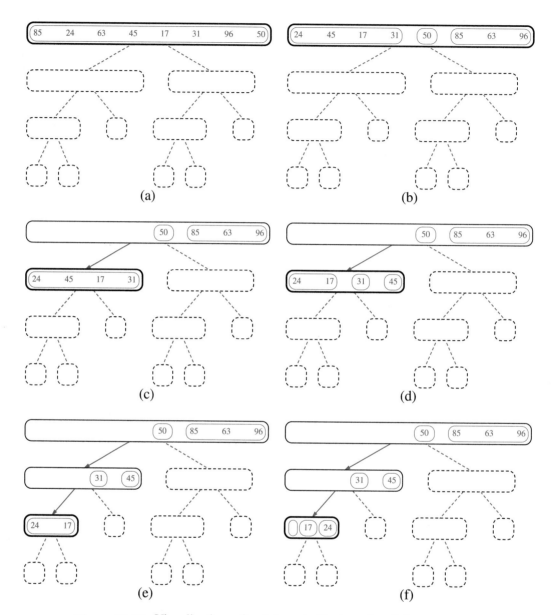

Figure 10.10: Visualization of quick-sort. Each node of the tree represents a recursive call. The nodes drawn with dashed lines represent calls that have not been made yet. The node drawn with thick lines represents the running invocation. The empty nodes drawn with thin lines represent terminated calls. The remaining nodes represent suspended calls (that is, active invocations that are waiting for a child invocation to return). Note the divide steps performed in (b), (d), and (f). (Continued in Figure 10.11.)

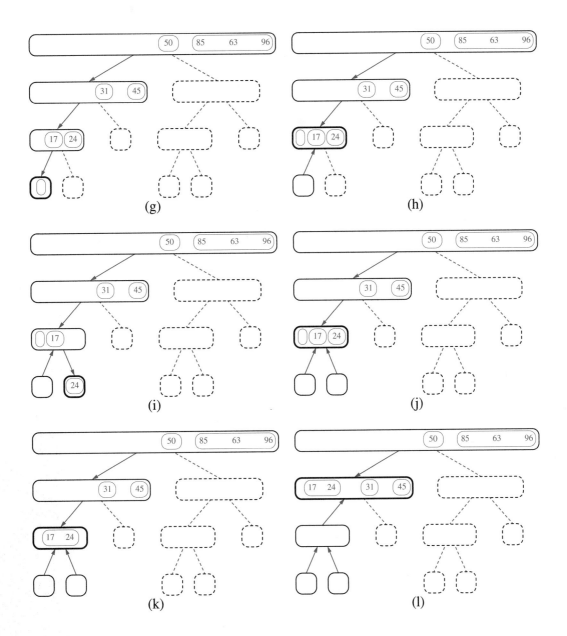

Figure 10.11: Visualization of an execution of quick-sort. Note the conquer step performed in (k). (Continued from Figure 10.10.)

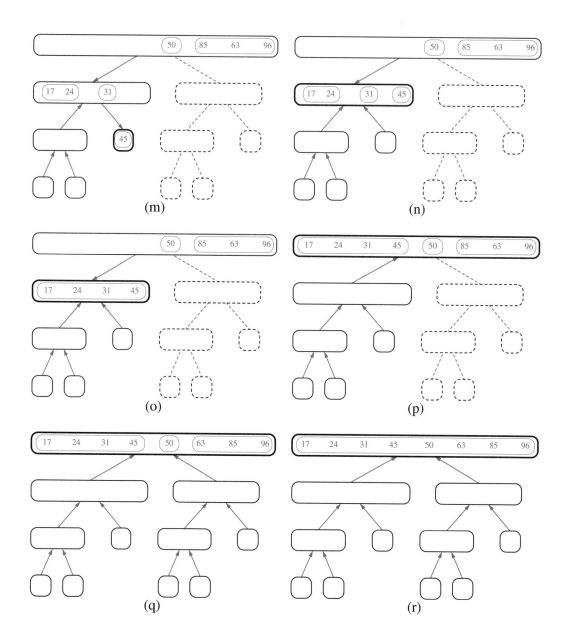

Figure 10.12: Visualization of an execution of quick-sort. Several invocations between (p) and (q) have been omitted. Note the conquer steps performed in (o)
and (r). (Continued from Figure 10.11.)

10.3.1 In-Place Quick-Sort

Recall from Section 7.3.4 that a sorting algorithm is ***in-place*** if it only uses a constant amount of memory in addition to that needed for the objects being sorted themselves. The merge-sort algorithm, as we have described it above, is not in-place, and making it be in-place requires a more complicated merging method than the one we discuss in Section 10.1.1. In-place sorting is not inherently difficult, however. For, as with heap-sort, quick-sort can be adapted to be in-place.

Performing the quick-sort algorithm in-place requires a bit of ingenuity, for we must use the input sequence itself to store the subsequences for all the recursive calls. We show algorithm inPlaceQuickSort(), which performs in-place quick-sort, in Code Fragment 10.6. Algorithm inPlaceQuickSort() assumes that the input sequence, S, has distinct elements. The reason for this restriction is explored in Exercise R-10.12. The extension to the general case is discussed in Exercise C-10.7. The algorithm accesses the elements of the input sequence, S, with rank-based methods. Hence, it runs efficiently provided S is implemented with an array.

Algorithm inPlaceQuickSort(S, a, b):

    Input: Sequence S of distinct elements; integers a and b

    Output: Sequence S with elements originally from ranks from a to b, inclusive, sorted in nondecreasing order from ranks a to b

    if $a \geq b$ **then return**   {empty subrange}

    $p \leftarrow S.\text{elemAtRank}(b)$ {pivot}

    $l \leftarrow a$ {will scan rightward}

    $r \leftarrow b - 1$ {will scan leftward}

    while $l \leq r$ **do**

        {find an element larger than the pivot}

        while $l \leq r$ **and** $S.\text{elemAtRank}(l) \leq p$ **do**

            $l \leftarrow l + 1$

        {find an element smaller than the pivot}

        while $r \geq l$ **and** $S.\text{elemAtRank}(r) \geq p$ **do**

            $r \leftarrow r - 1$

        if $l < r$ **then**

            $S.\text{swapElements}(S.\text{atRank}(l), S.\text{atRank}(r))$

    {put the pivot into its final place}

    $S.\text{swapElements}(S.\text{atRank}(l), S.\text{atRank}(b))$

    {recursive calls}

    inPlaceQuickSort($S, a, l - 1$)

    inPlaceQuickSort($S, l + 1, b$)

Code Fragment 10.6: In-place quick-sort for a sequence implemented with an array.

In-place quick-sort modifies the input sequence using swapElements() operations and does not explicitly create subsequences. Indeed, a subsequence of the input sequence is implicitly represented by a range of positions specified by a left-most rank *l* and a right-most rank *r*. The divide step is performed by scanning the sequence simultaneously from *l* forward and from *r* backward, swapping pairs of elements that are in reverse order, as shown in Figure 10.13. When these two indices "meet," subsequences *L* and *G* are on opposite sides of the meeting point. The algorithm completes by recursing on these two subsequences.

In-place quick-sort reduces the running time, caused by the creation of new sequences and the movement of elements between them, by a constant factor. We show a C++ implementation of in-place quick-sort in Code Fragment 10.7.

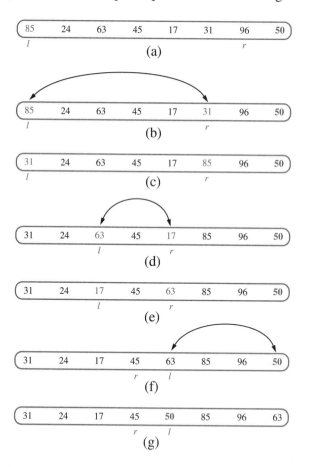

Figure 10.13: Divide step of in-place quick-sort. Index *l* scans the sequence from left to right, and index *r* scans the sequence from right to left. A swap is performed when *l* is at an element larger than the pivot and *r* is at an element smaller than the pivot. A final swap with the pivot completes the divide step.

```
template <typename Object, typename Sequence>
class QuickSort {                              // QuickSort class
protected:                                     // recursive utility
  void quickSortStep(Sequence& S, int leftBound, int rightBound);
public:
  void quickSort(Sequence& S);                 // main entry point
};

template <typename Object, typename Sequence>
void QuickSort<Object, Sequence>::             // recursive portion
quickSortStep(Sequence& S, int leftBound, int rightBound) {
  if (leftBound >= rightBound) return;         // 0 or 1 elements
  Object pivot = S.atRank(rightBound).element();  // select last as pivot
  int leftIndex = leftBound;                   // will scan rightward
  int rightIndex = rightBound − 1;             // will scan leftward
  while (leftIndex <= rightIndex) {
    while ((leftIndex <= rightIndex) &&        // scan right to larger
           S.atRank(leftIndex).element() <= pivot)
      leftIndex++;
    while ((rightIndex >= leftIndex) &&        // scan left to smaller
           S.atRank(rightIndex).element() >= pivot)
      rightIndex−−;
    if (leftIndex < rightIndex)                // both elements found
      S.swapElements(S.atRank(leftIndex), S.atRank(rightIndex));
  }                                            // until indices cross
                                               // pivot at leftIndex
  S.swapElements(S.atRank(leftIndex), S.atRank(rightBound));
  quickSortStep(S, leftBound, leftIndex−1);    // recur on both sides
  quickSortStep(S, leftIndex+1, rightBound);
}

template <typename Object, typename Sequence>
void QuickSort<Object, Sequence>::
quickSort(Sequence& S) {                       // main entry point
  if (S.size() <= 1) return;                   // 0 or 1 elements
  quickSortStep(S, 0, S.size()−1);             // call sort utility
}
```

Code Fragment 10.7: Class QuickSort, which defines the public function quickSort() for sorting a sequence using in-place quick-sort. The recursive utility function quickSortStep() does most of the work. It is assumed that the input sequence is implemented with an array and that its elements are distinct.

Unfortunately, the implementation of quick-sort shown in Code Fragment 10.7 is, technically speaking, not quite in-place, as it still requires more than a constant amount of additional space. Of course, we are using no additional space for the subsequences, and we are using only a constant amount of additional space for local variables (such as l and r). So, where does this additional space come from? It comes from the recursion, for, recalling Section 4.2.3, we note that we need space for a stack proportional to the depth of the recursion tree for quick-sort, which is at least $\log n$ and at most $n - 1$.

In order to make quick-sort truly in-place, we must implement it nonrecursively (and not use a stack). The key detail for such an implementation is that we need an in-place way of determining the bounds for the left and right boundaries of the "current" subsequence. Such a scheme is not too difficult, however, and we leave the details of this implementation to an exercise (C-10.5).

Running Time of Quick-Sort

We can analyze the running time of quick-sort with the same technique used for merge-sort in Section 10.1.1. Namely, we identify the time spent at each node of the quick-sort tree T (Figures 10.10, 10.11, and 10.12), and we sum up the running times for all the nodes.

The divide step and the conquer step of quick-sort are easy to implement in linear time. Thus, the time spent at a node v of T is proportional to the **input size** $s(v)$ of v, defined as the size of the sequence handled by the invocation of quick-sort associated with node v. Since subsequence E has at least one element (the pivot), the sum of the input sizes of the children of v is at most $s(v) - 1$.

Given a quick-sort tree T, let s_i denote the sum of the input sizes of the nodes at depth i in T. Clearly, $s_0 = n$, since the root r of T is associated with the entire sequence. Also, $s_1 \leq n - 1$, since the pivot is not propagated to the children of r. Next, consider s_2. If both children of r have nonzero input size, then $s_2 = n - 3$. Otherwise (one child of the root has zero size, the other has size $n - 1$), $s_2 = n - 2$. Thus, $s_2 \leq n - 2$. Continuing this line of reasoning, we obtain that $s_i \leq n - i$. As observed in Section 10.3, the height of T is $n - 1$ in the worst case. Thus, the worst-case running time of quick-sort is

$$O\left(\sum_{i=0}^{n-1} s_i\right), \quad \text{which is } O\left(\sum_{i=0}^{n-1}(n-i)\right) \quad \text{that is, } O\left(\sum_{i=1}^{n} i\right).$$

By Proposition 3.2, $\sum_{i=1}^{n} i$ is $O(n^2)$. Thus, quick-sort runs in $O(n^2)$ worst-case time.

Given its name, we would expect quick-sort to run quickly. However, the above quadratic bound indicates that quick-sort is slow in the worst case. Paradoxically, this worst-case behavior occurs for problem instances when sorting should be easy—if the sequence is already sorted. Moreover, one can show that quick-sort performs poorly even if the sequence is "almost" sorted.

Going back to our analysis, note that the best case for quick-sort on a sequence of distinct elements occurs when subsequences L and G happen to have roughly the same size. Indeed, in this case we save one pivot at each internal node and make two equal-sized calls for its children. Thus, we save 1 pivot at the root, 2 at level 1, 2^2 at level 2, and so on. That is, in the best case, we have

$$
\begin{aligned}
s_0 &= n \\
s_1 &= n-1 \\
s_2 &= n-(1+2) = n-3 \\
&\;\;\vdots \\
s_i &= n-(1+2+2^2+\cdots+2^{i-1}) = n-(2^i-1) \\
&\;\;\vdots
\end{aligned}
$$

Thus, in the best case, T has height $O(\log n)$ and quick-sort runs in $O(n \log n)$ time. We leave the justification of this fact as an exercise (R-10.10).

The informal intuition behind the expected behavior of quick-sort is that at each invocation the pivot will probably divide the input sequence about equally. Thus, we expect the average running time of quick-sort to be similar to the best-case running time, that is, $O(n \log n)$. We will see in the next section that introducing randomization makes quick-sort behave exactly as described above.

10.3.2 Randomized Quick-Sort

One common method for analyzing quick-sort is to assume that the pivot will always divide the sequence almost equally. We feel such an assumption would presuppose knowledge about the input distribution that is typically not available, however. For example, we would have to assume that we will rarely be given "almost" sorted sequences to sort, which are actually common in many applications. Fortunately, this assumption is not needed in order for us to match our intuition to quick-sort's behavior.

Since the goal of the partition step of the quick-sort function is to divide the sequence S almost equally, let us introduce randomization into the algorithm and pick a **random element** of the input sequence as the pivot. This variation of quick-sort is called **randomized quick-sort**. The following proposition shows that the expected running time of randomized quick-sort on a sequence with n elements is $O(n \log n)$. This expectation is taken over all the possible random choices the algorithm makes, and is independent of any assumptions about the distribution of the possible input sequences the algorithm is likely to be given.

Proposition 10.7: *The expected running time of randomized quick-sort on a sequence of size n is $O(n \log n)$.*

Justification: We make use of a simple fact from probability theory:

> *The expected number of times that a fair coin must be flipped until it shows "heads" k times is $2k$.*

Consider now a single recursive invocation of randomized quick-sort, and let m denote the size of the input sequence for this invocation. Say that this invocation is "good" if the pivot chosen is such that subsequences L and G have size at least $m/4$ and at most $3m/4$ each. Thus, since the pivot is chosen uniformly at random and there are $m/2$ pivots for which this invocation is good, the probability that an invocation is good is $1/2$ (the same as the probability that a coin will come up heads).

If a node v of the quick-sort tree T, as shown in Figure 10.14, is associated with a "good" recursive call, then the input sizes of the children of v are each $3s(v)/4$ at most (which is the same as $(s(v)/(4/3))$). If we take any path in T from the root to an external node, then the length of this path is at most the number of invocations that have to be made (at each node on this path) until achieving $\log_{4/3} n$ good invocations. Applying the probabilistic fact reviewed above, the expected number of invocations we must make until this occurs is $2\log_{4/3} n$. Thus, the expected length of any path from the root to an external node in T is $O(\log n)$. Recalling that the time spent at each level of T is $O(n)$, the expected running time of randomized quick-sort is $O(n \log n)$.   ∎

Actually, by using powerful facts from probability, we can show that the running time of randomized quick-sort is $O(n \log n)$ with high probability. We leave this analysis as an exercise (C-10.7) for the more mathematically inclined reader.

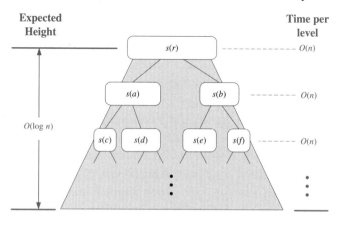

Total expected time: $O(n \log n)$

Figure 10.14: A visual time analysis of the quick-sort tree T.

10.4 A Lower Bound on Comparison-Based Sorting

Recapping our discussions on sorting to this point, we have described several methods with either a worst-case or expected running time of $O(n \log n)$ on an input sequence of size n. These methods include merge-sort and quick-sort, described in this chapter, as well as heap-sort, described in Section 7.3.4. A natural question to ask, then, is whether it is possible to sort any faster than in $O(n \log n)$ time.

In this section, we show that if the computational primitive used by a sorting algorithm is the comparison of two elements, then this is the best we can do—comparison-based sorting has an $\Omega(n \log n)$ worst-case lower bound on its running time. (Recall the notation $\Omega(\cdot)$ from Section 3.5.2.) To focus on the main cost of comparison-based sorting, let us only count the comparisons that a sorting algorithm performs. Since we want to derive a lower bound, this will be sufficient.

Suppose we are given a sequence $S = (x_0, x_1, \ldots, x_{n-1})$ that we wish to sort, and assume that all the elements of S are distinct (this is not a restriction since we are deriving a lower bound). Each time a sorting algorithm compares two elements x_i and x_j (that is, it asks, "is $x_i < x_j$?"), there are two outcomes: "yes" or "no." Based on the result of this comparison, the sorting algorithm may perform some internal calculations (which we are not counting here) and will eventually perform another comparison between two other elements of S, which again will have two outcomes. Therefore, we can represent a comparison-based sorting algorithm with a decision tree T (recall Example 6.4). That is, each internal node v in T corresponds to a comparison and the edges from node v' to its children correspond to the computations resulting from either a "yes" or "no" answer (see Figure 10.15).

It is important to note that the hypothetical sorting algorithm in question probably has no explicit knowledge of the tree T. We simply use T to represent all the possible sequences of comparisons that a sorting algorithm might make, starting from the first comparison (associated with the root) and ending with the last comparison (associated with the parent of an external node) just before the algorithm terminates its execution.

Each possible initial ordering, or **permutation**, of the elements in S will cause our hypothetical sorting algorithm to execute a series of comparisons, traversing a path in T from the root to some external node. Let us associate with each external node v in T, then, the set of permutations of S that cause our sorting algorithm to end up in v. The most important observation in our lower-bound argument is that each external node v in T can represent the sequence of comparisons for at most one permutation of S. The justification for this claim is simple: if two different permutations P_1 and P_2 of S are associated with the same external node, then there are at least two objects x_i and x_j, such that x_i is before x_j in P_1 but x_i is after x_j

in P_2. At the same time, the output associated with v must be a specific reordering of S, with either x_i or x_j appearing before the other. But if P_1 and P_2 both cause the sorting algorithm to output the elements of S in this order, then that implies there is a way to trick the algorithm into outputting x_i and x_j in the wrong order. Since this cannot be allowed by a correct sorting algorithm, each external node of T must be associated with exactly one permutation of S. We use this property of the decision tree associated with a sorting algorithm to prove the following result:

Proposition 10.8: *The running time of any comparison-based algorithm for sorting an n-element sequence is $\Omega(n \log n)$ in the worst case.*

Justification: The running time of a comparison-based sorting algorithm must be greater than or equal to the height of the decision tree T associated with this algorithm, as described above. (See Figure 10.15.) By the above argument, each external node in T must be associated with one permutation of S. Moreover, each permutation of S must result in a different external node of T. The number of permutations of n objects is $n! = n(n-1)(n-2)\cdots 2 \cdot 1$. Thus, T must have at least $n!$ external nodes. By Proposition 6.9, the height of T is at least $\log(n!)$. This immediately justifies the proposition, because there are at least $n/2$ terms that are greater than or equal to $n/2$ in the product $n!$; hence

$$\log(n!) \geq \log\left(\frac{n}{2}\right)^{\frac{n}{2}} = \frac{n}{2} \log \frac{n}{2},$$

which is $\Omega(n \log n)$.   ■

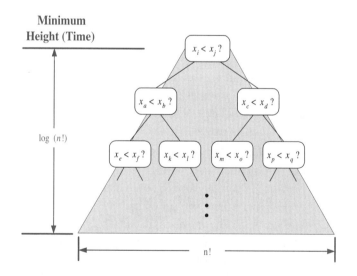

Figure 10.15: Visualizing the lower bound for comparison-based sorting.

10.5 Bucket-Sort and Radix-Sort

In the previous section, we show that $\Omega(n \log n)$ time is necessary, in the worst case, to sort an n-element sequence with a comparison-based sorting algorithm. A natural question to ask, then, is whether there are other kinds of sorting algorithms that can be designed to run asymptotically faster than $O(n \log n)$ time. Interestingly, such algorithms exist, but they require special assumptions about the input sequence to be sorted. Even so, such scenarios often arise in practice, so discussing them is worthwhile. In this section, we consider the problem of sorting a sequence of items, each a key-element pair.

10.5.1 Bucket-Sort

Consider a sequence S of n items whose keys are integers in the range $[0, N-1]$, for some integer $N \geq 2$, and suppose that S should be sorted according to the keys of the items. In this case, it is possible to sort S in $O(n+N)$ time. It might seem surprising, but this implies, for example, that if N is $O(n)$, then we can sort S in $O(n)$ time. Of course, the crucial point is that, because of the restrictive assumption about the format of the elements, we can avoid using comparisons.

The main idea is to use an algorithm called ***bucket-sort***, which is not based on comparisons, but on using keys as indices into a bucket array B that has entries from 0 to $N-1$. An item with key k is placed in the "bucket" $B[k]$, which itself is a sequence (of items with key k). After inserting each item of the input sequence S into its bucket, we can put the items back into S in sorted order by enumerating the contents of the buckets $B[0], B[1], \ldots, B[N-1]$ in order. We describe the bucket-sort algorithm in Code Fragment 10.8.

Algorithm bucketSort(S):
  Input: Sequence S of items with integer keys in the range $[0, N-1]$
  Output: Sequence S sorted in nondecreasing order of the keys

  let B be an array of N sequences, each of which is initially empty
  for each item x in S **do**
    let k be the key of x
    remove x from S and insert it at the end bucket (sequence) $B[k]$
  for $i \leftarrow 0$ to $N-1$ **do**
    for each item x in sequence $B[i]$ **do**
      remove x from $B[i]$ and insert it at the end of S

Code Fragment 10.8: Bucket-sort.

It is easy to see that bucket-sort runs in $O(n+N)$ time and uses $O(n+N)$ space. Hence, bucket-sort is efficient when the range N of values for the keys is small compared to the sequence size n, say $N = O(n)$ or $N = O(n\log n)$. Still, its performance deteriorates as N grows compared to n.

An important property of the bucket-sort algorithm is that it works correctly even if there are many different elements with the same key. Indeed, we described it in a way that anticipates such occurrences.

Stable Sorting

When sorting key-element items, an important issue is how equal keys are handled. Let $S = ((k_0, e_0), \ldots, (k_{n-1}, e_{n-1}))$ be a sequence of items. We say that a sorting algorithm is **stable** if, for any two items (k_i, e_i) and (k_j, e_j) of S, such that $k_i = k_j$ and (k_i, e_i) precedes (k_j, e_j) in S before sorting (that is, $i < j$), item (k_i, e_i) also precedes item (k_j, e_j) after sorting. Stability is important for a sorting algorithm because applications may want to preserve the initial ordering of elements with the same key.

Our informal description of bucket-sort in Code Fragment 10.8 does not guarantee stability. This is not inherent in the bucket-sort method itself, however, for we can easily modify our description to make bucket-sort stable, while still preserving its $O(n+N)$ running time. Indeed, we can obtain a stable bucket-sort algorithm by always removing the **first** element from sequence S and from the sequences $B[i]$ during the execution of the algorithm.

10.5.2 Radix-Sort

One of the reasons that stable sorting is so important is that it allows the bucket-sort approach to be applied to more general contexts than to sort integers. Suppose, for example, that we want to sort items that are pairs (k, l), where k and l are integers in the range $[0, N-1]$, for some integer $N \geq 2$. In a context such as this, it is natural to define an ordering on these items using the **lexicographical** (dictionary) convention, where $(k_1, l_1) < (k_2, l_2)$ if $k_1 < k_2$ or if $k_1 = k_2$ and $l_1 < l_2$ (Section 7.1.4). This is a pair-wise version of the lexicographic comparison function, usually applied to equal-length character strings (and it easily generalizes to tuples of d numbers for $d > 2$).

The **radix-sort** algorithm sorts a sequence of pairs such as S, by applying a stable bucket-sort on the sequence twice; first using one component of the pair as the ordering key and then using the second component. But which order is correct? Should we first sort on the k's (the first component) and then on the l's (the second component), or should it be the other way around?

Before we answer this question, we consider the following example.

Example 10.9: *Consider the following sequence S:*

$$S = ((3,3),(1,5),(2,5),(1,2),(2,3),(1,7),(3,2),(2,2)).$$

If we sort S stably on the first component, then we get the sequence

$$S_1 = ((1,5),(1,2),(1,7),(2,5),(2,3),(2,2),(3,3),(3,2)).$$

If we then stably sort this sequence S_1 using the second component, then we get the sequence

$$S_{1,2} = ((1,2),(2,2),(3,2),(2,3),(3,3),(1,5),(2,5),(1,7)),$$

which is not exactly a sorted sequence. On the other hand, if we first stably sort S using the second component, then we get the sequence

$$S_2 = ((1,2),(3,2),(2,2),(3,3),(2,3),(1,5),(2,5),(1,7)).$$

If we then stably sort sequence S_2 using the first component, then we get the sequence

$$S_{2,1} = ((1,2),(1,5),(1,7),(2,2),(2,3),(2,5),(3,2),(3,3)),$$

which is indeed sequence S lexicographically ordered.

So, from this example, we are led to believe that we should first sort using the second component and then again using the first component. This intuition is exactly right. By first stably sorting by the second component and then again by the first component, we guarantee that if two elements are equal in the second sort (by the first component), then their relative order in the starting sequence (which is sorted by the second component) is preserved. Thus, the resulting sequence is guaranteed to be sorted lexicographically every time. We leave the determination of how this approach can be extended to triples and other d-tuples of numbers to a simple exercise R-10.14. We can summarize this section as follows:

Proposition 10.10: *Let S be a sequence of n key-element items, each of which has a key $(k_1, k_2, \ldots, k_d)$, where k_i is an integer in the range $[0, N-1]$ for some integer $N \geq 2$. We can sort S lexicographically in time $O(d(n+N))$ using radix-sort.*

As important as it is, sorting is not the only interesting problem dealing with a total order relation on a set of elements. There are some applications, for example, that do not require an ordered listing of an entire set, but nevertheless call for some amount of ordering information about the set. Before we study such a problem (called "selection"), let us step back and briefly compare all of the sorting algorithms we have studied so far.

10.6   Comparison of Sorting Algorithms

At this point, it might be useful for us to take a breath and consider all the algorithms for sorting an n-element sequence that we have studied in this book. We have studied several methods, such as bubble-sort, insertion-sort, and selection-sort, that have $O(n^2)$-time behavior in the average and worst case. We have also studied several methods with $O(n\log n)$-time behavior, including heap-sort, merge-sort, and quick-sort. Finally, we have studied a special class of sorting algorithms, namely, the bucket-sort and radix-sort methods, that run in linear time for certain types of keys. Certainly, the bubble-sort and selection-sort algorithms are poor choices in any application, since they run in $\Theta(n^2)$ time even in the best case. But, of the remaining sorting algorithms, which is the best?

As with many things in life, there is no clear "best" sorting algorithm from the remaining candidates. The sorting algorithm best suited for a particular application depends on several properties of that application. We can offer some guidance and observations, therefore, based on the known properties of the "good" sorting algorithms.

Insertion-Sort

If implemented well, the running time of **insertion-sort** is $O(n+k)$, where k is the number of inversions (that is, the number of pairs of elements out of order). Thus, insertion-sort is an excellent algorithm for sorting small sequences (say, less than 50 elements), because insertion-sort is simple to program, and small sequences necessarily have few inversions. Also, insertion-sort is quite effective for sorting sequences that are already "almost" sorted. By "almost," we mean that the number of inversions is small. But the $O(n^2)$-time performance of insertion-sort makes it a poor choice outside of these special contexts.

Merge-Sort

Merge-sort, on the other hand, runs in $O(n\log n)$ time in the worst case, which is optimal for comparison-based sorting methods. Still, experimental studies have shown that, since it is difficult to make merge-sort run in-place, the overheads needed to implement merge-sort make it less attractive than the in-place implementations of heap-sort and quick-sort for sequences that can fit entirely in a computer's main memory area.

Even so, merge-sort is an excellent algorithm for situations where the input cannot all fit into main memory, but must be stored in blocks on an external memory device, such as a disk. In these contexts, the way that merge-sort processes runs of data in long merge streams makes the best use of all the data brought into main memory in a block from disk. Thus, for external memory sorting, the merge-sort algorithm tends to minimize the total number of disk reads and writes needed, which makes the merge-sort algorithm superior in such contexts.

Quick-Sort

Experimental studies have shown that if an input sequence can fit entirely in main memory, then the in-place versions of quick-sort and heap-sort run faster than merge-sort. In fact, quick-sort tends, on average, to beat heap-sort in these tests. So, *quick-sort* is an excellent choice as a general-purpose, in-memory sorting algorithm. Indeed, it is included in the qsort() sorting utility provided in C language libraries. Still, its $O(n^2)$ time worst-case performance makes quick-sort a poor choice in real-time applications where we must make guarantees on the time needed to complete a sorting operation.

Heap-Sort

In real-time scenarios where we have a fixed amount of time to perform a sorting operation and the input data can fit into main memory, the *heap-sort* algorithm is probably the best choice. It runs in $O(n \log n)$ worst-case time and can easily be made to execute in-place, using the vector-based implementation of a heap, as discussed in Section 7.3.2.

Bucket-Sort and Radix-Sort

Finally, if our application involves sorting by integer keys or d-tuples of integer keys, then *bucket-sort* or *radix-sort* is an excellent choice, for it runs in $O(d(n+N))$ time, where $[0, N-1]$ is the range of integer keys (and $d = 1$ for bucket sort). Thus, if $d(n+N)$ is "below" $n \log n$ (formally, $d(n+N)$ is $o(n \log n)$ using the little-oh notation from Section 3.5.2), then this sorting method should run faster than even quick-sort or heap-sort.

Thus, our study of all these different sorting algorithms provides us with a versatile collection of sorting methods in our algorithm engineering "toolbox."

10.7   Selection

There are a number of applications in which we are interested in identifying a single element in terms of its rank relative to an ordering of the entire set. Examples include identifying the minimum and maximum elements, but we may also be interested in, say, identifying the *median* element, that is, the element such that half of the other elements are smaller and the remaining half are larger. In general, queries that ask for an element with a given rank are called *order statistics*.

In this section, we discuss the general order-statistic problem of selecting the kth smallest element from an unsorted collection of n comparable elements. This is known as the *selection* problem. Of course, we can solve this problem by sorting the collection and then indexing into the sorted sequence at rank k. Using the best comparison-based sorting algorithms, this approach would take $O(n\log n)$ time, which is obviously an overkill for the cases where $k = 1$ or $k = n$ (or even $k = 2$, $k = 3$, $k = n-1$, or $k = n-5$), because we can easily solve the selection problem for these values of k in $O(n)$ time. Thus, a natural question to ask is whether we can achieve an $O(n)$ running time for all values of k (including the interesting case of finding the median, where $k = \lfloor n/2 \rfloor$).

10.7.1   Prune-and-Search

This may come as a small surprise, but we can indeed solve the selection problem in $O(n)$ time for any value of k. Moreover, the technique we use to achieve this result involves an interesting algorithmic design pattern. This design pattern is known as *prune-and-search* or *decrease-and-conquer*.

In applying this design pattern, we solve a given problem that is defined on a collection of n objects by pruning away a fraction of the n objects and recursively solving the smaller problem. When we have finally reduced the problem to one defined on a constant-sized collection of objects, then we solve the problem using some brute-force method. Returning back from all the recursive calls completes the construction. In some cases, we can avoid using recursion, in which case we simply iterate the prune-and-search reduction step until we can apply a brute-force method and stop. Incidentally, the binary search method described in Section 8.3.3 is an example of the prune-and-search design pattern.

10.7.2 Randomized Quick-Select

In applying the prune-and-search pattern to selection, we can design a simple and practical method, called ***randomized quick-select***, for finding the kth smallest element in an unordered sequence of n elements on which a total order relation is defined. Randomized quick-select runs in $O(n)$ ***expected*** time, taken over all possible random choices made by the algorithm, and this expectation does not depend whatsoever on any randomness assumptions about the input distribution. We note though that randomized quick-select runs in $O(n^2)$ time in the ***worst-case*** time, the justification of which is left as an exercise (R-10.17). We also provide an exercise (C-10.23) for designing a ***deterministic*** selection algorithm that runs in $O(n)$ ***worst-case*** time. This algorithm's existence is mostly of theoretical interest, however, since the constant factor hidden by the big-Oh is relatively large in this case.

Suppose we are given an unsorted sequence S of n comparable elements together with an integer $k \in [1, n]$. At a high level, the quick-select algorithm for finding the kth smallest element in S is similar in structure to the randomized quicksort algorithm described in Section 10.3.2. We pick an element x from S at random and use this as a "pivot" to subdivide S into three subsequences L, E, and G, storing the elements of S less than x, equal to x, and greater than x, respectively. This is the prune step. Then, based on the value of k, we then determine which of these sets to recur on. Randomized quick-select is described in Code Fragment 10.9.

Algorithm quickSelect(S, k):

Input: Sequence S of n comparable elements, and an integer $k \in [1, n]$
Output: The kth smallest element of S

if $n = 1$ **then**
    return the (first) element of S.
pick a random element x of S
remove all the elements from S and put them into three sequences:

- L, storing the elements in S less than x
- E, storing the elements in S equal to x
- G, storing the elements in S greater than x.

if $k \leq |L|$ **then**
    quickSelect(L, k)
else if $k \leq |L| + |E|$ **then**
    return x {each element in E is equal to x}
else
    quickSelect($G, k - |L| - |E|$)   {note the new selection parameter}

Code Fragment 10.9: Randomized quick-select algorithm.

10.7.3 Analyzing Randomized Quick-Select ⋆

We mentioned above that the randomized quick-select algorithm runs in expected $O(n)$ time. Fortunately, justifying this claim requires only the simplest of probabilistic arguments.

The Linearity of Expectation

The main probabilistic fact that we use is the **linearity of expectation**. This fact states that if X and Y are random variables and c is a number, then

$$E(X+Y) = E(X) + E(Y)$$

and

$$E(cX) = cE(X),$$

where we use $E(\mathcal{Z})$ to denote the expected value of the expression $\mathcal{Z}$.

Characterizing the Expected Time for Quick-Select

Let $t(n)$ denote the running time of randomized quick-select on a sequence of size n. Since the randomized quick-select algorithm depends on the outcome of random events, its running time, $t(n)$, is a random variable. We are interested in bounding $E(t(n))$, the expected value of $t(n)$. Say that a recursive invocation of randomized quick-select is "good" if it partitions S, so that the size of L and G is at most $3n/4$. Clearly, a recursive call is good with probability $1/2$. Let $g(n)$ denote the number of consecutive recursive invocations (including the present one) before getting a good invocation. Then

$$t(n) \le bn \cdot g(n) + t(3n/4),$$

where $b \ge 1$ is a constant (to account for the overhead of each call). We are, of course, focusing on the case where n is larger than 1, for we can easily characterize that $t(1) = b$ in a closed form. Applying the linearity of expectation property to the general case, then, we get

$$E(t(n)) \le E(bn \cdot g(n) + t(3n/4)) = bn \cdot E(g(n)) + E(t(3n/4)).$$

Since a recursive call is good with probability $1/2$, and whether a recursive call is good or not is independent of its parent call being good, the expected value of $g(n)$ is the same as the expected number of times we must flip a fair coin before it comes up "heads." This implies that $E(g(n)) = 2$. Thus, if we let $T(n)$ be a shorthand notation for $E(t(n))$ (the expected running time of the randomized quick-select algorithm), then we can write the case for $n > 1$ as

$$T(n) \le T(3n/4) + 2bn.$$

Obtaining a Closed Form Analysis

As with the merge-sort recurrence relation, we would like to convert this relation into a closed form. To do this, let us again iteratively apply this equation assuming n is large. So, for example, after two iterative applications, we get

$$T(n) \le T((3/4)^2 n) + 2b(3/4)n + 2bn.$$

At this point, we see that the general case is

$$T(n) \le 2bn \cdot \sum_{i=0}^{\lceil \log_{4/3} n \rceil} (3/4)^i.$$

In other words, the expected running time of randomized quick-select is $2bn$ times the sum of a geometric progression whose base is a positive number less than 1. Thus, by Proposition 3.1 on geometric summations, we obtain the result that $T(n)$ is $O(n)$. To summarize:

Proposition 10.11: *The expected running time of randomized quick-select on a sequence of size n is $O(n)$.*

As we mentioned earlier, there is a variation of quick-select that does not use randomization and runs in $O(n)$ worst-case time. Exercise C-10.23 walks the interested reader through the design and analysis of this algorithm.

10.8   Exercises

Reinforcement

R-10.1 Give a complete justification of Proposition 10.1.

R-10.2 In the merge-sort tree shown in Figures 10.2 through 10.5, some edges are drawn as arrows. What is the meaning of a downward arrow? How about an upward arrow?

R-10.3 Give a pseudo-code description of merge-sort that takes an array as its input and output, rather than a general sequence. (Note: You will probably need to use an auxiliary array as a "buffer.")

R-10.4 Show that the running time of the merge-sort algorithm on an n-element sequence is $O(n\log n)$, even when n is not a power of 2.

R-10.5 Suppose we are given two n-element sorted sequences A and B that should not be viewed as sets (that is, A and B may contain duplicate entries). Describe an $O(n)$-time method for computing a sequence representing the set $A\cup B$ (with no duplicates).

R-10.6 Show that $(X-A)\cup(X-B)=X-(A\cap B)$, for any three sets X,A, and B.

R-10.7 Provide pseudo-code descriptions for performing the insert() and remove() functions of the set ADT assuming we use sorted sequences to implement sets.

R-10.8 Suppose we modify the deterministic version of the quick-sort algorithm so that, instead of selecting the last element in an n-element sequence as the pivot, we choose the element at rank $\lfloor n/2 \rfloor$. What is the running time of this version of quick-sort on a sequence that is already sorted?

R-10.9 Suppose we modify the deterministic version of the quick-sort algorithm so that, instead of selecting the last element in an n-element sequence as the pivot, we choose the element at rank $\lfloor n/2 \rfloor$. Describe the kind of sequence that would cause this version of quick-sort to run in $\Theta(n^2)$ time.

R-10.10 Show that the best-case running time of quick-sort on a sequence of size n with distinct elements is $O(n\log n)$.

R-10.11 Give a pseudo-code description of the in-place version of quick-sort that is specialized to take an array as input, rather than a general sequence, and return that same array as output.

R-10.12 Suppose that algorithm inPlaceQuickSort() (Code Fragment 10.6) is executed on a sequence with duplicate elements. Show that, in this case, the algorithm correctly sorts the input sequence, but the result of the divide step may differ from the high-level description given in Section 10.3 and may result in inefficiencies. In particular, what happens in the partition step when there are elements equal to the pivot? Is the sequence E (storing the elements equal to the pivot) actually computed? Does the algorithm recur on the subsequences L and R, or on some other subsequences? What is the running time of the algorithm if all the elements of the input sequence are equal?

R-10.13 Which, if any, of the algorithms bubble-sort, heap-sort, merge-sort, and quick-sort are stable?

R-10.14 Describe a radix-sort method for lexicographically sorting a sequence S of triplets (k,l,m), where k, l, and m are integers in the range $[0, N-1]$, for some $N \geq 2$. How could this scheme be extended to sequences of d-tuples $(k_1, k_2, \ldots, k_d)$, where each k_i is an integer in the range $[0, N-1]$?

R-10.15 Is the bucket-sort algorithm in-place? Why or why not?

R-10.16 Give a pseudo-code description of an in-place quick-select algorithm.

R-10.17 Show that the worst-case running time of quick-select on an n-element sequence is $\Omega(n^2)$.

Creativity

C-10.1 Show how to implement function equals(B) on a set A (which tests whether $A = B$) in $O(|A| + |B|)$ time by means of a concrete class derived from the Merger class, assuming A and B are implemented with sorted sequences.

C-10.2 Give a concrete class derived from the Merger class for computing $A \oplus B$, which is the set of elements that are in A or B, but not in both.

C-10.3 Suppose that we implement the set ADT by representing each set using a balanced search tree. Describe and analyze algorithms for each of the functions in the set ADT.

C-10.4 Let A be a collection of objects. Describe an efficient method for converting A into a set. That is, remove all duplicates from A. What is the running time of this method?

C-10.5 Consider sets whose elements are (or can be mapped to) integers in the range $[0, N-1]$. A popular scheme for representing a set A of this type is by means of a Boolean vector, B, where we say that x is in A, if and only if, $B[x] = $ true. Since each cell of B can be represented with a single bit, B is sometimes referred to as a ***bit vector***. Describe efficient algorithms for performing the union(), intersection(), and subtraction() functions of the set ADT assuming this representation. What are the running times of these functions?

C-10.6★ Describe a nonrecursive, in-place version of the quick-sort algorithm. The algorithm should still be based on the same divide-and-conquer approach. (Hint: Think about how to "mark" the left and right boundaries of the current subsequence before making a recursive call from this one.)

C-10.7 Modify Algorithm inPlaceQuickSort() (Code Fragment 10.6) to efficiently handle the general case when the input sequence, S, may have duplicate keys.

C-10.8★ Show that randomized quick-sort runs in $O(n \log n)$ time with probability $1 - 1/n^2$. (Hint: Use the ***Chernoff bound*** that states that if we flip a coin k times, then the probability that we get fewer than $k/16$ heads is less than $2^{-k/8}$.)

C-10.9 Suppose we are given a sequence S of n elements, each of which is colored red or blue. Assuming S is represented as an array, give an in-place method for ordering S so that all the blue elements are listed before all the red elements. Can you extend your approach to three colors?

C-10.10 Suppose we are given an n-element sequence S, such that each element in S represents a different vote for class president, where each vote is given as an integer representing the student ID of the chosen candidate. Without making any assumptions about who is running or even how many candidates there are, design an $O(n \log n)$-time algorithm to see who wins the election S represents, assuming the candidate with the most votes wins.

C-10.11 Consider the voting problem from the previous exercise, but now suppose that we know the number $k < n$ of candidates running. Describe an $O(n \log k)$-time algorithm for determining who wins the election.

C-10.12 Show that any comparison-based sorting algorithm can be made to be stable, without affecting the asymptotic running time of this algorithm. (Hint: Change the way elements are compared with each other.)

C-10.13 Suppose we are given two sequences A and B of n elements, possibly containing duplicates, on which a total order relation is defined. Describe an efficient algorithm for determining if A and B contain the same set of elements (possibly in different orders). What is the running time of this method?

C-10.14 Suppose we are given a sequence S of n elements, each of which is an integer in the range $[0, n^2 - 1]$. Describe a simple method for sorting S in $O(n)$ time. (Hint: Think of alternate ways of viewing the elements.)

C-10.15 Let $S_1, S_2, \ldots, S_k$ be k different sequences whose elements have integer keys in the range $[0, N - 1]$, for some parameter $N \geq 2$. Describe an algorithm running in $O(n + N)$ time for sorting all the sequences (not as a union), where n denotes the total size of all the sequences.

C-10.16 Suppose we are given a sequence S of n elements, on which a total order relation is defined. Describe an efficient method for determining whether there are two equal elements in S. What is the running time of your method?

C-10.17 Let S be a sequence of n elements on which a total order relation is defined. An ***inversion*** in S is a pair of elements x and y, such that x appears before y in S but $x > y$. Describe an algorithm running in $O(n \log n)$ time for determining the ***number*** of inversions in S. (Hint: Try to modify the merge-sort algorithm to solve this problem.)

C-10.18 Let S be a sequence of n elements on which a total order relation is defined. Describe a comparison-based method for sorting S in $O(n + k)$ time, where k is the number of inversions in S (recall the definition of inversion from the previous problem). (Hint: Think of an in-place version of the insertion-sort algorithm that, after a linear-time preprocessing step, only swaps elements that are inverted.)

C-10.19 Give a sequence of n integers with $\Omega(n^2)$ inversions. (Recall the definition of inversion from Exercise C-10.17.)

C-10.20 Let A and B be two sequences of n integers each. Given an integer m, describe an $O(n \log n)$-time algorithm for determining if there is an integer a in A and an integer b in B, such that $m = a + b$.

C-10.21 Given a sequence S of n comparable elements, describe an efficient method for finding the $\lceil\sqrt{n}\rceil$ items whose rank in S is closest to that of the median. What is the running time of your method?

C-10.22 Bob has a set A of n nuts and a set B of n bolts, such that each nut in A has a unique matching bolt in B. Unfortunately, the nuts in A all look the same, and the bolts in B all look the same as well. The only kind of a comparison that Bob can make is to take a nut-bolt pair (a,b), such that $a \in A$ and $b \in B$, and test it to see if the threads of a are larger, smaller, or a perfect match with the threads of b. Describe an efficient algorithm for Bob to match up all of his nuts and bolts. What is the running time of this algorithm, in terms of nut-bolt tests that Bob must make?

C-10.23 This problem deals with the modification of the quick-select algorithm, so as to make it deterministic yet still run in $O(n)$ time on an n-element sequence. The idea is to modify the way we choose the pivot so that it is chosen deterministically, not randomly, as follows:

> Partition the set S into $\lceil n/5 \rceil$ groups of size 5 each (except possibly for one group). Sort each little set and identify the median element in this set. From this set of $\lceil n/5 \rceil$ "baby" medians, apply the selection algorithm recursively to find the median of the baby medians. Use this element as the pivot and proceed as in the quick-select algorithm.

Show that this deterministic method runs in $O(n)$ time by answering the following questions (please ignore floor and ceiling functions if that simplifies the mathematics, for the asymptotics are the same either way).

a. How many baby medians are less than or equal to the chosen pivot? How many are greater than or equal to the pivot?

b. For each baby median less than or equal to the pivot, how many other elements are less than or equal to the pivot? Is the same true for those greater than or equal to the pivot?

c. Argue why the method for finding the deterministic pivot and using it to partition S takes $O(n)$ time.

d. Based on these estimates, write a recurrence relation that bounds the worst-case running time $t(n)$ for this selection algorithm (note that in the worst case there are two recursive calls—one to find the median of the baby medians and one to then recur on the larger of L and G).

e. Using this recurrence relation, show by induction that $t(n)$ is $O(n)$.

C-10.24 Show how a deterministic $O(n)$-time selection algorithm can be used to design a quick-sort-like sorting algorithm that runs in $O(n \log n)$ ***worst-case*** time on an n-element sequence.

C-10.25 Given an unsorted sequence S of n comparable elements, and an integer k, give an $O(n \log k)$ expected-time algorithm for finding the $O(k)$ elements that have rank $\lceil n/k \rceil$, $2\lceil n/k \rceil$, $3\lceil n/k \rceil$, and so on.

Projects

P-10.1 Implement a nonrecursive version of the merge-sort algorithm. Perform a series of benchmarking time trials to test whether this method does indeed run in $O(n \log n)$ time, and write a short report describing the code and the results of these trials.

P-10.2 Design and implement a stable version of the bucket-sort algorithm for sorting a sequence of n elements with integer keys taken from the range $[0, N-1]$, for $N \geq 2$. The algorithm should run in $O(n+N)$ time. Perform a series of benchmarking time trials to test whether this method does indeed run in this time, for various values of n and N, and write a short report describing the code and the results of these trials.

P-10.3 Implement merge-sort and deterministic quick-sort and perform a series of benchmarking tests to see which one is faster. Your tests should include sequences that are very "random" looking, as well as ones that are "almost" sorted. Write a short report describing the code and the results of these trials.

P-10.4 Implement deterministic and randomized versions of the quick-sort algorithm and perform a series of benchmarking tests to see which one is faster. Your tests should include sequences that are very "random" looking as well as ones that are "almost" sorted. Write a short report describing the code and the results of these trials.

P-10.5 Implement an in-place version of insertion-sort and an in-place version of quick-sort. Perform benchmarking tests to determine the range of values of n where quick-sort is on average better than insertion-sort. Try to compare your algorithms on input sequences that are uniformly distributed and also on sequences that are "almost" sorted.

P-10.6 Design and implement an animation for one of the sorting algorithms described in this chapter. Your animation should illustrate the key properties

of this algorithm in an intuitive manner, and should be annotated with text
or sound so as to explain this algorithm to someone unfamiliar with it.
Write a short report describing this animation.

P-10.7   Implement the randomized quick-sort and quick-select algorithms. De-
         sign a series of benchmarking tests to test the relative speed of solving
         the selection problem either directly, by the quick-select method, or in-
         directly, by first sorting via the quick-sort method and then returning the
         element at the requested rank. Write a short report describing the code
         and the results of these trials.

P-10.8   Implement an extended set ADT that includes the functions union(B),
         intersect(B), subtract(B), size(), isEmpty(), plus the functions equals(B),
         contains(e), insert(e), and remove(e) with obvious meaning. You may
         use any representation you wish for sets, but your implementation must
         guarantee that no set contains any duplicate entries. Use a comparator,
         passed as an argument to a constructor, to test equality of elements.

Chapter Notes

Knuth's classic text on *Sorting and Searching* [59] contains an extensive history of the
sorting problem and algorithms for solving it, starting with the census card sorting machines of the late 19th century. Huang and Langston [50] describe how to merge two sorted
lists in-place in linear time. Our set ADT is derived from the set ADT of Aho, Hopcroft,
and Ullman [5]. The standard quick-sort algorithm is due to Hoare [47]. A tighter analysis of randomized quick-sort can be found in the book by Motwani and Raghavan [82].
Gonnet and Baeza-Yates [40] provide experimental comparisons and theoretical analyses
of a number of different sorting algorithms. The term "prune-and-search" comes originally from computational geometry literature (such as in the work of Clarkson [22] and
Megiddo [72, 73]). The term "decrease-and-conquer" is from Levitin [65].

Chapter

11

Text Processing

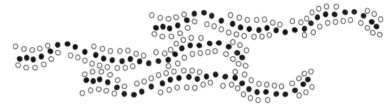

Contents

Document processing is rapidly becoming one of the dominant functions of computers. Computers are used to edit documents, to search documents, to transport documents over the Internet, and to display documents on printers and computer screens. Web "surfing" and Web searching are becoming significant and important computer applications, and many of the key computations in all of this document processing involve character strings and string pattern matching. For example, the Internet document formats HTML and XML are primarily text formats, with added tags for multimedia content. Making sense of the many terabytes of information on the Internet requires a considerable amount of text processing.

In this chapter, we study several of the fundamental text processing algorithms for quickly performing important string operations. We pay particular attention to algorithms for string searching and pattern matching, since these can often be computational bottlenecks in many document-processing applications. We also study some fundamental data structure and algorithmic issues involved in text processing, as well.

The progression of topics studied in this chapter continues to follow our abstract data type approach. The terminology and notation for the string ADT, which is used in this chapter, is defined in Section 11.1. It turns out that representing a string as an array of characters is quite simple and efficient, so we don't spend a lot of time on string representations. Nevertheless, the string ADT includes an interesting method for string pattern matching, and we study pattern matching algorithms in Section 11.2. In Section 11.3, we study the trie data structure, which is a tree-based structure that allows for fast searching in a collection of strings. We study an important text processing problem in Section 11.4, namely, the problem of compressing a document of text so that it fits more efficiently in storage or can be transmitted more efficiently over a network. We study another text processing problem in Section 11.5, which deals with how we can measure the similarity between two documents. All of these problems are topics that arise often in Internet computations, such as Web crawlers, search engines, document distribution, and information retrieval.

In addition to having interesting applications, the topics of this chapter also highlight some important algorithmic design patterns. In particular, in the section on pattern matching, we discuss the ***brute-force method***, which is often inefficient but has wide applicability. For text compression, we study the ***greedy method***, which often allows us to approximate solutions to hard problems, and for some problems (such as in text compression) actually gives rise to optimal algorithms. Finally, in discussing text similarity, we introduce the ***dynamic programming*** design pattern, which can be applied in some special instances to solve a problem in polynomial time that appears at first to require exponential time to solve.

11.1 String Operations

At the heart of text processing algorithms are methods for dealing with character strings. Character strings can come from a wide variety of sources, including scientific, linguistic, and Internet applications. Indeed, the following are examples of such strings:

$$P = \text{"CGTAAACTGCTTTAATCAAACGC"}$$
$$R = \text{"U.S. Men Win Soccer World Cup!"}$$
$$S = \text{"http://www.wiley.com/"}.$$

The first string, P, comes from DNA applications, the last string, S, is the Internet address (URL) for the Web site that accompanies this book, and the middle string, R, is a fictional news headline. In this section, we present some of the useful operations that are supported by the string ADT for processing strings such as these.

Substrings

Several of the typical string processing operations involve breaking large strings into smaller strings. In order to be able to speak about the pieces that result from such operations, we use the term **substring** of an m-character string P to refer to a string of the form $P[i]P[i+1]P[i+2]\cdots P[j]$, for some $0 \leq i \leq j \leq m-1$, that is, the string formed by the characters in P from index i to index j, inclusive. Technically, this means that a string is actually a substring of itself (taking $i = 0$ and $j = m-1$), so if we want to rule this out as a possibility, we must restrict the definition to **proper** substrings, which require that either $i > 0$ or $j < m-1$. To simplify the notation for referring to substrings, let us use $P[i..j]$ to denote the substring of P from index i to index j, inclusive. That is,

$$P[i..j] = P[i]P[i+1]\cdots P[j].$$

We use the convention that, if $i > j$, then $P[i..j]$ is equal to the **null string**, which has length 0. In addition, in order to distinguish some special kinds of substrings, let us refer to any substring of the form $P[0..i]$, for $0 \leq i \leq m-1$, as a **prefix** of P, and any substring of the form $P[i..m-1]$, for $0 \leq i \leq m-1$, as a **suffix** of P. For example, if we again take P to be the string of DNA given above, then "CGTAA" is a prefix of P, "CGC" is a suffix of P, and "TTAATC" is a (proper) substring of P. Note that the null string is a prefix and a suffix of any other string.

11.1.1   The STL String Class

Recall from Chapter 1 that C++ supports two types of strings. A C-style string is just an array of type char terminated by a null character '\0'. By themselves, C-style strings do not support complex string operations. The C++ Standard Template Library (STL) provides a complete string class. This class supports a bewildering number of string operations. We list just a few of them. In the following, let S denote the STL string object on which the operation is being performed, and let Q denote another STL string or a C-style string.

size(): Return the number of characters, n, of S.
Input: None; *Output:* int.

empty(): Return a Boolean indicating whether the string is empty.
Input: None; *Output:* bool.

operator[i]: Return the character at index i of S, without performing array bounds checking.
Input: int; *Output:* char.

at(i): Return the character at index i of S. An out_of_range exception is thrown if i is out of bounds.
Input: int; *Output:* char.

insert(i, Q): Insert string Q prior to index i in S and return a reference to the result.
Input: int i and string Q; *Output:* string&.

append(Q): Append string Q to the end of S and return a reference to the result.
Input: string; *Output:* string&.

erase(i, m): Remove m characters starting at index i and return a reference to the result.
Input: int i and m; *Output:* string&.

substr(i, m): Return the substring of S of length m starting at index i.
Input: int i and m; *Output:* string.

find(Q): If Q is a substring of S, return the index of the beginning of the first occurrence of Q in S, else return n, the length of S.
Input: String; *Output:* int.

c_str(): Returns a C-style string containing the contents of S..
Input: None; *Output:* char*.

Further Observations about STL Strings

By default a string is initialized to the empty string. A string may be initialized from another STL string or from a C-style string. It is not possible, however, to initialize an STL string from a single character. STL strings also support functions that return both forward and backward iterators. All operations that are defined in terms of integer indices have counterparts that are based on iterators.

The STL string class also supports assignment of one string to another. It provides relational operators, such as ==, <, >=, which are performed lexicographically. Strings can be concatenated using +, and we may append one string to another using +=. Strings can be input using >> and output using <<. The function getline(*in*, *S*) reads an entire line of input from the input stream *in* and assigns it to the string *S*.

The STL string class is actually a special case of a more general templated class, called basic_string<T>, which supports all the string operations but allows its elements to be of an arbitrary type, *T*, not just char. The STL string is just a short way of saying basic_string<char>. A "string of integers" could be defined as basic_string<int>.

Example 11.1: *Consider the following series of operations, which are performed on the string S =* "abcdefghijklmnop":

Operation	Output
S.size()	16
S.at(5)	'f'
S[5]	'f'
S + "qrs"	"abcdefghijklmnopqrs"
S == "abcdefghijklmnop"	true
S.find("ghi")	6
S.substr(4,6)	"efghij"
S.erase(4,6)	"abcdklmnop"
S.insert(1,"xxx")	"axxxbcdklmnop"
S += "xy"	"axxxbcdklmnopxy"
S.append("z")	"axxxbcdklmnopxyz"

With the exception of the find(*Q*) function, which we discuss in Section 11.2, all the above functions are easily implemented simply by representing the string as an array of characters.

11.2   Pattern Matching Algorithms

In the classic strings **pattern matching** problem, we are given a **text** string T of length n and a **pattern** string P of length m, and want to find whether P is a substring of T. The notion of a "match" is that there is a substring of T starting at some index i that matches P, character by character, so that $T[i] = P[0]$, $T[i+1] = P[1]$, ..., $T[i+m-1] = P[m-1]$. That is, $P = T[i..i+m-1]$. Thus, the output from a pattern matching algorithm could either be some indication that the pattern P does not exist in T or an integer indicating the starting index in T of a substring matching P. This is exactly the computation performed by the find() function of the STL string class. Alternatively, one may want to find all the indices where a substring of T matching P begins.

To allow for fairly general notions of a character string, we typically do not restrict the characters in T and P to explicitly come from a well-known character set, like the ASCII or Unicode character sets. Instead, we typically use the general symbol Σ to denote the character set, or **alphabet**, from which characters in T and P can come. This alphabet Σ can, of course, be a subset of the ASCII or Unicode character sets, but it could also be something more general and is even allowed to be infinite, like positive integers. Nevertheless, since most document processing algorithms are used in applications where the underlying character set is finite, we usually assume that the size of the alphabet Σ, denoted with $|\Sigma|$, is a fixed finite constant.

In this section, we present three pattern matching algorithms (with increasing levels of difficulty).

11.2.1   Brute Force

The **brute force** algorithmic design pattern is a powerful technique for algorithm design when we have something we wish to search for or when we wish to optimize some function. In applying this technique in a general situation, we typically enumerate all possible configurations of the inputs involved and pick the best of all these enumerated configurations.

Brute-Force Pattern Matching

In applying this technique to design the **brute-force pattern matching** algorithm, we derive what is probably the first algorithm that we might think of for solving the pattern matching problem—we simply test all the possible placements of P relative to T. This algorithm, shown in Code Fragment 11.1, is quite simple.

Algorithm BruteForceMatch(T,P):

    Input: Strings T (text) with n characters and P (pattern) with m characters

    Output: Starting index of the first substring of T matching P, or an indication that P is not a substring of T

    for $i \leftarrow 0$ **to** $n - m$ {for each candidate index in T} **do**

        $j \leftarrow 0$

        while $(j < m$ **and** $T[i+j] = P[j])$ **do**

            $j \leftarrow j + 1$

        if $j = m$ **then**

            return i

    return "There is no substring of T matching P."

Code Fragment 11.1: Brute-force pattern matching.

The brute-force pattern matching algorithm could not be simpler. It consists of two nested loops, with the outer loop indexing through all possible starting indices of the pattern in the text, and the inner loop indexing through each character of the pattern, comparing it to its potentially corresponding character in the text. Thus, the correctness of the brute-force pattern matching algorithm follows immediately from this exhaustive search approach.

Performance

The running time of brute-force pattern matching in the worst case is not good, however, because, for each candidate index in T, we can perform up to m character comparisons to discover that P does not match T at the current index. Referring to Code Fragment 11.1, we see that the outer for-loop is executed at most $n - m + 1$ times, and the inner loop is executed at most m times. Thus, the running time of the brute-force method is $O((n-m+1)m)$, which is simplified as $O(nm)$. Note that, when $m = n/2$, this algorithm has a quadratic running time $O(n^2)$.

Example 11.2: *Suppose we are given the text string*

$$T = \texttt{"abacaabaccabacabaabb"}$$

and the pattern string

$$P = \texttt{"abacab"}.$$

In Figure 11.1 we illustrate the execution of the brute-force pattern matching algorithm on T and P.

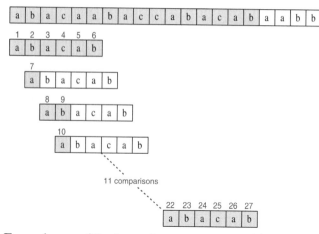

Figure 11.1: Example run of the brute-force pattern matching algorithm. The algorithm performs 27 character comparisons, indicated above with numerical labels.

11.2.2   The Boyer-Moore Algorithm

At first, we might feel that it is always necessary to examine every character in T in order to locate a pattern P as a substring. But this is not always the case, for the **Boyer-Moore (BM)** pattern matching algorithm, which we study in this section, can sometimes avoid comparisons between P and a sizable fraction of the characters in T. The only caveat is that, whereas the brute-force algorithm can work even with a potentially unbounded alphabet, the BM algorithm assumes the alphabet is of fixed, finite size. It works the fastest when the alphabet is moderately sized and the pattern is relatively long. Thus, the BM algorithm is ideal for searching words in documents. In this section, we describe a simplified version of the original algorithm by Boyer and Moore.

The main idea of the BM algorithm is to improve the running time of the brute-force algorithm by adding two potentially time-saving heuristics. Roughly stated, these heuristics are as follows:

Looking-Glass Heuristic: When testing a possible placement of P against T, begin the comparisons from the end of P and move backward to the front of P.

Character-Jump Heuristic: During the testing of a possible placement of P against T, a mismatch of text character $T[i] = c$ with the corresponding pattern character $P[j]$ is handled as follows. If c is not contained anywhere in P, then shift P completely past $T[i]$ (for it cannot match any character in P). Otherwise, shift P until an occurrence of character c in P gets aligned with $T[i]$.

We will formalize these heuristics shortly, but at an intuitive level, they work as an integrated team. The looking-glass heuristic sets up the other heuristic to allow us to avoid comparisons between P and whole groups of characters in T. In this case at least, we can get to the destination faster by going backwards, for if we encounter a mismatch during the consideration of P at a certain location in T, then we are likely to avoid lots of needless comparisons by significantly shifting P relative to T using the character-jump heuristic. The character-jump heuristic pays off big if it can be applied early in the testing of a potential placement of P against T.

Let us therefore get down to the business of defining how the character-jump heuristics can be integrated into a string pattern matching algorithm. To implement this heuristic, we define a function $\text{last}(c)$ that takes a character c from the alphabet and characterizes how far we may shift the pattern P if a character equal to c is found in the text that does not match the pattern. In particular, we define $\text{last}(c)$ as

- If c is in P, $\text{last}(c)$ is the index of the last (right-most) occurrence of c in P. Otherwise, we conventionally define $\text{last}(c) = -1$.

If characters can be used as indices in arrays, then the $\text{last}()$ function can be easily implemented as a look-up table. We leave the method for computing this table in $O(m + |\Sigma|)$ time, given P, as a simple exercise (R-11.6). This $\text{last}()$ function will give us all the information we need to perform the character-jump heuristic.

In Code Fragment 11.2, we show the BM pattern matching algorithm.

Algorithm BMMatch(T,P):

   Input: Strings T (text) with n characters and P (pattern) with m characters

   Output: Starting index of the first substring of T matching P, or an indication
       that P is not a substring of T

   compute function $\text{last}()$
   $i \leftarrow m - 1$
   $j \leftarrow m - 1$
   repeat
     if $P[j] = T[i]$ **then**
       if $j = 0$ **then**
         return i {a match!}
       else
         $i \leftarrow i - 1$
         $j \leftarrow j - 1$
     else
       $i \leftarrow i + m - \min(j, 1 + \text{last}(T[i]))$ { jump step }
       $j \leftarrow m - 1$
   until $i > n - 1$
   return "There is no substring of T matching P."

Code Fragment 11.2: The Boyer-Moore pattern matching algorithm.

The jump step is illustrated in Figure 11.2. In Figure 11.3, we illustrate the execution of the Boyer-Moore pattern matching algorithm on a similar input string as in Example 11.2.

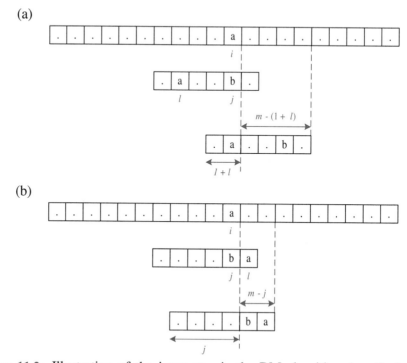

(a)

(b)

Figure 11.2: Illustration of the jump step in the BM algorithm (see Code Fragment 11.2), where we use the notation $l = \mathsf{last}(T[i])$. We distinguish two cases: (a) $1+l \leq j$, where we shift the pattern by $j-l$ units; (b) $j < 1+l$, where we shift the pattern by one unit.

The correctness of the BM pattern matching algorithm follows from the fact that each time the function makes a shift, it is guaranteed not to "skip" over any possible matches. For $\mathsf{last}(c)$ is the location of the ***last*** occurrence of c in P.

The worst-case running time of the BM algorithm is $O(nm + |\Sigma|)$. Namely, the computation of the $\mathsf{last}()$ function takes time $O(m + |\Sigma|)$ and the actual search for the pattern takes $O(nm)$ time in the worst case, the same as the brute-force algorithm. An example of a text-pattern pair that achieves the worst case is

$$T = \overbrace{aaaaaa \cdots a}^{n}$$
$$P = b\overbrace{aa \cdots a}^{m-1}.$$

The worst-case performance, however, is unlikely to be achieved for English text.

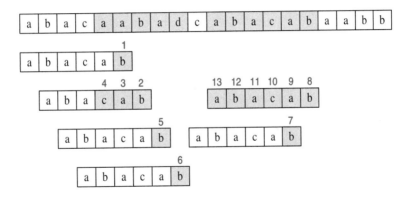

The last(c) function:

c	a	b	c	d
last(c)	4	5	3	−1

Figure 11.3: An illustration of the BM pattern matching algorithm. The algorithm performs 13 character comparisons, which are indicated with numerical labels.

Indeed, the BM algorithm is often able to skip over large portions of the text. (See Figure 11.4.) There is experimental evidence that on English text, the average number of comparisons done per text character is approximately 0.24 for a five-character pattern string. The payoff is not as great for binary strings or for very short patterns, however, in which case the KMP algorithm, discussed in Section 11.2.3, or, for very short patterns, the brute-force algorithm, may be better.

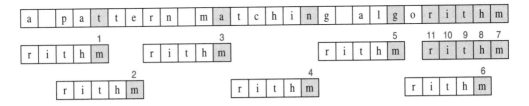

Figure 11.4: Execution of the Boyer-Moore algorithm on an English text and pattern, where a significant speedup is achieved. Note that not all text characters are examined.

A C++ implementation of the BM pattern matching algorithm is shown in Code Fragment 11.3.

```
                                                    // Boyer-Moore algorithm
int BMmatch(const string& text, const string& pattern) {
  vector<int> last = buildLastFunction(pattern);
  int n = text.size();
  int m = pattern.size();
  int i = m − 1;
  if (i > n − 1)                          // pattern longer than text?
    return −1;                            // ...then no match
  int j = m − 1;
  do {
    if (pattern[j] == text[i])
      if (j == 0) return i;               // found a match
      else {                              // looking-glass heuristic
        i−−; j−−;                         // proceed right-to-left
      }
    else {                                // character jump heuristic
      i = i + m − min(j, 1 + last[text[i]]);
      j = m − 1;
    }
  } while (i <= n − 1);
  return −1;                              // no match
}

                                          // construct function last
vector<int> buildLastFunction (const string& pattern) {
  const int N_ASCII = 128;                // number of ASCII characters
  int i;
  vector<int> last(N_ASCII);              // assume ASCII character set
  for (i = 0; i < N_ASCII; i++)           // initialize array
    last[i] = −1;
  for (i = 0; i < pattern.size(); i++) {
    last[pattern[i]] = i;                 // (implicit cast to ASCII code)
  }
  return last;
}
```

Code Fragment 11.3: The function BMmatch() implements the simplified Boyer-Moore (BM) pattern matching algorithm, which uses the looking-glass and character-jump heuristics. It returns the index of the beginning of the leftmost substring of the text matching the pattern, or −1 if there is no match. The auxiliary function buildLastFunction() returns an STL vector of size N_ASCII, storing the index of the last occurrence of each ASCII character in the pattern.

We have actually presented a simplified version of the Boyer-Moore (BM) algorithm. The original BM algorithm achieves running time $O(n+m+|\Sigma|)$ by using an alternative shift heuristic to the partially matched text string, whenever it shifts the pattern more than the character-jump heuristic. This alternative shift heuristic is based on applying the main idea from the Knuth-Morris-Pratt pattern matching algorithm, which we discuss next.

11.2.3 The Knuth-Morris-Pratt Algorithm

In studying the worst-case performance of the brute-force and BM pattern matching algorithms on specific instances of the problem, such as that given in Example 11.2, we should notice a major inefficiency. Specifically, we may perform many comparisons while testing a potential placement of the pattern against the text, yet, if we discover a pattern character that does not match in the text, then we throw away all the information gained by these comparisons and start over again from scratch with the next incremental placement of the pattern. The Knuth-Morris-Pratt (or "KMP") algorithm, discussed in this section, avoids this waste of information and, in so doing, it achieves a running time of $O(n+m)$, which is optimal in the worst case. That is, in the worst case any pattern matching algorithm will have to examine all the characters of the text and all the characters of the pattern at least once.

The Failure Function

The main idea of the KMP algorithm is to preprocess the pattern string P so as to compute a ***failure function*** f that indicates the proper shift of P so that, to the largest extent possible, we can reuse previously performed comparisons. Specifically, the failure function $f(j)$ is defined as the length of the longest prefix of P that is a suffix of $P[1..j]$ (note that we did ***not*** put $P[0..j]$ here). We also use the convention that $f(0) = 0$. Later, we will discuss how to compute the failure function efficiently. The importance of this failure function is that it "encodes" repeated substrings inside the pattern itself.

Example 11.3: *Consider the pattern string $P = $ "abacab" from Example 11.2. The Knuth-Morris-Pratt (KMP) failure function $f(j)$ for the string P is as shown in the following table:*

j	0	1	2	3	4	5
$P[j]$	a	b	a	c	a	b
$f(j)$	0	0	1	0	1	2

The KMP pattern matching algorithm, shown in Code Fragment 11.4, incrementally processes the text string T comparing it to the pattern string P. Each time there is a match, we increment the current indices. On the other hand, if there is a mismatch and we have previously made progress in P, then we consult the failure function to determine the new index in P where we need to continue checking P against T. Otherwise (there was a mismatch and we are at the beginning of P), we simply increment the index for T (and keep the index variable for P at its beginning). We repeat this process until we find a match of P in T or the index for T reaches n, the length of T (indicating that we did not find the pattern P in T).

Algorithm KMPMatch(T, P):

　　Input: Strings T (text) with n characters and P (pattern) with m characters

　　Output: Starting index of the first substring of T matching P, or an indication that P is not a substring of T

　　　$f \leftarrow$ KMPFailureFunction(P)　　　　　{construct the failure function f for P}

　　　$i \leftarrow 0$

　　　$j \leftarrow 0$

　　　while $i < n$ **do**

　　　　if $P[j] = T[i]$ **then**

　　　　　if $j = m - 1$ **then**

　　　　　　return $i - m + 1$　　　　{a match!}

　　　　　$i \leftarrow i + 1$

　　　　　$j \leftarrow j + 1$

　　　　else if $j > 0$ {no match, but we have advanced in P} **then**

　　　　　$j \leftarrow f(j - 1)$　　　　{j indexes just after prefix of P that must match}

　　　　else

　　　　　$i \leftarrow i + 1$

　　　return "There is no substring of T matching P."

Code Fragment 11.4: The KMP pattern matching algorithm.

The main part of the KMP algorithm is the while-loop, which performs a comparison between a character in T and a character in P each iteration. Depending upon the outcome of this comparison, the algorithm either moves on to the next characters in T and P, consults the failure function for a new candidate character in P, or starts over with the next index in T. The correctness of this algorithm follows from the definition of the failure function. Any comparisons that are skipped are actually unnecessary, for the failure function guarantees that all the ignored comparisons are redundant—they would involve comparing the same matching characters over again.

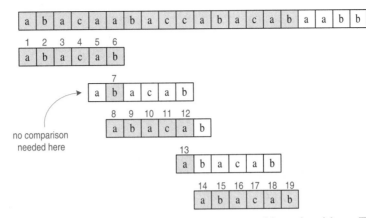

Figure 11.5: An illustration of the KMP pattern matching algorithm. The failure function f for this pattern is given in Example 11.3. The algorithm performs 19 character comparisons, which are indicated with numerical labels.

In Figure 11.5, we illustrate the execution of the KMP pattern matching algorithm on the same input strings as in Example 11.2. Note the use of the failure function to avoid redoing one of the comparisons between a character of the pattern and a character of the text. Also note that the algorithm performs fewer overall comparisons than the brute-force algorithm run on the same strings (Figure 11.1).

Performance

Excluding the computation of the failure function, the running time of the KMP algorithm is clearly proportional to the number of iterations of the while-loop. For the sake of the analysis, let us define $k = i - j$. Intuitively, k is the total amount by which the pattern P has been shifted with respect to the text T. Note that throughout the execution of the algorithm, we have $k \leq n$. One of the following three cases occurs at each iteration of the loop.

- If $T[i] = P[j]$, then i increases by 1, and k does not change, since j also increases by 1.
- If $T[i] \neq P[j]$ and $j > 0$, then i does not change and k increases by at least 1, since in this case k changes from $i - j$ to $i - f(j-1)$, which is an addition of $j - f(j-1)$, which is positive because $f(j-1) < j$.
- If $T[i] \neq P[j]$ and $j = 0$, then i increases by 1 and k increases by 1, since j does not change.

Thus, at each iteration of the loop, either i or k increases by at least 1 (possibly both); hence, the total number of iterations of the while-loop in the KMP pattern matching algorithm is at most $2n$. Achieving this bound, of course, assumes that we have already computed the failure function for P.

Constructing the KMP Failure Function

To construct the failure function, we use the function shown in Code Fragment 11.5, which is a "bootstrapping" process quite similar to the KMPMatch() algorithm. We compare the pattern to itself as in the KMP algorithm. Each time we have two characters that match, we set $f(i) = j + 1$. Note that, since we have $i > j$ throughout the execution of the algorithm, $f(j-1)$ is always defined when we need to use it.

Algorithm KMPFailureFunction(P):
  Input: String P (pattern) with m characters
  Output: The failure function f for P, which maps j to the length of the longest prefix of P that is a suffix of $P[1..j]$

  $i \leftarrow 1$
  $j \leftarrow 0$
  $f(0) \leftarrow 0$
  while $i < m$ **do**
    if $P[j] = P[i]$ **then**
        {we have matched $j + 1$ characters}
        $f(i) \leftarrow j + 1$
        $i \leftarrow i + 1$
        $j \leftarrow j + 1$
    else if $j > 0$ **then**
        {j indexes just after a prefix of P that must match}
        $j \leftarrow f(j-1)$
    else
        {we have no match here}
        $f(i) \leftarrow 0$
        $i \leftarrow i + 1$

Code Fragment 11.5: Computation of the failure function used in the KMP pattern matching algorithm. Note how the algorithm uses the previous values of the failure function to efficiently compute new values.

Algorithm KMPFailureFunction() runs in $O(m)$ time. Its analysis is analogous to that of algorithm KMPMatch(). Thus, we have:

Proposition 11.4: *The Knuth-Morris-Pratt algorithm performs pattern matching on a text string of length n and a pattern string of length m in $O(n+m)$ time.*

A C++ implementation of the KMP pattern matching algorithm is shown in Code Fragment 11.6.

```
                                                    // KMP algorithm
int KMPmatch(const string& text, const string& pattern) {
  int n = text.size();
  int m = pattern.size();
  vector<int> fail = computeFailFunction(pattern);
  int i = 0;                                         // text index
  int j = 0;                                         // pattern index
  while (i < n) {
    if (pattern[j] == text[i]) {
      if (j == m − 1)
        return i − m + 1;                            // found a match
      i++; j++;
    }
    else if (j > 0) j = fail[j − 1];
    else i++;
  }
  return −1;                                         // no match
}

vector<int> computeFailFunction(const string& pattern) {
  vector<int> fail(pattern.size());
  fail[0] = 0;
  int m = pattern.size();
  int j = 0;
  int i = 1;
  while (i < m) {
    if (pattern[j] == pattern[i]) {                  // j + 1 characters match
      fail[i] = j + 1;
      i++; j++;
    }
    else if (j > 0)                                  // j follows a matching prefix
      j = fail[j − 1];
    else {                                           // no match
      fail[i] = 0;
      i++;
    }
  }
  return fail;
}
```

Code Fragment 11.6: C++ implementation of the KMP pattern matching algorithm. The algorithm is expressed by two functions: KMPmatch() performs the matching and calls the auxiliary function computeFailFunction() to compute the failure function, represented as an STL vector. Method KMPmatch() indicates the absence of a match by returning the conventional value −1.

11.3 Tries

The pattern matching algorithms presented in the previous section speed up the search in a text by preprocessing the pattern (to compute the failure function in the KMP algorithm or the last function in the BM algorithm). In this section, we take a complementary approach, namely, we present string searching algorithms that preprocess the text. This approach is suitable for applications where a series of queries is performed on a fixed text, so that the initial cost of preprocessing the text is compensated by a speedup in each subsequent query (for example, a Web site that offers pattern matching in Shakespeare's *Hamlet* or a search engine that offers Web pages on the *Hamlet* topic).

A *trie* (pronounced "try") is a tree-based data structure for storing strings in order to support fast pattern matching. The main application for tries is in information retrieval. Indeed, the name "trie" comes from the word "re*trie*val." In an information retrieval application, such as a search for a certain DNA sequence in a genomic database, we are given a collection S of strings, all defined using the same alphabet. The primary query operations that tries support are pattern matching and *prefix matching*. The latter operation involves being given a string X, and looking for all the strings in S that contain X as a prefix.

11.3.1 Standard Tries

Let S be a set of s strings from alphabet Σ, such that no string in S is a prefix of another string. A *standard trie* for S is an ordered tree T with the following properties (see Figure 11.6):

- Each node of T, except the root, is labeled with a character of Σ.
- The ordering of the children of an internal node of T is determined by a canonical ordering of the alphabet Σ.
- T has s external nodes, each associated with a string of S, such that the concatenation of the labels of the nodes on the path from the root to an external node v of T yields the string of S associated with v.

Thus, a trie T represents the strings of S with paths from the root to the external nodes of T. Note the importance of assuming that no string in S is a prefix of another string. This ensures that each string of S is uniquely associated with an external node of T. We can always satisfy this assumption by adding a special character that is not in the original alphabet Σ at the end of each string.

Caution

An internal node in a standard trie T can have anywhere from 1 to d children, where d is the size of the alphabet. There is an edge going from the root r to one

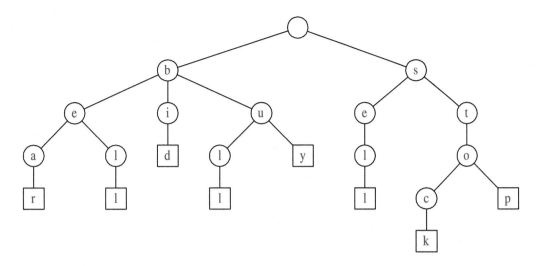

Figure 11.6: Standard trie for the strings {bear, bell, bid, bull, buy, sell, stock, stop}.

of its children for each character that is first in some string in the collection S. In addition, a path from the root of T to an internal node v at depth i corresponds to an i-character prefix $X[0..i-1]$ of a string X of S. In fact, for each character c that can follow the prefix $X[0..i-1]$ in a string of the set S, there is a child of v labeled with character c. In this way, a trie concisely stores the common prefixes that exist among a set of strings.

If there are only two characters in the alphabet, then the trie is essentially a binary tree, although some internal nodes may have only one child (that is, it may be an improper binary tree). In general, if there are d characters in the alphabet, then the trie will be a multi-way tree where each internal node has between 1 and d children. In addition, there are likely to be several internal nodes in a standard trie that have fewer than d children. For example, the trie shown in Figure 11.6 has several internal nodes with only one child. We can implement a trie with a tree storing characters at its nodes.

The following proposition provides some important structural properties of a standard trie.

Proposition 11.5: *A standard trie storing a collection S of s strings of total length n from an alphabet of size d has the following properties:*

- *Every internal node of T has at most d children*
- *T has s external nodes*
- *The height of T is equal to the length of the longest string in S*
- *The number of nodes of T is $O(n)$.*

The worst case for the number of nodes of a trie occurs when no two strings share a common nonempty prefix; that is, except for the root, all internal nodes have one child.

A trie T for a set S of strings can be used to implement a dictionary whose keys are the strings of S. Namely, we perform a search in T for a string X by tracing down from the root the path indicated by the characters in X. If this path can be traced and terminates at an external node, then we know X is in the dictionary. For example, in the trie in Figure 11.6, tracing the path for "bull" ends up at an external node. If the path cannot be traced or the path can be traced but terminates at an internal node, then X is not in the dictionary. In the example in Figure 11.6, the path for "bet" cannot be traced and the path for "be" ends at an internal node. Neither word is in the dictionary. Note that in this implementation of a dictionary, single characters are compared instead of the entire string (key). It is easy to see that the running time of the search for a string of size m is $O(dm)$, where d is the size of the alphabet. Indeed, we visit at most $m+1$ nodes of T and we spend $O(d)$ time at each node. For some alphabets, we may be able to improve the time spent at a node to be $O(1)$ or $O(\log d)$ by using a dictionary of characters implemented in a hash table or look-up table. However, since d is a constant in most applications, we can stick with the simple approach that takes $O(d)$ time per node visited.

From the above discussion, it follows that we can use a trie to perform a special type of pattern matching, called ***word matching***, where we want to determine whether a given pattern matches one of the words of the text exactly. (See Figure 11.7.) Word matching differs from standard pattern matching since the pattern cannot match an arbitrary substring of the text, but only one of its words. Using a trie, word matching for a pattern of length m takes $O(dm)$ time, where d is the size of the alphabet, independent of the size of the text. If the alphabet has constant size (as is the case for text in natural languages and DNA strings), a query takes $O(m)$ time, proportional to the size of the pattern. A simple extension of this scheme supports prefix matching queries. However, arbitrary occurrences of the pattern in the text (for example, the pattern is a proper suffix of a word or spans two words) cannot be efficiently performed.

To construct a standard trie for a set S of strings, we can use an incremental algorithm that inserts the strings one at a time. Recall the assumption that no string of S is a prefix of another string. To insert a string X into the current trie T, we first try to trace the path associated with X in T. Since X is not already in T and no string in S is a prefix of another string, we will stop tracing the path at an ***internal*** node v of T before reaching the end of X. We then create a new chain of node descendents of v to store the remaining characters of X. The time to insert X is $O(dm)$, where m is the length of X and d is the size of the alphabet. Thus, constructing the entire trie for set S takes $O(dn)$ time, where n is the total length of the strings of S.

s	e	e		a		b	e	a	r	?		s	e	l	l		s	t	o	c	k	!	
0	1	2	3	4	5	6	7	8	9	10	11	12	13	14	15	16	17	18	19	20	21	22	23

s	e	e		a		b	u	l	l	?		b	u	y		s	t	o	c	k	!	
24	25	26	27	28	29	30	31	32	33	34	35	36	37	38	39	40	41	42	43	44	45	46

b	i	d		s	t	o	c	k	!		b	i	d		s	t	o	c	k	!	
47	48	49	50	51	52	53	54	55	56	57	58	59	60	61	62	63	64	65	66	67	68

h	e	a	r		t	h	e		b	e	l	l	?		s	t	o	p	!
69	70	71	72	73	74	75	76	77	78	79	80	81	82	83	84	85	86	87	88

(a)

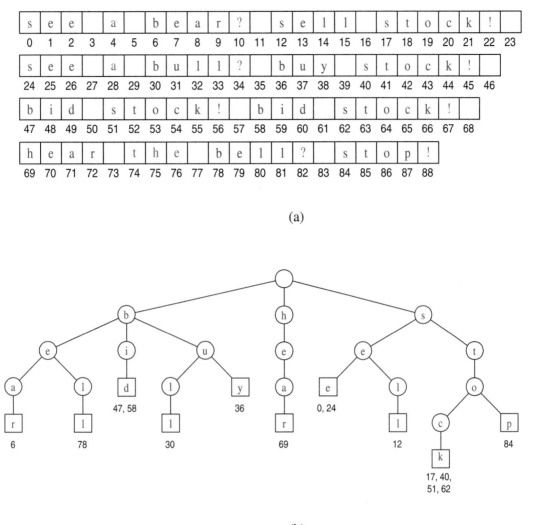

(b)

Figure 11.7: Word matching and prefix matching with a standard trie: (a) text to be searched; (b) standard trie for the words in the text (articles and prepositions, which are also known as *stop words*, excluded), with external nodes augmented with indications of the word positions.

There is a potential space inefficiency in the standard trie that has prompted the development of the **compressed trie**, which is also known (for historical reasons) as the **Patricia trie**. Namely, there are potentially a lot of nodes in the standard trie that have only one child, and the existence of such nodes is a waste. We discuss the compressed trie next.

11.3.2 Compressed Tries

A *compressed trie* is similar to a standard trie but it ensures that each internal node in the trie has at least two children. It enforces this rule by compressing chains of single-child nodes into individual edges. (See Figure 11.8.) Let T be a standard trie. We say that an internal node v of T is *redundant* if v has one child and is not the root. For example, the trie of Figure 11.6 has eight redundant nodes. Let us also say that a chain of $k \geq 2$ edges,

$$(v_0, v_1)(v_1, v_2) \cdots (v_{k-1}, v_k),$$

is *redundant* if

- v_i is redundant for $i = 1, \ldots, k-1$
- v_0 and v_k are not redundant.

We can transform T into a compressed trie by replacing each redundant chain $(v_0, v_1) \cdots (v_{k-1}, v_k)$ of $k \geq 2$ edges into a single edge (v_0, v_k), relabeling v_k with the concatenation of the labels of nodes $v_1, \ldots, v_k$.

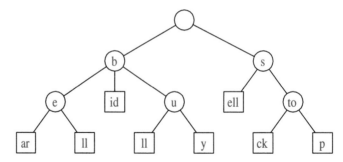

Figure 11.8: Compressed trie for the strings {bear, bell, bid, bull, buy, sell, stock, stop}. Compare this with the standard trie shown in Figure 11.6.

Thus, nodes in a compressed trie are labeled with strings, which are substrings of strings in the collection, rather than with individual characters. The advantage of a compressed trie over a standard trie is that the number of nodes of the compressed trie is proportional to the number of strings and not to their total length, as shown in the following proposition (compare with Proposition 11.5).

Proposition 11.6: *A compressed trie storing a collection S of s strings from an alphabet of size d has the following properties:*

- *Every internal node of T has at least two children and at most d children*
- *T has s external nodes*
- *The number of nodes of T is O(s).*

The attentive reader may wonder whether the compression of paths provides any significant advantage, since it is offset by a corresponding expansion of the node labels. Indeed, a compressed trie is truly advantageous only when it is used as an ***auxiliary*** index structure over a collection of strings already stored in a primary structure, and is not required to actually store all the characters of the strings in the collection.

Suppose, for example, that the collection S of strings is an array of strings $S[0]$, $S[1]$, ..., $S[s-1]$. Instead of storing the label X of a node explicitly, we represent it implicitly by a triplet of integers (i, j, k), such that $X = S[i][j..k]$; that is, X is the substring of $S[i]$ consisting of the characters from the jth to the kth included. (See the example in Figure 11.9. Also compare with the standard trie of Figure 11.7.)

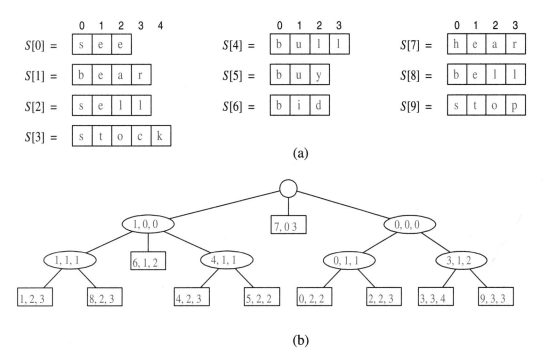

(a)

(b)

Figure 11.9: (a) Collection S of strings stored in an array. (b) Compact representation of the compressed trie for S.

This additional compression scheme allows us to reduce the total space for the trie itself from $O(n)$ for the standard trie to $O(s)$ for the compressed trie, where n is the total length of the strings in S and s is the number of strings in S. We must still store the different strings in S, of course, but we nevertheless reduce the space for the trie. In the next section, we present an application where the collection of strings can also be stored compactly.

11.3.3 Suffix Tries

One of the primary applications for tries is for the case when the strings in the collection S are all the suffixes of a string X. Such a trie is called the **suffix trie** (also known as a **suffix tree** or **position tree**) of string X. For example, Figure 11.10a shows the suffix trie for the eight suffixes of string "minimize." For a suffix trie, the compact representation presented in the previous section can be further simplified. Namely, the label of each vertex is a pair (i, j) indicating the string $X[i..j]$. (See Figure 11.10b.) To satisfy the rule that no suffix of X is a prefix of another suffix, we can add a special character, denoted with \$, that is not in the original alphabet Σ at the end of X (and thus to every suffix). That is, if string X has length n, we build a trie for the set of n strings $X[i..n-1]\$$, for $i = 0, \ldots, n-1$.

Caution

Saving Space

Using a suffix trie allows us to save space over a standard trie by using several space compression techniques, including those used for the compressed trie.

The advantage of the compact representation of tries now becomes apparent for suffix tries. Since the total length of the suffixes of a string X of length n is

$$1 + 2 + \cdots + n = \frac{n(n+1)}{2},$$

storing all the suffixes of X explicitly would take $O(n^2)$ space. Even so, the suffix trie represents these strings implicitly in $O(n)$ space, as formally stated in the following proposition.

Proposition 11.7: *The compact representation of a suffix trie T for a string X of length n uses $O(n)$ space.*

Construction

We can construct the suffix trie for a string of length n with an incremental algorithm like the one given in Section 11.3.1. This construction takes $O(dn^2)$ time because the total length of the suffixes is quadratic in n. However, the (compact) suffix trie for a string of length n can be constructed in $O(n)$ time with a specialized algorithm, different from the one for general tries. This linear-time construction algorithm is fairly complex, however, and is not reported here. Still, we can take advantage of the existence of this fast construction algorithm when we want to use a suffix trie to solve other problems.

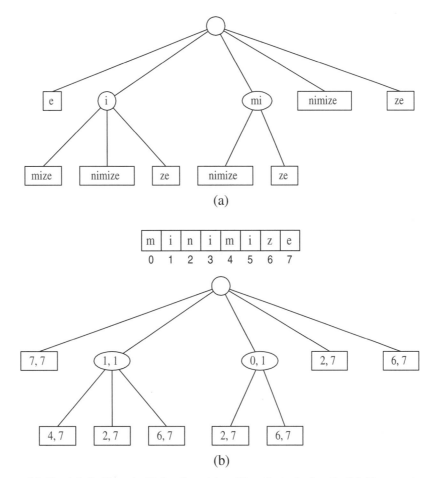

Figure 11.10: (a) Suffix trie T for the string $X = $ "minimize". (b) Compact representation of T, where pair (i, j) denotes $X[i..j]$.

Using a Suffix Trie

The suffix trie T for a string X can be used to efficiently perform pattern matching queries on text X. Namely, we can determine whether a pattern P is a substring of X by trying to trace a path associated with P in T. P is a substring of X, if and only if, such a path can be traced. The details of the pattern matching algorithm are given in Code Fragment 11.7, which assumes the following additional property on the labels of the nodes in the compact representation of the suffix trie:

> If node v has label (i, j) and Y is the string of length y associated with the path from the root to v (included), then $X[j - y + 1..j] = Y$.

This property ensures that we can easily compute the start index of the pattern in the text when a match occurs.

Algorithm suffixTrieMatch(T, P):

    Input: Compact suffix trie T for a text X and pattern P

    Output: Starting index of a substring of X matching P or an indication that P
       is not a substring of X

    $p \leftarrow P.\text{length}()$ { length of suffix of the pattern to be matched }
    $j \leftarrow 0$ { start of suffix of the pattern to be matched }
    $v \leftarrow T.\text{root}()$
    repeat
       $f \leftarrow$ **true** { flag indicating that no child was successfully processed }
       for each child w of v **do**
          $i \leftarrow \text{start}(v)$
          if $P[j] = T[i]$ **then**
             { process child w }
             $x \leftarrow \text{end}(w) - i + 1$
             if $p \leq x$ **then**
                { suffix is shorter than or of the same length of the node label }
                if $P[j..j + p - 1] = X[i..i + p - 1]$ **then**
                    return $i - j$ { match }
                else
                  return "P is not a substring of X"
             else
                { suffix is longer than the node label }
                if $P[j..j + x - 1] = X[i..i + x - 1]$ **then**
                    $p \leftarrow p - x$ { update suffix length }
                    $j \leftarrow j + x$ { update suffix start index }
                    $v \leftarrow w$
                    $f \leftarrow$ **false**
                    break out of the **for** loop
    until f **or** $T.\text{isExternal}(v)$
    return "P is not a substring of X"

Code Fragment 11.7: Pattern matching with a suffix trie. We denote the label of a node v with $(\text{start}(v), \text{end}(v))$, that is, the pair of indices specifying the substring of the text associated with v.

The correctness of algorithm suffixTrieMatch() follows from the fact that we search down the trie T, matching characters of the pattern P one at a time until one of the following events occurs:

- We completely match the pattern P
- We get a mismatch (caught by the termination of the for-loop without a break out)
- We are left with characters of P still to be matched after processing an external node.

Let m be the size of pattern P and d be the size of the alphabet. In order to determine the running time of algorithm suffixTrieMatch(), we make the following observations:

- We process at most $m + 1$ nodes of the trie
- Each node processed has at most d children
- At each node v processed, we perform at most one character comparison for each child w of v to determine which child of v needs to be processed next (which may possibly be improved by using a fast dictionary to index the children of v)
- We perform at most m character comparisons overall in the processed nodes
- We spend $O(1)$ time for each character comparison.

Performance

We conclude that algorithm suffixTrieMatch() performs pattern matching queries in $O(dm)$ time (and would possibly run even faster if we used a dictionary to index children of nodes in the suffix trie). Note that the running time does not depend on the size of the text X. Also, the running time is linear in the size of the pattern, that is, it is $O(m)$, for a constant-size alphabet. Hence, suffix tries are suited for repetitive pattern matching applications, where a series of pattern matching queries is performed on a fixed text.

We summarize the results of this section in the following proposition.

Proposition 11.8: *Let X be a text string with n characters from an alphabet of size d. We can perform pattern matching queries on X in $O(dm)$ time, where m is the length of the pattern, with the suffix trie of X, which uses $O(n)$ space and can be constructed in $O(dn)$ time.*

We explore another application of tries in the next subsection.

11.3.4 Search Engines

The World Wide Web contains a huge collection of text documents (Web pages). Information about these pages are gathered by a program called a **Web crawler**, which then stores this information in a special dictionary database. A Web **search engine** allows users to retrieve relevant information from this database, thereby identifying relevant pages on the Web containing given keywords. In this section, we present a simplified model of a search engine.

Inverted Files

The core information stored by a search engine is a dictionary, called an **inverted index** or **inverted file**, storing key-value pairs (w, L), where w is a word and L is a collection of pages containing word w. The keys (words) in this dictionary are called **index terms** and should be a set of vocabulary entries and proper nouns as large as possible. The elements in this dictionary are called **occurrence lists** and should cover as many Web pages as possible.

We can efficiently implement an inverted index with a data structure consisting of:

1. An array storing the occurrence lists of the terms (in no particular order).
2. A compressed trie for the set of index terms, where each external node stores the index of the occurrence list of the associated term.

The reason for storing the occurrence lists outside the trie is to keep the size of the trie data structure sufficiently small to fit in internal memory. Instead, because of their large total size, the occurrence lists have to be stored on disk.

With our data structure, a query for a single keyword is similar to a word matching query (see Section 11.3.1). Namely, we find the keyword in the trie and we return the associated occurrence list.

When multiple keywords are given and the desired output are the pages containing **all** the given keywords, we retrieve the occurrence list of each keyword using the trie and return their intersection. To facilitate the intersection computation, each occurrence list should be implemented with a sequence sorted by address or with a dictionary (see, for example, the generic merge computation discussed in Section 10.2).

In addition to the basic task of returning a list of pages containing given keywords, search engines provide an important additional service by **ranking** the pages returned by relevance. Devising fast and accurate ranking algorithms for search engines is a major challenge for computer researchers and electronic commerce companies.

11.4 Text Compression

In this section, we consider another text processing application, *text compression*. In this problem, we are given a string X defined over some alphabet, such as the ASCII or Unicode character sets, and we want to efficiently encode X into a small binary string Y (using only the characters 0 and 1). Text compression is useful in any situation where we are communicating over a low-bandwidth channel, such as a modem line or infrared connection, and we wish to minimize the time needed to transmit our text. Likewise, text compression is also useful for storing collections of large documents more efficiently, so as to allow for a fixed-capacity storage device to contain as many documents as possible.

The method for text compression explored in this section is the **Huffman code**. Standard encoding schemes, such as the ASCII and Unicode systems, use fixed-length binary strings to encode characters (with 7 bits in the ASCII system and 16 in the Unicode system). A Huffman code, on the other hand, uses a variable-length encoding optimized for the string X. The optimization is based on the use of character *frequencies*, where we have, for each character c, a count $f(c)$ of the number of times c appears in the string X. The Huffman code saves space over a fixed-length encoding by using short code-word strings to encode high-frequency characters and long code-word strings to encode low-frequency characters.

To encode the string X, we convert each character in X from its fixed-length code word to its variable-length code word, and we concatenate all these code words in order to produce the encoding Y for X. In order to avoid ambiguities, we insist that no code word in our encoding is a prefix of another code word in our encoding. Such a code is called a **prefix code**, and it simplifies the decoding of Y in order to get back X. (See Figure 11.11.) Even with this restriction, the savings produced by a variable-length prefix code can be significant, particularly if there is a wide variance in character frequencies (as is the case for natural language text in almost every spoken language).

Huffman's algorithm for producing an optimal variable-length prefix code for X is based on the construction of a binary tree T that represents the code. Each node in T, except the root, represents a bit in a code word, with each left child representing a "0" and each right child representing a "1." Each external node v is associated with a specific character, and the code word for that character is defined by the sequence of bits associated with the nodes in the path from the root of T to v. (See Figure 11.11.) Each external node v has a *frequency* $f(v)$, which is simply the frequency in X of the character associated with v. In addition, we give each internal node v in T a frequency, $f(v)$, that is the sum of the frequencies of all the external nodes in the subtree rooted at v.

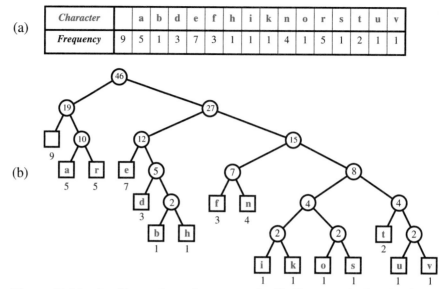

(a)

(b)

Figure 11.11: An illustration of an example Huffman code for the input string $X = $ "a fast runner need never be afraid of the dark": (a) frequency of each character of X; (b) Huffman tree T for string X. The code for a character c is obtained by tracing the path from the root of T to the external node where c is stored, and associating a left child with 0 and a right child with 1. For example, the code for 'a' is 010, and the code for 'f' is 1100.

11.4.1 The Huffman Coding Algorithm

The Huffman coding algorithm begins with each of the d distinct characters of the string X to encode, being the root node of a single-node binary tree. The algorithm proceeds in a series of rounds. In each round, the algorithm takes the two binary trees with the smallest frequencies and merges them into a single binary tree. It repeats this process until only one tree is left. (See Code Fragment 11.8.)

Each iteration of the while-loop in Huffman's algorithm can be implemented in $O(\log d)$ time using a priority queue represented with a heap. In addition, each iteration takes two nodes out of Q and adds one in, a process that will be repeated $d - 1$ times before exactly one node is left in Q. Thus, this algorithm runs in $O(n + d \log d)$ time. Although a full justification of this algorithm's correctness is beyond our scope here, we note that its intuition comes from a simple idea—any optimal code can be converted into an optimal code in which the code words for the two lowest-frequency characters, a and b, differ only in their last bit. Repeating the argument for a string with a and b replaced by a character c, gives the following:

Proposition 11.9: *Huffman's algorithm constructs an optimal prefix code for a string of length n with d distinct characters in $O(n + d \log d)$ time.*

Algorithm Huffman(X):

    Input: String X of length n with d distinct characters

    Output: Coding tree for X

    Compute the frequency $f(c)$ of each character c of X.

    Initialize a priority queue Q.

    for each character c in X **do**

        Create a single-node binary tree T storing c.

        Insert T into Q with key $f(c)$.

    while Q.size() > 1 **do**

        $f_1 \leftarrow Q$.minKey()

        $T_1 \leftarrow Q$.removeMin()

        $f_2 \leftarrow Q$.minKey()

        $T_2 \leftarrow Q$.removeMin()

        Create a new binary tree T with left subtree T_1 and right subtree T_2.

        Insert T into Q with key $f_1 + f_2$.

    return tree Q.removeMin()

Code Fragment 11.8: Huffman coding algorithm.

11.4.2 The Greedy Method

Huffman's algorithm for building an optimal encoding is an example of an application of an algorithmic design pattern called the ***greedy method***. This design pattern is applied to optimization problems, in which we are trying to construct some structure while minimizing or maximizing some property of that structure.

The general formula for the greedy method pattern is almost as simple as that for the brute-force method. In order to solve a given optimization problem using the greedy method, we proceed by making a sequence of choices. The sequence starts from some well-understood starting condition, and computes the cost for that initial condition. The pattern then asks that we iteratively make additional choices by identifying the decision that achieves the best cost improvement from all of the choices that are currently possible. This approach does not always lead to an optimal solution.

There are several problems that it does work for, however, and such problems are said to possess the ***greedy-choice*** property. This is the property that states that a global optimal condition can be reached by a series of locally optimal choices (that is, choices that are each the current best from among the possibilities available at the time), starting from a well-defined starting condition. The problem of computing an optimal variable-length prefix code is just one example of a problem that possesses the greedy-choice property.

11.5 Text Similarity Testing

A common text processing problem, which arises in genetics and software engineering, is to test the similarity between two text strings. In a genetics application, the two strings could correspond to two strands of DNA, which could, for example, come from two individuals, who we will consider genetically related if they have a long subsequence common to their respective DNA sequences. Likewise, in a software engineering application, the two strings could come from two versions of source code for the same program, and we may wish to determine which changes were made from one version to the next. Indeed, determining the similarity between two strings is considered such a common operation that the Unix/Linux operating systems come with a program, called `diff`, for comparing text files.

11.5.1 The Longest Common Subsequence Problem

There are several different ways we can define the similarity between two strings. Even so, we can abstract a simple, yet common, version of this problem using character strings and their subsequences. Given a string $X = x_0x_1x_2\cdots x_{n-1}$, a *subsequence* of X is any string that is of the form $x_{i_1}x_{i_2}\cdots x_{i_k}$, where $i_j < i_{j+1}$; that is, it is a sequence of characters that are not necessarily contiguous but are nevertheless taken in order from X. For example, the string *AAAG* is a subsequence of the string *CGATAATTGAGA*. Note that the concept of *subsequence* of a string is different from the concept of *substring* of a string defined in Section 11.1.

Caution

Problem Definition

The specific text similarity problem we address here is the *longest common subsequence* (LCS) problem. In this problem, we are given two character strings, $X = x_0x_1x_2\cdots x_{n-1}$ and $Y = y_0y_1y_2\cdots y_{m-1}$, over some alphabet (such as the alphabet $\{A,C,G,T\}$ common in computational genetics) and are asked to find a longest string S that is a subsequence of both X and Y.

One way to solve the longest common subsequence problem is to enumerate all subsequences of X and take the largest one that is also a subsequence of Y. Since each character of X is either in or not in a subsequence, there are potentially 2^n different subsequences of X, each of which requires $O(m)$ time to determine whether it is a subsequence of Y. Thus, this brute-force approach yields an exponential algorithm that runs in $O(2^n m)$ time, which is very inefficient. In this section, we discuss how to use an algorithmic design pattern called *dynamic programming* to solve the longest common subsequence problem much faster than this.

11.5.2 Dynamic Programming

There are few algorithmic techniques that can take problems that seem to require exponential time and produce polynomial-time algorithms to solve them. Dynamic programming is one such technique. In addition, the algorithms that result from applications of the dynamic programming technique are usually quite simple—often needing little more than a few lines of code to describe some nested loops for filling in a table.

The dynamic programming technique is used primarily for ***optimization*** problems, where we wish to find the "best" way of doing something. Often the number of different ways of doing that "something" is exponential, so a brute-force search for the best is computationally infeasible for all but the smallest problem sizes. We can apply the dynamic programming technique in such situations, however, if the problem has a certain amount of structure that we can exploit. This structure involves the following three components:

Simple Subproblems: There has to be some way of repeatedly breaking the global optimization problem into subproblems. Moreover, there should be a simple way of defining subproblems with just a few indices, like i, j, k, and so on.

Subproblem Optimization: An optimal solution to the global problem must be a composition of optimal subproblem solutions. We should not be able to find a globally optimal solution that contains suboptimal subproblems.

Subproblem Overlap: Optimal solutions to unrelated subproblems can contain subproblems in common.

Having given the general components of a dynamic programming algorithm, we next show how to apply it to the longest common subsequence problem.

11.5.3 Applying Dynamic Programming to the LCS Problem

We can solve the longest common subsequence problem much faster than exponential time using the dynamic programming technique. As mentioned above, one of the key components of the dynamic programming technique is the definition of simple subproblems that satisfy the subproblem optimization and subproblem overlap properties.

Recall that in the LCS problem, we are given two character strings, X and Y, of length n and m, respectively, and are asked to find a longest string S that is a subsequence of both X and Y. Since X and Y are character strings, we have a natural set of indices with which to define subproblems—indices into the strings X

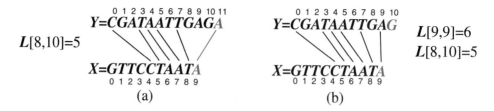

Figure 11.12: The two cases in the longest common subsequence algorithm: (a) $x_i = y_j$; (b) $x_i \neq y_j$. Note that the algorithm stores only the $L[i, j]$ values, not the matches.

and Y. Let us define a subproblem, therefore, as that of computing the value $L[i, j]$, which we will use to denote the length of a longest string that is a subsequence of both $X[0..i] = x_0x_1x_2 \ldots x_i$ and $Y[0..j] = y_0y_1y_2 \ldots y_j$. This definition allows us to rewrite $L[i, j]$ in terms of optimal subproblem solutions. This definition depends on which of the two following cases pertain. (See Figure 11.12.)

- $x_i = y_j$. In this case, we have a match between the last character of $X[0..i]$ and the last character of $Y[0..j]$. We claim that this character belongs to a longest common subsequence of $X[0..i]$ and $Y[0..j]$. To justify this claim, let us suppose it is not true. There has to be some longest common subsequence $x_{i_1}x_{i_2} \ldots x_{i_k} = y_{j_1}y_{j_2} \ldots y_{j_k}$. If $x_{i_k} = x_i$ or $y_{j_k} = y_j$, then we get the same sequence by setting $i_k = i$ and $j_k = j$. Alternately, if $x_{j_k} \neq x_i$, then we can get an even longer common subsequence by adding x_i to the end. Thus, a longest common subsequence of $X[0..i]$ and $Y[0..j]$ ends with x_i. Therefore, we set

$$L[i, j] = L[i-1, j-1] + 1 \quad \text{if } x_i = y_j.$$

- $x_i \neq y_j$. In this case, we cannot have a common subsequence that includes both x_i and y_j. That is, we can have a common subsequence end with x_i or one that ends with y_j (or possibly neither), but certainly not both. Therefore, we set

$$L[i, j] = \max\{L[i-1, j], L[i, j-1]\} \quad \text{if } x_i \neq y_j.$$

In order to make both of these equations make sense in the boundary cases when $i = 0$ or $j = 0$, we assign $L[i, -1] = 0$ for $i = -1, 0, 1, \ldots, n-1$ and $L[-1, j] = 0$ for $j = -1, 0, 1, \ldots, m-1$.

The above definition of $L[i, j]$ satisfies subproblem optimization, for we cannot have a longest common subsequence without also having longest common subsequences for the subproblems. Also, it uses subproblem overlap, because a subproblem solution $L[i, j]$ can be used in several other problems (namely, the problems $L[i+1, j]$, $L[i, j+1]$, and $L[i+1, j+1]$).

The LCS Algorithm

Turning this definition of $L[i, j]$ into an algorithm is actually quite straightforward. We initialize an $(n + 1) \times (m + 1)$ array, L, for the boundary cases when $i = 0$ or $j = 0$. Namely, we initialize $L[i, -1] = 0$ for $i = -1, 0, 1, \ldots, n - 1$ and $L[-1, j] = 0$ for $j = -1, 0, 1, \ldots, m - 1$. (This is a slight misuse of notation, since in reality, we would have to index the rows and columns of L starting with 0.) Then, we iteratively build up values in L until we have $L[n - 1, m - 1]$, the length of a longest common subsequence of X and Y. We give a pseudo-code description of how this approach results in a dynamic programming solution to the longest common subsequence (LCS) problem in Code Fragment 11.9.

Algorithm $\mathsf{LCS}(X, Y)$:

    Input: Strings X and Y with n and m elements, respectively

    Output: For $i = 0, \ldots, n - 1$, $j = 0, \ldots, m - 1$, the length $L[i, j]$ of a longest string that is a subsequence of both the string $X[0..i] = x_0 x_1 x_2 \cdots x_i$ and the string $Y[0..j] = y_0 y_1 y_2 \cdots y_j$

    for $i \leftarrow -1$ to $n - 1$ **do**

      $L[i, -1] \leftarrow 0$

    for $j \leftarrow 0$ to $m - 1$ **do**

      $L[-1, j] \leftarrow 0$

    for $i \leftarrow 0$ to $n - 1$ **do**

      for $j \leftarrow 0$ to $m - 1$ **do**

        if $x_i = y_j$ **then**

          $L[i, j] \leftarrow L[i - 1, j - 1] + 1$

        else

          $L[i, j] \leftarrow \max\{L[i - 1, j], L[i, j - 1]\}$

    return array L

Code Fragment 11.9: Dynamic programming algorithm for the LCS problem.

Performance

The running time of the algorithm of Code Fragment 11.9 is easy to analyze, for it is dominated by two nested for-loops, with the outer one iterating n times and the inner one iterating m times. Since the if-statement and assignment inside the loop each requires $O(1)$ primitive operations, this algorithm runs in $O(nm)$ time. Thus, the dynamic programming technique can be applied to the longest common subsequence problem, making a significant improvement over the exponential-time, brute-force solution to the LCS problem.

Algorithm LCS() (Code Fragment 11.9) computes the length of the longest common subsequence (stored in $L[n-1, m-1]$), but not the subsequence itself. As shown in the following proposition, a simple postprocessing step can extract the longest common subsequence from the array L returned by the algorithm.

Proposition 11.10: *Given a string X of n characters and a string Y of m characters, we can find the longest common subsequence of X and Y in $O(nm)$ time.*

Justification: Algorithm LCS() computes $L[n-1, m-1]$, the **length** of a longest common subsequence, in $O(nm)$ time. Given the table of $L[i, j]$ values, constructing a longest common subsequence is straightforward. One method is to start from $L[n, m]$ and work back through the table, reconstructing a longest common subsequence from back to front. At any position $L[i, j]$, we can determine whether $x_i = y_j$. If this is true, then we can take x_i as the next character of the subsequence (noting that x_i is **before** the previous character we found, if any), moving next to $L[i-1, j-1]$. If $x_i \neq y_j$, then we can move to the larger of $L[i, j-1]$ and $L[i-1, j]$. (See Figure 11.13.) We stop when we reach a boundary cell (with $i = -1$ or $j = -1$). This method constructs a longest common subsequence in $O(n+m)$ additional time. ∎

L	-1	0	1	2	3	4	5	6	7	8	9	10	11
-1	0	0	0	0	0	0	0	0	0	0	0	0	0
0	0	0	1	1	1	1	1	1	1	1	1	1	1
1	0	0	1	1	2	2	2	2	2	2	2	2	2
2	0	0	1	1	2	2	2	3	3	3	3	3	3
3	0	1	1	1	2	2	2	3	3	3	3	3	3
4	0	1	1	1	2	2	2	3	3	3	3	3	3
5	0	1	1	1	2	2	2	3	4	4	4	4	4
6	0	1	1	2	2	3	3	3	4	4	5	5	5
7	0	1	1	2	2	3	4	4	4	4	5	5	6
8	0	1	1	2	3	3	4	5	5	5	5	5	6
9	0	1	1	2	3	4	4	5	5	5	6	6	6

$$0\ 1\ 2\ 3\ 4\ 5\ 6\ 7\ 8\ 9\ 10\ 11$$
$$Y = CGATAATTGAGA$$

$$X = GTTCCTAATA$$
$$0\ 1\ 2\ 3\ 4\ 5\ 6\ 7\ 8\ 9$$

Figure 11.13: Illustration of the algorithm for constructing a longest common subsequence from the array L.

11.6   Exercises

Reinforcement

R-11.1 How many nonempty prefixes of the string $P =$"aaabbaaa" are also suffixes of P?

R-11.2 Draw a figure illustrating the comparisons done by the brute-force pattern matching algorithm for the case when the text is "aaabaadaabaaa" and the pattern is "aabaaa".

R-11.3 Repeat the previous problem for the BM pattern matching algorithm, not counting the comparisons made to compute the $last(c)$ function.

R-11.4 Repeat the previous problem for the KMP pattern matching algorithm, not counting the comparisons made to compute the failure function.

R-11.5 Compute a table representing the $last()$ function used in the BM pattern matching algorithm for the pattern string

"the quick brown fox jumped over a lazy cat"

assuming the following alphabet (which starts with the space character):

$$\Sigma = \{ \text{ ,a,b,c,d,e,f,g,h,i,j,k,l,m,n,o,p,q,r,s,t,u,v,w,x,y,z}\}.$$

R-11.6 Assuming that the characters in alphabet Σ can be enumerated and can index arrays, give an $O(m+|\Sigma|)$ time method for constructing the $last()$ function from an m-length pattern string P.

R-11.7 Compute a table representing the KMP failure function for the pattern string "cgtacgttcgtac".

R-11.8 Draw a standard trie for the following set of strings:

$$\{\text{abab, baba, ccccc, bbaaaa, caa, bbaacc, cbcc, cbca}\}.$$

R-11.9 Draw a compressed trie for the set of strings given in Exercise R-11.8.

R-11.10 Draw the compact representation of the suffix trie for the string

"minimize minime".

R-11.11 What is the longest prefix of the string "cgtacgttcgtacg" that is also a suffix of this string?

R-11.12 Draw the frequency array and Huffman tree for the following string:

> "dogs do not spot hot pots or cats".

R-11.13 Show the longest common subsequence array L for the two strings

$$X = \text{"skullandbones"}$$

$$Y = \text{"lullabybabies"}.$$

What is a longest common subsequence between these strings?

Creativity

C-11.1 Give an example of a text T of length n and a pattern P of length m that force the brute-force pattern matching algorithm to have a running time that is $\Omega(nm)$.

C-11.2 Give a justification of why the KMPFailureFunction() function (Code Fragment 11.5) runs in $O(m)$ time on a pattern of length m.

C-11.3 Show how to modify the KMP string pattern matching algorithm, in order to find *every* occurrence of a pattern string P that appears as a substring in T, while still running in $O(n+m)$ time. (Be sure to catch even those matches that overlap.)

C-11.4 Let T be a text of length n, and let P be a pattern of length m. Describe an $O(n+m)$-time method for finding the longest prefix of P that is a substring of T.

C-11.5 Say that a pattern P of length m is a *circular* substring of a text T of length n if there is an index $0 \le i < m$, such that $P = T[n-m+i..n-1] + T[0..i-1]$, that is, if P is a (normal) substring of T or P is equal to the concatenation of a suffix of T and a prefix of T. Give an $O(n+m)$-time algorithm for determining whether P is a circular substring of T.

C-11.6 The KMP pattern matching algorithm can be modified to run faster on binary strings by redefining the failure function as

$$f(j) = \text{the largest } k < j, \text{ such that } P[0..k-2]\widehat{p_k} \text{ is a suffix of } P[1..j],$$

where $\widehat{p_k}$ denotes the complement of the kth bit of P. Describe how to modify the KMP algorithm to be able to take advantage of this new failure function and also give a method for computing this failure function. Show that this method makes at most n comparisons between the text and the pattern (as opposed to the $2n$ comparisons needed by the standard KMP algorithm given in Section 11.2.3).

C-11.7 Modify the simplified BM algorithm presented in this chapter, using ideas from the KMP algorithm, so that it runs in $O(n+m)$ time.

C-11.8 Show how to perform prefix matching queries using a suffix trie.

C-11.9 Give an efficient algorithm for deleting a string from a standard trie and analyze its running time.

C-11.10 Give an efficient algorithm for deleting a string from a compressed trie and analyze its running time.

C-11.11 Describe an algorithm for constructing the compact representation of a suffix trie and analyze its running time.

C-11.12 Let T be a text string of length n. Describe an $O(n)$-time method for finding the longest prefix of T that is a substring of the reversal of T.

C-11.13 Describe an efficient algorithm to find the longest palindrome that is a suffix of a string T of length n. Recall that a *palindrome* is a string that is equal to its reversal. What is the running time of your algorithm?

C-11.14 Given a sequence $S = (x_0, x_1, x_2, \ldots, x_{n-1})$ of numbers, describe an $O(n^2)$-time algorithm for finding a longest subsequence $T = (x_{i_0}, x_{i_1}, x_{i_2}, \ldots, x_{i_{k-1}})$ of numbers, such that $i_j < i_{j+1}$ and $x_{i_j} > x_{i_{j+1}}$. That is, T is a longest decreasing subsequence of S.

C-11.15 Define the *edit distance* between two strings X and Y of length n and m, respectively, to be the number of edits that it takes to change X into Y. An edit consists of a character insertion, a character deletion, or a character replacement. For example, the strings "algorithm" and "rhythm" have edit distance 6. Design an $O(nm)$-time algorithm for computing the edit distance between X and Y.

C-11.16 Design a greedy algorithm for making change after someone buys some candy costing x cents and the customer gives the clerk \$1. Your algorithm should try to minimize the number of coins returned.

    a. Show that your greedy algorithm returns the minimum number of coins if the coins have denominations \$0.25, \$0.10, \$0.05, and \$0.01.

    b. Give a set of denominations for which your algorithm may not return the minimum number of coins. Include an example where your algorithm fails.

C-11.17 Anna has just won a contest that allows her to take n pieces of candy out of a candy store for free. Anna is old enough to realize that some candy is expensive, costing dollars per piece, while other candy is cheap, costing pennies per piece. The jars of candy are numbered $0, 1, \ldots, m-1$, so that jar j has n_j pieces in it, with a price of c_j per piece. Design an $O(n+m)$-time algorithm that allows Anna to maximize the value of the pieces of candy she takes for her winnings. Show that your algorithm produces the maximum value for Anna.

C-11.18 Let three integer arrays, A, B, and C, be given, each of size n. Given an arbitrary integer x, design an $O(n^2 \log n)$-time algorithm to determine if there exist numbers $a \in A$, $b \in B$, and $c \in C$, such that $x = a+b+c$. (Hint: Use brute force first to enumerate all pairs (a,b), such that $a \in A$ and $b \in B$.)

C-11.19★ Give an $O(n^2)$-time algorithm for the previous problem.

Projects

P-11.1 Write a simple line-based text editor, by storing each line of text in an STL string. Your editor should first input a text file, and then accept commands that ("i") insert one or more new lines, ("d") delete one or more lines, and ("s") substitute one text for another over a series of lines.

P-11.2 Perform an experimental analysis, using documents found on the Internet, of the efficiency (number of character comparisons performed) of the brute-force and KMP pattern matching algorithms for varying-length patterns.

P-11.3 Perform an experimental analysis, using documents found on the Internet, of the efficiency (number of character comparisons performed) of the brute-force and BM pattern matching algorithms for varying-length patterns.

P-11.4 Perform an experimental comparison of the relative speeds of the brute-force, KMP, and BM pattern matching algorithms. Document the time taken for coding up each of these algorithms as well as their relative running times on documents found on the Internet that are then searched using varying-length patterns.

P-11.5 Implement a compression and decompression scheme that is based on Huffman coding.

P-11.6 Create a class that implements a standard trie for a set of ASCII strings. The class should have a constructor that takes a list of strings as an argument, and the class should have a function that tests whether a given string is stored in the trie.

P-11.7 Create a class that implements a compressed trie for a set of ASCII strings. The class should have a constructor that takes a list of strings as an argument, and the class should have a function that tests whether a given string is stored in the trie.

P-11.8 Create a class that implements a prefix trie for an ASCII string. The class should have a constructor that takes a string and a function for pattern matching on the string as an argument.

P-11.9 Implement the simplified search engine described in Section 11.3.4 for the pages of a small Web site. Use all the words in the pages of the site as index terms, excluding stop words such as articles, prepositions, and pronouns.

P-11.10 Implement a search engine for the pages of a small Web site by adding a page-ranking feature to the simplified search engine described in Section 11.3.4. Your page-ranking feature should return the most relevant pages first. Use all the words in the pages of the site as index terms, excluding stop words, such as articles, prepositions, and pronouns.

Chapter Notes

The KMP algorithm is described by Knuth, Morris, and Pratt in their journal article [61], and Boyer and Moore describe their algorithm in a journal article published the same year [16]. In their article, however, Knuth *et al.* [61] also prove that the BM algorithm runs in linear time. More recently, Cole [23] shows that the BM algorithm makes at most $3n$ character comparisons in the worst case, and this bound is tight. All of the algorithms discussed above are also discussed in the book chapter by Aho [3], albeit in a more theoretical framework, including the methods for regular-expression pattern matching. The reader interested in further study of string pattern matching algorithms is referred to the book by Stephen [92] and the book chapters by Aho [3] and Crochemore and Lecroq [26].

The trie was invented by Morrison [81] and is discussed extensively in the classic *Sorting and Searching* book by Knuth [59]. The name "Patricia" is short for "Practical Algorithm to Retrieve Information Coded in Alphanumeric" [81]. McCreight [69] shows how to construct suffix tries in linear time. An introduction to the field of information retrieval, which includes a discussion of search engines for the Web is provided in the book by Baeza-Yates and Ribeiro-Neto [8].

Chapter

12

Graphs

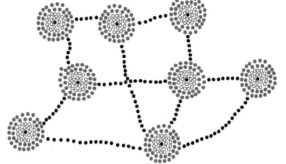

Contents

Greek mythology tells of an elaborate labyrinth that was built to house the monstrous part bull, part man, Minotaur. This labyrinth was so complex that neither beast nor human could escape it. No human, that is, until the Greek hero, Theseus, with the help of the king's daughter, Ariadne, decided to implement one of the algorithms discussed in this chapter. Theseus fastened a ball of thread to the door of the labyrinth and unwound it as he traversed the twisting passages in search of the monster. Theseus obviously knew about good algorithm design, for, after finding and defeating the beast, Theseus easily followed the string back out of the labyrinth to the loving arms of Ariadne.

Being able to determine which objects, such as labyrinth passages, are connected to which other objects may not always be as vitally important as it was in this story, but it is nevertheless fundamental. Connectivity information is present, for example, in city maps, where the objects are roads, and also in the routing tables for the Internet, where the objects are computers. Connectivity information is also present in the parent-child relationships defined by a binary tree, where the objects are tree nodes. Indeed, connectivity information can be defined by all kinds of relationships that exist between pairs of objects. The topic we study in this chapter—*graphs*—is therefore focused on representations and algorithms for dealing efficiently with such relationships. That is, a graph is a set of objects, called vertices, with a collection of pairwise connections between them. By the way, this notion of a "graph" should not be confused with bar charts and function plots, as these kinds of "graphs" are unrelated to the topic of this chapter.

Graphs have applications in a host of different domains, including mapping (in geographic information systems), transportation (in road and flight networks), electrical engineering (in circuits), and computer networking (in the connections of the Internet). Because applications for graphs are so widespread and diverse, people have developed a great deal of terminology to describe different components and properties of graphs. Fortunately, since most graph applications are relatively recent developments, this terminology is fairly intuitive.

Therefore, we begin this chapter by reviewing much of this terminology and presenting the graph ADT, including some elementary properties of graphs. Having given the graph ADT, we then present three main data structures for representing graphs in Section 12.2. As with trees, traversals are important computations for graphs, and we discuss such computations in Section 12.3. We discuss directed graphs in Section 12.4, where relationships have a given direction. This topic is not addressed in subsequent sections, however, so readers or instructors with limited time may skip Section 12.4. In Sections 12.5 through 12.7, we discuss weighted graphs, in which connections have a cost or distance associated with them. While weighted connections could be directed, in these sections we study the well-known shortest path and minimum spanning tree problems for undirected graphs.

12.1 The Graph Abstract Data Type

Viewed abstractly, a *graph* G is simply a set V of *vertices* and a collection E of pairs of vertices from V, called *edges*. Thus, a graph is a way of representing connections or relationships between pairs of objects from some set V. Incidentally, some books use different terminology for graphs and refer to what we call vertices as *nodes* and what we call edges as *arcs*. We use the terms "vertices" and "edges."

Edges in a graph are either *directed* or *undirected*. An edge (u, v) is said to be *directed* from u to v if the pair (u, v) is ordered, with u preceding v. An edge (u, v) is said to be *undirected* if the pair (u, v) is not ordered. Undirected edges are sometimes denoted with set notation, as $\{u, v\}$, but for simplicity we use the pair notation (u, v), noting that in the undirected case, the pair (u, v) is the same as (v, u). Graphs are typically visualized by drawing the vertices as ovals or rectangles and the edges as segments or curves connecting the vertices. The following are some examples of directed and undirected graphs.

Example 12.1: *We can visualize collaborations among the researchers of a certain discipline by constructing a graph whose vertices are associated with the researchers themselves, and whose edges connect pairs of vertices associated with researchers who have coauthored a paper or book. (See Figure 12.1.) Such edges are undirected because coauthorship is a* **symmetric** *relation; that is, if A has coauthored something with B, then B necessarily has coauthored something with A.*

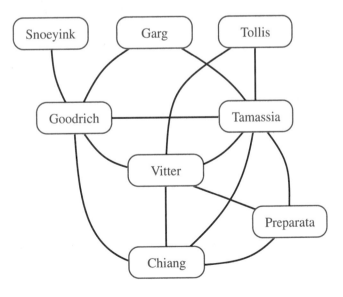

Figure 12.1: Graph of coauthorships among some authors.

Example 12.2: *We can associate, with an object-oriented program, a graph whose vertices represent the classes defined in the program, and whose edges indicate inheritance between classes. There is an edge from a vertex v to a vertex u if the class for v extends the class for u. Such edges are directed because the inheritance relation only goes in one direction (that is, it is* **asymmetric***).*

If all the edges in a graph are undirected, then we say the graph is an ***undirected graph***. Likewise, a ***directed graph***, also called a ***digraph***, is a graph whose edges are all directed. A graph that has both directed and undirected edges is often called a ***mixed graph***. Note that an undirected or mixed graph can be converted into an associated directed graph by replacing every undirected edge (u,v) with the pair of directed edges (u,v) and (v,u). It is often useful, however, to keep undirected and mixed graphs represented as they are, for such graphs have several applications, such as that of the following example.

Example 12.3: *A city map can be modeled by a graph whose vertices are intersections or dead-ends, and whose edges are stretches of streets without intersections. This graph has both undirected edges, which correspond to stretches of two-way streets, and directed edges, which correspond to stretches of one-way streets. Thus, in this way, a graph modeling a city map is a mixed graph.*

Example 12.4: *Physical examples of graphs are present in the electrical wiring and plumbing networks of a building. Such networks can be modeled as graphs, where each connector, fixture, or outlet is viewed as a vertex, and each uninterrupted stretch of wire or pipe is viewed as an edge. Such graphs are actually components of much larger graphs, namely the local power and water distribution networks. Depending on the specific aspects of these graphs that we are interested in, we may consider their edges as undirected or directed, for, in principle, water can flow in a pipe and current can flow in a wire in either direction.*

The two vertices joined by an edge are called the ***end vertices*** of the edge. The end vertices of an edge are also known as the ***endpoints*** of that edge. If an edge is directed, its first endpoint is called the ***origin*** and its second endpoint is called the ***destination*** of the edge.

Two vertices are said to be ***adjacent*** if they are endpoints of the same edge. An edge is said to be ***incident*** on a vertex if the vertex is one of the edge's endpoints. The ***outgoing edges*** of a vertex are the directed edges whose origin is that vertex. The ***incoming edges*** of a vertex are the directed edges whose destination is that vertex. The ***degree*** of a vertex v, denoted $\deg(v)$, is the number of incident edges of v. The ***in-degree*** and ***out-degree*** of a vertex v are the number of the incoming and outgoing edges of v, and are denoted $\operatorname{indeg}(v)$ and $\operatorname{outdeg}(v)$, respectively.

Example 12.5: *We can study air transportation by constructing a graph G, called a* **flight network**, *whose vertices are associated with airports, and whose edges are associated with flights. (See Figure 12.2.) In graph G, the edges are directed because a given flight has a specific travel direction (from the origin airport to the destination airport). The endpoints of an edge e in G correspond respectively to the origin and destination for the flight corresponding to e. Two airports are adjacent in G if there is a flight that flies between them, and an edge e is incident upon a vertex v in G if the flight for e flies to or from the airport for v. The outgoing edges of a vertex v correspond to the outbound flights from v's airport, and the incoming edges correspond to the inbound flights to v's airport. Finally, the in-degree of a vertex v of G corresponds to the number of inbound flights to v's airport, and the out-degree of a vertex v in G corresponds to the number of outbound flights.*

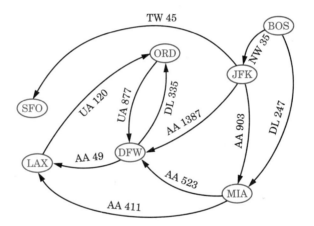

Figure 12.2: Example of a directed graph representing a flight network. The endpoints of edge UA 120 are LAX and ORD; hence, LAX and ORD are adjacent. The in-degree of DFW is 3, and the out-degree of DFW is 2.

The definition of a graph refers to the group of edges as a ***collection***, not a ***set***, thus allowing for two undirected edges to have the same end vertices, and for two directed edges to have the same origin and the same destination. Such edges are called ***parallel edges*** or ***multiple edges***. Parallel edges can occur in a flight network (Example 12.5), in which case multiple edges between the same pair of vertices could indicate different flights operating on the same route at different times of the day. Another special type of edge is one that connects a vertex to itself. Namely, we say that an edge (undirected or directed) is a ***self-loop*** if its two endpoints coincide. A self-loop may occur in a graph associated with a city map (Example 12.3), where it would correspond to a "circle" (a curving street that returns to its starting point).

With few exceptions, like those mentioned above, graphs do not have parallel edges or self-loops. Such graphs are said to be *simple*. Thus, we can usually say that the edges of a simple graph are a *set* of vertex pairs (and not just a collection). Throughout this chapter, we shall assume that a graph is simple unless otherwise

Caution

specified. This assumption simplifies the presentation of data structures and algorithms for graphs. Extending the results of this chapter to general graphs that admit self-loops and/or parallel edges is straightforward, though the details can be tedious.

We explore, in the propositions that follow, a few important properties of the vertex degrees and of the number of edges in a graph. These properties relate the number of vertices and edges to each other and to the degrees of the vertices in a graph.

Proposition 12.6: *If G is a graph with m edges, then*

$$\sum_{v \in G} \deg(v) = 2m.$$

Justification: An edge (u, v) is counted twice in the above summation; once by its endpoint u and once by its endpoint v. Thus, the total contribution of the edges to the degrees of the vertices is twice the number of edges.   ■

Proposition 12.7: *If G is a directed graph with m edges, then*

$$\sum_{v \in G} indeg(v) = \sum_{u \in G} outdeg(u) = m.$$

Justification: In a directed graph, an edge (u, v) contributes one unit to the out-degree of its origin u and one unit to the in-degree of its destination v. Thus, the total contribution of the edges to the out-degrees of the vertices is equal to the number of edges, and similarly for the out-degrees.   ■

Proposition 12.8: *Let G be a simple graph with n vertices and m edges. If G is undirected, then $m \leq n(n-1)/2$, and if G is directed, then $m \leq n(n-1)$.*

Justification: Suppose that G is undirected. Since no two edges can have the same endpoints and there are no self-loops, the maximum degree of a vertex in G is $n-1$ in this case. Thus, by Proposition 12.6, $2m \leq n(n-1)$. Now suppose that G is directed. Since no two edges can have the same origin and destination, and there are no self-loops, the maximum in-degree of a vertex in G is $n-1$ in this case. Thus, by Proposition 12.7, $m \leq n(n-1)$.   ■

Put another way, Proposition 12.8 states that a simple graph with n vertices has $O(n^2)$ edges.

A *path* of a graph is a sequence of alternating vertices and edges that starts at a vertex and ends at a vertex, such that each edge is incident to its predecessor and successor vertex. A *cycle* is a path whose start and end vertices are the same. We say that a path is *simple* if each vertex in the path is distinct, and we say that a cycle is *simple* if each edge in the cycle is distinct and each vertex is distinct, except for the first and last one. A *directed path* is a path whose edges are all directed and traversed along their direction. A *directed cycle* is defined similarly. For example, in the flight network of Figure 12.2, (BOS, NW 35, JFK, AA 1387, DFW) is a directed simple path, and (LAX, UA 120, ORD, UA 877, DFW, AA 49, LAX) is a directed simple cycle.

Example 12.9: *Given a graph G representing a city map (see Example 12.3), we can model a couple driving from their home to dinner at a recommended restaurant as traversing a path though G. If they know the way, and don't accidentally go through the same intersection twice, then they traverse a simple path in G. Likewise, we can model the entire trip the couple takes, from their home to the restaurant and back, as a cycle. If they go home from the restaurant in a completely different way than how they went, not even going through the same intersection twice, then their entire round trip is a simple cycle. Finally, if they travel along one-way streets for their entire trip, then we can model their night out as a directed cycle.*

A *subgraph* of a graph G is a graph H whose vertices and edges are subsets of the vertices and edges of G, respectively. For example, in the flight network of Figure 12.2, vertices BOS, JFK, and MIA, and edges AA 903 and DL 247 form a subgraph. A *spanning subgraph* of G is a subgraph of G that contains all the vertices of the graph G. A graph is *connected* if, for any two vertices, there is a path between them. If a graph G is not connected, its maximal connected subgraphs are called the *connected components* of G. A *forest* is a graph without cycles. A *tree* is a connected forest, that is, a connected graph without cycles. Note that this definition of a tree is somewhat different from the one given in Chapter 6. Namely, in the context of graphs, a tree has no root. Whenever there is ambiguity, the trees of Chapter 6 should be referred to as *rooted trees*, while the trees of this chapter should be referred to as *free trees*. The connected components of a forest are (free) trees. A *spanning tree* of a graph is a spanning subgraph that is a (free) tree.

| Caution |

Example 12.10: *Perhaps the most talked about graph today is the Internet, which can be viewed as a graph whose vertices are computers and whose (undirected) edges are communication connections between pairs of computers on the Internet. The computers and the connections between them in a single domain, like wiley.com, form a subgraph of the Internet. If this subgraph is connected, then two*

users on computers in this domain can send e-mail to one another without having their information packets ever leave their domain. Suppose the edges of this subgraph form a spanning tree. This implies that, if even a single connection goes down (for example, because someone pulls a communication cable out of the back of a computer in this domain), then this subgraph will no longer be connected.

There are a number of simple properties of trees, forests, and connected graphs. We explore a few of them in the following proposition.

Proposition 12.11: *Let G be an undirected graph with n vertices and m edges. Then we have the following:*

- *If G is connected, then $m \geq n - 1$.*
- *If G is a tree, then $m = n - 1$.*
- *If G is a forest, then $m \leq n - 1$.*

We leave the justification of this proposition as an exercise (C-12.1).

12.1.1   Graph Functions

As an abstract data type, a graph is a positional container of elements that are stored at the graph's vertices and edges. Namely, the **positions** in a graph are its vertices and edges. Hence, we can store elements in a graph at either its vertices or its edges (or both). In terms of a C++ implementation, this implies that we can define Vertex and Edge interfaces that each extend the Position interface. Recall that a position has an element() method, which returns the element that is stored at this position. We also use specialized iterators for vertices and edges, called VertexIterator and EdgeIterator, respectively.

Since a graph is a positional container (Section 6.1.3), the graph ADT supports the member functions size(), isEmpty(), elements(), positions(), replaceElement(p, o), and swapElements(p, q), where p and q denote positions, and o denotes an object (that is, an element).

Graphs are a much richer abstract data type than those we have discussed in previous chapters. Their richness derives mostly from the fact that two different kinds of positions (vertices and edges) help define a graph. So as to present the functions for the graph ADT in as organized a way as possible, we divide the graph functions into three main categories: general functions, functions dealing with directed edges, and functions for updating and modifying graphs. In addition, in order to simplify the presentation, we denote a vertex position with v, an edge position with e, and an object (element) stored at a vertex or edge with o. Also, we do not discuss error conditions that may occur.

General Functions

We begin by describing the fundamental functions for a graph, which ignore the direction of the edges. Each of the following functions returns global information about a graph G:

> numVertices(): Return the number of vertices in G.
>
> numEdges(): Return the number of edges in G.
>
> vertices(): Return an iterator of the vertices of G.
>
> edges(): Return an iterator of the edges of G.

Unlike a tree (which has a root), a graph has no special vertex. Hence, we have a method that returns an arbitrary vertex of the graph:

> aVertex(): Return a vertex of G.

The following accessor functions take vertex and edge positions as arguments:

> degree(v): Return the degree of v.
>
> adjacentVertices(v): Return an iterator of the vertices adjacent to v.
>
> incidentEdges(v): Return an iterator of the edges incident upon v.
>
> endVertices(e): Return an array of size 2 storing the end vertices of e.
>
> opposite(v, e): Return the endpoint of edge e distinct from v.
>
> areAdjacent(v, w): Return whether vertices v and w are adjacent.

Functions Dealing with Directed Edges

When we allow for some or all of the edges in a graph to be directed, then there are several additional functions we should include in the graph ADT. We begin with some functions for dealing specifically with directed edges.

> directedEdges(): Return an iterator of all directed edges.
>
> undirectedEdges(): Return an iterator of all undirected edges.
>
> destination(e): Return the destination of the directed edge e.
>
> origin(e): Return the origin of the directed edge e.
>
> isDirected(e): Return true if and only if the edge e is directed.

In addition, the existence of directed edges requires that we have ways of relating vertices and edges in terms of directions:

inDegree(v): Return the in-degree of v.

outDegree(v): Return the out-degree of v.

inIncidentEdges(v): Return an iterator of all the incoming edges to v.

outIncidentEdges(v): Return an iterator of all the outgoing edges from v.

inAdjacentVertices(v): Return an iterator of all the vertices adjacent to v along incoming edges to v.

outAdjacentVertices(v): Return an iterator of all the vertices adjacent to v along outgoing edges from v.

Functions for Updating Graphs

We can also allow for update functions that add or delete edges and vertices:

insertEdge(v, w, o): Insert and return an undirected edge between vertices v and w, storing the object o at this position.

insertDirectedEdge(v, w, o): Insert and return a directed edge from vertex v to vertex w, storing the object o at this position.

insertVertex(o): Insert and return a new (isolated) vertex storing the object o at this position.

removeVertex(v): Remove vertex v and all its incident edges.

removeEdge(e): Remove edge e.

makeUndirected(e): Make edge e undirected.

reverseDirection(e): Reverse the direction of directed edge e.

setDirectionFrom(e, v): Make edge e directed away from vertex v.

setDirectionTo(e, v): Make edge e directed into vertex v.

We also assume that a graph provides type definitions for each of the various types such as Graph::Vertex, Graph::Edge, Graph::VertexIterator, and so on.

There are admittedly a lot of functions in the graph ADT. The number of functions is, to a certain extent, unavoidable, however, since graphs are such rich structures. Graphs support two kinds of positions—vertices and edges—and even then allow for edges to be either directed or undirected. We need to have different functions for accessing and updating all these different positions, as well as dealing with the relationships that can exist between these different positions.

12.2 Data Structures for Graphs

There are several ways to realize the graph ADT with a concrete data structure. In this section, we discuss three popular approaches, usually referred to as the *edge list* structure, the *adjacency list* structure, and the *adjacency matrix* structure. In all the three representations, we use a container (a list or vector, for example) to store the vertices of the graph. Regarding the edges, there is a fundamental difference between the first two structures and the latter. The edge list structure and the adjacency list structure store only the edges actually present in the graph, while the adjacency matrix stores a placeholder for every pair of vertices (whether there is an edge between them or not). As we will explain in this section, this difference implies that, for a graph G with n vertices and m edges, an edge list or adjacency list representation uses $O(n+m)$ space, whereas an adjacency matrix representation uses $O(n^2)$ space.

12.2.1 The Edge List Structure

The *edge list* structure is possibly the simplest, though not the most efficient, representation of a graph G. A schematic illustration of the edge list structure for a directed graph G is shown in Figure 12.3.

Vertex Objects

A vertex v of G storing an element o is explicitly represented by a vertex object. All such vertex objects are stored in a container V, which would typically be a list, vector, or dictionary. If we represent V as a vector, for example, then we would naturally think of the vertices as being numbered. If we represent V as a dictionary, on the other hand, then we would naturally think of each vertex as being identified by a key that we associate with it. It is also useful for this dictionary to support the locator pattern (see Section 8.5). Note that the elements of container V are the vertex positions of graph G.

The vertex object for a vertex v storing element o has data members for:

- A reference to element o
- Counters for the number of incident undirected edges, incoming directed edges, and outgoing directed edges
- A reference to the position (or locator) of the vertex-object in container V.

The distinguishing feature of the edge list structure is not how it represents vertices, however, but the way in which it represents edges. In this structure, an edge e of G

storing an element o is explicitly represented by an edge object. The edge objects are stored in a container E, which would typically be a list, vector, or dictionary (possibly supporting the locator pattern).

Edge Objects

The edge object for an edge e storing element o has data members for:

- A reference to element o
- A Boolean indicator of whether e is directed or undirected
- References to the vertex objects in V associated with the endpoint vertices of e (if the edge e is undirected) or to the origin and destination vertices of e (if the edge e is directed)
- A reference to the position (or locator) of the edge-object in container E.

The Edge List

The reason this structure is called the **edge list** structure is that the simplest and most common implementation of the container E is with a list. Even so, in order to be able to conveniently search for specific objects associated with edges, we may wish to implement E with a dictionary, in spite of our calling this the "edge list." We may also wish to implement the container V as a dictionary for the same reason. Still, in keeping with tradition, we call this structure the edge list structure.

The main feature of the edge list structure is that it provides direct access from edges to the vertices they are incident upon. This allows us to define simple algorithms for implementing the different edge-based functions of the graph ADT (for example, functions endVertices(), origin(), and destination()). We can simply access the appropriate data members of the given edge object to implement each such method.

Nevertheless, the "inverse" operation—that of accessing the edges that are incident upon a vertex—requires an exhaustive inspection of all the edge objects in container E. That is, in order to determine which edges are incident to a vertex v, we must examine all the edges in the edge list and check, for each one, if it happens to be incident to v. Thus, for example, function incidentEdges(v) runs in time proportional to the number of edges in the graph, not in time proportional to the degree of vertex v. In fact, even to check if two vertices v and w are adjacent using the areAdjacent(v,w) function, requires that we search the entire edge list looking for the edge (v,w) or (w,v). Moreover, since removing a vertex involves removing all of its incident edges, the function removeVertex() also requires a complete search of the edge list, E.

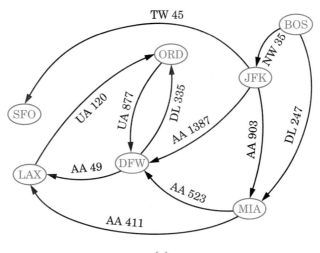

(a)

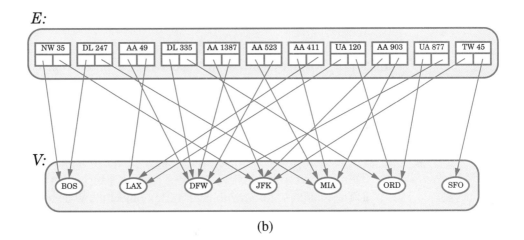

(b)

Figure 12.3: (a) A directed graph G; (b) schematic representation of the edge list structure for G. To avoid clutter, we do not show the following fields of the vertex objects: the three counters for the incident edges and the reference to the position (or locator) of the vertex-object in container V. Also, we do not show the following fields of the edge objects: the Boolean direction indicator and the reference to the position (or locator) of the edge-object in container E. Finally, we visualize the elements stored in the vertex and edge objects with the element names, instead of actual references to the element objects.

Performance

Table 12.1 summarizes the performance of the edge-list implementation of a graph.

Operation	Time
size, isEmpty, replaceElement, swapElements	$O(1)$
numVertices, numEdges, aVertex	$O(1)$
vertices	$O(n)$
edges, directedEdges, undirectedEdges	$O(m)$
elements, positions	$O(n+m)$
endVertices, opposite, origin, destination, isDirected, degree, inDegree, outDegree	$O(1)$
incidentEdges, inIncidentEdges, outIncidentEdges, adjacentVertices, inAdjacentVertices, outAdjacentVertices, areAdjacent	$O(m)$
insertVertex, insertEdge, insertDirectedEdge, removeEdge, makeUndirected, reverseDirection, setDirectionFrom, setDirectionTo	$O(1)$
removeVertex	$O(m)$

Table 12.1: Running times of the functions of a graph implemented with an edge list, where V and E are realized with doubly linked lists. The space used is $O(n+m)$, where n is the number of vertices and m is the number of edges.

Details for selected functions of the graph ADT are as follows:

- Functions numVertices(), numEdges(), and size() are implemented in $O(1)$ time by returning V.size(), E.size(), and V.size() $+E$.size(), respectively.
- The counters stored with each vertex object allow us to perform, in constant time, functions degree(), inDegree(), and outDegree().
- Functions vertices() and edges() are implemented by calling V.elements() and E.elements(), respectively.
- We implement iterators directedEdges() and undirectedEdges() by calling E.elements() and only returning those edges that are of the correct type.
- Since the containers V and E are lists implemented with a doubly linked list, we can insert vertices, and insert and remove edges, in $O(1)$ time.
- Functions incidentEdges(), inIncidentEdges(), outIncidentEdges(), adjacent-Vertices(), inAdjacentVertices(), outAdjacentVertices(), and areAdjacent() all take $O(m)$ time, because we must inspect all edges to determine which edges are incident upon a vertex v.
- The update function removeVertex(v) takes $O(m)$ time, since it requires that we inspect all the edges to find and remove those incident upon v.

12.2.2 The Adjacency List Structure

The ***adjacency list*** structure for a graph G extends the edge list structure, adding extra information that supports direct access to the incident edges (and thus to the adjacent vertices) of each vertex. While the edge list structure views the edge-vertex incidence relation only from the point of view of the edges, the adjacency list structure considers it from both viewpoints. This symmetric approach allows us to use the adjacency list structure to implement a number of vertex functions of the graph ADT much faster than what is possible with the edge list structure, even though these two representations both use an amount of space proportional to the number of vertices and edges in the graph. We illustrate the adjacency list structure of a directed graph in Figure 12.4. The adjacency list structure includes all the structural components of the edge list structure plus the following:

- A vertex object v holds a reference to a container $I(v)$, called the ***incidence container*** of v, storing references to the edges incident on v. If directed edges are allowed, $I(v)$ is partitioned into $I_{in}(v)$, $I_{out}(v)$, and $I_{un}(v)$, which store the in-coming, out-going, and undirected edges incident to v, respectively.
- The edge object for an edge (u, v) holds references to the positions (or locators) of the edge in the incidence containers $I(u)$ and $I(v)$.

The Adjacency List

Traditionally, the incidence container $I(v)$ for a vertex v is realized by means of a list, which is why we call this way of representing a graph the ***adjacency list*** structure. Still, there may be some contexts where we wish to represent an incidence container $I(v)$ as, say, a dictionary or a priority queue, so let us stick with thinking of $I(v)$ as a generic container of edge objects. If we want to support a graph representation that can represent a graph G potentially containing both directed and undirected edges, then we have, for each vertex, three incidence containers, $I_{in}(v)$, $I_{out}(v)$, and $I_{un}(v)$, that store references to the edge objects associated with the directed incoming, directed outgoing, and undirected edges incident on v, respectively.

The adjacency list structure provides direct access both from the edges to the vertices and from the vertices to their incident edges. Being able to provide access between vertices and edges in both directions allows us to speed up the performance of a number of the graph functions by using an adjacency list structure instead of an edge list structure. For a vertex v, the space used by the incidence container of v is proportional to the degree of v, that is, it is $O(\deg(v))$. Thus, by Proposition 12.6, the space requirement of the adjacency list structure is $O(n + m)$.

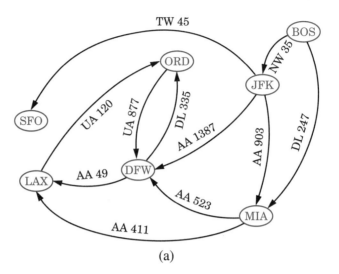

(a)

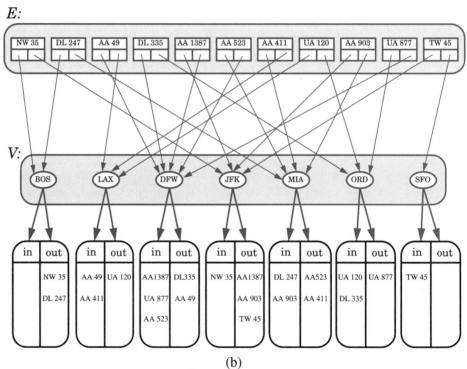

(b)

Figure 12.4: (a) A directed graph *G*; (b) schematic representation of the adjacency list structure of *G*. As in Figure 12.3, we do not show various fields of the vertex and edge objects, and we visualize the elements of containers with names instead of objects. Also, we only show the incidence containers for directed edges, since there are no undirected edges in this graph.

Performance

Table 12.2 summarizes the performance of the adjacency list representation of a graph, assuming that V, E, and the incident structures are all implemented with linked lists.

Note that all of the functions of the graph ADT that can be implemented with the edge list structure in $O(1)$ time can also be implemented in $O(1)$ time for the adjacency list structure using essentially the same algorithms. In addition, the adjacency list structure provides improved running time for the following functions:

- The functions that return iterators of incident edges or adjacent vertices for a vertex v take time proportional to their output size, that is, $O(\deg(v))$ time.
- Method areAdjacent(u,v) can be performed by inspecting either the incidence container of u or that of v. By choosing the smaller of the two, we get $O(\min(\deg(u),\deg(v)))$ running time.
- Method removeVertex(v) requires the inspection of the incidence container of v, and thus takes $O(\deg(v))$ time.

Operation	Time
size, isEmpty, replaceElement, swapElements	$O(1)$
numVertices, numEdges, aVertex	$O(1)$
vertices	$O(n)$
edges, directedEdges, undirectedEdges	$O(m)$
elements, positions	$O(n+m)$
endVertices, opposite, origin, destination, isDirected, degree, inDegree, outDegree	$O(1)$
incidentEdges(v), inIncidentEdges(v), outIncidentEdges(v), adjacentVertices(v), inAdjacentVertices(v), outAdjacentVertices(v)	$O(\deg(v))$
areAdjacent(u,v)	$O(\min(\deg(u),\deg(v)))$
insertVertex, insertEdge, insertDirectedEdge, removeEdge, makeUndirected, reverseDirection, setDirectionFrom, setDirectionTo	$O(1)$
removeVertex(v)	$O(\deg(v))$

Table 12.2: Running times for the functions of a graph implemented with an adjacency list structure, where containers V and E and the incidence containers are realized with lists, which are, in turn, implemented with doubly linked lists. We denote with n and m the number of vertices and edges of the graph, respectively. The space used is $O(n+m)$.

As we will see in future sections, the improvement of an adjacency list over an edge list is quite useful, for the adjacency list structure allows us to perform several iterator functions for a vertex v in $O(\deg(v))$ time, as opposed to the $O(m)$ time performance for the edge list structure. Note that we can further improve the running time of the areAdjacent(u,v) function if we implement the container E with a fast dictionary whose keys are pairs of vertices. We explore this approach in further detail in an exercise (C-12.4).

12.2.3   The Adjacency Matrix Structure

Like the adjacency list structure, the ***adjacency matrix*** representation of a graph also extends the edge-structure with an additional component. In this case, we augment the edge list with a matrix (a two-dimensional array) A that allows us to determine adjacencies between pairs of vertices in constant time. As we shall see, achieving this speedup comes at a price in the space usage of the data structure.

In the adjacency matrix representation, we think of the vertices as being the integers in the set $\{0, 1, \ldots, n-1\}$ and the edges as being pairs of such integers. This allows us to store references to edges in the cells of a two-dimensional $n \times n$ array A. Specifically, the adjacency matrix representation extends the edge list structure as follows (see Figure 12.5):

- A vertex object v also stores a distinct integer key in the range $0, 1, \ldots, n-1$, called the ***index*** of v. To simplify the discussion, we may refer to the vertex with index i simply as "vertex i."

- We keep a two-dimensional $n \times n$ array A, such that the cell $A[i,j]$ holds a reference to the edge object e that goes from the vertex with index i to the vertex with index j, if such an edge exists. If the edge e, connecting vertices i and j, is undirected, then we store references to e in both $A[i,j]$ and $A[j,i]$. If there is no edge from vertex i to vertex j, then $A[i,j]$ references NULL (or a special object indicating that this cell is associated with no edge).

The adjacency matrix A allows us to perform the function areAdjacent(v,w) in $O(1)$ time. We achieve this performance by accessing the vertices v and w to determine their respective indices i and j, and then testing whether the cell $A[i,j]$ references NULL. This performance achievement is counteracted by an increase in the space usage, however, which is now $O(n^2)$, and in the running time of other functions. For example, the vertex functions, such as incidentEdges(), adjacent-Vertices(), inAdjacentVertices(), and outAdjacentVertices(), now require that we examine an entire row or column of array A, which takes $O(n)$ time. Moreover, any vertex insertions or deletions now require creating a whole new array A, of larger or smaller size, respectively, which takes time $O(n^2)$.

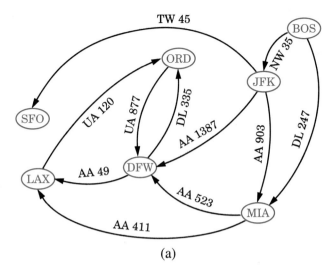

(a)

0	1	2	3	4	5	6
BOS	DFW	JFK	LAX	MIA	ORD	SFO

(b)

	0	1	2	3	4	5	6
0	Ø	Ø	NW 35	Ø	DL 247	Ø	Ø
1	Ø	Ø	Ø	AA 49	Ø	DL 335	Ø
2	Ø	AA 1387	Ø	Ø	AA 903	Ø	TW 45
3	Ø	Ø	Ø	Ø	Ø	UA 120	Ø
4	Ø	AA 523	Ø	AA 411	Ø	Ø	Ø
5	Ø	UA 877	Ø	Ø	Ø	Ø	Ø
6	Ø	Ø	Ø	Ø	Ø	Ø	Ø

(c)

Figure 12.5: Schematic representation of the adjacency matrix structure: (a) directed graph G; (b) numbering of the vertices of G; (c) adjacency matrix A for G.

Performance

Table 12.3 summarizes the performance of the adjacency matrix implementation of a graph. From this table we observe that the adjacency list structure is superior to the adjacency matrix in space, and is superior in time for all functions except for the areAdjacent() function.

Operation	Time
size, isEmpty, replaceElement, swapElements	$O(1)$
numVertices, numEdges, aVertex	$O(1)$
vertices	$O(n)$
edges, directedEdges, undirectedEdges	$O(m)$
elements, positions	$O(n+m)$
endVertices, opposite, origin, destination, isDirected, degree, inDegree, outDegree	$O(1)$
incidentEdges, inIncidentEdges, outIncidentEdges, adjacentVertices, inAdjacentVertices, outAdjacentVertices	$O(n)$
areAdjacent	$O(1)$
insertEdge, insertDirectedEdge, removeEdge, makeUndirected, reverseDirection, setDirectionFrom, setDirectionTo	$O(1)$
insertVertex, removeVertex	$O(n^2)$

Table 12.3: Running times of the functions of a graph implemented with an adjacency matrix. We denote the number of vertices and edges of the graph with n and m respectively. The space used is $O(n^2)$.

Historically, the adjacency matrix was the first representation used for graphs. We should not find this fact surprising, however, for the adjacency matrix has a natural appeal as a mathematical structure (for example, an undirected graph has a symmetric adjacency matrix). The adjacency list structure came later, with its natural appeal in computing due to its faster functions for most algorithms (many algorithms do not use function areAdjacent()) and its space efficiency.

Most of the graph algorithms we examine in this book will run efficiently when acting upon a graph stored using the adjacency list representation. In some cases, however, a trade-off occurs, where graphs with few edges are most efficiently processed with an adjacency list structure and graphs with many edges are most efficiently processed with an adjacency matrix structure.

Next, we explore a fundamental kind of algorithmic operation that we might wish to perform on a graph—traversing the edges and the vertices of that graph.

12.3 Graph Traversal

A *traversal* is a systematic procedure for exploring a graph by examining all of its vertices and edges. A traversal is efficient if it visits all the vertices and edges in time proportional to their number, that is, in linear time. In this section and the next, we consider two efficient traversals of undirected graphs, called depth-first search and breadth-first search, respectively. In Section 12.4.1, we extend these techniques to traversals of directed graphs.

12.3.1 Depth-First Search

The first traversal algorithm we consider is *depth-first search* (DFS) in an undirected graph. Depth-first search is useful for performing a number of computations on graphs, including finding a path from one vertex to another, determining whether or not a graph is connected, and computing a spanning tree of a connected graph. In this section, we explain how DFS works and how it can be used.

Depth-first search in an undirected graph G is analogous to wandering in a labyrinth with a string and a can of paint without getting lost. We begin at a specific starting vertex s in G, which we initialize by fixing one end of our string to s and painting s as "visited." The vertex s is now our "current" vertex—call our current vertex u. We then consider an (arbitrary) edge (u, v) incident to the current vertex u. If the edge (u, v) leads us to an already visited (that is, painted) vertex v, we immediately return to vertex u. If, on the other hand, (u, v) leads us to an unvisited vertex v, then we unroll our string, and go to v. We then paint v as "visited," and make it the current vertex, repeating the above computation. Eventually, we will get to a "dead-end," that is, a current vertex u, such that all the edges incident on u lead to vertices already visited. Thus, taking any edge incident on u, will cause us to return to u. To get out of this impasse, we roll our string back up, backtracking along the edge that brought us to u, going back to a previously visited vertex v. We then make v our current vertex and repeat the above computation for any edges incident upon v that we have not looked at before. If all of v's incident edges lead to visited vertices, then we again roll up our string and backtrack to the vertex we came from to get to v, and repeat the procedure at that vertex. Thus, we continue to backtrack along the path that we have traced so far until we find a vertex that has yet unexplored edges, take one such edge, and continue the traversal. The process terminates when our backtracking leads us back to the start vertex s, and there are no more unexplored edges incident on s. This simple process traverses the edges of G in an elegant, systematic way. An example of a depth-first search traversal is shown in Figure 12.6.

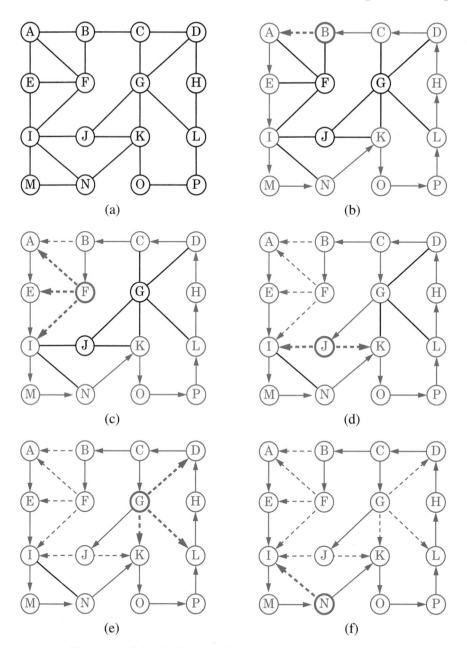

Figure 12.6: Example of depth-first search traversal on a graph starting at vertex *A*. Discovery edges are shown with solid lines and back edges are shown with dashed lines: (a) input graph; (b) path of discovery edges traced from A until back edge (B,A) is hit; (c) reaching F, which is a dead end; (d) after backtracking to C, resuming with edge (C,G), and hitting another dead end, J; (e) after backtracking to G; (f) after backtracking to N.

We can visualize a DFS traversal by orienting the edges along the direction in which they are explored during the traversal, distinguishing the edges used to discover new vertices, called *discovery edges*, or *tree edges*, from those that lead to already visited vertices, called *back edges*. (See Figure 12.6f.) In the analogy above, discovery edges are the edges where we unroll our string when we traverse them, and back edges are the edges where we immediately return without unrolling any string. As we will see, the discovery edges form a spanning tree of the connected component of the starting vertex s. We call the edges not in this tree "back edges" because, assuming that the tree is rooted at the start vertex, each such edge leads back from a vertex in this tree to one of its ancestors in the tree.

The pseudo-code for a DFS traversal starting at a vertex v follows our analogy with string and paint. We use recursion to implement the string analogy, and we assume that we have a mechanism (the paint analogy) to determine if a vertex or edge has been explored or not, and to label the edges as discovery edges or back edges. This mechanism will require additional space and may affect the running time of the algorithm. A pseudo-code description of the recursive DFS algorithm is given in Code Fragment 12.1.

Algorithm DFS(G,v):
>   *Input:* A graph G and a vertex v of G
>   *Output:* A labeling of the edges as discovery edges and back edges
>
>   **for all** edges e in G.incidentEdges(v) **do**
>   **if** edge e is unexplored **then**
> $w \leftarrow G$.opposite(v,e)
>   **if** vertex w is unexplored **then**
>   label e as a discovery edge
>   recursively call DFS(G,w)
>   **else**
>   label e as a back edge

Code Fragment 12.1: The depth-first search algorithm.

There are a number of observations that we can make about the depth-first search algorithm, many of which derive from the way the DFS algorithm partitions the edges of the undirected graph G into two groups, the discovery edges and the back edges. For example, since back edges always connect a vertex v to a previously visited vertex u, each back edge implies a cycle in G, consisting of the discovery edges from u to v plus the back edge (u,v).

Proposition 12.12, which follows, identifies some other important properties of the depth-first search traversal method.

Proposition 12.12: *Let G be an undirected graph on which a DFS traversal starting at a vertex s has been performed. Then:*

- *The traversal visits all vertices in the connected component of s*
- *The discovery edges form a spanning tree of the connected component of s.*

Justification: Suppose, for the sake of contradiction, there is a vertex v in s's connected component not visited, and let w be the first unvisited vertex on some path from s to v (of course, we may have $v = w$). Since w is the first unvisited vertex on this path, it has a neighbor u that was visited. But when we visited u, we must have considered the edge (u, w); hence, it cannot be correct that w is unvisited. Therefore, there are no unvisited vertices in s's connected component.

Since we only mark edges when we go to unvisited vertices, we will never form a cycle with discovery edges, that is, discovery edges form a tree. Moreover, this is a spanning tree because, as we have just seen, the depth-first search visits each vertex in the connected component of s.   ■

In terms of its running time, depth-first search is an efficient method for traversing a graph. Note that DFS is called exactly once on each vertex, and that every edge is examined exactly twice, once from each of its end vertices. Thus, if n_s vertices and m_s edges are in the connected component of vertex s, a DFS starting at s runs in $O(n_s + m_s)$ time, provided the following conditions are satisfied:

- The graph is represented by a data structure with the following performance:
  - function incidentEdges(v) takes $O(\text{degree}(v))$ time
  - functions hasNext() and nextEdge() of the EdgeIterator, returned by incidentEdges(v), each take $O(1)$ time
  - function opposite(v, e) takes $O(1)$ time.

  The adjacency list structure satisfies the above properties, but the adjacency matrix structure does not.
- We have a way to "mark" a vertex or edge as explored, and to test if a vertex or edge has been explored in $O(1)$ time. One way to do such marking is to allow additional attributes to be associated with edges and vertices of the graph, as will be discussed below. Another way is to use an auxiliary hash table to store the explored vertices and edges. This scheme satisfies the condition in the probabilistic sense, because a hash table supports the mark (insert) and test (find) operations in $O(1)$ **expected** time (see Section 8.2).

By Proposition 12.12 and the above discussion, we can solve a number of interesting problems for an undirected graph, as summarized below.

Proposition 12.13: *Let G be a graph with n vertices and m edges represented with an adjacency list. A DFS traversal of G can be performed in $O(n + m)$ time. Also, $O(n + m)$-time algorithms, based on DFS, exist for the following:*

- *Testing whether G is connected*
- *Computing a spanning tree of G, if G is connected*
- *Computing the connected components of G*
- *Computing a path between two given vertices of G, or reporting that no such path exists*
- *Computing a cycle in G, or reporting that G has no cycles.*

The justification of Proposition 12.13 is based on algorithms that use the depth-first search algorithm or slightly modified versions of the DFS algorithm as subroutines. We explore the details in some interesting, but not too difficult, exercises.

The Decorator Pattern

Marking the explored vertices in a DFS traversal is an example of the **decorator** software engineering design pattern. This pattern is used to add attributes or "decorations" to existing objects. Each attribute is identified by a specific decoration object, a, which acts as a kind of key identifying this attribute. Intuitively, the attribute a is the "name" of the decoration, and we then allow this attribute to take on different values for the different objects that are decorated with a attributes. The use of decorations is motivated by the need of some algorithms and data structures to add extra variables, or temporary scratch data, to objects that do not normally have such variables. Hence, a decoration is an attribute-value pair that can be dynamically attached to an object. Unlike the key-element pairs that were used in dictionaries, a decoration value is not limited to a single fixed type, and instead is a polymorphic type.

For example, nodes in an AVL tree or red-black tree could be decorated with height or color attributes, respectively. In our DFS example, we would like to have "decorable" vertices and edges with a **status** attribute, which could be set to either **visited** or **unvisited**. We can realize the decorator pattern in our graphs by assuming that the vertices and edges of our graphs support the following additional member functions of a **decorable object**:

$\text{has}(a)$: Tests whether the object has attribute a.

$\text{get}(a)$: Returns the value of attribute a.

$\text{set}(a, x)$: Sets to x the value of attribute a.

$\text{destroy}(a)$: Removes attribute a and its associated value.

Polymorphic Objects

The above functions can be implemented by storing at each vertex and edge a dictionary whose key-elements pairs are the attributes and their values. Although in principle, the attribute could be any type that would be suitable for use as a key, we will use attributes of type string in our examples.

The goal of implementing decorations supporting multiple value types poses an interesting problem. To illustrate this problem, let us suppose that we wished to design an algorithm that associated with each vertex of the graph an integer weight and a string label. One way to do this might be to associate a dictionary data structure with each vertex of the graph. Given a vertex v with an associated dictionary, we might then consider storing its associated weight and label using the following dictionary insertion functions.

```
v.insert("weight", 10);
v.insert("label", "my label");
```

The problem is that, in order to define a dictionary, it is necessary to specify the type of both the keys and elements. The keys are strings, but in one case the element is an integer and in the other case it is a string. Since C++ is a strongly typed programming language, such type variation is not allowed.

To solve this problem, we need to design a ***polymorphic*** element type (Section 2.2.2). We define a generic Object class, and we derive other classes, each of which holds a single value of some given type. In addition to a constructor, each derived type provides a member function getValue(), which retrieves this value. In Code Fragment 12.2, we present an example of such a polymorphic class Object, and provide two derived classes, Integer, which stores a single int value, and String, which stores a single string value. Of course, it would be easy to extend this class structure to store many other types, including bool, char, float, and double.

Returning to our dictionary example, we could now define a dictionary associated with vertex v, whose associated element is a pointer to an Object, or ObjectPtr. We then create new objects, either of type Integer or String, and store pointers to these objects in the dictionary. Since both of these classes are derived from class Object, the resulting pointers are subtypes of ObjectPtr. When we retrieve an object, we then cast the object pointer to the appropriate type, and then get its value. Since weights are always associated with integers, and labels are always associated with strings, we know which type of cast to perform in each case. In order to safely perform this task in C++ and catch possible errors, a ***dynamic cast*** (Section 2.2.4) is used, as shown in Code Fragment 12.3.

```
class Object {                                         // generic object
public:
    virtual ~Object() { }                              // virtual destructor
    int      intValue()    const throw(BadCastException); // get integer value
    string   stringValue() const throw(BadCastException); // get string value
};

class Integer : public Object {                        // integer object
private:
    int value;                                         // integer value
public:
    Integer(int v = 0) { value = v; }                  // constructor
    int getValue() const { return value; }             // get the value
};

class String : public Object {                         // string object
private:
    string value;                                      // string value
public:
    String(const string& v = "") { value = v; }        // constructor
    string getValue() const { return value; }          // get the value
};
                                                       // get Integer's value
int Object::intValue() const throw(BadCastException)
{
    const Integer* p = dynamic_cast<const Integer*>(this);
    if (p == NULL) throw BadCastException("intValue() from non-Integer");
    return p->getValue();
}
                                                       // get String's value
string Object::stringValue() const throw(BadCastException)
{
    const String* p = dynamic_cast<const String*>(this);
    if (p == NULL) throw BadCastException("stringValue() from non-String");
    return p->getValue();
}
```

Code Fragment 12.2: Class Object, which represents a generic object, and derived classes Integer and String, which store a single element of type int and string, respectively.

```
Object* ip = new Integer(10);                    // create integer object
Object* sp = new String("mylabel");              // create string object
v.insertItem("weight", ip);                      // store in v's dictionary
v.insertItem("label", sp);
// ...
Object* op = v.find("weight").element();         // retrieve weight
const Integer* p = dynamic_cast<const Integer*>(op); // cast to Integer*
int w = p->getValue();                           // get its value
```

Code Fragment 12.3: Example use of Object with a polymorphic dictionary.

Because the operations of casting and value extraction occur naturally in combination, we define member functions intValue() and stringValue() of class Object for extracting these values. These functions throw an exception if an attempt is made to extract one type from a pointer to an object of a different type. (See Code Fragment 12.2.) An example of the use of decorations based on polymorphic objects will be presented in the next section.

A Generic DFS Implementation in C++

In Code Fragments 12.4 and 12.5, we show a C++ implementation of a generic depth-first search traversal by means of a class called DFS. Its behavior can be specialized for a particular application by redefining function initialize(), which activates the computation, and the following functions, which are called at various times by the recursive template function dfsTraversal().

- startVisit(Vertex v): called at the start of the execution of dfsTraversal().
- traverseDiscovery(Edge e, Vertex v): called when a discovery edge e out of v is traversed.
- traverseBack(Edge e, Vertex v): called when a back edge e out of v is traversed.
- isDone(): called to determine whether to end the traversal early.
- finishVisit(Vertex v): called when all the incident edges of v have been traversed.
- result(): called to return the output of dfsTraversal().

Using the Template Method Pattern for DFS

Our generic depth-first search traversal is based on the template method pattern (see Section 6.3.5), which describes a generic computation mechanism that can be specialized by redefining certain steps.

The mechanism used to identify the vertices and edges that have been already visited (explored) during the traversal is encapsulated in the calls to functions isVisited(), markVisited(), and MarkUnvisited(). Our implementation (see Code Fragment 12.5) assumes that the vertices and edges support the decorator pattern. Each vertex and edge is associated with a decoration attribute called "status." The associated value is a pointer to one of two dynamically allocated objects, visited and unvisited. The contents of these two objects is of no concern to us. We simply use the fact that their pointer values differ to distinguish between visited and unvisited vertices and edges. Alternatively, we could use a dictionary of vertex and edge positions and store the visited vertices and edges in it.

To do anything interesting with function dfsTraversal(), we must extend the DFS class and redefine some of the auxiliary functions of Code Fragment 12.5 to perform some computation on the graph. This approach conforms to the template method pattern, for these functions specialize the behavior of the template function dfsTraversal().

Code Fragments 12.6 through 12.8 illustrate extensions of the dfsTraversal() function. Class ConnectivityTesterDFS (Code Fragment 12.6), for instance, tests whether the graph is connected. It counts the vertices reachable by a DFS traversal starting at a vertex and compares this number with the total number of vertices of the graph. The graph is connected if all the vertices were reached.

Class FindPathDFS (Code Fragment 12.7) finds a path between a pair of given start vertex s and target vertex t. It performs a depth-first search traversal beginning at the start vertex. We maintain the path of discovery edges from the start vertex to the current vertex, represented as a sequence. When we encounter an unexplored vertex, we add it to the end of the path. When we encounter the target vertex, we set a flag pathDetected indicating that a path has been detected. When we finish processing a vertex, if it contributes to the path (pathDetected is true), it is kept in the sequence, and otherwise it is removed.

Class FindCycleDFS (Code Fragment 12.8) finds a cycle in the connected component of a given vertex v, by performing a depth-first search traversal from v. As in FindPathDFS, the current discovery edges are stored in a sequence. The cycle is detected as soon as the first back edge is seen. This event is indicated by setting the flag variable cycleDetected, saving the vertex at the start of the cycle in cycleStart, and adding this back edge to the sequence. The discovery edges starting from the root of the DFS tree to cycleStart are not part of the cycle, and this "tail" is removed when the DFS traversal is finished.

```
template <typename Graph>
class DFS {
protected:                                            // local types
  typedef typename Graph::Vertex        Vertex;
  typedef typename Graph::Edge          Edge;
  typedef typename Graph::VertexIterator VertexIterator;
  typedef typename Graph::EdgeIterator  EdgeIterator;
protected:                                            // member data
  const Graph& G;                                     // the graph
  Object *visited, *unvisited;                         // decorator values
public:
  DFS(const Graph& g) : G(g)                          // constructor
    { visited = new Object; unvisited = new Object; }
  void initialize() {                                 // initialize a new DFS
    VertexIterator V = G.vertices();                  // unmark everything
    while (V.hasNext()) markUnvisited(V.nextVertex());
    EdgeIterator E = G.edges();
    while (E.hasNext()) markUnvisited(E.nextEdge());
  }
  virtual ~DFS()
    { delete visited; delete unvisited; }              // destructor
protected:                                            // marking utilities
  void dfsTraversal(const Vertex& v) {                 // generic DFS search
    startVisit(v);                                     // visit v
    markVisited(v);                                    // mark v visited
    EdgeIterator inEdges = G.incidentEdges(v);
    while (inEdges.hasNext()) {                         // try all its edges
      Edge e = inEdges.nextEdge();
      if (!isVisited(e)) {                             // new edge?
        markVisited(e);                                // mark it visited
        Vertex w = G.opposite(v, e);                   // get next vertex
        if (!isVisited(w)) {                           // unexplored?
          traverseDiscovery(e, v);                     // let's discover it
          if (!isDone())
            dfsTraversal(w);                           // continue traversal
        }
        else                                           // explored
          traverseBack(e, v);                          // process back edge
      }
    }
    finishVisit(v);                                    // all done
  }
  // ... (insert overriden functions and marking utilities here)
};
```

Code Fragment 12.4: Class DFS, which performs a generic DFS traversals of a graph. (Continued in Code Fragment 12.5.)

```
protected:                                          // overridden functions
  virtual void startVisit(const Vertex& v) { }      // first visit to v
  virtual void finishVisit(const Vertex& v) { }     // finished with v
                                                    // discover edge e
  virtual void traverseDiscovery(const Edge& e, const Vertex& from) { }
                                                    // back edge e
  virtual void traverseBack(const Edge& e, const Vertex& from) { }
  virtual bool isDone() const { return false; }     // done early?
protected:                                          // marking utilities
  void markVisited(const Vertex& v)    { v.set("status", visited); }
  void markVisited(const Edge& e)      { e.set("status", visited); }
  void markUnvisited(const Vertex& v)  { v.set("status", unvisited); }
  void markUnvisited(const Edge& e)    { e.set("status", unvisited); }
  bool isVisited(const Vertex& v)      { return v.get("status") == visited; }
  bool isVisited(const Edge& e)        { return e.get("status") == visited; }
```

Code Fragment 12.5: Auxiliary functions for specializing the template function dfsTraversal() and the Vertex and edge marking utility functions of class DFS (Continued from Code Fragment 12.4).

```
template <typename Graph>
class ConnectivityTesterDFS : public DFS<Graph> { // test connectivity
protected:                                          // local types
  typedef typename Graph::Vertex Vertex;
private:
  int reached;                                      // how many verts reached
protected:                                          // overriden functions
  virtual void startVisit(const Vertex& v)          // count visited vertex
    { reached++; }
public:
  ConnectivityTesterDFS(const Graph& g)             // constructor
    : DFS<Graph>(g) { }
  bool run() {                                      // main entry point
    initialize();                                   // initialize DFS
    reached = 0;                                    // init vertex count
    if (!G.isEmpty()) {
      Vertex v = G.aVertex();                       // select any vertex
      dfsTraversal(v);                              // start DFS here
    }
    return (reached == G.numVertices());            // visit all => connected
  }
};
```

Code Fragment 12.6: Specialization of class DFS to test if the graph is connected.

```
template <typename Graph>
class FindPathDFS : public DFS<Graph> {          // find a path by DFS
protected:                                        // local types
  typedef typename Graph::Vertex         Vertex;
  typedef typename Graph::VertexSequence VertexSequence;
private:                                           // local data
  Vertex            target;                        // the target vertex
  bool              pathDetected;                  // is target found?
  VertexSequence    path;                          // path storage
protected:                                         // overridden functions
  virtual void startVisit(const Vertex& v) {       // visit vertex
    path.insertLast(v);                            // insert into path
    if (v == target)                               // target vertex seen?
      pathDetected = true;                         // path is detected
  }
  virtual void finishVisit(const Vertex& v) {      // done with vertex
    if (!pathDetected)
      path.remove(path.last());                    // remove if not on path
  }
  virtual bool isDone() const                      // are we done yet?
    { return pathDetected; }
public:
  FindPathDFS(const Graph& g)                      // constructor
    : DFS<Graph>(g), path() { }
                                                    // find path from s to t
  VertexSequence run(const Vertex& s, const Vertex& t) {
    initialize();                                  // initialize DFS
    target = t;                                    // t is the target
    path = VertexSequence();                       // reset path sequence
    pathDetected = false;
    dfsTraversal(s);                               // do the search
    return path;                                   // return the path
  }
};
```

Code Fragment 12.7: Specialization of class DFS to find a path between the start vertex *s* and a target vertex *t*. The variable pathDetected is set as soon as *t* is discovered and is used to control which vertices are kept in the final path sequence.

```
template <typename Graph>
class FindCycleDFS : public DFS<Graph> {
protected:                                          // local types
  typedef typename Graph::Vertex        Vertex;
  typedef typename Graph::Edge          Edge;
  // ... (other Graph typenames omitted)
private:                                             // local data
  bool              cycleDetected;                   // cycle detected?
  Vertex            cycleStart;                       // start of cycle
  EdgeSequence      cycle;                            // cycle storage
protected:                                           // overrriden functions
  virtual void finishVisit(const Vertex& v) {        // finished with vertex
    if ((!cycle.isEmpty()) && (!cycleDetected))      // not building a cycle?
      cycle.remove(cycle.last());                    // remove this edge
  }
  virtual void traverseDiscovery(const Edge& e, const Vertex& from)
    { if (!cycleDetected) cycle.insertLast(e); }     // add edge to sequence
  virtual void traverseBack(const Edge& e, const Vertex& from) {
    if (!cycleDetected) {                            // no cycle yet?
      cycleDetected = true;                          // cycle is now detected
      cycle.insertLast(e);                           // insert back edge
      cycleStart = G.opposite(from, e);              // save starting vertex
    }
  }
  virtual bool isDone() const { return cycleDetected; } // done yet?
public:
  FindCycleDFS(const Graph& g) : DFS<Graph>(g) { }   // constructor
  EdgeSequence run(const Vertex& s) {                // find a cycle from s
    initialize();                                    // initialize DFS
    cycle = EdgeSequence();                          // create cycle sequence
    cycleDetected = false;
    dfsTraversal(s);                                 // do the search
    if (!cycle.isEmpty() && s != cycleStart) {       // found a cycle?
      EdgeSeqPosIterator pi = cycle.positions();
      while (pi.hasNext()) {                         // remove the tail
        EdgeSeqPosition ep = pi.next();
        cycle.remove(ep);                            // ...up to cycleStart
        if (G.areIncident(cycleStart, ep.element())) break;
      }
    }
    return cycle;                                    // return the cycle
  }
};
```

Code Fragment 12.8: Specialization of class DFS to find a cycle in the connected component of the start vertex.

12.3.2 Breadth-First Search

In this section, we consider the ***breadth-first search*** (BFS) traversal algorithm. Like DFS, BFS traverses a connected component of a graph, and in so doing, defines a useful spanning tree. BFS is less "adventurous" than DFS, however. Instead of wandering the graph, BFS proceeds in rounds and subdivides the vertices into ***levels***. BFS can also be thought of as a traversal using a string and paint, with BFS unrolling the string in a more conservative manner.

BFS starts at vertex s, which is at level 0, and defines the "anchor" for our string. In the first round, we let out the string the length of one edge, and we visit all the vertices we can reach without unrolling the string any farther. In this case, we visit, and paint as "visited," the vertices adjacent to the start vertex s—these vertices are placed into level 1. In the second round, we unroll the string the length of two edges and we visit all the new vertices we can reach without unrolling our string any farther. These new vertices, which are adjacent to level 1 vertices and not previously assigned to a level, are placed into level 2, and so on. The BFS traversal terminates when every vertex has been visited.

Pseudo-code for a BFS starting at a vertex s is shown in Code Fragment 12.9. We use auxiliary space to label edges, mark visited vertices, and store containers associated with levels. That is, the containers L_0, L_1, L_2, and so on, store the nodes that are in level 0, level 1, level 2, and so on. These containers could, for example, be implemented as queues. They also allow BFS to be nonrecursive.

Algorithm BFS(s):

    initialize container L_0 to contain vertex s

    $i \leftarrow 0$

    while L_i is not empty **do**

      create container L_{i+1} to initially be empty

      for each vertex v in L_i **do**

        for each edge e incident on v **do**

          if edge e is unexplored **then**

            let w be the other endpoint of e

            if vertex w is unexplored **then**

              label e as a discovery edge

              insert w into L_{i+1}

            else

              label e as a cross edge

      $i \leftarrow i+1$

        Code Fragment 12.9: The breadth-first search algorithm.

We illustrate a BFS traversal in Figure 12.7.

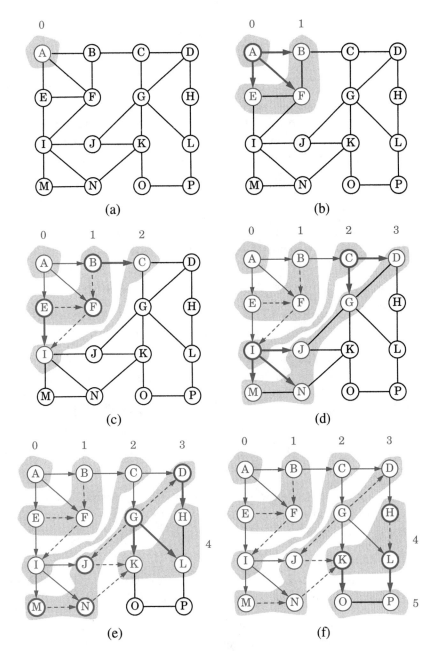

Figure 12.7: Example of a breadth-first search traversal, where the edges incident on a vertex are explored by the alphabetical order of the adjacent vertices. The discovery edges are shown with solid lines and the cross edges are shown with dashed lines: (a) graph before the traversal; (b) discovery of level 1; (c) discovery of level 2; (d) discovery of level 3; (e) discovery of level 4; (f) discovery of level 5.

One of the nice properties of the BFS approach is that, in performing the BFS traversal, we can label each vertex by the length of a shortest path (in terms of the number of edges) from the start vertex s. In particular, if vertex v is placed into level i by a BFS starting at vertex s, then the length of a shortest path from s to v is i.

As with DFS, we can visualize the BFS traversal by orienting the edges along the direction in which they are explored during the traversal, and by distinguishing the edges used to discover new vertices, called ***discovery edges***, from those that lead to already visited vertices, called ***cross edges***. (See Figure 12.7f.) As with the DFS, the discovery edges form a spanning tree, which in this case we call the BFS tree. We do not call the nontree edges "back edges" in this case, however, for none of them connects a vertex to one of its ancestors. Every nontree edge connects a vertex v to another vertex that is neither v's ancestor nor its descendent.

The BFS traversal algorithm has a number of interesting properties, some of which we explore in the proposition that follows.

Proposition 12.14: *Let G be an undirected graph on which a BFS traversal starting at vertex s has been performed. Then*

- *The traversal visits all vertices in the connected component of s.*
- *The discovery-edges form a spanning tree T, which we call the BFS tree, of the connected component of s.*
- *For each vertex v at level i, the path of the BFS tree T between s and v has i edges, and any other path of G between s and v has at least i edges.*
- *If (u,v) is an edge that is not in the BFS tree, then the level numbers of u and v differ by at most 1.*

We leave the justification of this proposition as an exercise (C-12.13). The analysis of the running time of BFS is similar to that of DFS, which implies the following.

Proposition 12.15: *Let G be a graph with n vertices and m edges represented with the adjacency list structure. A BFS traversal of G takes $O(n+m)$ time. Also, $O(n+m)$-time algorithms based on BFS exist for the following problems:*

- *Testing whether G is connected*
- *Computing a spanning tree of G, if G is connected*
- *Computing the connected components of G*
- *Given a start vertex s of G, computing, for every vertex v of G, a path with the minimum number of edges between s and v, or reporting that no such path exists.*
- *Computing a cycle in G, or reporting that G has no cycles.*

12.4 Directed Graphs

In this section, we study directed graphs. Recall that a directed graph, which is also known as a *digraph*, is a graph whose edges are all directed.

Comparing BFS and DFS for Directed and Undirected Graphs

As we show in this section, BFS and DFS can be extended to directed graphs. We should stress, however, that these algorithms have both similarities and differences when respectively applied to directed graphs and undirected graphs. The BFS traversal is better at finding shortest paths in an undirected graph (where distance is measured by the number of edges), and this property still holds for directed graphs. Also, for undirected graphs, BFS produces a spanning tree, such that all the nontree edges are cross edges, but this property does not hold for directed BFS. The DFS traversal is better for answering complex connectivity questions, such as determining if every pair of vertices in an undirected graph can be connected by two disjoint paths. Also, it produces a spanning tree of an undirected graph, such that all the nontree edges are back edges, which is a property that does not hold for directed DFS.

Reachability

One of the most fundamental issues with directed graphs is the notion of *reachability*, which deals with determining where we can get to in a directed graph. A traversal in a directed graph always goes along directed paths, that is, paths where all the edges are traversed according to their respective directions. Given vertices u and v of a digraph $\vec{G}$, we say that u *reaches* v (and v is *reachable* from u) if $\vec{G}$ has a directed path from u to v. We also say that a vertex v reaches an edge (w, z) if v reaches the origin vertex w of the edge.

A digraph $\vec{G}$ is *strongly connected* if, for any two vertices u and v of $\vec{G}$, u reaches v and v reaches u. A *directed cycle* of $\vec{G}$ is a cycle where all the edges are traversed according to their respective directions. (Note that $\vec{G}$ may have a cycle consisting of two edges with opposite direction between the same pair of vertices.) A digraph $\vec{G}$ is *acyclic* if it has no directed cycles. (See Figure 12.8 for examples.)

The *transitive closure* of a digraph $\vec{G}$ is the digraph $\vec{G}^*$, such that the vertices of $\vec{G}^*$ are the same as the vertices of $\vec{G}$, and $\vec{G}^*$ has an edge (u, v), whenever $\vec{G}$ has a directed path from u to v. That is, we define $\vec{G}^*$ by starting with the digraph $\vec{G}$ and adding in an extra edge (u, v) for each u and v, such that v is reachable from u (and there isn't already an edge (u, v) in $\vec{G}$).

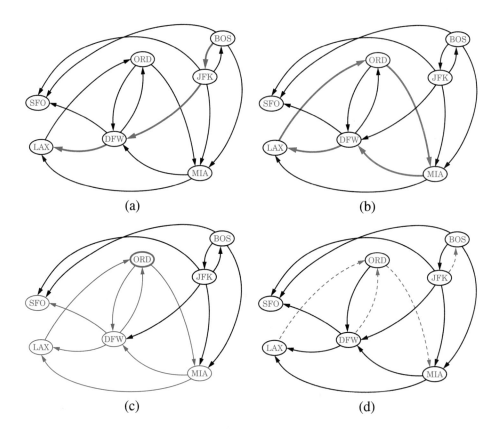

(a)   (b)

(c)   (d)

Figure 12.8: Examples of reachability in a digraph: (a) a directed path from BOS to LAX is drawn in blue; (b) a directed cycle (ORD, MIA, DFW, LAX, ORD) is shown in blue; its vertices induce a strongly connected subgraph; (c) the subgraph of the vertices and edges reachable from ORD is shown in blue; (d) removing the dashed blue edges gives an acyclic digraph.

Interesting problems that deal with reachability in a digraph $\vec{G}$ include the following:

- Given vertices u and v, determine whether u reaches v.
- Find all the vertices of $\vec{G}$ that are reachable from a given vertex s.
- Determine whether $\vec{G}$ is strongly connected.
- Determine whether $\vec{G}$ is acyclic.
- Compute the transitive closure $\vec{G}^*$ of $\vec{G}$.

In the remainder of this section, we explore some efficient algorithms for solving these problems.

12.4.1 Traversing a Digraph

As with undirected graphs, we can explore a digraph in a systematic way with methods akin to the depth-first search (DFS) and breadth-first search (BFS) algorithms previously defined for undirected graphs (Sections 12.3.1 and 12.3.2). Such explorations can be used, for example, to answer reachability questions. The directed depth-first search and breadth-first search methods we develop in this section for performing such explorations are very similar to their undirected counterparts. In fact, the only real difference is that the directed depth-first search and breadth-first search methods only traverse edges according to their respective directions.

The directed version of DFS starting at a vertex v can be described by the recursive algorithm in Code Fragment 12.10. (See Figure 12.9.)

Algorithm DirectedDFS(v):

    Mark vertex v as visited.

    for each outgoing edge (v, w) of v **do**

        if vertex w has not been visited **then**

            Recursively call DirectedDFS(w).

Code Fragment 12.10: The DirectedDFS algorithm.

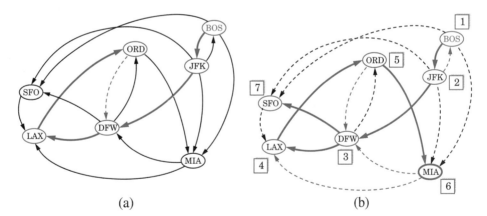

(a)   (b)

Figure 12.9: An example of a DFS in a digraph: (a) intermediate step, where, for the first time, an already visited vertex (DFW) is reached; (b) the completed DFS. The tree edges are shown with solid blue lines, the back edges are shown with dashed blue lines, and the forward and cross edges are shown with dashed black lines. The order in which the vertices are visited is indicated by a label next to each vertex. The edge (ORD,DFW) is a back edge, but (DFW,ORD) is a forward edge. Edge (BOS,SFO) is a forward edge, and (SFO,LAX) is a cross edge.

A DFS on a digraph $\vec{G}$ partitions the edges of $\vec{G}$ reachable from the starting vertex into **tree edges** or **discovery edges**, which lead us to discover a new vertex, and **nontree edges**, which take us to a previously visited vertex. The tree edges form a tree rooted at the starting vertex, called the **depth-first search** tree, and there are three kinds of nontree edges:

- **back edges**, which connect a vertex to an ancestor in the DFS tree
- **forward edges**, which connect a vertex to a descendent in the DFS tree
- **cross edges**, which connect a vertex to a vertex that is neither its ancestor nor its descendent.

Refer back to Figure 12.9b to see an example of each type of nontree edge.

Proposition 12.16: *Let $\vec{G}$ be a digraph. Depth-first search on $\vec{G}$ starting at a vertex s visits all the vertices of $\vec{G}$ that are reachable from s. Also, the DFS tree contains directed paths from s to every vertex reachable from s.*

Justification: Let V_s be the subset of vertices of $\vec{G}$ visited by DFS starting at vertex s. We want to show that V_s contains s and every vertex reachable from s belongs to V_s. Suppose now, for the sake of a contradiction, that there is a vertex w reachable from s that is not in V_s. Consider a directed path from s to w, and let (u,v) be the first edge on such a path taking us out of V_s, that is, u is in V_s but v is not in V_s. When DFS reaches u, it explores all the outgoing edges of u, and thus must also reach vertex v via edge (u,v). Hence, v should be in V_s, and we have obtained a contradiction. Therefore, V_s must contain every vertex reachable from s.   ∎

Analyzing the running time of the directed DFS method is analogous to that for its undirected counterpart. In particular, a recursive call is made for each vertex exactly once, and each edge is traversed exactly once (from its origin). Hence, if n_s vertices and m_s edges are reachable from vertex s, a directed DFS starting at s runs in $O(n_s + m_s)$ time, provided the digraph is represented with a data structure that supports constant-time vertex and edge methods. The adjacency list structure satisfies this requirement, for example.

By Proposition 12.16, we can use DFS to find all the vertices reachable from a given vertex, and hence to find the transitive closure of $\vec{G}$. That is, we can perform a DFS, starting from each vertex v of $\vec{G}$, to see which vertices w are reachable from v, adding an edge (v,w) to the transitive closure for each such w. Likewise, by repeatedly traversing digraph $\vec{G}$ with a DFS, starting in turn at each vertex, we can easily test whether $\vec{G}$ is strongly connected. Namely, $\vec{G}$ is strongly connected if each DFS visits all the vertices of $\vec{G}$.

Thus, we may immediately derive the proposition that follows.

Proposition 12.17: *Let $\vec{G}$ be a digraph with n vertices and m edges. The following problems can be solved by an algorithm that traverses $\vec{G}$ n times using DFS, runs in $O(n(n+m))$ time, and uses $O(n)$ auxiliary space:*

- *Computing, for each vertex v of $\vec{G}$, the subgraph reachable from v*
- *Testing whether $\vec{G}$ is strongly connected*
- *Computing the transitive closure $\vec{G}^*$ of $\vec{G}$.*

Testing for Strong Connectivity

Actually, we can determine if a directed graph $\vec{G}$ is strongly connected much faster than this, by using two depth-first searches. We begin by performing a DFS of our directed graph $\vec{G}$ starting at an arbitrary vertex s. If there is any vertex of $\vec{G}$ that is not visited by this DFS, and is not reachable from s, then the graph is not strongly connected. So, if this first DFS visits each vertex of $\vec{G}$, then we reverse all the edges of $\vec{G}$ (using the reverseDirection method) and perform another DFS starting at s in this "reverse" graph. If every vertex of $\vec{G}$ is visited by this second DFS, then the graph is strongly connected, for each of the vertices visited in this DFS can reach s. Since this algorithm makes just two DFS traversals of $\vec{G}$, it runs in $O(n+m)$ time.

Directed Breadth-First Search

As with DFS, we can extend breadth-first search (BFS) to work for directed graphs. The algorithm still visits vertices, level by level, and partitions the set of edges into **tree edges** (or **discovery edges**), which together form a directed **breadth-first search** tree rooted at the start vertex, and **nontree edges**. Unlike the directed DFS method, however, the directed BFS method only leaves two kinds of nontree edges: **back edges**, which connect a vertex to one of its ancestors, and **cross edges**, which connect a vertex to another vertex that is neither its ancestor nor its descendent. There are no forward edges, which is a fact we explore in an exercise (C-12.9).

12.4.2 Transitive Closure

In this section, we explore an alternative technique for computing the transitive closure of a digraph. Let $\vec{G}$ be a digraph with n vertices and m edges. We compute the transitive closure of $\vec{G}$ in a series of rounds. We initialize $\vec{G}_0 = \vec{G}$. We also arbitrarily number the vertices of $\vec{G}$ as $v_1, v_2, \ldots, v_n$. We then begin the computation of the rounds, beginning with round 1. In a generic round k, we construct digraph $\vec{G}_k$ starting with $\vec{G}_k = \vec{G}_{k-1}$ and adding to $\vec{G}_k$ the directed edge (v_i, v_j) if digraph $\vec{G}_{k-1}$ contains both the edges (v_i, v_k) and (v_k, v_j). In this way, we will enforce a simple rule embodied in the proposition that follows.

Proposition 12.18: *For* $i = 1, \ldots, n$, *digraph* $\vec{G}_k$ *has an edge* (v_i, v_j), *if and only if, digraph* $\vec{G}$ *has a directed path from* v_i *to* v_j, *whose intermediate vertices (if any) are in the set* $\{v_1, \ldots, v_k\}$. *In particular,* $\vec{G}_n$ *is equal to* $\vec{G}^*$, *the transitive closure of* $\vec{G}$.

Proposition 12.18 suggests a simple algorithm for computing the transitive closure of $\vec{G}$ that is based on the series of rounds we described above. This algorithm is known as the ***Floyd-Warshall algorithm***, and its pseudo-code is given in Code Fragment 12.11. From this pseudo-code, we can easily analyze the running time of the Floyd-Warshall algorithm, assuming that the data structure representing G supports functions areAdjacent() and insertDirectedEdge() in $O(1)$ time. The main loop is executed n times and the inner loop considers each of $O(n^2)$ pairs of vertices, performing a constant-time computation for each one. Thus, the total running time of the Floyd-Warshall algorithm is $O(n^3)$.

Algorithm FloydWarshall($\vec{G}$):
    Input: A digraph $\vec{G}$ with n vertices
    Output: The transitive closure $\vec{G}^*$ of $\vec{G}$

    let $v_1, v_2, \ldots, v_n$ be an arbitrary numbering of the vertices of $\vec{G}$
    $\vec{G}_0 \leftarrow \vec{G}$
    for $k \leftarrow 1$ to n **do**
        $\vec{G}_k \leftarrow \vec{G}_{k-1}$
        for each i, j in $\{1, \ldots, n\}$ with $i \neq j$ and $i, j \neq k$ **do**
            if both edges (v_i, v_k) and (v_k, v_j) are in $\vec{G}_{k-1}$ **then**
                add edge (v_i, v_j) to $\vec{G}_k$ (if it is not already present)
    return $\vec{G}_n$

Code Fragment 12.11: Pseudo-code for the Floyd-Warshall algorithm. This algorithm computes the transitive closure $\vec{G}^*$ of G by incrementally computing a series of digraphs $\vec{G}_0, \vec{G}_1, \ldots, \vec{G}_n$, where for $k = 1, \ldots, n$.

This description is actually an example of an algorithmic design pattern known as dynamic programming, which is discussed in more detail in Section 11.5.2. From the above description and analysis, we may immediately derive the following proposition.

Proposition 12.19: *Let* $\vec{G}$ *be a digraph with n vertices, and let* $\vec{G}$ *be represented by a data structure that supports lookup and update of adjacency information in* $O(1)$ *time. Then the Floyd-Warshall algorithm computes the transitive closure* $\vec{G}^*$ *of* $\vec{G}$ *in* $O(n^3)$ *time.*

We illustrate an example run of the Floyd-Warshall algorithm in Figure 12.10.

The running time of the Floyd-Warshall algorithm might appear to be slower than performing a DFS of a directed graph from each of its vertices, but this depends upon the representation of the graph. If a graph is represented using an adjacency matrix, then running the DFS method once on a directed graph $\vec{G}$ takes $O(n^2)$ time (we explore the reason for this in an exercise). Thus, running DFS n times takes $O(n^3)$ time, which is no better than a single execution of the Floyd-Warshall algorithm, but the Floyd-Warshall algorithm would be much simpler to implement. Nevertheless, if the graph is represented using an adjacency list structure, then running the DFS algorithm n times would take $O(n(n+m))$ time to compute the transitive closure. Even so, if the graph is **dense**, that is, if it has $\Theta(n^2)$ edges, then this approach still runs in $O(n^3)$ time and is more complicated than a single instance of the Floyd-Warshall algorithm. The only case where repeatedly calling the DFS method is better, is when the graph is not dense and is represented using an adjacency list structure.

12.4.3 Directed Acyclic Graphs

Directed graphs without directed cycles are encountered in many applications. Such a digraph is often referred to as a **directed acyclic graph**, or **DAG**, for short. Applications of such graphs include the following:

- Inheritance between classes of a C++ program
- Prerequisites between courses of a degree program
- Scheduling constraints between the tasks of a project.

Example 12.20: *In order to manage a large project, it is convenient to break it up into a collection of smaller tasks. The tasks, however, are rarely independent, because scheduling constraints exist between them. (For example, in a house building project, the task of ordering nails obviously precedes the task of nailing shingles to the roof deck.) Clearly, scheduling constraints cannot have circularities, because they would make the project impossible. (For example, in order to get a job you need to have work experience, but in order to get work experience you need to have a job.) The scheduling constraints impose restrictions on the order in which the tasks can be executed. Namely, if a constraint says that task a must be completed before task b is started, then a must precede b in the order of execution of the tasks. Thus, if we model a feasible set of tasks as vertices of a directed graph, and we place a directed edge from v to w whenever the task for v must be executed before the task for w, then we define a directed acyclic graph.*

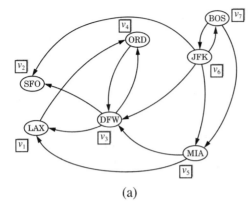
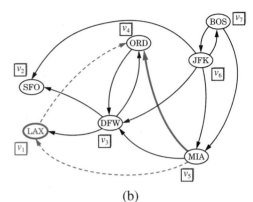

(a)   (b)

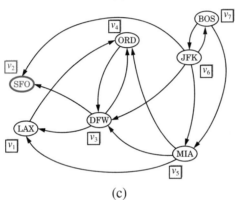
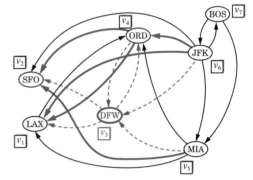

(c)   (d)

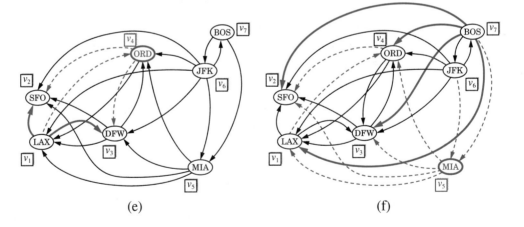

(e)   (f)

Figure 12.10: Sequence of digraphs computed by the Floyd-Warshall algorithm: (a) initial digraph $\vec{G} = \vec{G}_0$ and numbering of the vertices; (b) digraph $\vec{G}_1$; (c) $\vec{G}_2$; (d) $\vec{G}_3$; (e) $\vec{G}_4$; (f) $\vec{G}_5$. Note that $\vec{G}_5 = \vec{G}_6 = \vec{G}_7$. If digraph $\vec{G}_{k-1}$ has the edges (v_i, v_k) and (v_k, v_j), but not the edge (v_i, v_j), in the drawing of digraph $\vec{G}_k$, we show edges (v_i, v_k) and (v_k, v_j) with dashed blue lines, and edge (v_i, v_j) with a thick blue line.

The above example motivates the following definition. Let $\vec{G}$ be a digraph with n vertices. A **topological ordering** of $\vec{G}$ is an ordering $v_1, \ldots, v_n$ of the vertices of $\vec{G}$, such that for every edge (v_i, v_j) of $\vec{G}$, $i < j$. That is, a topological ordering is an ordering such that any directed path in $\vec{G}$ traverses vertices in increasing order. (See Figure 12.11.) Note that a digraph may have multiple topological orderings.

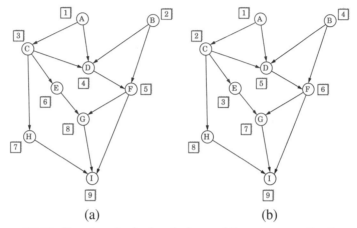

(a)   (b)

Figure 12.11: Two topological orderings of the same acyclic digraph.

Proposition 12.21: $\vec{G}$ *has a topological ordering, if and only if, it is acyclic.*

Justification: The necessity (the "only if" part of the statement) is easy to demonstrate. Suppose $\vec{G}$ is topologically ordered. Assume, for the sake of a contradiction, that $\vec{G}$ has a cycle consisting of edges $(v_{i_0}, v_{i_1}), (v_{i_1}, v_{i_2}), \ldots, (v_{i_{k-1}}, v_{i_0})$. Because of the topological ordering, we must have $i_0 < i_1 < \cdots < i_{k-1} < i_0$, which is clearly impossible. Thus, $\vec{G}$ must be acyclic.

We now argue the sufficiency of the condition (the "if" part). Suppose $\vec{G}$ is acyclic. We will give an algorithmic description of how to build a topological ordering for $\vec{G}$. Since $\vec{G}$ is acyclic, $\vec{G}$ must have a vertex with no incoming edges (that is, with in-degree 0). Let v_1 be such a vertex. Indeed, if v_1 did not exist, then in tracing a directed path from an arbitrary start vertex, we would eventually encounter a previously visited vertex, thus contradicting the acyclicity of $\vec{G}$. If we remove v_1 from $\vec{G}$, together with its outgoing edges, the resulting digraph is still acyclic. Hence, the resulting digraph also has a vertex with no incoming edges, and we let v_2 be such a vertex. By repeating this process until the digraph becomes empty, we obtain an ordering $v_1, \ldots, v_n$ of the vertices of $\vec{G}$. Because of the above construction, if (v_i, v_j) is an edge of $\vec{G}$, then v_i must be deleted before v_j can be deleted, and thus $i < j$. Thus, $v_1, \ldots, v_n$ is a topological ordering. ∎

Proposition 12.21's justification suggests an algorithm (Code Fragment 12.12), called ***topological sorting***, for computing a topological ordering of a digraph.

Algorithm TopologicalSort($\vec{G}$):

    Input: A digraph $\vec{G}$ with n vertices.

    Output: A topological ordering $v_1, \ldots, v_n$ of $\vec{G}$.

    Let S be an initially empty stack.

    for each vertex u of $\vec{G}$ **do**

        Let incounter(u) be the in-degree of u.

        if incounter$(u) = 0$ **then**

            S.push(u)

    $i \leftarrow 1$

    while S is not empty **do**

        $u \leftarrow S$.pop()

        Let u be vertex number i in the topological ordering.

        $i \leftarrow i + 1$

        for each outgoing edge (u, w) of u **do**

            incounter$(w) \leftarrow$ incounter$(w) - 1$

            if incounter$(w) = 0$ **then**

                S.push(w)

Code Fragment 12.12: Pseudo-code for the topological sorting algorithm. (We show an example application of this algorithm in Figure 12.12.)

Proposition 12.22: *Let $\vec{G}$ be a digraph with n vertices and m edges. The topological sorting algorithm runs in $O(n+m)$ time using $O(n)$ auxiliary space, and either computes a topological ordering of $\vec{G}$ or fails to number some vertices, which indicates that $\vec{G}$ has a directed cycle.*

Justification: The initial computation of in-degrees and setup of the incounter variables can be done with a simple traversal of the graph, which takes $O(n+m)$ time. We use the decorator pattern to associate counter attributes with the vertices. Say that a vertex u is ***visited*** by the topological sorting algorithm when u is removed from the stack S. A vertex u can be visited only when incounter$(u) = 0$, which implies that all its predecessors (vertices with outgoing edges into u) were previously visited. As a consequence, any vertex that is on a directed cycle will never be visited, and any other vertex will be visited exactly once. The algorithm traverses all the outgoing edges of each visited vertex once, so its running time is proportional to the number of outgoing edges of the visited vertices. Therefore, the algorithm runs in $O(n+m)$ time. Regarding the space usage, observe that the stack S and the incounter variables attached to the vertices use $O(n)$ space.   ∎

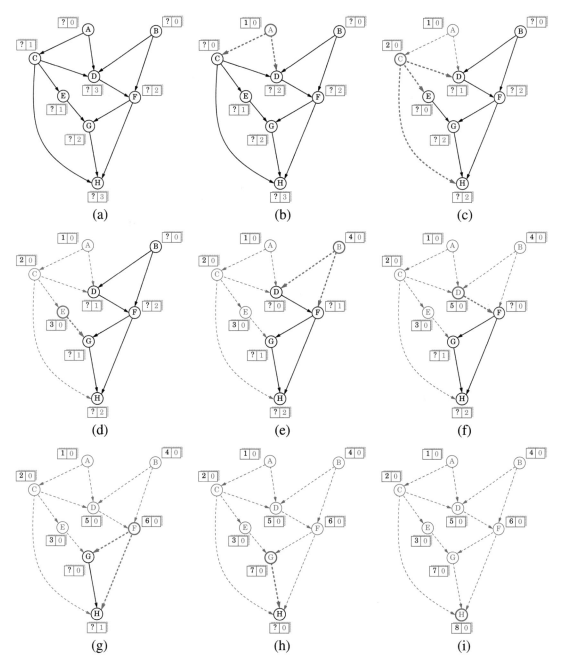

Figure 12.12: Example of a run of algorithm TopologicalSort (Code Fragment 12.12): (a) initial configuration; (b–i) after each while-loop iteration. The vertex labels show the vertex number and the current incounter value. The edges traversed are shown with dashed blue arrows. Thick lines denote the vertex and edges examined in the current iteration.

Testing if a Directed Graph is Acyclic

As a side effect, the topological sorting algorithm of Code Fragment 12.12 also tests whether the input digraph $\vec{G}$ is acyclic. Indeed, if the algorithm terminates without ordering all the vertices, then the subgraph of the vertices that have not been ordered must contain a directed cycle. (See Figure 12.13.)

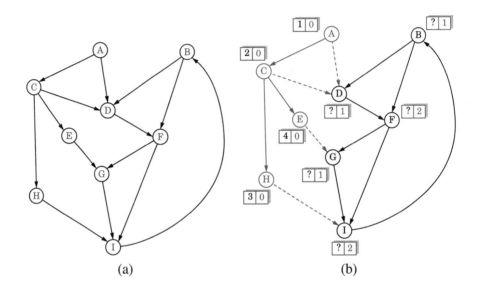

(a)   (b)

Figure 12.13: Detecting a directed cycle: (a) input digraph; (b) after algorithm TopologicalSort (Code Fragment 12.12) terminates, the subgraph of the vertices with undefined number contains a directed cycle.

Next we present an application of directed graph traversal.

12.4.4 Application: Garbage Collection ⋆

In languages like C and C++ the memory space for objects is explicitly allocated and deallocated by the programmer. If it is not done correctly, explicit memory-allocation can be a source of errors. In contrast, other languages, like Java, place the burden of memory management on the run-time environment. A Java programmer does not have to explicitly deallocate the memory for some object when its life is over. Instead, a ***garbage collector*** mechanism deallocates the memory for such objects.

Let us consider how such a system would operate.

Determining Live Objects

Recall that dynamic objects are allocated from the system's memory heap (see Section 4.3.3). In addition, the running program stores its local variables on the runtime stack (see Section 4.2.3). Since the local variables can point to objects in the memory heap, all the variables and objects in the runtime stacks of the running program are called *root objects*. All those objects that can be reached, either directly or indirectly, by following pointers or references that start from a root object are called *live objects*. The live objects are the active objects currently being used by the running program; these objects should *not* be deallocated. For example, a running program may store a pointer to a sequence S in a variable that is implemented using a doubly linked list. The pointer variable to S is a root object, while the object for S is a live object, as are all the node objects that are referenced from this object and all the elements that are referenced from these node objects.

From time to time, the runtime system may notice that free space in the memory heap is becoming scarce. At such times, the system may elect to reclaim the space being used for objects that are no longer live. This reclamation process is known as *garbage collection*. There are several different algorithms for garbage collection, but one of the most used is the *mark-sweep algorithm*. Let us consider the steps needed to implement a garbage collection algorithm based on this algorithm.

The Mark-Sweep Algorithm

In the mark-sweep garbage collection algorithm, we associate, with each object, a *mark bit* that identifies if that object is live or not. When we determine at some point that garbage collection is needed, we suspend the execution of the program and clear all of the mark bits of objects currently allocated in the memory heap. We then trace, through the runtime stack of the currently running program, and mark all of the (root) objects in this stack as "live." We must then determine all of the other live objects—the ones that are reachable from the root objects. To do this efficiently, we should use the directed-graph version of the depth-first search traversal. In this case, each object in the memory heap is viewed as a vertex in a directed graph, and a pointer or reference from one object to another is viewed as an edge. By performing a directed DFS from each root object, we can correctly identify and mark each live object. This process is known as the "mark" phase. Once this process is complete, we scan through the memory heap and reclaim any space that is being used for an object that has not been marked. This scanning process is known as the "sweep" phase, and when it completes, we resume running the suspended program. Thus, the mark-sweep garbage collection algorithm will reclaim unused space in time proportional to the number of live objects and their pointers plus the size of the memory heap.

Performing DFS In-place

The mark-sweep algorithm is an effective way of reclaiming unused space in the memory heap, but there is an important issue we must face during the mark phase. Since we are probably reclaiming memory space at a time when free memory is scarce, we must take special care not to use much extra space during the garbage collection itself. The trouble is that the DFS algorithm, as we have described it, can use as much extra space as there are vertices in the graph. In the case of garbage collection, the vertices in our graph are the objects in the memory heap. We probably don't have this much memory to use, so our only alternative is to find a way to perform DFS in-place rather than recursively, that is, we must perform DFS using only a constant amount of additional storage. Fortunately, it is possible to perform DFS in-place.

The main idea for performing DFS in-place is to simulate the recursion stack using the edges of the graph (which, in the case of garbage collection, corresponds to object references). Whenever we traverse an edge from a visited vertex v to a new vertex w, we change the edge (v, w) stored in v's adjacency list to point back to v's parent in the DFS tree. When we return back to v (simulating the return from the "recursive" call at w), we can now switch the edge we modified to point back to w as it did before. Of course, we need to have some way of identifying which edge we need to change back. One possibility is to number the references going out of v as 1, 2, and so on, and store, in addition to the mark bit (which we are using for the "visited" tag in our DFS), a count identifier that tells us which edges we have modified.

Of course, using a count identifier requires an extra word of storage per object. This extra word can be avoided in some implementations, however. For example, many implementations of the Java runtime system represent an object as a composition of a reference with a type identifier (which indicates the object's type) and a reference to the other objects or data fields for this object. Since the type reference is always supposed to be the first element of the composition in such implementations, this reference can be used to "mark" the edge that is changed when leaving an object v and going to some object w in the DFS. The reference at v that refers to the type of v is swapped with the reference at v that refers to w. On returning to v, it is possible to identify the edge (v, w) that was changed, because it is the first reference in the composition for v, and the position of the reference to v's type identifies the place where this edge belongs in v's adjacency list. Thus, whether the edge-swapping trick or a count identifier is used, it is possible to implement DFS in-place without affecting its asymptotic running time.

12.5   Weighted Graphs

As we saw in Section 12.3.2, the breadth-first search strategy can be used to find a shortest path from some starting vertex to every other vertex in a connected graph. This approach makes sense in cases where each edge is as good as any other, but there are many situations where this approach is not appropriate. For example, we might be using a graph to represent a computer network (such as the Internet), and we might be interested in finding the fastest way to route a data packet between two computers. In this case, it is probably not appropriate for all the edges to be equal to each other, for some connections in a computer network are typically much faster than others (for example, some edges might represent slow phone-line connections while others might represent high-speed, fiber-optic connections). Likewise, we might want to use a graph to represent the roads between cities, and we might be interested in finding the fastest way to travel cross-country. In this case, it is again probably not appropriate for all the edges to be equal to each other, for some inter-city distances will likely be much larger than others. Thus, it is natural to consider graphs whose edges are not weighted equally.

A **weighted graph** is a graph that has a numeric (for example, integer) label $w(e)$ associated with each edge e, called the **weight** of edge e. We show an example of a weighted graph in Figure 12.14.

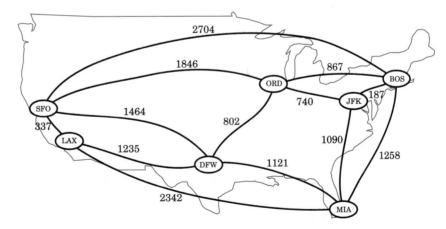

Figure 12.14: A weighted graph whose vertices represent major U.S. airports and whose edge weights represent distances in miles. This graph has a path from JFK to LAX of total weight 2,777 (going through ORD and DFW). This is the minimum weight path in the graph from JFK to LAX.

12.6   Shortest Paths

Let G be a weighted graph. The **length** (or weight) of a path is the sum of the weights of the edges of P. That is, if $P = ((v_0, v_1), (v_1, v_2), \ldots, (v_{k-1}, v_k))$, then the length of P, denoted $w(P)$, is defined as

$$w(P) = \sum_{i=0}^{k-1} w((v_i, v_{i+1})).$$

The **distance** from a vertex v to a vertex u in G, denoted $d(v, u)$, is the length of a minimum length path (also called **shortest path**) from v to u, if such a path exists.

The convention is that $d(v, u) = +\infty$ if there is no path at all from v to u in G. Even if there is a path from v to u in G, the distance from v to u may not be defined, however, if there is a cycle in G whose total weight is negative. For example, suppose vertices in G represent cities, and the weights of edges in G represent how much money it costs to go from one city to another. If someone were willing to actually pay us to go from say JFK to ORD, then the "cost" of the edge (JFK,ORD) would be negative. If someone else were willing to pay us to go from ORD to JFK, then there would be a negative-weight cycle in G and distances would no longer be defined. That is, anyone can now build a path (with cycles) in G from any city A to another city B that first goes to JFK and then cycles as many times as he or she likes from JFK to ORD and back, before going on to B. The existence of such paths allows us to build arbitrarily low negative-cost paths (and in this case make a fortune in the process). But distances cannot be arbitrarily low negative numbers. Thus, any time we use edge weights to represent distances, we must be careful not to introduce any negative-weight cycles.

Suppose we are given a weighted graph G, and we are asked to find a shortest path from some vertex v to each other vertex in G, viewing the weights on the edges as distances. In this section, we explore efficient ways of finding all such shortest paths. The first algorithm we discuss is for the common case when all the edge weights in G are nonnegative (that is, $w(e) \geq 0$ for each edge e of G); hence, we know in advance that there are no negative-weight cycles in G. Recall that the special case of computing a shortest path when all weights are 1 was solved with the BFS algorithm presented in Section 12.3.2. An interesting approach for solving this **single-source** problem is based on the **greedy method** (Section 11.4.2). Recall that in this pattern we solve a problem by repeatedly selecting the best choice from among those available in each iteration. This paradigm can often be used when we are trying to optimize some cost function over a collection of objects. We can add objects to our collection, one at a time, always picking the next one that optimizes the function from among those yet to be chosen.

12.6.1   Dijkstra's Algorithm

The main idea in applying the greedy method pattern to the single-source shortest-path problem is to perform a "weighted" breadth-first search starting at v. In particular, we can use the greedy method to develop an algorithm that iteratively grows a "cloud" of vertices out of v, with the vertices entering the cloud in order of their distances from v. Thus, in each iteration, the next vertex chosen is the vertex outside the cloud that is closest to v. The algorithm terminates when no more vertices are outside the cloud, at which point we have a shortest path from v to every other vertex of G. This approach is a simple, but nevertheless powerful, example of the greedy method design pattern.

A Greedy Method for Finding Shortest Paths

Applying the greedy method to the single-source, shortest-path problem, results in an algorithm known as ***Dijkstra's algorithm***. When applied to other graph problems, however, the greedy method may not necessarily find the best solution (such as in the so-called ***traveling salesman problem***, in which we wish to find the shortest path that visits all the vertices in a graph exactly once). Nevertheless, there are a number of situations in which the greedy method allows us to compute the best solution. In this chapter, we discuss two such situations: computing shortest paths and constructing a minimum spanning tree.

In order to simplify the description of Dijkstra's algorithm, we assume, in the following, that the input graph G is undirected (that is, all its edges are undirected) and simple (that is, it has no self-loops and no parallel edges). Hence, we denote the edges of G as unordered vertex pairs (u, z).

Caution

In Dijkstra's algorithm for finding shortest paths, the cost function we are trying to optimize in our application of the greedy method is also the function that we are trying to compute—the shortest path distance. This may at first seem like circular reasoning, until we realize that we can actually implement this approach by using a "bootstrapping" trick, consisting of using an approximation to the distance function we are trying to compute, which will be equal to the true distance in the end.

Edge Relaxation

Let us define a label $D[u]$ for each vertex u in V, which we use to approximate the distance in G from v to u. The meaning of these labels is that $D[u]$ will always store the length of the best path we have found ***so far*** from v to u. Initially, $D[v] = 0$ and $D[u] = +\infty$ for each $u \neq v$, and we define the set C, which is our "***cloud***" of vertices, to initially be the empty set $\emptyset$. At each iteration of the algorithm, we select a vertex u not in C with smallest $D[u]$ label, and we pull u into C. In the very first iteration, we will, of course, pull v into C. Once a new vertex u is pulled into C, we then update the label $D[z]$ of each vertex z that is adjacent to u and is outside of C, to reflect the fact that there may be a new and better way to get to z via u. This update operation is known as a *relaxation* procedure, for it takes an old estimate and checks if it can be improved to get closer to its true value. (A metaphor for why we call this a relaxation comes from a spring that is stretched out and then "relaxed" back to its true resting shape.) In the case of Dijkstra's algorithm, the relaxation is performed for an edge (u, z), such that we have computed a new value of $D[u]$ and wish to see if there is a better value for $D[z]$ using the edge (u, z). The specific edge relaxation operation is as follows:

Edge Relaxation:

$$\textbf{if } D[u] + w((u,z)) < D[z] \textbf{ then}$$
$$D[z] \leftarrow D[u] + w((u,z))$$

We give the pseudo-code for Dijkstra's algorithm in Code Fragment 12.13. Note that we use a priority queue Q to store the vertices outside of the cloud C.

Algorithm ShortestPath(G, v):

> *Input:* A simple undirected weighted graph G with nonnegative edge weights, and a distinguished vertex v of G.
>
> *Output:* A label $D[u]$, for each vertex u of G, such that $D[u]$ is the length of a shortest path from v to u in G
>
> Initialize $D[v] \leftarrow 0$ and $D[u] \leftarrow +\infty$ for each vertex $u \neq v$.
> Let a priority queue Q contain all the vertices of G using the D labels as keys.
> **while** Q is not empty **do**
>> {pull a new vertex u into the cloud}
>> $u \leftarrow Q.\text{removeMin}()$
>> **for** each vertex z adjacent to u such that z is in Q **do**
>>> {perform the *relaxation* procedure on edge (u, z)}
>>> **if** $D[u] + w((u,z)) < D[z]$ **then**
>>> $D[z] \leftarrow D[u] + w((u,z))$
>>> Change to $D[z]$ the key of vertex z in Q.
>
> **return** the label $D[u]$ of each vertex u

Code Fragment 12.13: Dijkstra's algorithm for the single-source shortest path problem.

Figures 12.15 and 12.16 show several iterations of Dijkstra's algorithm.

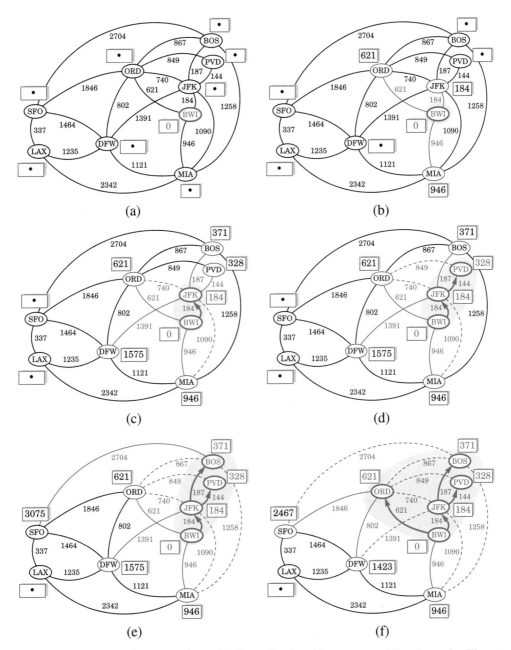

Figure 12.15: An execution of Dijkstra's algorithm on a weighted graph. The start vertex is BWI. A box next to each vertex v stores the label $D[v]$. The symbol • is used instead of $+\infty$. The edges of the shortest-path tree are drawn as thick blue arrows, and for each vertex u outside the "cloud" we show the current best edge for pulling in u with a solid blue line. (Continued in Figure 12.16.)

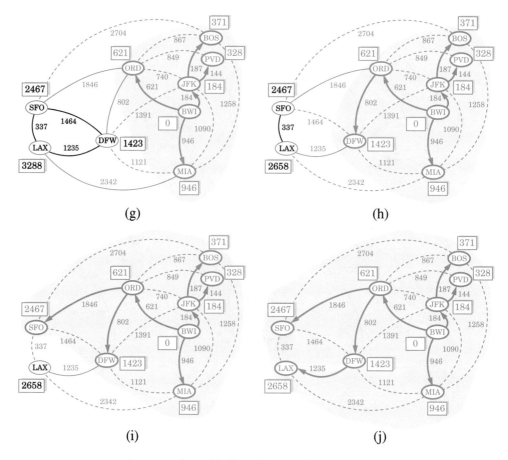

(g)

(h)

(i)

(j)

Figure 12.16: An execution of Dijkstra's algorithm. (Continued from Figure 12.15.)

Why It Works

The interesting, and possibly even a little surprising, aspect of the Dijkstra algorithm is that, at the moment a vertex u is pulled into C, its label $D[u]$ stores the correct length of a shortest path from v to u. Thus, when the algorithm terminates, it will have computed the shortest-path distance from v to every vertex of G. That is, it will have solved the single-source shortest path problem.

It is probably not immediately clear why Dijkstra's algorithm correctly finds the shortest path from the start vertex v to each other vertex u in the graph. Why is it that the distance from v to u is equal to the value of the label $D[u]$ at the time vertex u is pulled into the cloud C (which is also the time u is removed from the priority queue Q)? The answer to this question depends on there being no negative-weight edges in the graph, for it allows the greedy method to work correctly, as we show in the proposition that follows.

Proposition 12.23: *In Dijkstra's algorithm, whenever a vertex u is pulled into the cloud, the label D[u] is equal to d(v,u), the length of a shortest path from v to u.*

Justification: Suppose that $D[t] > d(v,t)$ for some vertex t in V, and let u be the *first* vertex the algorithm pulled into the cloud C (that is, removed from Q), such that $D[u] > d(v,u)$. There is a shortest path P from v to u (for otherwise $d(v,u) = +\infty = D[u]$). Let us therefore consider the moment when u is pulled into C, and let z be the first vertex of P (when going from v to u) that is not in C at this moment. Let y be the predecessor of z in path P (note that we could have $y = v$). (See Figure 12.17.) We know, by our choice of z, that y is already in C at this point. Moreover, $D[y] = d(v,y)$, since u is the *first* incorrect vertex. When y was pulled into C, we tested (and possibly updated) $D[z]$ so that we had, at that point,

$$D[z] \le D[y] + w((y,z)) = d(v,y) + w((y,z)).$$

But since z is the next vertex on the shortest path from v to u, this implies that

$$D[z] = d(v,z).$$

But we are now at the moment when we are picking u, not z, to join C; hence,

$$D[u] \le D[z].$$

It should be clear that a subpath of a shortest path is itself a shortest path. Hence, since z is on the shortest path from v to u,

$$d(v,z) + d(z,u) = d(v,u).$$

Moreover, $d(z,u) \ge 0$ because there are no negative-weight edges. Therefore,

$$D[u] \le D[z] = d(v,z) \le d(v,z) + d(z,u) = d(v,u).$$

But this contradicts the definition of u; hence, there can be no such vertex u. ∎

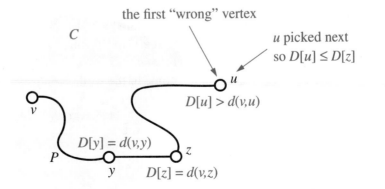

Figure 12.17: A schematic illustration for the justification of Proposition 12.23.

The Running Time of Dijkstra's Algorithm

In this section, we analyze the time complexity of Dijkstra's algorithm. We denote the number of vertices and edges of the input graph G with n and m respectively. We assume that the edge weights can be added and compared in constant time. Because of the high level of the description we gave for Dijkstra's algorithm in Code Fragment 12.13, analyzing its running time requires that we give more details on its implementation. Specifically, we should indicate the data structures used and how they are implemented.

Let us first assume that we are representing the graph G using an adjacency list structure. This data structure allows us to step through the vertices adjacent to u during the relaxation step in time proportional to their number. It still does not settle all the details for the algorithm, however, for we must say more about how to implement the other principle data structure in the algorithm—the priority queue Q.

An efficient implementation of the priority queue Q uses a heap (see Section 7.3). This allows us to extract the vertex u with smallest D label (call to the removeMin() function) in $O(\log n)$ time. As noted in the pseudo-code, each time we update a $D[z]$ label, we need to update the key of z in the priority queue. If Q is implemented as a heap, then this key update can, for example, be done by first removing and then inserting z with its new key. If our priority queue Q supports the locator pattern (see Section 7.4), then we can easily implement such key updates in $O(\log n)$ time, since a locator for vertex z would allow Q to have immediate access to the item storing z in the heap (see Section 7.4). Assuming this implementation of Q, Dijkstra's algorithm runs in $O((n+m)\log n)$ time.

Referring back to Code Fragment 12.13, the details of the running-time analysis are as follows:

- Inserting all the vertices in Q with their initial key value can be done in $O(n \log n)$ time by repeated insertions, or in $O(n)$ time using bottom-up heap construction (see Section 7.3.5).
- At each iteration of the **while** loop, we spend $O(\log n)$ time to remove vertex u from Q, and $O(\text{degree}(v)\log n)$ time to perform the relaxation procedure on the edges incident on u.
- The overall running time of the **while** loop is

$$\sum_{v \in G} (1 + \text{degree}(v)) \log n,$$

which is $O((n+m)\log n)$ by Proposition 12.6.

Note that if we wish to express the running time as a function of n only, then it is $O(n^2 \log n)$ in the worst case.

An Alternative Implementation for Dijkstra's Algorithm

Let us now consider an alternative implementation for the priority queue Q using an unsorted sequence. This, of course, requires that we spend $\Omega(n)$ time to extract the minimum element, but it allows for very fast key updates, provided Q supports the locator pattern (Section 7.4). Specifically, we can implement each key update done in a relaxation step in $O(1)$ time—we simply change the key value once we locate the item in Q to update. Hence, this implementation results in a running time that is $O(n^2 + m)$, which can be simplified to $O(n^2)$ since G is simple.

Comparing the Two Implementations

We have two choices for implementing the priority queue in Dijkstra's algorithm: a locator-based heap implementation, which yields $O((n+m)\log n)$ running time, and a locator-based unsorted sequence implementation, which yields an $O(n^2)$-time algorithm. Since both implementations would be fairly simple to code up, they are about equal in terms of the programming sophistication needed. These two implementations are also about equal in terms of the constant factors in their worst-case running times. Looking only at these worst-case times, we prefer the heap implementation when the number of edges in the graph is small (that is, when $m < n^2/\log n$), and we prefer the sequence implementation when the number of edges is large (that is, when $m > n^2/\log n$).

Proposition 12.24: *Given a simple undirected weighted graph G with n vertices and m edges, such that the weight of each edge is nonnegative, and a vertex v of G, Dijkstra's algorithm computes the distance from v to all other vertices of G in $O((n+m)\log n)$ worst-case time, or, alternatively, in $O(n^2)$ worst-case time.*

In Exercise R-12.16, we explore how to modify Dijkstra's algorithm to output a tree T rooted at v, such that the path in T from v to a vertex u is a shortest path in G from v to u.

Programming Dijkstra's Algorithm in C++

Having given a pseudo-code description of Dijkstra's algorithm, let us now present C++ code for performing Dijkstra's algorithm, assuming we are given an undirected graph with positive integer weights. We express the algorithm by means of a class Dijkstra (Code Fragments 12.15 and 12.16), which declares the function weight(e) to extract the weight of edge e. Class Dijkstra provides a constructor, which is given the graph, and it provides a function run(s), which runs Dijkstra's algorithm starting at the source vertex s.

The main computation of Dijkstra's algorithm is performed by function run(), given in Code Fragment 12.16. A priority queue Q, supporting locator-based functions (Section 7.4.1), is used to store the unprocessed vertices according to their distance from the source. We insert a vertex u into Q with function insert(), which returns the locator ℓ of u in Q. When edge relaxation is performed, the distance associated with a vertex may change to a new value d, and hence it is necessary to access this locator and perform replaceKey(ℓ, d), to inform the priority queue of the change in distance.

In order to access priority queue locators with each vertex, we "attach" to each vertex u its locator in Q. This is done using the decorator design pattern (Section 12.3.1). Recall that each decoration value is a pointer to an Object or one of its subtypes. For this reason we introduce a "class wrapper," called LocatorX shown in Code Fragment 12.14. It is derived from Object, and it stores a priority queue locator as its only data member. The actual locator value is obtained in getLoc() by extracting the attribute value, casting the resulting Object pointer to a pointer to LocatorX, and then calling the member function getValue() to access its value.

```
class LocatorX : public Object {            // PQ Locator wrapper
private:
    Locator loc;                            // the locator
public:
    LocatorX(const Locator& l)              // constructor
        { loc = l; }
    Locator getValue() const                // return its value
        { return loc; }
};
```

Code Fragment 12.14: Class LocatorX, which is used by Dijkstra to "wrap" a priority queue locator in a subtype of Object, so that it can be used as a vertex attribute. (See Code Fragment 12.15 and 12.16.)

In order to simplify access to vertex decorations and priority queue locators, we define a number of convenience functions. Functions setLoc(v) and getLoc(v) assign and retrieve a locator attribute to a vertex v, respectively. Similarly, setDist(v) sets the integer distance attribute associated with vertex v. Instead of using an additional data structure for the labels $D[u]$, we exploit the fact that $D[u]$ is the key of vertex u in Q, and thus $D[u]$ can be retrieved given the locator of u in Q. This online distance extraction is done in function getDist(ℓ).

After execution, each vertex of the graph is decorated with its distance from the source vertex s, using the label "dist." We use the polymorphic objects introduced in Section 12.3.1 for storing decorations. Thus, the distance to a vertex v can be extracted with v.get("dist")->intValue(). This offline distance extraction is done by the public function getDist(v).

```
template <typename Graph>
class Dijkstra {
protected:                                      // local types
  typedef typename Graph::Vertex        Vertex;
  // ... (other graph types omitted)
  typedef PriorityQueue::Locator        Locator;
  // ... (insert LocatorX here)
  enum { INFINITE = INT_MAX };                  // infinite weight
protected:                                      // member data
  const Graph&    graph;                        // the graph
  PriorityQueue   Q;                            // the priority queue
public:
  Dijkstra(const Graph& g) : graph(g) { }       // constructor
  int getDist(const Vertex& u) const            // final distance to u
    { return u.get("dist")->intValue(); }
protected:                                      // local utilities
  int weight(const Edge& e) const               // get edge weight
    { return e.get("weight")->intValue(); }
  void setDist(const Vertex& v, int d)          // set vertex distance
    { v.set("dist", new Integer(d)); }
  void setLoc(const Vertex& v, const Locator& loc)  // set v's locator
    { v.set("loc", new LocatorX(loc)); }
  bool hasLoc(const Vertex& v) const            // does v have locator?
    { return v.has("loc"); }
  Locator getLoc(const Vertex& v) const         // get v's locator
    { return dynamic_cast<LocatorX*>(v.get("loc"))->getValue(); }
  void destroyLoc(const Vertex& v) {            // remove locator attrib
    LocatorX* p = dynamic_cast<LocatorX*>(v.get("loc"));
    delete p;                                   // delete locator object
    v.destroy("loc");                           // delete attribute
  }
  Vertex getVertex(const Locator& loc) const    // get locator vertex
    { return loc.element(); }
  int getDist(const Locator& loc) const         // get vertex distance
    { return loc.key(); }
  // ... (insert run() here)
};
```

Code Fragment 12.15: Class Dijkstra implementing Dijkstra's algorithm. (Continued in Code Fragment 12.16.)

```
public:
  void run(const Vertex& s) {                            // run Dijkstra's alg
    VertexIterator vertices = graph.vertices();
    while (vertices.hasNext()) {                          // initialize vertices
      Vertex u = vertices.nextVertex();
      int u_dist = INFINITE;                             // distance = infinity
      if (u == s) u_dist = 0;                            // ...except source
      setDist(u, u_dist);
      Locator u_loc = Q.insertItem(u_dist, u);           // put vertex into Q
      setLoc(u, u_loc);                                  // save its locator
    }
    while (!Q.isEmpty()) {                               // main processing loop
      Locator  u_loc   = Q.min();                        // get closest vertex
      Vertex   u       = getVertex(u_loc);
      int      u_dist  = getDist(u_loc);                 // ...and its distance
      Q.remove(u_loc);                                   // remove it from Q
      setDist(u, u_dist);                                // set final distance
      destroyLoc(u);                                     // remove the locator
      if (u_dist == INFINITE) continue;                  // ignore if unreachable
      EdgeIterator edges = graph.incidentEdges(u);
      while (edges.hasNext()) {                          // visit u's neighbors
        Edge e = edges.nextEdge();
        Vertex z = graph.opposite(u,e);
        if (hasLoc(z)) {                                 // if z is not finished
          int      e_weight = weight(e);                 // get edge weight
          Locator  z_loc    = getLoc(z);
          int      z_dist   = getDist(z_loc);            // get distance to z
          if (u_dist + e_weight < z_dist)                // relaxation of (u,z)
            Q.replaceKey(z_loc, u_dist + e_weight);
        }
      }
    }
  }
}
```

Code Fragment 12.16: Function run() of class Dijkstra, which runs Dijkstra's algorithm starting at source vertex *s*. Although this function is long enough that it should be defined outside the class, we have left it in the class to simplify notation. (Continued from Code Fragment 12.15.)

12.7 Minimum Spanning Trees

Suppose we wish to connect all the computers in a new office building using the least amount of cable. We can model this problem using a weighted graph G whose vertices represent the computers, and whose edges represent all the possible pairs (u, v) of computers, where the weight $w((v, u))$ of edge (v, u) is equal to the amount of cable needed to connect computer v to computer u. Rather than computing a shortest path tree from some particular vertex v, we are interested in finding a (free) tree T that contains all the vertices of G and has the minimum total weight over all such trees instead. Methods for finding such a tree are the focus of this section.

Problem Definition

Given a weighted undirected graph G, we are interested in finding a tree T that contains all the vertices in G and minimizes the sum

$$w(T) = \sum_{(v,u) \in T} w((v, u)).$$

A tree such as this, that contains every vertex of a connected graph G, is said to be a ***spanning tree***, and the problem of computing a spanning tree T with smallest total weight is known as the ***minimum spanning tree*** (or ***MST***) problem.

The development of efficient algorithms for the minimum spanning tree problem predates the modern notion of computer science itself. In this section, we discuss two algorithms for solving the MST problem. These algorithms are all classic applications of the ***greedy method***, which, as was discussed briefly in the previous section, is based on choosing objects to join a growing collection by iteratively picking an object that minimizes some cost function. The first algorithm we discuss is Kruskal's algorithm, which "grows" the MST in clusters by considering edges in order of their weights. The second algorithm we discuss is the Prim-Jarník algorithm, which grows the MST from a single root vertex, much in the same way as Dijkstra's shortest-path algorithm.

As in Section 12.6.1, in order to simplify the description of the algorithms, we

Caution

assume, in the following, that the input graph G is undirected (that is, all its edges are undirected) and simple (that is, it has no self-loops and no parallel edges). Hence, we denote the edges of G as unordered vertex pairs (u, z).

Before we discuss the details of these algorithms, however, let us give a crucial fact about minimum spanning trees that forms the basis of the algorithms.

A Crucial Fact about Minimum Spanning Trees

The two MST algorithms we discuss are based on the greedy method, which, in this case, depends crucially on the following fact. (See Figure 12.18.)

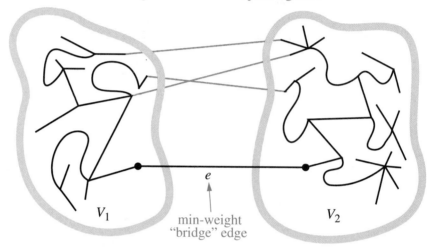

Figure 12.18: An illustration of the crucial fact about minimum spanning trees.

Proposition 12.25: *Let G be a weighted connected graph, and let V_1 and V_2 be a partition of the vertices of G into two disjoint nonempty sets. Furthermore, let e be an edge in G with minimum weight from among those with one endpoint in V_1 and the other in V_2. There is a minimum spanning tree T that has e as one of its edges.*

Justification: Let T be a minimum spanning tree of G. If T does not contain edge e, the addition of e to T must create a cycle. Therefore, there is some edge f of this cycle that has one endpoint in V_1 and the other in V_2. Moreover, by the choice of e, $w(e) \leq w(f)$. If we remove f from $T \cup \{e\}$, we obtain a spanning tree whose total weight is no more than before. Since T was a minimum spanning tree, this new tree must also be a minimum spanning tree.   ∎

In fact, if the weights in G are distinct, then the minimum spanning tree is unique. We leave the justification of this less crucial fact to an exercise (C-12.17). In addition, note that Proposition 12.25 remains valid even if the graph G contains negative-weight edges or negative-weight cycles, unlike the algorithms we presented for shortest paths.

12.7.1 Kruskal's Algorithm

The reason Proposition 12.25 is so important is that it can be used as the basis for building a minimum spanning tree. In Kruskal's algorithm, it is used to build the minimum spanning tree in clusters. Initially, each vertex is in its own cluster all by itself. The algorithm then considers each edge in turn, ordered by increasing weight. If an edge e connects two different clusters, then e is added to the set of edges of the minimum spanning tree, and the two clusters connected by e are merged into a single cluster. If, on the other hand, e connects two vertices that are already in the same cluster, then e is discarded. Once the algorithm has added enough edges to form a spanning tree, it terminates and outputs this tree as the minimum spanning tree.

We give pseudo-code for Kruskal's MST algorithm in Code Fragment 12.17 and we show the working of this algorithm in Figures 12.19, 12.20, and 12.21.

Algorithm Kruskal(G):

    Input: A simple connected weighted graph G with n vertices and m edges

    Output: A minimum spanning tree T for G

  for each vertex v in G **do**

    Define an elementary cluster $C(v) \leftarrow \{v\}$.

  Initialize a priority queue Q to contain all edges in G, using the weights as keys.

  $T \leftarrow \emptyset$ {T will ultimately contain the edges of the MST}

  while T has fewer than $n - 1$ edges **do**

    $(u, v) \leftarrow Q$.removeMin()

    Let $C(v)$ be the cluster containing v, and let $C(u)$ be the cluster containing u.

    if $C(v) \neq C(u)$ **then**

      Add edge (v, u) to T.

      Merge $C(v)$ and $C(u)$ into one cluster, that is, union $C(v)$ and $C(u)$.

  return tree T

      Code Fragment 12.17: Kruskal's algorithm for the MST problem.

As mentioned before, the correctness of Kruskal's algorithm follows from the crucial fact about minimum spanning trees, Proposition 12.25. Each time Kruskal's algorithm adds an edge (v, u) to the minimum spanning tree T, we can define a partitioning of the set of vertices V (as in the proposition) by letting V_1 be the cluster containing v and letting V_2 contain the rest of the vertices in V. This clearly defines a disjoint partitioning of the vertices of V and, more importantly, since we are extracting edges from Q in order by their weights, e must be a minimum-weight edge with one vertex in V_1 and the other in V_2. Thus, Kruskal's algorithm always adds a valid minimum spanning tree edge.

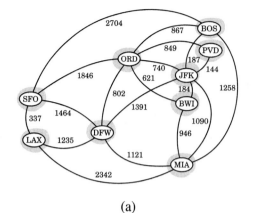
(a)

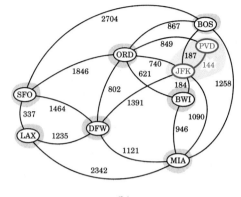
(b)

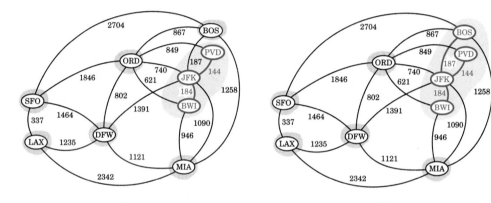
(c)

(d)

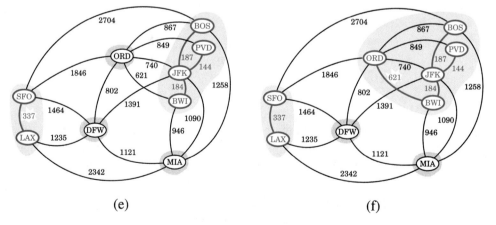
(e)

(f)

Figure 12.19: Example of an execution of Kruskal's MST algorithm on a graph with integer weights. We show the clusters as shaded regions and we highlight the edge being considered in each iteration. (Continued in Figure 12.20.)

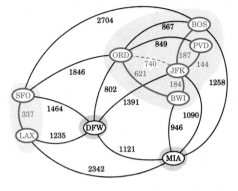

(g)

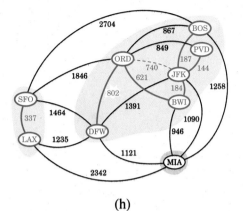

(h)

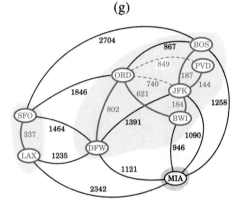

(i)

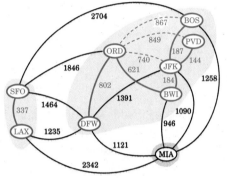

(j)

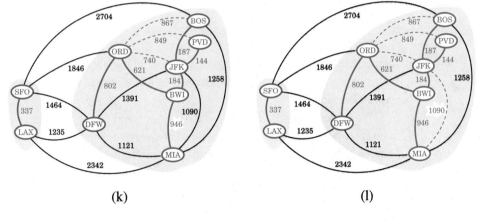

(k)

(l)

Figure 12.20: An example of an execution of Kruskal's MST algorithm. Rejected edges are shown dashed. (Continued from Figure 12.19.)

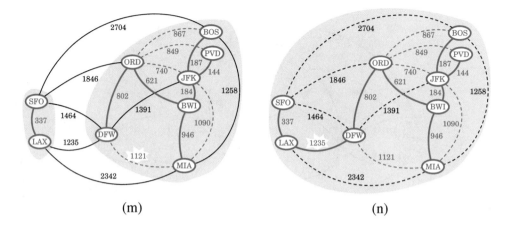

(m)   (n)

Figure 12.21: Example of an execution of Kruskal's MST algorithm. The edge considered in (n) merges the last two clusters, which concludes this execution of Kruskal's algorithm. (Continued from Figure 12.20.)

The Running Time of Kruskal's Algorithm

In this section, we analyze the time complexity of Kruskal's algorithm. We denote the number of vertices and edges of the input graph G with n and m, respectively. We assume that the edge weights can be compared in constant time. Because of the high level of the description we gave for Kruskal's algorithm in Code Fragment 12.17, analyzing its running time requires that we give more details on its implementation. Specifically, we should indicate the data structures used and how they are implemented.

We implement the priority queue Q using a heap. Thus, we can initialize Q in $O(m \log m)$ time by repeated insertions, or in $O(m)$ time using bottom-up heap construction (see Section 7.3.5). In addition, at each iteration of the **while** loop, we can remove a minimum-weight edge in $O(\log m)$ time, which actually is $O(\log n)$, since G is simple.

We represent each cluster C with an unordered list of vertices, which could, for example, be implemented with a linked list. Also, we store, with each vertex v, a reference to its cluster $C(v)$. With this representation, testing whether $C(u) \neq C(v)$ takes $O(1)$ time. When we need to merge two clusters, $C(u)$ and $C(v)$, we move the elements of the *smaller* cluster into the larger one and update the cluster references of the vertices in the smaller cluster. Since we can simply add the elements of the smaller cluster at the end of the list for the larger cluster, merging two clusters takes time proportional to the size of the smaller cluster. That is, merging clusters $C(u)$ and $C(v)$ takes $O(\min\{|C(u)|, |C(v)|\})$ time.

Proposition 12.26: *Consider an execution of Kruskal's algorithm on a graph with n vertices, where clusters are represented with sequences and with cluster references at each vertex. The total time spent merging clusters is $O(n\log n)$.*

Justification: We observe that each time a vertex is moved to a new cluster, the size of the cluster containing the vertex at least doubles. Let $t(v)$ be the number of times that vertex v is moved to a new cluster. Since the maximum cluster size is n,

$$t(v) \leq \log n.$$

The total time spent merging clusters in Kruskal's algorithm can be obtained by summing up the work done on each vertex, which is proportional to

$$\sum_{v \in G} t(v) \leq n\log n.$$

■

Using Proposition 12.26 and arguments similar to those used in the analysis of Dijkstra's algorithm, we conclude that the total running time of Kruskal's algorithm is $O((n+m)\log n)$, which can be simplified as $O(m\log n)$ since G is simple and connected.

Proposition 12.27: *Given a simple connected weighted graph G, with n vertices and m edges, Kruskal's algorithm constructs a minimum spanning tree for G in $O(m\log n)$ time.*

12.7.2   The Prim-Jarník Algorithm

In the Prim-Jarník algorithm, we grow a minimum spanning tree from a single cluster starting from some "root" vertex v. The main idea is similar to that of Dijkstra's algorithm. We begin with some vertex v, defining the initial "cloud" of vertices C. Then, in each iteration, we choose a minimum-weight edge $e = (v, u)$, connecting a vertex v in the cloud C to a vertex u outside of C. The vertex u is then brought into the cloud C and the process is repeated until a spanning tree is formed. Again, the crucial fact about minimum spanning trees comes to play, because, by always choosing the smallest-weight edge joining a vertex inside C to one outside C, we are assured of always adding a valid edge to the MST.

To efficiently implement this approach, we can take another cue from Dijkstra's algorithm. We maintain a label $D[u]$ for each vertex u outside the cloud C, so that $D[u]$ stores the weight of the best current edge for joining u to the cloud C. These

Algorithm PrimJarnik(*G*):

   Input: A weighted connected graph *G* with *n* vertices and *m* edges
   Output: A minimum spanning tree *T* for *G*

Pick any vertex *v* of *G*
$D[v] \leftarrow 0$
for each vertex $u \neq v$ **do**
   $D[u] \leftarrow +\infty$
Initialize $T \leftarrow \emptyset$.
Initialize a priority queue *Q* with an item $((u, \text{null}), D[u])$ for each vertex *u*, where
(u, null) is the element and $D[u])$ is the key.
while *Q* is not empty **do**
   $(u, e) \leftarrow Q.\text{removeMin}()$
   Add vertex *u* and edge *e* to *T*.
   for each vertex *z* adjacent to *u* such that *z* is in *Q* **do**
      {perform the relaxation procedure on edge (u, z)}
      if $w((u, z)) < D[z]$ **then**
         $D[z] \leftarrow w((u, z))$
         Change to $(z, (u, z))$ the element of vertex *z* in *Q*.
         Change to $D[z]$ the key of vertex *z* in *Q*.
return the tree *T*

Code Fragment 12.18: The Prim-Jarník algorithm for the MST problem.

labels allow us to reduce the number of edges that we must consider in deciding which vertex will be next to join the cloud. We give the pseudo-code in Code Fragment 12.18.

   Let *n* and *m* denote the number of vertices and edges of the input graph *G*, respectively. The implementation issues for the Prim-Jarník algorithm are similar to those for Dijkstra's algorithm. If we implement the priority queue *Q* as a heap that supports the locator-based priority queue functions (see Section 7.4), we can extract the vertex *u* in each iteration in $O(\log n)$ time. In addition, we can update each $D[z]$ value in $O(\log n)$ time, as well, which is a computation considered at most once for each edge (u, z). The other steps in each iteration can be implemented in constant time. Thus, the total running time is $O((n+m)\log n)$, which is $O(m\log n)$. Hence, we can summarize as follows:

Proposition 12.28: *Given a simple connected weighted graph G with n vertices and m edges, the Prim-Jarník algorithm constructs a minimum spanning tree for G in $O(m\log n)$ time.*

   We illustrate the Prim-Jarník algorithm in Figures 12.22 and 12.23.

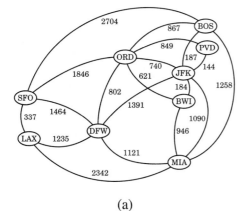
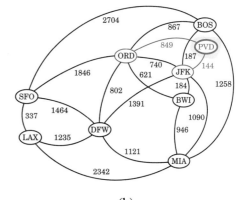

(a)

(b)

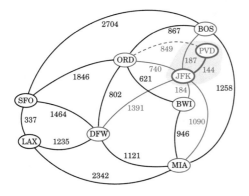
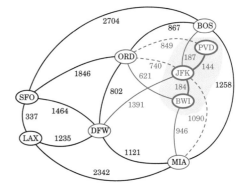

(c)

(d)

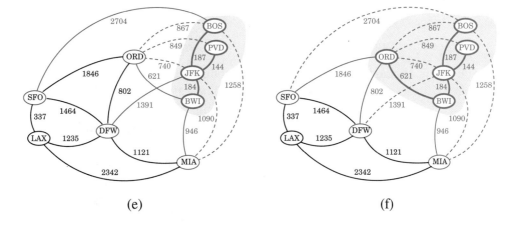

(e)

(f)

Figure 12.22: An illustration of the Prim-Jarník algorithm. (Continued in Figure 12.23.)

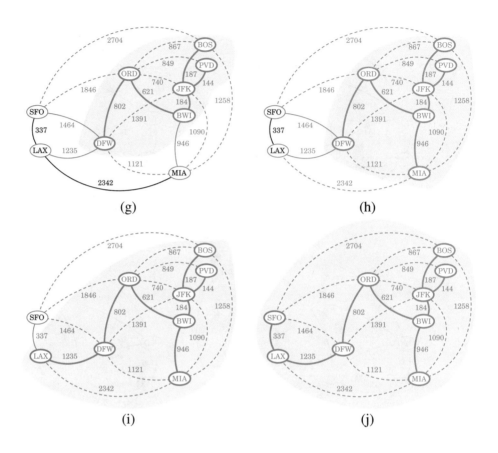

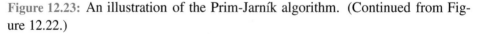

Figure 12.23: An illustration of the Prim-Jarník algorithm. (Continued from Figure 12.22.)

A Comparison of the Above MST Algorithms

Although each of the above algorithms for computing minimum spanning trees has the same worst-case running time, both algorithms have relatively small constant factors in their asymptotic running times. Each one achieves this running time using different data structures and different approaches to building the minimum spanning tree.

Concerning auxiliary data structures, Kruskal's algorithm uses a priority queue to store edges, and a collection of sets, implemented with lists, to store clusters. The Prim-Jarník algorithm uses only a priority queue, to store vertex-edge pairs. Thus, from an ease of programming viewpoint, the Prim-Jarník algorithm is preferable. Indeed, the Prim-Jarník algorithm is so similar to Dijkstra's algorithm that an implementation of Dijkstra's algorithm could be converted into an implementation for the Prim-Jarník algorithm without much effort.

12.8   Exercises

Reinforcement

R-12.1 Draw a simple undirected graph G that has 12 vertices, 18 edges, and 3 connected components. Why would it be impossible to draw G with 3 connected components if G had 66 edges?

R-12.2 Let G be a simple connected graph with n vertices and m edges. Explain why $O(\log m)$ is $O(\log n)$.

R-12.3 Draw a simple connected directed graph with 8 vertices and 16 edges, such that the in-degree and out-degree of each vertex is 2. Show that there is a single (nonsimple) cycle that includes all the edges of your graph, that is, you can trace all the edges in their respective directions without ever lifting your pencil. (Such a cycle is called an ***Euler tour***.)

R-12.4 Repeat the previous problem and then remove one edge from the graph. Show that now there is a single (nonsimple) path that includes all the edges of your graph. (Such a path is called an ***Euler path***.)

R-12.5 Bob loves foreign languages and wants to plan his course schedule for the following years. He is interested in the following nine language courses: LA15, LA16, LA22, LA31, LA32, LA126, LA127, LA141, and LA169. The course prerequisites are:

- LA15: (none)
- LA16: LA15
- LA22: (none)
- LA31: LA15
- LA32: LA16, LA31
- LA126: LA22, LA32
- LA127: LA16
- LA141: LA22, LA16
- LA169: LA32.

Find the sequence of courses that allows Bob to satisfy all the prerequisites.

R-12.6 Suppose we represent a graph G having n vertices and m edges with the edge list structure. Why, in this case, does the insertVertex() function run in $O(1)$ time while the removeVertex() function runs in $O(m)$ time?

R-12.7 Let *G* be a graph whose vertices are the integers 1 through 8, and let the adjacent vertices of each vertex be given by the table below:

vertex	adjacent vertices
1	(2, 3, 4)
2	(1, 3, 4)
3	(1, 2, 4)
4	(1, 2, 3, 6)
5	(6, 7, 8)
6	(4, 5, 7)
7	(5, 6, 8)
8	(5, 7)

Assume that, in a traversal of *G*, the adjacent vertices of a given vertex are returned in the same order as they are listed in the above table.

a. Draw *G*.
b. Give the sequence of vertices of *G* visited using a DFS traversal starting at vertex 1.
c. Give the sequence of vertices visited using a BFS traversal starting at vertex 1.

R-12.8 Would you use the adjacency list structure or the adjacency matrix structure in each of the following cases? Justify your choice.

a. The graph has 10,000 vertices and 20,000 edges, and it is important to use as little space as possible.
b. The graph has 10,000 vertices and 20,000,000 edges, and it is important to use as little space as possible.
c. You need to answer the query areAdjacent() as fast as possible, no matter how much space you use.

R-12.9 Explain why the DFS traversal runs in $\Theta(n^2)$ time on an *n*-vertex simple graph that is represented with the adjacency matrix structure.

R-12.10 Draw the transitive closure of the directed graph shown in Figure 12.2.

R-12.11 Compute a topological ordering for the directed graph drawn with solid edges in Figure 12.8d.

R-12.12 Can we use a queue instead of a stack as an auxiliary data structure in the topological sorting algorithm shown in Code Fragment 12.12?

R-12.13 Draw a simple, connected, weighted graph with 8 vertices and 16 edges, each with unique edge weights. Identify one vertex as a "start" vertex and illustrate a running of Dijkstra's algorithm on this graph.

R-12.14 Show how to modify the pseudo-code for Dijkstra's algorithm for the case when the graph may contain parallel edges and self-loops.

R-12.15 Show how to modify the pseudo-code for Dijkstra's algorithm for the case when the graph is directed and we want to compute shortest **directed paths** from the source vertex to all the other vertices.

R-12.16 Show how to modify the pseudo-code for Dijkstra's algorithm to not only output the distance from v to each vertex in G, but also to output a tree T rooted at v, such that the path in T from v to a vertex u is actually a shortest path in G from v to u.

R-12.17 There are eight small islands in a lake, and the state wants to build seven bridges to connect them so that each island can be reached from any other one via one or more bridges. The cost of constructing a bridge is proportional to its length. The distances between pairs of islands are given in the following table.

	1	2	3	4	5	6	7	8
1	-	240	210	340	280	200	345	120
2	-	-	265	175	215	180	185	155
3	-	-	-	260	115	350	435	195
4	-	-	-	-	160	330	295	230
5	-	-	-	-	-	360	400	170
6	-	-	-	-	-	-	175	205
7	-	-	-	-	-	-	-	305
8	-	-	-	-	-	-	-	-

Find which bridges to build so that the total construction cost is minimum.

R-12.18 Draw a simple, connected, undirected, weighted graph with 8 vertices and 16 edges, each with unique edge weights. Illustrate the execution of Kruskal's algorithm on this graph. (Note that there is only one minimum spanning tree for this graph.)

R-12.19 Repeat the previous problem for the Prim-Jarník algorithm.

R-12.20 Consider the unsorted sequence implementation of the priority queue Q used in Dijkstra's algorithm. What is, in this case, the best-case running time of Dijkstra's algorithm $\Omega(n^2)$ on an n-vertex graph? (Hint: Consider the size of Q each time the minimum element is extracted.)

R-12.21 Describe the meaning of the graphical conventions used in Figure 12.6 illustrating a DFS traversal. What do the colors blue and black refer to? What do the arrows signify? How about thick lines and dashed lines?

R-12.22 Repeat Exercise R-12.21 for Figure 12.7 illustrating a BFS traversal.

R-12.23 Repeat Exercise R-12.21 for Figure 12.9 illustrating a directed DFS traversal.

R-12.24 Repeat Exercise R-12.21 for Figure 12.10 illustrating the Floyd-Warshall algorithm.

R-12.25 Repeat Exercise R-12.21 for Figure 12.12 illustrating the topological sorting algorithm.

R-12.26 Repeat Exercise R-12.21 for Figures 12.15 and 12.16 illustrating Dijkstra's algorithm.

R-12.27 Repeat Exercise R-12.21 for Figures 12.19 and 12.21 illustrating Kruskal's algorithm.

R-12.28 Repeat Exercise R-12.21 for Figures 12.22 and 12.23 illustrating the Prim-Jarník algorithm.

Creativity

C-12.1 Justify Proposition 12.11.

C-12.2 Describe the details of an $O(n+m)$-time algorithm for computing **all** the connected components of an undirected graph G with n vertices and m edges.

C-12.3 Let T be the spanning tree rooted at the start vertex produced by the depth-first search of a connected, undirected graph G. Argue why every edge of G, not in T, goes from a vertex in T to one of its ancestors, that is, it is a **back edge**.   (Hint: Suppose that such a nontree edge is a cross edge, and argue, based upon the order the DFS visits the end vertices of this edge.)

C-12.4 Suppose we wish to represent an n-vertex graph G using the edge list structure, assuming that we identify the vertices with the integers in the set $\{0, 1, \ldots, n-1\}$. Describe how to implement the container E to support $O(\log n)$-time performance for the areAdjacent() function. How are you implementing the function in this case?

C-12.5 Tamarindo University and many other schools worldwide are doing a joint project on multimedia. A computer network is built to connect these schools using communication links that form a free tree. The schools decide to install a file server at one of the schools to share data among all the schools. Since the transmission time on a link is dominated by the link setup and synchronization, the cost of a data transfer is proportional to the number of links used. Hence, it is desirable to choose a "central" location for the file server. Given a free tree T and a node v of T, the *eccentricity* of v is the length of a longest path from v to any other node of T. A node of T with minimum eccentricity is called a *center* of T.

    a. Design an efficient algorithm that, given an n-node free tree T, computes a center of T.

    b. Is the center unique? If not, how many distinct centers can a free tree have?

C-12.6 Show that, if T is a BFS tree produced for a connected graph G, then, for each vertex v at level i, the path of T between s and v has i edges, and any other path of G between s and v has at least i edges. (Hint: Justify this by induction on the length of a shortest path from the start vertex.)

C-12.7 The time delay of a long-distance call can be determined by multiplying a small fixed constant by the number of communication links on the telephone network between the caller and callee. Suppose the telephone network of a company named RT&T is a free tree. The engineers of RT&T want to compute the maximum possible time delay that may be experienced in a long-distance call. Given a free tree T, the *diameter* of T is the length of a longest path between two nodes of T. Give an efficient algorithm for computing the diameter of T.

C-12.8 A company named RT&T has a network of n switching stations connected by m high-speed communication links. Each customer's phone is directly connected to one station in his or her area. RT&T has developed a prototype video-phone system that allows two customers to see each other during a phone call. In order to have acceptable image quality, however, the number of links used to transmit video signals between the two parties cannot exceed four. Suppose that RT&T's network is represented by a graph. Design an efficient algorithm that computes, for each station, the set of stations it can reach using no more than four links.

C-12.9 Explain why there are no forward nontree edges with respect to a BFS tree constructed for a directed graph. (Hint: Suppose there is such an edge and show why it would not be a nontree edge.)

C-12.10 An independent set of an undirected graph $G = (V, E)$ is a subset I of V, such that no two vertices in I are adjacent. That is, if $u, v \in I$, then $(u, v) \notin E$. A ***maximal independent set*** M is an independent set, such that, if we were to add any additional vertex to M, then it would not be independent any more. Every graph has a maximal independent set. (Can you see this? This question is not part of the exercise, but it is worth thinking about.) Give an efficient algorithm that computes a maximal independent set for a graph G. What is this method's running time?

C-12.11 An ***Euler tour*** of a directed graph $\vec{G}$ with n vertices and m edges is a cycle that traverses each edge of $\vec{G}$ exactly once according to its direction. Such a tour always exists if $\vec{G}$ is connected and the in-degree equals the out-degree of each vertex in $\vec{G}$. Describe an $O(n+m)$-time algorithm for finding an Euler tour of such a digraph $\vec{G}$.

C-12.12 Let G be an undirected graph G with n vertices and m edges. Describe an $O(n+m)$-time algorithm for traversing each edge of G exactly once in each direction.

C-12.13 Justify Proposition 12.14.

C-12.14 Give an example of an n-vertex simple graph G that causes Dijkstra's algorithm to run in $\Omega(n^2 \log n)$ time when its implemented with a heap for the priority queue.

C-12.15 Give an example of a weighted directed graph $\vec{G}$ with negative-weight edges, but no negative-weight cycle, such that Dijkstra's algorithm incorrectly computes the shortest-path distances from some start vertex v.

C-12.16 Consider the following greedy strategy for finding a shortest path from vertex ***start*** to vertex ***goal*** in a given connected graph.

> 1: Initialize ***path*** to ***start***.
> 2: Initialize ***VisitedVertices*** to {***start***}.
> 3: If ***start=goal***, return ***path*** and exit. Otherwise, continue.
> 4: Find the edge (***start,v***) of minimum weight such that ***v*** is adjacent to ***start*** and ***v*** is not in ***VisitedVertices***.
> 5: Add ***v*** to ***path***.
> 6: Add ***v*** to ***VisitedVertices***.
> 7: Set ***start*** equal to ***v*** and go to step 3.

Does this greedy strategy always find a shortest path from ***start*** to ***goal***? Either explain intuitively why it works, or give a counter example.

C-12.17 Show that, if all the weights in a connected weighted graph G are distinct, then there is exactly one minimum spanning tree for G.

C-12.18 Design an efficient algorithm for finding a ***longest*** directed path from a vertex s to a vertex t of an acyclic weighted digraph $\vec{G}$. Specify the graph representation used and any auxiliary data structures used. Also, analyze the time complexity of your algorithm.

C-12.19 Suppose you are given a diagram of a telephone network, which is a graph G whose vertices represent switching centers, and whose edges represent communication lines between two centers. The edges are marked by their bandwidth. The bandwidth of a path is the bandwidth of its lowest bandwidth edge. Give an algorithm that, given a diagram and two switching centers a and b, will output the maximum bandwidth of a path between a and b.

C-12.20 NASA wants to link n stations spread over the country using communication channels. Each pair of stations has a different bandwidth available, which is a known *a priori*. NASA wants to select $n-1$ channels (the minimum possible) in such a way that all the stations are linked by the channels and the total bandwidth (defined as the sum of the individual bandwidths of the channels) is maximum. Give an efficient algorithm for this problem and determine its worst-case time complexity. Consider the weighted graph $G = (V, E)$, where V is the set of stations and E is the set of channels between the stations. Define the weight $w(e)$ of an edge $e \in E$ as the bandwidth of the corresponding channel.

C-12.21 Suppose you are given a ***timetable***, which consists of:

- A set $\mathcal{A}$ of n airports, and for each airport $a \in \mathcal{A}$, a minimum connecting time $c(a)$
- A set $\mathcal{F}$ of m flights, and the following, for each flight $f \in \mathcal{A}$:
  - Origin airport $a_1(f) \in \mathcal{A}$
  - Destination airport $a_2(f) \in \mathcal{A}$
  - Departure time $t_1(f)$
  - Arrival time $t_2(f)$.

Describe an efficient algorithm for the flight scheduling problem. In this problem, we are given airports a and b, and a time t, and we wish to compute a sequence of flights that allows one to arrive at the earliest possible time in b when departing from a at or after time t. Minimum connecting times at intermediate airports should be observed. What is the running time of your algorithm as a function of n and m?

C-12.22 Let $\vec{G}$ be a weighted digraph with n vertices. Design a variation of Floyd-Warshall's algorithm for computing the lengths of the shortest paths from every vertex to every other vertex. Your algorithm should run in $O(n^3)$ time.

C-12.23 As your reward for saving the Kingdom of Bigfunnia from the evil monster, "Exponential Asymptotic," the king has given you the opportunity to earn a big reward. Behind the castle there is a maze, and along each corridor of the maze there is a bag of gold coins. The amount of gold in each bag varies. You will be given the opportunity to walk through the maze, picking up bags of gold. You may enter only through the door marked "ENTER" and exit through the door marked "EXIT." (These are distinct doors.) While in the maze you may not retrace your steps. Each corridor of the maze has an arrow painted on the wall. You may only go down the corridor in the direction of the arrow. There is no way to traverse a "loop" in the maze. You will receive a map of the maze, including the amount of gold in and the direction of each corridor. Describe an algorithm to help you pick up the most gold.

C-12.24 Suppose we are given a directed graph $\vec{G}$ with n vertices, and let M be the $n \times n$ adjacency matrix corresponding to $\vec{G}$.

    a. Let the product of M with itself (M^2) be defined for $1 \leq i, j \leq n$, as follows:

$$M^2(i, j) = M(i, 1) \odot M(1, j) \oplus \cdots \oplus M(i, n) \odot M(n, j),$$

    where "$\oplus$" is the Boolean **or** operator and "$\odot$" is Boolean **and**. Given this definition, what does $M^2(i, j) = 1$ imply about the vertices i and j? What if $M^2(i, j) = 0$?

    b. Suppose M^4 is the product of M^2 with itself. What do the entries of M^4 signify? How about the entries of $M^5 = (M^4)(M)$? In general, what information is contained in the matrix M^p?

    c. Now suppose that $\vec{G}$ is weighted and assume the following:

      1: for $1 \leq i \leq n, M(i, i) = 0$.
      2: for $1 \leq i, j \leq n, M(i, j) = weight(i, j)$ if $(i, j) \in E$.
      3: for $1 \leq i, j \leq n, M(i, j) = \infty$ if $(i, j) \notin E$.

    Also, let M^2 be defined, for $1 \leq i, j \leq n$, as follows:

$$M^2(i, j) = \min\{M(i, 1) + M(1, j), \ldots, M(i, n) + M(n, j)\}.$$

    If $M^2(i, j) = k$, what may we conclude about the relationship between vertices i and j?

Projects

P-12.1 Write a class implementing a simplified graph ADT that has only functions relevant to undirected graphs and does not include update functions, using the adjacency matrix structure. Your class should include a constructor method that takes two containers (for example, sequences)—a container V of vertex elements and a container E of pairs of vertex elements—and produces the graph G that these two containers represent.

P-12.2 Implement the simplified graph ADT described in Project P-12.1, using the adjacency list structure.

P-12.3 Implement the simplified graph ADT described in Project P-12.1, using the edge list structure.

P-12.4 Extend the class of Project P-12.2 to support update functions.

P-12.5 Extend the class of Project P-12.2 to support all the functions of the graph ADT (including functions for directed edges).

P-12.6 Implement a generic BFS traversal using the template method pattern.

P-12.7 Implement the topological sorting algorithm.

P-12.8 Implement the Floyd-Warshall transitive closure algorithm.

P-12.9 Design an experimental comparison of repeated DFS traversals versus the Floyd-Warshall algorithm for computing the transitive closure of a digraph.

P-12.10 Implement Kruskal's algorithm assuming that the edge weights are integers.

P-12.11 Implement the Prim-Jarník algorithm assuming that the edge weights are integers.

P-12.12 Perform an experimental comparison of two of the minimum spanning tree algorithms discussed in this chapter (Kruskal and Prim-Jarník). Develop an extensive set of experiments to test the running times of these algorithms using randomly generated graphs.

Chapter Notes

The depth-first search method is a part of the "folklore" of computer science, but Hopcroft and Tarjan [48, 96] are the ones who showed how useful this algorithm is for solving several different graph problems. Knuth [58] discusses the topological sorting problem. The simple linear-time algorithm that we describe for determining if a directed graph is strongly connected is due to Kosaraju. The Floyd-Warshall algorithm appears in a paper by Floyd [34] and is based upon a theorem of Warshall [102]. The mark-sweep garbage collection method we describe is one of many different algorithms for performing garbage collection. We encourage the reader interested in further study of garbage collection to examine the book by Jones [53]. To learn about different algorithms for drawing graphs, please see the book chapter by Tamassia [94], the annotated bibliography of Di Battista *et al.* [28], or the book by Di Battista *et al.* [29]. The first known minimum spanning tree algorithm is due to Barůvka [9], and was published in 1926. The Prim-Jarník algorithm was first published in Czech by Jarník [52] in 1930 and in English in 1957 by Prim [87]. Kruskal published his minimum spanning tree algorithm in 1956 [62]. The reader interested in further study of the history of the minimum spanning tree problem is referred to the paper by Graham and Hell [43]. The current asymptotically fastest minimum spanning tree algorithm is a randomized method of Karger, Klein, and Tarjan [54] that runs in $O(m)$ expected time.

Dijkstra [30] published his single-source, shortest path algorithm in 1959. The reader interested in further study of graph algorithms is referred to the books by Ahuja, Magnanti, and Orlin [6], Cormen, Leiserson, and Rivest [25], Even [32], Gibbons [38], Mehlhorn [75], and Tarjan [97], and the book chapter by van Leeuwen [99]. Incidentally, the running time for the Prim-Jarník algorithm, and also that of Dijkstra's algorithm, can actually be improved to be $O(n \log n + m)$ by implementing the queue Q with either of two more sophisticated data structures, the "Fibonacci Heap" [36] or the "Relaxed Heap" [31]. The reader interested in these implementations is referred to the papers that describe the implementation of these structures, and how they can be applied to the shortest-path and minimum spanning tree problems.

Appendix

Useful Mathematical Facts

In this appendix we give several useful mathematical facts. We begin with some combinatorial definitions and facts.

Logarithms and Exponents

The logarithm function is defined as

$$\log_b a = c \qquad \text{if} \qquad a = b^c.$$

The following identities hold for logarithms and exponents:

1. $\log_b ac = \log_b a + \log_b c$
2. $\log_b a/c = \log_b a - \log_b c$
3. $\log_b a^c = c \log_b a$
4. $\log_b a = (\log_c a)/\log_c b$
5. $b^{\log_c a} = a^{\log_c b}$
6. $(b^a)^c = b^{ac}$
7. $b^a b^c = b^{a+c}$
8. $b^a/b^c = b^{a-c}$

In addition, we have the following:

Proposition A.1: *If $a > 0$, $b > 0$, and $c > a + b$, then*

$$\log a + \log b \leq 2\log c - 2.$$

The **_natural logarithm_** function $\ln x = \log_e x$, where $e = 2.71828\ldots$, is the value of the following progression:

$$e = 1 + \frac{1}{1!} + \frac{1}{2!} + \frac{1}{3!} + \cdots.$$

In addition,

$$e^x = 1 + \frac{x}{1!} + \frac{x^2}{2!} + \frac{x^3}{3!} + \cdots$$

$$\ln(1 + x) = x - \frac{x^2}{2!} + \frac{x^3}{3!} - \frac{x^4}{4!} + \cdots.$$

There are a number of useful inequalities relating to these functions (which derive from these definitions).

Proposition A.2: *If* $x > -1$,

$$\frac{x}{1+x} \le \ln(1+x) \le x.$$

Proposition A.3: *For* $0 \le x < 1$,

$$1 + x \le e^x \le \frac{1}{1-x}.$$

Proposition A.4: *For any two positive real numbers* x *and* n,

$$\left(1 + \frac{x}{n}\right)^n \le e^x \le \left(1 + \frac{x}{n}\right)^{n+x/2}.$$

Integer Functions and Relations

The "floor" and "ceiling" functions are defined respectively as follows:

1. $\lfloor x \rfloor$ = the largest integer less than or equal to x.
2. $\lceil x \rceil$ = the smallest integer greater than or equal to x.

The **modulus** function is defined for integers $a \ge 0$ and $b > 0$ as

$$a \bmod b = a - \left\lfloor \frac{a}{b} \right\rfloor b.$$

The **factorial** function is defined as

$$n! = 1 \cdot 2 \cdot 3 \cdot \cdots \cdot (n-1)n.$$

The binomial coefficient is

$$\binom{n}{k} = \frac{n!}{k!(n-k)!},$$

which is equal to the number of different **combinations** one can define by choosing k different items from a collection of n items (where the order does not matter). The name "binomial coefficient" derives from the **binomial expansion**:

$$(a+b)^n = \sum_{k=0}^{n} \binom{n}{k} a^k b^{n-k}.$$

We also have the following relationships.

Proposition A.5: *If* $0 \le k \le n$, *then*

$$\left(\frac{n}{k}\right)^k \le \binom{n}{k} \le \frac{n^k}{k!}.$$

Proposition A.6 (Stirling's Approximation):

$$n! = \sqrt{2\pi n} \left(\frac{n}{e}\right)^n \left(1 + \frac{1}{12n} + \varepsilon(n)\right),$$

where $\varepsilon(n)$ *is* $O(1/n^2)$.

The ***Fibonacci progression*** is a numeric progression such that $F_0 = 0$, $F_1 = 1$, and $F_n = F_{n-1} + F_{n-2}$ for $n \ge 2$.

Proposition A.7: *If* F_n *is defined by the Fibonacci progression, then* F_n *is* $\Theta(g^n)$, *where* $g = (1 + \sqrt{5})/2$ *is the so-called* **golden ratio**.

Summations

There are a number of useful facts about summations.

Proposition A.8: *Factoring summations:*

$$\sum_{i=1}^{n} af(i) = a \sum_{i=1}^{n} f(i),$$

provided a *does not depend upon* i.

Proposition A.9: *Reversing the order:*

$$\sum_{i=1}^{n} \sum_{j=1}^{m} f(i,j) = \sum_{j=1}^{m} \sum_{i=1}^{n} f(i,j).$$

One special form of summation is a ***telescoping sum***:

$$\sum_{i=1}^{n} (f(i) - f(i-1)) = f(n) - f(0),$$

which arises often in the amortized analysis of a data structure or algorithm.

The following are some other facts about summations that arise often in the analysis of data structures and algorithms.

Proposition A.10:

$$\sum_{i=1}^{n} i = \frac{n(n+1)}{2}.$$

Proposition A.11:

$$\sum_{i=1}^{n} i^2 = \frac{n(n+1)(2n+1)}{6}.$$

Proposition A.12: *If $k \geq 1$ is an integer constant, then*

$$\sum_{i=1}^{n} i^k \text{ is } \Theta(n^{k+1}).$$

Another common summation is the **geometric sum**

$$\sum_{i=0}^{n} a^i,$$

for any fixed real number $0 < a \neq 1$.

Proposition A.13:

$$\sum_{i=0}^{n} a^i = \frac{1 - a^{n+1}}{1 - a}$$

for any real number $0 < a \neq 1$.

Proposition A.14:

$$\sum_{i=0}^{\infty} a^i = \frac{1}{1 - a}$$

for any real number $0 < a < 1$.

There is also a combination of the two common forms, called the **linear exponential** summation, which has the following expansion:

Proposition A.15: *For $0 < a \neq 1$, and $n \geq 2$,*

$$\sum_{i=1}^{n} ia^i = \frac{a - (n+1)a^{(n+1)} + na^{(n+2)}}{(1 - a)^2}.$$

The nth **harmonic number** H_n is defined as

$$H_n = \sum_{i=1}^{n} \frac{1}{i}.$$

Proposition A.16: *If H_n is the nth harmonic number, then H_n is $\ln n + \Theta(1)$.*

Basic Probability

We review some basic facts from probability theory. The most basic is that any statement about a probability is defined upon a *sample space* S, which is defined as the set of all possible outcomes from some experiment. We leave the terms "outcomes" and "experiment" undefined in any formal sense.

Example A.17: *Consider an experiment that consists of the outcome from flipping a coin five times. This sample space has 2^5 different outcomes, one for each different ordering of possible flips that can occur.*

Sample spaces can also be infinite, as the following example illustrates.

Example A.18: *Consider an experiment that consists of flipping a coin until it comes up heads. This sample space is infinite, with each outcome being a sequence of i tails followed by a single flip that comes up heads, for $i \in \{1, 2, 3, \ldots\}$.*

A *probability space* is a sample space S together with a probability function Pr that maps subsets of S to real numbers in the interval $[0, 1]$. It mathematically captures the notion of the probability of certain "events" occurring. Formally, each subset A of S is called an *event*, and the probability function Pr is assumed to possess the following basic properties with respect to events defined from S:

1. $\Pr(\emptyset) = 0$.
2. $\Pr(S) = 1$.
3. $0 \leq \Pr(A) \leq 1$, for any $A \subseteq S$.
4. If $A, B \subseteq S$ and $A \cap B = \emptyset$, then $\Pr(A \cup B) = \Pr(A) + \Pr(B)$.

Two events A and B are *independent* if

$$\Pr(A \cap B) = \Pr(A) \cdot \Pr(B).$$

A collection of events $\{A_1, A_2, \ldots, A_n\}$ is *mutually independent* if

$$\Pr(A_{i_1} \cap A_{i_2} \cap \cdots \cap A_{i_k}) = \Pr(A_{i_1}) \Pr(A_{i_2}) \cdots \Pr(A_{i_k}).$$

for any subset $\{A_{i_1}, A_{i_2}, \ldots, A_{i_k}\}$.

The *conditional probability* that an event A occurs, given an event B, is denoted as $\Pr(A|B)$, and is defined as the ratio

$$\frac{\Pr(A \cap B)}{\Pr(B)},$$

assuming that $\Pr(B) > 0$.

An elegant way for dealing with events is in terms of **random variables**. Intuitively, random variables are variables whose values depend upon the outcome of some experiment. Formally, a **random variable** is a function X that maps outcomes from some sample space S to real numbers. An **indicator random variable** is a random variable that maps outcomes to the set $\{0,1\}$. Often, in data structure and algorithm analysis, we use a random variable X to characterize the running time of a randomized algorithm. In this case, the sample space S is defined by all possible outcomes of the random sources used in the algorithm.

We are most interested in the typical, average, or "expected" value of such a random variable. The **expected value** of a random variable X is defined as

$$\mathbf{E}(X) = \sum_x x \Pr(X = x),$$

where the summation is defined over the range of X (which in this case is assumed to be discrete).

Proposition A.19 (The Linearity of Expectation): *Let X and Y be two arbitrary random variables. Then*

$$\mathbf{E}(X + Y) = \mathbf{E}(X) + \mathbf{E}(Y).$$

Example A.20: *Let X be a random variable that assigns the outcome of the roll of two fair dice to the sum of the number of dots showing. Then $\mathbf{E}(X) = 7$.*

Justification: *To justify this claim, let X_1 and X_2 be random variables corresponding to the number of dots on each die. Thus, $X_1 = X_2$ (i.e., they are two instances of the same function) and $\mathbf{E}(X) = \mathbf{E}(X_1 + X_2) = \mathbf{E}(X_1) + \mathbf{E}(X_2)$. Each outcome of the roll of a fair die occurs with probability $1/6$. Thus*

$$\mathbf{E}(X_i) = \frac{1}{6} + \frac{2}{6} + \frac{3}{6} + \frac{4}{6} + \frac{5}{6} + \frac{6}{6} = \frac{7}{2},$$

for $i = 1, 2$. Therefore, $E(X) = 7$. ∎

Two random variables X and Y are **independent** if

$$\Pr(X = x | Y = y) = \Pr(X = x),$$

for all real numbers x and y.

Proposition A.21: *If two random variables X and Y are independent, then*

$$\mathbf{E}(XY) = \mathbf{E}(X)\mathbf{E}(Y).$$

Example A.22: *Let X be a random variable that assigns the outcome of a roll of two fair dice to the product of the number of dots showing. Then $E(X) = 49/4$.*

Justification: Let X_1 and X_2 be random variables denoting the number of dots on each die. The variables X_1 and X_2 are clearly independent; hence

$$E(X) = E(X_1 X_2) = E(X_1)E(X_2) = (7/2)^2 = 49/4.$$

∎

Useful Mathematical Techniques

To determine whether a function is little-oh or little-omega of another, it is sometimes helpful to apply the following rule.

Proposition A.23 (L'Hôpital's Rule): *If we have $\lim_{n \to \infty} f(n) = +\infty$ and we have $\lim_{n \to \infty} g(n) = +\infty$, then $\lim_{n \to \infty} f(n)/g(n) = \lim_{n \to \infty} f'(n)/g'(n)$, where $f'(n)$ and $g'(n)$ denote the derivatives of $f(n)$ and $g(n)$ respectively.*

In deriving an upper or lower bound for a summation, it is often useful to *split a summation* as follows:

$$\sum_{i=1}^{n} f(i) = \sum_{i=1}^{j} f(i) + \sum_{i=j+1}^{n} f(i).$$

Another useful technique is to **bound a sum by an integral**. If f is a nondecreasing function, then, assuming the following terms are defined,

$$\int_{a-1}^{b} f(x)\,dx \leq \sum_{i=a}^{b} f(i) \leq \int_{a}^{b+1} f(x)\,dx.$$

There is a general form of recurrence relation that arises in the analysis of divide-and-conquer algorithms:

$$T(n) = aT(n/b) + f(n),$$

for constants $a \geq 1$ and $b > 1$.

Proposition A.24: *Let $T(n)$ be defined as above. Then*

1. *If $f(n)$ is $O(n^{\log_b a - \varepsilon})$, for some constant $\varepsilon > 0$, then $T(n)$ is $\Theta(n^{\log_b a})$.*
2. *If $f(n)$ is $\Theta(n^{\log_b a} \log^k n)$, for a fixed nonnegative integer $k \geq 0$, then $T(n)$ is $\Theta(n^{\log_b a} \log^{k+1} n)$.*
3. *If $f(n)$ is $\Omega(n^{\log_b a + \varepsilon})$, for some constant $\varepsilon > 0$, and if $af(n/b) \leq cf(n)$, then $T(n)$ is $\Theta(f(n))$.*

This proposition is known as the ***master method*** for characterizing divide-and-conquer recurrence relations asymptotically.

Bibliography

[1] G. M. Adel'son-Vel'skii and Y. M. Landis, "An algorithm for the organization of information," *Doklady Akademii Nauk SSSR*, vol. 146, pp. 263–266, 1962. English translation in *Soviet Math. Dokl.*, **3**, 1259–1262.

[2] A. Aggarwal and J. S. Vitter, "The input/output complexity of sorting and related problems," *Commun. ACM*, vol. 31, pp. 1116–1127, 1988.

[3] A. V. Aho, "Algorithms for finding patterns in strings," in *Handbook of Theoretical Computer Science* (J. van Leeuwen, ed.), vol. A. Algorithms and Complexity, pp. 255–300, Amsterdam: Elsevier, 1990.

[4] A. V. Aho, J. E. Hopcroft, and J. D. Ullman, *The Design and Analysis of Computer Algorithms*. Reading, MA: Addison-Wesley, 1974.

[5] A. V. Aho, J. E. Hopcroft, and J. D. Ullman, *Data Structures and Algorithms*. Reading, MA: Addison-Wesley, 1983.

[6] R. K. Ahuja, T. L. Magnanti, and J. B. Orlin, *Network Flows: Theory, Algorithms, and Applications*. Englewood Cliffs, NJ: Prentice Hall, 1993.

[7] K. Arnold and J. Gosling, *The Java Programming Language*. The Java Series, Reading, Mass.: Addison-Wesley, 1996.

[8] R. Baeza-Yates and B. Ribeiro-Neto, *Modern Information Retrieval*. Reading, Mass.: Addison-Wesley, 1999.

[9] O. Baruvka, "O jistem problemu minimalnim," *Praca Moravske Prirodovedecke Spolecnosti*, vol. 3, pp. 37–58, 1926. (in Czech).

[10] R. Bayer, "Symmetric binary B-trees: Data structure and maintenance," *Acta Informatica*, vol. 1, no. 4, pp. 290–306, 1972.

[11] R. Bayer and McCreight, "Organization of large ordered indexes," *Acta Inform.*, vol. 1, pp. 173–189, 1972.

[12] J. L. Bentley, "Programming pearls: Writing correct programs," *Communications of the ACM*, vol. 26, pp. 1040–1045, 1983.

[13] J. L. Bentley, "Programming pearls: Thanks, heaps," *Communications of the ACM*, vol. 28, pp. 245–250, 1985.

[14] G. Booch, *Object-Oriented Analysis and Design with Applications*. Redwood City, CA: Benjamin/Cummings, 1994.

[15] C. B. Boyer and U. C. Merzbach, *A History of Mathematics*. New York: John Wiley & Sons, Inc., 2nd ed., 1991.

[16] R. S. Boyer and J. S. Moore, "A fast string searching algorithm," *Communications of the ACM*, vol. 20, no. 10, pp. 762–772, 1977.

[17] G. Brassard, "Crusade for a better notation," *SIGACT News*, vol. 17, no. 1, pp. 60–64, 1985.

[18] T. Budd, *An Introduction to Object-Oriented Programming.* Reading, Mass.: Addison-Wesley, 1991.

[19] T. Budd, *C++ for Java Programmers.* Reading, Mass.: Addison-Wesley, 1999.

[20] L. Cardelli and P. Wegner, "On understanding types, data abstraction and polymorphism," *ACM Computing Surveys*, vol. 17, no. 4, pp. 471–522, 1985.

[21] S. Carlsson, "Average case results on heapsort," *BIT*, vol. 27, pp. 2–17, 1987.

[22] K. L. Clarkson, "Linear programming in $O(n3^{d^2})$ time," *Inform. Process. Lett.*, vol. 22, pp. 21–24, 1986.

[23] R. Cole, "Tight bounds on the complexity of the Boyer-Moore pattern matching algorithm," *SIAM Journal on Computing*, vol. 23, no. 5, pp. 1075–1091, 1994.

[24] D. Comer, "The ubiquitous B-tree," *ACM Comput. Surv.*, vol. 11, pp. 121–137, 1979.

[25] T. II. Cormen, C. E. Leiserson, and R. L. Rivest, *Introduction to Algorithms.* Cambridge, MA: MIT Press, 1990.

[26] M. Crochemore and T. Lecroq, "Pattern matching and text compression algorithms," in *The Computer Science and Engineering Handbook* (A. B. Tucker, Jr., ed.), ch. 8, pp. 162–202, CRC Press, 1997.

[27] S. A. Demurjian, Sr., "Software design," in *The Computer Science and Engineering Handbook* (A. B. Tucker, Jr., ed.), ch. 108, pp. 2323–2351, CRC Press, 1997.

[28] G. Di Battista, P. Eades, R. Tamassia, and I. G. Tollis, "Algorithms for drawing graphs: an annotated bibliography," *Comput. Geom. Theory Appl.*, vol. 4, pp. 235–282, 1994.

[29] G. Di Battista, P. Eades, R. Tamassia, and I. G. Tollis, *Graph Drawing: Algorithms for Geometric Representations of Graphs.* Englewood Cliffs, NJ: Prentice Hall, 1998.

[30] E. W. Dijkstra, "A note on two problems in connexion with graphs," *Numerische Mathematik*, vol. 1, pp. 269–271, 1959.

[31] J. R. Driscoll, H. N. Gabow, R. Shrairaman, and R. E. Tarjan, "Relaxed heaps: An alternative to Fibonacci heaps with applications to parallel computation.," *Commun. ACM*, vol. 31, pp. 1343–1354, 1988.

[32] S. Even, *Graph Algorithms.* Potomac, Maryland: Computer Science Press, 1979.

[33] R. Fleischer, B. Moret, and E. Meineche Schmidt, eds., *Experimental Algorithms: From Algorithm Design to Robust and Efficient Software*, vol. 2547 of *Lecture Notes in Computer Science.* Springer-Verlag, 2002.

[34] R. W. Floyd, "Algorithm 97: Shortest path," *Communications of the ACM*, vol. 5, no. 6, p. 345, 1962.

[35] R. W. Floyd, "Algorithm 245: Treesort 3," *Communications of the ACM*, vol. 7, no. 12, p. 701, 1964.

[36] M. L. Fredman and R. E. Tarjan, "Fibonacci heaps and their uses in improved network optimization algorithms," *J. ACM*, vol. 34, pp. 596–615, 1987.

[37] E. Gamma, R. Helm, R. Johnson, and J. Vlissides, *Design Patterns: Elements of Reusable Object-Oriented Software.* Reading, Mass.: Addison-Wesley, 1995.

[38] A. M. Gibbons, *Algorithmic Graph Theory.* Cambridge, UK: Cambridge University Press, 1985.

[39] A. Goldberg and D. Robson, *Smalltalk-80: The Language.* Reading, Mass.: Addison-Wesley, 1989.

[40] G. H. Gonnet and R. Baeza-Yates, *Handbook of Algorithms and Data Structures in Pascal and C*. Reading, Mass.: Addison-Wesley, 1991.

[41] G. H. Gonnet and J. I. Munro, "Heaps on heaps," *SIAM Journal on Computing*, vol. 15, no. 4, pp. 964–971, 1986.

[42] M. T. Goodrich, M. Handy, B. Hudson, and R. Tamassia, "Accessing the internal organization of data structures in the JDSL library," in *Proc. Workshop on Algorithm Engineering and Experimentation* (M. T. Goodrich and C. C. McGeoch, eds.), vol. 1619 of *Lecture Notes Comput. Sci.*, pp. 124–139, Springer-Verlag, 1999.

[43] R. L. Graham and P. Hell, "On the history of the minimum spanning tree problem," *Annals of the History of Computing*, vol. 7, no. 1, pp. 43–57, 1985.

[44] R. L. Graham, D. E. Knuth, and O. Patashnik, *Concrete Mathematics*. Reading, Mass.: Addison-Wesley, 1989.

[45] L. J. Guibas and R. Sedgewick, "A dichromatic framework for balanced trees," in *Proc. 19th Annu. IEEE Sympos. Found. Comput. Sci.*, Lecture Notes Comput. Sci., pp. 8–21, Springer-Verlag, 1978.

[46] Y. Gurevich, "What does $O(n)$ mean?," *SIGACT News*, vol. 17, no. 4, pp. 61–63, 1986.

[47] C. A. R. Hoare, "Quicksort," *The Computer Journal*, vol. 5, pp. 10–15, 1962.

[48] J. E. Hopcroft and R. E. Tarjan, "Efficient algorithms for graph manipulation," *Communications of the ACM*, vol. 16, no. 6, pp. 372–378, 1973.

[49] C. S. Horstmann, *Computing Concepts with C++ Essentials*. Ney York: John Wiley and Sons, 2nd ed., 1998.

[50] B. Huang and M. Langston, "Practical in-place merging," *Communications of the ACM*, vol. 31, no. 3, pp. 348–352, 1988.

[51] J. JáJá, *An Introduction to Parallel Algorithms*. Reading, Mass.: Addison-Wesley, 1992.

[52] V. Jarnik, "O jistem problemu minimalnim," *Praca Moravske Prirodovedecke Spolecnosti*, vol. 6, pp. 57–63, 1930. (in Czech).

[53] R. E. Jones, *Garbage Collection: Algorithms for Automatic Dynamic Memory Management*. John Wiley and Sons, 1996.

[54] D. R. Karger, P. Klein, and R. E. Tarjan, "A randomized linear-time algorithm to find minimum spanning trees," *Journal of the ACM*, vol. 42, pp. 321–328, 1995.

[55] R. M. Karp and V. Ramachandran, "Parallel algorithms for shared memory machines," in *Handbook of Theoretical Computer Science* (J. van Leeuwen, ed.), pp. 869–941, Amsterdam: Elsevier/The MIT Press, 1990.

[56] P. Kirschenhofer and H. Prodinger, "The path length of random skip lists," *Acta Informatica*, vol. 31, pp. 775–792, 1994.

[57] D. E. Knuth, *Fundamental Algorithms*, vol. 1 of *The Art of Computer Programming*. Reading, MA: Addison-Wesley, 1st ed., 1968.

[58] D. E. Knuth, *Fundamental Algorithms*, vol. 1 of *The Art of Computer Programming*. Reading, MA: Addison-Wesley, 2nd ed., 1973.

[59] D. E. Knuth, *Sorting and Searching*, vol. 3 of *The Art of Computer Programming*. Reading, MA: Addison-Wesley, 1973.

[60] D. E. Knuth, "Big omicron and big omega and big theta," in *SIGACT News*, vol. 8, pp. 18–24, 1976.

[61] D. E. Knuth, J. H. Morris, Jr., and V. R. Pratt, "Fast pattern matching in strings," *SIAM Journal on Computing*, vol. 6, no. 1, pp. 323–350, 1977.

[62] J. B. Kruskal, Jr., "On the shortest spanning subtree of a graph and the traveling salesman problem," *Proc. Amer. Math. Soc.*, vol. 7, pp. 48–50, 1956.

[63] N. G. Leveson and C. S. Turner, "An investigation of the Therac-25 accidents," *IEEE Computer*, vol. 26, no. 7, pp. 18–41, 1993.

[64] R. Levisse, "Some lessons drawn from the history of the binary search algorithm," *The Computer Journal*, vol. 26, pp. 154–163, 1983.

[65] A. Levitin, "Do we teach the right algorithm design techniques?," in *30th ACM SIGCSE Symp. on Computer Science Education*, pp. 179–183, 1999.

[66] S. Lippmann, *Essential C++*. Reading, Mass.: Addison-Wesley, 2000.

[67] S. Lippmann and J. Lajoie, *C++ Primer*. Reading, Mass.: Addison-Wesley, 3rd ed., 1998.

[68] B. Liskov and J. Guttag, *Abstraction and Specification in Program Development*. Cambridge, Mass./New York: The MIT Press/McGraw-Hill, 1986.

[69] E. M. McCreight, "A space-economical suffix tree construction algorithm," *Journal of Algorithms*, vol. 23, no. 2, pp. 262–272, 1976.

[70] C. J. H. McDiarmid and B. A. Reed, "Building heaps fast," *Journal of Algorithms*, vol. 10, no. 3, pp. 352–365, 1989.

[71] C. C. McGeoch, "Experimental analysis of algorithms," in *Handbook of Global Optimization* (P. M. Pardalos and H. E. Romeijn, eds.), vol. 2, Kluwer Academic Press, 2002.

[72] N. Megiddo, "Linear-time algorithms for linear programming in R^3 and related problems," *SIAM J. Comput.*, vol. 12, pp. 759–776, 1983.

[73] N. Megiddo, "Linear programming in linear time when the dimension is fixed," *J. ACM*, vol. 31, pp. 114–127, 1984.

[74] K. Mehlhorn, *Data Structures and Algorithms 1: Sorting and Searching*, vol. 1 of *EATCS Monographs on Theoretical Computer Science*. Heidelberg, Germany: Springer-Verlag, 1984.

[75] K. Mehlhorn, *Data Structures and Algorithms 2: Graph Algorithms and NP-Completeness*, vol. 2 of *EATCS Monographs on Theoretical Computer Science*. Heidelberg, Germany: Springer-Verlag, 1984.

[76] K. Mehlhorn and S. Näher, *LEDA: a Platform for Combinatorial and Geometric Computing*. Cambridge, UK: Cambridge University Press, 1999.

[77] K. Mehlhorn and A. Tsakalidis, "Data structures," in *Handbook of Theoretical Computer Science* (J. van Leeuwen, ed.), vol. A. Algorithms and Complexity, pp. 301–341, Amsterdam: Elsevier, 1990.

[78] S. Meyers, *More Effective C++*. Reading, Mass.: Addison-Wesley, 1996.

[79] S. Meyers, *Effective C++*. Reading, Mass.: Addison-Wesley, 2nd ed., 1998.

[80] M. H. Morgan, *Vitruvius: The Ten Books on Architecture*. New York: Dover Publications, Inc., 1960.

[81] D. R. Morrison, "PATRICIA—practical algorithm to retrieve information coded in alphanumeric," *Journal of the ACM*, vol. 15, no. 4, pp. 514–534, 1968.

[82] R. Motwani and P. Raghavan, *Randomized Algorithms*. New York, NY: Cambridge University Press, 1995.

[83] D. R. Musser and A. Saini, *STL Tutorial and Reference Guide: C++ Programming with the Standard Template Library*. Reading, Mass.: Addison-Wesley, 1996.

[84] T. Papadakis, J. I. Munro, and P. V. Poblete, "Average search and update costs in skip lists," *BIT*, vol. 32, pp. 316–332, 1992.

[85] P. V. Poblete, J. I. Munro, and T. Papadakis, "The binomial transform and its application to the analysis of skip lists," in *Proceedings of the European Symposium on Algorithms (ESA)*, pp. 554–569, 1995.

[86] I. Pohl, *C++ For C Programmers*. Reading, Mass.: Addison-Wesley, 3rd ed., 1999.

[87] R. C. Prim, "Shortest connection networks and some generalizations," *Bell Syst. Tech. J.*, vol. 36, pp. 1389–1401, 1957.

[88] W. Pugh, "Skip lists: a probabilistic alternative to balanced trees," *Commun. ACM*, vol. 33, no. 6, pp. 668–676, 1990.

[89] H. Samet, *The Design and Analysis of Spatial Data Structures*. Reading, MA: Addison-Wesley, 1990.

[90] R. Schaffer and R. Sedgewick, "The analysis of heapsort," *Journal of Algorithms*, vol. 15, no. 1, pp. 76–100, 1993.

[91] R. Sedgewick and P. Flajolet, *An Introduction to the Analysis of Algorithms*. Reading, Mass.: Addison-Wesley, 1996.

[92] G. A. Stephen, *String Searching Algorithms*. World Scientific Press, 1994.

[93] B. Stroustrup, *The C++ Programming Language*. Reading, Mass.: Addison-Wesley, 3rd ed., 1997.

[94] R. Tamassia, "Graph drawing," in *Handbook of Discrete and Computational Geometry* (J. E. Goodman and J. O'Rourke, eds.), ch. 44, pp. 815–832, Boca Raton, FL: CRC Press LLC, 1997.

[95] R. Tarjan and U. Vishkin, "An efficient parallel biconnectivity algorithm," *SIAM J. Comput.*, vol. 14, pp. 862–874, 1985.

[96] R. E. Tarjan, "Depth first search and linear graph algorithms," *SIAM Journal on Computing*, vol. 1, no. 2, pp. 146–160, 1972.

[97] R. E. Tarjan, *Data Structures and Network Algorithms*, vol. 44 of *CBMS-NSF Regional Conference Series in Applied Mathematics*. Philadelphia, PA: Society for Industrial and Applied Mathematics, 1983.

[98] A. B. Tucker, Jr., *The Computer Science and Engineering Handbook*. CRC Press, 1997.

[99] J. van Leeuwen, "Graph algorithms," in *Handbook of Theoretical Computer Science* (J. van Leeuwen, ed.), vol. A. Algorithms and Complexity, pp. 525–632, Amsterdam: Elsevier, 1990.

[100] J. S. Vitter, "Efficient memory access in large-scale computation," in *Proc. 8th Sympos. Theoret. Aspects Comput. Sci.*, Lecture Notes Comput. Sci., Springer-Verlag, 1991.

[101] J. S. Vitter and P. Flajolet, "Average-case analysis of algorithms and data structures," in *Algorithms and Complexity* (J. van Leeuwen, ed.), vol. A of *Handbook of Theoretical Computer Science*, pp. 431–524, Amsterdam: Elsevier, 1990.

[102] S. Warshall, "A theorem on boolean matrices," *Journal of the ACM*, vol. 9, no. 1, pp. 11–12, 1962.

[103] J. W. J. Williams, "Algorithm 232: Heapsort," *Communications of the ACM*, vol. 7, no. 6, pp. 347–348, 1964.

[104] M. R. Williams, *A History of Computing Technology*. Prentice-Hall, Inc., 1985.

[105] D. Wood, *Data Structures, Algorithms, and Performance*. Reading, Mass.: Addison-Wesley, 1993.